Critical Acclaim for another title by Paul Bonner, *PC/Computing Customizing Windows 3.1*

"Bonner has the rare gift of being able to explain technical matters in readable and enlightening fashion. It's a book to work with as you learn how to do the remarkable feats that Bonner describes."

—Hugh Anderson, *The Montreal Gazette*

"Paul Bonner...has written a remarkable book on how to customize Windows 3.1. By the time you finish the book and its accompanying diskette, you should be able to make Windows do precisely what you want it to do. If you have an interest in programming and use Windows 3.1, you will find this book invaluable."

—Hugh Bayless, *Monterey Bay Users Group-PC*

"...wordsmith Bonner has created a delightful guide...*PC/Computing Customizing Windows 3.1* will be a boon to the weathered programmer. Definitely a buy recommendation."

—John Cartmell, Jr., *Selected Book Review*

"*PC/Computing Customizing Windows 3.1*...fills an important vacancy in the 'How To' category of books written about Windows 3.1. A 'must have' for any Windows user."

—Bob Bloom, *The Atlanta Windows Users Group*

"An extremely useful chapter outlines usability guidelines that should be carved in stone and kept near the terminal of any software developer...it's one of the best primers on basic concepts available. Bonner teaches that programming is more than the mastery of a particular computer language; rather, it's an approach to problem-solving applicable across a multitude of computer languages and programs. If you want a glimpse inside this procedure in action, you won't find a better place to look."

—Paul A. Gilster, *CompuServe*

PC MAGAZINE
VISUAL BASIC
UTILITIES

PC MAGAZINE VISUAL BASIC UTILITIES

PAUL BONNER

ZIFF-DAVIS PRESS
EMERYVILLE, CALIFORNIA

Development Editor	Robert Hummel
Copy Editor	Kandy Arnold
Technical Reviewer	Dan Appleman
Project Coordinator	Kim Haglund
Proofreader	Cort Day
Cover Design	Tom Morgan/Blue Design, San Francisco
Book Design	Tom Morgan/Blue Design, San Francisco
Word Processing	Howard Blechman, Cat Haglund, and Allison Levin
Page Layout	Tony Jonick, Anna L. Marks, and Cat Haglund
Indexer	Ted Laux

Ziff-Davis Press books are produced on a Macintosh computer system with the following applications: FrameMaker®, Microsoft® Word, QuarkXPress®, Adobe Illustrator®, Adobe Photoshop®, Adobe Streamline™, MacLink®*Plus*, Aldus® FreeHand™, Collage Plus™.

Ziff-Davis Press
5903 Christie Avenue
Emeryville, CA 94608

ISBN 1-56276-106-4

Manufactured in the United States of America
10 9 8 7 6 5 4 3 2 1

Dedicated to my mother and to the memory of my father, who together taught me to value work, independence, and love.

CONTENTS AT A GLANCE

TABLE OF CONTENTS

ACKNOWLEDGMENTS

PC Magazine Visual Basic Utilities could not have been completed without the assistance of countless people, beginning with the many MSBASIC forum members on CompuServe who assisted in my Visual Basic education over the past several years. Among them, Jonathan Zuck, Jim Ferguson, Costas Kistos, Nelson Ford, Keith Funk, Keith Pleas, and Jeff Simms deserve special mention for their unceasing willingness to share their knowledge and experience.

I'd also like to thank Neal B. Scott and Gary Wisniewski for making tangible contributions to this book in the form of code that they created and placed in the public domain. Neal contributed the ZIP file-reading routines used in Chapter 3, without which VB ZIP Shell would not have been possible, and Gary not only created the File Manager drag-and-drop client custom control used in Chapter 4, but also twice modified it at my request.

I would also like to thank all those who worked with me on this book. The list starts with Rob Hummel, who originally conceived the Utilities series and who guides each series book to fruition. Rob's clear vision and uncommon good sense helped keep me on track throughout this project. I also feel genuine gratitude toward Dan Appleman, whose brilliant technical editing and immense knowledge of Visual Basic helped me solve countless problems. Finally, I'd like to thank Kandy Arnold, copy editor, for her fine line editing, Cindy Hudson, my publisher, for believing in this book and staying with it, and Kim Haglund and everyone else at Ziff-Davis Press who contributed to the book's design, production, and marketing.

Finally, my eternal thanks to Betsy for putting up with me through another one.

INTRODUCTION

This book is the story of my love affair with Visual Basic. Like any love story, it includes a few trials and a few tribulations, but it also includes many moments of pure delight.

Visual Basic makes the simple things—data entry screens, application prototypes and simple database programs—so easy that that there is a natural tendency to think of it as a tool that can only do the simple things. But for the more adventurous user who is willing to look under the covers to find out why things happen the way they do in Visual Basic, and who is willing to push past the limits of Visual Basic's built-in capabilities, Visual Basic turns out to be much more than a simple tool for simple applications. In the hands of that sort of user, Visual Basic is an ideal tool for system utilities, or for automating other applications, or for customizing the operation of the entire Windows system. In fact, with the help of an occasional custom control or dynamic link library, I believe that Visual Basic is the fastest, easiest, and most efficient tool for nearly every Windows programming task.

The eight projects presented in *PC Magazine Visual Basic Utilities* are designed to serve two purposes. First, each is intended to stand on its own as a useful utility. So even if you choose to never read a word of this book's text, and never examine a line of the source code that it presents, the eight utilities included on the companion disk should be valuable additions to your Windows environment.

I hope, however, that anyone who cracks the cover will discover that the utilities presented herein also fulfill the book's second mission: to illustrate valuable and often underdocumented Visual Basic programming techniques, and moreover, to document the entire process of building Windows applications in Visual Basic.

Each chapter guides the reader through that process, from the initial planning phase in which I outline the goals for each utility, through the design of its user interface and data structures, and then step by step through the process of writing its program code. In each chapter I describe the technical hurdles that I encountered in the course of each project, and how I overcame them.

■ WHO THIS BOOK IS FOR

All of the utilities presented here were designed to push the limits of Visual Basic. This book is not intended for novices or newcomers to Visual Basic programming, although it could serve well as an adjunct to a standard introductory text. Instead, my goal was to show readers who are already familiar with Visual Basic's core capabilities and perhaps frustrated by its limitations how those capabilities can be extended and those limitations overcome, so that they can fully explore the possibilities of this remarkable programming tool.

To that end, most of the projects presented here make extensive use of Windows application programming interface (API) functions. The Windows API is a treasure trove for Visual Basic programmers, but it can also be very daunting. Although there are finally some good references to the Windows API for Visual Basic programmers, it is still very difficult to know where to begin when approaching the API, and a bit scary. API functions are much less intuitive, and far more finicky, than Visual Basic's built-in capabilities. I know that the first few times I made use of API functions, I did so with my fingers crossed and a fire extinguisher on hand. So, one of my goals in *PC Magazine Visual Basic Utilities* was to document the processes of identifying the API functions needed for a project, incorporating them in your project code, and testing them to ensure that they work as expected.

Some of the projects included here also make use of custom controls or custom dynamic link libraries (DLLs) in order to access Windows functions that are not available from within Visual Basic itself. Custom controls and DLLs are enormously useful devices for the Visual Basic programmer. However, I've made only limited use of them in this book, preferring in most cases to demonstrate how the effects one might achieve with a custom control or DLL can be achieved with Visual Basic code and API calls alone.

■ THE UTILITIES

The utilities presented in this book are designed to serve a wide range of purposes.

Chapter 1 presents VB Code Librarian, a source code library designed to simplify the process of adding standard routines to Visual Basic projects. It provides a repository for the standard routines one uses time and time again in developing Visual Basic applications—routines for centering forms, accessing .INI files, creating standard message boxes, and the like. It also demonstrates high-speed sequential file access routines, techniques for indexing sorted list boxes, and use of the Windows clipboard.

Title Bar Clock, presented in Chapter 2, is a system utility that makes extensive use of Windows API functions to maintain a constant display of the current date and time on the title bar of the active Windows application. This chapter is a strong lesson in the use of Windows API calls, and in avoiding the pitfalls that can arise whenever your application needs to manipulate other applications.

Chapter 3 presents VB ZIP Shell, a Windows front end to PKWARE's shareware file compression utilities PKZIP and PKUNZIP. In addition to providing a Windows interface to these DOS utilities, it demonstrates a number of valuable techniques, including reading the contents of ZIP files from within Windows, running DOS applications in hidden windows, and techniques for building multiple-document-interface applications.

VB Q, the utility presented in Chapter 4, is a print queue for Windows that allows the user to print any document file either immediately or at a specified time. It demonstrates use of the Windows Registration Database and of SHELL.DLL, shows how to build Wizard-like dialogs that guide users through difficult tasks, provides a variety of techniques for interacting with other applications, and includes a custom control that allows any Visual Basic application to accept drag-and-drop messages from File Manager.

Chapter 5 presents VB Typographer, which allows the user to view the entire character set of any installed font in any size or style, and to print sample pages for any or all fonts. It demonstrates a wide range of useful techniques for working with multiple fonts, wrapping text, and interacting with a printer.

Clips, presented in Chapter 6, is a multiple clipboard utility that stores all text that you copy to the Windows clipboard, and enables you to edit captured text and combine text from multiple clipboard operations. It includes a custom DLL that enables Visual Basic applications to monitor clipboard operations.

DeskMenu, the utility presented in Chapter 7, presents a pop-up hierarchical menu of Program Manager groups and items whenever you click the right mouse button on the Windows desktop. It demonstrates use of Program Manager's dynamic data exchange interface, techniques for tracking pop-up menus and loading menu controls at runtime, and it includes a custom DLL for monitoring mouse clicks on the desktop window.

Finally, Chapter 8 presents VB MAKer, which uses Visual Basic's Access database engine to maintain a database of custom controls which it uses to assist the user in creating new Visual Basic project files. It demonstrates a variety of database techniques employing Visual Basic's data control, provides a method for simulating a data-aware list box control, and illustrates a method for searching the DOS path.

The companion disk also includes a number of additional programs. These include PKZIP 1.10 for use with VB ZIP Shell (please note, however, that PKZIP and PKUNZIP are shareware—you are obligated to pay a registration fee if you use them); DRAGDROP.ZIP, which contains the public domain File Manager drag-and-drop client custom control used by VB Q; the source and compiled code for WinFo, a window information utility I wrote to assist in the development of Title Bar Clock; and finally, the complete source code for the VB Utilities Installer installation program.

Chapter 8 is followed by two appendices. Appendix A lists a number of custom controls, development tools, and books that I've found useful in my Visual Basic programming experience, and Appendix B provides instructions for installing the applications and source code that you'll find on the companion disk.

With the right tools and the right approach, nearly anything is possible in Visual Basic. The chapters that follow simply show how I found the tools and the approaches necessary to complete eight projects, each of which started with the question, "I wonder if *this* is possible." I hope you find that they make for interesting reading.

C H A P T E R

1

RECYCLING YOUR CODE WITH VB CODE LIBRARIAN

VB Code Librarian helps you maintain a library of subroutines and functions that can be reused in any Visual Basic development project.

Every subroutine or function that you create has the potential to serve as an endlessly reusable component, callable by any other routine that needs its services. You might start off just trying to save yourself a couple of lines of typing, but in the process create a routine which you'll be able to reuse dozens or hundreds of times.

Therefore, every time you write a line of code, you create an opportunity to save yourself development, programming, and debugging time in the future.

In practice, of course, not every subroutine you create turns out to be quite that recyclable, but depending upon your coding style and the kinds of applications you write, many can be. You may have written, for instance, a routine for centering a form on the screen, or for reading information from a private .INI file, or for

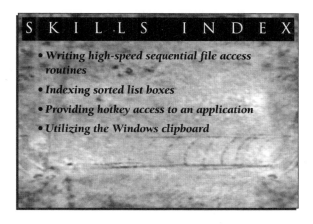

SKILLS INDEX

- *Writing high-speed sequential file access routines*
- *Indexing sorted list boxes*
- *Providing hotkey access to an application*
- *Utilizing the Windows clipboard*

extracting a file name from a full path name, any one of which you might make use of time after time in the course of a large development project.

As you move on to other projects, chances are good that you'll want to make use of many of these same routines. In theory at least, there is no reason why you can't—in fact, it makes great sense to do so. Unfortunately, though, Visual Basic doesn't provide a good way to import routines from one project into another. In fact, it makes it darned difficult.

There are ways to do it. You could, for instance, add the forms or modules in which the routines you need are located to your current project, but even after you've hunted down those files and used the Add File command to bring them in, this method is fraught with inconvenience and peril. If you leave those files attached to your current project, you risk the possibility of inadvertently introducing changes in them, and thus corrupting the source code of the previous project for which they were originally created. Moreover, because Visual Basic compiles all the code in a project's files when it creates an .EXE, not just the routines that are actually used, the size of your application's .EXE file may grow disproportionately if you only utilize a few of the routines from the imported modules or forms.

The other alternative—detaching the imported files once you've copied the routines that you need into a different module—eliminates these problems, but is both clumsy and, like the former method, prone to error. For one thing, you can't actually copy routines from one module to another, because Visual Basic doesn't allow two module-level routines to have the same name. So, instead, you must first *cut* the routine from the original file before *pasting* it into the new file, reintroducing the possibility of corrupting the original file should you later, in a moment of confusion, tell Visual Basic to save the changes in the original file before closing it. Moreover, with this method there is always the possibility that you will neglect to copy a global function declaration or constant needed by the routine that you are importing, since those are stored in the Declarations section of a module, not with the routines that actually use them. As a result, having (1) added the file that originally contained the routine to your project, (2) cut the routine from the original file, (3) pasted the routine into a module belonging to the current file, and (4) removed the original file from the project (and having repeated Steps 2 and 3 for however many routines you wish to move into your project), you may find that you have to start over again at Step 1 to retrieve a global declaration that you omitted the first time you went through the procedure.

There are other ways to move routines from one project to another, of course, but none are particularly satisfying. You can, for instance, open module files, or form files saved by using the ASCII Save option in a text editor such as Notepad and copy the routines you want into your destination file, or you can resort to retyping the routines in your new project, using a paper printout as your guide. But neither method is as direct or as error-free as anyone would like for an operation such as this.

Having explored and grown dissatisfied with each of these methods over the course of many Visual Basic development projects, I found myself yearning for a better way. What Visual Basic needed, I decided, was a routine library that would provide a way to store and later access frequently used routines. Out of that yearning came the utility presented in this chapter, VB Code Librarian.

■ USING VB CODE LIBRARIAN

VB Code Librarian automates and simplifies the process of moving functions and routines between projects. It allows you to build a library of reusable routines, then makes them easily available for use in any Visual Basic project. Moreover, it does so without exposing the projects for which the routines were originally developed to the danger of source code corruption, and without forcing you to open one file after another in search of an elusive routine.

■ Accessing Library Routines

A code library, as I've defined it for the purposes of VB Code Librarian, is a collection of routines or functions that can be reused in any Visual Basic development project. There are two distinct steps to using a code library: The first is the library-building step, through which you add one or more routines or functions to the library, and the second is the library-access step, whereby you move a routine or function from the library into a new development project. I designed VB Code Librarian to assist the user in both these steps.

It stands to reason that you can't use library routines that you haven't entered, so the process of building a library—by adding at least one entry to it—must precede that of accessing the library. However, since the fundamental underlying concept of a code library is that the routines it contains will only be entered once but used many times, I elected to make the access process the more convenient, by making it the default action when VB Code Librarian starts. To that end, the first thing you see when VB Code Librarian launches is a list box containing the titles of all the routines that have already been added to the library, as shown in Figure 1.1.

*VB Code
Librarian's
main screen*

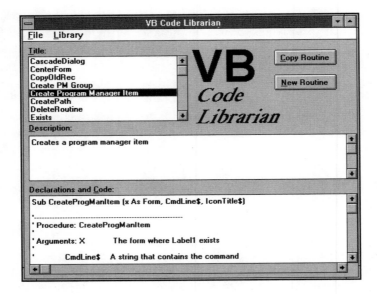

You'll see two edit boxes beneath the Title list box. VB Code Librarian uses the upper edit box to display a description of the routine whose title is currently selected, and the lower edit box to display the routine's complete source code. The contents of both are editable, so you can change the description or update the code at any time.

To use a routine from the Library in a Visual Basic project, you need merely select its title in the Title list box and then click the Copy Routine button (or choose the Copy Routine item on the Library menu). VB Code Librarian will react by displaying the message box shown in Figure 1.2, telling you that the code for the selected routine has been copied to the clipboard.

Once the code is on the clipboard, you can paste it into your current Visual Basic project merely by placing the cursor in the Declarations section of either a code module or a form and pressing Shift+Insert.

That's all there is to making use of existing library routines.

Creating Library Routines

The process of creating a new library entry is nearly as simple. Like the library access process, it makes use of the Windows clipboard.

To create a new library entry, you call up the VB Code Librarian New Routine screen, either by selecting the New Routine item on the Library menu, or by pressing the New Routine button on VB Code Librarian's main screen. Then you assign a name to the new routine, followed first by a description, and then by the routine's declarations and code.

VB Code Librarian uses this message to confirm that the selected routine has been copied to the clipboard.

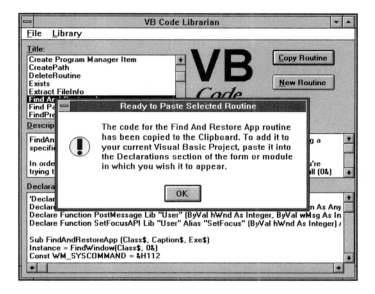

This can all be done manually, if you so desire, by typing the necessary information into each field, but you'll generally find it more efficient to use the Windows clipboard to copy the new routine's declarations and code into the library. For instance, suppose that you have created a routine to center a form on the screen, and have decided that it would be a good candidate for inclusion in the library, since the routine could be of value in many projects. You might start by highlighting the entire routine (including its Sub...End Sub or Function...End Function lines) in the Visual Basic code editor, and then selecting the Edit Copy command to place the routine's code onto the clipboard. Next, you would activate VB Code Librarian, press the New Routine button or select its corresponding menu item, and type a name for the routine into the first edit field (labeled Title) on the New Routine form. Then you might tab down to the Description field, and type a description of the routine, such as the following:

CenterForm centers a form on the screen. It accepts one parameter: the name of the form to be centered.

Finally, you would tab twice to get to the Code field and press Shift+Insert to paste the text of the routine from the clipboard. Once you had done so, the screen would resemble that shown in Figure 1.3.

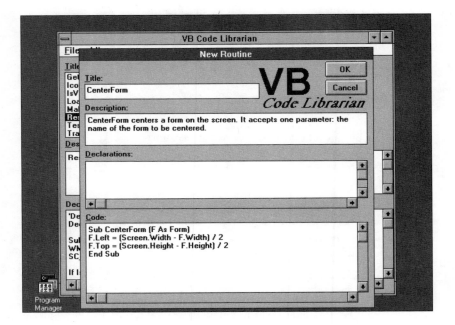

If the routine that you're adding to the library made use of external functions (such as calls to the Windows API) or global variables, or otherwise needed to make entries in the Declarations section of the form or module to which it was being added, there would be one additional step involved. You would have to copy the declarations used by the routine into the Declarations field of the New Routine form. You can do so before or after you copy the code, and the order makes no difference to VB Code Librarian, just as long as you put the declarations in the Declarations field and the code in the Code field. When you later use the Library to copy the routine to the clipboard, and then paste it into another Visual Basic project, everything that you entered into the Declarations field on the New Routine form will be added to the Declarations section of the target form or module, preceded by a comment line reading "'Declarations for RoutineTitle" (where RoutineTitle is the title you've given the routine). Meanwhile, everything you've entered into the Code field will be added to the target form or module as a new subroutine or function.

Sometimes you'll want to add a suite of routines to the library, consisting of several functions or subroutines that work together to achieve some end. For instance, you might have a series of interdependent routines to extract the file root, file extension, and path from a fully qualified file name. You can add linked routines to the library in either of two ways: by adding each as a separate entry to the library, or by combining them in a single entry, giving them a shared title and description, and simply pasting each routine's code into the Code field, one after the other. When you later paste the code into a new project, Visual Basic will parse it into a series of separate routines.

Aside from creating new routines and accessing existing ones, the only other user interface functions offered by VB Code Librarian are an option on the Code menu to delete the currently selected routine from the Library, and About box and Exit options on the File menu, which present copyright information and exit the program, respectively.

■ HOTKEY ACCESS

Use of VB Code Librarian—no matter whether you're building the library or making use of its contents—involves considerable switching back and forth between VB Code Librarian and the Visual Basic development environment. This led me to want to provide hotkey access between the two, so that one hotkey would make VB Code Librarian pop up, while another would activate the Visual Basic development environment.

Unfortunately, Visual Basic doesn't provide a built-in hotkey capability. Moreover, while the Windows 3.1 API includes a function called SetWindowsHookEx that can be used to install a systemwide keyboard filter, thereby creating a hotkey for an application, the function must be called by a dynamic link library (DLL), and thus cannot be accessed directly from within Visual Basic.

(Several third-party add-ons for Visual Basic, including MicroHelp Inc.'s VB Tools and Crescent Software Inc.'s QuickPak Professional for Windows, include custom controls—Visual Basic-specific dynamic link libraries—that act as a wrapper for the SetWindowsHookEx function, allowing you to assign a hotkey to an application. However, since my intent was to design all the projects in this book so that they could be used and edited without recourse to third-party products, it wasn't possible to use these solutions in VB Code Librarian.)

Nevertheless, I still wanted hotkey access if it was at all possible. As it turned out, I found a way to do so through a most unlikely source: the Program Manager. One of

Program Manager's least noted features is its Shortcut Key facility, which is accessed through the File Properties dialog box. When you assign a Shortcut Key combination to an icon in Program Manager, pressing that keystroke combination while you're working with Program Manager will launch the application. That's a nice trick, but at first glance it doesn't seem to really solve the problem, since having to activate Program Manager is even less convenient than switching directly between VB Code Librarian or the Visual Basic development environment using the Task Manager or the Windows Alt+Tab task-switch key.

It turns out, however, that the Program Manager Shortcut Keys play a different role if Program Manager isn't the active application. If you've launched an application from Program Manager, you can activate it at any time by pressing its hotkey, no matter what other application is active (as long as the hotkey doesn't conflict with a shortcut key used by the active application). So if you've assigned Shift+Control+L to VB Library and Shift+Control+V to the Visual Basic development environment, you can switch between them instantly by pressing their hotkeys, as long as you've launched them both from within Program Manager.

Its dependence upon an application having been launched from within Program Manager keeps this from being an ideal method for providing hotkey access to Visual Basic applications. Merely having assigned a shortcut key to an application isn't enough—Program Manager will ignore your attempts to use the shortcut key if you launched the application using some other method, such as double-clicking on its executable file in File Manager. But in general this method should provide satisfactory results—at least until such time when a future version of Visual Basic provides access to the SetWindowsHookEx function or otherwise enables hotkey assignment.

■ AUTOMATION ISSUES

VB Code Librarian, as described here, is a much simpler application than I originally imagined it would be.

Initially, I thought that VB Code Librarian should be much more automated than it turned out to be. For instance, I felt that the New Routine screen should automatically copy whichever routine was visible in the Visual Basic code window. Instead, in the final version of the application presented in this chapter, the burden of copying the new routine's code to the clipboard is left with the user. Similarly, I initially believed that once you had pressed the Copy Routine button, VB Code Librarian should automatically switch to Visual Basic and paste the code into the active form or module, whereas in the final version it merely places the code onto the clipboard and requires that you select an insertion point and issue the paste command.

My initial plans for the application were certainly within the realm of possibility. However, as the program developed I came to view them as both inappropriate and impractical. For instance, I could have had the New Routine procedure automatically copy the code of the currently visible routine in the Visual Basic code editor, but it wouldn't be able to determine which declarations from the form's or module's Declarations section should go with that routine. Moreover, if the routine that was visible in Visual Basic at the time I activated the New Routine procedure wasn't the one I wanted to add to the library, I would end up with code in the library that I didn't want. Similarly, while it wouldn't have been a great deal of trouble to program the access procedure to guess the form or module into which I wanted to paste a newly copied routine, that guess certainly wouldn't have been correct every time, and undoing a mistaken guess might prove to be difficult. Since my basic philosophy about automation is that any program that tries to guess what you want to do has to be right at least 95 percent of the time before its wrong guesses become tolerable, neither of these automation measures seemed advisable. Thus, VB Code Librarian ended up being a simpler, and I believe better, program than I originally envisioned.

INSIDE VB CODE LIBRARIAN

VB Code Librarian's source code is spread across three files: SELFORM.FRM, consisting of the application's main screen and code to support it, ADDFORM.FRM, consisting of the New Routines dialog box and code to support it, and LIBMOD.BAS, a code-only module containing a variety of subroutines.

Form Design

Both of VB Code Librarian's *screen forms* are relatively simple. Its main *screen*, SELFORM.FRM, is equipped with a resizable border, minimize and maximize buttons, and a standard Control menu. The *form* features the Title list box and two text box controls, one used to display a routine's description, and the other its code. The Sorted property of the Title list box is set to True (so that the titles will be displayed in alphabetical order), as is the *Multiline* property of both text boxes. The Description text box is equipped with a vertical scroll bar, so that Description text is word-wrapped, while the Code text box is equipped with both horizontal and vertical scroll bars, so that it can display long lines of code without wrapping them.

The Form_Resize event for SelectForm adjusts the width of the Description and Title text box *fields,* and both the height and width of the *Code* field, in response to changes in the size of SelectForm. Thus, if you maximize the form, the width of the Description field and the height of the Code and Description fields will increase dramatically, as shown in Figure 1.4, allowing you to view much more of their contents at one time than with the default sizes. Similarly, if you reduce the size of the form, the width of all three fields will be reduced in an attempt to make all three fields usable and leave their scroll bars visible, even when SelectForm has been reduced to a small fraction of its normal size.

FIGURE 1.4

SelectForm's Form_Resize event increases the width of the Description field and both the height and width of the Code field in response to the user maximizing or otherwise increasing the size of the form.

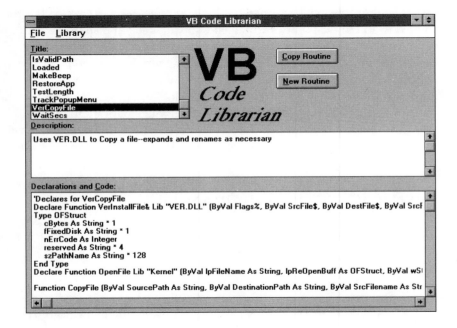

SelectForm also includes two buttons, labeled New Routine and Copy Routine, which are members of a single control array called Command1, and two menus, labeled File and Library. The File menu offers the option of exiting the program or viewing an About box, while the Library menu offers the option to copy the selected routine, delete the selected routine, or add a new routine.

AddForm, the only other form used by VB Code Librarian, is designed to be displayed as a modal dialog box. As such, it is equipped with a non-resizable border and lacks a control menu or minimize or maximize buttons. It features four text box controls, all of which are members of a control array called Text1, and two buttons, both members of a control array called Command1. The four elements in the Text1 array are the Title field, the Description field, the Code field, and the Declarations field, array elements 0 through 3, respectively; while the Command1 control array consists of the OK and Cancel buttons, array elements 0 and 1.

Both forms feature a pair of labels used to form a colorful "VB Code Librarian" logo, as well as labels equipped with access keys for each text box control and for the Title list box. The tab order for each form is set so that the label for each text box or list box immediately precedes it, so that when you press the access key for, for instance, the *Declarations:* label on SelectForm (Alt+D is its access key, as indicated by the underline beneath the D in the label's caption), the input focus jumps to the next control in the tab order which can accept input—the Declarations text box.

- ### Event-driven Code
  Like any good Windows application, VB Code Librarian is event-driven. Aside from a brief flurry of activity during the program's initialization process, the application's code executes only in response to user actions. Hence, the program's operation can be segmented into six distinct functions: Initialization, Selecting a Routine, Modifying a Routine, Deleting a Routine, Saving a New Routine, and Copying a Routine.

- # INITIALIZATION
  During its initialization process, VB Code Librarian declares several global variables, most of which are found in the Declarations section of LIBMOD.BAS. The majority of these variables aren't used during the initialization process; they're simply declared here so that they'll be available globally. Hence, I'll describe them and explain their use in the context of the routines which make use of them.

  Two of the global declarations are of great interest in the initialization routine, however: an empty string array called Routines( ) that, after redimensioning, will be used to hold the names of all the routines in the library, and RecCounter, an integer variable that will be used to keep track of the number of entries in the library.

  VB Code Librarian's initialization is controlled by the Form_Load procedure for SelectForm, the application's main window. This routine is responsible for populating the Title list box with the titles of all the library entries, and then selecting the first entry in the list and populating the Code and Description fields to reflect that selection.

  From the beginning of this project I felt that the most intuitive way to provide access to the routines stored in the library was to have the user select from a list of routine titles or names. Given that, it seemed obvious that the contents of the Title list box could serve as an index to the routine descriptions and code, and that as long as VB Code Librarian maintained a complete list of the routine titles in memory, which it does in the Routines( ) string array, there was no need for it also to keep all the code and descriptions in memory at once. Accordingly, I elected to store the contents of the Title list box in a separate disk file from those of the Code and Description text boxes.

The titles are stored in a sequential ASCII file called LIB.IDX, while the descriptions and code are stored in a sequential ASCII file called LIBCODE.ASC. The first line in the LIB.IDX file is a number corresponding to the total number of entries in the library. Then the titles of each entry follow, one to a line.

After initializing the value of some global variables, the Form_Load procedure for SelectForm calls a subroutine called GetFiles, which is located in LIBMOD.BAS. I created GetFiles as a subroutine, rather than as inline code for the Form_Load routine, because I expected that it would end up being called from several points in the program, whenever there arose a need to reload the list of titles into the Routines( ) array.

▪ **The GetFiles Routine**

GetFiles's first task is to determine the number of records, or library entries, recorded in LIB.IDX, so that the Routines( ) string array can be redimensioned to a number large enough to hold each routine's title. There are many ways to count the number of entries in a sequential ASCII file, but the simplest and fastest is to have the routine that saves the entries use the first line of the file to record the number of entries. That's the method that VB Code Librarian uses.

Accordingly, GetFiles begins by opening LIB.IDX for input and reading the first line of the file into a variable called C$. It redimensions Routines( ) to hold the number of records indicated by the value of C$, and then proceeds to read each routine title from LIB.IDX, assigning each to an element of the Routines( ) array. In addition, GetFiles adds each title to the Title list box on SelectForm, and sets the ItemData property for each item added to the list box to the value of the list box's NewIndex property:

```
Open Path$ + "Lib.IDX" For Input As F
Input #F, C$
RecCounter = Val(C$)
ReDim Routines(RecCounter)
For X = 1 To RecCounter
    Input #F, Routines(X)
    SelectForm.Titles.AddItem Routines(X)
    SelectForm.Titles.ItemData(SelectForm.Titles.NewIndex) = X
Next
Close F
```

In designing SelectForm, I set the sorted property of the Title list box to *True*, so that the list of titles would appear in alphabetical order. By doing so, however, I raised the issue of whether VB Code Librarian would determine which data record in LIBCODE.ASC should be loaded into the Code and Description fields when the user selected a title, since the Listbox.ListIndex property, which one would normally use for this purpose, would return the selected item's place in the sorted order, not in the natural order. (In other words, a routine which was called AAA#1 Quick Sort Routine might appear first in the sorted list, even though it was the 20th entry in the Library, and thus its ListIndex property would return a value of 1, rather than the value of 20 that would be needed to locate the correct code for that title.)

One way to solve the problem would be to compare the text of the list box item selected by the user to every item in the Routines( ) array until a match was found, and thus determine the selected title's place in the array. But in addition to being inelegant, that approach would fail should the library ever contain two routines with the same title, since it would always return the description and code of the first such routine. Giving different routines the same title may not be particularly clever, but nonetheless the user shouldn't be punished for it.

Instead, I opted to use the NewIndex and ItemData properties of the Title list box to obtain and record the record number of each library entry. A list box's NewIndex property always indicates the index of the most-recently added entry in a list box, while the list box's ItemData property can be used to assign additional data to a list box item. This data won't be visible in the list box, but can be obtained by evaluating the ItemData property. So as each routine is added to the list box, the GetFiles routine sets the ItemData property for the newly added list box item to the value of the list box's NewIndex property, as follows:

```
SelectForm.Titles.ItemData(SelectForm.Titles.NewIndex)
```

When VB Code Librarian later needs to determine which record has been selected in the Title list box to find the library entry's description and code, it can do so simply by examining the selected list box item's ItemData property, as follows:

```
Index = Titles.ItemData(Titles.ListIndex)
```

Once GetFiles completes loading the Title list box and the Routines( ) array, it returns control to the SelectForm Form_Load procedure, which concludes by selecting the first item in the Title list box (checking first to make sure that the list box isn't empty—in which case it would do nothing):

```
If Titles.ListCount Then Titles.ListIndex = 0
```

Selecting this item triggers the Titles_Click event, which is performed whenever a selection is made in the Title list box. Thus, the initialization process ends by launching the routine selection process.

■ SELECTING A ROUTINE

Two things must happen whenever a selection is made in the Title list box. First, VB Code Librarian has to determine whether the description or code of the previously selected (and thus currently visible) routine has changed and, if so, offer the user the chance to record the changes to disk. Next, it has to locate the description and code for the newly selected routine and display them in SelectForm's Code and Description text box fields.

The Titles_Click routine takes care of its first responsibility by calling a subroutine called Check_Changes, which evaluates the value of a global integer flag, called OldChoiceChanged, to determine whether the contents of either the code or description fields has changed. If so, it proceeds as described below in the section entitled "Modifying a Routine."

Once that chore is complete, Titles_Click uses the two-line procedure shown previously to determine the index number of the newly selected title, and then begins to search the LIBCODE.ASC file for its code.

Searching a sequential text file such as LIBCODE.ASC can be a slow process, especially when any individual entry has the potential to occupy dozens or even hundreds of lines, as might a large Visual Basic routine. The slowest part of the process is not the actual reading of the file from disk, but rather the string comparisons which are necessary to locate and identify the text for which the application is searching—especially since after a few selections, most if not all of LIBCODE.ASC will probably have already been read into your disk cache.

Accordingly, in designing the format of the LIBCODE.ASC file, I attempted to incorporate elements that would speed this process as much as possible. Routines appear in LIBCODE.ASC in the order in which they were entered into the library. The description of each routine is preceded by an index tag containing its index number surrounded by square brackets (so that the fifth routine is preceded by [5]), and followed by a line which reads [Code]. The routine's code begins immediately after that tag, and is itself followed by a tag which reads [Stop], after which the index tag for the following routine appears. In addition, I assigned the string [Code] to a global constant called CodeStart, and the string [Stop] to a global constant called CodeEnd, so that I could more easily refer to them throughout the application.

Thus, a printout of one simple routine from LIBCODE.ASC might look like this:

```
[6]
WaitSecs delays program execution for a specified number of seconds.
[Code]
Sub WaitSecs (secs)
    start! = Timer
    While Timer < start! + secs
    Temp = DoEvents()
    Wend
End Sub
[Stop]
```

The search routine opens the LIBCODE.ASC file, and then begins to read through it in search of the index tag for the newly selected routine, as follows:

```
Look$ = "[" & Index & "]"
Do While C$ <> Look$
    Line Input #F, C$
Loop
```

The structure of this loop differs from the standard example code that you'll find in the Visual Basic manuals, which recommend a structure like the following for loops utilizing Line Input#:

```
Do While Not EOF(F)
    Input #1, C$
    If C$=Look$ Then Exit Do
Loop
```

The recommended usage has the good grace to check to see whether an end-of-file flag has been set, but in so doing introduces an additional comparison for each iteration of the loop. The structure of LIBCODE.ASC, as described above, dictates that the routine won't encounter an end-of-file marker before finding *Look$* unless the file has been damaged. Thus I decided to forgo the *EOF()* check for the three Line Input loops in the Titles_Click procedure, instead relying on a simple On Error routine which, when called, informs the user that an error has occurred in reading the routine, thus eliminating a redundant string comparison within each loop without endangering the application's stability.

Once the index tag has been found, the routine reinitializes *C$* as an empty string. It then starts to build the routine's description, by reading LIBCODE.ASC until it arrives at the [*Code*] tag, adding each line that it reads to *C$*. In doing so, it makes use of two global constants—*CRLF$*, which consists of a carriage return and line feed which the routine adds to each line as it is read, and *CodeStart$* (the [*Code*] tag):

```
Line Input #F, C$
Do While C$<> Codestart$
    D$ = D$ + C$ + CRLF$
    Line input #F, C$
Loop
```

Finally, the Titles_Click routine reinitializes *C$* and *D$*, and then reads the routine's code and places it in the Code field, using the same procedures as for the Description field:

```
Line Input #F, C$
Do While C$<> CodeEnd$
    D$ = D$ + C$ +CRLF$
    Line Input #F, C$
Loop
Code = D$
```

By minimizing the number of string comparisons in each of these loops, VB Code Librarian achieves very good performance, with little or no discernible difference between the time it takes to retrieve and display the code for the first routine in LIB-CODE.ASC and that of the last, even when the library file contains dozens of routines.

■ MODIFYING A ROUTINE

Presumably, if the user modifies a routine's code or description, he or she doesn't want to lose those modifications. Therefore, VB Code Librarian has to be aware that a modification has occurred, and offer the user the opportunity to save the changes to disk before it reads the next routine into memory. Thus, I created a global integer flag called OldChoiceChanged, and added a single line of code to the Change events for the Code and Description text boxes, which sets the value of OldChoiceChanged to *True* when a modification is made to the contents of either field. (The Titles_Click routine resets OldChoiceChanged to *False* after reading in a new record from disk, so it will only have a value of *True* if the current record has been changed.)

The fields called Code and Description on SelectForm are both editable text boxes, which means that the user can modify their contents at any time. When the contents of either field are modified, the code for the field's Change event (either Description_Change or Code_Change) sets the global integer flag OldChoiceChanged to *True*.

Whenever the user selects a new item in the Title list box, or initiates the process of adding a routine to the library, or attempts to exit the program, VB Code Librarian calls the Check_Changes subroutine (which is stored in LIBMOD.BAS). Check_Changes evaluates the contents of the OldChoiceChanged flag, and, if it is equal to *True*, opens the message box shown in Figure 1.5 to determine if the user wishes to save the changed entry before proceeding.

VB Code Librarian uses this message box to determine if the user wishes to save changes to library entries.

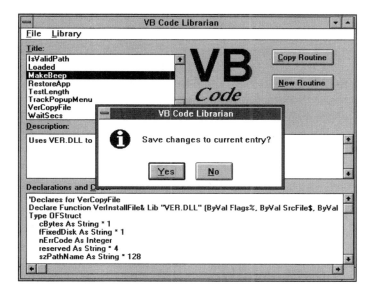

If the user clicks the message box's Yes button, Check_Changes calls a routine called LibSave to save the changed LIBCODE.ASC file. Otherwise, it returns control to the calling routine.

The simple sequential ASCII nature of LIBCODE.ASC, and the random length of its records, precludes the possibility of altering only the changed routine's data on disk. Instead, LibSave has to rewrite the entire LIBCODE.ASC file whenever a record is changed. It starts by opening the current LIBCODE.ASC file for input and a second file, CODEFILE.TMP, for output. (At this point it also copies LIB.IDX to a temporary file called LIB1.IDX. While there would seem to be no need to create a new copy of the index file here, since only the contents of the LIBCODE.ASC file are being changed, LibSave, along with several other routines, utilizes a subroutine called CleanUpFiles to manage temporary files, and CleanUpFiles needs to find both

CODEFILE.TMP and LIB1.IDX on the disk. Next, it loops through all the records in the library, writing the index tag for each record to CODEFILE.TMP and then comparing the record number to the value of the current record (which it obtains using the same two-line method described above). If the record number is the same as that of the current (changed) record, LibSave saves its contents as follows:

```
Print #F, SelectForm.Description.Text
Print #F, CodeStart$
Print #F, SelectForm.Code.Text
Print #F, CodeEnd$
```

Otherwise, it calls a subroutine called CopyOldRec, which copies the old contents of the record from LIBCODE.ASC to CODEFILE.TMP.

It might seem that it would make sense to have CopyOldRec perform the process of saving each routine's index tag at the same time that it saves its contents, rather than having LibSave write the tag to disk. But I also planned to use the CopyOldRec routine following the deletion of a record, in which case the index numbers of some routines would change. Thus, it made more sense to have each routine that calls CopyOldRec (LibSave and DeleteRecord) save the index tag for the library entry being copied, and simply let CopyOldRec handle the process of copying the library entry's code and description.

■ THE COPYOLDREC ROUTINE

I designed CopyOldRec to be called once for each record being copied from LIB-CODE.ASC to CODEFILE.TMP. It begins by determining which record it should copy, using the value of the integer variable *RecordNum*, and searching for that record's data in LIBCODE.ASC, as follows:

```
Look$ = "[" & RecordNum & "]"
Do While C$ <> Look$
   Input #J, C$
Loop
```

Once the record has been located, CopyOldRec reads its code and description line by line, and outputs each line to CODEFILE.TMP:

```
Line Input #J, C$
Do While C$ <> CodeEnd$
   Print #F, C$
   Line Input #J, C$
Loop
```

CopyOldRec makes no distinction between a routine's code and description, treating them as a single entity that lies between *Look$* (the routine's index tag) and the *CodeEnd$* tag. It concludes by writing *CodeEnd$* to CODEFILE.TMP, and then returns control to the LibSave procedure.

Once every record in the library has been saved to CODEFILE.TMP, LibSave calls the CleanUpFiles routine which first deletes any old backup versions of LIB.IDX and LIBCODE.ASC that it finds, then renames LIB.IDX and LIBCODE.ASC with the .BAK extensions, and finally renames the temporary files LIB1.IDX and CODEFILE.TMP to LIB.IDX and LIBCODE.ASC, respectively. CleanUpFiles also is used by the VB Code Librarian routines responsible for adding new routines and deleting routines, as described below.

Thus concludes the process of modifying a routine.

■ DELETING A ROUTINE

VB Code Librarian calls the DeleteRoutine subroutine in LIBMOD.BAS when the user selects the Delete Routine item on the Library menu.

Since record deletions are permanent, DeleteRoutine starts by posting a message box that asks whether the user really wants to delete the selected routine, as shown in Figure 1.6.

If the user indicates that he or she wishes to proceed with deleting the selected record, DeleteRoutine opens LIB1.IDX and writes a revised list of titles to it, leaving out the title of the selected record and decreasing the total count of records by one.

Next, DeleteRoutine needs to save the code and descriptions of all the records except the current one to a new file. So, it opens LIBCODE.ASC for input and CODE-FILE.TMP for output and, using much the same procedure as the LibSave routine discussed above, copies the code and description data of each library entry from the former to the latter, using the CopyOldRec routine to actually copy the data.

The only significant difference between DeleteRoutine and LibSave is that Delete-Routine needs to decrease the index tag record number of each entry that follows the newly deleted routine. It does so by comparing the index number of the currently selected (newly deleted) entry with that of the entry whose data is being written:

```
For RecordNum = 1 To RecCounter
Select Case RecordNum
Case Is < Index
   Header$ = "[" & RecordNum & "]"
   Print #F, Header$
   CopyOldRec
```

```
Case Is = Index                'Do nothing
Case Is > Index
    Header$ = "[" & RecordNum - 1 & "]"
    Print #F, Header$
    CopyOldRec
End Select
Next RecordNum
```

Like LibSave, DeleteRoutine concludes by calling CleanUpFiles.

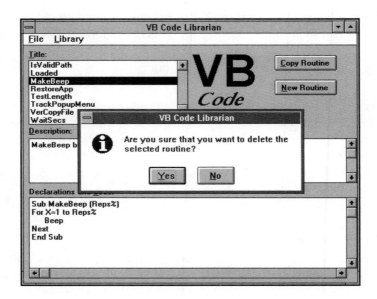

■ SAVING A NEW ROUTINE

The process of saving a new routine, which is initiated when the user clicks the OK button on the New Routine dialog box, is managed by a function called SaveNewRoutine.

■ The SaveNewRoutine Function

I wanted to have VB Code Librarian perform a pair of safety checks before saving the new record to disk, and to abort the process of adding the record if either check fails. Accordingly, I defined SaveNewRoutine as a function which returns an integer value, rather than as a simple subroutine. Doing so allows the Command1_Click procedure to evaluate the result returned by SaveNewRoutine to determine what step it should take next.

Before a new record is actually saved to disk, SaveNewRoutine begins by checking to make sure that there is something to save. If all four text fields on AddForm are empty it exits, returning a value of *False*, which indicates to the Command1_Click procedure that AddForm can unload itself without performing any additional steps.

Next, the SaveNewRoutine function checks the contents of the Title field to make sure that the user has given the routine a title. If not, it posts a message box imploring the user to give the routine a title, and then exits, returning a value of 1, which the Command1_Click procedure uses as an indication that it should exit without unloading AddForm, thus giving the user a chance to add a title to the Title field.

Once SaveNewRoutine has completed these checks and determined that there is something to save and a title under which to save it, it opens a temporary file, giving it the by now familiar name LIB1.IDX, and writes the list of titles to it, appending the new routine's title to the end of the list and increasing the record counter at the beginning of the list by one.

Next, SaveNewRoutine saves the new routine's code and description. Since these have to be appended to the end of the existing data in LIBCODE.ASC, SaveNewRoutine doesn't need to use CopyOldRec to copy individual routines from LIBCODE.ASC to CODEFILE.TMP. Instead, it simply copies the entire LIBCODE.ASC file to CODE-FILE.TMP, and then opens CODEFILE.TMP in Append mode. It then writes the index tag for the new record, followed by the contents of the Title field, followed by *Code-Start$*. Then, it evaluates the contents of the Declarations field on the New Routine dialog box. If the field is not empty, it writes a line consisting of the string '*Declares for* followed by the routine's title, to create an identifying comment for the routine's declarations, and then writes out the declarations for the routine, followed by *CRLF$*.

Finally, SaveNewRoutine writes out the contents of the Code field, followed by *CodeEnd$*, then calls CleanUpFiles to process the temporary and backup files and returns a value of *True*, which the Command1_Click procedure interprets as an indication that the routine has been saved. The Command1_Click procedure responds by clearing the Title list box on SelectForm and calling GetFiles to load a new list of titles (thus ensuring that the new routine appears in the list), and then selects the new routine by setting SelectForm.Titles.ListIndex equal to SelectForm.Titles.NewIndex. (The NewIndex property of a list box points to its most recently added item.) Finally it unloads AddForm, leaving the new routine selected in the Title list box.

■ COPYING A ROUTINE

The last of VB Code Librarian's functions is the one that gives it an excuse for being: that of copying a routine's declarations and code to the clipboard so that they may be pasted into a new Visual Basic project.

This process, which is launched when the user clicks the Copy Routine button or selects the Copy Routine item on the Library menu, is about as simple you can get. It simply issues the command Clipboard.SetText Code.Text to copy the text of the SelectForm Code field (which contains both the routine's code and its declarations) to the clipboard, and then creates the message box shown in Figure 1.2 to inform the user that the code is ready to be pasted into the new Visual Basic project.

Once the text of the routine's code and declarations has been placed on the clipboard, the user can paste it into his or her Visual Basic project simply by placing the cursor at the bottom of a form or module's Declarations section and issuing the Paste command. Visual Basic automatically parses the text as if it were being typed at the keyboard, storing the declarations (preceded by the identifying comment described above) in the Declarations section, and creating a new subroutine or function for each Sub...End Sub or Function...End Function block in the routine's code. The routine's title and description are not pasted into the project, since their purpose is to identify and explain the use of the routine in the library, not in an actual programming project.

■ SUMMARY

VB Code Librarian provides a simple and efficient solution to the problem of moving routines from one Visual Basic project to another. While its effective use requires some discipline and foresight—the best time to add a routine to the library is when you create it, not when you need it for another project—it provides a flexible solution to a vexing problem.

One upgrade you may wish to make to this program is to add file-selection routines to enable it to work with multiple library files. Given the performance limitations of sequential access files, creating multiple small library files segregated by routine type might provide more satisfactory results than endlessly appending new routines to a single library file. For instance, UI.LIB for user interface routines, WINAPI.LIB for Windows API declarations and calls, and FILEIO.LIB for file-oriented routines.

SAMPLE LIBRARY ON DISK

The companion disk to *PC Magazine Visual Basic Utilities* includes sample library files (LIB.IDX and LIBCODE.ASC) containing 12 or more routines for performing a variety of common Visual Basic programming tasks. If these are of no interest to you, you can either delete them one by one or simply delete LIB.IDX and LIBCODE.ASC, in which case the application will create new, empty library files the next time it is run. ∎

REUSABLE CODE

The underlying premise of VB Code Librarian is that it is possible—and, indeed, relatively easy—to write reusable code in Visual Basic, code that can be taken from one project and used in another. Doing so isn't always an effortless task, but by observing a few simple rules you can greatly increase the reusability of every routine you write.

Whenever possible, pass variables identifying forms and controls to your library routines, rather than identifying them explicitly within the routine.

In other words, you should write your CenterForm routine like this:

```
Sub CenterForm (F As Form)
F.Left = (Screen.Width - F.Width) / 2
F.Top = (Screen.Height - F.Height) / 2
End Sub
```

rather than like this:

```
Sub CenterForm ()
NamedForm.Left = (Screen.Width - NamedForm.Width) / 2
NamedForm.Top = (Screen.Height - NamedForm.Height) / 2
End Sub
```

Another key to writing code that can be easily reused is to identify clearly in the Declarations section of your forms and modules what routine uses which declarations. You'll still have to remember to include those declarations when you add the routine to the library, but at least a few well-placed comments will give you a clue as to which declarations are needed to make a routine work.

Still, no matter what steps you take, there will be times when the code you write won't be particularly portable—when it will be more convenient, or simpler, or result in faster performance, to place project-specific references in a routine's code. Nevertheless, routines written in such a manner may still be good candidates for inclusion in VB Code Librarian's library if you believe that you'll have need of a similar routine in the future. Even if you only use them as a template, and have to tinker extensively with the code to make it work well in a new project, in many cases doing so will still be faster than creating an entire routine from scratch. In addition, the ability that VB Code Librarian gives you to edit the description, declarations, and code of library routines means that, once a routine has been added to the library, you have an opportunity to "globalize" it without any danger of corrupting the source code of the project for which it was originally written.   ∎

E N D N O T E

CREATING PROGRAM MANAGER SHORTCUT KEYS

Creating a Shortcut Key for an application that has been installed as a Program Manager icon is quite simple. You need merely highlight the application's icon, then select the Properties item on Program Manager's File menu. When you do so, Program Manager opens its Program Item Properties dialog box, which contains four editable text fields, one each for the program's title, command line, working directory, and Shortcut Key field, then press the key combination that you want to use as the Shortcut Key for the selected application. You can use any letter, number, or special character in combination with the Control+Alt, Control+Shift, or Control+Alt+Shift keys as a shortcut key, and Program Manager will warn you if the combination that you've entered has already been assigned to another application.   ∎

VB CODE LIBRARIAN

```
' * * * * * * * * * * * * * * *
' Chapter 1 Listing
' VB Code Librarian
' Copyright (c) 1993, Paul Bonner
' PC Magazine Visual Basic Utilities
' * * * * * * * * * * * * * * *
' ASCII Listing of SELECTFRM.FRM
' * * * * * * * * * * * * * * *
VERSION 2.00
Begin Form SelectForm
    BackColor          =    &H00C0C0C0&
    Caption            =    "VB Code Librarian"
    DrawStyle          =    1   'Transparent
    ForeColor          =    &H00000040&
    Height             =    6465
    Icon               =    SELFORM.FRX:0000
    Left               =    1620
    LinkTopic          =    "Form1"
    ScaleHeight        =    5775
    ScaleWidth         =    7800
    Top                =    1230
    Width              =    7920
    Begin CommandButton Command1
        Caption            =    "&Copy Routine"
        Height             =    375
        Index              =    1
        Left               =    5880
        TabIndex           =    7
        Top                =    240
        Width              =    1455
    End
    Begin CommandButton Command1
        Caption            =    "&New Routine"
        Height             =    375
        Index              =    0
        Left               =    5880
        TabIndex           =    8
        Top                =    840
        Width              =    1455
    End
```

```
Begin ListBox Titles
    BackColor       =     &H00FFFFFF&
    ForeColor       =     &H00000000&
    Height          =     1590
    Left            =     120
    Sorted          =     -1    'True
    TabIndex        =     1
    Top             =     360
    Width           =     3615
End
Begin TextBox Description
    BackColor       =     &H00FFFFFF&
    ForeColor       =     &H00000000&
    Height          =     1095
    Left            =     120
    MultiLine       =     -1    'True
    ScrollBars      =     2     'Vertical
    TabIndex        =     3
    Top             =     2280
    Width           =     7455
End
Begin TextBox Code
    BackColor       =     &H00FFFFFF&
    ForeColor       =     &H00000000&
    Height          =     1935
    Left            =     120
    MultiLine       =     -1    'True
    ScrollBars      =     3     'Both
    TabIndex        =     6
    Top             =     3720
    Width           =     7455
End
Begin Label Label1
    AutoSize        =     -1    'True
    BackColor       =     &H00C0C0C0&
    Caption         =     "&Title:"
    Height          =     195
    Index           =     4
    Left            =     120
    TabIndex        =     0
    Top             =     120
    Width           =     450
End
Begin Label Label1
    AutoSize        =     -1    'True
    BackColor       =     &H00C0C0C0&
    Caption         =     "&Description:"
    Height          =     195
```

```
      Index           =     3
      Left            =     120
      TabIndex        =     2
      Top             =     2000
      Width           =     1095
      WordWrap        =     -1    'True
   End
   Begin Label Label1
      AutoSize        =     -1    'True
      BackColor       =     &H00C0C0C0&
      Caption         =     "Declarations and &Code:"
      Height          =     195
      Index           =     2
      Left            =     120
      TabIndex        =     4
      Top             =     3480
      Width           =     2010
   End
   Begin Label Label1
      BackColor       =     &H00C0C0C0&
      BackStyle       =     0     'Transparent
      Caption         =     "VB"
      FontBold        =     -1    'True
      FontItalic      =     0     'False
      FontName        =     "Arial"
      FontSize        =     54
      FontStrikethru  =     0     'False
      FontUnderline   =     0     'False
      ForeColor       =     &H00400000&
      Height          =     1095
      Index           =     1
      Left            =     3960
      TabIndex        =     9
      Top             =     0
      Width           =     1695
   End
   Begin Label Label1
      BackColor       =     &H00C0C0C0&
      BackStyle       =     0     'Transparent
      Caption         =     "Code Librarian"
      FontBold        =     -1    'True
      FontItalic      =     -1    'True
      FontName        =     "MS Serif"
      FontSize        =     24
      FontStrikethru  =     0     'False
      FontUnderline   =     0     'False
      ForeColor       =     &H00000040&
      Height          =     975
```

```
         Index                =    0
         Left                 =    3960
         TabIndex             =    5
         Top                  =    1080
         Width                =    2295
      End
      Begin Menu FileMenu
         Caption              =    "&File"
         Begin Menu fileItem
            Caption           =    "&Exit"
            Index             =    0
         End
         Begin Menu fileItem
            Caption           =    "-"
            Index             =    1
         End
         Begin Menu fileItem
            Caption           =    "&About"
            Index             =    2
         End
      End
      Begin Menu mCode
         Caption              =    "&Library"
         Begin Menu codeItem
            Caption           =    "&Copy Routine"
            Index             =    0
         End
         Begin Menu codeItem
            Caption           =    "&New Routine"
            Index             =    1
         End
         Begin Menu codeItem
            Caption           =    "&Delete Routine"
            Index             =    2
         End
      End
   End
End
```

LISTING

SELECT.FRM CODE LISTING

```
' * * * * * * * * * * * * * * *
' SELECTFRM.FRM Code Listing
' * * * * * * * * * * * * * * *
'Copyright (c) 1993, Paul Bonner
'PC Magazine Visual Basic Utilities
DefInt A-Z
Option Explicit

Sub Code_Change ()
' * * * * * * * * * * * * * * *
'Set flag to indicate code has been changed
' * * * * * * * * * * * * * * *
  OldChoiceChanged = True
End Sub

Sub CodeItem_Click (Index As Integer)
' * * * * * * * * * * * * * * *
'Library menu procedures
' * * * * * * * * * * * * * * *
Select Case Index
Case 0
  Command1(1) = True  'Copy selected, so click Copy button
Case 1
  Command1(0) = True   'New selected, click New button
Case 2
  DeleteRoutine         'Delete selected, so call DeleteRoutine
End Select
End Sub

Sub Command1_Click (Index As Integer)
Dim rName$, M$, X
' * * * * * * * * * * * * * * *
'Processes button clicks for Copy Routine and
'New Routine buttons
' * * * * * * * * * * * * * * *
Select Case Index
Case 0    'New Routine button was pushed
  Check_Changes  'Determine if current record has changed
  CenterDialog AddForm, Me  'Center AddForm over SelectForm
  AddForm.Show 1           'Show AddForm Modally
Case 1    'Copy Routine button was pushed
  If Titles.ListCount = 0 Then Exit Sub
  Clipboard.SetText Code.Text  'Put Code on Clipboard
  rName$ = Titles.Text
  M$ = "The code for the " + rName$ + " routine has been copied to the ⇔
    Clipboard. To add it to your current Visual Basic Project,"
  M$ = M$ + " paste it into the Declarations section of the form or module ⇔
    in which you wish it to appear."
  X = MsgBox(M$, 48, "Ready to Paste Selected Routine")
End Select
End Sub

Sub Description_Change ()
```

```
' * * * * * * * * * * * * * * *
'Set flag to indicate description has been changed
' * * * * * * * * * * * * * * *
OldChoiceChanged = True
End Sub

Sub fileItem_Click (Index As Integer)
' * * * * * * * * * * * * * *
'File menu procedures
' * * * * * * * * * * * * * *
Select Case Index
Case 0                  'Exit item selected
  Unload SelectForm
Case 1                  'Separator bar--can't be selected
Case 2                  'About item selected
  MsgBox "VB Code Librarian 1.0" + CRLF$ + "Copyright © 1993, Paul Bonner" + ⇔
      CRLF$ + "PC Magazine Visual Basic Utilities" + CRLF$ + "All Rights ⇔
      Reserved.", 64, "VB Code Librarian"
End Select
End Sub

Sub Form_Load ()
' * * * * * * * * * * * * * * *
'Set Path$ variable, appending backslash if necessary
' * * * * * * * * * * * * * * *
Path$ = App.Path
If Right$(Path$, 1) <> "\" Then Path$ = Path$ + "\"
' * * * * * * * * * * * * * * *
'Initialize CRLF$ as carriage return and line feed
' * * * * * * * * * * * * * * *
CRLF$ = Chr$(13) + Chr$(10)
' * * * * * * * * * * * * * * *
'Move SelectForm to center of screen
' * * * * * * * * * * * * * * *
CenterForm Me
' * * * * * * * * * * * * * * *
'Initialize variable used to track previous listbox selection
' * * * * * * * * * * * * * * *
OldChoice = -1
' * * * * * * * * * * * * * * *
'Load Title listbox
' * * * * * * * * * * * * * * *
GetFiles
' * * * * * * * * * * * * * * *
'Select first item in listbox
' * * * * * * * * * * * * * * *
If Titles.ListCount Then Titles.ListIndex = 0
End Sub

Sub Form_QueryUnload (Cancel As Integer, UnloadMode As Integer)
    Check_Changes
End Sub

Sub Form_Resize ()
 Dim W, H
 W = Width - (2 * Code.Left)
 If W < 800 Then W = 800
 Description.Width = W
 Code.Width = W
 If W < 3736 Then Titles.Width = W:  Else Titles.Width = 3735
 H = Height - (Code.Top + 800)
 If H > 1200 Then Code.Height = H
End Sub
```

```
Sub Titles_Click ()
Dim F, Index, Look$, C$, D$
' * * * * * * * * * * * *
'Exit if selected item hasn't changed
' * * * * * * * * * * * *
If Titles.ListIndex = OldChoice Then Exit Sub
' * * * * * * * * * * * *
'Determine if contents of current record have changed
' * * * * * * * * * * * * * * *
Check_Changes
' * * * * * * * * * * * * * *
'Display hourglass cursor
' * * * * * * * * * * * * * *
Screen.MousePointer = 11
' * * * * * * * * * * * * * *
'Set OldChoice to newly selected item
' * * * * * * * * * * * * * *
OldChoice = Titles.ListIndex
' * * * * * * * * * * * * * *
'Open code file
' * * * * * * * * * * * *
F = FreeFile
On Error GoTo FileError
Open Path$ + "LIBCODE.ASC" For Input As F
' * * * * * * * * * * * * * *
'Find index number of selected routine
' * * * * * * * * * * * * *
Index = Titles.ItemData(Titles.ListIndex)
' * * * * * * * * * * * * *
'Set Look$ to select item's index tag
' * * * * * * * * * * * * *
Look$ = "[" & Index & "]"
' * * * * * * * * * * * * *
'Find item's header
' * * * * * * * * * * * *
Do While C$ <> Look$
    Line Input #F, C$
Loop
C$ = ""
' * * * * * * * * * * * * * *
'Read item's description
' * * * * * * * * * * * * * *
Line Input #F, C$
Do While C$ <> CodeStart$
    D$ = D$ + C$ + CRLF$
    Line Input #F, C$
Loop
Description = D$
' * * * * * * * * * * * *
'Read Code
' * * * * * * * * * * * * *
D$ = ""
C$ = ""
Line Input #F, C$
Do While C$ <> CodeEnd$
    D$ = D$ + C$ + CRLF$
    Line Input #F, C$
Loop
Code = D$
' * * * * * * * * * * * * *
'Close file
' * * * * * * * * * * * *
Close F
' * * * * * * * * * * * *
```

```
'Restore standard pointer
' * * * * * * * * * * * * *
Screen.MousePointer = 1
' * * * * * * * * * * * * *
'Set record-changed flag to false
' * * * * * * * * * * * * *
OldChoiceChanged = False
' * * * * * * * * * * * * *
'Exit label used by FileError: routine
BackDoor:
Exit Sub
' * * * * * * * * * * * * *
'Handling routine for file read errors
' * * * * * * * * * * * * *
FileError:
MsgBox "File error attempting to read LIBCODE.ASC."
Resume BackDoor
End Sub
Sub Titles_DblClick ()
Command1(1) = True
End Sub
```

LISTING

ASCII LISTING OF ADDFORM.FRM

```
' * * * * * * * * * * * * * * *
' ASCII Listing of ADDFORM.FRM
' * * * * * * * * * * * * * * *
VERSION 2.00
Begin Form AddForm
    BackColor      =     &H00C0C0C0&
    BorderStyle    =     1    'Fixed Single
    Caption        =     "New Routine"
    ControlBox     =     0    'False
    Height         =     6420
    Left           =     1095
    LinkTopic      =     "Form2"
    MaxButton      =     0    'False
    MinButton      =     0    'False
    ScaleHeight    =     6015
    ScaleWidth     =     6870
    Top            =     1125
    Width          =     6990
    Begin TextBox Text1
        BackColor      =     &H00FFFFFF&
        ForeColor      =     &H00000000&
        Height         =     1170
```

```
      Index            =     3
      Left             =     120
      MultiLine        =     -1    'True
      ScrollBars       =     3    'Both
      TabIndex         =     5
      Top              =     2445
      Width            =     6615
   End
   Begin TextBox Text1
      BackColor        =     &H00FFFFFF&
      ForeColor        =     &H00000000&
      Height           =     780
      Index            =     1
      Left             =     120
      MultiLine        =     -1    'True
      TabIndex         =     3
      Top              =     1275
      Width            =     6615
   End
   Begin TextBox Text1
      BackColor        =     &H00FFFFFF&
      ForeColor        =     &H00000000&
      Height           =     375
      Index            =     0
      Left             =     120
      TabIndex         =     1
      Top              =     555
      Width            =     4095
   End
   Begin CommandButton Command1
      Caption          =     "OK"
      Height           =     375
      Index            =     0
      Left             =     5760
      TabIndex         =     8
      Top              =     40
      Width            =     975
   End
   Begin CommandButton Command1
      Cancel           =     -1    'True
      Caption          =     "Cancel"
      Height           =     375
      Index            =     1
      Left             =     5760
      TabIndex         =     9
      Top              =     480
      Width            =     975
   End
```

```
Begin TextBox Text1
    BackColor       =       &H00FFFFFF&
    ForeColor       =       &H00000000&
    Height          =       1935
    Index           =       2
    Left            =       120
    MultiLine       =       -1   'True
    ScrollBars      =       3    'Both
    TabIndex        =       7
    Top             =       3960
    Width           =       6615
End
Begin Label Label1
    AutoSize        =       -1   'True
    BackColor       =       &H00C0C0C0&
    Caption         =       "&Declarations:"
    Height          =       195
    Index           =       5
    Left            =       120
    TabIndex        =       4
    Top             =       2160
    Width           =       1140
    WordWrap        =       -1   'True
End
Begin Label Label1
    BackColor       =       &H00C0C0C0&
    BackStyle       =       0    'Transparent
    Caption         =       "Code Librarian"
    FontBold        =       -1   'True
    FontItalic      =       -1   'True
    FontName        =       "MS Serif"
    FontSize        =       18
    FontStrikethru  =       0    'False
    FontUnderline   =       0    'False
    ForeColor       =       &H00000040&
    Height          =       375
    Index           =       4
    Left            =       4200
    TabIndex        =       11
    Top             =       840
    Width           =       3015
End
Begin Label Label1
    BackColor       =       &H00C0C0C0&
    BackStyle       =       0    'Transparent
    Caption         =       "VB"
    FontBold        =       -1   'True
    FontItalic      =       0    'False
```

```
        FontName           =      "Arial"
        FontSize           =      45
        FontStrikethru     =      0      'False
        FontUnderline      =      0      'False
        ForeColor          =      &H00400000&
        Height             =      855
        Index              =      3
        Left               =      4200
        TabIndex           =      10
        Top                =      0
        Width              =      1215
     End
     Begin Label Label1
        AutoSize           =      -1     'True
        BackColor          =      &H00C0C0C0&
        Caption            =      "&Code:"
        Height             =      195
        Index              =      2
        Left               =      120
        TabIndex           =      6
        Top                =      3720
        Width              =      1095
        WordWrap           =      -1     'True
     End
     Begin Label Label1
        AutoSize           =      -1     'True
        BackColor          =      &H00C0C0C0&
        Caption            =      "Descri&ption:"
        Height             =      195
        Index              =      1
        Left               =      120
        TabIndex           =      2
        Top                =      1030
        Width              =      1095
        WordWrap           =      -1     'True
     End
     Begin Label Label1
        AutoSize           =      -1     'True
        BackColor          =      &H00C0C0C0&
        Caption            =      "&Title:"
        Height             =      195
        Index              =      0
        Left               =      120
        TabIndex           =      0
        Top                =      310
        Width              =      450
     End
  End
End
```

LISTING

ADDFORM.FRM CODE LISTING

```
' * * * * * * * * * * * * * * *
' ADDFORM.FRM Code Listing
' * * * * * * * * * * * * * * *
'Copyright (c) 1993, Paul Bonner
'PC Magazine Visual Basic Utilities
DefInt A-Z
Option Explicit

Sub Command1_Click (Index As Integer)
' * * * * * * * * * * * * *
'If OK button pushed
'Select next action based on result
'of SaveNewRoutine() function
' * * * * * * * * * * * * *
If Index = 0 Then
   Select Case SaveNewRoutine()
   Case Is = False     'Nothing to save--do nothing
   Case Is = True      'Routine was saved--select
                       'it in Title listbox
      SelectForm.Titles.Clear
      GetFiles
      If SelectForm.Titles.ListCount Then
      SelectForm.Titles.ListIndex=SelectForm.Titles.NewIndex
      End If
Case Is = 1           'Routine needs a title--so exit
  Exit Sub
End Select
End If
Unload AddForm        'Return to SelectForm
End Sub


Function SaveNewRoutine () As Integer
Dim F, C$, X, Header$
' * * * * * * * * * * * * *
'Make sure there's something to save
' * * * * * * * * * * * * *
If Text1(0) + Text1(1) + Text1(2) + Text1(3) = "" Then
   SaveNewRoutine = False
   Exit Function
End If
' * * * * * * * * * * * * *
'Make sure the routine is titled
' * * * * * * * * * * * * *
If Text1(0) = "" Then
   MsgBox "Please give this routine a title!"
   SaveNewRoutine = 1
   Exit Function
End If
' * * * * * * * * * * * * *
'Save Title
' * * * * * * * * * * * * *
F = FreeFile
Open Path$ + "Lib1.IDX" For Output Access Write As #F
C$ = Trim(Str$(RecCounter + 1))
```

```
Print #F, C$
For X = 1 To RecCounter
    Print #F, Routines(X)
Next
Print #F, Text1(0)
Close F
' * * * * * * * * * * * *
'Append Description, Declarations and Code
' * * * * * * * * * * *
If RecCounter > 0 Then FileCopy Path$ + "LIBCODE.ASC", Path$ + "CODEFILE.TMP"
F = FreeFile
Open Path$ + "CODEFILE.TMP" For Append As #F
Header$ = "[" & RecCounter + 1 & "]"
Print #F, Header$
Print #F, Text1(1)        'Write Title
Print #F, CodeStart$
If Text1(3) <> "" Then    'Write Declarations
    Print #F, "'Declares for " & Text1(0)
    Print #F, Text1(3)
    Print #F, CRLF$
End If
Print #F, Text1(2)        'Write Code
Print #F, CodeEnd$
Close F
CleanUpFiles
SaveNewRoutine = True
End Function
```

LISTING

LIBCODE.BAS

```
' * * * * * * * * * * * * *
' LIBCODE.BAS Code Listing
' * * * * * * * * * * * * *
'Copyright (c) 1993, Paul Bonner
'PC Magazine Visual Basic Utilities
DefInt A-Z
Option Explicit
Global Routines() As String    'array of routine names
Global Path$                   'application path
Global OldChoice As Integer    'previously selected routine
Global OldChoiceChanged As Integer 'flags change in current record
Global RecCounter As Integer   'tracks number of records
Global CRLF$                   'carriage return/line feed holder
Global Const CodeStart$ = "[Code]"  'used in LIBCODE.ASC to separate ⇔
    description and code
Global Const CodeEnd$ = "[Stop]"    'end of code marker for LIBCODE.ASC
' * * * * * * * * * * * * *
'Module level variables used in file-handling routines
' * * * * * * * * * * * * *
Dim F As Integer               'file handle
Dim J As Integer               'file handle
Dim RecordNum As Integer       'identifies current record
```

```
Sub CenterDialog (TopForm As Form, BottomForm As Form)
Dim L, T
' * * * * * * * * * * * * *
'Routine to center one form on top of another
' * * * * * * * * * * * * *
L = BottomForm.Left + (BottomForm.Width - TopForm.Width) / 2
If L + TopForm.Width > Screen.Width Then L = Screen.Width - TopForm.Width
If L < 0 Then L = 0
TopForm.Left = L
T = BottomForm.Top + (BottomForm.Height - TopForm.Height) / 2
If T + TopForm.Height > Screen.Height Then T = Screen.Height - TopForm.Height
If T < 0 Then T = 0
TopForm.Top = T
End Sub

Sub CenterForm (F As Form)
' * * * * * * * * * * * * *
'Routine to center a form on screen
' * * * * * * * * * * * * *
F.Left = (Screen.Width - F.Width) / 2
F.Top = (Screen.Height - F.Height) / 2
End Sub

Sub Check_Changes ()
Dim SaveIt%
' * * * * * * * * * * * * *
'If current record has changed and the listbox isn't empty
'give user a chance to save the file
' * * * * * * * * * * * * *
If OldChoiceChanged And SelectForm.Titles.ListCount <> 0 Then
  SaveIt% = MsgBox("Save changes to current entry?", 68, "VB Code Librarian")
    If SaveIt% = 6 Then LibSave      'User clicked Yes button, so save it
    OldChoiceChanged = False
End If
End Sub

Sub CleanUpFiles ()
Dim X%
' * * * * * * * * * * * * *
'Kill old backups
'Backup current files
'Make temp files current
' * * * * * * * * * * * * *
On Error Resume Next
Kill Path$ + "LibIdx.Bak"
Kill Path$ + "LibCode.Bak"
Name Path$ + "Lib.IDX" As Path$ + "LibIdx.Bak"
Name Path$ + "LibCode.Asc" As Path$ + "LibCode.Bak"
Name Path$ + "Lib1.IDX" As Path$ + "Lib.IDX"
Name Path$ + "CodeFile.Tmp" As Path$ + "LibCode.Asc"
X% = DoEvents()
End Sub

Sub CopyOldRec ()
Dim Look$, C$
' * * * * * * * * * * * * *
'Used to copy old contents of record to new file
' * * * * * * * * * * * * *
Look$ = "[" & RecordNum & "]"
' * * * * * * * * * * * * *
'Find index tag
' * * * * * * * * * * * * *
Do While C$ <> Look$
    Input #J, C$
```

```
Loop
' * * * * * * * * * * * *
'Read and copy old Description and Code
' * * * * * * * * * * * *
On Error GoTo ErrStop
Line Input #J, C$
Do While C$ <> CodeEnd$
    Print #F, C$
    Line Input #J, C$
Loop
' * * * * * * * * * * * *
'Backdoor for error-handling routine
' * * * * * * * * * * * *
ErrDoor:
' * * * * * * * * * * * *
'Add [Stop] tag at end of code
' * * * * * * * * * * * *
Print #F, CodeEnd$
Exit Sub


' * * * * * * * * * * * *
'Error-handling routine
' * * * * * * * * * * * *
ErrStop:
Resume ErrDoor
End Sub

Sub DeleteRoutine ()
Dim X, Index, C$, Header$
' * * * * * * * * * * * *
'Exit if Titles listbox is empty
' * * * * * * * * * * * *
If SelectForm.Titles.ListCount = 0 Then Exit Sub
' * * * * * * * * * * * *
'Confirm user wants to delete
' * * * * * * * * * * * *
X = MsgBox("Are you sure that you want to delete the selected routine?", 68, ⇔
     "VB Code Librarian")
If X <> 6 Then Exit Sub
' * * * * * * * * * * * *
'Identify record to delete
' * * * * * * * * * * * *
Index = SelectForm.Titles.ItemData (SelectForm.Titles.ListIndex)
' * * * * * * * * * * * *
'Save titles
' * * * * * * * * * * * *
F = FreeFile
Open Path$ + "Lib1.IDX" For Output Access Write As #F Len = 4096
' * * * * * * * * * * * *
'Decrease record counter by one
' * * * * * * * * * * * *
C$ = Trim(Str$(RecCounter - 1))
Print #F, C$
' * * * * * * * * * * * *
'Write out all titles except deleted one
' * * * * * * * * * * * *
For X = 1 To RecCounter
  If X <> Index Then Print #F, Routines(X)
Next
Close F
' * * * * * * * * * * * *
'Open input and output files for
'descriptions and code
' * * * * * * * * * * * *
```

```
F = FreeFile
Open Path$ + "CODEFILE.TMP" For Output Access Write As #F Len = 4096
J = FreeFile
Open Path$ + "LIBCODE.ASC" For Input As #J
' * * * * * * * * * * * *
'Loop through all records
'Save all except the deleted record
'Decrease the index number for all
'records above the current record.
' * * * * * * * * * * * *
For RecordNum = 1 To RecCounter
Select Case RecordNum
Case Is < Index
  Header$ = "[" & RecordNum & "]"
  Print #F, Header$
  CopyOldRec
Case Is = Index          'Deleted record, do nothing
Case Is > Index
  Header$ = "[" & RecordNum - 1 & "]"
  Print #F, Header$
  CopyOldRec
End Select
Next RecordNum
Close F
Close J
' * * * * * * * * * * * *
'Now clean up files
' * * * * * * * * * * * *
CleanUpFiles
' * * * * * * * * * * * *
'Clear titles listbox, repopulate, and select first item
' * * * * * * * * * * * *
SelectForm.Titles.Clear
GetFiles
If SelectForm.Titles.ListCount Then SelectForm.Titles.ListIndex = 0
End Sub

Sub GetFiles ()
Dim C$, X, Y
' * * * * * * * * * * * *
'Open Titles file
' * * * * * * * * * * * *
F = FreeFile
On Error GoTo IDXNotFound
Open Path$ + "Lib.IDX" For Input As F
' * * * * * * * * * * * *
'Input total records
' * * * * * * * * * * * *
Input #F, C$
RecCounter = Val(C$)
' * * * * * * * * * * * *
'Redimension Routines() array to hold
'titles of all records
' * * * * * * * * * * * *
ReDim Routines(RecCounter)
' * * * * * * * * * * * *
'Read record titles
' * * * * * * * * * * * *
For X = 1 To RecCounter
    Input #F, Routines(X)
' * * * * * * * * * * * *
'Add title to listbox, with BigTab$ and RecordNum appended
' * * * * * * * * * * * *
  SelectForm.Titles.AddItem Routines(X) '+ BigTab$ & X
```

```
   SelectForm.Titles.ItemData(SelectForm.Titles.NewIndex) = X
Next
Close F
BackDoor:
Exit Sub
' * * * * * * * * * * * *
'Error-handling routine
'Give user chance to create a new
'index file if error trying to read old one
' * * * * * * * * * * * *
IDXNotFound:
Y = MsgBox(Path$ + "LIB.IDX Not Found. Create new library?", 20, "VB Code ⇔
    Librarian")
If Y <> 6 Then End
RecCounter = 0
Resume BackDoor
End Sub

Sub LibSave ()
Dim Index, Header$
' * * * * * * * * * * * *
'Create LIB1.IDX so that CleanUpFiles doesn't clobber index
' * * * * * * * * * * * *
Name Path$ + "Lib.IDX" As Path$ + "Lib1.IDX"
' * * * * * * * * * * * *
'Determine which record has been changed
' * * * * * * * * * * * *
Index = SelectForm.Titles.ItemData(OldChoice)
' * * * * * * * * * * * *
'Save Descriptions & Code
' * * * * * * * * * * * *
F = FreeFile
Open Path$ + "CodeFile.Tmp" For Output Access Write As #F Len = 4096
J = FreeFile
Open Path$ + "LibCode.Asc" For Input As #J
For RecordNum = 1 To RecCounter
    Header$ = "[" & RecordNum & "]"
    Print #F, Header$
' * * * * * * * * * * * *
'If RecordNum=the changed record, save the changed data
'otherwise copy the old data for this record
' * * * * * * * * * * * *
    If RecordNum = Index Then
        Print #F, SelectForm.Description.Text
        Print #F, CodeStart$
        Print #F, SelectForm.Code.Text
        Print #F, CodeEnd$
    Else
        CopyOldRec
    End If
Next RecordNum
Close J
Close F
' * * * * * * * * * * * *
'Now clean up files
' * * * * * * * * * * * *
Clean UpFiles
End Sub
```

2

TITLE BAR CLOCK

Title Bar Clock puts the current time and date on the title bar of the active Windows application,

updating it each minute.

I t isn't difficult for your PC to supply you with the current date and time. Along with everything else that it does in the course of an average workday, a PC maintains a constant check on the current time and date. It might not be as accurate as a fine Rolex (or even a cheap Swatch, for that matter), but it does always have at least some notion of the time and date, and

it maintains that awareness without detracting at all from its capability to perform other tasks.

Unfortunately, getting a PC to share that knowledge without disrupting its other activities is difficult—even from within a multitasking environment like Windows. Sure, you can open up a DOS window and type **TIME** and **DATE** at the command line, but the answers you'll get are snapshots—the time and date at the moment you typed those commands—not a constantly updating display.

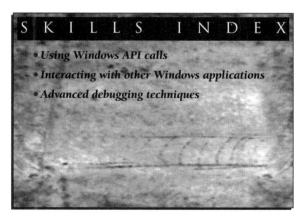

SKILLS INDEX

- *Using Windows API calls*
- *Interacting with other Windows applications*
- *Advanced debugging techniques*

Within Windows itself, you can run the Clock accessory to obtain an ongoing report of the time and date. But in many ways the Clock accessory is an unsatisfactory timepiece. You certainly don't want to run it as a full-screen application; PCs remain a bit expensive for full-time use as desk clocks. You can run it as an icon, but all too frequently another application ends up obscuring the clock at exactly those moments when you want to check the time or date, so you still have to interrupt what you're doing to bring the Clock icon or window to the foreground.

Version 3.1 of Clock, which shipped with Windows 3.1, was improved by the addition of an "Always on Top" menu item which, when selected, keeps the Clock window on top of all other open windows, even that of the active application. This provides a big boost to Clock's usefulness, because it means that the time and date are always available to you at a glance, as shown in Figure 2.1. Nevertheless, it is not a perfect solution. Always on Top windows can be annoying, since they usually obscure part of the active application's screen.

FIGURE 2.1

The Clock accessory's Always On Top mode makes it more useful, but also can be annoying when it obscures vital screen information.

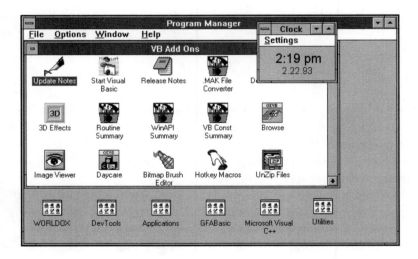

One way to eliminate that annoying aspect of Clock's Always on Top mode is to reduce the size of its window until it is not much thicker than a menu bar, and then move it over an empty part of the active application's menu bar and title bar. This ensures that the time display doesn't obscure any part of the screen that you need to see. Unfortunately, unless you run every application in full-screen mode, as soon as you switch to another application you'll probably have to reposition, and perhaps also resize, the Clock to make it as unobtrusive in the active application as it was in the former one.

Although positioning the Clock accessory above the menu and title bar areas of another application's window isn't an entirely satisfactory solution, it did start me on the path of finding a more ideal one, by reminding me of a public-domain utility for the Macintosh that I had seen once or twice. This utility maintained a constant display of the current time on the Macintosh's menu bar. That kind of thing is possible on the Macintosh because there is only one menu bar no matter how many applications are running or how large the dimensions of the screen. The application with the input focus simply takes over and modifies the Macintosh's System menu bar (which starts at the top left corner of the screen and stretches across the screen). In contrast, each Windows application creates its own menu bar, and it is not uncommon to have multiple menu bars visible on-screen at once, even though only one application has the input focus.

As I recalled this Macintosh utility, I began to wonder if something similar might not be possible under Windows. Specifically, I wondered whether a Visual Basic application could periodically get control and add a display of the current time and date to the menu bar or title bar of the active application. It certainly seemed possible that a combination of a timer control and calls to the Windows API functions could be used to obtain and modify the title bar caption. I didn't know, however, whether a utility like this could be made reliable enough and fast enough to avoid destablizing Windows or degrading the overall system performance. As demonstrated by Title Bar Clock, the utility presented in this chapter, the answer is yes.

■ USING TITLE BAR CLOCK

Title Bar Clock boasts about as simple a user interface as is possible for a Windows application. It launches as a minimized window, so that it appears as an icon at the bottom of the screen, and immediately starts doing its thing—displaying the current date and time in the title bar of the main window of whatever application is active, as shown by Figure 2.2.

When you activate another application, Title Bar Clock removes the time and date display from the caption of the window on which it had been displayed, and adds it to the main window of the newly activated application.

If you double-click on Title Bar Clock's icon to open up its window, it temporarily stops its title bar modifications, and instead displays the time and date centered on its own window, as shown in Figure 2.3. The window is resizable, and the time and date display will remain centered on it no matter how large or small you make it. Minimize Title Bar Clock again, and it returns to the task of keeping the time and date displayed on the active window's title bar.

FIGURE 2.2

Title Bar Clock, visible in icon form at the lower-left of the screen, maintains a display of the time and date on the active window's title bar.

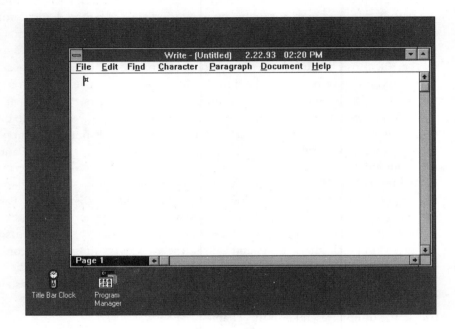

That is about the limit of Title Bar Clock's user-interface and function set. The only other thing you can do with it is shut it down, by selecting the Close item on its Control menu.

■ INSIDE TITLE BAR CLOCK

The first decision I made upon beginning the Title Bar Clock project was to have it display the time and date on the active window's title bar rather than on its menu bar, as was the case with the Macintosh utility which inspired this project.

There were several reasons for this. For one thing, displaying the time and date on the menu bar would have been inappropriate to the menu bar's purpose as a user-interface element. Menu bar items should do something. When selected, they should either launch an action (in which case an exclamation point should be appended to the end of the menu item's text), or, more commonly, they should reveal a drop-down menu.

FIGURE 2.3

When you open Title Bar Clock's window it becomes a run-of-the-mill clock application, discontinuing its title bar manipulations until you minimize it again.

In addition, and perhaps more importantly, adding the time and date to the menu bar as false menu items would have consumed more system resources than simply modifying the title bar text. Windows must track every item on a menu bar and be prepared to react to the user's selection of any item and, to do so, it devotes some of its system resource memory to this task, whereas title bar text is treated as a static string that requires no significant resources to maintain.

Finally, use of the menu bar would have had unseemly effects with applications whose menu bars are already quite long. In many cases, appending the time and date as new items to the end of the menu bar would cause the menu bar to wrap to a second bar (as it does if you make any application's window narrower than the width of its menu bar). I personally detest working with wrapped menu bars; I consider them to be ugly, difficult to use, and wasteful of screen real estate, so I certainly didn't want to write a utility which would cause them to appear more often.

Putting the time and date on the title bar allowed me to avoid all these problems. I could simply append the time and date to the current text of the active window's title bar, avoiding any user-interface confusion, waste of system resources, or unnecessary wrapping of the menu bar.

Of course, no matter which location I chose, I knew I had to go considerably beyond the limits of Visual Basic's internal command set to make Title Bar Clock work. Visual Basic's internal command set allows an application to control the appearance and contents of its own title bar and menu bar, but not those of any other application. To manipulate either the title bar or menu bars of another application, you've got to make calls to the Windows API (application programming interface), using Visual Basic's Declare statement to identify the API functions or subroutines that will be used in your application.

■ Three Little API Calls

Some research into the Windows API (for more information about using the Windows API, see the Endnote, "Windows API Functions") allowed me to identify three functions which form the functional core of Title Bar Clock: GetActiveWindow, GetWindowText, and SetWindowText. The GetActiveWindow function returns the handle of the active window (the window that has the input focus), while GetWindowText returns the caption of a specified window, and SetWindowText sets a specified window's title bar caption to a specified string.

With these functions in hand, the heart of Title Bar Clock's workings became clear: To maintain a display of the current time and date on the caption of the active window's application, Title Bar Clock periodically would have to call GetActiveWindow to identify the active window, then use the handle returned by that call to call GetWindowText, and finally append the time and date (as returned by Visual Basic's Now( ) function) to the string returned by that function and pass them, along with the handle returned by GetActiveWindow, to SetWindowText. A standard timer control could easily provide the periodicity required, so it appeared that the project would be child's play to program.

Thus, I thought my code would look something like this:

```
Sub Timer1_Timer
wHand%=GetActiveWindow()
T%=GetWindowText(wHand%, OldText$, 72)
NewText$=OldText$+Spacer$+Format(Now, "ShortDate") ⟺
    + Spacer$ + Format(Now, "hh:mm am/pm")
T%=SetWindowText(wHand%, NewText$)
End Sub
```

Of course, I knew that I would have to dimension *OldText$* in advance as a fixed-length string, because any string that you pass to an API routine for modification must be of fixed length, and fill *Spacer$* with several spaces so that the time and date would be visibly separate from each other and from the original window caption. I

then decided that an appropriate interval for the timer would be about 500 ms, giving the timer routine the opportunity to execute twice a second.

In addition, I realized that if Title Bar Clock had already placed a time and date in
the caption, it would have to strip the old time and date before adding the new time
and date. Otherwise, the caption would simply get longer and longer each time the
routine was performed. It also made sense to only update the title bar if the caption
that the routine was going to put there had changed since the last time the routine
was performed.

The first problem was easy to solve. I simply added a string called *FakeSpace$*,
which holds a single *CHR$(160)*, to the definition of the string *NewText$*, inserting it
immediately before the first *Spacer$*, so that the statement assigning *NewText$*'s value
now read:

```
NewText$=OldText$ + FakeSpace$ + Spacer$ +... etc., etc.
```

CHR$(160) is a space with its high order bit set (32 + 128). It looks just like a
space on-screen, but easily can be detected as distinct from a standard space, which
is defined as *CHR$(32)*, by using the ASC or INSTR functions in Visual Basic. In addi-
tion, it is very unlikely to be found in a window caption unless Title Bar Clock puts it
there. Thus, Title Bar Clock is able to strip off the old time and date display from the
window title as follows:

```
I%=Instr(OldText$,FakeSpace)
If I% Then OldText$=Left$(OldText$,I%-1)
```

Then, once Title Bar Clock defined *NewText$* to include the time and date, I added
the following check to ensure that the new caption wasn't identical to the old one before calling the SetWindowText function.

```
If NewText$<>OldText$ Then SetWindowText WinHand%,NewText$
```

Finally, when a different window is made active, Title Bar Clock must strip the
time and date display from the caption of the previous window before adding it to
the new window's title bar. To do so, I created a variable called *OldwHandle%* to keep
track of the active window from timer event to timer event. If the handle returned by
the GetActiveWindow function isn't equal to *OldwHandle%*, Title Bar Clock resets the
caption of the *OldwHandle%* window by looking for *FakeSpace$* and stripping it and
everything that follows it from the caption. Then it resets the value of *OldwHandle%*
to point to the handle returned by GetActiveWindow, and adds the time and date to
the new window's title bar.

The statements we've been discussing compose the functional heart of Title Bar Clock. And, in fact, if I hadn't encountered any surprises along the way, they would have been sufficient to handle its primary chore of displaying the time and date on the title bar of the active window. But, as it turned out, there were a few unexpected complications. Some of these arose from decisions that I made about how I wanted Title Bar Clock to work, and others were required to overcome some inconsistencies in the way that various applications create and maintain their windows. Both varieties are worthy of discussion.

■ Time Out for Aesthetics

Initially, I planned to have Title Bar Clock display the current time down to the second, and update its display each second. But as I experimented with early prototypes of the utility, I discovered that while it was well within the realm of possibility to update the time each second without imposing a performance penalty on other applications, the result was not aesthetically pleasing. The title bar would seem to flicker as its caption was rewritten once a second to display the current time. I decided to forgo the seconds part of the display, so that the utility would only update the title bar caption once per minute, eliminating the annoying flicker.

(Should you desire to have Title Bar Clock display seconds as well as minutes and hours, you can do so very simply by modifying a single line in the FixTitle routine.

The line currently reads:

```
NewText$ = NewText$ + FakeSpace$ + Spacer$ + Format(Now, "Short Date") + ⇔
    Spacer$ + Format(Now, "hh:mm am/pm")
```

Changing the *hh:mm am/pm* to *hh:mm:ss am/pm* will force Title Bar Clock to display the current second along with the hour and minutes.)

I also found another aesthetic flaw associated with Title Bar Clock's use of GetActiveWindow. The time-date display moved constantly to whatever little window or dialog box momentarily gained the input focus. For instance, if an application opened a dialog box, which popped up another dialog box which in turn generated yet another dialog box, the time-date display would continue to move to whichever dialog box had the input focus. This proved almost as annoying as the flicker that had been caused by updating the time display every second. I wanted Title Bar Clock to be as unobtrusive as it was useful and, to me, the best way to make it unobtrusive was to leave its time-date display in the title bar of the application's main window, rather than moving it to whatever child window or dialog box happened to gain the input focus for a second or two.

■ **Parents and Children**

For Title Bar Clock to ignore pop-up windows and dialog boxes, it had to know a little bit about the way that Windows applications create windows.

In general, every Windows application has one top-level window that can claim ownership for all the other windows created by that application. When the top-level window is closed, all the windows that it owns should also close, and the application's execution terminate.

A top-level window can own many windows, consisting of everything from simple message boxes to complex dialog boxes to MDI (multiple-document-interface) child windows. The top-level window is the *parent* of all the windows that it owns directly, and those windows are referred to as its children. In addition, a child of the top-level window may itself have one or more child windows, which may in turn have child windows themselves.

I wanted Title Bar Clock to ignore all child windows and maintain its display of the time and date on the active application's top-level window. To do so, the utility had to be capable of determining whether the window identified by the GetActiveWindow call (the active window) was itself a top-level window, and, if not, to identify the top-level window to which the active window belonged.

To achieve this, I chose the GetParent function, which returns a 0 if the specified window has no parent, or if it does have one, returns the handle of its parent.

The call to GetParent is very simple. You need merely supply it with the handle of the window whose parent you wish to identify. So, to identify the parent of the active window, you can use the following code:

```
WinHand%=GetActiveWindow()
Parent% = GetParent(WinHand%)
```

Of course, a single call to GetParent isn't always sufficient for Title Bar Clock's purpose. Because the parent of the active window might itself be a child of the top-level window, or even of another child window, Title Bar Clock must identify the top-level window, the parent of all parents for an application. Doing so would be simple with most Windows development tools; by using a combination of the EnumWindows and EnumChildWindows Windows API functions you could easily identify the top-level window. However, both functions use a call-back procedure, a Windows facility which is not normally available from within Visual Basic. Therefore, Title Bar Clock has to determine the top-level window in a different way. It does so by means of a simple DO LOOP that makes multiple calls to GetParent until the function returns a value of 0, indicating that the specified window has no parent and thus, presumably, is the top-level window for the application. The code for this follows:

```
Parent% = GetParent(WinHand%)
Do While Parent%
OldParent% = Parent%
Parent% = GetParent%(OldParent%)
Loop
If Parent% Then OldParent%=Parent%
```

Once the loop has been completed, the variable *OldParent%* should contain the handle of the active application's top-level window. This routine isn't infallible. Some applications which utilize highly non-structured ways of structuring windows can fool it. But it does succeed in the vast majority of cases, and doesn't reduce system stability even in those cases when it doesn't succeed.

■ Exception Handling

Once I had determined how Title Bar Clock could identify the top-level window, I thought that I had a straight run to the finish line in front of me, since it appeared that Title Bar Clock could add the date and time to the active window's caption with just a few lines of code. However, with the help of some spectacular crashes that not only brought Title Bar Clock to a halt but also crashed Windows, I soon discovered that the situation was a little more complex than that.

It became apparent that for every rule about how windows are created, there are at least a few major applications that violate it. In some cases, an application's top-level window will be a captionless one, and, as I learned from the aforementioned crashes, Windows doesn't react at all well to the use of SetWindowText with such a window. In fact, it misbehaves in a most insidious way. Instead of crashing immediately, it posts a General Protection Fault message box, citing the application whose caption Title Bar Clock was trying to modify as the offending application, and giving you the option of ignoring the error or closing the application. If you decided to ignore the error, Windows functions normally until you attempt to close the application cited in the error box—at which point Windows crashes to the DOS prompt without so much as a fare-thee-well. Obviously, this was a problem that had to be solved.

In other cases, an application's top-level window will be invisible, and thus there is no benefit to be gained from attempting to modify its caption. Instead, Title Bar Clock has to recognize this and instead change the title of the window's first visible child.

Finally, there is Visual Basic, which violates more of the standard window-handling procedures than any other application I've encountered. For one thing, the real top-level window in the Visual Basic development environment is invisible, and the window that you might think is the top-level window—the one that's captioned "Microsoft Visual Basic (design)" and which contains Visual Basic's menu bar, Control menu, and minimize and maximize buttons—isn't the parent of any of the other windows. Meanwhile, each form in a compiled Visual Basic application (except, thank goodness, for MDI child forms), is an independent, parentless window, with no apparent relation to any other form used by the application. So, for example, if your application uses a modal pop-up custom dialog box, the dialog box is for all intents and purposes a top-level window; it has no parent, and there is no way to neatly identify the window above which it has appeared as an application's true top-level window.

Once I figured out what was going on in each of these cases, I was able to add safety checks or workarounds to the routine that Title Bar Clock uses to modify the top-level window's caption—at least, in every case except for that of compiled Visual Basic applications, where I was never able to find a way to trace the parentage of the windows they create back to a visible top-level window. As a result, Title Bar Clock adds the time and date to the caption of whatever window is active in a compiled Visual Basic application.

The hard part was figuring out what was causing the problems. At first all I knew was that my early prototypes of Title Bar Clock weren't always performing as I expected. Windows crashed every time I tried to load Lotus Notes with Title Bar Clock running in the background and, despite the attempts Title Bar Clock made to identify the top-level window, the time and date appeared on whatever window had the input focus in the Visual Basic development environment, rather than on its main window.

Since Title Bar Clock was relying on the GetParent( ) Windows API function to identify the top-level window, I began to suspect that the problems it was encountering had to do with window parentage. I knew that many Windows applications make use of invisible windows, and it seemed possible that this might be the source of the problem if GetParent was returning a pointer to an invisible window.

The problem was how to test that suspicion. I needed more information about the window hierarchy of the applications that were causing problems with Title Bar Clock, and it wasn't easy to find. You won't find a family tree of all the windows used by an application in its documentation, and there is obviously no visible evidence of invisible windows.

I decided that the only way out was to write a little utility to obtain the needed information. The result, which I call Window Info, simply reports the handle, caption, and classname of the window under the mouse cursor, its immediate parent (if any), and its progenitor (the parent of all its parents), as shown in Figure 2.4. I won't spend a lot of time discussing Window Info here, because I'm not sure that it has any use beyond debugging Title Bar Clock, but for additional information about the Window Info utility, see the Endnote, "Window Info.")

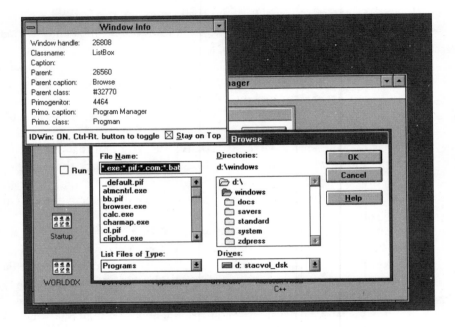

FIGURE 2.4

The Window Info utility, included on the accompanying disk, provided useful information during the process of debugging Title Bar Clock.

The information provided by Window Info turned out to be exactly the information that I needed to debug Title Bar Clock. Sure enough, when I used it to explore the window hierarchy of the applications that were causing problems for Title Bar Clock, it began to identify invisible, captionless windows as the parents or progenitors of the visible windows.

■ Handling Phantoms

Having discovered the source of the problem—the presence of invisible, captionless, top-level windows—I realized that I would have to add code to handle it. Once again, I turned to the Windows API, in which I found a function to address each of the problems: IsWindowVisible, (which returns a value of *True* if the specified window is visible or *False* if it is not), and GetWindowTextLength (which returns the number of characters in the specified window's caption).

I incorporated these functions into a few lines of code that execute immediately after the code that identifies the active window's top-level parent. If a parent has been identified, its handle will have been stored in the variable *OldParent%*. These lines check to make sure that *OldParent%* is visible and that it has a caption. If so, the variable *WinHand%*, which is used to identify the target window, is reset to equal the value of *OldParent%*, so that *WinHand%* now points to the top-level window. Otherwise, *WinHand%* is unchanged.

```
If OldParent% Then
IfGetWindowTextLength(OldParent%)<>FalseAndIsWindowVisible(OldParent%)<>⇔
    False Then WinHand% = OldParent%
End If
```

■ The Visual Basic Kludge

The workaround just discussed solved the problems that caused Title Bar Clock to crash with applications that have hidden or captionless top-level windows, but it didn't completely eliminate the problems it was encountering with the Visual Basic development environment. In fact, since the top-level development environment window is invisible (and captionless, too), this little workaround merely ensured that the time and date display would continue to pop up on whatever Visual Basic development environment window was active: the project window, a form under construction, a code window, the Debug window, and so on.

Since the Visual Basic development environment was the only application I found that encountered this problem when used with Title Bar Clock, and since I wanted to use the two together, I decided that the solution was to include a special-case code that would treat the Visual Basic development environment differently than any other application. In other words, a kludge.

I wanted this little kludge to substitute the handle of the main development environment window (the window that includes the Visual Basic title bar and menu) for that of any other window that was created by the Visual Basic development environment. To do so, Title Bar Clock had to (1) determine whether the Visual Basic development environment was running, (2) determine if the active window was created by the development environment, and if so, (3) substitute the handle of the main Visual Basic window for that of the active window before proceeding to add the time and date to its caption.

Step 1 was simple, thanks to the Windows API function FindWindow. FindWindow accepts two parameters, the class name of the window being sought, and its caption. (Before a Windows application can create a new window it must define its window class—a set of attributes describing the appearance and behavior of the window. The class name is among those attributes). You have the option of passing FindWindow both the class name and caption parameters or either one alone, in which case you must pass a null value (0&) for the other parameter. Now, as demonstrated by Title Bar Clock, captions can change, so passing a specific caption to FindWindow, which only works if it finds an exact match, is not particularly effective. However, a window's class name doesn't change, so as long as you know the class name of the window that you're trying to find, FindWindow should always be able to locate it.

Ah, but there's the rub. How do you find a window's class name? The Windows API has a GetClassName function, but it requires the window's handle as a parameter. If Title Bar Clock already had the handle, it wouldn't need the class name. Here again, my little Window Info utility came in handy. Because it reports the handle and class name of any window that the mouse cursor passes over, I was able to use it to determine the class name of the main development environment window, which turned out to be *wndclass_desked_gsk*. Since a window's class name never changes (unlike its handle, which Windows assigns on the fly as the window is created), there was no need for Title Bar Clock to attempt to determine the main development window's class name at runtime; instead, I was able to hard code it into the application.

Once I had learned the class name of the development environment window, I could use FindWindow to determine its handle, completing Step 1.

The next step, determining if the active window was created by the Visual Basic development environment, uses two more API calls: GetWindowWord and GetModule-FileName. GetWindowWord can be used to retrieve a variety of information about a given window. Title Bar Clock uses it to determine the active window's instance handle, which identifies the application which registered the window's window class. Next, Title Bar Clock calls GetModuleFileName, passing it the window's instance handle, to determine the DOS file name of the application which created the active window.

Step 2 of Title Bar Clock's kludge for the Visual Basic development environment concludes by determining whether the string returned by GetModuleFileName contains "VB.EXE," which would indicate that the active window was indeed created by the Visual Basic development environment. If so, then Title Bar Clock performs Step 3, substituting the handle of the main development environment window (as returned by the call to FindWindow) for the handle of the active window.

The code for the development environment workaround looks like this:

```
VBEnv% = FindWindow("wndclass_desked_gsk", 0&)
If VBEnv% Then
  GW% = GetWindowWord(WinHand%, GWW_HINSTANCE)
```

```
  MF% = GetModuleFileName(GW%, OldText, 72)
  If InStr(OldText, "VB.EXE") Then OldParent% = VBEnv%
End If
```

I elected to have Title Bar Clock call FindWindow at every timer event, and only call the GetWindowWord/GetModuleFileName sequence if FindWindow returned a handle for the development environment window, because a pair of timing loops that I used to test the procedure indicated that the former method was marginally faster. (1,000 repetitions of the FindWindow function takes about .44 seconds on my 80386-based PC, compared to about .55 seconds for the other sequence.)

All in all, the Visual Basic workaround looks simple when you reduce it to a half dozen lines of code, but it took a good while to write. I initially tried a different approach—thinking that I could compare the class name of the active window to that used by the Visual Basic development environment to designate screen forms, but my Window Info utility revealed that the class names of windows created by Visual Basic (ThunderForm) don't change when they're compiled. In other words, both the run-time version and the development version of a Visual Basic form have the "Thunder-Form" class name, so if I excluded all windows with that class name from Title Bar Clock's ministrations, it would not work with any application produced by Visual Basic. Or, if I had specified that Title Bar Clock should automatically affix the time and date to the development environment main window if the active window was of the ThunderForm class, then it would do so even if the active window belonged to a compiled Visual Basic application. I wanted the workaround to come into play only if the active window was actually created by the development environment, and the GetModuleFileName method described above was the only way to do so.

■ Assembling the Pieces

In the course of adding the safety checks and workarounds that I've described to Title Bar Clock, I pulled most of the actual title bar manipulation routines out of the Timer event and put them in a subroutine called FixTitle. This enabled me to use the same block of code for two purposes: to strip the time-date display from a no-longer-active window, and to affix it to an active window. This was accomplished simply by having the Timer event call FixTitle with two parameters: the handle of the window whose caption is to be manipulated, and a True/False flag indicating whether the time and date is to be added to the window's caption.

The five-hundred-millisecond timer interval allows Title Bar Clock to keep up with even the most frantic window-switching. However, the low priority of timer events also creates the possibility that the target window may be destroyed in the interval between the Timer event's call to GetActiveWindow and the FixTitle routine's attempt to modify its caption. This could result in FixTitle attempting to add or remove the time or date to the caption of a window which no longer exists, an instruction that Windows might find indigestible. To eliminate this problem, I chose to precede the title bar manipulation sequence with a call to the Windows API function IsWindow, which indicates whether a given window handle is valid. IsWindow returns a value of zero (or False) if the handle isn't valid, so Title Bar Clock only proceeds with its title bar manipulation when IsWindow returns a value other than False.

■ SCREEN FORM DESIGN

Given the simple nature of Title Bar Clock's user interface, its form design was equally simple. Title Bar Clock uses only a single form, named VBClockForm, containing one timer control (Timer1) and two labels (Label1 and Label2). The timer control is enabled at startup, with an interval of 500 ms, and the autosize property of both labels is set to True.

ENDNOTE

PC CLOCK ACCURACY

There's one problem with displaying the time and date that Title Bar Clock can't solve: Your PC is a lousy timepiece. The internal clocks of most PCs gain or lose several seconds per day. As the months and years go by, the time reflected by your PC's internal clock may be off by many minutes. The only solution to this is to reset the time and date regularly, using a more accurate source to obtain the correct time.

Even given the inaccuracy of a PC's internal clock, I imagine you'll find Title Bar Clock to be a very convenient and useful utility. In fact, in some ways it might even be all the more useful because of this inaccuracy. If you use the time-keeping capabilities of your PC for any critical applications, you had better know what time your PC *thinks* it is, especially if its notion of the time is significantly in error. ▪

ENDNOTE

WINDOWS API FUNCTIONS

The Windows API is a treasure trove. Nearly everything that Windows does, and everything that defines what Windows is, is available for your examination and manipulation through the 700-plus functions and subroutines that make up the Windows application programming interface. On the other hand, the Windows API also can be a minefield. As described above, mistakes in use of the Windows API can crash your application, or any other application with which it happens to be interacting, or Windows itself. So the wise Visual Basic programmer proceeds very carefully while exploring the Windows API.

Until recently, there was almost no information about the Windows API geared toward Visual Basic programmers. If you wanted to experiment with calling API functions from within Visual Basic, you pretty much had to figure out for yourself how to transfer the C-language-oriented descriptions in the *Windows Programmer's Reference* (or any other guide to the Windows API) to use the API functions with Visual Basic— a task that many Visual Basic programmers understandably like to avoid. Fortunately, that situation has begun to change recently. The Professional Toolkit version of Visual Basic includes a pair of Windows help files that describe the API functions and present the correct syntax for calling them from within Visual Basic. Although the descriptions are still oriented toward C-language programmers, having all the declarations available is a big help. For more heavy-duty help, however, you'll want to check out *PC Magazine Visual Basic Programmer's Guide to the Windows API* by Dan Appleman, published by Ziff-Davis Press, which is worth its weight in gold to any Visual Basic programmer. ∎

THE WINDOW INFO UTILITY

The little utility program called Window Info that I used to debug Title Bar Clock took only an hour or so to write—partly because most of the API calls that it uses are also used by VB Clock, and thus I had already figured out their correct syntax and usage, and partly because I had a model. The utility was inspired by a public-domain utility called VBFindID, written by Costas Kitsos and available through the MSBASIC forum on CompuServe. VBFindID reports the control ID, handle, class name, and caption of any window that the mouse passes over. However, it doesn't report any information about the window's parentage, so I needed to extend its capabilities to obtain the data needed by Title Bar Clock.

Because VBFindID was written in Turbo Pascal for Windows rather than in Visual Basic, I had to start from scratch to write Window Info. The utility uses an endless DoEvents() loop (a loop that executes whenever no other event is waiting in Windows) to make calls to the Windows API functions GetCursorPos and WindowFromPoint. The former returns a point data structure consisting of the X and Y coordinates of the mouse cursor, while the latter identifies the topmost window that contains that point. Once the window handle has been obtained, Window Info uses the same API methods as Title Bar Clock to identify the window's caption and parentage.

Window Info has two other interesting features. The first is that the user can elect to have it function as a stay-on-top window (like the Windows 3.1 Clock accessory). In addition, Window Info uses calls to the Windows API function GetAsyncKeyState to create a systemwide hotkey that allows the user to toggle the utility's reporting functions on or off by holding down the Control key and clicking the right mouse button. This method, which was initially described by Jonathan Zuck in an article in *Windows Tech Journal*, uses more processing time than is desirable in a general-purpose application, but seems acceptable for special-purpose use, such as a debugging tool like Window Info. Its chief advantages over the Program Manager Shortcut Key method employed by VB Librarian are that it works even if the utility wasn't launched by Program Manager and that it supports the use of any key combination, including mouse clicks, not just the Control and Alt key combinations offered by the Program Manager facility.

While there isn't space here to describe Window Info's code in detail, complete commented source code is included on the disk which accompanies this book. ∎

LAUNCHING TITLE BAR CLOCK AT WINDOWS STARTUP

There are at least two good reasons to install Title Bar Clock in your Program Manager Startup folder and leave it there. The first is that doing so ensures that Title Bar Clock will run every time you start Windows, so that the time and date will always be available to you on the title bar of the active window. The other is that launching Title Bar Clock at startup and leaving it running loads into memory a copy of the Visual Basic runtime DLL (VBRUN200.DLL), used by every Visual Basic application. While this adds a couple of extra seconds to the time it takes to launch Windows, it subsequently reduces the time it takes to launch any other compiled Visual Basic application by the same amount. Thus, all your other Visual Basic applications will launch more quickly when Title Bar Clock is running. ∎

ADDING FUNCTIONS TO TITLE BAR CLOCK

Title Bar Clock can be expanded in several ways. It would be fairly simple, for instance, to incorporate an alarm feature into the application, so that it could notify you (either through a title bar message or a standard Windows message box), for instance, when it was time for an appointment. To make this change, you would have to give Title Bar Clock a facility for entering appointment times, and then have it check to see if any of those times had been reached during its Timer event processing.   ■

LISTING

TITLE BAR CLOCK

```
'   * * * * * * * * * * * * * * * * * * * * * * * * * * * * *
'   * Title Bar Clock
'   * Copyright (c) 1993, Paul Bonner
'   * PC Magazine Visual Basic Utilities
'   *
'   * VBCLOCK.FRM
'   *  ASCII Form Listing
VERSION 2.00
Begin Form VBClockForm
   BackColor       =   &H00C0C0C0&
   Caption         =   "Title Bar Clock"
   FillColor       =   &H00C0C0C0&
   FillStyle       =   0   'Solid
   FontBold        =   -1  'True
   FontItalic      =   0   'False
   FontName        =   "Arial"
   FontSize        =   8.25
   FontStrikethru  =   0   'False
   FontUnderline   =   0   'False
   Height          =   1620
   Icon            =   VBCLOCK.FRX:0000
   Left            =   3375
   LinkTopic       =   "Form1"
   ScaleHeight     =   1215
   ScaleWidth      =   3510
   Top             =   4410
   Width           =   3630
   Begin Timer Timer1
      Interval     =   500
      Left         =   0
      Top          =   0
   End
   Begin Label Label2
      AutoSize        =   -1  'True
      BackStyle       =   0   'Transparent
      Caption         =   "Label2"
      FontBold        =   0   'False
      FontItalic      =   0   'False
      FontName        =   "Arial"
      FontSize        =   8.25
      FontStrikethru  =   0   'False
      FontUnderline   =   0   'False
      Height          =   210
      Left            =   360
      TabIndex        =   1
      Top             =   600
      Width           =   480
   End
   Begin Label Label1
      AutoSize        =   -1  'True
      BackColor       =   &H00C0C0C0&
      BackStyle       =   0   'Transparent
      Caption         =   "Label 1"
      FontBold        =   -1  'True
```

```
         FontItalic        =    0      'False
         FontName          =    "Arial"
         FontSize          =    12
         FontStrikethru    =    0      'False
         FontUnderline     =    0      'False
         Height            =    285
         Left              =    360
         TabIndex          =    0
         Top               =    240
         Width             =    825
      End
   End
End
'   * * * * * * * * * * * * * * * * * * * * * * * * * *
'   * Declarations section: VBCLOCK.FRM
'   * * * * * * * * * * * * * * * * * * * * * * * * * *
DefInt A-Z
Option Explicit
Declare Function GetWindowText Lib "User" (ByVal hWnd As Integer, ByVal⇔
   lpString As String, ByVal aint As Integer) As Integer
Declare Function GetWindowTextLength Lib "User" (ByVal hWnd As Integer) As⇔
   Integer
Declare Sub SetWindowText Lib "User" (ByVal hWnd As Integer, ByVal lpString⇔
   As String)
Declare Function GetActiveWindow Lib "User" () As Integer
Declare Function IsIconic Lib "User" (ByVal hWnd As Integer) As Integer
Declare Function GetParent Lib "User" (ByVal hWnd As Integer) As Integer
Declare Function IsWindow Lib "User" (ByVal hWnd As Integer) As Integer
Declare Function IsWindowVisible Lib "User" (ByVal hWnd As Integer) As Integer
Declare Function FindWindow Lib "user" (ByVal Class As Any, ByVal Caption As⇔
   Any) As Integer
Declare Function GetWindowWord Lib "User" (ByVal hWnd As Integer, ByVal⇔
   nIndex As Integer) As Integer
Const GWW_HINSTANCE = (-6)
Declare Function GetModuleFileName Lib "Kernel" (ByVal hModule As Integer,⇔
   ByVal lpFilename As String, ByVal nSize As Integer) As Integer
Dim OldText As String * 73
Dim wHandle%
Dim OldTarget%
Dim OldWinHand%

Sub Form_Load ()
'   * * * * * * * * * * * * * * * * * * * * * * * * * *
'   * as VB Clock loads
'   * first set Label1 to display the current time,
'   * then set on Label2 to display the copyright info,
'   * then minimize the VB Clock window
'   * * * * * * * * * * * * * * * * * * * * * * * * * *
Label1.Caption = Format(Now, "Short Date") + "  " + Format(Now, "hh:mm:ss⇔
   am/pm")
Label2.Caption = "Copyright (c) 1992 Paul Bonner" + Chr$(13) + Chr$(10) + "PC⇔
   Magazine Visual Basic Utilities"
WindowState = 1
End Sub

Sub Form_Resize ()
'   * * * * * * * * * * * * * * * * * * * * * * * * * *
'   * whenever the form is resized,
'   * center the label that displays
'   * the time, date, and copyright notice
'   * * * * * * * * * * * * * * * * * * * * * * * * * *
Label1.Left = (Width / 2) - (Label1.Width / 2)
Label2.Left = (Width / 2) - (Label2.Width / 2)
Label1.Top = (Height / 2) - (((Label1.Height + Label2.Height) / 2) +⇔
```

```
      (Label2.Height / 2))
Label2.Top = Label1.Top + Label1.Height + 30
End Sub

Sub Timer1_Timer ()
'    * * * * * * * * * * * * * * * * * * * * * * * *
'    * begin by getting
'    * the handle of the active window.
'    * if it has changed since the last timer event
'    * call FixTitle, telling it to remove the time from
'    * the previous target window.
'    * * * * * * * * * * * * * * * * * * * * * * * *
wHandle% = GetActiveWindow()
If wHandle% <> OldWinHand% Then
   FixTitle OldTarget%, False
   OldTarget% = wHandle%
   OldWinHand% = wHandle%
End If
'    * * * * * * * * * * * * * * * * * * * * * * * *
'    * next, check to see whether VB Clock is minimized
'    * * * * * * * * * * * * * * * * * * * * * * * *
Select Case WindowState
   Case Is = 1     'minimized
'    * * * * * * * * * * * * * * * * * * * * * * * *
'    * if  VB Clock is minimized
'    * check to see if the active window is iconic
'    * if so, exit
'    * otherwise, call FixTitle again, telling it to display
'    * the time in the active window's title bar
'    * * * * * * * * * * * * * * * * * * * * * * * *
   If IsIconic(wHandle%) Then Exit Sub
   FixTitle wHandle%, True
Case Else  'not minimized
'    * * * * * * * * * * * * * * * * * * * * * * * *
'    * if  VB Clock is not minimized,
'    * update the caption for Label1 on the VB Clock form
'    * to display the current time
'    * * * * * * * * * * * * * * * * * * * * * * * *
   wHandle% = GetActiveWindow()
   If wHandle% <> OldWinHand% Then
      FixTitle OldTarget%, False
      OldTarget% = wHandle%
   End If
   Label1 = Format(Now, "Short Date") + "  " + Format(Now, "hh:mm:ss am/pm")
End Select
End Sub

Sub FixTitle (WinHand%, ShowTime%)
Dim FakeSpace$, Spacer$, X, Parent%, Progenitor%, OldActive%
Dim VBEnv%, GW%, MF%, TempVar$, NewText$
FakeSpace$ = Chr$(160)          'not a space char, but alt-160
Spacer$ = String$(3, 32)
'    * * * * * * * * * * * * * * * * * * * * * * * *
'    * FixTitle takes two parameters--the title of the
'    * window, and a true/false flag indicating
'    * whether it should display the current
'    * time in the window's title
'    * * * * * * * * * * * * * * * * * * * * * * * *
'    * Make sure the window handle is still valid
'    * If so, try to get the handle of the active window's
'    * parent window.
'    * * * * * * * * * * * * * * * * * * * * * * * *
If IsWindow(WinHand%) <> False Then
   Parent% = GetParent(WinHand%)
```

```
'   * * * * * * * * * * * * * * * * * * * * * * * * * *
'   * If the active window has a parent, and
'   * if the parent is visible and it has a caption, loop
'   * until you get to the parent of all parents
'   * * * * * * * * * * * * * * * * * * * * * * * * * *
Do While Parent%
  Progenitor% = Parent%
  Parent% = GetParent%(Progenitor%)
Loop
If Parent% Then Progenitor% = Parent%

'   * * * * * * * * * * * * * * * * * * * * * * * * * *
'   * Kludge for VB Dev environment.
'   * Substitute top editor window for
'   * hidden patriarch if VB dev env active.
'   * * * * * * * * * * * * * * * * * * * * * * * * * *
VBEnv% = FindWindow("wndclass_desked_gsk", 0&)
If VBEnv% Then
  GW% = GetWindowWord(WinHand%, GWW_HINSTANCE)
  MF% = GetModuleFileName(GW%, OldText, 72)
  If InStr(OldText, "VB.EXE") Then Progenitor% = VBEnv%
End If
'   * * * * * * * * * * * * * * * * * * * * * * * * * *
'   * If there is a parent and it has a caption and its
'   * window is visible then make it the target window
'   * * * * * * * * * * * * * * * * * * * * * * * * * *
If Progenitor% Then
  If GetWindowTextLength(Progenitor%) <> False And
       IsWindowVisible(Progenitor%) <> False Then WinHand%
       = Progenitor%
End If
'   * * * * * * * * * * * * * * * * * * * * * * * * * *
' * next, get the caption of the active window (or its parent). if it doesn't
'   * have one, exit the sub
'   * * * * * * * * * * * * * * * * * * * * * * * * * *
TempVar% = GetWindowText(WinHand%, OldText, 72)
If TempVar% = False Then Exit Sub
'   * * * * * * * * * * * * * * * * * * * * * * * * * *
'   * otherwise, strip off the null character (CHR$(0) from
'   * the end of the fixed length string that contains the
'   * caption
'   * * * * * * * * * * * * * * * * * * * * * * * * * *
TempVar% = InStr(OldText, Chr$(0))
If TempVar% <> False Then OldText = Left$(OldText, TempVar% - 1)
'   * * * * * * * * * * * * * * * * * * * * * * * * * *
'   * now set the new caption equal to the old caption
'   * and look to see if the new caption contains a
'   * FakeSpace$. if so, strip off the time
'   * * * * * * * * * * * * * * * * * * * * * * * * * *
NewText$ = OldText
TempVar% = InStr(NewText$, FakeSpace$)
If TempVar% <> False Then NewText$ = Left$(NewText$, TempVar% - 1)
'   * * * * * * * * * * * * * * * * * * * * * * * * * *
'   * next strip off any extra spaces from the new caption
'   * string and, if ShowTime% is True, add the time and
'   * date to the new caption string
'   * * * * * * * * * * * * * * * * * * * * * * * * * *
NewText$ = Trim$(NewText$)
If ShowTime% = True Then
NewText$ = NewText$ + FakeSpace$ + Spacer$ + Format(Now, "Short Date") ⇔
```

```
                   + Spacer$ + Format(Now, "hh:mm am/pm")
             End If
      '     * * * * * * * * * * * * * * * * * * * * * * * * *
      '     * finally, if the window handle is still valid, and the
      '     * window is visible, and the new caption isn't the same
      '     * as the old caption
      '     * set the window's title to the new caption
      '     * and record the target window's handle
      '     * * * * * * * * * * * * * * * * * * * * * * * * *
         If IsWindowVisible(WinHand%) <> False And RTrim(OldText) <> NewText$ Then
             SetWindowText WinHand%, NewText$
             OldTarget% = WinHand%
         End If
      End If
      End Sub
```

3

VB ZIP SHELL

VB ZIP Shell provides a complete Windows front end for the MS-DOS command line utilities PKZIP and PKUNZIP.

Along with all the benefits that come from making the move from MS-DOS to Windows, there are a few losses. Perhaps the most notable of these is that the command line utilities that once seemed the epitome of convenience suddenly become very inconvenient to use. Rather than typing a command at the MS-DOS prompt and immediately seeing the results of your ef-

forts, you've got to open up an MS-DOS command shell window before issuing the command to start your utilty. Not only is it an added step, but it also negates the user-interface advantages that you would receive from working with a Windows-based utility.

Given this situation, you have several options: You can rewrite an MS-DOS utility as a Windows application yourself, attempting to duplicate all of the features of the MS-DOS application under Windows. You can wait for the

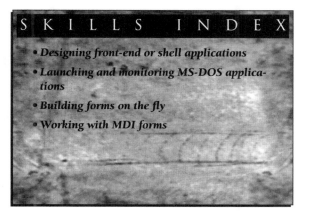

SKILLS INDEX

• *Designing front-end or shell applications*

• *Launching and monitoring MS-DOS applications*

• *Building forms on the fly*

• *Working with MDI forms*

vendor who created the MS-DOS application to rewrite it. Or you can write an application that provides a Windows front end to the utility. While the first two choices have the advantage of leaving you with a true Windows application, they also require either a significant programming effort on your part (in the case of the first option) or significant patience (in the case of the second). The third option—writing a Windows-based front end for the utility—has the disadvantage of still requiring a shell-to-MS-DOS operation, but it requires far less patience or programming effort than the others, and thus is frequently the most practical choice. Moreover, by using a few simple techniques, you can entirely hide the fact that the Windows-based front-end application is driving a command line MS-DOS–based utility, thus leaving it, from the user's perspective, indistinguishable from a true Windows-based application. With a little Visual Basic programming, you can obtain transparent access to MS-DOS command line utilities from within Windows.

VB ZIP Shell, the project presented in this chapter, is a Windows-based front-end application for the popular shareware file-compression and -decompression utilities PKZIP and PKUNZIP, from PkWare Inc. (Copies of both utilities are provided on the disk that accompanies this book. You are required to register these utilities and pay the appropriate shareware fee to PkWare if you continue to use them beyond a brief trial period.)

Beyond its obvious value for users of PKZIP and PKUNZIP, VB ZIP Shell demonstrates several useful techniques that should be readily adaptable for use with nearly any MS-DOS–based command line utility. These include the capability of a Visual Basic application to launch an MS-DOS application from a hidden window, to pause its own execution until the MS-DOS application exits, and to provide the user with a report of any error messages or other information provided by the MS-DOS utility.

■ USING VB ZIP SHELL

VB ZIP Shell operates as a standard Windows multiple-document-interface (MDI) application. Like any other MDI application, VB ZIP Shell allows the user to work with multiple documents at one time. Each document is viewed in a separate MDI child window located in the client area of the MDI parent window. In this case, the documents in question are ZIP files, and the MDI parent window is the main VB ZIP Shell window.

VB ZIP Shell allows you to work with two kinds of documents: existing ZIP files from which you wish to extract one or more compressed files, and new ZIP files to which you wish to add files. In addition, it allows you to update existing ZIP files, or add new files to them. You can work simultaneously with any mix of existing and new ZIP files, with the options that are available to you at any one time changing depending upon the kind of file that is represented by the active document window.

When VB ZIP Shell launches, its client area is empty, but a menu bar, button bar, and status line are all visible to the user, as shown in Figure 3.1.

The client area of VB ZIP Shell window is empty at start-up.

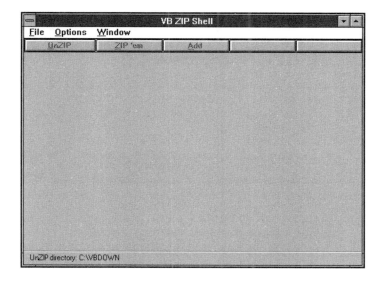

Because there is no active document window at start-up, the toolbar buttons across the top of the screen are grayed out. Similarly, the window-manipulation options on VB ZIP Shell's Window menu, activated when you use the Open item on the File menu to open an existing ZIP file or the New item to create a new one, are also grayed.

Selecting the New item to create a new ZIP file causes a small dialog box titled New ZIP File to appear, as shown in Figure 3.2. This dialog is used to name the new ZIP file and to indicate the disk and directory in which it is to be stored.

Once you've provided a name and a location for the new ZIP file, VB ZIP Shell opens a new MDI child window, the title bar of which reflects the new archive's full path and file name. But the new ZIP file hasn't been created yet—instead, the newly opened window is intended to allow you to designate the files to be placed in the ZIP file. Once you have done so, click the button labeled "ZIP 'em" to create the ZIP file.

FIGURE 3.2

The New ZIP
File dialog box
is used to name
a new archive
and to indicate
where it is to
be stored.

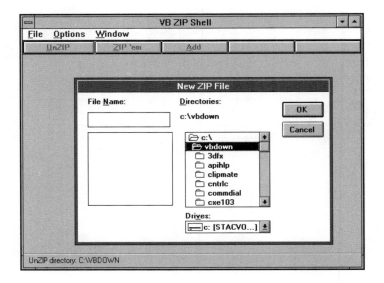

The New ZIP File window contains a standard list box, holding the list of items to zip (compress), as well as the standard file, directory, and drive list controls used to select those items. The file list box allows multiple selections, so you can highlight a series of files from a single directory. To add them to the list of files to be zipped, simply click the Add File button on VB ZIP Shell's toolbar. Entire directories or even entire drives also may be designated for zipping. To indicate this, the caption on the Add File button will change to Add Dir. when the directory list control is active, and to Add Drive when the drive list control is active. To indicate that you want to add all the files in, for instance, C:\VB2\ZIPREAD to a ZIP file, highlight that directory in the directory list box and then click the Add Dir. button. A new entry, reading C:\VB2\Z-IPREAD*.* will be added to the list of items to be zipped, as shown in Figure 3.3. Similarly, if you clicked the Add Drive button while drive C was highlighted in the drive list control, an entry reading *C:*.** would be added to the list of items to zip.

Of course, in addition to creating new ZIP archives, VB ZIP Shell extracts files from existing ZIP files. When you select the Open option from the utility's File menu, a dialog box appears that allows you to select the ZIP file that you wish to open, as shown in Figure 3.4.

FIGURE 3.3

The VB ZIP Shell can be used to compress entire directories or drives, in addition to single or multiple files.

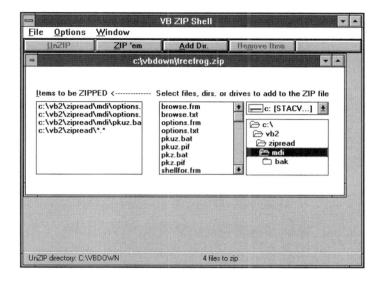

FIGURE 3.4

The Open ZIP File dialog box is used to select the ZIP file that you wish to open.

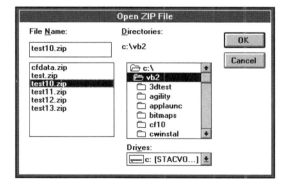

After you select the file that you wish to open, VB ZIP Shell creates and displays a new MDI child window. Once again, the new window's caption reflects the name of the ZIP file and its MS-DOS path. The new window contains only a single list box instead of the several controls found in windows that represent new ZIP files. This list box displays the contents of the ZIP file, showing the name, creation time and date, compressed size, expanded size, and compression ratio of each file in the archive.

When the ZIP file is first opened, the leftmost button on VB ZIP Shell's toolbar reads UnZIP All. This option expands all the files in the archive at once. Once you select a file in the list box, however, the toolbar button's caption changes to read UnZIP Selected, as shown in Figure 3.5.

VB ZIP Shell allows you to pick and choose the files that you want to expand.

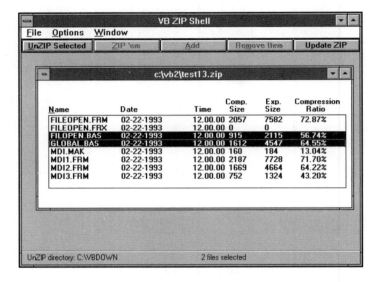

Use the rightmost button on the toolbar, labeled Update ZIP, to add new files to the existing ZIP file, or to refresh the files in the ZIP archive so that it contains the most current versions of those files. When you select the Update ZIP button, the window displaying the existing ZIP file is transformed into a new ZIP window: The list box displaying the ZIP archive files is reduced in width and its contents updated so that only the names of the files contained in the ZIP archive are displayed. In addition, file list, directory, and drive controls are added to the window so that you can select additional items to add to the archive. Finally, the toolbar buttons change to those used with a new ZIP file. At this point, you can select the ZIP 'em button to refresh the current contents of the ZIP file, add new files to the list, or remove any files from the list that you don't want to have refreshed during the PKZIP operation.

■ Other User-interface Elements

Using VB ZIP Shell, you can open any mix of new and existing ZIP files. As described, the captions of the toolbar buttons change according to the type of file represented by the active MDI child window. Thus, you can open an existing file, create a new ZIP file, and then reactivate the existing file by clicking on its window, and the toolbar buttons will always reflect the options valid for the file represented by the active window.

VB ZIP Shell's Window menu offers the four more-or-less standard options for arranging MDI child windows: Cascade, Tile Horizontally, Tile Vertically, and Arrange Icons. In addition, it maintains a list of all open MDI child windows; you can switch from one window to another by selecting their names from this list.

The Options menu, meanwhile, contains three items which are used to set the command line options that will be sent to PKZIP or PKUNZIP. Selecting the first item, ZIP Options, opens the dialog box shown in Figure 3.6.

FIGURE 3.6

The ZIP Options dialog box is used to set the command line options that will be sent to PKZIP.

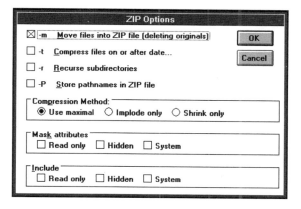

The second item, UnZIP Options, produces a similar dialog box that is used to set PKUNZIP options, while the third item, UnZIP Path, is used to indicate the directory in which unzipped (decompressed) files should be stored.

Finally, in addition to its toolbar and menus, VB ZIP Shell uses a status bar at the bottom of the screen to indicate the directory to which files will be Unzipped. And, depending upon whether the active MDI child window represents a new or existing ZIP file, it displays the number of files that you've selected in the existing ZIP file or the number of items that you've added to the new ZIP file, respectively.

After you have selected the files that you want to zip or unzip, click the appropriate toolbar button to launch the operation. The VB ZIP Shell launches PKZIP or PKUNZIP as a hidden background process, passing it the command line switches needed to achieve the results you've indicated. The VB ZIP Shell's cursor turns into an hourglass and a flashing message appears on the status line informing you that it

is zipping or unzipping files. After PKZIP or PKUNZIP exits, VB ZIP Shell displays a
dialog box that reports whether the files were zipped or unzipped, as shown in Figure 3.7. Any problems that occurred during the PKZIP or PKUNZIP operation will be
indicated in this report.

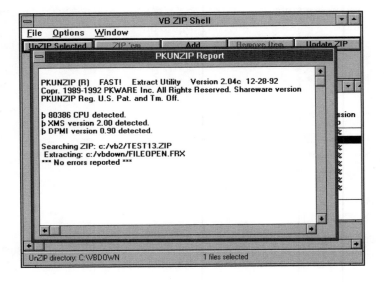

FIGURE 3.7

*The VB ZIP
Shell posts a
report like this
one to show the
results of any
PKZIP or
PKUNZIP
operation.*

Like any shell program, VB ZIP Shell adds some overhead to using PKZIP and
PKUNZIP. It uses more memory than the MS-DOS command line utility alone, and a
skilled user of the MS-DOS utility can undoubtedly produce results a little faster from
the command line than by loading VB ZIP Shell, negotiating its menus, selecting files
from list boxes, and then finally pressing the ZIP or UnZIP button to fire up PKZIP or
PKUNZIP. But VB ZIP Shell also offers some very real benefits in compensation for its
relatively minor overhead: the capability to work simultaneously with multiple ZIP
files, the capability to preview the contents of a ZIP file before running PKUNZIP, and
the sure knowledge that, as long as you click the correct check boxes on the ZIP or
UnZIP Options screens, VB ZIP Shell will send the correct command line switches to
PKZIP or PKUNZIP—eliminating the need to remember and type correctly the rather
obscure syntax of PKZIP and PKUNZIP's command switches. These benefits, at least
in my view, more than outweigh any minor overhead imposed by VB ZIP Shell.

INSIDE VB ZIP SHELL

To the user, VB ZIP Shell looks and acts like a completely independent Windows application. But from a programmer's point of view, it is anything but independent. A shell utility's operations are necessarily subordinate to the needs of the MS-DOS command line utility that it drives. Thus, nearly every design decision made in this project reflects the limitations and expectations of PKZIP and PKUNZIP.

The most sophisticated looking aspects of the application were both the simplest design decisions to make and the easiest to implement. For instance, the decision to make VB ZIP Shell an MDI application, capable of simultaneously opening multiple ZIP files, was an obvious way to add value to the application.

In contrast, the most difficult aspects of the application-design process were those that look the most prosaic in operation—launching PKZIP or PKUNZIP in the background, and reporting the results of the operation to the user.

Design Goals

As I approached this project, my primary goal was to "Windows-ize" PKZIP and PKUNZIP. I wanted VB ZIP Shell to make them look and act as much like true Windows utilities as possible. The first and most obvious step was to eliminate the need for the user ever to have to type anything resembling a standard MS-DOS command line instruction, such as:

```
PKZIP -jR -rP -m TESTFILE.ZIP C:\TESTDIR\*.*
```

(This command line would instruct PKZIP to create a ZIP file called TESTFILE.ZIP in the current directory, to add all the files except read-only files (-jR) in C:\TESTDIR and any subdirectories (-r) below that directory into the ZIP file, to store the path of each file (the P flag after the -r), and to delete the files from the disk (-m) once they had been added to the ZIP file.)

To avoid having the user compose a command line, VB ZIP Shell needed to provide a way for the user to:

- Indicate whether he or she wanted to work with a new or existing ZIP file

- Specify all the command options expected by PKZIP and PKUNZIP through standard Windows controls

- Launch PKZIP or PKUNZIP automatically

To further make the operations appear more Windows-like, I wanted to mask the fact that VB ZIP Shell must shell to MS-DOS to run PKZIP and PKUNZIP. After all, what kind of a Windows utility would VB ZIP Shell be if every time you turned around it was opening an MS-DOS window on screen? The obvious solution was to launch PKZIP and PKUNZIP as hidden applications. But doing so imposed two additional requirements on VB ZIP Shell: It had to be able to determine when the hidden MS-DOS session that it launched terminated, and it had to be able to report any problems that occurred during the PKZIP or the PKUNZIP operation.

Finally, VB ZIP Shell needed to be able to display the contents of existing ZIP files in a window. Otherwise, there would be no way to selectively unzip files. I originally planned to have VB ZIP Shell provide this capability by running PKUNZIP in the background with the correct command line switch to generate a listing of the ZIP file's contents. The VB ZIP Shell would capture PKUNZIP's output and display it on screen. In the early stages of this project, however, I had the good fortune to stumble upon a set of public-domain routines for reading ZIP file directories that had been uploaded to the CompuServe MSBASIC forum by their author, Neal B. Scott. Scott's routines were written for use with Microsoft Corp.'s PDS 7.1 (a BASIC-language development system for MS-DOS), but were simple to convert for use with Visual Basic, and proved far more efficient than shelling out to MS-DOS to generate a ZIP file directory.

▪ Specifying Command Line Parameters

PKZIP and PKUNZIP both support a huge and often bewildering array of command line switches. These switches control a multitude of options, such as the types of files that are to be included in the zip or the unzip operation, whether files in subdirectories of the currect directory are to be zipped, whether subdirectory structures stored in a ZIP file are to be expanded, and whether a ZIP file is password-protected. These options are implemented through command line switches, each of which consists of one or more letters and is preceded by a dash.

For the most part, these options can be combined freely. A few are mutually exclusive; for instance, you can only specify one compression method for a ZIP file, but most of the others can be combined in nearly any order. That doesn't mean that every combination will work—PKZIP or PKUNZIP may ignore some switches if you provide an incompatible combination—but they can be combined freely without hanging up either utility.

To provide a better interface for these switches, VB ZIP Shell needs to map them to standard Windows controls. The Windows control that comes the closest to a command line on-off toggle switch is a check box, so I elected to use check box controls to present most of the options. However, for those switches where the user can pick only one out of a set of options, such as compression method or file-extraction order,

I used radio (option) buttons, which are specifically designed to present mutually exclusive choices.

While this mapping works well and is easy to understand for anyone who knows how to operate standard Windows applications, it isn't a perfect fit. Sometimes I had to squeeze a little bit tightly to get the PKZIP and the PKUNZIP options to fit into the pattern. For instance, on the UnZIP Options screen, the Files to UnZIP group box offers three option button choices: All files, New and out of date files, and New files only. (For those not familar with PKUNZIP's options, the second option describes the -*n* flag, which extracts both those files from the ZIP file that are newer than files with the same name in the destination directory and those that do not currently exist in the destination directory, while the third option (representing the -*f* flag) will extract only files for which older versions exist in the destination directory.)

After initially implementing these options as check boxes, I decided to change them into option buttons, because the second and third options can't be combined. But doing so meant that I had to offer a third choice (the All Files option) when in fact PKUNZIP doesn't have any such command line switch. Instead, it assumes you want to extract all files unless you specify one of the other two flags. The only purpose of the All Files option button is to switch off the other two options. Nevertheless, this mapping worked fairly well overall, despite some occasional awkwardness.

Once I had determined how to present these command line options to the user, VB ZIP Shell still needed a way to interpret the user's choices, and to convert them to the actual command line switches used by PKZIP and PKUNZIP.

It made sense to have the choices that the user made on the options screens apply to all zip or unzip operations, and, with one exception, to save them to disk and load them again the next time that VB ZIP Shell is run. (The exception is the setting that indicates that only files created on or after a specified date are to be zipped. Leaving this option switched on could result in PKZIP not zipping the files that the user specified in a subsequent VB ZIP Shell session if the user forgot having turned on the option. Moreover, there didn't seem to be much reason to save this setting, since the user would likely want to change the specified date during most sessions anyway. So I elected to switch this setting off when saving the settings to disk.)

I created a pair of global integer arrays, called *zO*() and *uZO*(), to record the choices the user made, and wrote a pair of simple ASCII file routines to read and write the contents of those arrays to files called ZIPOPT.DAT and UNZIPOPT.DAT.

That took care of storing the options, but VB ZIP Shell still had to turn them into a command line for PKZIP and PKUNZIP. To do that, I wrote a subroutine called

BuildString, which evaluates the contents of the zO( ) and uZO( ) arrays and translates them into two strings called *zOpts$* and *uzOpts$*.

For check box items on the options screens, the two zO( ) and uzO( ) arrays simply store the value of each check box when the user clicks the OK button to close the options screen. So, if a check box was checked, the array will hold a value of 1 in the item representing that option. If it was unchecked, the array will hold a value of 0.

The VB ZIP Shell uses the 0 element of the zO( ) array to store the value of the check box lableled Move Files into ZIP, which corresponds to the -m command line switch, so BuildString( ) uses this simple statement to determine whether or not to add the switch to the zOpts$:

```
If zO(0) = 1 Then zOpts$ = zOpts$ + "-m "
```

The values of Option buttons are stored a little differently. Since one member of any option button group must be selected (and no more than one can be selected), a single element of the array is used to store the index number of the selected button in each option button group. For instance, element four of the zO( ) array is used to store the value of the compression method option button group. In that group, the Use Maximal button has an index value of 0, the Implode Only button has a value of 1, and the Shrink Only button has a value of 2. So BuildString( ) uses this simple test to determine which compression method command line switch to add to the PKZIP command line:

```
Select Case zO(4)
Case 0
   zOpts$ = zOpts$ + "-ex "
Case 1
   zOpts$ = zOpts$ + "-ei "
Case 2
   zOpts$ = zOpts$ + "-es "
End Select
```

Finally, both of the options screens include at least one group of options that corresponds to a single command line flag followed by one or more additional flags, depending upon the check boxes that the user has selected. For instance, the Mask Attributes group on the Zip Option screen is used to indicate whether PKZIP should mask hidden, system, or read-only files (in other words, treat them as normal writable files). If the user has checked any of these boxes, then the command line must include the -j flag, which is then followed by an additional flag for each box that the user checked: an *h* for hidden files, an *s* for system files, and an *r* for read-only files.

BuildString( ) uses the following routine to create the correct command line switch out of the contents of elements five through seven of the zO( ) array, which hold the values of the three check boxes:

```
If zO(5) + zO(6) + zO(7) > 0 Then
    zOpts$ = zOpts$ + "-j"
    If zO(5) = 1 Then zOpts$ = zOpts$ + "h"
    If zO(6) = 1 Then zOpts$ = zOpts$ + "s"
    If zO(7) = 1 Then zOpts$ = zOpts$ + "r"
    zOpts$ = zOpts$ + " "
End If
```

In short, BuildString( ) first determines if the total value of the three array elements exceeds 0, in which case it adds the -j flag to the command line. Next it examines each value to see whether its associated flag should be added to the command line, and then finally it adds a space to the end of the -jXXX flag. BuildString( ) uses the same methods to build uzOpts$.

To ensure that the zOpts$ and uzOpts$ strings always reflect the user's most recent choices, VB ZIP Shell calls BuildString( ) as the program loads (to build the strings using the values stored in ZIPOPT.DAT and UNZIPOPT.DAT) and then again every time the user clicks the OK button to close one of the option screens.

■ Launching PKZIP and PKUNZIP

Using a Windows-based front end to drive an MS-DOS command line utility always presents some problems. The Windows application must be able to launch the command line utility, pass it all the parameters that it requires, and then pause its own operation until the command line utility has finished its work.

For the most part, these were simple problems to solve. PKZIP and PKUNZIP both require multiple command line parameters: the name of the ZIP file that is to be compressed or decompressed, any command line option switches that the user wishes to set, and a list of the files that are to be extracted from or added to the ZIP file. I used a string array called ZipFil$( ) to keep track of the names of all the open ZIP files, and the BuildString( ) function described above ensures that the command line parameters always reflect the user's current choices.

Files to be added to or extracted from a ZIP file are normally specified by entering each file's name on the command line. Thus, adding the files STORY1.TXT, STORY2.TXT, and STORY3.TXT to a ZIP file called TEST.ZIP would require the following command:

```
PKZIP TEST.ZIP STORY1.TXT STORY2.TXT STORY3.TXT
```

However, PKZIP and PKUNZIP also accept another method of specifying files: an ASCII text file listing the names of each file that should be compressed or expanded. So, if you create a file called PKLIST.TXT, containing the names of the three files listed above, you could substitute the name of that file for the separately listed names by typing:

```
PKZIP TEST.ZIP @PKLIST.TXT
```

The @ symbol informs PKZIP or PKUNZIP that the file name that follows it is a ZIP list file which it should read, not a file to be compressed or decompressed.

I elected to use this method to pass the list of files that are to be zipped or unzipped, rather than simply appending each file's name to the command line, because otherwise the command line could become inordinately long if the user specified a large number of files to zip or unzip.

Thus, when the user presses the ZIP 'em or UnZIP button, VB ZIP Shell creates a simple text file named PKLIST.LIS and adds to it the names of all the files that are to be zipped or unzipped.

I had initially planned to use the Visual Basic Shell( ) function for the actual job of launching PKZIP and PKUNZIP. However, the VB Shell didn't support another of my design goals—that of launching the application from a hidden window. To meet this goal, I elected to use the Windows API function WinExec( ).

WinExec( )'s syntax is essentially identical to that of VB Shell( ), but it offers the additional capability to run an application from a hidden window. WinExec( ) returns an integer representing the task ID of the application that has been launched, or an error value if it was unable to launch the application.

Both Shell( ) and WinExec( ) return immediately once they've attempted to launch the specified application; neither has any built-in option to pause the calling application's operation until the launched application has terminated. Fortunately, however, the task ID returned by WinExec( ) can be used in a call to the GetModuleUsage( ) function. This function returns a value of True if the specified task is currently running, or a value of False if it is not. By calling GetModuleUsage( ) in a loop that terminates only when the function returns a value of False, you can pause the operation of an application such as VB ZIP Shell until the specified task has completed its operation.

Thus, VB ZIP Shell uses the following code to launch PKZIP and PKUNZIP. WinExec( ) is passed two parameters: *S$*, containing the complete command line (including the parameter string composed by BuildString( ) and a reference to @PKLIST.LIS) and a 0, indicating that the application is to be launched from a hidden window).

```
Temp% = WinExec(S$, 0)
If Temp% < 32 Then
   MsgBox "Can't launch S$", 48, "VB ZIP Shell"
   Exit Sub
End If
While GetModuleUsage(Temp%)
   Wait% = DoEvents()
   ToggleLabel Flag%
Wend
```

The call to DoEvents( ) in the While loop gives PKZIP and PKUNZIP a chance to run. The loop continues until GetModuleUsage( ) returns a value of zero (or False), indicating that the application launched by WinExec( ) has terminated.

- ## More Features, More Work

My desire to have PKZIP and PKUNZIP run in the background, completely hidden from the user, imposed additional requirements upon VB ZIP Shell. Not only did VB ZIP Shell have to pause to allow PKZIP or PKUNZIP to do its work, but it also had to be capable of reporting the results of the operation and any errors that occurred during it to the user. Moreover, with the command line utility hidden, the user wouldn't be able to see prompts from PKZIP or PKUNZIP in order to respond to them. Thus, VB ZIP Shell had to prevent—in advance—any errors that would require PKZIP or PKUNZIP to pause and wait for user input.

Fortunately, the intelligent design of PKZIP and PKUNZIP made most of these problems relatively easy to solve. For instance, extensive testing revealed only one circumstance where PKUNZIP paused for user input, and none for PKZIP.

The one situation that causes PKUNZIP to pause occurs when it has been instructed to extract a compressed file from a ZIP file when a file of the same name already exists in the destination directory and the user has not included the -o (overwrite existing files) switch on the command line. In that case, PKUNZIP posts a warning message such as this:

Warning! file: RPT.MAK already exists. Overwrite (y/n)?

Having posted the warning, PKUNZIP waits until the user types a Y or N before continuing. That's fine when PKUNZIP's output is visible, but since I intended to have VB ZIP Shell run PKUNZIP in a hidden window, the user wouldn't see the prompt and, thus, PKUNZIP would wait forever for a response that it wasn't going to get.

It was clear that the best way to prevent this situation from arising was to have VB ZIP Shell check whether the user had set the overwrite-file switch prior to each PKUNZIP operation. If not, it checks each of the files that the user has selected for unzipping to see if a file of the same name already exists in the destination directory. If a duplicate file exists, VB ZIP Shell uses the message box shown in Figure 3.8 to ask if the user wishes to overwrite the existing file.

The VB ZIP Shell uses this message box to determine if it should overwrite an existing file with a file that is about to be decompressed.

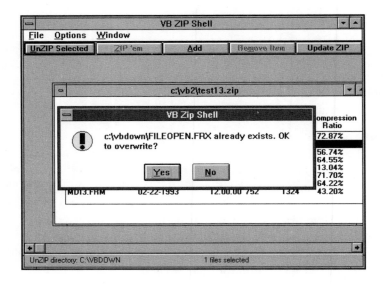

If the user replies that the file should be overwritten, VB ZIP Shell adds the -o switch to the command line, and then checks the next file in the selection list. If the user indicates that a file is not to be overwritten, VB ZIP Shell deselects it in the list box—thereby removing it from the list of files to be unzipped. This ensures that PKUNZIP will never receive the order to unzip a file that already exists in the destination directory without having the overwrite switch set.

To determine whether a file of the same name already exists in the destination directory, I wrote a brief function called Exists%( ). The function takes one parameter—a fully qualified file name consisting of the destination directory and the name of the file, and returns an integer value of either True (if the file exists) or False (if it doesn't).

```
Function Exists%(F$)
On Error GoTo NF
Exists% = True
If FileLen(F$) > -1 Then Exit Function
NF:
      Exists% = False
```

```
      Resume Next
End Function
```

As you can see, the Exists%() function uses the Visual Basic FileLen function and an error-handling routine as the test for a file's existence. Passing FileLen the name of a non-existent file causes a File Not Found error. The On Error statement catches that error and transfers control to the statement following the label *NF*, where the value of Exists% is set to True. Execution then resumes at the statement after the one that caused the error.

In this case, since the error occurred on the condition side of an If-Then statement, the next statement is the action command Exit Function, which immediately follows the Then keyword in the If-Then statement. (This caused me some problems in debugging the Exists%() routine, because I intially expected that Visual Basic would jump to the beginning of a new program line, or at least to a colon (:) statement seperator, in its search for the Next statement following the Resume Next command. Apparently, however, Visual Basic's internal parsing treats a statement entered as

```
IF  X  =  5  THEN  Y  =  2
```

as if you had typed

```
IF  X  =  5  Then
    Y  =  2
End  If
```

Thus, the action part of the If-Then statement is the Next statement.)

In addition to preventing errors in this manner, I wanted VB ZIP Shell to be capable of reporting the results of the PKZIP or the PKUNZIP operation to the user: How many files were zipped or unzipped, how much space was saved, and whether any errors occurred.

PKZIP and PKUNZIP report this information to the user by sending text to the MS-DOS window like this:

```
PKUNZIP (R)      FAST!     Extract Utility     Version 1.1     03-15-90
Copr. 1989-1990 PKWARE Inc. All Rights Reserved. PKUNZIP/h for help
PKUNZIP Reg. U.S. Pat. and Tm. Off.
Searching ZIP: c:/vb2/TEST.ZIP
Exploding: c:/vb2/RPTFORM.FRM
UnShrinking: c:/vb2/RPT.MAK
```

Since the user wouldn't be able to see this information as it is displayed in the hidden window, VB ZIP Shell needed another way to capture it and present it to the user. It seemed obvious that the way to accomplish this was to use MS-DOS's redirection capabilities to send the text that PKZIP and PKUNZIP would normally display on screen to a text file, and then have VB ZIP Shell present the contents of that file to the user once the ZIP or UnZIP operation was complete.

You can redirect the output of a utility from the MS-DOS command line very easily, by adding a greater than (>) symbol, followed by the name of the file that is to receive the text. For instance, the following command line would send the text output from PKUNZIP to a file called PK.TXT:

```
pkunzip test.zip rpt.mak >pk.txt
```

Thus, it seemed that a command such as WINEXEC(S$,0) where S$ contains "pkunzip test.zip rpt.mak >pk.txt" should accomplish the same task. However, for reasons that remain unclear to me, redirection does not work with MS-DOS .EXEs launched from within Windows by using WinExec( ) or Shell( ). Further experimentation revealed, though, that if WinExec( ) or Shell( ) is used to launch a batch program that in turn launches the .EXE with a redirection command, the output will be redirected. Thus, VB ZIP Shell does not launch PKZIP or PKUNZIP directly. Instead, it launches one of two batch programs, PKZ.BAT or PKUZ.BAT, both of which contain just three lines of code.

PKZ.BAT looks like this:

```
pkzip %1 %2 %3 %4 %5 %6 %7 %8 %9 >pk.txt
if errorLevel 0 echo *** No errors reported *** >>pk.txt
exit
```

This command launches PKZIP with up to nine parameters and uses the redirection command to channel PKZIP's output to a file called PK.TXT. Then, if the MS-DOS error-level flag is equal to zero, indicating that no errors occurred in the PKZIP operation, it appends the text " *** No errors reported ***" to PK.TXT. Finally, it issues an EXIT command to close the hidden MS-DOS Window.

PKUZ.BAT is identical, except that it launches PKUNZIP rather than PKZIP.

The VB ZIP Shell launches these batch files with the command line:

```
WinExec(S$,0)
where S$ has been defined as follows:
S$ = "PKUZ.BAT " + CurrOpts$ + " " + ZipFil$(AF%) + " " + Dest$ + " @PKLIST.LIS"
```

CurrOpts$* contains the current zip or unzip options, while *ZipFil$(AF%) contains the name of the ZIP file, *Dest$* contains the destination path, and PKLIST.LIS contains the list of files that are to be zipped or unzipped.

To make the process run more smoothly, I used Windows's PIFEDIT.EXE to create
PIF files for both PKZ.BAT and PKUZ.BAT. These PIF files use default values for all
settings with two exceptions: I checked the Close Window on Exit box to ensure that
the hidden MS-DOS window would close when the batch program issued the EXIT
command, and I used the Advanced Settings dialog box to set the Background Priority multitasking option to 5,000. This gives PKZIP and PKUNZIP a much larger share
of Windows's processing time, even though they are running in background hidden
windows, than the default background priority of 50. As a result, they can accomplish their tasks nearly as quickly as when they run in the foreground from an MS-
DOS command line window.

After the batch file has issued the EXIT command, thus terminating the task
launched by WinExec( ), VB ZIP Shell displays the contents of the PK.TXT file in the
PKZIP Report window. Because PK.TXT is a simple ASCII file, VB ZIP Shell is able to
do so by using a simple line input routine that loops until it reaches the end of the
file, as follows:

```
On Error GoTo RptError
G = FreeFile
Open "PK.Txt" For Input As G
Do While Not EOF(G)
    Line Input #G, C$
    i% = InStr(C$, "imploding")
    If i% Then
        Temp% = InStr(C$, "(")
        C$ = Left$(C$, i% + 10) + Mid$(C$, Temp%)
    End If
    D$ = D$ + C$ + Chr$(13) + Chr$(10)
Loop
Close G
Kill "PK.TXT"
Load UnZipReport
CenterForm UnZipReport
UnZipReport.Text1 = D$
Screen.MousePointer = 1
UnZipReport.Show 1
```

The only unusual aspect to this routine is that as it reads each line it searches the
text for the word "Imploding" and, if it is found, chops out the middle of the line.
This is done purely for cosmetic reasons. PKZIP repeatedly displays the percentage of
an implosion operation completed as it compresses a file, using control characters to
locate the percentage indicator at the same screen location. After I wrote the first version of this routine, I discovered that these characters make a mess of the display

when loaded into a text box, so I simply determined where they occurred in the line and used Visual Basic's Instr( ) and Mid$( ) functions to chop them out.

This little cosmetic fix was the last piece in the puzzle of VB ZIP Shell's capability to launch and control PKZIP and PKUNZIP. With the ZIP reporting facility complete, VB ZIP Shell was able to launch either utility from a hidden MS-DOS window, control its operation through command line parameters, preventing in advance any errors that might hang up its operation, and report the results of the operation to the user.

■ Reading ZIP Files

One of VB ZIP Shell's more impressive tricks is its capability to read and display the contents of ZIP files in a list box without having to run PKUNZIP to obtain the list. It's one I can take no credit for—I just got lucky here. Shortly after I began work on VB ZIP Shell, Neal B. Scott posted a file called ZIPREA.ZIP in Library 2 of the MSBASIC forum on CompuServe. ZIPREA.ZIP contained a series of routines for reading ZIP files from PDS 7.1 that Scott had written and graciously placed in the public domain. I was able to adapt these routines for use with Visual Basic in a matter of minutes.

The problem with reading ZIP files from within Basic is that they are in binary format and, like any binary file, difficult if not impossible to decipher unless you have a map of the file's layout. Fortunately, PKWARE includes a complete description of ZIP file layout in APPNOTE.TXT, a text file included in the PKZIP 1.1 package. Scott's routines locate and decipher the file directory within a ZIP file based on this information. The archive's directory lists the name of each file in the ZIP archive, the PKUNZIP version needed to extract it, the compression method used for that file, the date and time the file was last modified, and the file's compressed and uncompressed sizes.

All this information is stored in binary format. So Scott's routines include several conversion functions, including functions for converting the high- and low-order bits of binary data to unsigned integers and unsigned words, and functions for converting MS-DOS's representations of dates and times to formatted strings.

The key routine in Scott's collection is called ReadZip( ). This routine makes use of a user-defined type called LocalFileHeaderType that is used to store the data from the ZIP file's local file directory. LocalFileHeaderType is defined as follows:

```
Type LocalFileHeaderType
    ver As String * 2        'versionneededtoextract
    generalpurposebitflag As String * 2
    method As String * 2     'compressionmethod
    modtime As String * 2      'lastmodfiletime
    moddate As String * 2      'lastmodfiledate
    crc32 As String * 4
```

```
    cSize As String * 4      'compressedsize
    uncSize As String * 4     'uncompressedsize
    fNameLen As String * 2     'filenamelength
    xFieldLen  As String * 2    'ExtraFieldLength
End Type
```

I modified Scott's ReadZip() subroutine slightly to include references to the active form, which VB ZIP Shell passes as it calls the subroutine. ReadZip() uses the Get# function to read the binary ZIP file, as shown below:

```
Sub ReadZip (F As Form)
If ZipFil$(AF%) = "" Then Exit Sub
Dim HeaderSignature              As String * 4
Dim LFH          As LocalFileHeaderType
Dim ZipBuf%
ZipBuf% = FreeFile
F.List1.Clear
Open ZipFil$(AF%) For Binary As ZipBuf%
'get 1st header
Dim CurByte&
CurByte& = 1
Get #ZipBuf%, CurByte&, HeaderSignature
CurByte& = CurByte& + Len(HeaderSignature)
Do While HeaderSignature = "PK "          '0x04034b50
    Get #ZipBuf%, CurByte&, LFH
    LFH.moddate = STRDate2DOS$(Date$)
    LFH.modtime = STRTime2DOS$("12.00.00")
    Put #ZipBuf%, CurByte&, LFH
    CurByte& = CurByte& + Len(LFH)
    Dim TempfNameLen&
    TempfNameLen& = UnsignedInt&(LFH.fNameLen)
    Dim FileName$
    FileName$ = Space$(TempfNameLen&)
    Get #ZipBuf%, , FileName$
    CurByte& = CurByte& + Len(FileName$)
    Dim xFieldLen&
    xFieldLen& = UnsignedInt&(LFH.xFieldLen)
    Dim TempExtraField$
    TempExtraField$ = Space$(xFieldLen&)
    Get #ZipBuf%, , TempExtraField$
    CurByte& = CurByte& + Len(TempExtraField$)
    Dim TempcSize#
    TempcSize# = UnsignedWORD#(LFH.cSize)
    CurByte& = CurByte& + TempcSize#
    AddFile FileName$, LFH, F
    'get next file name
    Get #ZipBuf%, CurByte&, HeaderSignature
```

```
    CurByte& = CurByte& + Len(HeaderSignature)
Loop
Close #ZipBuf%
End Sub
```

I wrote a routine called AddFile() to make use of the information ReadZip() obtains. This routine adds the information about each file obtained by ReadZip() to the list box on the active form. In addition, it seemed that it would be useful to have VB ZIP Shell indicate how much each file had been compressed by expressing the size of the compressed file as a percentage of its uncompressed size. This information was easy to determine simply by dividing the file's compressed size by its uncompressed size. However, since it's possible, although not common, to compress a file whose length is zero, AddFile() first had to determine whether the file's uncompressed size was greater than zero to avoid a Division by Zero error when it calculated the compression percentage.

```
Sub AddFile (FileName$, LFH As LocalFileHeaderType, F As Form)
Dim D%, Per$
Do While Len(FileName$) < 12
    FileName$ = FileName$ + " "
Loop
If UnsignedWORD#(LFH.uncSize) > 0 Then
    Per$ = Format$(1 - UnsignedWORD#(LFH.cSize) / ⇔
       UnsignedWORD#(LFH.uncSize), "Percent")
End If
F.List1.AddItem FileName$ & hT$ & DOSDate2STR$(LFH.moddate) ⇔
    & hT$ & DOSTime2STR$(LFH.modtime) & hT$ & ⇔
    UnsignedWORD#(LFH.cSize) & hT$ & ⇔
    UnsignedWORD#(LFH.uncSize) & hT$ & Per$
End Sub
```

The routines that VB ZIP Shell uses to read ZIP files are specific to files created by PKZIP. But the general methods and type conversions that Scott developed can be adapted to read any binary file, as long as you have a description of the file's format in hand.

The VB ZIP Shell uses modified versions of Scott's ZIP-reading routines, which are all found in the project's ZIPREAD.BAS file. In addition, the companion disk includes a file called PDS_ZIP.ZIP that contains Scott's complete original routines.

■ Form Design Issues

Early in the design process, I made two key decisions about VB ZIP Shell's screen forms. The first was to use an MDI interface, allowing the user to work with multiple ZIP files at once. Again, this was a way of adding value to the application with relatively little effort. Visual Basic makes the process of building an MDI application very simple. First, I used an MDI form, rather than a standard form, for VB ZIP Shell's start-up form. Then I used the form-properties setting to change the form used to display ZIP files into an MDI child form.

Of course, it isn't enough to merely create an MDI application; you also have to keep track of data about each MDI child window and your application has to be capable of discerning which child window is active. To do so, I took advantage of the fact that Visual Basic treats forms as objects, and allows you to create additional forms at runtime in the same way you can create additional members of a control array at runtime.

The MDI child form that VB ZIP Shell uses to display ZIP files is called UnZipper, so VB ZIP Shell includes a declaration that reads

```
Global zForm( )   As New UnZipper
```

to identify zForm( ) as an array of UnZipper forms. Then it uses the Tag property of each member in that array (every control and form object has a Tag property that the program can use to keep track of information about the object) to store each form's index number. Thus, a procedure invoked by zForm(6) can use the construct Me.Tag to pass its index number (6) to a subroutine.

I adapted the methods used by the MDI Notepad example application to keep track of MDI child windows. First, I defined a data type called FormState to track information about each child window. The definition of form state follows:

```
Type FormState
    Dirty As Integer        'contents changed?
    Deleted As Integer      'Form # can be reused?
    zType As Integer        'newZip or openZip
End Type
```

The VB ZIP Shell uses FormState.Dirty to track whether the contents of the list of files to be added to a new ZIP file have been modified. The VB ZIP Shell creates a FormState variable, called *fState,* when the New ZIP form is created, and initializes its Dirty flag to False. It then sets fState.Dirty to True when the user adds files to the contents of the list box. For instance, when the user double-clicks on a file in the file list to add it to the File to ZIP list box, VB ZIP Shell executes the following statements:

```
List1.AddItem File1
fState(Me.Tag).Dirty = True
```

The Dirty flag is reset to False when the user compresses the file.

The VB ZIP Shell uses an array called zForm( ) to keep track of open ZIP files. At start-up, zForm( ) is empty. It is redimensioned to hold one element the first time a ZIP file is created or opened, then redimensioned again to hold two elements when a second file is opened, and so on. This is an easy way to track forms, but it has the unfortunate side effect of creating an ever-growing array, because the size of the array increases every time a ZIP file is opened or created.

The VB ZIP Shell uses the Deleted flag to solve this problem. When the user closes a ZIP file, the Deleted flag for the array element that represents that file is set to True. In a process modeled after one in the MDI Notepad example, VB ZIP Shell loops through all the elements of the array looking for one whose Deleted flag is True prior to increasing the size of the array. If it finds a deleted entry, it simply reuses that element to represent the new form, rather than creating a new element.

The VB ZIP Shell uses a function called GetOpenCounter to look for deleted array elements. The function takes no parameters, and returns an integer flag indicating the index number of the first Deleted element, or a value of False if no deleted elements were found.

```
Function GetOpenCounter () As Integer
Dim X
For X = 1 To zFormCount
    If fState(X).Deleted = True Then
        fState(X).Dirty = False
        fState(X).Deleted = False
        GetOpenCounter = X
        Exit Function
    End If
Next
End Function
```

The zType flag in the FormState variable indicates whether the form represents a new ZIP file or an existing one. The VB ZIP Shell uses the value of this flag to update the toolbar buttons when a new child window is activated.

Finally, VB ZIP Shell uses an integer variable called *AF%* to keep track of the active MDI child form, and a string array called ZipFil$() to track the ZIP file associated with each open window.

The procedure that VB ZIP Shell executes when the user selects the new item from the File menu shows how all these values are initialized when a new ZIP file is created. First VB ZIP Shell calls GetOpenCounter() to determine if it can reuse an existing element in the zForm() array. If GetOpenCounter() returns a value greater than zero, the new form is assigned to the array element with that value. Otherwise, VB ZIP Shell creates new elements in the zForm(),and the fState() and ZipFil$() arrays, using the ReDim Preserve command to preserve their existing contents:

```
Test = GetOpenCounter()
If Test > 0 Then
    Set F = zForm(Test)
    fState(Test).zType = NewZip
    AF% = Test
Else
    zFormCount = zFormCount + 1
    ReDim Preserve zForm(zFormCount)
    ReDim Preserve fState(zFormCount)
    ReDim Preserve ZipFil$(zFormCount)
    Set F = zForm(zFormCount)
    fState(zFormCount).zType = NewZip
    AF% = zFormCount
End If
```

When the user attempts to close a form, the form's Form_QueryUnload procedure checks and updates the values of these variables, as follows:

```
If fState(Me.Tag).Dirty = True Then
  If MsgBox("Abandon changes to this ZIP file?", 36, "VB ⇔
    ZIP Shell") <> 6 Then Cancel = True
End If
fState(Me.Tag).Deleted = True
fState(Me.Tag).zType = False
```

This procedure creates the message box shown in Figure 3.9 if the form's Dirty flag is True.

■ Runtime Form Assembly

My second key form-design decision was to have VB ZIP Shell do most of the work of building the two options forms and the forms used to display new and existing ZIP files at runtime. I decided to do this, rather than completely building the forms in advance, for two reasons: First, this approach cut down on the number of files in the project, by allowing me to use a single form, named Options, to present both options screens, and a single form named UnZipper to present both new and existing ZIP files. In contrast, if I had completely built all four forms at runtime, the project would have needed separate .FRM files for each of the four forms.

More importantly, runtime assembly of these forms provided me with a great deal of flexibility in the design process. User-interface design, in my experience, is usually an iterative process, not one that I can complete *in toto* prior to writing any code. For example, I initially planned to use check boxes for the -f and -n options on the UnZIP options screen. When later I decided to use option buttons to represent those items, I needed only to change a few lines of code to effect the change, rather than having to modify the form's layout using Visual Basic's form-design tools.

FIGURE 3.9

The Form_Query-
Unload routine
offers the user
the opportunity
to cancel the
form-unload
process if the
contents of a
ZIP file have
been changed.

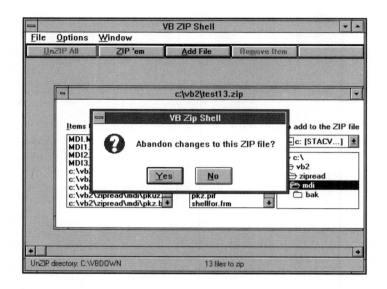

I was also able to add to the number of options presented on these forms, or remove options that I had decided not to implement in this version of VB ZIP Shell,
again merely by modifying a few lines of code, rather than by having to re-layout the
screens.

Figure 3.10 shows how the design-time layout of the options screen works. It contains a single check box on the form itself, three frames, and two buttons. The first
frame contains a single check box, the second frame contains a single option button,
and the third frame contains one check box and one option button.

What isn't immediately apparent is that I used the Properties window to identify
each of the check boxes and option buttons as the zero element of a control array.
This allows VB ZIP Shell to use the Load command to create new elements of each
control array at runtime.

When the user selects either the UnZIP Options… or ZIP Options… items on the
Options menu, VB ZIP Shell sets a global variable called OptionsMode% to the index
number of the menu item selected (0 in the case of ZIP Options… or 1 in the case of
UnZIP Options…). Then it loads the Options form, centers it on screen by calling a

FIGURE 3.10

The Options
form contains
only a rough
prototype of
the final design
for the two
Options
screens. The
final layout
isn't performed
until VB ZIP
Shell loads the
form.

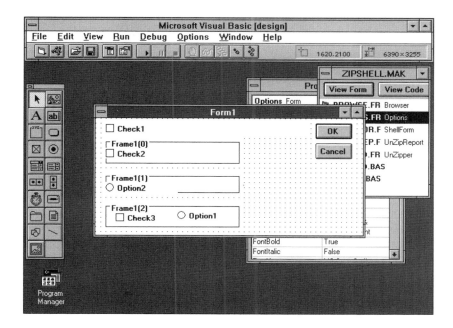

subroutine known as CenterForm, and finally issues the Show command to display the form:

```
OptionsMode% = Index
Load Options
CenterForm Options
Options.Show 1
```

The Form_Load procedure for the Options form does the actual work of creating the form on the fly. Because this procedure is called before the form is shown, the user only sees the final, completed form.

The Options form's Form_Load procedure starts by examining the value of Options-Mode%, to determine whether to build a ZIP Options or UnZIP Options form. If the value is equal to zero, it starts the form-building process, as follows:

```
Caption = "ZIP Options"
For FF = 1 To 3
    Load xBox(FF)
    xBox(FF).Top = xBox(FF - 1).Top + 400
    xBox(FF).Visible = True
    xBox(FF).TabIndex = FF
Next
```

These instructions create three additional check boxes on the form, position them at 400 twip intervals below the first check box, make them visible, and set their tab index. Next, the procedure sets the value of a variable called T% equal to FF, and then assigns captions to all four of the check boxes on the form:

```
T% = FF
xBox(0).Caption = "-m    &Move files into ZIP file (deleting originals)"
xBox(1).Caption = "-t    &Compress files on or after date..."
xBox(2).Caption = "-r    &Recurse subdirectories"
xBox(3).Caption = "-P    &Store pathnames in ZIP file"
```

The procedure then assigns a caption to the topmost frame on the form, positions and sizes the frame, assigns the frame's tab index, and calls a subroutine called Add-Opt1 to create two additional option buttons in the frame:

```
'draw compression method box
Frame1(1).Caption = "Com&pression Method:"
Frame1(1).Left = xBox(0).Left
Frame1(1).Height = 600
Frame1(1).Width = Width - 500
Frame1(1).Top = xBox(FF - 1).Top + 400
Frame1(1).TabIndex = T%: T% = T% + 1
Option2(0).Top = 260
Option2(0).Left = 260
Option2(0).Caption = "Use maximal"
Option2(0).Width = TextWidth(Option2(0).Caption) + 300
Option2(0).TabIndex = T%: T% = T% + 1
AddOpt1 Option2(1), Option2(0), "Implode only", T%: T% = T% + 1
AddOpt1 Option2(2), Option2(1), "Shrink only", T%: T% = T% + 1
```

The AddOpt1 subroutine takes four parameters: the control that it is to add to the Options form, the previous control from which it positions the new control, the caption for the new control, and the new control's tab index:

```
Sub AddOpt1 (C As Control, Pre As Control, Cap$, TI%)
Load C
C.Visible = True
C.Top = Pre.Top
C.Left = Pre.Left + Pre.Width + 200
C.Caption = Cap$
C.Width = TextWidth(C.Caption) + 300
C.TabIndex = TI%
End Sub
```

The Form_Load procedure continues to add new controls until the form is completely assembled. Then it executes the following lines to set the tab index of the form's two command buttons, and adjusts the height of the form:

```
For X = 0 To 1
```

```
    ShellForm.Command2(X).TabIndex = T%: T% = T% + 1
Next
Height = Frame1(2).Top + Frame1(2).Height + 600
```

The Form_Load procedure uses similar code to assemble the UnZIP Options form.

One of the key elements of this procedure is its rigorous redefinition of each control's tab index as it is loaded. This ensures that the tab key will always advance the cursor to the next control as expected, while failing to redefine the tab index in this manner results in a very disordered tab order.

■ OPERATIONAL FLEXIBILITY

My original plan for VB ZIP Shell didn't include the capability to add new files to existing ZIP files. However, once I started to assemble the application, it became clear that this would be a useful capability.

It wasn't until I started to add this capability—which is accessed through the Update ZIP toolbar button—that I realized the final benefit of this method of asssembling forms on the fly. The basic UnZipper form used to represent both new and existing ZIP files contains all the controls needed for either operation: a list box for listing the files in the ZIP contents of existing ZIP files, or for listing the files that are to be added to a new ZIP file, plus file, directory, and drive list boxes for selecting files that are to be added to a new ZIP file, and three labels used to explain the information presented in those controls, as shown in Figure 3.11.

When a new ZIP file is created, VB ZIP Shell sets the visible property for all four list boxes and one of the labels to True. When an existing ZIP file is opened, all controls except the first list box and the other two labels are made invisible. These controls are also sized and positioned at the time the window is created.

There are only two real differences, then, between a window that contains a new ZIP file and one that contains an existing one: which controls are visible and the value of the zType variable of the fState array element that represents that window. The VB ZIP Shell updates its toolbar command buttons in accordance with the value of the zType variable. Therefore, all I had to do to allow updates to an existing ZIP file was change the value of the existing ZIP file's zType variable to indicate that it is a new ZIP file, hide the controls on the MDI child window that are used to present existing ZIP files, and make visible the controls used with new ZIP files. (Well, I also had to reduce the size of the primary list box that is used with both types of files, and remove all the information from that list except for the file names, but you get the point... .)

FIGURE 3.11
Final layout of the UnZipper form doesn't occur until the form is loaded. This allows the same form to be used to represent new and existing ZIP files.

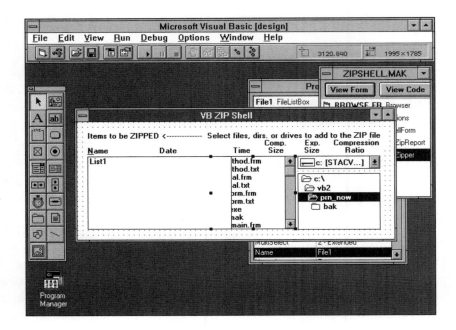

In contrast, if I had designed separate forms to represent new and existing ZIP files, VB ZIP Shell would have had to load a new form into memory, redimension all of its arrays to make room for the new form, hide the existing form, transfer the list of the ZIP file's current contents from the old form to the new form's list box, and then unload the old form. While not an onerous task, doing so would certainly have been more complicated than merely issuing a few form redesign commands such as these:

```
fState(AF%).zType = NewZip
HideC F.List1
'Fix Layout
F.List1.Width = 2495
ShowC F.List1
F.File1.Pattern = "*.*"
ShowC F.File1
ShowC F.Dir1
ShowC F.Drive1
HideC F.Label1(0)
HideC F.Label1(1)
F.Label2.Top = F.List1.Top - (F.Label2.Height + 45)
ShowC F.Label2
F.Width = F.Dir1.Left + F.Dir1.Width + (F.List1.Left * 2)
```

The ShowC and HideC commands in this listing invoke a pair of subroutines, called ShowC( ) and HideC( ), which simply turn on or turn off visible property for the specified form. For instance, ShowC( )'s listing is as follows:

```
Sub ShowC (C As Control)
C.Visible = True
End Sub
```

I wrote these routines just to shorten the Form_Load procedure's listing, but obviously each instance of ShowC Control or HideC Control could be replaced by Control.Visible=True or Control.Visible=False.

Once the form's controls have been repositioned, the procedure calls a subroutine called UpdateLabels that updates the toolbar command buttons based on the value of the specified form's FormType.zType variable:

```
UpdateLabels zForm(AF%)
```

These examples demonstrate the flexibility that Visual Basic applications can gain from performing final form layout at runtime, rather than at design time. While this process is somewhat slower than using fully designed forms, you can all but eliminate any performance degradation associated with it by performing layout changes before a form is shown or while the controls being manipulated are hidden.

■ Command Line Parameters

One final VB ZIP Shell feature that I haven't discussed is its capability to open an existing ZIP file specified on the command line at the time that VB ZIP Shell is launched. I wanted to be able to launch VB ZIP Shell by double-clicking on a ZIP file in the File Manager, so I added code for handling command line parameters to the Form_Load procedure for ShellForm (VB ZIP Shell's start-up form) and then used File Manager's Associate facility to associate files bearing the extension .ZIP with ZIPSHELL.EXE. Once the association was created, Windows would automatically run VB ZIP Shell whenever I attempted to "run" a ZIP file (either by double-clicking on it in File Manager, or by typing a file name with a .ZIP extension in the Program Manager's File Run dialog box).

The Form_Load procedure for ShellForm (VB ZIP Shell's start-up form) examines the Command$ variable that Visual Basic uses to pass command line parameters. If Command$ is not empty, VB ZIP Shell sets a global variable called Startup$, equal to Command$, and then triggers the file-open procedure from the File menu, as follows:

```
If Command$ <> "" Then
   Startup$ = Command$
```

```
    FileItem_Click (1)
End If
```

The file-open procedure uses the value of Startup$ to determine whether it should display the Browser form which VB ZIP Shell uses for file selection. If Startup$ is empty, the procedure loads and displays the Browser form. Otherwise, it sets the value of the first element of the ZipFil$( ) array equal to Startup$, then sets Startup$ equal to an empty string (so that future calls to the file-open procedure will display the Browser):

```
If Startup$ = "" Then
    Browser.Show 1
Else
    ZipFil$(AF%) = Startup$
    Startup$ = ""
End If
```

I had to use Startup$ to represent the contents of Command$ because Command$ is read-only at runtime. The file-open procedure needed to be able to empty the string, because otherwise VB ZIP Shell would attempt to open the file specified by Command$ every time it called the file-open procedure. The behavior I wanted was to have the file specified in Command$ opened only the first time the file-open procedure was called, so I needed to use a writable variable, such as Startup$, to pass the contents of Command$.

■ Enhancing VB ZIP Shell

There are several avenues you might wish to explore in terms of enhancing VB ZIP Shell. First, you might want to increase the number of PKZIP and PKUNZIP options that it supports. The current version offers support for the most commonly used PKZIP and PKUNZIP command line switches, but you might find you need to add support for others. The on-the-fly design of the Options screen should speed that process nicely.

The VB ZIP Shell doesn't explicitly support version 2.04 of the PKZIP and PKUN-ZIP utilities. While it can certainly drive the upwardly compatible new versions, it isn't equipped to handle their new features, such as archives that span multiple disks.

Finally, there is plenty of room for enhancing VB ZIP Shell's user interface. One place you might want to start is the dialog box that appears when you select the UnZIP Path… item on the Options screen. Currently, VB ZIP Shell simply calls the Visual Basic InputBox$( ) function to obtain a new destination path from the user, and hence has little control over the appearance of the dialog box. It would be easy work to instead call a new form. Then you could select a destination path from a directory list box rather than having to type in the path, and you could offer the option to create a new directory from within the dialog box.

Other possible user-interface enhancements would be the option to have VB ZIP Shell automatically delete a ZIP file after extracting all files from it, the addition of a status bar on the Options screens in which VB ZIP Shell could present more detailed explanations of each available option, and the addition of an on-line Help file.

■ SUMMARY

The VB ZIP Shell provides an effective Windows interface to the MS-DOS command line utilities PKZIP and PKUNZIP. In the process, it demonstrates a number of valuable techniques for creating bridges between Windows and the MS-DOS–based utilities we can't quite leave behind.

The code for VB ZIP Shell is too long, and the event-driven interactions of its MDI interface are necessarily too convoluted to provide a detailed explanation of each of its procedures. What I've tried to do in this chapter is discuss the highlights of the application, and present solutions to the trickier problems that arise in building a utility of this type. The comments in the code listing that follows should fill in any gaps in my explanations.

LISTING

ZSHELL.BAS

```
'    * * * * * * * * * * * * * * * * * * * * * * * * **
'    VB ZIP Shell
'    Copyright (c) 1993, Paul Bonner
'    PC Magazine Visual Basic Utilities
'    * * * * * * * * * * * * * * * * * * * * * * * * **

'    * * * * * * * * * * * * * * * * * * * * * * * * **
'    ZSHELL.BAS
'    Copyright (c) 1993, Paul Bonner
'    PC Magazine Visual Basic Lab Notes
'    * * * * * * * * * * * * * * * * * * * * * * * * **
DefInt A-Z
Option Explicit
'    * * * * * * * * * * * * * * * * * * * * * * * * **
'    Define API functions used to launch & monitor
'    PKUZ.BAT and PKZ.BAT
'    * * * * * * * * * * * * * * * * * * * * * * * * **
Declare Function GetModuleUsage Lib "Kernel" (ByVal hModule As Integer) As ⇔
    Integer
Declare Function WinExec Lib "Kernel" (ByVal lpCmdLine As String, ByVal ⇔
    nCmdShow As Integer) As Integer
'    * * * * * * * * * * * * * * * * * * * * * * * * **
'    Define FormState type
'    * * * * * * * * * * * * * * * * * * * * * * * * **
Type FormState
    Dirty As Integer      'contents changed?
    Deleted As Integer    'Form # can be reused?
    zType As Integer      'newZip or openZip
End Type
'    * * * * * * * * * * * * * * * * * * * * * * * * **
'    Define Global variables
'    * * * * * * * * * * * * * * * * * * * * * * * * **
Global Startup$    'command line parameter
Global Const NewZip = 1
Global Const OldZip = 2
Global hT$    'Tab
Global uzOpts$, zOpts$
Global fState()  As FormState
Global zForm()   As New UnZipper
Global zFormCount As Integer
Global AF%   'form counter
Global AP$   'application path
Global zO(10) 'zip options array
Global uzO(9) 'unzip options array
Global ZipFil$()    'ZIP file name
Global Dest$    'unzip directory
Global Source$    'source directory used by file open
Global OptionsMode% 'indicates which option screen to show
Global sDate$    'start date for "ZIP on or after" ops


Sub BuildString ()
'    * * * * * * * * * * * * * * * * * * * * * * * * **
'    Routine to assemble options strings
```

```
'    * * * * * * * * * * * * * * * * * * * * * * * * * **
zOpts$ = ""
uzOpts$ = ""
Dim X, sd$
'    * * * * * * * * * * * * * * * * * * * * * * * * * **
'    Strip date separator from sDate$
'    * * * * * * * * * * * * * * * * * * * * * * * * * **
For X = 1 To Len(sDate$)
If Mid$(sDate$, X, 1) <> "/" Then
   sd$ = sd$ + Mid$(sDate$, X, 1)
End If
Next X
'    * * * * * * * * * * * * * * * * * * * * * * * * * **
'    Build Zip Options string
'    * * * * * * * * * * * * * * * * * * * * * * * * * **
If zO(0) = 1 Then zOpts$ = zOpts$ + "-m "
If zO(1) = 1 Then zOpts$ = zOpts$ + "-t" + sd$ + " "
If zO(2) = 1 Then zOpts$ = zOpts$ + "-r "
If zO(3) = 1 Then zOpts$ = zOpts$ + "-P "
Select Case zO(4)
Case 0
   zOpts$ = zOpts$ + "-ex "
Case 1
   zOpts$ = zOpts$ + "-ei "
Case 2
   zOpts$ = zOpts$ + "-es "
End Select
If zO(5) + zO(6) + zO(7) > 0 Then
   zOpts$ = zOpts$ + "-j"
   If zO(5) = 1 Then zOpts$ = zOpts$ + "h"
   If zO(6) = 1 Then zOpts$ = zOpts$ + "s"
   If zO(7) = 1 Then zOpts$ = zOpts$ + "r"
   zOpts$ = zOpts$ + " "
End If
If zO(8) + zO(9) + zO(10) > 0 Then
   zOpts$ = zOpts$ + "-w"
   If zO(8) = 1 Then zOpts$ = zOpts$ + "h"
   If zO(9) = 1 Then zOpts$ = zOpts$ + "s"
   If zO(10) = 1 Then zOpts$ = zOpts$ + "r"
   zOpts$ = zOpts$ + " "
End If
'    * * * * * * * * * * * * * * * * * * * * * * * * * **
'    Build UnZip Options string
'    * * * * * * * * * * * * * * * * * * * * * * * * * **
If uZO(0) = 1 Then uzOpts$ = uzOpts$ + "-t "
If uZO(1) = 1 Then uzOpts$ = uzOpts$ + "-d "
If uZO(2) = 1 Then uzOpts$ = uzOpts$ + "-o "
If uZO(4) = 1 Then uzOpts$ = uzOpts$ + "-n "
If uZO(5) = 1 Then uzOpts$ = uzOpts$ + "-f "
If uZO(6) + uZO(7) + uZO(8) > 0 Then
   uzOpts$ = uzOpts$ + "-j"
   If uZO(6) = 1 Then uzOpts$ = uzOpts$ + "h"
   If uZO(7) = 1 Then uzOpts$ = uzOpts$ + "s"
   If uZO(8) = 1 Then uzOpts$ = uzOpts$ + "r"
   uzOpts$ = uzOpts$ + " "
End If
Select Case uZO(9)
Case 0
   uzOpts$ = uzOpts$ + "-ec "
Case 1
   uzOpts$ = uzOpts$ + "-ed "
Case 2
   uzOpts$ = uzOpts$ + "-ee "
Case 3
```

```
    uzOpts$ = uzOpts$ + "-en "
Case 4
    uzOpts$ = uzOpts$ + "-es "

End Select
zOpts$ = Trim(zOpts$)
uzOpts$ = Trim(uzOpts$)
End Sub

Sub CenterForm (F As Form)
'   * * * * * * * * * * * * * * * * * * * * * * * * * **
'   Center specified form on screen
'   * * * * * * * * * * * * * * * * * * * * * * * * * **
F.Left = (Screen.Width - F.Width) / 2
F.Top = (Screen.Height - F.Height) / 2
End Sub

Function CheckForExistingFiles (F As Form, D$) As Integer
'   * * * * * * * * * * * * * * * * * * * * * * * * * **
'   Routine checks to see whether any files to be
'   unzipped already exist in destination directory.
'   * * * * * * * * * * * * * * * * * * * * * * * * * **
Dim i, X%, Fil$, L&, Check%
If Right$(Trim(D$), 1) <> "\" Then D$ = D$ + "\"
'   * * * * * * * * * * * * * * * * * * * * * * * * * **
'   Check each selected file in Files to Unzip list box
'   * * * * * * * * * * * * * * * * * * * * * * * * * **
For i = 0 To F.List1.ListCount - 1
    If F.List1.Selected(i) Then
 Fil$=Trim(Left$(F.List1.List(i),InStr(Trim(F.List1.List(i)),hT$)-1))
'   * * * * * * * * * * * * * * * * * * * * * * * * * **
'   Correct reversed directory separator
'   * * * * * * * * * * * * * * * * * * * * * * * * * **
        X% = InStr(2, Fil$, "/")
        If X% Then Fil$ = Mid$(Fil$, X% + 1)
        X% = InStr(Fil$, "/")
        Do While X%
            Fil$ = Left$(Fil$, X% - 1) + "\" + Mid$(Fil$, X% + 1)
            X% = InStr(Fil$, "/")
        Loop
'   * * * * * * * * * * * * * * * * * * * * * * * * * **
'   Call Exists% function to determine if file exists
'   * * * * * * * * * * * * * * * * * * * * * * * * * **
        If Exists%(D$ + Fil$) = True Then
        Check% = MsgBox(D$ + Fil$ + " already exists. Okay to overwrite?", ⇔
52, "VB ZIP Shell")
'   * * * * * * * * * * * * * * * * * * * * * * * * * **
'   Deselect file if user doesn't want to overwrite
'   * * * * * * * * * * * * * * * * * * * * * * * * * **
            If Check% = 7 Then
                F.List1.Selected(i) = False
                F.List1.Refresh
            End If
        End If
    End If
Next i
If F.List1.SelCount = 0 Then F.List1.ListIndex = 0
'   * * * * * * * * * * * * * * * * * * * * * * * * * **
'   Return value indicating number of files to unzip
'   * * * * * * * * * * * * * * * * * * * * * * * * * **
CheckForExistingFiles = F.List1.SelCount
End Function

Sub DoItNow (Flag%, S$)
```

```
'   * * * * * * * * * * * * * * * * * * * * * * * * * * * * **
'    Launches and monitors PKZ.BAT and PKUZ.BAT
'    Accepts two parameters:
'      Flag% indicates type of operation--used to toggle
'         status bar label
'      S$ contains command line
'   * * * * * * * * * * * * * * * * * * * * * * * * * * * * **
Dim Temp%, Wait%, G, i%, C$, D$, F As Form
Set F = ShellForm.ActiveForm
'   * * * * * * * * * * * * * * * * * * * * * * * * * * * * **
'    Launch app specified in S$ in a hidden window
'   * * * * * * * * * * * * * * * * * * * * * * * * * * * * **
Temp% = WinExec(S$, 0)   '0 = launch hidden
'   * * * * * * * * * * * * * * * * * * * * * * * * * * * * **
'    Report error if launch failed
'   * * * * * * * * * * * * * * * * * * * * * * * * * * * * **'
If Temp% < 32 Then
    MsgBox "Can't launch S$", 48, "VB ZIP Shell"
    Exit Sub
End If
'   * * * * * * * * * * * * * * * * * * * * * * * * * * * * **
'    Disable Edit and Window menus
'   * * * * * * * * * * * * * * * * * * * * * * * * * * * * **
ToggleMenus False
'   * * * * * * * * * * * * * * * * * * * * * * * * * * * * **
'    Wait while hidden app executes
'    flashing status bar message all the while
'   * * * * * * * * * * * * * * * * * * * * * * * * * * * * **
While GetModuleUsage(Temp%)
    Wait% = DoEvents()
    ToggleLabel Flag%
Wend
'   * * * * * * * * * * * * * * * * * * * * * * * * * * * * **
'    Delete list of files to ZIP or unZIP
'   * * * * * * * * * * * * * * * * * * * * * * * * * * * * **
Kill "PKLIST.LIS"
'   * * * * * * * * * * * * * * * * * * * * * * * * * * * * **
'    Restore status bar label
'   * * * * * * * * * * * * * * * * * * * * * * * * * * * * **
ToggleLabel 2
ShellForm.Label2 = F.List1.SelCount & "files selected"
On Error GoTo RptError
'   * * * * * * * * * * * * * * * * * * * * * * * * * * * * **
'    Open and read report
'   * * * * * * * * * * * * * * * * * * * * * * * * * * * * **
G = FreeFile
Open "PK.Txt" For Input As G
Do While Not EOF(G)
    Line Input #G, C$
    i% = InStr(C$, "imploding")
    If i% Then
        Temp% = InStr(C$, "(")
        C$ = Left$(C$, i% + 10) + Mid$(C$, Temp%)
    End If
    D$ = D$ + C$ + Chr$(13) + Chr$(10)
Loop
Close G
'   * * * * * * * * * * * * * * * * * * * * * * * * * * * * **
'    Delete report file, then display report screen
'   * * * * * * * * * * * * * * * * * * * * * * * * * * * * **
Kill "PK.TXT"
ToggleMenus True
Load UnZipReport
CenterForm UnZipReport
```

```
UnZipReport.Text1 = D$
On Error GoTo 0
Screen.MousePointer = 1
UnZipReport.Show 1
BackDoor:
Exit Sub
RptError:
   MsgBox "Error reading ZIP report", 48, "VB ZIP Shell"
   Screen.MousePointer = 1
   Resume BackDoor
End Sub

Function Exists% (F$)
'    * * * * * * * * * * * * * * * * * * * * * * * * * * * **
'    Check for existence of F$
'    * * * * * * * * * * * * * * * * * * * * * * * * * * * **
On Error GoTo NF
Exists% = True
If FileLen(F$) > -1 Then Exit Function
NF:
   Exists% = False
   Resume Next
End Function

Function GetOpenCounter () As Integer
'    * * * * * * * * * * * * * * * * * * * * * * * * * * * **
'    Try to find an open array element
'    * * * * * * * * * * * * * * * * * * * * * * * * * * * **
Dim X
For X = 1 To zFormCount
   If fState(X).Deleted = True Then
      fState(X).Dirty = False
      fState(X).Deleted = False
      GetOpenCounter = X
      Exit Function
   End If
Next
End Function

Sub GetOptions ()
'    * * * * * * * * * * * * * * * * * * * * * * * * * * * **
'    Read previously saved options and dest path
'    * * * * * * * * * * * * * * * * * * * * * * * * * * * **
Dim F, z$, X
F = FreeFile
On Error GoTo ReError
'    * * * * * * * * * * * * * * * * * * * * * * * * * * * **
'    Get Unzip Path
'    * * * * * * * * * * * * * * * * * * * * * * * * * * * **
z$ = AP$ + "ZShell.DAT"
Open z$ For Input As F
   Input #F, Dest$
Close F
'    * * * * * * * * * * * * * * * * * * * * * * * * * * * **
'    Get Zip Options
'    * * * * * * * * * * * * * * * * * * * * * * * * * * * **
F = FreeFile
z$ = AP$ + "ZIPOPT.DAT"
Open z$ For Input As F
For X = 0 To UBound(zO)
   Input #F, zO(X)
Next
'    * * * * * * * * * * * * * * * * * * * * * * * * * * * **
'    sDate$ isn't stored/so we initialize it here
```

```
'    * * * * * * * * * * * * * * * * * * * * * * * * * * **
zO(1) = 0
sDate$ = Format(Now, "Short Date")
Close F
'    * * * * * * * * * * * * * * * * * * * * * * * * * * **
'    Get UnZip Options
'    * * * * * * * * * * * * * * * * * * * * * * * * * * **
F = FreeFile
z$ = AP$ + "UNZIPOPT.DAT"
Open z$ For Input As F
For X = 0 To UBound(uZO)
   Input #F, uZO(X)
Next
Close F

Re:
On Error GoTo 0
'    * * * * * * * * * * * * * * * * * * * * * * * * * * **
'    Create options strings
'    * * * * * * * * * * * * * * * * * * * * * * * * * * **
BuildString
Exit Sub

ReError:
   Close F
   Resume Re
End Sub

Sub HideC (C As Control)
'    * * * * * * * * * * * * * * * * * * * * * * * * * * **
'    Hide specified control
'    * * * * * * * * * * * * * * * * * * * * * * * * * * **
C.Visible = False
End Sub

Function IsValidPath (DestPath$, ByVal DefaultDrive$) As Integer
Dim Tmp$, Drive$, legalChar$, backpos, forepos, Temp$, i, periodpos, length
'    * * * * * * * * * * * * * * * * * * * * * * * * * * **
'    Checks validity of specified path
'    adapted from SetupKit project in the
'    sample code that accompanies VB 2.0
'    Professional Toolkit
'    Returns True if path valid, False if not
'    * * * * * * * * * * * * * * * * * * * * * * * * * * **

    DestPath$ = Trim(DestPath$)
'    * * * * * * * * * * * * * * * * * * * * * * * * * * **
'    ' Check Default Drive Parameter
'    * * * * * * * * * * * * * * * * * * * * * * * * * * **
    If Right$(DefaultDrive$, 1) <> ":" Or Len(DefaultDrive$) <> 2 Then
      GoTo parseErr
    End If
'    * * * * * * * * * * * * * * * * * * * * * * * * * * **
'    Insert default drive if path begins with root backslash
'    * * * * * * * * * * * * * * * * * * * * * * * * * * **
    If Left$(DestPath$, 1) = "\" Then
    DestPath$ = DefaultDrive + DestPath$
    End If
'    * * * * * * * * * * * * * * * * * * * * * * * * * * **
'    Check for invalid characters
'    * * * * * * * * * * * * * * * * * * * * * * * * * * **
    On Error Resume Next
    Tmp$ = Dir$(DestPath$)
    If Err <> 0 Then
```

```
      GoTo parseErr
      End If
'     * * * * * * * * * * * * * * * * * * * * * * * * **
'     Check for wildcard characters and spaces
'     * * * * * * * * * * * * * * * * * * * * * * * * **
      If (InStr(DestPath$, "*") <> 0) GoTo parseErr
      If (InStr(DestPath$, "?") <> 0) GoTo parseErr
      If (InStr(DestPath$, " ") <> 0) GoTo parseErr
'     * * * * * * * * * * * * * * * * * * * * * * * * **
'     Check position of colon
'     * * * * * * * * * * * * * * * * * * * * * * * * **
      If Mid$(DestPath$, 2, 1) <> Chr$(58) Then GoTo parseErr
'     * * * * * * * * * * * * * * * * * * * * * * * * **
'     Insert root backslash if needed
'     * * * * * * * * * * * * * * * * * * * * * * * * **
      If Len(DestPath$) > 2 Then
      If Right$(Left$(DestPath$, 3), 1) <> "\" Then
   DestPath$ = Left$(DestPath$, 2) + "\" + Right$(DestPath$, Len(DestPath$) ⇔
      - 2)
      End If
      End If
'     * * * * * * * * * * * * * * * * * * * * * * * * **
'     Check destination drive validity
'     * * * * * * * * * * * * * * * * * * * * * * * * **
      Drive$ = Left$(DestPath$, 1)
      ChDrive (Drive$)          ' Try to change to the dest drive
      If Err <> 0 Then GoTo parseErr
'     * * * * * * * * * * * * * * * * * * * * * * * * **
'     Add final backslash
'     * * * * * * * * * * * * * * * * * * * * * * * * **
      If Right$(DestPath$, 1) <> "\" Then
      DestPath$ = DestPath$ + "\"
      End If
'     * * * * * * * * * * * * * * * * * * * * * * * * **
'     Root dir is a valid dir
'     * * * * * * * * * * * * * * * * * * * * * * * * **
      If Len(DestPath$) = 3 Then
      If Right$(DestPath$, 2) = ":\" Then
      GoTo ParseOK
      End If
      End If

'     * * * * * * * * * * * * * * * * * * * * * * * * **
'     Check for repeated Slash
'     * * * * * * * * * * * * * * * * * * * * * * * * **
      If InStr(DestPath$, "\\") <> 0 Then GoTo parseErr

'     * * * * * * * * * * * * * * * * * * * * * * * * **
'     Check for illegal directory names
'     * * * * * * * * * * * * * * * * * * * * * * * * **
      legalChar$ = "!#$%&'()-0123456789@ABCDEFGHIJKLMNOPQRSTUVWXYZ^_`{}~."
      backpos = 3
      forepos = InStr(4, DestPath$, "\")
      Do
      Temp$ = Mid$(DestPath$, backpos + 1, forepos - backpos - 1)

'     * * * * * * * * * * * * * * * * * * * * * * * * **
'     Test for illegal characters
'     * * * * * * * * * * * * * * * * * * * * * * * * **
      For i = 1 To Len(Temp$)
      If InStr(legalChar$, UCase$(Mid$(Temp$, i, 1))) = 0 Then GoTo parseErr
      Next i

'     * * * * * * * * * * * * * * * * * * * * * * * * **
```

```
'    Check combinations of periods and lengths
'    * * * * * * * * * * * * * * * * * * * * * * * * **
     periodpos = InStr(Temp$, ".")
     length = Len(Temp$)
     If periodpos = 0 Then
     If length > 8 Then GoTo parseErr    ' Base too long
     Else
     If periodpos > 9 Then GoTo parseErr     ' Base too long
     If length > periodpos + 3 Then GoTo parseErr   ' Extension too long
   If InStr(periodpos + 1, Temp$, ".") <> 0 Then GoTo parseErr' Two periods ⇔
     not allowed
     End If

     backpos = forepos
     forepos = InStr(backpos + 1, DestPath$, "\")
     Loop Until forepos = 0
'    * * * * * * * * * * * * * * * * * * * * * * * * **
'    No errors found. Report path is valid
'    * * * * * * * * * * * * * * * * * * * * * * * **
ParseOK:
     IsValidPath = True
     Exit Function


'    * * * * * * * * * * * * * * * * * * * * * * * * **
'    Error found. Report path is invalid
'    * * * * * * * * * * * * * * * * * * * * * * * * **
parseErr:
     IsValidPath = False
End Function

Sub ShowC (C As Control)
'    * * * * * * * * * * * * * * * * * * * * * * * * **
'    Make specified control visible
'    * * * * * * * * * * * * * * * * * * * * * * * * **
C.Visible = True
End Sub

Sub ToggleLabel (Flag As Integer)
'    * * * * * * * * * * * * * * * * * * * * * * * * **
'    Flash "Zipping" or "UnZipping" message while PKZIP/PKUNZIP
'    runs in the hidden window.
'    Flag indicates which operation, or if Flag = 2, that ToggleLabel
'    should reinitialize the static variable Dot% which it uses to
'    add a changing number of periods to the end of the flashing label
'    * * * * * * * * * * * * * * * * * * * * * * * * **
Dim X, i, L$
Static Dot%
If Flag = 2 Then Dot% = 0: Exit Sub     'operation complete
If Dot% < 3 Then Dot% = 3
If Flag = True Then
   L$ = "UnZipping files" + String$(Dot%, ".")
Else
   L$ = "Zipping files" + String$(Dot%, ".")
End If
'    * * * * * * * * * * * * * * * * * * * * * * * * **
'    Call DoEvents() often, letting PKZIP/PKUNZIP do their thing
'    * * * * * * * * * * * * * * * * * * * * * * * * **
For X = 1 To 5: i = DoEvents(): Next     'delay loop
ShellForm.Label2 = L$
Dot% = Dot% + 1
If Dot% = 43 Then Dot% = 3
End Sub


Sub ToggleMenus (Flag%)
```

```
'    * * * * * * * * * * * * * * * * * * * * * * * * * * * **
'    Enable or disable menus
'    * * * * * * * * * * * * * * * * * * * * * * * * * * * **
Dim Wait%
For Wait% = 0 To 1
   ShellForm.TopMenu(Wait%).Enabled = Flag%
Next
ShellForm.winMenu.Enabled = Flag%
End Sub

Sub UpdateLabels (F As Form)
'    * * * * * * * * * * * * * * * * * * * * * * * * * * * **
'    Update toolbar button labels to reflect current file type
'    * * * * * * * * * * * * * * * * * * * * * * * * * * * **
Select Case fState(F.Tag).zType

Case Is = 1     'NewZip
'    * * * * * * * * * * * * * * * * * * * * * * * * * * * **
'    New ZIP file
'    * * * * * * * * * * * * * * * * * * * * * * * * * * * **
   ShellForm.Command2(2).Enabled = True
   ShellForm.Command2(0).Enabled = False
   ShellForm.Command2(3).Caption = "Re&move Item"
   If F.List1.ListCount > 0 Then
       ShellForm.Command2(1).Enabled = True
       ShellForm.Command2(3).Enabled = True
   Else
       ShellForm.Command2(3).Enabled = False
       ShellForm.Command2(1).Enabled = False
   End If
   ShellForm.Command2(4).Caption = ""
   ShellForm.Command2(4).Enabled = False
   ShellForm.Label2 = F.List1.ListCount & " files to zip"

Case Is = 2     'OldZip
'    * * * * * * * * * * * * * * * * * * * * * * * * * * * **
'    Existing ZIP file
'    * * * * * * * * * * * * * * * * * * * * * * * * * * * **
   Dim X
   ShellForm.Command2(0).Enabled = True
   For X = 1 To 3
       ShellForm.Command2(X).Enabled = False
   Next
   ShellForm.Command2(4).Caption = "Update ZIP"
   ShellForm.Command2(4).Enabled = True
   If F.List1.SelCount > 0 Then
       ShellForm.Command2(0).Caption = "&UnZIP Selected"
   Else
       ShellForm.Command2(0).Caption = "&UnZIP All"
   End If
   ShellForm.Label2 = F.List1.SelCount & " files selected"
Case Else
End Select
End Sub

Sub WindowMenuCheck (Closing%)
'    * * * * * * * * * * * * * * * * * * * * * * * * * * * **
'    Updates Window menu
'    Closing parameter is set to True by QueryUnload procedure of
'    UnZipper form to indicate that the form is about to
'    close, so value of T% should be adjusted to reflect the form's
'    imminent departure
'    * * * * * * * * * * * * * * * * * * * * * * * * * * * **
Dim T%, X
```

```
Select Case Closing%
Case Is = False
    T% = 1
Case Is = True
    T% = 2
End Select
'    * * * * * * * * * * * * * * * * * * * * * * * * * * * **
'    Disable Windows menu if Forms.Count is not greater than T%
'    * * * * * * * * * * * * * * * * * * * * * * * * * * * **
For X = 0 To 3
    ShellForm.wMenu(X).Enabled = Forms.Count > T%
Next
End Sub


'    * * * * * * * * * * * * * * * * * * * * * * * * * * * **
'    SHELLFRM.FRM
'    Copyright (c) 1993, Paul Bonner
'    PC Magazine Visual Basic Lab Notes
'    * * * * * * * * * * * * * * * * * * * * * * * * * * * **
VERSION 2.00
Begin MDIForm ShellForm
    Caption         =    "VB ZIP Shell    12/17/92   10:17 am"
    Height          =    6180
    Icon            =    SHELLFOR.FRX:0000
    Left            =    1245
    LinkTopic       =    "MDIForm1"
    Top             =    1230
    Width           =    8040
    Begin PictureBox Picture2
        Align           =    2    'Align Bottom
        BackColor       =    &H00C0C0C0&
        BorderStyle     =    0    'None
        Height          =    330
        Left            =    0
        ScaleHeight     =    330
        ScaleWidth      =    7920
        TabIndex        =    6
        Top             =    5160
        Width           =    7920
        Begin Line Line2
            BorderColor     =    &H00808080&
            X1              =    5280
            X2              =    7440
            Y1              =    240
            Y2              =    240
        End
        Begin Label Label2
            AutoSize        =    -1    'True
            BackStyle       =    0    'Transparent
            Caption         =    "Label2"
            FontBold        =    0    'False
            FontItalic      =    0    'False
            FontName        =    "MS Sans Serif"
            FontSize        =    8.25
            FontStrikethru  =    0    'False
            FontUnderline   =    0    'False
            Height          =    195
            Left            =    4200
            TabIndex        =    8
            Top             =    60
            Width           =    480
        End
        Begin Label Label1
            AutoSize        =    -1    'True
```

```
        BackColor         =      &H00C0C0C0&
        Caption           =      "Label1"
        FontBold          =      0      'False
        FontItalic        =      0      'False
        FontName          =      "MS Sans Serif"
        FontSize          =      8.25
        FontStrikethru    =      0      'False
        FontUnderline     =      0      'False
        Height            =      255
        Left              =      120
        TabIndex          =      7
        Top               =      60
        Width             =      480
     End
     Begin Line Line1
        BorderColor       =      &H00FFFFFF&
        X1                =      840
        X2                =      4920
        Y1                =      120
        Y2                =      120
     End
End
Begin PictureBox Picture1
     Align             =      1      'Align Top
     BackColor         =      &H00C0C0C0&
     Height            =      330
     Left              =      0
     ScaleHeight       =      300
     ScaleWidth        =      7890
     TabIndex          =      0
     Top               =      0
     Width             =      7920
     Begin CommandButton Command2
        Caption           =      "&UnZIP"
        Enabled           =      0      'False
        Height            =      300
        Index             =      0
        Left              =      0
        TabIndex          =      5
        Top               =      0
        Width             =      1665
     End
     Begin CommandButton Command2
        Caption           =      "&ZIP 'em"
        Enabled           =      0      'False
        Height            =      300
        Index             =      1
        Left              =      1680
        TabIndex          =      4
        Top               =      0
        Width             =      1560
     End
     Begin CommandButton Command2
        Caption           =      "&Add"
        Enabled           =      0      'False
        Height            =      300
        Index             =      2
        Left              =      3240
        TabIndex          =      3
        Top               =      0
        Width             =      1560
     End
     Begin CommandButton Command2
        Caption           =      "  "
```

```
        Enabled            =     0     'False
        Height             =     300
        Index              =     3
        Left               =     4800
        TabIndex           =     2
        Top                =     0
        Width              =     1560
     End
     Begin CommandButton Command2
        Caption            =     " "
        Enabled            =     0     'False
        Height             =     300
        Index              =     4
        Left               =     6360
        TabIndex           =     1
        Top                =     0
        Width              =     1560
     End
  End
  Begin Menu TopMenu
     Caption            =     "&File"
     Index              =     0
     Begin Menu fileItem
        Caption            =     "&New"
        Index              =     0
     End
     Begin Menu fileItem
        Caption            =     "&Open"
        Index              =     1
     End
     Begin Menu fileItem
        Caption            =     "&Close"
        Index              =     2
     End
     Begin Menu fileItem
        Caption            =     "-"
        Index              =     3
     End
     Begin Menu fileItem
        Caption            =     "&About VB ZIP Shell..."
        Index              =     4
     End
     Begin Menu fileItem
        Caption            =     "E&xit"
        Index              =     5
     End
  End
  Begin Menu TopMenu
     Caption            =     "&Options"
     Index              =     1
     Begin Menu optItem
        Caption            =     "&ZIP Options..."
        Index              =     0
     End
     Begin Menu optItem
        Caption            =     "&UnZIP Options..."
        Index              =     1
     End
     Begin Menu optItem
        Caption            =     "UnZip &Path..."
        Index              =     2
     End
  End
  Begin Menu winMenu
```

```
        Caption             =    "&Window"
        WindowList          =    -1   'True
        Begin Menu wMenu
            Caption         =    "&Cascade"
            Index           =    0
        End
        Begin Menu wMenu
            Caption         =    "Tile &Horizontally"
            Index           =    1
        End
        Begin Menu wMenu
            Caption         =    "Tile &Vertically"
            Index           =    2
        End
        Begin Menu wMenu
            Caption         =    "&Arrange Icons"
            Index           =    3
        End
    End
End
DefInt A-Z
Option Explicit

Sub Command2_Click (Index As Integer)
Dim F As Form, G, i, Opt$, S$, Temp%, C$, t$, CurrOpts$   'D$, Wait%
AF% = ActiveForm.Tag
Set F = ActiveForm
'   * * * * * * * * * * * * * * * * * * * * * * * * * * * * * **
'   Evaluate toolbar button clicks
'   * * * * * * * * * * * * * * * * * * * * * * * * * * * * * **
Select Case Index
Case 0      'UnZip
    If F.List1.ListIndex = -1 Then Exit Sub
'   * * * * * * * * * * * * * * * * * * * * * * * * * * * * * **
'   If UnZip All was pressed, select all entries in list box
'   * * * * * * * * * * * * * * * * * * * * * * * * * * * * * **
If F.List1.SelCount = 0 Then
        For i = 0 To F.List1.ListCount - 1
        F.List1.Selected(i) = True
        Next
    End If
    Screen.MousePointer = 11
'   * * * * * * * * * * * * * * * * * * * * * * * * * * * * * **
'   If overwrite files option not set,
'   call CheckExistingFiles to avoid File Already Exists errors
'   * * * * * * * * * * * * * * * * * * * * * * * * * * * * * **

    If Not InStr(uzOpts$, "-o") > 0 Then
        Temp% = CheckForExistingFiles(F, Dest$)
'   * * * * * * * * * * * * * * * * * * * * * * * * * * * * * **
'   If there are still files to unzip, add -o to current options
'   * * * * * * * * * * * * * * * * * * * * * * * * * * * * * **
        If Temp% > 0 Then
        CurrOpts$ = "-o " + uzOpts$
        Else
        Screen.MousePointer = 1
        Exit Sub
        End If
    Else
        CurrOpts$ = uzOpts$
    End If
'   * * * * * * * * * * * * * * * * * * * * * * * * * * * * * **
'   Write out list of files to unzip
'   * * * * * * * * * * * * * * * * * * * * * * * * * * * * * **
```

```
      G = FreeFile
      Open "PKLIST.LIS" For Output As G
      For i = 0 To F.List1.ListCount - 1
         If F.List1.Selected(i) Then
   Print #G, Left$(F.List1.List(i), InStr(Trim(F.List1.List(i)), hT$) - 1)
         End If
      Next i
      Close G
'   * * * * * * * * * * * * * * * * * * * * * * * * * * * **
'   Build command line, call DoItNow to run command line
'   * * * * * * * * * * * * * * * * * * * * * * * * * * * **
      S$ = "PKUZ.BAT " + CurrOpts$ + " " + ZipFil$(AF%) + " " + Dest$ + " ⇔
      @PKLIST.LIS"
      DoItNow True, S$

Case 1
'   * * * * * * * * * * * * * * * * * * * * * * * * * * * **
'      ZIP button selected
'   * * * * * * * * * * * * * * * * * * * * * * * * * * * **
      If F.List1.ListIndex = -1 Then Exit Sub
      G = FreeFile
      Screen.MousePointer = 11
      Open "PKLIST.LIS" For Output As G
'   * * * * * * * * * * * * * * * * * * * * * * * * * * * **
'      Build list of files to zip
'   * * * * * * * * * * * * * * * * * * * * * * * * * * * **
      Dim ReCurse%
      For i = 0 To F.List1.ListCount - 1
         Print #G, Trim(F.List1.List(i))
         If InStr(F.List1.List(i), "*") Then ReCurse% = True
      Next i
      Close G
      CurrOpts$ = zOpts$
'   * * * * * * * * * * * * * * * * * * * * * * * * * * * **
'      Eliminate -r -p from options if user hasn't added any
'      directories or drives to ZIP file--prevents accidental recursion
'      and unnecessary storage of path names in ZIP
'   * * * * * * * * * * * * * * * * * * * * * * * * * * * **
   If ReCurse% <> True Then
         i = InStr(CurrOpts$, "-r ")
      If i > 0 Then CurrOpts$ = Left$(CurrOpts$, i - 1) + Mid$(CurrOpts$, i + 3)
         i = InStr(CurrOpts$, "-P ")
      If i > 0 Then CurrOpts$ = Left$(CurrOpts$, i - 1) + Mid$(CurrOpts$, i + 3)
      End If
'   * * * * * * * * * * * * * * * * * * * * * * * * * * * **
'      Build command line, call DoItNow to execute
'   * * * * * * * * * * * * * * * * * * * * * * * * * * * **
      S$ = "PKZ.BAT " + CurrOpts$ + " " + ZipFil$(AF%) + " " + "@PKLIST.LIS"
      DoItNow False, S$
      fState(F.Tag).Dirty = False

Case 2      'Add
'   * * * * * * * * * * * * * * * * * * * * * * * * * * * **
'      Add files to ZIP
'   * * * * * * * * * * * * * * * * * * * * * * * * * * * **
      C$ = ShellForm.Command2(2).Caption
'   * * * * * * * * * * * * * * * * * * * * * * * * * * * **
'      Add selected file
'   * * * * * * * * * * * * * * * * * * * * * * * * * * * **
   If C$ = "&Add File" Then
         For i = 0 To F.File1.ListCount - 1
         If F.File1.Selected(i) Then
         F.List1.AddItem t$ + F.File1.List(i)
         F.File1.Selected(i) = False
```

```
      End If
      Next i
'     * * * * * * * * * * * * * * * * * * * * * * * * * * * **
'     Add selected directory
'     * * * * * * * * * * * * * * * * * * * * * * * * * * * **
   ElseIf C$ = "&Add Dir." Then
      t$ = F.Dir1.List(F.Dir1.ListIndex)
      If Right$(t$, 1) <> "\" Then t$ = t$ + "\"
      F.List1.AddItem t$ + "*.*"
'     * * * * * * * * * * * * * * * * * * * * * * * * * * * **
'     Add selected drive
'     * * * * * * * * * * * * * * * * * * * * * * * * * * * **
   ElseIf C$ = "&Add Drive" Then
      t$ = F.Drive1.List(F.Drive1.ListIndex)
      If Len(t$) > 2 Then t$ = Left$(t$, 2) + "\*.*"
      F.List1.AddItem t$
   End If
   If F.List1.ListCount > 0 Then F.List1.ListIndex = F.List1.NewIndex
   fState(F.Tag).Dirty = True

Case 3
'  * * * * * * * * * * * * * * * * * * * * * * * * * * * **
'   Remove files from ZIP
'  * * * * * * * * * * * * * * * * * * * * * * * * * * * **
   If F.List1.SelCount > 0 Then
   For i = F.List1.ListCount - 1 To 0 Step -1
      If F.List1.Selected(i) Then F.List1.RemoveItem i
   Next i
   For i = 0 To F.List1.ListCount - 1
      F.List1.Selected(i) = False
   Next
   End If
   UpdateLabels zForm(AF%)

Case 4
'  * * * * * * * * * * * * * * * * * * * * * * * * * * * **
'   Update old ZIP
'   Start by converting type to NewZip
'   and hide list box to prevent screen flashing
'  * * * * * * * * * * * * * * * * * * * * * * * * * * * **
   fState(AF%).zType = NewZip
   HideC F.List1
   Dim x, Sp%
   For x = 0 To F.List1.ListCount - 1
'  * * * * * * * * * * * * * * * * * * * * * * * * * * * **
'   Strip spaces & tabs from list box contents
'  * * * * * * * * * * * * * * * * * * * * * * * * * * * **
      Sp% = InStr(F.List1.List(x), Chr$(32))
      If Sp% = 0 Then Sp% = InStr(F.List1.List(x), Chr$(9))
      If Sp% > 0 Then
      F.List1.List(x) = Left$(F.List1.List(x), Sp% - 1)
      End If
'     * * * * * * * * * * * * * * * * * * * * * * * * * * * **
'     Fix directory separator--PKUNZIP stores it in reverse
'     * * * * * * * * * * * * * * * * * * * * * * * * * * * **
      Sp% = InStr(F.List1.List(x), "/")
      If Sp% > 0 Then
      F.List1.List(x) = "\" + Left$(F.List1.List(x), Sp% - 1) + "\" + ⇔
   Mid$(F.List1.List(x), Sp% + 1)
      End If
   Next x
'  * * * * * * * * * * * * * * * * * * * * * * * * * * * **
'   Rearrange controls
'  * * * * * * * * * * * * * * * * * * * * * * * * * * * **
```

```
    F.List1.Width = 2495
    ShowC F.List1
    F.File1.Pattern = "*.*"
    ShowC F.File1
    ShowC F.Dir1
    ShowC F.Drive1
    HideC F.Label1(0)
    HideC F.Label1(1)
    F.Label2.Top = F.List1.Top - (F.Label2.Height + 45)
    ShowC F.Label2
    F.Width = F.Dir1.Left + F.Dir1.Width + (F.List1.Left * 2)
'    * * * * * * * * * * * * * * * * * * * * * * * * * * * * **
'     Fix labels on toolbar buttons
'     set focus to Files to Zip list box
'     and update Windows menu
'    * * * * * * * * * * * * * * * * * * * * * * * * * * * * **
    UpdateLabels zForm(AF%)
    zForm(AF%).File1.SetFocus
    WindowMenuCheck False
Case Else
End Select
End Sub

Sub FileItem_Click (Index As Integer)
'    * * * * * * * * * * * * * * * * * * * * * * * * * * * * **
'     Process file menu selections
'    * * * * * * * * * * * * * * * * * * * * * * * * * * * * **
Dim F As Form, Test, x, CRLF$
Select Case Index
Case 0     'New
'    * * * * * * * * * * * * * * * * * * * * * * * * * * * * **
'     New ZIP file
'     Call GetOpenCounter to determine if can reuse existing array
'     elements or need new one
'    * * * * * * * * * * * * * * * * * * * * * * * * * * * * **
    Test = GetOpenCounter()
    If Test > 0 Then
       Set F = zForm(Test)
       fState(Test).zType = NewZip
       AF% = Test
    Else
       zFormCount = zFormCount + 1
       ReDim Preserve zForm(zFormCount)
       ReDim Preserve fState(zFormCount)
       ReDim Preserve ZipFil$(zFormCount)
       Set F = zForm(zFormCount)
       fState(zFormCount).zType = NewZip
       AF% = zFormCount
    End If
'    * * * * * * * * * * * * * * * * * * * * * * * * * * * * **
'     Show Browser form to get file name
'    * * * * * * * * * * * * * * * * * * * * * * * * * * * * **
    Browser.Show 1
    If ZipFil$(AF%) = "" Then fState(AF%).Deleted = True: Exit Sub
    F.Tag = AF%
    F.List1.Clear
'    * * * * * * * * * * * * * * * * * * * * * * * * * * * * **
'     Show New Zip form
'     and arrange controls on it
'    * * * * * * * * * * * * * * * * * * * * * * * * * * * * **
    zForm(AF%).Show
    F.Caption = ZipFil$(AF%)
    F.List1.Width = 2495
    ShowC F.List1
```

```
            F.File1.Pattern = "*.*"
            ShowC F.File1
            ShowC F.Dir1
            ShowC F.Drive1
            HideC F.Label1(0)
            HideC F.Label1(1)
            F.Label2.Top = F.List1.Top - (F.Label2.Height + 45)
            ShowC F.Label2
            F.Width = F.Dir1.Left + F.Dir1.Width + (F.List1.Left * 2)
            WindowMenuCheck False

      Case 1      'Open
      '  * * * * * * * * * * * * * * * * * * * * * * * * * * * **
      '    Open existing ZIP
      '    Call GetOpenCounter to determine if can reuse existing array
      '    elements or need new one
      '  * * * * * * * * * * * * * * * * * * * * * * * * * * * **
            Test = GetOpenCounter()
            If Test > 0 Then
                Set F = zForm(Test)
                fState(Test).zType = OldZip
                AF% = Test
            Else
                zFormCount = zFormCount + 1
                ReDim Preserve zForm(zFormCount)
                ReDim Preserve fState(zFormCount)
                ReDim Preserve ZipFil$(zFormCount)
                Set F = zForm(zFormCount)
                fState(zFormCount).zType = OldZip
                AF% = zFormCount
            End If
      '  * * * * * * * * * * * * * * * * * * * * * * * * * * * **
      '    Check contents of Startup$
      '    Show browser unless Startup$ contains a ZIP file name
      '    passed on the command line
      '  * * * * * * * * * * * * * * * * * * * * * * * * * * * **
            If StartUp$ = "" Then
                Browser.Show 1
            Else
                ZipFil$(AF%) = StartUp$
                StartUp$ = ""
            End If
      '  * * * * * * * * * * * * * * * * * * * * * * * * * * * **
      '    Exit sub if user canceled Browser
      '  * * * * * * * * * * * * * * * * * * * * * * * * * * * **
            If ZipFil$(AF%) = "" Then fState(AF%).Deleted = True: Exit Sub
      '  * * * * * * * * * * * * * * * * * * * * * * * * * * * **
      '    Otherwise, show the new MDI window and arrange controls
      '  * * * * * * * * * * * * * * * * * * * * * * * * * * * **
            zForm(AF%).Show
            F.Tag = AF%
            F.Caption = ZipFil$(AF%)
            F.List1.Width = 6975
            HideC F.File1
            HideC F.Dir1
            HideC F.Drive1
            HideC F.Label2
            ShellForm.Command2(2).Caption = "&Add"
            ShellForm.Command2(2).Enabled = True
            If ZipFil$(AF%) = "" Then Exit Sub
            F.List1.Clear
            ShowC F.List1
            ShowC F.Label1(0)
            ShowC F.Label1(1)
```

```
      Screen.MousePointer = 11
'     * * * * * * * * * * * * * * * * * * * * * * * * * * **
'     Add ZIP file contents to List1
'     * * * * * * * * * * * * * * * * * * * * * * * * * * **
      ReadZip F
      F.List1.Visible = True
      F.Width = F.List1.Width + (F.List1.Left * 2)
      WindowMenuCheck False
      Screen.MousePointer = 1

Case 2
'     * * * * * * * * * * * * * * * * * * * * * * * * * * **
'     Close button
'     * * * * * * * * * * * * * * * * * * * * * * * * * * **
      If Forms.Count = 1 Then Exit Sub
      Set F = ActiveForm
      Unload F
      For x = 0 To 4
          ShellForm.Command2(x).Enabled = False
      Next
Case 3      'Separator

Case 4      'About item
'     * * * * * * * * * * * * * * * * * * * * * * * * * * **
'     Show About box
'     * * * * * * * * * * * * * * * * * * * * * * * * * * **
   CRLF$ = Chr$(13) + Chr$(10)
   x = MsgBox("VB ZIP Shell" + CRLF$ + "Copyright (c) 1993, Paul Bonner" + ⇔
      CRLF$ + "PC Magazine Visual Basic Utilities" + CRLF$ + "All rights ⇔
      reserved.", 64, "VB ZIP Shell")
Case 5      'Exit
'     * * * * * * * * * * * * * * * * * * * * * * * * * * **
'     Attempt to end program--MDI child form QueryUnload procedure
'     will give user chance to halt process if any form is dirty
'     * * * * * * * * * * * * * * * * * * * * * * * * * * **
      End
End Select
End Sub

Sub MDIForm_Load ()
'     * * * * * * * * * * * * * * * * * * * * * * * * * * **
'     Program start-up code
'     * * * * * * * * * * * * * * * * * * * * * * * * * * **
AP$ = App.Path
If Right$(AP$, 1) <> "\" Then AP$ = AP$ + "\"
hT$ = Chr$(9)
'     * * * * * * * * * * * * * * * * * * * * * * * * * * **
'     Get previously saved options
'     * * * * * * * * * * * * * * * * * * * * * * * * * * **
GetOptions
If Dest$ = "" Then Dest$ = App.Path
'     * * * * * * * * * * * * * * * * * * * * * * * * * * **
'     Update labels
'     * * * * * * * * * * * * * * * * * * * * * * * * * * **
Label1 = "UnZip directory: " + Dest$
Label2 = ""
Source$ = Dest$
'     * * * * * * * * * * * * * * * * * * * * * * * * * * **
'     Center form
'     * * * * * * * * * * * * * * * * * * * * * * * * * * **
CenterForm Me
WindowMenuCheck False
'     * * * * * * * * * * * * * * * * * * * * * * * * * * **
'     If ZIP file passed on command line
```

```
'    pass its name to the File Open procedure  * * * * * * * * **
'    * * * * * * * * * * * * * * * * * * * * * * * * * * * * * **
If Command$ <> "" Then
    Startup$ = Command$
    FileItem_Click (1)
End If
End Sub

Sub optItem_Click (Index As Integer)  * * * * * * * * * * * * **
'    * * * * * * * * * * * * * * * * * * * * * * * * * * * * * **
'    Process Option menu selections  * * * * * * * * * * * * * **
'    * * * * * * * * * * * * * * * * * * * * * * * * * * * * * **
Dim D$
Select Case Index
Case Is < 2  * * * * * * * * * * * * * * * * * * * * * * * * * **
'    * * * * * * * * * * * * * * * * * * * * * * * * * * * * * **
'    User-selected Zip Options or UnZip Options item  * * * * **
'    * * * * * * * * * * * * * * * * * * * * * * * * * * * * * **
    OptionsMode% = Index
    Load Options
    CenterForm Options
    Options.Show 1

Case Else  * * * * * * * * * * * * * * * * * * * * * * * * * * **
'    * * * * * * * * * * * * * * * * * * * * * * * * * * * * * **
'    User select Unzip Path item
'    so get the new destination and store it  * * * * * * * * **
'    * * * * * * * * * * * * * * * * * * * * * * * * * * * * * **
  D$ = InputBox$("Enter destination path for Unzipped files:", "VB ZIP ⇔
    Shell", Dest$)
    If D$ <> "" Then Dest$ = D$:  Else D$ = Dest$
    Label1 = "UnZip directory: " + UCase$(D$)
    Dim Z$, F
    F = FreeFile
    Z$ = AP$ + "ZShell.DAT"
    On Error Resume Next
    Open Z$ For Output As F
    Print #F, Dest$
    On Error GoTo 0
End Select
End Sub

Sub Picture2_Resize ()  * * * * * * * * * * * * * * * * * * * **
'    * * * * * * * * * * * * * * * * * * * * * * * * * * * * * **
'    Resize 3D border lines for status bar
'    when the status bar is resized in respose to form resize
'    * * * * * * * * * * * * * * * * * * * * * * * * * * * * * **
Line1.X1 = 0
Line1.Y1 = 10
Line1.Y2 = 10
Line1.X2 = Picture2.Width
Line2.X1 = 0
Line2.Y1 = 0
Line2.Y2 = 0
Line2.X2 = Picture2.Width
End Sub

Sub wMenu_Click (Index As Integer)  * * * * * * * * * * * * * **
'    * * * * * * * * * * * * * * * * * * * * * * * * * * * * * **
'    Process Window arrange commands  * * * * * * * * * * * * **
'    * * * * * * * * * * * * * * * * * * * * * * * * * * * * * **
ShellForm.Arrange Index
End Sub
```

OPTIONS.FRM

```
'    * * * * * * * * * * * * * * * * * * * * * * * * * * **
'    OPTIONS.FRM
'    Copyright (c) 1993, Paul Bonner
'    PC Magazine Visual Basic Utilities
'    * * * * * * * * * * * * * * * * * * * * * * * * * * **
VERSION 2.00
Begin Form Options
   BorderStyle      =   3  'Fixed Double
   Caption          =   "Form1"
   ControlBox       =   0    'False
   Height           =   3255
   Left             =   1620
   LinkTopic        =   "Form1"
   MaxButton        =   0    'False
   MinButton        =   0    'False
   ScaleHeight      =   2850
   ScaleWidth       =   6270
   Top              =   2100
   Width            =   6390
   Begin Frame Frame1
      Caption       =     "Frame1(2)"
      Height        =     615
      Index         =     2
      Left          =     240
      TabIndex      =     7
      Top           =     2040
      Width         =     3135
      Begin OptionButton Option1
         Caption       =     "Option1"
         Height        =     375
         Index         =     0
         Left          =     1680
         TabIndex      =     9
         Top           =     120
         Width         =     1215
      End
      Begin CheckBox Check3
         Caption       =     "Check3"
         Height        =     255
         Index         =     0
         Left          =     240
         TabIndex      =     8
         Top           =     240
         Width         =     1215
      End
   End
   Begin Frame Frame1
      Caption       =     "Frame1(1)"
      Height        =     495
      Index         =     1
      Left          =     240
      TabIndex      =     4
      Top           =     1320
      Width         =     3135
```

```
        Begin OptionButton Option2
            Caption          =       "Option2"
            Height           =       255
            Index            =       0
            Left             =       0
            TabIndex         =       5
            Top              =       240
            Width            =       1695
        End
    End
    Begin Frame Frame1
        Caption          =       "Frame1(0)"
        Height           =       615
        Index            =       0
        Left             =       240
        TabIndex         =       3
        Top              =       480
        Width            =       3135
        Begin CheckBox Check2
            Caption          =       "Check2"
            Height           =       255
            Index            =       0
            Left             =       0
            TabIndex         =       6
            Top              =       240
            Width            =       1215
        End
    End
    Begin CommandButton Command1
        Caption          =       "Cancel"
        Height           =       375
        Index            =       1
        Left             =       5160
        TabIndex         =       2
        Top              =       600
        Width            =       855
    End
    Begin CommandButton Command1
        Caption          =       "OK"
        Default          =       -1    'True
        Height           =       375
        Index            =       0
        Left             =       5160
        TabIndex         =       1
        Top              =       120
        Width            =       855
    End
    Begin CheckBox xBox
        Caption          =       "Check1"
        Height           =       255
        Index            =       0
        Left             =       240
        TabIndex         =       0
        Top              =       120
        Width            =       4695
    End
End
DefInt A-Z
Option Explicit
Dim Loaded%

Sub AddOpt1 (C As Control, Pre As Control, Cap$, TI%)
'    * * * * * * * * * * * * * * * * * * * * * * * * * * * * * **
'    Add specified control to form, locating it relative
```

```
'   to previous control, add caption and set tab order
'    * * * * * * * * * * * * * * * * * * * * * * * * **
Load C
C.Visible = True
C.Top = Pre.Top
C.Left = Pre.Left + Pre.Width + 200
C.Caption = Cap$
C.Width = TextWidth(C.Caption) + 300
C.TabIndex = TI%
End Sub

Sub Command1_Click (Index As Integer)
Select Case Index
Case 0      'OK
'    * * * * * * * * * * * * * * * * * * * * * * * * **
'    User checked okay, so evaluate and save selections,
'    Then build options string
'    * * * * * * * * * * * * * * * * * * * * * * * * **
    EvalSels
    SaveSels
    BuildString
Case 1      'Cancel
End Select
Unload Options
End Sub

Sub EvalSels ()
'    * * * * * * * * * * * * * * * * * * * * * * * * **
'    Build options array from user selections
'    * * * * * * * * * * * * * * * * * * * * * * * * **

Dim X
Select Case OptionsMode%
'    * * * * * * * * * * * * * * * * * * * * * * * * **
'    ZIP Options screen
'    * * * * * * * * * * * * * * * * * * * * * * * * **
Case 0
    For X = 0 To 3
        Zo(X) = xBox(X)
    Next
    For X = 0 To 2
        If Option2(X) Then Zo(4) = X
    Next
    For X = 5 To 7
        Zo(X) = Check2(X - 5)
    Next
    For X = 8 To 10
        Zo(X) = Check3(X - 8)
    Next
'    * * * * * * * * * * * * * * * * * * * * * * * * **
'    UnZIP Options screen
'    * * * * * * * * * * * * * * * * * * * * * * * * **
Case 1
    For X = 0 To 2
        uZo(X) = xBox(X)
    Next
    For X = 6 To 8
        uZo(X) = Check2(X - 6)
    Next
    For X = 0 To 4
        If Option2(X) Then uZo(9) = X
    Next
    For X = 3 To 5
        Select Case Option1(X - 3)
```

```
        Case True
        uZo(X) = 1
        Case Else
        uZo(X) = 0
        End Select
    Next
End Select
End Sub

Sub Form_Load ()
Dim FF, T%, X
'   * * * * * * * * * * * * * * * * * * * * * * * * * * * **
'    Build form based on OptionsMode%
'   * * * * * * * * * * * * * * * * * * * * * * * * * * * **
Select Case OptionsMode%
'   * * * * * * * * * * * * * * * * * * * * * * * * * * * **
'    Build ZIP Options form
'   * * * * * * * * * * * * * * * * * * * * * * * * * * * **
Case 0
    Caption = "ZIP Options"
'   * * * * * * * * * * * * * * * * * * * * * * * * * * * **
'    Load check boxes, set location, tab order, captions
'   * * * * * * * * * * * * * * * * * * * * * * * * * * * **
    For FF = 1 To 3
        Load xBox(FF)
        xBox(FF).Top = xBox(FF - 1).Top + 400
        xBox(FF).Visible = True
        xBox(FF).TabIndex = FF
    Next
    T% = FF
    xBox(0).Caption = "-m    &Move files into ZIP file (deleting originals)"
    xBox(1).Caption = "-t     &Compress files on or after date..."
    xBox(2).Caption = "-r     &Recurse subdirectories"
    xBox(3).Caption = "-P     &Store pathnames in ZIP file"
'   * * * * * * * * * * * * * * * * * * * * * * * * * * * **
'    Draw compression method box, and add option buttons
'   * * * * * * * * * * * * * * * * * * * * * * * * * * * **
    Frame1(1).Caption = "Com&pression Method:"
    Frame1(1).Left = xBox(0).Left
    Frame1(1).Height = 600
    Frame1(1).Width = Width - 500
    Frame1(1).Top = xBox(FF - 1).Top + 400
    Frame1(1).TabIndex = T%: T% = T% + 1
    Option2(0).Top = 260
    Option2(0).Left = 260
    Option2(0).Caption = "Use maximal"
    Option2(0).Width = TextWidth(Option2(0).Caption) + 300
    Option2(0).TabIndex = T%: T% = T% + 1
    AddOpt1 Option2(1), Option2(0), "Implode only", T%: T% = T% + 1
    AddOpt1 Option2(2), Option2(1), "Shrink only", T%: T% = T% + 1
'   * * * * * * * * * * * * * * * * * * * * * * * * * * * **
'    Build Mask Attributes box, add check box controls
'   * * * * * * * * * * * * * * * * * * * * * * * * * * * **
    Frame1(0).Caption = "Mas&k attributes"
    Frame1(0).Left = xBox(0).Left
    Frame1(0).Height = 600
    Frame1(0).Width = Width - 500
    Frame1(0).Top = Frame1(1).Top + Frame1(1).Height + 200
    Frame1(0).TabIndex = T%: T% = T% + 1
    Check2(0).Top = 260
    Check2(0).Left = 260
    Check2(0).Caption = "Read only"
    Check2(0).Width = TextWidth(Check2(0).Caption) + 300
    Check2(0).TabIndex = T%: T% = T% + 1
```

```
    AddOpt1 Check2(1), Check2(0), "Hidden", T%: T% = T% + 1
    AddOpt1 Check2(2), Check2(1), "System", T%: T% = T% + 1
'   * * * * * * * * * * * * * * * * * * * * * * * * * * * * * *
'    Build Include Files box, add check boxes, hide option button
'   * * * * * * * * * * * * * * * * * * * * * * * * * * * * * *
    Option1(0).Visible = False
    Frame1(2).Caption = "&Include"
    Frame1(2).Left = xBox(0).Left
    Frame1(2).Height = 600
    Frame1(2).Width = Width - 500
    Frame1(2).Top = Frame1(0).Top + Frame1(0).Height + 200
    Frame1(2).TabIndex = T%: T% = T% + 1
    Check3(0).Top = 260
    Check3(0).Left = 260
    Check3(0).Caption = "Read only"
    Check3(0).Width = TextWidth(Check3(0).Caption) + 300
    Check3(0).TabIndex = T%: T% = T% + 1
    AddOpt1 Check3(1), Check3(0), "Hidden", T%: T% = T% + 1
    AddOpt1 Check3(2), Check3(1), "System", T%: T% = T% + 1
    For X = 0 To 1
        ShellForm.Command2(X).TabIndex = T%: T% = T% + 1
    Next
    Height = Frame1(2).Top + Frame1(2).Height + 600

Case Else
'   * * * * * * * * * * * * * * * * * * * * * * * * * * * * * *
'    Build UnZip Options form
'   * * * * * * * * * * * * * * * * * * * * * * * * * * * * * *
    Caption = "UnZIP Options"
'   * * * * * * * * * * * * * * * * * * * * * * * * * * * * * *
'    Load check boxes, position them, set tab order, add captions
'   * * * * * * * * * * * * * * * * * * * * * * * * * * * * * *
    For FF = 1 To 2
        Load xBox(FF)
        xBox(FF).Top = xBox(FF - 1).Top + 400
        xBox(FF).Visible = True
        xBox(FF).TabIndex = FF
    Next
    T% = FF
    xBox(0).Caption = "-t     &Test ZIPfile integrity"
    xBox(1).Caption = "-d     Create &directories stored in ZIP"
    xBox(2).Caption = "-o     &Overwrite existing files"
'   * * * * * * * * * * * * * * * * * * * * * * * * * * * * * *
'    Build Mask Attributes box, add check box controls
'   * * * * * * * * * * * * * * * * * * * * * * * * * * * * * *
    Frame1(0).Caption = "&Mask attributes"
    Frame1(0).Left = xBox(0).Left
    Frame1(0).Height = 600
    Frame1(0).Width = Width - 500
    Frame1(0).Top = xBox(FF - 1).Top + 400
    Frame1(0).TabIndex = T%: T% = T% + 1
    Check2(0).Top = 260
    Check2(0).Left = 260
    Check2(0).Caption = "Read only"
    Check2(0).Width = TextWidth(Check2(0).Caption) + 300
    Check2(0).TabIndex = T%: T% = T% + 1
    AddOpt1 Check2(1), Check2(0), "Hidden", T%: T% = T% + 1
    AddOpt1 Check2(2), Check2(1), "System", T%: T% = T% + 1
'   * * * * * * * * * * * * * * * * * * * * * * * * * * * * * *
'    Build Extract Order box, add option buttons
'   * * * * * * * * * * * * * * * * * * * * * * * * * * * * * *
    Frame1(1).Caption = "&Extract in order of:"
    Frame1(1).Left = xBox(0).Left
    Frame1(1).Height = 600
```

```
   Frame1(1).Width = Width - 500
   Frame1(1).Top = Frame1(0).Top + Frame1(0).Height + 200
   Frame1(1).TabIndex = T%: T% = T% + 1
   Option2(0).Top = 260
   Option2(0).Left = 260
   Option2(0).Caption = "CRC"
   Option2(0).Width = TextWidth(Option2(0).Caption) + 300
   Option2(0).TabIndex = T%: T% = T% + 1
   AddOpt1 Option2(1), Option2(0), "Date", T%: T% = T% + 1
   AddOpt1 Option2(2), Option2(1), "Ext", T%: T% = T% + 1
   AddOpt1 Option2(3), Option2(2), "Name", T%: T% = T% + 1
   AddOpt1 Option2(4), Option2(3), "Size", T%: T% = T% + 1
'   * * * * * * * * * * * * * * * * * * * * * * * * * * * **
'   Build Files to Extract box, hide check box, add option buttons
'   * * * * * * * * * * * * * * * * * * * * * * * * * * * **
   Frame1(2).Left = xBox(0).Left
   Frame1(2).Height = 660
   Frame1(2).Width = Width - 500
   Frame1(2).Top = Frame1(1).Top + Frame1(1).Height + 200
   Frame1(2).TabIndex = T%: T% = T% + 1
   Frame1(2).Caption = "&Files to UnZip:"
   Check3(0).Visible = False
   Option1(0).Top = 260
   Option1(0).Left = 260
   Option1(0).Caption = "All"
   Option1(0).Width = TextWidth(Option1(0).Caption) + 300
   Option1(0).TabIndex = T%: T% = T% + 1
 AddOpt1 Option1(1), Option1(0), "-n New && out of date files only", T%: ⇔
    T% = T% + 1
 AddOpt1 Option1(2), Option1(1), "-f new files only", T%: T% = T% + 1
   Frame1(2).Visible = True
   For X = 0 To 1
       Command1(X).TabIndex = T%: T% = T% + 1
   Next
   Height = Frame1(2).Top + Frame1(2).Height + 600
End Select
'   * * * * * * * * * * * * * * * * * * * * * * * * * * * **
'   Retrieve saved options
'   * * * * * * * * * * * * * * * * * * * * * * * * * * * **
GetSels
End Sub

Sub GetSels ()
Dim X
'   * * * * * * * * * * * * * * * * * * * * * * * * * * * **
'   Set screen controls to reflect current values of options array
'   * * * * * * * * * * * * * * * * * * * * * * * * * * * **
Select Case OptionsMode%
'   * * * * * * * * * * * * * * * * * * * * * * * * * * * **
'   ZIP Options screen
'   * * * * * * * * * * * * * * * * * * * * * * * * * * * **
Case 0
   For X = 0 To 3
       xBox(X) = Zo(X)
   Next
   Option2(Zo(4)) = True
   For X = 5 To 7
       Check2(X - 5) = Zo(X)
   Next
   For X = 8 To 10
       Check3(X - 8) = Zo(X)
   Next
'   * * * * * * * * * * * * * * * * * * * * * * * * * * * **
'   UnZIP Options screen
```

```
'    * * * * * * * * * * * * * * * * * * * * * * * * **
Case 1
    For X = 0 To 2
        xBox(X) = uZo(X)
    Next
    For X = 6 To 8
        Check2(X - 6) = uZo(X)
    Next
        Option2(uZo(9)) = True
    For X = 3 To 5
        If uZo(X) = 1 Then Option1(X - 3) = True
    Next
End Select
End Sub

Sub SaveSels ()
'    * * * * * * * * * * * * * * * * * * * * * * * * **
'    Save user selections to disk
'    * * * * * * * * * * * * * * * * * * * * * * * * **
Dim f, X, Z$
On Error GoTo SvErr
f = FreeFile
Select Case OptionsMode%
'    * * * * * * * * * * * * * * * * * * * * * * * * **
'    ZIP Options screen
'    * * * * * * * * * * * * * * * * * * * * * * * * **
Case 0
    Z$ = AP$ + "ZIPOPT.DAT"
    Open Z$ For Output As f
    For X = 0 To UBound(Zo, 1)
        Print #f, Zo(X)
    Next
'    * * * * * * * * * * * * * * * * * * * * * * * * **
'    UnZIP Options screen
'    * * * * * * * * * * * * * * * * * * * * * * * * **
Case 1
    Z$ = AP$ + "UNZIPOPT.DAT"
    Open Z$ For Output As f
    For X = 0 To UBound(uZo, 1)
        Print #f, uZo(X)
    Next
End Select
SE:
Close f
Exit Sub
SvErr:
Resume SE
End Sub

Sub xBox_Click (Index As Integer)
'    * * * * * * * * * * * * * * * * * * * * * * * * **
'    Special handler for Starting Date check box on Zip Option screen
'    * * * * * * * * * * * * * * * * * * * * * * * * **
If Options.Visible = False Then Exit Sub
Dim D$
On Error Resume Next
Select Case Index
Case 1
'    * * * * * * * * * * * * * * * * * * * * * * * * **
'    Get starting date when user clicks check box
'    * * * * * * * * * * * * * * * * * * * * * * * * **

    If OptionsMode% = 0 And xBox(Index) = 1 Then
        D$ = sDate$
```

```
      sDate$ = InputBox("Enter the starting date for the files that you wish ⇔
         to include in the ZIP", "Enter Date", D$)
      End If
End Select
End Sub
```

LISTING

BROWSER.FRM

```
'    * * * * * * * * * * * * * * * * * * * * * * * * * * **
'    BROWSER.FRM
'    Copyright (c) 1993, Paul Bonner
'    PC Magazine Visual Basic Utilities
'    * * * * * * * * * * * * * * * * * * * * * * * * * * **
VERSION 2.00
Begin Form Browser
   BorderStyle      =     3   'Fixed Double
   Caption          =     "Browse"
   ControlBox       =     0   'False
   Height           =     4050
   Left             =     2355
   LinkTopic        =     "Form1"
   MaxButton        =     0   'False
   MinButton        =     0   'False
   ScaleHeight      =     3645
   ScaleWidth       =     5910
   Top              =     2070
   Width            =     6030
   Begin TextBox Text1
      Height        =     360
      Left          =     240
      TabIndex      =     1
      Text          =     "Text1"
      Top           =     480
      Width         =     1935
   End
   Begin CommandButton Command1
      Cancel        =     -1   'True
      Caption       =     "Cancel"
      Height        =     375
      Index         =     1
      Left          =     4800
      TabIndex      =     8
      Top           =     720
      Width         =     975
   End
   Begin CommandButton Command1
      Caption       =     "OK"
      Default       =     -1   'True
      Height        =     375
      Index         =     0
      Left          =     4800
      TabIndex      =     7
      Top           =     240
```

```
            Width               =      975
         End
         Begin FileListBox File1
            Height              =      1785
            Left                =      240
            Pattern             =      "*.ZIP"
            TabIndex            =      2
            Top                 =      960
            Width               =      1995
         End
         Begin DriveListBox Drive1
            Height              =      315
            Left                =      2520
            TabIndex            =      6
            Top                 =      3120
            Width               =      1995
         End
         Begin DirListBox Dir1
            Height              =      1830
            Left                =      2520
            TabIndex            =      4
            Top                 =      960
            Width               =      1995
         End
         Begin Label Label2
            Caption             =      "&Drives:"
            Height              =      255
            Index               =      1
            Left                =      2520
            TabIndex            =      5
            Top                 =      2900
            Width               =      2055
         End
         Begin Label Label3
            Caption             =      "Label3"
            Height              =      255
            Left                =      2400
            TabIndex            =      9
            Top                 =      480
            Width               =      2175
         End
         Begin Label Label2
            Caption             =      "&Directories:"
            Height              =      255
            Index               =      0
            Left                =      2400
            TabIndex            =      3
            Top                 =      120
            Width               =      2055
         End
         Begin Label Label1
            AutoSize            =      -1    'True
            Caption             =      "File &Name:"
            Height              =      195
            Left                =      240
            TabIndex            =      0
            Top                 =      120
            Width               =      915
         End
      End
End
DefInt A-Z
Option Explicit

Sub Command1_Click (Index As Integer)
```

```
'       * * * * * * * * * * * * * * * * * * * * * * * * * **
'       Process commands in browse dialog box
'       * * * * * * * * * * * * * * * * * * * * * * * * * **
Dim Dot
Select Case Index
Case 0
   Dim F$, dStart, F1$
   F$ = Text1
'       * * * * * * * * * * * * * * * * * * * * * * * * * **
'       Look for directory change command
'       * * * * * * * * * * * * * * * * * * * * * * * * * **
   If F$ = ".." Then Dir1.Path = F$: Exit Sub
'       * * * * * * * * * * * * * * * * * * * * * * * * * **
'       Look for wildcards or directory path data
'       * * * * * * * * * * * * * * * * * * * * * * * * * **
   If InStr(F$, "*") Or InStr(F$, "\") Or InStr(F$, ":") Then
      For dStart = Len(Text1) To 1 Step -1
         F1$ = Mid$(F$, dStart, 1)
         If F1$ = "\" Or F1$ = ":" Then Exit For
      Next
'       * * * * * * * * * * * * * * * * * * * * * * * * * **
'       If Text1 contains path data, set drive and dir
'       * * * * * * * * * * * * * * * * * * * * * * * * * **
      If dStart > 0 Then
         If Mid$(F$, 2, 1) = ":" Then Drive1.Drive = Left$(F$, 1)
         F1$ = F$
'       * * * * * * * * * * * * * * * * * * * * * * * * * **
'       Check validity of path
'       * * * * * * * * * * * * * * * * * * * * * * * * * **
         If IsValidPath(F1$, Left$(Drive1, 2)) Then
            On Error Resume Next
            Dir1.Path = F$
            File1.Path = F$
            On Error GoTo 0
         End If
'       * * * * * * * * * * * * * * * * * * * * * * * * * **
'       Use value of Text1 to identify file pattern
'       * * * * * * * * * * * * * * * * * * * * * * * * * **
         F$ = Text1
   If Mid$(F$, dStart + 1) <> "" Then File1.Pattern = Mid$(F$, dStart + 1)
      Else
         File1.Pattern = F$
      End If
      dStart = 0
      Text1 = ""
   End If
'       * * * * * * * * * * * * * * * * * * * * * * * * * **
'       Identify target file
'       * * * * * * * * * * * * * * * * * * * * * * * * * **
   ZipFil$(af%) = RTrim$(File1.Path)
 If Right$(ZipFil$(af%), 1) <> "\" Then ZipFil$(af%) = ZipFil$(af%) + "\"
'       * * * * * * * * * * * * * * * * * * * * * * * * * **
'       Handler for new ZIPs
'       * * * * * * * * * * * * * * * * * * * * * * * * * **
   If fState(af%).zType = NewZip Then
      If Text1 = "" Then ZipFil$(af%) = "": Exit Sub
      ZipFil$(af%) = ZipFil$(af%) + Text1
      Dot = InStr(ZipFil$(af%), ".")
      If Dot = 0 Then ZipFil$(af%) = ZipFil$(af%) + ".ZIP"
'       * * * * * * * * * * * * * * * * * * * * * * * * * **
'       Handler for existing Zips
'       * * * * * * * * * * * * * * * * * * * * * * * * * **
   Else
      If File1 <> "" Then
```

```
          ZipFil$(af%) = ZipFil$(af%) + File1
      Else
          If Text1 = "" Then Exit Sub
          If InStr(Text1, "\") Then
              ZipFil$(af%) = Text1
          Else
              ZipFil$(af%) = File1.Path + "\" + Text1
          End If
      End If
      If Exists(ZipFil$(af%)) = False Then
          Dot = MsgBox(ZipFil$(af%) + " not found.", 48, "VB ZIP Shell")
          ZipFil$(af%) = ""
          Exit Sub
      End If
   End If
'   * * * * * * * * * * * * * * * * * * * * * * * * * **
'   Identify source path
'   * * * * * * * * * * * * * * * * * * * * * * * * * **
   Source$ = File1.Path
Case Else          'Cancel button
   ZipFil$(af%) = ""
End Select
Unload Browser
End Sub

Sub Dir1_Change ()
File1.Path = Dir1.Path
Text1 = ""
Label3 = Dir1.Path
End Sub

Sub Dir1_Click ()
Dim P$
P$ = Dir1.List(Dir1.ListIndex)
If File1.Path <> P$ Then
   File1.Path = P$
   Text1 = ""
   Label3 = P$
End If
End Sub

Sub Drive1_Change ()
On Error GoTo DriveError
Dir1.Path = Drive1.Drive
Dir1.Refresh
Exit Sub
DriveError:
   MsgBox "Drive Not Ready", 48, "VB ZIP Shell"
   Resume Next
End Sub

Sub Drive1_KeyUp (KeyCode As Integer, Shift As Integer)
'VB Drive_Change event misses changes initiated by keystroke, so
'pick them up here
Dir1.Path = Drive1.Drive
End Sub

Sub File1_Click ()
Text1 = File1
End Sub

Sub File1_DblClick ()
   Command1(0).Value = True
End Sub
```

```
Sub Form_Load ()
'    * * * * * * * * * * * * * * * * * * * * * * * * * **
'    Set caption and arrange controls based on whether this is
'    a new or existing ZIP
'    * * * * * * * * * * * * * * * * * * * * * * * * * **
ZipFil$(af%) = ""
If fState(af%).zType = NewZip Then
    Text1 = ""
    Caption = "New ZIP file"
    Label1 = "File &Name:"
    Text1.Visible = True
    File1.Enabled = False
Else
    Text1 = ""
    Caption = "Open ZIP file"
    Label1 = "File &Name:"
End If
Label3 = Dir1.Path
Drive1.Drive = Left$(Source$, 1)
Dir1.Path = Source$
End Sub
```

LISTING

ZIPREAD.FRM

```
'    * * * * * * * * * * * * * * * * * * * * * * * * * **
'    ZIPREAD.FRM
'    Copyright (c) 1993, Paul Bonner
'    PC Magazine Visual Basic Utilities
'    * * * * * * * * * * * * * * * * * * * * * * * * * **
VERSION 2.00
Begin Form UnZipper
    BackColor        =    &H00FFFFFF&
    Caption          =    "VB ZIP Shell "
    Height           =    3285
    Icon             =    ZIPREAD.FRX:0000
    Left             =    1140
    LinkTopic        =    "Form1"
    MDIChild         =    -1    'True
    ScaleHeight      =    2880
    ScaleWidth       =    7425
    Top              =    2130
    Visible          =    0      'False
    Width            =    7545
    Begin ListBox List1
        BackColor        =    &H00FFFFFF&
        ForeColor        =    &H00000000&
        Height           =    1785
        Left             =    240
        MultiSelect      =    2      'Extended
        TabIndex         =    3
        Top              =    840
        Visible          =    0      'False
```

```
      Width              =      3375
   End
   Begin FileListBox File1
      BackColor          =      &H00FFFFFF&
      Height             =      1785
      Hidden             =      -1   'True
      Left               =      3120
      MultiSelect        =      2    'Extended
      System             =      -1   'True
      TabIndex           =      2
      Top                =      840
      Visible            =      0    'False
      Width              =      1995
   End
   Begin DriveListBox Drive1
      BackColor          =      &H00FFFFFF&
      Height             =      315
      Left               =      5160
      TabIndex           =      1
      Top                =      840
      Visible            =      0    'False
      Width              =      1935
   End
   Begin DirListBox Dir1
      BackColor          =      &H00FFFFFF&
      Height             =      1380
      Left               =      5160
      TabIndex           =      0
      Top                =      1260
      Visible            =      0    'False
      Width              =      1935
   End
   Begin Label Label1
      BackColor          =      &H00FFFFFF&
      Caption            =      "&Name                    Date ⇔
   Time        Size         Size          Ratio"
      Height             =      255
      Index              =      0
      Left               =      240
      TabIndex           =      6
      Top                =      600
      Width              =      6855
   End
   Begin Label Label1
      BackColor          =      &H00FFFFFF&
      Caption            =      "                                   ⇔
   Comp.        Exp.         Compression"
      Height             =      195
      Index              =      1
      Left               =      240
      TabIndex           =      5
      Top                =      420
      Width              =      6975
   End
   Begin Label Label2
      BackColor          =      &H00FFFFFF&
      Caption            =      "&Items to be ZIPPED <-------------- Select ⇔
   files, dirs. or drives to add to the ZIP file"
      Height             =      255
      Left               =      240
      TabIndex           =      4
      Top                =      240
      Width              =      6975
   End
```

```
End
DefInt A-Z
Option Explicit

Sub Dir1_Change ()
File1.Path = Dir1.Path
File1.Refresh
End Sub

Sub Dir1_GotFocus ()
ShellForm.Command2(2).Caption = "&Add Dir."
ShellForm.Command2(3).Enabled = False
End Sub

Sub Drive1_Change ()
On Error Resume Next
Dir1.Path = Drive1
Dir1.Refresh
End Sub

Sub Drive1_GotFocus ()
ShellForm.Command2(3).Enabled = False
ShellForm.Command2(2).Caption = "&Add Drive"
End Sub

Sub File1_DblClick ()
'    * * * * * * * * * * * * * * * * * * * * * * * * * * **
'    Add current file to List1
'    * * * * * * * * * * * * * * * * * * * * * * * * * * **
List1.AddItem File1
fState(Me.Tag).Dirty = True
End Sub

Sub File1_GotFocus ()
ShellForm.Command2(2).Caption = "&Add File"
ShellForm.Command2(3).Enabled = False
End Sub

Sub Form_Activate ()
'    * * * * * * * * * * * * * * * * * * * * * * * * * * **
'    Update toolbar buttons to reflect current file type
'    * * * * * * * * * * * * * * * * * * * * * * * * * * **

    UpdateLabels Me
End Sub

Sub Form_QueryUnload (Cancel As Integer, UnloadMode As Integer)
'    * * * * * * * * * * * * * * * * * * * * * * * * * * **
'    Check if Form is dirty--cancel if user doesn't want to
'    lose changes
'    * * * * * * * * * * * * * * * * * * * * * * * * * * **
If fState(Me.Tag).Dirty = True Then
  If MsgBox("Abandon changes to this ZIP file?", 36, "VB ZIP Shell") <> 6 ⇔
    Then Cancel = True
End If
'    * * * * * * * * * * * * * * * * * * * * * * * * * * **
'    Otherwise, delete this form
'    and disable toolbar buttons
'    * * * * * * * * * * * * * * * * * * * * * * * * * * **
fState(Me.Tag).Deleted = True
fState(Me.Tag).zType = False
Dim X
For X = 0 To 4
    ShellForm.Command2(X).Enabled = False
```

```
Next X
ShellForm.Label2 = ""
Set zForm(Me.Tag) = Nothing
End Sub

Sub Form_Unload (Cancel As Integer)
'   * * * * * * * * * * * * * * * * * * * * * * * * * * * **
'   Update Windows menu--True parameter tells WindowMenuCheck
'   that a form is being unloaded
'   * * * * * * * * * * * * * * * * * * * * * * * * * * * **
WindowMenuCheck True
End Sub

Sub List1_Click ()
'   * * * * * * * * * * * * * * * * * * * * * * * * * * * **
'   Update toolbar buttons
'   * * * * * * * * * * * * * * * * * * * * * * * * * * * **
UpdateLabels Me
End Sub

Sub List1_GotFocus ()
ShellForm.Command2(2).Enabled = False
End Sub

Sub List1_LostFocus ()
ShellForm.Command2(2).Enabled = True
End Sub
```

LISTING

UNZIPPER.FRM

```
'   * * * * * * * * * * * * * * * * * * * * * * * * * * * **
'   UNZIPPER.FRM
'   Copyright (c) 1993, Paul Bonner
'   PC Magazine Visual Basic Utilities
'   * * * * * * * * * * * * * * * * * * * * * * * * * * * **
VERSION 2.00
Begin Form UnZipReport
    BackColor       =   &H00C0C0C0&
    BorderStyle     =   3   'Fixed Double
    Caption         =   "PKUNZIP Report"
    Height          =   4710
    Left            =   1440
    LinkTopic       =   "Form2"
    MaxButton       =   0   'False
    MinButton       =   0   'False
    ScaleHeight     =   4305
    ScaleWidth      =   7050
    Top             =   2385
    Width           =   7170
    Begin TextBox Text1
        Height      =   4095
        Left        =   120
        MultiLine   =   -1  'True
```

```
        ScrollBars        =     3    'Both
        TabIndex          =     0
        Text              =     "Text1"
        Top               =     120
        Width             =     6735
    End
End
DefInt A-Z
Option Explicit
```

ZIPREAD.BAS

```
'     * * * * * * * * * * * * * * * * * * * * * * * * * * * *
'     ZIPREAD.BAS
'     Copyright (c) 1993, Paul Bonner
'     PC Magazine Visual Basic Utilities
'     PDS 7.1 routines developed and placed in public domain
'     by Neal B. Scott
'     Adapted for use with Visual Basic 2.0 by Paul Bonner
'     Complete ZIP file layout can be found in APPNOTE.TXT,
'     as distributed by PKWARE Inc.
'     * * * * * * * * * * * * * * * * * * * * * * * * * * * *
DefInt A-Z
Option Explicit
'     * * * * * * * * * * * * * * * * * * * * * * * * * * * *
'     Define type for reading ZIP file directory
'     * * * * * * * * * * * * * * * * * * * * * * * * * * * *
Type LocalFileHeaderType
     ver    As String * 2      'versionneededtoextract
     generalpurposebitflag   As String * 2
     method         As String * 2     'compressionmethod
     modtime        As String * 2     'lastmodfiletime
     moddate        As String * 2     'lastmodfiledate
     crc32          As String * 4
     cSize          As String * 4     'compressedsize
     uncSize        As String * 4     'uncompressedsize
     fNameLen       As String * 2     'filenamelength
     xFieldLen      As String * 2     'ExtraFieldLength
End Type

Sub AddFile (FileName$, LFH As LocalFileHeaderType, F As Form)
'     * * * * * * * * * * * * * * * * * * * * * * * * * * * *
'     Add file to list box
'     pad file name to make it look pretty
'     compute percentage saved for non-zero length files
'     * * * * * * * * * * * * * * * * * * * * * * * * * * * *
Dim D%, Per$
Do While Len(FileName$) < 12
    FileName$ = FileName$ + " "
Loop
If UnsignedWORD#(LFH.uncSize) > 0 Then
Per$=Format$(1-UnsignedWORD#(LFH.cSize)/UnsignedWORD#(LFH.uncSize),⇔
    "Percent")
```

```
End If
F.List1.AddItem FileName$ & hT$ & DOSDate2STR$(LFH.moddate) & hT$ & ⇔
    DOSTime2STR$(LFH.modtime) & hT$ & UnsignedWORD#(LFH.cSize) & hT$ & ⇔
    UnsignedWORD#(LFH.uncSize) & hT$ & Per$
End Sub

Function DOSDate2STR$ (AA$)    'MSDOSDate2STR$Date$
'    * * * * * * * * * * * * * * * * * * * * * * * * * **
'    Convert binary data to Date
'    * * * * * * * * * * * * * * * * * * * * * * * * * **


'    * * * * * * * * * * * * * * * * * * * * * * * * * **
'    First get the year
'    * * * * * * * * * * * * * * * * * * * * * * * * * **
Dim DateInt&
DateInt& = UnsignedInt&(AA$)
Dim FourDigitYr%
FourDigitYr% = (DateInt& \ 512) + 1980
Dim FormattedYear$
FormattedYear$ = "19" + Right$("0" + LTrim$(Str$(FourDigitYr%)), 2)


'    * * * * * * * * * * * * * * * * * * * * * * * * * **
'    Now the month
'    * * * * * * * * * * * * * * * * * * * * * * * * * **
DateInt& = DateInt& - (FourDigitYr% - 1980) * 512
Dim TwoDigitMonth%
TwoDigitMonth% = (DateInt& \ 32)
Dim FormattedMonth$
FormattedMonth$ = Right$("0" + LTrim$(Str$(TwoDigitMonth%)), 2)
'    * * * * * * * * * * * * * * * * * * * * * * * * * **
'    Now the day
'    * * * * * * * * * * * * * * * * * * * * * * * * * **
DateInt& = DateInt& - TwoDigitMonth% * 32
Dim TwoDigitDay%
TwoDigitDay% = DateInt&
Dim FormattedDay$
FormattedDay$ = Right$("0" + LTrim$(Str$(TwoDigitDay%)), 2)
'    * * * * * * * * * * * * * * * * * * * * * * * * * **
'    Put it all together
'    * * * * * * * * * * * * * * * * * * * * * * * * * **
DOSDate2STR$ = FormattedMonth$ + "-" + FormattedDay$ + "-" + FormattedYear$
End Function

Function DOSTime2STR$ (AA$)    'MSDOSTime2STRTime$
'    * * * * * * * * * * * * * * * * * * * * * * * * * **
'    Convert binary data to Time
'    * * * * * * * * * * * * * * * * * * * * * * * * * **


'    * * * * * * * * * * * * * * * * * * * * * * * * * **
'    First get the hour
'    * * * * * * * * * * * * * * * * * * * * * * * * * **
Dim TimeInt&
TimeInt& = UnsignedInt&(AA$)
Dim TwoDigitHour%
TwoDigitHour% = TimeInt& \ 2048
Dim FormattedHour$
FormattedHour$ = Right$("0" + LTrim$(Str$(TwoDigitHour%)), 2)


'    * * * * * * * * * * * * * * * * * * * * * * * * * **
'    Now get the minutes
'    * * * * * * * * * * * * * * * * * * * * * * * * * **
TimeInt& = TimeInt& - (TwoDigitHour% * 2048&)
```

```
Dim TwoDigitMinutes%
TwoDigitMinutes% = (TimeInt& \ 32)
Dim FormattedMinutes$
FormattedMinutes$ = Right$("0" + LTrim$(Str$(TwoDigitMinutes%)), 2)

'    * * * * * * * * * * * * * * * * * * * * * * * * **
'    Now get the seconds
'    * * * * * * * * * * * * * * * * * * * * * * * * **
TimeInt& = TimeInt& - TwoDigitMinutes% * 32
Dim TwoDigitSeconds%
TwoDigitSeconds% = TimeInt& * 2
Dim FormattedSeconds$
FormattedSeconds$ = Right$("0" + LTrim$(Str$(TwoDigitSeconds%)), 2)

'    * * * * * * * * * * * * * * * * * * * * * * * * **
'    Now put it all together
'    * * * * * * * * * * * * * * * * * * * * * * * * **
DOSTime2STR$ = FormattedHour$ + "." + FormattedMinutes$ + "." + ⇔
    FormattedSeconds$
End Function

Sub ReadZip (F As Form)
'    * * * * * * * * * * * * * * * * * * * * * * * * **
'    Routine for binary read of ZIP file
'    * * * * * * * * * * * * * * * * * * * * * * * * **
If ZipFil$(AF%) = "" Then Exit Sub
Dim HeaderSignature    As String * 4
Dim LFH    As LocalFileHeaderType
Dim ZipBuf%
ZipBuf% = FreeFile
F.List1.Clear
Open ZipFil$(AF%) For Binary As ZipBuf%
'    * * * * * * * * * * * * * * * * * * * * * * * * **
'    Get header of 1st file
'    * * * * * * * * * * * * * * * * * * * * * * * * **
Dim CurByte&
CurByte& = 1
Get #ZipBuf%, CurByte&, HeaderSignature
CurByte& = CurByte& + Len(HeaderSignature)
Do While HeaderSignature = "PK"      '0x04034b50
    Get #ZipBuf%, CurByte&, LFH
    LFH.moddate = STRDate2DOS$(Date$)
    LFH.modtime = STRTime2DOS$("12.00.00")
    Put #ZipBuf%, CurByte&, LFH
    CurByte& = CurByte& + Len(LFH)
    Dim TempfNameLen&
    TempfNameLen& = UnsignedInt&(LFH.fNameLen)
    Dim FileName$
    FileName$ = Space$(TempfNameLen&)
    Get #ZipBuf%, , FileName$
    CurByte& = CurByte& + Len(FileName$)
    Dim xFieldLen&
    xFieldLen& = UnsignedInt&(LFH.xFieldLen)
    Dim TempExtraField$
    TempExtraField$ = Space$(xFieldLen&)
    Get #ZipBuf%, , TempExtraField$
    CurByte& = CurByte& + Len(TempExtraField$)
    Dim TempcSize#
    TempcSize# = UnsignedWORD#(LFH.cSize)
    CurByte& = CurByte& + TempcSize#
'    * * * * * * * * * * * * * * * * * * * * * * * * **
'    Add to list box
'    * * * * * * * * * * * * * * * * * * * * * * * * **
    AddFile FileName$, LFH, F
```

```
'    * * * * * * * * * * * * * * * * * * * * * * * * * * * **
'    Get next file name
'    * * * * * * * * * * * * * * * * * * * * * * * * * * * **
   Get #ZipBuf%, CurByte&, HeaderSignature
   CurByte& = CurByte& + Len(HeaderSignature)
Loop
Close #ZipBuf%
End Sub

Function STRDate2DOS$ (AA$)   'STRDate2MSDOSDate$
'    * * * * * * * * * * * * * * * * * * * * * * * * * * * **
'    Convert date to binary
'    * * * * * * * * * * * * * * * * * * * * * * * * * * * **
Dim TwoDigitMonth%
TwoDigitMonth% = Val(Left$(AA$, 2))
Dim TwoDigitDay%
TwoDigitDay% = Val(Mid$(AA$, 4, 2))
Dim FourDigitYr%
FourDigitYr% = Val(Right$(AA$, 4))
Dim Temp&
Temp& = (FourDigitYr% - 1980) * 512 + (TwoDigitMonth% * 32) + TwoDigitDay%
Dim High&
High& = Temp& \ 256
Dim Low&
Low& = Temp& - High& * 256
Dim HighByte$
HighByte$ = Chr$(High&)
Dim LowByte$
LowByte$ = Chr$(Low&)
STRDate2DOS$ = LowByte$ + HighByte$
End Function

Function STRTime2DOS$ (AA$)   'STRTime2MSDOSTime$
'    * * * * * * * * * * * * * * * * * * * * * * * * * * * **
'    Convert time to binary
'    * * * * * * * * * * * * * * * * * * * * * * * * * * * **
Dim TwoDigitHour%
TwoDigitHour% = Val(Left$(AA$, 2))
Dim TwoDigitMinutes%
TwoDigitMinutes% = Val(Mid$(AA$, 4, 2))
Dim TwoDigitSeconds%
TwoDigitSeconds% = Val(Mid$(AA$, 7))
Dim Temp&
Temp&=(TwoDigitHour%*2048&)+TwoDigitMinutes%*32+(TwoDigitSeconds%\2)
Dim High&
High& = Temp& \ 256
Dim Low&
Low& = Temp& - High& * 256
Dim HighByte$
HighByte$ = Chr$(High&)
Dim LowByte$
LowByte$ = Chr$(Low&)
STRTime2DOS$ = LowByte$ + HighByte$
End Function

Function UnsignedInt& (AA$)
'    * * * * * * * * * * * * * * * * * * * * * * * * * * * **
'    Convert string to unsigned int
'    * * * * * * * * * * * * * * * * * * * * * * * * * * * **
Dim Value&
Value& = Asc(Right$(AA$, 1)) * 256&
Value& = Value& + Asc(Left$(AA$, 1))
UnsignedInt& = Value&
End Function
```

```
Function UnsignedWORD# (AA$)
'    * * * * * * * * * * * * * * * * * * * * * * **
'    Convert string to unsigned word
'    * * * * * * * * * * * * * * * * * * * * * * **
Dim Value#
Value# = Asc(Mid$(AA$, 4, 1)) * 256# * 256# * 256#
Value# = Value# + Asc(Mid$(AA$, 3, 1)) * 256# * 256#
Value# = Value# + Asc(Mid$(AA$, 2, 1)) * 256#
Value# = Value# + Asc(Mid$(AA$, 1, 1))
UnsignedWORD# = Value#
End Function
```

4

VB Q

Visual Basic Q provides queued or instant printing of documents from nearly any Windows application.

Printing in Windows is anything but fun. Mostly, it's tedious. Printing from many applications seems to take forever, and generally once you start printing a job, you can forget about doing anything else with that application until the printing is completed—few Windows applications provide the opportunity to print in the background. Worst of all, you generally don't have any choice about suffering through this. There's no easy way to tell PageMaker, Word, Windows, Excel, or any other application: "Print this file when I go out to lunch," or "Print these 10 files overnight and have them ready for me in the morning."

Windows 3.1's File Manager helps a little bit—but only a little bit. You can highlight a file in File Manager, then select the Print item from File Manager's File menu, and File Manager will launch the application associated with that file, print the file, and then shut down the application. That

SKILLS INDEX

- **Using Windows 3.1's Registration Database and File Associations**
- **Implementing the File Manager's drag-and-drop support**
- **Interacting with other Windows applications**
- **Providing transparent access to dialog boxes from other applications**
- **Designing "wizards" to guide users through difficult procedures**

sequence sounds pretty nifty, but there are two problems with it. First, few application developers bother to use the Windows 3.1 Registration Database to tell File Manager how to print the files created by their applications, and second, even if they do, you still have to sit there while the file is being printed; there's no Print Later menu item.

VB Q is designed to solve these problems. It can automate the printing of nearly any document created by a Windows application, and allows you to specify exactly when that printing is to take place.

■ A HANDFUL OF PRINT METHODS

One of Windows 3.1's hidden treasures is its facility, known as the Registration Database, whereby an application can provide Windows with the information Windows needs to open or print that application's documents.

The concept is simple. The Registration Database stores the command line parameters or DDE commands needed to launch an application and to open or print its documents. Once the parameters have been recorded in the Registration Database, you should be able to open any file of the specified type by double-clicking on it in File Manager, or to print it by selecting the file and then selecting the Print item from File Manager's File menu.

To make things even simpler, Windows 3.1 provides a simple mechanism for an application to register itself (that is, to add its parameter information to the Registration Database) at the time you install the application.

Unfortunately, there are two problems with this scenario. First, few developers take advantage of the Registration Database in their Windows installation routines. You can get around this failure by using the RegEdit utility included with Windows 3.1 to enter the necessary information yourself, but that won't help you solve the second problem, which is that many—indeed most—applications don't provide a mechanism for passing the command to print a file through either the command line parameters or the DDE commands. Almost all Windows applications will open their documents if you include the name of the document you wish to open on the command line as you start the application, but not many offer any facility to specify that the document should be printed immediately upon being opened.

Without a Registration Database entry telling it how to print a file, File Manager is helpless. If you try to use File Manager to print a file for which that information is lacking, all you get is an error message like that in Figure 4.1.

FIGURE 4.1

Without the
proper
Registration
Database
information,
File Manager
can't print a file.

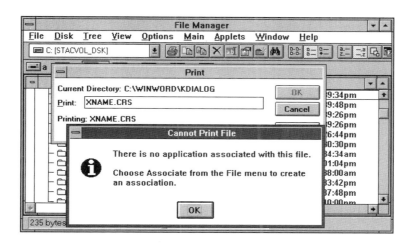

Eventually, more applications will probably support the Registration Database by adding a command line Print This File switch or a DDE Print command, and so more files will be printable directly from within File Manager. But while Microsoft might be willing to be patient on this score, I'm not. And so, while VB Q will take advantage of the information in the Registration Database about how to print a file, it doesn't give up like File Manager if that information doesn't exist. Instead, it provides a mechanism for you to tell VB Q the steps it needs to take to print a file of nearly any type in the absence of Registration Database information.

That method is simplicity itself. VB Q opens the document to be printed by launching the application with which it is associated, passing it the name of the document on the command line. Next it issues the keyboard commands (such as **Alt+FP{ENTER}**) that the application needs to print an open document. (How does VB Q know how to do all this? Because the first time you attempt to use it to print a file with an extension for which no information is specified in the Registration Database, VB Q asks you to identify the application that should be used to print the file and to specify the key sequence used to access that application's print command.) After the document has been printed, VB Q instructs the application to shut down.

This alternative method for printing files for which the Registration Database won't serve is referred to as VB Q Keys throughout VB Q's code and user interface.

The capability to print files that File Manager can't is VB Q's first big advantage. The second is that, unlike File Manager, VB Q allows you to specify *when* those files should be printed. You can tell VB Q to print files immediately as fast as you add them to its queue, or to wait until a specified time and then begin printing all the files in its queue.

■ USING VB Q

I designed VB Q to be as simple to use as possible. Generally, you only need to supply two pieces of information to start using it: the file or files that it should print, and whether those files should be printed immediately or at a later time. (In addition, the first time you attempt to print a file of any given type, you may have to supply VB Q with information about how files with that extension are to be printed.)

VB Q's main screen, which appears when you launch the application, contains a single list box under a label that reads Files to print:, a button (initially disabled) that is captioned View Report, a status bar with two messages reading, respectively, "0 files in queue" and "Print mode not set," and four top-level menus, labeled File, Edit, Schedule and Help. This screen is shown in Figure 4.2.

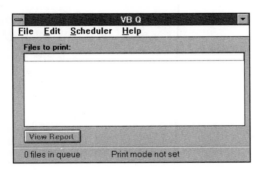

The File menu contains one menu item, labeled Exit, which is used to shut down VB Q. The Edit menu contains three items: VB Q Keys…, Registration Database…, and Remove File. The first two allow you to edit the current VB Q Keys or Registration Database settings for printing files of any given type, or to create settings for a new file type.

The Schedule menu also contains three items. The first, labeled Set Print Time…, is used to set the time at which VB Q should print any files in its queue. The second and third items, which are isolated from the first by a separator bar, are toggle switches for VB Q's two operational modes: Scheduled Print and Immediate Print. When you select either of these, a check mark appears next to the item to indicate that it is active, or the check mark is removed if the selected mode was already active.) In addition, if you select the Scheduled Print item without having previously set the print time, the Set Print Time dialog box appears, as shown in Figure 4.3.

The Set Print Time dialog box is used to indicate the time at which VB Q should print the files in its queue.

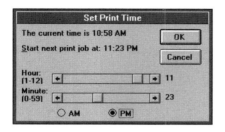

Finally, the Help menu contains a single item, labeled About VB Q..., which is used to access VB Q's About box.

▪ Adding Files to the Queue

You'll notice that none of VB Q's menu items actually allow you to select the files that you want to print. Instead, VB Q is designed to work in conjunction with the Windows 3.1 File Manager. To add files to VB Q, you drag them from File Manager (or any other application that uses the File Manager drag-drop server protocol) into its window or onto its icon to indicate that they are to be printed.

When you drop a file into VB Q, it checks quickly to ensure that it knows how to print the file. As long as information on how to print files with the same extension as the dropped file exists in either the Registration Database or VBQ.INI (where VB Q Keys data is stored), the file is added to the Files to print list box, as shown in Figure 4.4. VB Q automatically sorts the files in the list box according to their extension.

If, on the other hand, VB Q can't locate the information that it needs in the Registration Database or its VB Q Keys data, it opens a dialog box labeled VB Q Trail Guide to inform you of the problem and to present several possible solutions, as shown in Figure 4.5.

VB Q's Trail Guide dialog box is modeled after the wizards, helpers, and such that have appeared in many commercial Windows applications over the past year or so. The Trail Guide dialog box is intended to explain your options when a problem occurs, and to guide you through the process of solving the problem.

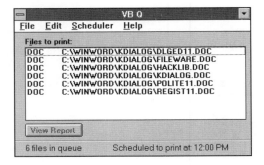

FIGURE 4.4

*The Files to
print list box
lists the files
that you've
dragged into
VB Q from File
Manager.*

FIGURE 4.5

*The VB Q Trail
Guide presents
several options
if you ask VB
Q to process a
file that it
doesn't know
how to print.*

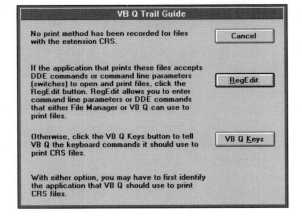

The Trail Guide dialog box presents three options: You can Cancel the dialog box, in which case the file in question won't be added to VB Q's print queue; or you can use either RegEdit or VB Q Keys to enter information about printing files of this type.

When you click the RegEdit button, VB Q launches the Windows 3.1 Registration Editor, navigates to its Add File Type dialog box, and fills in some of the information required by the Registration Editor, as shown in Figure 4.6. But you'll have to enter the command line parameters or DDE commands that the application requires to print a file on demand, since VB Q has no way of determining that information by itself.

The RegEdit option has the advantage of working with both the File Manager and VB Q. Once you've entered the correct data into the Registration Database, you'll be able to print files of the specified type either by dragging them into VB Q or by selecting the Print item on the File Manager's Print menu.

VB Q launches the Registration Editor and fills in some of the information it requires when you click the RegEdit button on the VB Q Trail Guide dialog box.

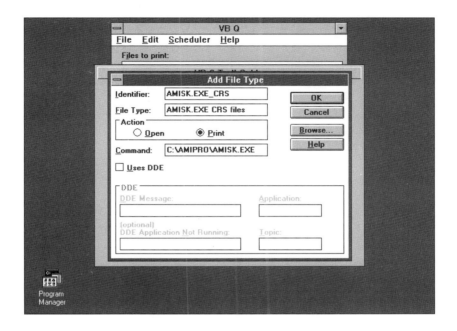

Unfortunately, the RegEdit option can't be used with all applications, since many applications don't provide a DDE or command line interface to their print function. Thus, VB Q provides a second option, that of specifying VB Q Keys information for the application which should be used to print files of the specified type.

When you select the VB Q Keys button, VB Q opens up a new dialog box labeled VB Q Keys for XXX Files (where .XXX is the three-letter extension of the file that you're trying to print). This dialog box, shown in Figure 4.7, allows you to specify the keyboard commands that VB Q should use to print files within the application associated with the extension .XXX. A series of eight buttons along the bottom of the box allows you to enter special characters such as Tab, Alt, and Enter into the VB Q Keys command string.

To enter VB Q Keys data for an application, you'll have to be familiar enough with the application to recall its exact keyboard command sequence for printing open files. If you are not certain, the best course at that point is to launch the application and open a document, then use keyboard commands to tell the application to print the open file, writing down each command as you issue it.

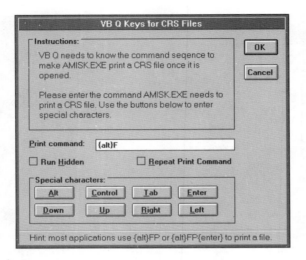

FIGURE 4.7

The VB Q Keys dialog box lets you specify the commands that VB Q needs to send to make a specific application print an open document.

The VB Q Keys screen also allows you to specify that the application be run in a hidden window. Otherwise, VB Q runs applications with which it intends to interact in a standard window, which can be rather annoying if you're trying to work on something else while VB Q is printing files from its queue. Selecting this option ensures that the application's main window will be hidden when VB Q runs it, so that generally the most evidence you'll see of it is a quick flash of a Print dialog box. But this also means that you won't necessarily know if a print command that VB Q issues fails, and this of course makes it much harder to diagnose what went wrong because you can't see the application's window. Thus, I recommend that you select this option only after having used VB Q to print several documents in standard, visible windows with the application. Doing so should ensure that the VB Q Keys entry for the application is correct. Even so, there isn't a 100-percent guarantee that the application will print correctly with a hidden main window, but in most cases it will as long as you've first tested the VB Q Keys print command for that application and determined that it works correctly.

The final item on the VB Q Keys screen is a check box labeled Repeat Print Command. Selecting this box tells VB Q Keys that the application discards print commands issued while a document is being loaded. This is atypical behavior, but some applications do this, and as a result, VB Q ends up shutting down the application without the specified document having been printed. When the Repeat Print Command box is checked, VB Q issues the print command repeatedly until the application responds to the command, thus enabling VB Q to force printing even in applications that discard a print command received while a document is loading. However, checking this box for an application that does not require it could result in many copies of a document being printed—not just one—so this box should be checked only if you've observed VB Q shutting down a particular application before it has had the chance to print the specified file.

■ File Associations

Before it allows you to specify RegEdit or VB Q Keys information for a file type, VB Q checks to see if there is an application associated with files which have that extension. If not, it runs File Manager in a hidden window, navigates to its Associate dialog box, and presents that dialog box at the center of the screen. This process allows you to identify the application which you want to use to print the file, as shown in Figure 4.8.

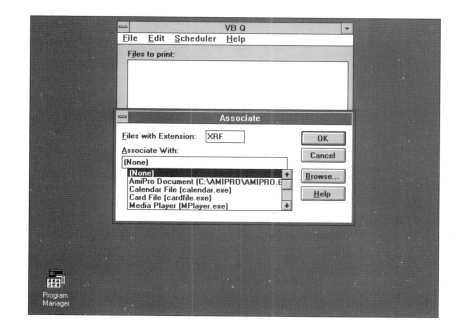

FIGURE 4.8

VB Q uses the File Manager's Associate facility to let you identify the application that it should use to print files of the selected type.

- ## The VB Q Report

Once you've told VB Q what files you wish to print, it will attempt to print them, either immediately if you've selected the Immediate Print mode, or at the scheduled time if you've selected the Scheduled Print mode.

Once each file has been printed, VB Q enables the View Report button on its main screen, as shown in Figure 4.9.

FIGURE 4.9

After VB Q has printed the files in its queue list, the View Report button is enabled.

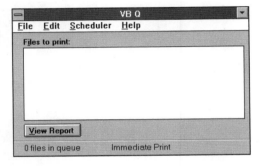

If you select the View Report button, VB Q's main form expands to show two additional list boxes, one labeled Printed and the other labeled Not Printed. The files that were printed correctly will be listed in the Printed list box, while any files for which VB Q detected an error during the print process will appear in the Not Printed list box, as shown in Figure 4.10.

You can drag files out of either of these list boxes into the Files to print list box to reprint them. In addition, you can double-click on a file in the Not Printed dialog box. When you do so, VB Q will identify the error that occurred during printing and suggest how you can fix it, as shown in Figure 4.11.

The Clear Report button can be used to clear the contents of both report list boxes and to close the report. Alternately, you can use the Remove File item on VB Q's Edit menu to remove one by one files from these lists or from the Files to Print list.

At the beginning of this section I said that VB Q was designed to be as simple as possible to use. That is a large caveat, and indeed there are some aspects of getting applications to work with VB Q that are not entirely straightforward. But VB Q attempts to guide you through the trickier aspects of that process by means of Trail Guides and informative dialog boxes. Moreover, once you have figured out the correct print method for files of any given type, you'll never have to edit or enter that information again. Instead, you'll be able to print files of that type at any time simply by dragging them into VB Q.

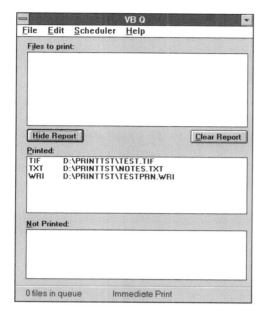

FIGURE 4.10

The VB Q print report lists the files that it has printed and any which it was unable to print.

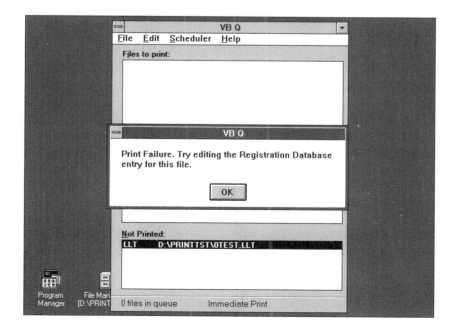

FIGURE 4.11

VB Q records errors that occur during printing and suggests how they might be resolved.

INSIDE VB Q

My goal with VB Q was to supplement Windows 3.1's standard facilities for printing. As such, it works in conjunction with the Registration Database, the File Manager, the Print Manager (if you've elected to use the Windows spooler), and the standard print functions of your Windows applications, rather than by attempting to replace any of them.

This approach allows VB Q to enhance Windows's standard print facilities, and to overcome some of their shortcomings, without having to undertake any of the more difficult chores that they perform (such as interacting with a printer).

The development process for VB Q was an iterative one. I started by seeking only to provide queued printing for the same files that the File Manager can print, using the information in the Registration Database. But as I proceeded, and became more aware of the limitations of the Registration Database's print support and the widespread failure of application developers to provide Registration Database information for their files, it became clear that my initial goal was insufficient to produce a useful utility. As a result, I felt compelled to add several features to VB Q to overcome these limitations.

Some of the limitations were simple to address. For instance, the ShellExecute command from SHELL.DLL, which is used to instruct Windows 3.1 either to open or to print a file, wasn't designed for unattended printing. It passes the command to print a file to the application with which the file is associated, but doesn't attempt to deal with the Print options/confirmation box that most applications open when you issue the print command. In other words, ShellExecute simply issues the print command, leaving it up to the user to close the dialog box before printing actually commences. That's fine if you're sitting there at the computer ready to respond to the dialog box, but VB Q needed a way to shut the dialog box automatically to allow for unattended printing.

To solve this problem, I wrote a brief routine called ClosePrintDialog() that VB Q calls immediately after issuing the ShellExecute command. The command examines the title of the active window, using the GetWindowText() API function. If the five leftmost characters read Print and the sixth character is either a CHR$(0) or a CHR$(160) (in case Titlebar Clock is running and has appended the time to the window's caption), the ClosePrintDialog routine sends an Enter keystroke to the dialog box to close it and start the printing process, as shown in the following code fragment:

```
Sub ClosePrintDialog ()
Dim T%, wTxt As String * 64
T% = GetWindowText(GetActiveWindow(), wTxt, 63)
If InStr(wTxt, Chr$(0)) = 6 Or InStr(wTxt, Chr$(160)) = 6 Then
```

```
    If Left$(wTxt, 5) = "Print" Then SendKeys ("~")
End If
End Sub
```

Next, I began to realize how few applications add the prerequisite information on how to print their files to the Registration Database at installation time, so I wanted to provide a way for the user to supply that information. The simplest way to do so would have been to simply execute REGEDIT.EXE and let the user fill in all the prerequisite data, but this seemed rather ungainly since it would have required the user both to know which print commands the application in question would respond to and to understand fully the less than obvious workings of REGEDIT. For instance, I couldn't do much about the first requirement—the user has to know the print commands that his or her application requires—but I could simplify the process of using REGEDIT and have VB Q fill in some of the other data that it requires.

REGEDIT's Add File Type dialog box requires the user to enter both a unique keyword called an Identifier to describe a new file type, and a text description called a File Type that will be displayed in both REGEDIT's list of file types and the File Manager's Associate dialog box, as shown in Figure 4.12. Furthermore, the Associate dialog box must be used to link files with a specified extension to the File Type text description before ShellExecute can be used to open or print a file.

FIGURE 4.12

REGEDIT's Add File Type dialog box is used to add new file types to the Registration Database.

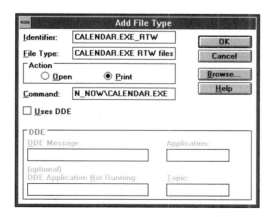

I saw that I could simplify this process considerably by having VB Q automatically fill in the Identifier and File Type fields, and automatically add an association between the file extensions and the File Type to WIN.INI (where File Manager stores its list of file associations). But to do so, VB Q had to be able to launch REGEDIT, navigate to the Add File Type screen, fill in those fields, and then leave the cursor positioned correctly for the user to fill in the remaining data.

To make this process as smooth as possible, I employed a technique of launching REGEDIT in a hidden window, then issuing it the commands necessary to open the Add File Type dialog box and to display it on screen. (This technique was first demonstrated on CompuServe's MSBASIC forum by Jeff Simms, who used it to access the File Manager's Format dialog box from within a Visual Basic application. In VB Q, I've adapted his technique for use with both REGEDIT's Add File Type dialog box and the File Manager's Associate dialog box.)

The routine that does this is called BorrowDialog. It accepts six parameters: the name of the form that calls the function, the class name of the application's main window, the name of the application's .EXE file, the ID number for the menu command that will be used to access the dialog box, the caption of the target dialog box, and a string containing any additional commands that should be sent to the dialog via a SendKeys command. The routine is shown here:

```
Sub BorrowDialog (F As Form, Class$, TargetExe$, cID%, dCaption$, Send$)
Dim TargetWnd, I%, wFlag, wnd%, X, Y
'    **********************************
'    First see if app is running
'    **********************************
TargetWnd = FindWindow(Class$, 0&)
'    **********************************
'    If not launch app in a hidden window
'    **********************************
    If TargetWnd = 0 Then
        I% = WinExec(TargetExe$, 0)
        TargetWnd = FindWindow(Class$, 0&)
        If TargetWnd = 0 Then
            MsgBox "Unable to launch" + TargetExe$ + "."
            Exit Sub
        End If
        wFlag = 1
    End If
'    **********************************
'    Lock desktop window update to
'    prevent screen redraws while dialog box is
'    drawn and centered on screen
'    **********************************
    I% = LockWindowUpdate(GetDesktopWindow())
'    **********************************
'    send menu command to open target dialog
'    **********************************
    I% = PostMessage(TargetWnd, WM_COMMAND, cID%, 0)
'    **********************************
'    call CenterDialog routine to center it
'    **********************************
    CenterDialog dCaption$
'    **********************************
'    Send any additional commands specified in call
'    **********************************
    If Send$ <> "" Then SendKeys Send$
'    **********************************
```

```
'   Unlock screen
'   ********************************
    I% = LockWindowUpdate(0)
'   ********************************
'   Pause until dialog closes
'   ********************************
    wnd% = GetActiveWindow()
    While IsWindow(wnd%)
        X = DoEvents()
    Wend
    X = DoEvents()
'   ********************************
'   If the app wasn't already running when we started
'   shut it down now
'   ********************************
    If wFlag Then
        wFlag = 0
        I% = PostMessage(TargetWnd, WM_CLOSE, 0, 0)
    End If
        While IsWindow(TargetWnd)
            X = DoEvents()
        Wend
X = DoEvents()
I% = SetActiveWindow(F.hWnd)
End Sub
```

■ The CenterDialog Routine

The CenterDialog routine called in the middle of BorrowDialog is quite simple. It uses the GetWindowRect API function to obtain the current layout of the dialog that it is to center on screen. (GetWindowRect returns a Rect structure consisting of four integers indicating the left, right, top, and bottom edges of the specified window.) Then it obtains the same information for the desktop window (which occupies the entire viewable screen) and centers the dialog box over the desktop window as follows:

```
targetWdth% = lpDlgRect.Right - lpDlgRect.Left
TargetHght% = lpDlgRect.Bottom - lpDlgRect.Top
GetWindowRect GetDesktopWindow(), lpDskRect
Scrwdth% = lpDskRect.Right - lpDskRect.Left
Scrhght% = lpDskRect.Bottom - lpDskRect.Top
X% = (Scrwdth% - TargetWdth%) / 2
Y% = (Scrhght% - TargetHght%) / 2
SetWindowPos wnd%, 0, X%, Y%, 0, 0, SWP_NOZORDER Or SWP_NOSIZE
```

The final statement in CenterDialog calls the Windows API function SetWindows-Pos, instructing it to reposition the dialog to screen coordinates X%, Y% without changing its size or its position in the window list.

As structured, the BorrowDialog routine is nearly universally applicable; you can adapt it to make a selected dialog box from almost any other application pop up as if it belonged to your application. However, it has two important, and not always ready-at-hand, prerequisites. You must know the class name of the application's main window and the ID number of the menu command that activates the dialog box you wish to "borrow."

■ Listing Menu IDs

I was able to obtain the class name of REGEDIT's main window using the Window Info utility (described in Chapter 2) that I wrote to assist in debugging Title Bar Clock, but Window Info doesn't provide any information about a window's menus. Fortunately, however, there is a series of simple Window API functions that can be used to obtain a list of menu IDs for any given window. These are GetMenu(), GetMenuItemCount(), GetSubMenu(), and GetMenuItemID(), all of which are found in USER.EXE. The declarations for these routines are as follows:

```
Declare Function GetMenu Lib "User" (ByVal hWnd As Integer) As Integer
DeclareFunctionGetMenuItemCountLib"User"(ByValhMenuAsInteger)AsInteger
Declare Function GetMenuItemID Lib "User" (ByVal hMenu As Integer, ByVal ⇔
    nPos As Integer) As Integer
Declare Function GetSubMenu Lib "User" (ByVal hMenu As Integer, ByVal nPos ⇔
    As Integer) As Integer
```

I put these functions to use in a routine called ListFMMenus, which simply dumps a list of the menu's IDs for a specified menu to a list box.

In the code that follows, the initial GetMenu call returns the handle for REGEDIT's main menu bar. The subsequent GetSubMenu call returns the handle of REGEDIT's Edit menu (all the menu functions are zero-based, so the first submenu, File, is Number 0, while the second, Edit, is Number 1). The GetMenuItemCount call returns an integer indicating how many items appear on the Edit menu, and then the For-Next loop that immediately follows uses GetMenuItemID to obtain and print the ID of each item.

```
Sub ListRegEditMenus()
Dim FmhWnd, I%, fmMenu%, X, V%, Y%
I% = WinExec("REGEDIT", 0)
FmhWnd = FindWindow("Registration Editor", 0&)
fmMenu% = GetMenu(FmhWnd)
'Get Edit Menu
fmMenu% = GetSubMenu(fmMenu%, 1)
X% = GetMenuItemCount(fmMenu%)
Form1.List1.Additem Str$(X%) & "items on menu..."
For V% = 1 To X%
    Y% = GetMenuItemID(fmMenu%, V%)
    Form1.List1.Additem Str$(Y%)
Next V%
Exit Sub
```

The output from this routine is shown in Figure 4.13.

FIGURE 4.13

*The ListRegEdit-
Menus function
outputs a list of
menu IDs to the
Debug window*

Add File Type is the first item on the Edit menu, so its ID was the first one listed: 1056. Once I had this number, and the class name of REGEDIT's main window (Registration Editor), I was able to use BorrowDialog() to pop up Registration Editor's Add File Type dialog box as if it were part of VB Q itself.

VB Q uses the Send$ parameter of BorrowDialog() to fill in the Identifier and File Type fields of the Add File Type dialog box, and specify the application that should be associated with this file type. I had two reasons for doing this. The first was benevolent. The purpose of these fields isn't always particularly clear, so I wanted to save the user the trouble of having to fill them out. Secondly, before VB Q could make use of the new Registration Database entry, it had to make another entry to the database linking the file extension associated with the new file type to the Identifier specified in the Add File Type dialog box, such as

`.INI=NOTEPAD_INI`

The easiest way to do this was to have VB Q fill in the Identifier and File Type fields and caution the user not to change them.

VB Q passes BorrowDialog() the following string in the Send$ parameter

```
Send$ = TargetApp$ + "_" + Ext$ + Chr$(9) + TargetApp$ + " " + Ext$ + ⇔
    "files{TAB}{RIGHT}{TAB}%U%B" + UCase$(Left$(Ret, InStr(Ret, " "))) + ⇔
    "~%C{RIGHT} "
```

This complex-looking string is actually easy to understand once you recall that BorrowDialog() sends it verbatim to the dialog box using Visual Basic's SendKeys function, and understand the contents of the variables contained in the string: TargetApp$ contains the name, minus its file extension, of the .EXE file with which the data file is to be associated; Ext$ contains the data file's extension; and Ret contains the full name and path of the .EXE file.

The dialog box opens with the input cursor located in its Identifier field, so it receives the name (minus extension) of the executable file, followed by an underscore, followed by the extension of the file type being added to the Registration Database. Chr$(9) is the tab character, so the first Chr$(9) tabs the cursor to the File Type field, which then receives the file name, followed by a space, followed by the document extension, followed by "files". Then the cursor tabs to the dialog's Action field, and the {RIGHT} command is used to select Print. Next, an Alt+U is sent to turn off the "Uses DDE" check box, and then an Alt+B is sent to activate the Browse button, which opens a standard Browse dialog box identical to the one used by the Program Manager. The next part of Send$ inserts the full path and name of the executable file for documents of this type into the Browse dialog box, followed by an Enter. At this point, REGEDIT automatically copies the data entered in the Browse dialog box to the Command field, and Send$ concludes by sending an Alt+C to move to that field, and then a {RIGHT} to position the cursor to the right of the executable program's file name.

All the user has to do at this point is enter the command line parameter that the application uses to immediately print a file or, if the application uses DDE, clear the command field, check the Uses DDE box, and enter the proper DDE commands in the fields below. Since the majority of applications don't accept DDE commands to print files, I elected to assume that the application doesn't and let the user tell REGEDIT otherwise if it does.

■   **Borrowing File Manager Dialog Boxes**
As noted above, VB Q checks to ensure that a file association exists for the file type the user is trying to print prior to executing REGEDIT. If no association exists, VB Q uses BorrowDialog() to give the user access to File Manager's Associate dialog box prior to running REGEDIT.

Since Jeff Simm's original example code for this technique used the File Manager, I expected that I would be able to borrow the File Manager's dialog boxes just as simply as I had REGEDIT's. However, I use several third-party File Manager extensions on my system, and in the course of building VB Q, I discovered that some of them do not unload properly when the File Manager is run in a hidden window and then unloaded via the PostMessage WM_Close method used by BorrowDialog(). Worse, by remaining in memory, the extensions caused a General Protection Fault (GPF) the next time the File Manager was loaded.

I couldn't determine where the fault lay here. The File Manager Extensions API is known to be buggy, so that could be at fault, but all the extensions in question unload properly when the File Manager is run normally and unloaded via a mouse or keyboard action. Be that as it may, GPFs are unacceptable, so after experimenting a bit and discovering that the error could be avoided by unloading the extension DLLs after the File Manager unloads, I added a bit of File Manager-specific code to BorrowDialog() that searches out and destroys any File Manager extensions left in memory after the File Manager unloads.

I inserted this code into BorrowDialog() immediately after the PostMessage WM_Close command.

```
If TargetExe$ = "WINFILE.EXE" Then
' **********************************
'    wait for File Manager to unload
' **********************************
        X = GetModuleHandle("WINFILE.EXE")
        While X > 0
          Y = DoEvents()
          X = GetModuleHandle("WINFILE.EXE")
        Wend
' **********************************
'    Clean up any File Manager Extensions that didn't unload normally
' **********************************
        Dim AddOns As String * 255
        Dim Spacer%, Dllname$
' **********************************
'    Null parameter for keyname in a GetPrivateProfileString call
'    retrieves entire list, separated by CHR$(0)'s
' **********************************
  X = GetPrivateProfileString("AddOns", 0&, "", AddOns, 254, "WINFILE.INI")
        Spacer% = InStr(AddOns, Chr$(0))
        Do While Spacer% > 0
          Dllname$ = Left$(AddOns, Spacer% - 1)
' **********************************
'    GetModuleHandle for DLL
'    Call FreeModule to unload it
' **********************************
          X = GetModuleHandle(Dllname$)
          If X > 0 Then FreeModule (X)
' **********************************
' list of keys ends with double null, so...
' **********************************
```

```
        If Mid$(AddOns, Spacer% + 1, 1) = Chr$(0) Then Exit Do
'  ***********************************
'  Otherwise, find the next key
'  ***********************************
        AddOns = Mid$(AddOns, Spacer% + 1)
        Spacer% = InStr(AddOns, Chr$(0))
    Loop
    Screen.MousePointer = 1
End If
```

The routine uses GetPrivateProfileString to obtain a list of all the File Manager extensions from WINFILE.INI, which are listed in standard .INI fashion under a key named [AddOns]. Once the routine has obtained the list, it uses GetModuleHandle to obtain a handle for each DLL that is still in memory, and then uses FreeModule to unload them from memory.

FreeModule is a powerful function, not to be used lightly. It is safe to use here since there is no reason for a File Manager extension to be present in memory if the File Manager is not, but otherwise it should be used with extreme caution. There are few ways to make your system unstable faster than by using FreeModule indiscriminately. It should be called only when you are absolutely certain that neither any of the currently executing tasks nor Windows itself has any reason to expect that the module you're unloading is still in memory.

By using BorrowDialog(), I was able to link REGEDIT's Add File Type dialog box and the File Manager's dialog box to VB Q Keys, thus providing a way for the user to specify Registration Database information for those applications whose vendors had failed to do so. Unfortunately, the more I experimented with REGEDIT the more I realized that there was a reason why most vendors don't supply Registration Database data for their applications: Their applications don't support the print methods offered by the Registration Database. In other words, for most Windows applications there is no combination of command line parameters or DDE commands that will force the application to open and print a file and then shut down without user intervention.

This left me with two options. I could confine VB Q to the relatively trivial task of printing, on a delayed basis, those files that the File Manager can print directly, or I could attempt to broaden its support for those applications whose documents the File Manager can't print by offering VB Q users another method of automating printing. Since many of the applications whose printing I wanted to automate for my own needs were among the group with which the File Manager is helpless, I decided to take the more ambitious route, and thus VB Q Keys was born.

∎ VB Q KEYS

The VB Q Keys concept is simple: to automate the process of opening any document for which an association exists by passing its name on the command line to the application with which it is associated, selecting the File Print command to print the file, and then finally shutting the file down. It's easy to do that from the keyboard for nearly any Windows application, and so it seemed that it should be possible to automate the process from within VB Q.

Initially I thought that VB Q Keys would have to obtain three pieces of data from the user: (1) the command used by the target application to open a file; (2) the command it uses to print a file; and (3) the command used to shut down the target application. Experimentation revealed, however, that there is nearly universal support for passing the name of a document file to be opened on the command line among Windows applications, and that a WM_CLOSE message can be used to shut down almost all Windows applications.

Thus, VB Q Keys only requires the user to specify the print command used by the application. For what it's worth, I probably could have eliminated even this requirement, since the Print-command sequence for a Windows application is almost always ALT+FP or ALT+FP{Enter}. VB Q could have assumed it was the former, and then sent an {Enter} to close any dialog box that didn't disappear right away after the ALT+FP command was issued. But in addition to ensuring that VB Q can access the print function of any oddball applications that don't use these common sequences, requiring the user to specify the Print command allows the adventurous to use the VB Q Keys facility to set additional options in an application's Print Dialog box. For instance, in Microsoft Word for Windows, a VB Q Keys sequence of

```
{alt}FP{alt}C2{alt}G1{tab}10{enter}
```

would result in Word printing two copies of pages one through ten of the open document.

Furthermore, having the user specify the print sequence underlines the notion that this sort of automation is not bulletproof. While I didn't want to cause the user any undue anxiety, I also didn't want to give the impression that VB Q would automatically work perfectly with every application. It demands of the user some willingness to experiment, and having the user specify the command keys makes that clearer than would having VB Q make assumptions about them.

Once I had decided to use this approach of having the user specify the Print command, VB Q needed a way to (1) obtain a Print command from the user and (2) transmit that command to the target application.

The obvious solution to the second requirement was to use Visual Basic's Send-Keys function to send the target application the keystrokes necessary to make it print an open file. So that meant that either the user would have to enter the correct syntax for a SendKeys command string—which can be rather tricky, given SendKeys's use of special symbols for many command keys (such as + for Shift)—or that the program would have to translate whatever commands the user entered into a SendKeys command string.

I elected to have the user enter the command string in a sort of pseudo-SendKeys code that VB Q translates into the real thing. To help the user along, I included a series of shortcut buttons for entering command keys on the VB Q Keys screen. For instance, rather than requiring the user to remember that SendKeys uses a percent sign to indicate that the Alt key should be pressed (so that SendKeys "%F" sends Alt+F), the VB Q Keys screen includes a button labeled Alt that inserts the string {alt} into the text box in which the user is entering the command string. This not only makes it easy for the user to enter these commands, but also presents them in a way that is more easily understood. A string such as "{alt}F{alt}O{tab}{space}{enter}" is easier for a user unused to SendKeys syntax to decipher than is "%F%O{TAB} ~."

Later, when VB Q is ready to send the command string to the target application, it calls a subroutine called SendCommandString which translates the pseudocode entered by the user into the actual code needed to make SendKeys function correctly. The key (no pun intended) to VB Q's capability to translate these command strings is a two-dimensional string array called Keys$(). The Keys$() array is initialized in a routine called InitKeys() as VB Q loads.

```
Sub InitKeys()
Keys$(0, 0) = "{alt}"
Keys$(0, 1) = "%"
Keys$(1, 0) = "{control}"
Keys$(1, 1) = "{^}"
Keys$(2, 0) = "{tab}"
Keys$(2, 1) = UCase$(Keys$(2, 0))
Keys$(3, 0) = "{enter}"
Keys$(3, 1) = "~"
Keys$(4, 0) = "{down}"
Keys$(4, 1) = UCase$(Keys$(4, 0))
Keys$(5, 0) = "{up}"
Keys$(5, 1) = UCase$(Keys$(5, 0))
Keys$(6, 0) = "{right}"
Keys$(6, 1) = UCase$(Keys$(6, 0))
Keys$(7, 0) = "{left}"
```

```
Keys$(7, 1) = UCase$(Keys$(7, 0))
End Sub
```

As you can see, the Keys() array consists of eight pairs of strings. The first element in each pair is the string which will be entered into the text box on the VB Q Keys screen when the user presses the button associated with that element, while the second element in each pair is the actual SendKeys command for the key.

The eight shortcut buttons on the VB Q Keys screen compose a control array called Command2, with index numbers running from 0 to 7. The buttons correspond to the Keys$() elements with the same index numbers, so button 0 is used to enter the {alt} string, button 1 to enter the {control} string, and so on. By maintaining this correspondence, VB Q can determine the string that it is to enter into the list box by using the index number of the command button that the user pressed to identify the appropriate Keys$() string.

```
Sub Command2_Click (Index As Integer)
Text1.SelText = Keys$(Index, 0)
Text1.SetFocus
End Sub
```

This routine responds to the user clicking a shortcut button by inserting the Keys$() string corresponding to that button into the text box. If the user has highlighted any text in the text box prior to clicking the shortcut key, the highlighted text is replaced by the Keys$() string. Otherwise, the Keys$() string is inserted at the active location of the text box's vertical-bar cursor, and the selection point is automatically moved to the end of the newly entered text.

When the user closes the VB Q Keys dialog box, VB Q writes the contents of the text box to a private .INI file, along with the values of the two check boxes on the screen, using the Windows API function WritePrivateProfileString:

```
a$ = "Extensions"
F$ = "VBQ.INI"
X% = WritePrivateProfileString(a$, Ext$ + "_Print", Text1, F$)
X%=WritePrivateProfileString(a$,Ext$+"_Hidden",Str$(Check1.Value),F$)
X%=WritePrivateProfileString(a$,Ext$+"_Repeat",Str$(Check2.Value),F$)
```

Ext$ contains the file extension of the files with which the VB Q Keys command will be used. Thus, an entry in VBQ.INI that tells VBQ how to print .TIF files using ZSoft's PhotoFinish might look like this:

```
TIF_Print={alt}FP{enter}
TIF_Hidden=1
TIF_Repeat=0
```

The .INI file does not need to store the name of the program used to print these files, since that information is already recorded in the Extensions section of WIN.INI. Using the same example, your WIN.INI file might include an entry such as the following that associates .TIF files with PhotoFinish:

```
tif=C:\PHOTO\PHOTO.EXE ^.TIF
```

At print time, VB Q uses a routine called SendCommandString to translate the VB Q Keys entry for an application into the correct SendKeys syntax and to send that command to the application. SendCommandString accepts two parameters: the VB Q Keys string (Key$) that it is to send to the target application, and the handle of the target application's main window (wHand%). The SendCommandString procedure simply loops through the Keys$() array, replacing each instance of the X,0 element of the array that it finds in Key$ with an X,1 element, as follows:

```
For X% = 0 To 7
    L% = Len(Keys$(X%, 0))
    I% = InStr(Key$, Keys$(X%, 0))
    Do While I%
      Key$ = Left$(Key$, I% - 1) + Keys$(X%, 1) + Mid$(Key$, I% + L%)
      I% = InStr(Key$, Keys$(X%, 0))
    Loop
Next
```

Once that process is complete, SendCommandString() uses the Windows API function SetActiveWindow to activate the target window, and then issues the Send-Keys command to send the Print command to the target.

```
I% = SetActiveWindow(wHand%)
SendKeys Key$
```

■ The KeysPrint Routine

So far, so good. VB Q could obtain a Print command string from the user, store it, and translate it for sending to the target application. All that remained was to ensure that the command string was sent to the target application at the right time, and that VB Q shut down the target application once it had completed printing. These are jobs I intended to perform with a function called KeysPrint. Both of these seemed to be simple tasks, but in fact they turned out to be gnawingly difficult.

If you're wondering why no one else has written an application to do this—or why Microsoft chose not to go the route adding universal printing support to its File Manager—I learned why in writing the KeysPrint function. The final code for the function may seem fairly straightforward, but what you see below reveals only a small fraction of the work that went into this routine. It doesn't show the hundreds of lines of code I wrote and then discarded in pursuing endless blind alleys and dead-end streets attempting to fulfill what seemed like a simple set of requirements.

In fact, each of KeysPrint's tasks (launching the application, issuing a user-specified Print command, and shutting down the application) was simple to accomplish, as long as they were taken separately. The tough part was putting them all together and making sure that VB Q performed them all at the right time. For instance, the command to print the file can't be sent until the application has loaded the file and is ready to accept menu commands. Otherwise, the application might ignore the command, and the file will never get printed. Similarly, the command to shut down the application can't be sent until the application has finished printing the file. Otherwise, the application might terminate the print job prematurely, resulting in an incomplete print job.

These kinds of problems are easy to solve when you're sitting in front of your PC's screen. Windows applications provide plenty of visual clues about their status, making it very unlikely that you'll inadvertently shut down an application in the middle of a print job or not notice that the application is not responding to the Print command that you just attempted to issue. The key here was to make VB Q respond to those same visual clues.

The KeysPrint() function takes three parameters (the full name of the file to be printed, the name of the application that is to be used to print it, and the extension of the file to be printed) and returns a value of either 33 if the function detects no errors in the printing process or –5 if an error occurs. (I selected these values to correspond with the values returned by ShellExecute, the Windows API function that VB Q uses to print files using data from the Registration Database. ShellExecute returns a value greater than 32 if it succeeds in printing a file, or less than 32 if it fails.)

The function begins by determining whether it should launch the application specified by Exe$ in a hidden or visible window. To do so, it calls a function called Get-Pvt, passing it a string composed of the document's extension concatenated with "_Private". GetPvt reads the VBQ.INI file and returns the contents of the specified entry, so for .DOC files it would return the contents of the DOC_Private entry.

If GetPvt returns a string whose value is 1, KeysPrint() calls the Windows API WinExec function, passing it the name of the application to launch and the file that the application is to open, followed by the constant SW_HIDE, which tells WinExec that the application should be launched in a hidden window. Otherwise, KeysPrint() simply calls the Visual Basic Shell function to launch the application in a normal window.

```
Function KeysPrint (F$, Exe$, Ext$) As Integer
'    * returns either 33 (success) or -5 (failure)
```

```
Dim X%, Y%, wHand%, A%, B%, Ini$
On Error GoTo Failed
Ini$ = GetPvt(Ext$ + "_Hidden")
Select Case Val(Ini$)
Case Is = 1 ' Run Hidden
   X% = WinExec(Exe$ + " " + F$, SW_HIDE)
Case Else   ' Run Visible
   X% = Shell(Exe$ + " " + F$, 1)
End Select
On Error Resume Next
```

Once it has issued the command to launch the application, KeysPrint() calls DoEvents() to allow the application a chance to load. At this point, KeysPrint() needs to determine the window handle for the application's main window, since it will need that handle first to activate the window and later to shut down the application.

It would appear at first that KeysPrint() could obtain the window's handle simply by calling the Windows function GetActiveWindow(). There are several conditions, however, that can make that method unreliable. For instance, if the user has activated another application, which could happen during the DoEvents() call, the wrong window will be identified. Moreover, some applications open a child window to tell you that they're loading a file. A simple GetActiveWindow() call would return the handle of the child window, not its parent as intended.

The trick, then, was to ensure that KeysPrint() identified the correct window. To do so, it has to first wait for any child windows of the "Loading CHUCKLES.DOC" ilk to close, and then identify the target application's main window.

KeysPrint() accomplishes the first task by calling a WaitForMsgBoxClose routine. This routine determines if the active window is a standard message box window. If so, it waits for that window to close before returning to the KeysPrint() routine. Otherwise, it returns immediately.

```
Sub WaitForMsgBoxClose ()
'   * Delay execution until standard windows message box
'     * or BORDLG closes
Dim cName As String * 80, Y%, X%, c$
Y% = GetActiveWindow()
X% = GetClassName(Y%, cName, 79)
c$ = UCASE$(Left$(cName, 3))
If c$ = "#32" Or c$ = ("BOR" Then
   Do While IsWindow(Y%)
      X% = DoEvents()
   Loop
End If
End Sub
```

WaitForMsgBoxClose starts by obtaining the handle of the active window. Then it obtains the class name of that window, and examines the first three characters in its name. Standard Windows message boxes have the class name #32770, while message boxes created with Borland's C++ have the class name BORDLG, so WaitForMsgBox looks for either BOR or #32 in its search for a message box. If it determines that a message box is the active window, it enters a Do Loop in which it calls DoEvents() repeatedly until the window is closed.

Once the message box (if any) has closed, KeysPrint() resumes its search for the target application's main window. It uses the Windows API function GetWindow to cycle through the entire windows list, calling the GetWindowWord function for each window to determine if its instance handle is equal to the instance handle returned by the Shell() or WinExec() function that was used to launch the target application. Once it finds a window associated with the target application's task, it looks for the owner of that window to identify the target application's main window.

```
'give app a chance to load
Y% = DoEvents()
'wait for its main window to become activated
wHand% = 0
'    * wait for a "loading" msgbox to close
WaitForMsgBoxClose
Y% = Form1.hWnd
Y% = GetWindow(Y%, GW_HwndFirst)
' * now loop, until you find a window associated with task
Do While wHand% = 0
   If GetWindowWord(Y%, GWW_Hinstance) = X% Then
      wHand% = GetWindow(Y%, GW_OWNER)
      If wHand% = 0 Then wHand% = Y%
   End If
   A% = DoEvents()
   Y% = GetWindow(Y%, GW_HwndNext)
   If Y% = 0 Then Y% = GetWindow(Form1.hWnd, GW_HwndFirst)
Loop
```

Once any loading message boxes are closed, the target application should be ready to accept a Print command. Thus, once it has identified the target application's main window, KeysPrint() should be able to call GetPvt to obtain the VB Q Keys Print command string for the target application and then call SendCommandString to send the string to the target. However, there is a huge difference between "should be able to" and "can," and testing revealed that some Windows applications don't follow this simple rule. Instead, they display their main window immediately and then load the document file specified on the command line without displaying a message box to tell the user what they're doing. As a result, it appears to KeysPrint() that they are ready to accept a Print command long before they actually are ready to do so.

I went round and round with this, trying to determine when applications that behave in this manner are ready to accept a Print command. I experimented with various API calls to determine if the main window was enabled (and thus ready for mouse or keyboard input), or if its main menu bar was enabled, or if the Print item on its File menu was enabled, but in at least one case (WINGIF.EXE, a shareware graphics application from SuperSet Software Corp.) the application passed all of these tests even though it was in fact not ready to accept a Print command.

All in all, I probably wrote and then discarded a couple hundred lines of code representing five or six different methods for determining when WINGIF.EXE was ready to accept a command. Each failed. So in the end I was forced to resort to the kludgey (but guaranteed to be effective) method of sending the print command repeatedly until the application responds to it. So KeysPrint() sends the Print command, waits a bit to see what happens, and then sends it again if the application hasn't responded by opening a Print dialog box.

This method works with WINGIF, but causes other applications that don't need multiple commands to print several copies of each document. That wasn't what I wanted, so I had to make repeated issuing of the Print command an option, user-selectable on the VB Q Keys screen, which should be used only with applications that appear to ignore VB Q's Print command when the option is not selected.

KeysPrint() uses the Windows API function GetLastActivePopup to determine when the target application responds to the Print command. GetLastActivePopup returns the handle of a specified window's most recently active pop-up child window, or the handle of the target window if it doesn't own any pop-up menus.

The KeysPrint() Print command sequence begins with a call to GetPvt to obtain the VB Q Keys command for the target application. Then KeysPrint() calls GetLastActivePopup to determine the handle of the most recent pop-up window prior to actually issuing the Print command. Next, it sends the command string to the active window and calls DoEvents() to allow the application's Print dialog box to close.

Once the command string has been sent, KeysPrint() checks the VBQ.INI file to determine if the Print command is to be repeated for this application. If so, it enters a loop that it will not exit until GetLastActivePopup returns a value other than the value it returned before the Print command was issued (indicating that the application has responded to the Print command). Inside the loop, it calls DoEvents repeatedly while incrementing a counter called L%. Every time L% reaches 1,000, KeysPrint sends the Print command to the target window and then resets L%'s value to 1 and begins all over again.

```
Ini$ = GetPvt(Ext$ + "_Print")
A% = GetLastActivePopup(wHand%)
SendCommandString Ini$, wHand%
X% = DoEvents()
'      *Kludge for apps that ignore Print command while loading file
Ini$ = GetPvt(Ext$ + "_Repeat")
If Val(Ini$) = 1 Then
    Dim L%
    Ini$ = GetPvt(Ext$ + "_Print")
    Do While GetLastActivePopup(wHand%) = A%
        L% = L% + 1
        Y% = DoEvents()
        If L% = 1000 Then
            SendCommandString Ini$, wHand%:
            L% = 1
        End If
    Loop
End If
```

Once the Print command has been issued once (for applications that don't require repeated commands) or several times (when the user has selected the Repeated option), KeysPrint() calls WaitForMsgBoxClose again to determine if the target application has opened a new message box, such as the "Printing CHUCKLES.DOC" box posted by many applications while they are printing. If so, the WaitForMsgBoxClose routine pauses execution until the message box window closes. Otherwise, KeysPrint() is ready for a sprint to the finish line. All it has to do now is shut down the target application and then wait for it to close.

KeysPrint() uses the Windows's API PostMessage function to instruct the target application to close, and then it generates a Do Loop with repeated calls to the IsWindow() API function to determine whether the application has in fact closed. While in that loop, KeysPrint calls a simple function, CloseSaveChangesDialog, which is identical to WaitForMsgBoxClose except that it sends an N character to any message box that it finds, rather than simply waiting for the message box to close. This process is designed to close any "Save changes before closing" dialog boxes that the application might post prior to shutting down.

```
WaitForMsgBoxClose
X% = PostMessage(wHand%, WM_CLOSE, 0, 0)
While IsWindow(wHand%)
    X% = DoEvents()
    CloseSaveChangesDialog
Wend
KeysPrint = 33
kpRE:
```

```
Exit Function
Failed:
    KeysPrint = -5
    Resume kpRE
End Function
```

That concludes the KeysPrint() function, and with it, the toughest part of the VB Q project.

■ FUNDAMENTAL TECHNIQUES

So far, this discussion has centered entirely on overcoming limitations in Windows's standard print facilities. Although those weren't the only challenges in developing VB Q, they were fortunately the hardest ones. VB Q also had to interact with several standard Windows facilities, including the Registration Database and the File Manager drag-and-drop API, as well as perform several other functions.

■ Accessing the Registration Database

Windows 3.1 includes seven functions, all found in SHELL.DLL, for interacting with the Registration Database. These are: RegCloseKey, RegCreateKey, RegDeleteKey, RegEnumKey, RegOpenKey, RegQueryValue, and RegSetValue. Each of these is callable from within Visual Basic, although in researching this project I was unable to find any published listing of the Visual Basic declarations for these functions. I was able to determine their correct syntax from the C-language declarations described in the Windows 3.1 SDK Help file that accompanies Visual Basic Professional Toolkit, along with a hint or two from MSBASIC forum denizen Jonathan Zuck. The declarations for all seven functions are included in VBQMOD.BAS, although VB Q makes use of just five of them.

Once you have the declarations, the Registration Database functions are remarkably easy to use. The database stores data in a hierarchically structured tree which includes a file extension entry for each file type in the database. The extension entries appear as follows:

```
.PCX=PBRUSH
```

The value of each extension entry is known as an identifier. Information on how to open or print a file is stored under its identifier, as follows:

```
PBRUSH=Paintbrush Picture
    shell
        print
            command=pbrush.exe /p %1
```

Thus, to determine whether the Registration Database includes the data needed to print a file, you must first search for its extension to obtain the file type's identifier, and then search for the \shell\print\command associated with it.

Each of the Registration Database functions returns a value of zero (defined as Error_Success) if the function succeeds, or a nonzero value if it fails. So an application can call each function in sequence, testing for a nonzero response after each call, as demonstrated in the CheckReg() function. VB Q uses CheckReg() to determine if there is a Print command entry in the Registration Database for files with a specified extension.

```
Function CheckReg (Ext$) As Integer
Dim x&, NewKey&, KeyName$, Y&, Result$
Const lRes& = 80
Result$ = String$(lRes&, 0)
KeyName$ = "." + Ext$
'exit if Ext$ not listed in Registration Database
If RegOpenKey(HKEY_Classes_ROOT,KeyName$,NewKey&)<>Error_Success Then⇔
    Exit Function
'get Identifier for this key
x& = RegQueryValue(NewKey&, 0&, Result$, lRes&)
Y& = RegCloseKey(NewKey&)
'Exit if no identifier found
If x& <> Error_Success Then Exit Function
'get print command
Result$ = Left$(Result$, InStr(Result$, Chr$(0)) - 1) + "\shell\print"
'exit if no print command
If RegOpenKey(HKEY_Classes_ROOT, Result$, NewKey&)<>Error_Success Then⇔
    Exit Function 'GoTo Fail
Y& = RegCloseKey(NewKey&)
CheckReg = True
End Function
```

CheckReg() begins by calling RegOpenKey in an attempt to open a key consisting of a dot followed by the current file extension (so the key would be .DOC for files with a .DOC extension). The function exits if that call fails. Otherwise, CheckReg() calls RegQueryValue to obtain the value of that key, and again exits if the function fails. It then concatenates the value returned by RegQueryKey with \shell\print and attempts to open a key with that name. If that attempt is successful, CheckReg() returns a value of True. Otherwise, it returns a value of False.

■ **Drag-and-Drop Support from the File Manager**
One of the neater innovations in Windows 3.1 was the File Manager drag-and-drop API, which allows the user to drag files from the File Manager into applications written to take advantage of this API. VB Q relies upon this capability as the sole means by which the user can indicate the files that VB Q is to print.

To use the File Manager drag-and-drop API, an application must first call the DragAcceptFiles() function in SHELL.DLL to indicate that one or more of its windows is able to receive dropped files. Once it has done so, the File Manager will send the application a WM_DROPFILES message whenever the user releases files over the specified window. At that point, the application must acknowledge the dropped message by calling the DragQueryFile() function to determine the names of all the files that the user dropped into it.

The drag-and-drop API is very simple—except for one thing. Visual Basic normally intercepts the WM_DROPFILES message (along with any other messages sent to your application) and discards it (because Visual Basic doesn't contain any facility for handling drag-and-drop messages). Thus, to take advantage of this capability, your application has to circumvent Visual Basic's default message-handling procedure.

In my previous book, *PC/Computing Customizing Windows 3.1,* I described a method for intercepting drag-and-drop messages by calling Windows's PeekMessage() function in an endless DoEvents() loop, and initially I planned on using the same method with VB Q. However, shortly before I began work on VB Q, I came across a better way to access this drag-and-drop capability: a free Visual Basic custom control called DRAGDROP.VBX.

DRAGDROP.VBX was created by Gary Wisniewski of Apex Software, maker of Agility/VB, a fine database-management custom control. Wisniewski posted the control in CompuServe's MSBASIC forum, along with a message stating that it may be freely distributed. As if that weren't enough, he also twice made minor modifications to the control at my request, so I am deeply indebted to him.

The advantage of using DRAGDROP.VBX rather than the DoEvents()/PeekMessage() method of accessing the File Manager drag-and-drop API is that doing so eliminates the need to write any code to support this facility. Instead, the control automatically calls DragAcceptFiles() for the form into which it is placed, and automatically handles drag-and-drop events. When the user drops files into a form containing a DRAGDROP.VBX control, the control's DROP event is fired. The control's PointX and PointY properties indicate the location at which the files were dropped, its FileCount property indicates how many files were dropped, and its FileName array indicates the names of all the dropped files.

When the user drops files into VB Q, the program calls the DragDropEvent() subroutine. This subroutine loops through the list of dropped files, checking each file's extension first against the Registration Database and then, if the extension is not found in the Registration Database, against the VB Q Keys data in VBQ.INI. If neither source contains instructions for printing files with that extension, the user is given the option of entering either Registration Database or VB Q Keys information for that extension. If the user fails to do so, files with that extension won't be printed. Otherwise, if VB

Q finds printing instructions for files with that extension, the file name is added to the list of files to be printed.

```
Sub DragDropEvent ()
Dim x%, ExtPt%, fCount%, Valid%
Dim Ret As String * 255
'Get drop file names
fCount% = Form1.DragDrop1.FileCount
ReDim dFile$(fCount%)
For x% = 1 To fCount%
    dFile(x%) = Form1.DragDrop1.FileName(x% - 1)
Next
'    * Disable control while files being checked
Form1.DragDrop1.Enabled = False
'    * Check files
For x% = 0 To fCount%
'    * Get extension
    ExtPt% = InStr(dFile$(x%), ".")
    If ExtPt% Then
        Ext$ = Mid$(dFile$(x%), ExtPt% + 1)
'    * Check for reg db or vbq keys entry for ext$
        Valid% = ValidFile%(Ext$)
        If Not Valid% Then
            NoMethod.Show 1
            Form1.SetFocus
'    * check again
            Valid% = ValidFile%(Ext$)
        End If
        If Not Valid% Then
            MsgBox dFile$(x%) + " won't be printed", 48, "VB Q"
        Else
            Form1.List1.AddItem Ext$ + Chr$(9) + dFile$(x%)
        End If
    End If
Next
'    * Re-enable control
Form1.DragDrop1.Enabled = True
'    * Update counter label
CountQFiles
'    * Form1.Label2 = Form1.List1.ListCount & " files in queue"
End Sub
```

The actual job of checking whether printing instructions are available for files with a specified extension is performed by VB Q's ValidFile%() function. It starts by calling the CheckReg() function. If CheckReg can't find printing information for the extension in the Registration Database, ValidFile% calls the CheckPrivate() function, which searches for print instructions for the extension in VBQ.INI.

```
Function ValidFile% (Ext$)
Dim Valid%
Valid% = CheckReg(Ext$)
If Not Valid% Then Valid% = CheckPrivate(Ext$)
ValidFile% = Valid%
End Function
```

■ **Entering and Monitoring Time**

In addition to keeping track of the files that the user wishes to print, VB Q has to know when the files are to be printed.

VB Q uses a variable called StartTime of a custom type called Start to keep track of the print time the user enters on the Set Print Time form. The Start type is defined as follows:

```
Type Start
    Hour As Integer
    Minute As Integer
End Type
```

When the user closes the SetPrintTime dialog box, VB Q examines the value of the two scroll bars used to set the print time, as well as the two option buttons used to indicate AM or PM, and sets the value of StartTime accordingly.

```
StartTime.Hour = Hscroll1(0).Value
If Option1(1) = True And StartTime.Hour <> 12 Then StartTime.Hour = ⇔
    StartTime.Hour + 12
If Option1(0) = True And StartTime.Hour = 12 Then StartTime.Hour = ⇔
    StartTime.Hour = 0
StartTime.Minute = Hscroll1(1).Value
```

VB Q uses a timer control with an interval of two seconds to determine whether the time has come for it to print the specified files. The timer event routine starts by checking whether there are any files in the queue list box to print. If not, it exits immediately.

If there are files to print, the timer routine checks the caption of Label3 on VB Q's main form (Form1). This label always reflects the current print mode; it will read "Immediate Print" if VB Q is set to print files immediately, or "Scheduled to print at:" followed by the scheduled printing time if the user has selected the Scheduled Print option on the Schedule menu. If the user hasn't yet selected a print mode, the label will read "Print mode not set." The timer isn't enabled until the user has selected a print mode, so the timer event routine will never find this caption.

The use of the label control by the timer event routine illustrates an important point: Control properties can play the part of global variables in a Visual Basic application. Originally I intended to use a global variable to track the print mode, but since I also wanted to use Label3 to indicate the print mode at all times, I realized that there was no need to maintain a separate global variable for this purpose: Label3 could serve as the global variable. While this method isn't ideal for all situations (as reading control properties is slower than evaluating variables, this method would hamper time-critical

functions), in many cases you can simplify your program considerably without any significant performance hit by using control properties in lieu of variables.

```
Sub Timer1_Timer ()
Dim S%
'    * Check count
If list1.ListCount = 0 Then Exit Sub
'    * Check print method (boolean check)
S% = (Left$(Label3, 4) = "Sche")
'    * If scheduled print, check time--exit if not time yet
If S% Then
IfStartTime.Hour<Hour(Now)AndStartTime.Minute<Minute(Now)ThenExitSub
End If
'    * If immediate or time
'    * Print everything in list1
Do While List1.ListCount > 0
    PrintTopItem
    ClosePrintDialog
Loop
'    * Turn off the scheduled check mark, since the job is done
'    * reset caption
If S% Then
    ScheduleMenuSelection 2
    Caption = "VB Q"
End If
End Sub
```

If VB Q is in immediate mode or the scheduled print time has arrived, the timer
event routine loops through the list of files in the queue, calling the PrintTopItem routine once for each file. Next, the timer routine calls the ClosePrintDialog routine,
which shuts any Print dialog boxes posted by applications that weren't designed for
unattended printing. Finally, it calls ScheduleMenuSelection to turn off the scheduled
print mode.

The PrintTopItem routine checks first to see if the topmost file in the queue list
box is to be printed using data from the Registration Database. If so, it calls the Windows API function ShellExecute(), which instructs Windows to use Registration Database information to open or print a file, passing it the name of the file to print (A$)
and an instruction (SW_MINIMIZE) to run the application in a minimized window:

```
ExtPt% = ShellExecute(Form1.hWnd, "Print", A$, 0&, App.Path, SW_MINIMIZE)
```

Once the Print command has been received, Windows launches the application associated with the file specified in A$, instructs it to print the file, and then shuts down
the application.

If there is no Registration Database print method for the file, the PrintTopItem routine checks to see if there is a VB Q Keys method. If so, it calls the KeysPrint routine.
Otherwise, it adds the file to the Files Not Printed list.

Once PrintTopItem has finished examining and printing the file, it activates the View Report button used to view the lists of files that have been printed or which VB Q was unable to print.

■ FORM DESIGN ISSUES

Designing VB Q's forms was fairly straightforward. The only unusual thing about any of the forms is the amount of text presented in some of VB Q's dialog boxes. Since some of the tasks VB Q asks the user to perform, such as defining VB Q Keys or editing the Registration Database, are complex, I sought to simplify the tasks as much as possible by surrounding them with rich informational dialog boxes that fully explain the choices available to the user.

The logic of this is clear: You can reduce the complexity of a task by fully explaining each step. Nevertheless, few programmers regularly apply this logic to their programs. Instead, in a holdover from the days when every byte of computer memory was precious, many programmers seem to pride themselves on the terseness of their dialog-box prompts. Memory isn't that precious anymore, and certainly a few extra words in a dialog box are well worth the memory they consume if they simplify a program enough to eliminate some support calls.

As an example of how difficult this tradition of terseness can make things for the user, consider the standard Associate dialog box posted by the File Manager (see Figure 4.8).

This dialog box is about as uninformative as you can get. Any user who doesn't fully understand the process of associating files will undoubtedly be completely lost when confronted with it.

To smooth out this process, VB Q precedes every appearance of the Associate dialog box with the VB Q Trail Guide dialog box shown in Figure 4.14, which simply explains the intended purpose of the Associate dialog box, and provides a hint on how it should be used.

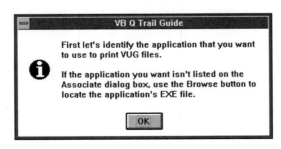

FIGURE 4.14

The VB Q Trail Guide dialog box is designed to simplify use of the Associate dialog box.

ENHANCING VB Q

Several enhancements to VB Q suggest themselves almost immediately. For example, it would be useful to be able to save queue lists and recall them for later use, and to designate files that are to be printed each day. Also, additional error-checking might be useful in the KeysPrint routine to ensure that VB Q can print files from any Windows application, and extensions to the VB Q Keys pseudocode language might allow the user to exercise more control over the appearance and layout of documents printed in VB Q.

LISTING

VB Q

```
'   *   *   *   *   *   *   *   *   *   *   *   *   *   *   *   *   *   *   *   *   *   *   *   *   *   *
'   VBQMAIN.FRM
'   Copyright (c) 1993 by Paul Bonner
'   PC Magazine Visual Basic Utilities
'   *   *   *   *   *   *   *   *   *   *   *   *   *   *   *   *   *   *   *   *   *   *   *   *   *   *

Version 2.0
Begin Form Form1
    AutoRedraw        =      -1   'True
    BackColor         =      &H00C0C0C0&
    BorderStyle       =      1   'Fixed Single
    Caption           =      "VB Q"
    Height            =      7005
    Icon              =      VBQ_MAIN.FRX:0000
    Left              =      2385
    LinkTopic         =      "Form1"
    MaxButton         =      0   'False
    ScaleHeight       =      6315
    ScaleWidth        =      5520
    Top               =      1065
    Width             =      5640
    Begin DragDrop DragDrop1
        Left          =      4200
        Top           =      4200
    End
    Begin CommandButton Command1
        Caption       =      "&Clear Report"
        Height        =      315
        Left          =      4080
        TabIndex      =      7
        Top           =      2220
        Visible       =      0   'False
        Width         =      1335
    End
    Begin Timer Timer1
        Interval      =      2000
        Left          =      3720
        Top           =      4200
    End
    Begin PictureBox Picture1
        Align         =      2   'Align Bottom
        BackColor     =      &H00C0C0C0&
        BorderStyle   =      0   'None
        Height        =      375
        Left          =      0
        ScaleHeight   =      375
        ScaleWidth    =      5520
        TabIndex      =      8
        Top           =      5940
        Width         =      5520
        Begin Line Line1
            BorderColor   =      &H00FFFFFF&
            Index         =      1
            X1            =      3600
```

```
                  X2              =     4800
                  Y1              =     0
                  Y2              =     0
               End
               Begin Line Line1
                  BorderColor     =     &H00808080&
                  Index           =     0
                  X1              =     1080
                  X2              =     2280
                  Y1              =     0
                  Y2              =     0
               End
               Begin Label Label3
                  AutoSize        =     -1    'True
                  BackColor       =     &H00C0C0C0&
                  Caption         =     "Label3"
                  FontBold        =     0     'False
                  FontItalic      =     0     'False
                  FontName        =     "MS Sans Serif"
                  FontSize        =     9.75
                  FontStrikethru  =     0     'False
                  FontUnderline   =     0     'False
                  Height          =     240
                  Left            =     2280
                  TabIndex        =     10
                  Top             =     60
                  Width           =     615
               End
               Begin Label Label2
                  AutoSize        =     -1    'True
                  BackColor       =     &H00C0C0C0&
                  Caption         =     "Label2"
                  FontBold        =     0     'False
                  FontItalic      =     0     'False
                  FontName        =     "MS Sans Serif"
                  FontSize        =     9.75
                  FontStrikethru  =     0     'False
                  FontUnderline   =     0     'False
                  Height          =     240
                  Left            =     240
                  TabIndex        =     9
                  Top             =     60
                  Width           =     615
               End
            End
            Begin CommandButton Command5
               Caption         =     "View Report"
               Enabled         =     0     'False
               Height          =     315
               Left            =     240
               TabIndex        =     2
               Top             =     2220
               Width           =     1335
            End
            Begin ListBox List2
               Enabled         =     0     'False
               Height          =     1395
               Index           =     1
               Left            =     240
               TabIndex        =     4
               Top             =     2880
               Width           =     5175
            End
            Begin ListBox List2
```

```
      Enabled             =     0     'False
      Height              =     1200
      Index               =     0
      Left                =     240
      TabIndex            =     6
      Top                 =     4680
      Width               =     5175
   End
   Begin ListBox List1
      BackColor           =     &H00FFFFFF&
      DragIcon            =     VBQ_MAIN.FRX:0302
      Height              =     1785
      Left                =     240
      Sorted              =     -1    'True
      TabIndex            =     1
      Top                 =     360
      Width               =     5175
   End
   Begin Label Label1
      AutoSize            =     -1    'True
      BackColor           =     &H00C0C0C0&
      Caption             =     "&Printed:"
      Enabled             =     0     'False
      Height              =     195
      Index               =     2
      Left                =     240
      TabIndex            =     3
      Top                 =     2640
      Width               =     675
   End
   Begin Label Label1
      AutoSize            =     -1    'True
      BackColor           =     &H00C0C0C0&
      Caption             =     "&Not Printed:"
      Enabled             =     0     'False
      Height              =     195
      Index               =     1
      Left                =     240
      TabIndex            =     5
      Top                 =     4440
      Width               =     1035
   End
   Begin Label Label1
      AutoSize            =     -1    'True
      BackColor           =     &H00C0C0C0&
      Caption             =     "&Files to print:"
      DragIcon            =     VBQ_MAIN.FRX:0604
      Height              =     195
      Index               =     0
      Left                =     240
      TabIndex            =     0
      Top                 =     120
      Width               =     1125
   End
   Begin Menu fMenu
      Caption             =     "&File"
      Begin Menu fItem
         Caption          =     "&Exit"
         Index            =     0
      End
   End
   Begin Menu EditMenu
      Caption             =     "&Edit"
      Begin Menu editItem
```

```
                    Caption          =      "VB Q &Keys..."
                    Index            =      0
              End
              Begin Menu editItem
                    Caption          =      "Registration &Database..."
                    Index            =      1
              End
              Begin Menu editItem
                    Caption          =      "&Remove File"
                    Index            =      2
              End
        End
        Begin Menu schMenu
              Caption            =      "&Scheduler"
              Begin Menu sItem
                    Caption          =      "Set Print &Time..."
                    Index            =      0
              End
              Begin Menu sItem
                    Caption          =      "-"
                    Index            =      1
              End
              Begin Menu sItem
                    Caption          =      "&Scheduled Print"
                    Index            =      2
              End
              Begin Menu sItem
                    Caption          =      "&Immediate Print"
                    Index            =      3
              End
        End
        Begin Menu HelpMenu
              Caption            =      "&Help"
              Begin Menu HelpItem
                    Caption          =      "&About VB Q..."
              End
        End
End
DefInt A-Z
Option Explicit


Sub Command1_Click () 'Clear Report
Dim X%
X% = MsgBox("Clear contents of the report list boxes?", 52, "VB Q")
If X% <> 6 Then Exit Sub
For X% = 0 To 1
    List2(X%).Clear
Next
' * * * * * * * * * * * * * * * * * * * * * * * * * * * *
' * Trigger the Close report button
' * * * * * * * * * * * * * * * * * * * * * * * * * * * *
Command5.Value = True
' * * * * * * * * * * * * * * * * * * * * * * * * * * * *
' * Disable report controls
' * * * * * * * * * * * * * * * * * * * * * * * * * * * *
ToggleReport False
' * * * * * * * * * * * * * * * * * * * * * * * * * * * *
' * Disable the View Report button
' * * * * * * * * * * * * * * * * * * * * * * * * * * * *
Command5.Enabled = False
End Sub

Sub Command5_Click () 'Hide/Show report
```

```
Dim X%
' * * * * * * * * * * * * * * * * * * * * * * * * * *
' * Determine action based on form height
' * * * * * * * * * * * * * * * * * * * * * * * * * *
Select Case Height
Case Is = 3600
   Height = 7000
   Command5.Caption = "&Hide Report"
   Command1.Visible = True
' * * * * * * * * * * * * * * * * * * * * * * * * * *
' * Enable report controls
' * * * * * * * * * * * * * * * * * * * * * * * * * *
ToggleReport True
Case Else
   Height = 3600
   Command5.Caption = "&View Report"
   Command1.Visible = False
' * * * * * * * * * * * * * * * * * * * * * * * * * *
' * Disable report controls
' * * * * * * * * * * * * * * * * * * * * * * * * * *
ToggleReport False
End Select
End Sub

Sub DragDrop1_Drop (PointX As Long, PointY As Long)
' * * * * * * * * * * * * * * * * * * * * * * * * * *
' * Call handler for FM drag-and-drop event
' * * * * * * * * * * * * * * * * * * * * * * * * * *
DragDropEvent
End Sub

Sub editItem_Click (Index As Integer)
' * * * * * * * * * * * * * * * * * * * * * * * * * *
' * Call handler for edit menu selections
' * * * * * * * * * * * * * * * * * * * * * * * * * *
EditMenuSelection Index
End Sub

Sub fItem_Click (Index As Integer)
Select Case Index
Case 0    'Exit
   End
End Select
End Sub

Sub Form_DragOver (Source As Control, X As Single, Y As Single, State As ⇔
   Integer)
' * * * * * * * * * * * * * * * * * * * * * * * * * *
' * Set icon for dragging from report over form
' * * * * * * * * * * * * * * * * * * * * * * * * * *
Source.DragIcon = Label1(0).DragIcon
End Sub

Sub Form_Load ()
' * * * * * * * * * * * * * * * * * * * * * * * * * *
' * Center form on screen (with room for report)
' * * * * * * * * * * * * * * * * * * * * * * * * * *
Left = (Screen.Width - Width) / 2
Top = (Screen.Height - 7000) / 2
Height = 3600
' * * * * * * * * * * * * * * * * * * * * * * * * * *
' * Assign drag icons
' * * * * * * * * * * * * * * * * * * * * * * * * * *
List2(0).DragIcon = Label1(0).DragIcon
```

```
List2(1).DragIcon = List2(0).DragIcon
' * * * * * * * * * * * * * * * * * * * * * * * * * * *
' * Draw status bar lines
' * * * * * * * * * * * * * * * * * * * * * * * * * * *
DrawStatusBarLines Me
' * * * * * * * * * * * * * * * * * * * * * * * * * * *
' * Init globals
' * * * * * * * * * * * * * * * * * * * * * * * * * * *
CRLF$ = Chr$(13) + Chr$(10)
StartTime.Hour = -1
' * * * * * * * * * * * * * * * * * * * * * * * * * * *
' * Read vb q keys values
' * * * * * * * * * * * * * * * * * * * * * * * * * * *
InitKeys
' * * * * * * * * * * * * * * * * * * * * * * * * * * *
' * Set labels and timer
' * * * * * * * * * * * * * * * * * * * * * * * * * * *
CountQFiles
Label3 = "Print mode not set"
Timer1.Enabled = False
End Sub

Sub Form_Resize ()
Form1.Caption = "VB Q"
' * * * * * * * * * * * * * * * * * * * * * * * * * * *
' * Change caption if form is minimized/restored
' * * * * * * * * * * * * * * * * * * * * * * * * * * *
Select Case WindowState
Case 1
    If Left$(Label3, 6) = "Print " Then
        Form1.Caption = "VB Q"
    Else
        Form1.Caption = "VB Q" + Chr(10) + Chr$(13) + Label3
    End If
Case Else
End Select
End Sub

Sub HelpItem_Click ()
' * * * * * * * * * * * * * * * * * * * * * * * * * * *
' * Display copyright notice
' * * * * * * * * * * * * * * * * * * * * * * * * * * *
Dim X%
X% = MsgBox("VB Q -- A Print Queue for Windows 3.1" + CRLF$ + "Copyright (c) ⇔
    1993, by Paul Bonner" + CRLF$ + "PC Magazine Visual Basic Utilities", ⇔
    64, "About VB Q")
End Sub

Sub List1_DragDrop (Source As Control, X As Single, Y As Single)
' * * * * * * * * * * * * * * * * * * * * * * * * * * *
' * Handler for drag-drop from report
' * * * * * * * * * * * * * * * * * * * * * * * * * * *
List1.AddItem Source.List(Source.ListIndex)
Source.RemoveItem Source.ListIndex
' * * * * * * * * * * * * * * * * * * * * * * * * * * *
' * Close report if no files remain there
' * * * * * * * * * * * * * * * * * * * * * * * * * * *
If List2(0).ListCount = 0 And List2(1).ListCount = 0 Then
    Command5.Value = True
    Command5.Enabled = False
End If
' * * * * * * * * * * * * * * * * * * * * * * * * * * *
' * Update Files in Queue counter
' * * * * * * * * * * * * * * * * * * * * * * * * * * *
```

```
        CountQFiles
        End Sub

        Sub List1_DragOver (Source As Control, X As Single, Y As Single, State As ⇔
           Integer)
        '   * * * * * * * * * * * * * * * * * * * * * * * * * *
        '   * Change dragicon to show that files can be dropped here
        '   * * * * * * * * * * * * * * * * * * * * * * * * * *
        Source.DragIcon = List1.DragIcon
        End Sub

        Sub List1_GotFocus ()
        '   * * * * * * * * * * * * * * * * * * * * * * * * * *
        '   * Identify active list for edit menu handler
        '   * * * * * * * * * * * * * * * * * * * * * * * * * *
        Set ActiveList = List1
        End Sub

        Sub List2_DblClick (Index As Integer)
        '   * * * * * * * * * * * * * * * * * * * * * * * * * *
        '   * Explain not printed files
        '   * * * * * * * * * * * * * * * * * * * * * * * * * *
        Select Case Index
        Case 0
            Dim I%, A$
            I% = List2(0).ItemData(List2(0).ListIndex)
            Select Case I%
                Case Is = -10
                A$ = "No print method on record for this file"
                Case Is = -5
            A$ = "Print Failure. Try editing the VB Q Keys entry for this file type."
                Case Is > 0 < 33
            A$ = "Print Failure. Try editing the Registration Database entry for ⇔
            this file."
                Case Else
                A$ = "Unknown print failure."
                End Select
            MsgBox A$
        Case 1
        End Select

        End Sub

        Sub List2_GotFocus (Index As Integer)
        '   * * * * * * * * * * * * * * * * * * * * * * * * * *
        '   * Identify active list for edit menu handler
        '   * * * * * * * * * * * * * * * * * * * * * * * * * *
        Set ActiveList = List2(Index)
        End Sub

        Sub List2_MouseDown (Index As Integer, Button As Integer, Shift As Integer, ⇔
           X As Single, Y As Single)
        '   * * * * * * * * * * * * * * * * * * * * * * * * * *
        '   * Initiate file drag
        '   * * * * * * * * * * * * * * * * * * * * * * * * * *
        List2(Index).Drag 1
        End Sub

        Sub sItem_Click (Index As Integer)
        '   * * * * * * * * * * * * * * * * * * * * * * * * * *
        '   * Call Schedule menu handler
        '   * * * * * * * * * * * * * * * * * * * * * * * * * *
        ScheduleMenuSelection Index
        End Sub
```

```
Sub Timer1_Timer ()
Dim S%
'   * * * * * * * * * * * * * * * * * * * * * * * * * * * *
'   * Check count
'   * * * * * * * * * * * * * * * * * * * * * * * * * * * *
If List1.ListCount = 0 Then Exit Sub
'   * * * * * * * * * * * * * * * * * * * * * * * * * * * *
'   * Check print mode
'   * * * * * * * * * * * * * * * * * * * * * * * * * * * *
S% = Left$(Label3, 4) = "Sche"
If S% Then   ' If scheduled print, check time
  If StartTime.Hour < Hour(Now) And StartTime.Minute < Minute(Now) Then ⇔
    Exit Sub
End If
'   * * * * * * * * * * * * * * * * * * * * * * * * * * * *
'   * If immediate mode or time to print,
'   * print everything in List1
'   * * * * * * * * * * * * * * * * * * * * * * * * * * * *
Do While List1.ListCount > 0
    PrintTopItem
    ClosePrintDialog
Loop
'   * * * * * * * * * * * * * * * * * * * * * * * * * * * *
'   * Turn off the scheduled check mark, since the job
'   * is done, and reset caption
'   * * * * * * * * * * * * * * * * * * * * * * * * * * * *
If S% Then
    ScheduleMenuSelection 2
    Caption = "VB Q"
End If
End Sub
```

LISTING

NOMETHOD

```
'   * * * * * * * * * * * * * * * * * * * * * * * * * * * *
'   NOMETHOD.FRM
'   Copyright © 1993 by Paul Bonner
'   PC Magazine Visual Basic Utilities
'   * * * * * * * * * * * * * * * * * * * * * * * * * * * *
VERSION 2.00
Begin Form NoMethod
    BackColor       =   &H00C0C0C0&
    BorderStyle     =   3   'Fixed Double
    Caption         =   "VB Q Trail Guide"
    ControlBox      =   0   'False
    Height          =   4905
    Left            =   1815
    LinkTopic       =   "Form2"
    MaxButton       =   0    'False
    MinButton       =   0    'False
    ScaleHeight     =   4500
    ScaleWidth      =   6180
```

```
    Top               =      1650
    Width             =      6300
    Begin CommandButton Command1
        Cancel         =      -1    'True
        Caption        =      "Cancel"
        Height         =      360
        Index          =      2
        Left           =      4560
        TabIndex       =      2
        Top            =      240
        Width          =      1395
    End
    Begin CommandButton Command1
        Caption        =      "VB Q &Keys"
        Height         =      360
        Index          =      1
        Left           =      4560
        TabIndex       =      1
        Top            =      2760
        Width          =      1395
    End
    Begin CommandButton Command1
        Caption        =      "&RegEdit"
        Height         =      360
        Index          =      0
        Left           =      4560
        TabIndex       =      0
        Top            =      1320
        Width          =      1395
    End
    Begin Label Label3
        BackColor      =      &H00C0C0C0&
        Caption        =      "Label3"
        Height         =      1575
        Left           =      240
        TabIndex       =      5
        Top            =      2760
        Width          =      4095
    End
    Begin Label Label2
        BackColor      =      &H00C0C0C0&
        Caption        =      "Label2"
        Height         =      1455
        Left           =      240
        TabIndex       =      4
        Top            =      1080
        Width          =      4095
    End
    Begin Label Label1
        BackColor      =      &H00C0C0C0&
        Caption        =      "Label1"
        Height         =      615
        Left           =      240
        TabIndex       =      3
        Top            =      240
        Width          =      4095
    End
End
DefInt A-Z
Option Explicit

Sub Command1_Click (Index As Integer)
If Index <> 2 Then    'If not Cancel
    Dim ExtPt%, Ret As String * 255, Temp$
```

```
'   * * * * * * * * * * * * * * * * * * * * * * * * * * *
'   * Check to see if an association recorded in WIN.INI
'   * * * * * * * * * * * * * * * * * * * * * * * * * * *
ExtPt% = GetProfileString("Extensions", Ext$, "DOG", Ret, 254)
'   * * * * * * * * * * * * * * * * * * * * * * * * * * *
'   * If not, get one
'   * * * * * * * * * * * * * * * * * * * * * * * * * * *
    If Left$(Ret$, 3) = "DOG" Then
    Temp$ = "First let's identify the application that you want to use to ⇔
    print " + Ext$ + " files."
     Temp$ = Temp$ + CRLF$ + CRLF$ + "If the application you want isn't ⇔
    listed in the dialog box, use the Browse button to locate the ⇔
    application's .EXE file."
        MsgBox Temp$, 64, "VB Q Trail Guide"
        BorrowDialog Me, "WFS_Frame", "WINFILE.EXE", 103, "Associate", ""
        ExtPt% = GetProfileString("Extensions", Ext$, "DOG", Ret, 254)
        If Left$(Ret, 3) = "DOG" Then Exit Sub
    End If
    TargetApp$ = BuildTarget(Ret)
End If
Select Case Index
Case 0      'RegEdit button
  Temp$ = "Registration Editor will run so you can add the command to print ⇔
    " + Ext$ + " files." + CRLF$ + CRLF$ + "Caution: Do not change the value ⇔
    that VB Q enters into the 'Identifier' field on the Add File Type dialog ⇔
    box."
    MsgBox Temp$, 64, "VB Q Trail Guide"
    Dim Send$
  Send$ = TargetApp$ + "_" + Ext$ + Chr$(9) + TargetApp$ + " " + Ext$ + " ⇔
    files{TAB}{RIGHT}{TAB}%U%B" + UCase$(Left$(Ret, InStr(Ret, " "))) + ⇔
    "~%C{RIGHT}  "
  BorrowDialog Me, "Registration Editor", "REGEDIT.EXE", 1056, "Add File ⇔
    Type", Send$
    ExtPt% = AddExtToReg(Ext$, TargetApp$)
Case 1      ' VB Q Keys button
    Special.Show 1
Case Else     'Cancel
End Select
TargetApp$ = ""
Unload Me
End Sub


Sub Form_Load ()
CenterForm Me
Label1 = "No print method has been recorded for files with the extension " + ⇔
    Ext$ + "."
Label2 = "If the application that prints these files accepts DDE commands or ⇔
    command line parameters (switches) to open and print files, click the ⇔
    RegEdit button."
Label2 = Label2 + " RegEdit allows you to enter command line parameters or ⇔
    DDE commands that either File Manager or VB Q can use to print files."
Label3 = "Otherwise, click the VB Q Keys button to tell VB Q the keyboard ⇔
    commands it should use to print " + Ext$ + " files."
Label3 = Label3 + CRLF$ + CRLF$ + CRLF$ + "With either option, you may first ⇔
    have to identify the application that VB Q should use to print " + Ext$ ⇔
    + " files."
End Sub
```

LISTING

SPECIAL FORM

```
'   *  *  *  *  *  *  *  *  *  *  *  *  *  *  *  *  *  *  *  *  *  *  *  *  *  *  *  *
'   SPECIAL.FRM
'   Copyright (c) 1993 by Paul Bonner
'   PC Magazine Visual Basic Utilities
'   *  *  *  *  *  *  *  *  *  *  *  *  *  *  *  *  *  *  *  *  *  *  *  *  *  *  *  *
VERSION 2.00
Begin Form Special
    BackColor       =    &H00C0C0C0&
    BorderStyle     =    3   'Fixed Double
    Caption         =    "VB Q Keys"
    ControlBox      =    0      'False
    Height          =    5625
    Left            =    1020
    LinkTopic       =    "Form2"
    MaxButton       =    0      'False
    MinButton       =    0      'False
    ScaleHeight     =    5220
    ScaleWidth      =    6255
    Top             =    1110
    Width           =    6375
    Begin CheckBox Check2
        BackColor       =    &H00C0C0C0&
        Caption         =    "&Repeat Print Command"
        Height          =    360
        Left            =    2760
        TabIndex        =    6
        Top             =    3000
        Width           =    2295
    End
    Begin CheckBox Check1
        BackColor       =    &H00C0C0C0&
        Caption         =    "Run &Hidden"
        Height          =    360
        Left            =    240
        TabIndex        =    5
        Top             =    3000
        Width           =    1575
    End
    Begin Frame Frame2
        BackColor       =    &H00C0C0C0&
        Caption         =    "Instructions:"
        Height          =    2295
        Left            =    240
        TabIndex        =    0
        Top             =    120
        Width           =    4815
        Begin Label Label2
            BackColor       =    &H00C0C0C0&
            FontBold        =    0      'False
            FontItalic      =    0      'False
            FontName        =    "MS Sans Serif"
            FontSize        =    9.75
            FontStrikethru  =    0      'False
            FontUnderline   =    0      'False
```

```
      Height            =     1695
      Left              =     240
      TabIndex          =     1
      Top               =     360
      Width             =     4455
   End
End
Begin PictureBox Picture1
   Align             =     2   'Align Bottom
   BackColor         =     &H00C0C0C0&
   BorderStyle       =     0   'None
   Height            =     360
   Left              =     0
   ScaleHeight       =     360
   ScaleWidth        =     6255
   TabIndex          =     17
   Top               =     4860
   Width             =     6255
   Begin Line Line1
      BorderColor       =     &H00FFFFFF&
      Index             =     1
      X1                =     3840
      X2                =     5040
      Y1                =     0
      Y2                =     120
   End
   Begin Line Line1
      BorderColor       =     &H00808080&
      Index             =     0
      X1                =     1560
      X2                =     2760
      Y1                =     0
      Y2                =     60
   End
   Begin Label Label3
      BackColor         =     &H00C0C0C0&
      Caption           =     "Label3"
      FontBold          =     0     'False
      FontItalic        =     0     'False
      FontName          =     "MS Sans Serif"
      FontSize          =     9.75
      FontStrikethru    =     0     'False
      FontUnderline     =     0     'False
      Height            =     255
      Left              =     240
      TabIndex          =     18
      Top               =     60
      Width             =     6135
   End
End
Begin Frame Frame1
   BackColor         =     &H00C0C0C0&
   Caption           =     "Special characters:"
   Height            =     1215
   Left              =     240
   TabIndex          =     3
   Top               =     3480
   Width             =     4815
   Begin CommandButton Command2
      Caption           =     "&Left"
      Height            =     315
      Index             =     7
      Left              =     3480
      TabIndex          =     14
```

```
            Top             =       720
            Width           =       930
      End
      Begin CommandButton Command2
            Caption         =       "&Right"
            Height          =       315
            Index           =       6
            Left            =       2400
            TabIndex        =       13
            Top             =       720
            Width           =       930
      End
      Begin CommandButton Command2
            Caption         =       "&Up"
            Height          =       315
            Index           =       5
            Left            =       1320
            TabIndex        =       12
            Top             =       720
            Width           =       930
      End
      Begin CommandButton Command2
            Caption         =       "&Down"
            Height          =       315
            Index           =       4
            Left            =       120
            TabIndex        =       11
            Top             =       720
            Width           =       930
      End
      Begin CommandButton Command2
            Caption         =       "&Alt"
            Height          =       315
            Index           =       0
            Left            =       120
            TabIndex        =       7
            Top             =       300
            Width           =       930
      End
      Begin CommandButton Command2
            Caption         =       "&Control"
            Height          =       315
            Index           =       1
            Left            =       1320
            TabIndex        =       8
            Top             =       300
            Width           =       930
      End
      Begin CommandButton Command2
            Caption         =       "&Tab"
            Height          =       315
            Index           =       2
            Left            =       2400
            TabIndex        =       9
            Top             =       300
            Width           =       930
      End
      Begin CommandButton Command2
            Caption         =       "&Enter"
            Height          =       315
            Index           =       3
            Left            =       3480
            TabIndex        =       10
            Top             =       300
```

```
              Width            =      930
         End
      End
      Begin CommandButton Command1
         Cancel               =      -1    'True
         Caption              =      "Cancel"
         Height               =      375
         Index                =      1
         Left                 =      5280
         TabIndex             =      16
         Top                  =      840
         Width                =      795
      End
      Begin CommandButton Command1
         Caption              =      "OK"
         Default         ⸍     =      -1    'True
         Height               =      375
         Index                =      0
         Left                 =      5280
         TabIndex             =      15
         Top                  =      240
         Width                =      795
      End
      Begin TextBox Text1
         Height               =      285
         Left                 =      1800
         TabIndex             =      4
         Text                 =      "Text1"
         Top                  =      2640
         Width                =      3255
      End
      Begin Label Label1
         BackColor            =      &H00C0C0C0&
         Caption              =      "&Print command:"
         Height               =      255
         Index                =      1
         Left                 =      240
         TabIndex             =      2
         Top                  =      2640
         Width                =      1575
      End
   End
End
DefInt A-Z
Option Explicit

Sub Check1_Click ()
' * * * * * * * * * * * * * * * * * * * * * * * * * * * *
' * Warn user to use Run Hidden only
' * after VB Q Keys for this app are debugged
'
' * Skip warning if form is loading
' * * * * * * * * * * * * * * * * * * * * * * * * * * * *
If Me.Visible = False Then Exit Sub
If Check1 = 1 Then
  MsgBox "Select the Run Hidden option only if you're sure that this VB Q ⇔
    Keys print command works reliably.", 48, "VB Q Keys"
End If
End Sub

Sub Check1_GotFocus ()
Label3 = "Use this option only if you're sure the print command works reliably."
End Sub

Sub Check2_Click ()
```

```
'   * * * * * * * * * * * * * * * * * * * * * * * * * * *
'   * Warn user to use Repeat Print command
'   * only after extensive testing

'   * Skip warning if form is loading
'   * * * * * * * * * * * * * * * * * * * * * * * * * * *
If Me.Visible = False Then Exit Sub
If Check2 = 1 Then
  MsgBox "Note: You should select the Repeat Print Command option only if ⇔
     this application ignores print commands while loading a file.", 48, "VB ⇔
     Q Keys"
End If
End Sub

Sub Check2_GotFocus ()
Label3 = "Use to send print commands repeatedly to apps. that require it."
End Sub

Sub Command1_Click (Index As Integer)
Select Case Index
Case 0      'OK
   Dim X%, A$, F$
'   * * * * * * * * * * * * * * * * * * * * * * * * * * *
'   * VB Q Keys entry is required
'   * * * * * * * * * * * * * * * * * * * * * * * * * * *
      If Text1 = "" Then
         MsgBox "You must fill in this field", 48, "VB Q"
         Exit Sub
      End If
   A$ = "Extensions"
   F$ = "VBQ.INI"
'   * * * * * * * * * * * * * * * * * * * * * * * * * * *
'   * Save VBQ.INI data
'   * * * * * * * * * * * * * * * * * * * * * * * * * * *
   X% = WritePrivateProfileString(A$, Ext$ + "_Print", Text1, F$)
X%=WritePrivateProfileString(A$,Ext$+"_Hidden",Str$(Check1.Value),F$)
X%=WritePrivateProfileString(A$,Ext$+"_Repeat",Str$(Check2.Value),F$)
Case 1     'Cancel
End Select
Unload Me
End Sub

Sub Command1_GotFocus (Index As Integer)
Select Case Index
Case 0
   Label3 = "Click OK to save the changes you've made"
Case 1
   Label3 = "Click Cancel to abandon the changes you've made."
End Select
End Sub

Sub Command2_Click (Index As Integer)
'   * * * * * * * * * * * * * * * * * * * * * * * * * * *
'   * Insert Keys$() associated with this button
'   * * * * * * * * * * * * * * * * * * * * * * * * * * *
Text1.SelText = Keys$(Index, 0)
Text1.SetFocus
End Sub

Sub Command2_GotFocus (Index As Integer)
Label3 = "Click this key to insert " + Keys$(Index, 0) + "."
End Sub

Sub Form_Load ()
```

```
Caption = "VB Q Keys for " + Ext$ + " Files"
CenterForm Me
Select Case EditSpecial%
Case False      ' New VB Q Keys entry
    Text1 = ""
Case Else       ' Existing entry
    Text1 = GetPvt(Ext$ + "_Print")
    Check1.Value = Val(GetPvt(Ext$ + "_Hidden"))
    Check2.Value = Val(GetPvt(Ext$ + "_Repeat"))
    EditSpecial% = False
End Select
Dim X%
DrawStatusBarLines Me      ' Draw 3D lines
Label2 = "VB Q needs to know the command sequence to make " + TargetApp$ + ⇔
    " print a " + Ext$ + " file once it is opened."
Label2 = Label2 + CRLF$ + CRLF$ + "Please enter the command " + TargetApp$ + ⇔
    " needs to print a " + Ext$ + " file. Use the buttons below to enter ⇔
    special characters."
End Sub

Sub Text1_GotFocus ()
Dim X%
Dim L$
'   * * * * * * * * * * * * * * * * * * * * * * * * * * * * *
'   * Place hint in status bar
'   * * * * * * * * * * * * * * * * * * * * * * * * * * * * *
Label3 = "Hint: most applications use {alt}FP or {alt}FP{enter} to print a ⇔
    file."
End Sub
```

LISTING

TIME FORM

```
'   * * * * * * * * * * * * * * * * * * * * * * * * * * * * *
'   TIMEFORM.FRM
'   Copyright (c) 1993 by Paul Bonner
'   PC Magazine Visual Basic Utilities
'   * * * * * * * * * * * * * * * * * * * * * * * * * * * * *
VERSION 2.00
Begin Form TimeForm
    BackColor       =    &H00C0C0C0&
    BorderStyle     =    3   'Fixed Double
    Caption         =    "Set Print Time"
    ControlBox      =    0   'False
    Height          =    2775
    Left            =    2205
    LinkTopic       =    "Form2"
    MaxButton       =    0   'False
    MinButton       =    0   'False
    ScaleHeight     =    2370
    ScaleWidth      =    4515
    Top             =    2370
    Width           =    4635
    Begin OptionButton Option1
```

```
      BackColor           =     &H00C0C0C0&
      Caption             =     "PM"
      Height              =     255
      Index               =     1
      Left                =     2160
      TabIndex            =     12
      Top                 =     2040
      Width               =     1215
   End
   Begin OptionButton Option1
      BackColor           =     &H00C0C0C0&
      Caption             =     "AM"
      Height              =     255
      Index               =     0
      Left                =     960
      TabIndex            =     11
      Top                 =     2040
      Width               =     1215
   End
   Begin HScrollBar HScroll1
      Height              =     255
      Index               =     1
      Left                =     840
      Max                 =     59
      TabIndex            =     5
      Top                 =     1680
      Value               =     1
      Width               =     2535
   End
   Begin HScrollBar HScroll1
      Height              =     255
      Index               =     0
      Left                =     840
      Max                 =     12
      Min                 =     1
      TabIndex            =     3
      Top                 =     1200
      Value               =     1
      Width               =     2535
   End
   Begin CommandButton Command1
      Cancel              =     -1      'True
      Caption             =     "Cancel"
      Height              =     375
      Index               =     1
      Left                =     3360
      TabIndex            =     1
      Top                 =     600
      Width               =     975
   End
   Begin CommandButton Command1
      Caption             =     "OK"
      Default             =     -1      'True
      Height              =     375
      Index               =     0
      Left                =     3360
      TabIndex            =     0
      Top                 =     120
      Width               =     975
   End
   Begin Label Label2
      BackStyle           =     0      'Transparent
      Caption             =     "Hour: (1-12)"
      Height              =     375
```

```
      Index           =     3
      Left            =     120
      TabIndex        =     10
      Top             =     1080
      Width           =     600
   End
   Begin Label Label2
      BackStyle       =     0     'Transparent
      Caption         =     "Minute: (0-59)"
      Height          =     375
      Index           =     2
      Left            =     120
      TabIndex        =     9
      Top             =     1525
      Width           =     765
   End
   Begin Label Label4
      AutoSize        =     -1    'True
      BackStyle       =     0     'Transparent
      Caption         =     "Label4"
      Height          =     195
      Left            =     120
      TabIndex        =     8
      Top             =     120
      Width           =     585
   End
   Begin Label Label3
      AutoSize        =     -1    'True
      BackStyle       =     0     'Transparent
      Caption         =     "Label3"
      Height          =     195
      Left            =     2040
      TabIndex        =     7
      Top             =     480
      Width           =     585
   End
   Begin Label Label2
      BackStyle       =     0     'Transparent
      Caption         =     "Label2"
      Height          =     195
      Index           =     1
      Left            =     3480
      TabIndex        =     6
      Top             =     1680
      Width           =     585
   End
   Begin Label Label2
      BackStyle       =     0     'Transparent
      Caption         =     "Label2"
      Height          =     195
      Index           =     0
      Left            =     3480
      TabIndex        =     4
      Top             =     1200
      Width           =     585
   End
   Begin Label Label1
      AutoSize        =     -1    'True
      BackStyle       =     0     'Transparent
      Caption         =     "&Start next print job at:"
      Height          =     195
      Left            =     120
      TabIndex        =     2
      Top             =     480
```

```
        Width            =    1875
      End
End
DefInt A-Z
Option Explicit

Sub Command1_Click (Index As Integer)
Select Case Index
Case 0      'ok
    StartTime.Hour = Hscroll1(0).Value
'   * * * * * * * * * * * * * * * * * * * * * * * *
'   * Correct for AM/PM and hour=0
'   * * * * * * * * * * * * * * * * * * * * * * * *
  If Option1(1) = True And StartTime.Hour <> 12 Then StartTime.Hour = ⇔
    StartTime.Hour + 12
  If Option1(0) = True And StartTime.Hour = 12 Then StartTime.Hour = ⇔
    StartTime.Hour = 0
    StartTime.Minute = Hscroll1(1).Value
Case 1      'cancel
End Select
    Unload Me
End Sub

Sub Form_Load ()
CenterForm Me
Dim SP%, N$
'   * * * * * * * * * * * * * * * * * * * * * * * *
'   * Display current hour
'   * * * * * * * * * * * * * * * * * * * * * * * *
N$ = Str$(Now)
SP% = InStr(N$, " ")
N$ = Mid$(N$, SP% + 1)
SP% = InStr(N$, ":")
Hscroll1(0).Value = Val(Left$(N$, SP% - 1))
'   * * * * * * * * * * * * * * * * * * * * * * * *
'   * Display current Minute
'   * * * * * * * * * * * * * * * * * * * * * * * *
N$ = Mid$(N$, SP% + 1)
SP% = InStr(N$, ":")
Hscroll1(1).Value = Val(Left$(N$, SP% - 1))
'   * * * * * * * * * * * * * * * * * * * * * * * *
'   * Update scroll bar labels and status bar
'   * * * * * * * * * * * * * * * * * * * * * * * *
UpDateLabels
Label4 = "The current time is " + Format$(Now, "Medium Time")
If InStr(Format(Now, "Medium Time"), "PM") Then
    Option1(1) = True
Else
    Option1(0) = True
End If
End Sub

Sub HScroll1_Change (Index As Integer)
'   * * * * * * * * * * * * * * * * * * * * * * * *
'   * Display changes in scroll bar labels and status bar
'   * * * * * * * * * * * * * * * * * * * * * * * *
UpDateLabels
End Sub

Sub HScroll1_Scroll (Index As Integer)
UpDateLabels
End Sub

Sub Option1_Click (Index As Integer)
```

```
'   * * * * * * * * * * * * * * * * * * * * * * * * * *
'   * Display changes in scroll bar labels and status bar
'   * * * * * * * * * * * * * * * * * * * * * * * * * *
UpDateLabels
End Sub

Sub UpDateLabels ()
'   * * * * * * * * * * * * * * * * * * * * * * * *
'   * Display current time selection
'   * * * * * * * * * * * * * * * * * * * * * * * *
Dim sHour%, sMinute%, N$
'   * * * * * * * * * * * * * * * * * * * * * * * *
'   * Label for Hour scroll bar
'   * * * * * * * * * * * * * * * * * * * * * * * *
Label2(0) = Trim(Str$(Hscroll1(0).Value))
'   * * * * * * * * * * * * * * * * * * * * * * * *
'   * Label for Minute scroll bar
'   * * * * * * * * * * * * * * * * * * * * * * * *
Label2(1) = Trim(Str$(Hscroll1(1).Value))
sHour% = Val(Label2(0))
If Option1(1) = True Then sHour% = sHour% + 12
sMinute% = Val(Label2(1))
If sHour% = 12 Then sHour% = 0
If sHour% = 24 Then sHour% = sHour% - 12
'   * * * * * * * * * * * * * * * * * * * * * * * *
'   * Status bar label
'   * * * * * * * * * * * * * * * * * * * * * * * *
Label3 = Format$(sHour% & ":" & Label2(1), "Medium Time")
End Sub
```

LISTING

VB Q EXEC

```
'   * * * * * * * * * * * * * * * * * * * * * * * * * *
'   VBQEXEC.BAS
'   Copyright (c) 1993 by Paul Bonner
'   PC Magazine Visual Basic Utilities
'   * * * * * * * * * * * * * * * * * * * * * * * * * *
DefInt A-Z
Option Explicit
'   * * * * * * * * * * * * * * * * * * * * * * * * * *
'   * Declares to run hidden apps, center and control them
'   * * * * * * * * * * * * * * * * * * * * * * * * * *
Type Rect
    Left As Integer
    Top As Integer
    Right As Integer
    Bottom As Integer
End Type
Declare Sub SetWindowPos Lib "User" (ByVal hWnd As Integer, ByVal ⇔
    hWndInsertAfter As Integer, ByVal X As Integer, ByVal Y As Integer, ⇔
    ByVal cx As Integer, ByVal cy As Integer, ByVal wFlags As Integer)
Declare Sub GetWindowRect Lib "User" (ByVal hWnd As Integer, lpRect As Rect)
Declare Function IsWindow Lib "User" (ByVal hWnd As Integer) As Integer
```

```
Declare Function WinExec Lib "Kernel" (ByVal lpCmdLine As String, ByVal ⇔
   nCmdShow As Integer) As Integer
Declare Function SetActiveWindow Lib "User" (ByVal hWnd As Integer) As Integer
Declare Function GetActiveWindow Lib "User" () As Integer
Declare Function LockWindowUpdate Lib "User" (ByVal hwndLock As Integer) As ⇔
   Integer
Declare Function GetDesktopWindow Lib "User" () As Integer
Declare Function FindWindow Lib "User" (ByVal lpClassName As Any, ByVal ⇔
   lpWindowName As Any) As Integer
Declare Function PostMessage Lib "User" (ByVal hWnd As Integer, ByVal wMsg ⇔
   As Integer, ByVal wParam As Integer, ByVal lParam As Long) As Integer
Global Const WM_COMMAND = &H111
Global Const WM_CLOSE = &H10
Dim wFlag%
Dim lpDlgRect As Rect
Dim lpDskRect As Rect
Const SWP_NOSIZE = &H1
Const SWP_NOZORDER = &H4
' * * * * * * * * * * * * * * * * * * * * * * * * * *
' * Declares to get menu IDs
' * * * * * * * * * * * * * * * * * * * * * * * * * *
Declare Function GetMenu Lib "User" (ByVal hWnd As Integer) As Integer
Declare Function GetMenuItemCount Lib "User" (ByVal hMenu As Integer) As Integer
Declare Function GetMenuItemID Lib "User" (ByVal hMenu As Integer, ByVal ⇔
   nPos As Integer) As Integer
Declare Function GetSubMenu Lib "User" (ByVal hMenu As Integer, ByVal nPos ⇔
   As Integer) As Integer
' * * * * * * * * * * * * * * * * * * * * * * * * * *
' * Declares to unload pesky FM Extensions
' * * * * * * * * * * * * * * * * * * * * * * * * * *
Declare Sub FreeModule Lib "Kernel" (ByVal hLibModule%)
Declare Function GetModuleHandle Lib "Kernel" (ByVal lpModuleName$) As Integer

Sub BorrowDialog (F As Form, Class$, TargetExe$, cID%, dCaption$, Send$)
Dim TargetWnd, I%, wnd%, X, Y
' * * * * * * * * * * * * * * * * * * * * * * * * * *
' * Attempt to locate window of specified class
' * * * * * * * * * * * * * * * * * * * * * * * * * *
TargetWnd = FindWindow(Class$, 0&)
   If TargetWnd = 0 Then
' * * * * * * * * * * * * * * * * * * * * * * * * * *
' * If can't locate, try to launch Exe
' * * * * * * * * * * * * * * * * * * * * * * * * * *
I% = WinExec(TargetExe$, 0)
      TargetWnd = FindWindow(Class$, 0&)
      If TargetWnd = 0 Then
      MsgBox "Unable to launch " + TargetExe$ + "."
      Exit Sub
      End If
   End If
' * * * * * * * * * * * * * * * * * * * * * * * * * *
' * Stop screen update
' * * * * * * * * * * * * * * * * * * * * * * * * * *
I% = LockWindowUpdate(GetDesktopWindow())
' * * * * * * * * * * * * * * * * * * * * * * * * * *
' * Instruct app to display desired dialog box
' * then center dialog on screen, send it specified keys
' * and unlock window update
' * * * * * * * * * * * * * * * * * * * * * * * * * *
I% = PostMessage(TargetWnd, WM_COMMAND, cID%, 0)
   CenterDialog dCaption$
   If Send$ <> "" Then SendKeys Send$
   I% = LockWindowUpdate(0)
' * * * * * * * * * * * * * * * * * * * * * * * * * *
```

```
'    * Wait for dialog box to close
'    * * * * * * * * * * * * * * * * * * * * * * * * * *
wnd% = GetActiveWindow()
    While IsWindow(wnd%)
        X = DoEvents()
    Wend
    X = DoEvents()
'    * * * * * * * * * * * * * * * * * * * * * * * * * *
'    * Shut down app
'    * * * * * * * * * * * * * * * * * * * * * * * * * *
I% = PostMessage(TargetWnd, WM_CLOSE, 0, 0)
    While IsWindow(TargetWnd)
        X = DoEvents()
    Wend
'    * * * * * * * * * * * * * * * * * * * * * * * * * *
'    * Shut down those pesky File Manager extensions
'    * * * * * * * * * * * * * * * * * * * * * * * * * *
If TargetExe$ = "WINFILE.EXE" Then
'    * * * * * * * * * * * * * * * * * * * * * * * * * *
'    * Wait for File Manager to unload
'    * * * * * * * * * * * * * * * * * * * * * * * * * *
X = GetModuleHandle("WINFILE.EXE")
        While X > 0
        Y = DoEvents()
        X = GetModuleHandle("WINFILE.EXE")
        Wend
'    * * * * * * * * * * * * * * * * * * * * * * * * * *
'    * Clean up any File Manager Extensions that didn't unload normally
'    * * * * * * * * * * * * * * * * * * * * * * * * * *
Dim AddOns As String * 255
        Dim Spacer%, Dllname$
'    * * * * * * * * * * * * * * * * * * * * * * * * * *
' * Null parameter for keyname retrieves entire list, separated by CHR$(0)'s
'    * * * * * * * * * * * * * * * * * * * * * * * * * *
X = GetPrivateProfileString("AddOns", 0&, "", AddOns, 254, "WINFILE.INI")
        Spacer% = InStr(AddOns, Chr$(0))
        Do While Spacer% > 0
        Dllname$ = Left$(AddOns, Spacer% - 1)
        X = GetModuleHandle(Dllname$)
        If X > 0 Then FreeModule (X)
'    * * * * * * * * * * * * * * * * * * * * * * * * * *
'    * List of keys ends with double null, so...
'    * * * * * * * * * * * * * * * * * * * * * * * * * *
If Mid$(AddOns, Spacer% + 1, 1) = Chr$(0) Then Exit Do
'    * * * * * * * * * * * * * * * * * * * * * * * * * *
'    * Otherwise, find the next key
'    * * * * * * * * * * * * * * * * * * * * * * * * * *
AddOns = Mid$(AddOns, Spacer% + 1)
        Spacer% = InStr(AddOns, Chr$(0))
        Loop
        screen.MousePointer = 1
End If
X = DoEvents()
I% = SetActiveWindow(F.hWnd)
End Sub

Sub CenterDialog (WinText As String)
Dim X%, wnd%, wdth%, hght%, Scrwdth%, Scrhght%, Y%
'    * * * * * * * * * * * * * * * * * * * * * * * * * *
'    * Exit if can't find dialog
'    * * * * * * * * * * * * * * * * * * * * * * * * * *
Do
   If FindWindow(0&, WinText) Then Exit Do
   X% = DoEvents()
```

```
Loop
wnd% = GetActiveWindow()
'  * * * * * * * * * * * * * * * * * * * * * * * * *
'  * Get dialog's dimensions
'  * * * * * * * * * * * * * * * * * * * * * * * * *
GetWindowRect wnd%, lpDlgRect
wdth% = lpDlgRect.Right - lpDlgRect.Left
hght% = lpDlgRect.Bottom - lpDlgRect.Top
'  * * * * * * * * * * * * * * * * * * * * * * * * *
'  * Get screen dimensions
'  * * * * * * * * * * * * * * * * * * * * * * * * *
GetWindowRect GetDesktopWindow(), lpDskRect
Scrwdth% = lpDskRect.Right - lpDskRect.Left
Scrhght% = lpDskRect.Bottom - lpDskRect.Top
'  * * * * * * * * * * * * * * * * * * * * * * * * *
'  * Determine coordinates to center dialog
'  * * * * * * * * * * * * * * * * * * * * * * * * *
X% = (Scrwdth% - wdth%) / 2
Y% = (Scrhght% - hght%) / 2
'  * * * * * * * * * * * * * * * * * * * * * * * * *
'  * Move dialog to those coordinates
'  * * * * * * * * * * * * * * * * * * * * * * * * *
SetWindowPos wnd%, 0, X%, Y%, 0, 0, SWP_NOZORDER Or SWP_NOSIZE
End Sub

Sub ListFMMenus ()
'  * * * * * * * * * * * * * * * * * * * * * * * * *
'  * Routine to list File Manager File menu item IDs
'  * used in developing project / code not called in
'  * final project
'  * (LIST1.SORTED should be false for this to work)
'  * * * * * * * * * * * * * * * * * * * * * * * * *
    Dim FmhWnd, I%, wFlag, fmMenu%, X, V%, Y%
    FmhWnd = FindWindow("WFS_Frame", 0&)

    If FmhWnd = 0 Then
     I% = WinExec("Winfile", 0)
     FmhWnd = FindWindow("WFS_Frame", 0&)
        If FmhWnd = 0 Then
            MsgBox "Unable to launch File Manager"
            Exit Sub
        End If
     wFlag = 1
    End If

fmMenu% = GetMenu(FmhWnd)
'  * * * * * * * * * * * * * * * * * * * * * * * * *
'  * Get File Menu
'  * * * * * * * * * * * * * * * * * * * * * * * * *
fmMenu% = GetSubMenu(fmMenu%, 0)
X = GetMenuItemCount(fmMenu%)
Form1.List1.AddItem Str$(X) & " items on menu..."
For V% = 1 To X
    Y% = GetMenuItemID(fmMenu%, V%)
    Form1.List1.AddItem Str$(Y%)
Next V%
Exit Sub

End Sub

Sub ListRegEditMenus ()
'  * * * * * * * * * * * * * * * * * * * * * * * * *
'  * Routine to list RegEdit Edit menu item IDs
'  * used in developing project / code not called in
```

```
'    * final project
'    * (LIST1.SORTED should be false for this to work)
'    * * * * * * * * * * * * * * * * * * * * * * * * * *
     Form1.List1.Sorted = False
     Dim ReghWnd, I%, wFlag, fmMenu%, X, V%, Y%
     ReghWnd = FindWindow("Registration Editor", 0&)
     If ReghWnd = 0 Then
       I% = WinExec("REGEDIT", 1)
       ReghWnd = FindWindow("Registration Editor", 0&)
          If ReghWnd = 0 Then
                MsgBox "Unable to launch REGEDIT.EXE"
                Exit Sub
          End If
        wFlag = 1
     End If
fmMenu% = GetMenu(ReghWnd)
'    * * * * * * * * * * * * * * * * * * * * * * * * * *
'    * Get second menu
'    * * * * * * * * * * * * * * * * * * * * * * * * * *
fmMenu% = GetSubMenu(fmMenu%, 1)
X = GetMenuItemCount(fmMenu%)
Form1.List1.AddItem Str$(X) & "items on menu..."
For V% = 0 To X - 1
    Y% = GetMenuItemID(fmMenu%, V%)
    Form1.List1.AddItem Str$(Y%)
Next V%
Exit Sub
End Sub
```

LISTING

VP Q MOD

```
'    * * * * * * * * * * * * * * * * * * * * * * * * * *
'    VBQMOD.BAS
'    Copyright (c) 1993 by Paul Bonner
'    PC Magazine Visual Basic Utilities
'    * * * * * * * * * * * * * * * * * * * * * * * * * *
DefInt A-Z
Option Explicit
'    * * * * * * * * * * * * * * * * * * * * * * * * * *
'    * Global variables
'    * * * * * * * * * * * * * * * * * * * * * * * * * *
Global keys$(7, 1)    'vb q keys keywords
Global dFile$()       'drop files array
Global Ext$           'Extension of current file
Global EditSpecial%   'True/False flag for Special--editing or creating new
Global TargetApp$     'app that will do the printing for Ext$
Global CRLF$          'carriage return/line feed
Global ActiveList As Control  'active form1 list box
Type Start
    Hour As Integer
    Minute As Integer
End Type
Global StartTime As Start    'scheduled print time
```

```
'   * * * * * * * * * * * * * * * * * * * * *
'   * Declarations for reading WIN.INI
'   * * * * * * * * * * * * * * * * * * * * *
Declare Function GetProfileString Lib "Kernel" (ByVal lpAppName As String, ⇔
    ByVal lpKeyName As String, ByVal lpDefault As String, ByVal ⇔
    lpReturnedString As String, ByVal nSize As Integer) As Integer
'   * * * * * * * * * * * * * * * * * * * * *
'   * Declares for using private Ini file
'   * * * * * * * * * * * * * * * * * * * * *
Declare Function GetPrivateProfileString Lib "Kernel" (ByVal ⇔
    lpApplicationName As String, ByVal lpKeyName As Any, ByVal lpDefault As ⇔
    String, ByVal lpReturnedString As String, ByVal nSize As Integer, ByVal ⇔
    lpFileName As String) As Integer
Declare Function WritePrivateProfileString Lib "Kernel" (ByVal ⇔
    lpApplicationName As String, ByVal lpKeyName As String, ByVal lpString ⇔
    As String, ByVal lplFileName As String) As Integer
'   * * * * * * * * * * * * * * * * * * * * *
'   * Declarations for ShellExecute
'   * * * * * * * * * * * * * * * * * * * * *
Declare Function ShellExecute Lib "Shell.dll" (ByVal hWnd%, ByVal lpszOp$, ⇔
    ByVal lpszFile$, ByVal lpszParams As Any, ByVal lpszDir$, ByVal ⇔
    fsShowCnd%) As Integer
Declare Function IsIconic Lib "User" (ByVal hWnd%) As Integer
Declare Function ShowWindow Lib "User" (ByVal hWnd%, ByVal nCmdShow%) As Integer
Global Const SW_MAXIMIZE = 3
Global Const SW_RESTORE = 9
Global Const SW_MINIMIZE = 6
Global Const SW_HIDE = 0
'   * * * * * * * * * * * * * * * * * * * * *
'   * Declarations for Registration Database
'   * * * * * * * * * * * * * * * * * * * * *
Declare Function RegOpenKey Lib "SHELL.DLL" (ByVal lpOpenKeyHand&, ByVal ⇔
    KeyName$, lpNewKeyHand&) As Long
Declare Function RegQueryValue Lib "SHELL.DLL" (ByVal lpOpenKeyHand&, ByVal ⇔
    KeyName As Any, ByVal lpRes As String, lenResBuff&) As Long
Declare Function RegCloseKey Lib "SHELL.DLL" (lpNewKeyHand&) As Long
Declare Function RegCreateKey Lib "SHELL.DLL" (ByVal lpOpenKeyHand&, ByVal ⇔
    KeyName$, lpNewKeyHand&) As Long
Declare Function RegSetValue Lib "SHELL.DLL" (ByVal lpOpenKeyHand&, ByVal ⇔
    SubKey As Any, ByVal fdwType&, ByVal KeyText$, ByVal lenKeyText&) As Long
Declare Function RegEnumKey Lib "SHELL.DLL" (ByVal lpOpenKeyHand&, ByVal ⇔
    SubKeyIndex As Integer, ByVal KeyText$, ByVal lenKeyText&) As Long
Declare Function RegDeleteKey Lib "SHELL.DLL" (ByVal lpOpenKeyHand&, ByVal ⇔
    SubKey As Any) As Long
Const Reg_SZ = 1
Const Error_Success = 0
Const HKEY_Classes_ROOT = 1
'   * * * * * * * * * * * * * * * * * * * * *
'   * Declares used by ClosePrintDiaog
'   * * * * * * * * * * * * * * * * * * * * *
Declare Function GetWindowText Lib "User" (ByVal hWnd As Integer, ByVal ⇔
    lpString As String, ByVal aint As Integer) As Integer
'   * * * * * * * * * * * * * * * * * * * * *
'   * Declares for KeysPrint method
'   * * * * * * * * * * * * * * * * * * * * *
Declare Function GetWindowWord Lib "User" (ByVal hWnd%, ByVal nIndex%) As ⇔
    Integer
Global Const GWW_Hinstance = (-6)
Declare Function GetLastActivePopup Lib "User" (ByVal hwndOwnder%) As Integer
Declare Function GetWindow Lib "User" (ByVal hWnd%, ByVal wCmd%) As Integer
Global Const GW_HWndFirst = 0
Global Const GW_HWNDNext = 2
Global Const GW_OWNER = 4
Global Const GW_CHILD = 5
```

```
Declare Function GetClassName Lib "User" (ByVal hWnd%, ByVal lpClassName$, ⇔
    ByVal nMaxCount%) As Integer
Declare Function SetFocusAPI Lib "User" Alias "SetFocus" (ByVal hWnd As ⇔
    Integer) As Integer

Function AddExtToReg (Ext$, TargetApp$) As Integer
' * * * * * * * * * * * * * * * * * * * * * * * * * * * * *
' * Add new file extension to Registration Database
' * * * * * * * * * * * * * * * * * * * * * * * * * * * * *
Dim x&, NewKey&, KeyName$, Y&, lRes&, Result As String
Result = String$(80, 0)
lRes& = Len(Result)
AddExtToReg = True
KeyName = TargetApp$ + "_" + Ext$
x& = RegOpenKey(HKEY_Classes_ROOT, KeyName$, NewKey&)
Y& = RegCloseKey(NewKey&)
If x& <> Error_Success Then AddExtToReg = False: Exit Function
x& = RegCreateKey(HKEY_Classes_ROOT, "." + Ext$, NewKey&)
If x& <> Error_Success Then AddExtToReg = False
KeyName$ = TargetApp + "_" + Ext$
lRes& = Len(KeyName$)
x& = RegSetValue(NewKey&, 0&, Reg_SZ, KeyName$, lRes&)
If x& <> Error_Success Then AddExtToReg = False
Y& = RegCloseKey(NewKey&)
End Function

Function BuildTarget (Ret As String) As String
' * * * * * * * * * * * * * * * * * * * * * * * * * * * * *
' * Extract .EXE file name from fully qualified file name
' * * * * * * * * * * * * * * * * * * * * * * * * * * * * *
Dim Y%
TargetApp$ = UCase$(Left$(Ret, InStr(Ret, " ")))
For Y% = Len(TargetApp$) To 1 Step -1
  If Mid$(TargetApp$, Y%, 1) = "\" Then TargetApp$ = Mid$(TargetApp$, Y% + ⇔
    1): Exit For
Next
BuildTarget = Trim(TargetApp$)
End Function

Sub CenterForm (F As Form)
F.Left = (Screen.Width - F.Width) / 2
F.Top = (Screen.Height - F.Height) / 2
End Sub

Sub CheckAssoc (Ext$, Ret As String)
' * * * * * * * * * * * * * * * * * * * * * * * * * * * * *
' * Look for extension in WIN.INI
' * if not found, open borrow Associate dialog box
' * * * * * * * * * * * * * * * * * * * * * * * * * * * * *
Dim ExtPt%, Temp$
ExtPt% = GetProfileString("Extensions", Ext$, "DOG", Ret, 254)
If Left$(Ret$, 3) = "DOG" Then
  Temp$ = "First let's identify the application that you want to use to ⇔
    print " + Ext$ + " files."
  Temp$ = Temp$ + CRLF$ + CRLF$ + "If the application you want isn't listed ⇔
    on the Associate dialog box, use the Browse button to locate the ⇔
    application's .EXE file."
  MsgBox Temp$, 64, "VB Q Trail Guide"
  BorrowDialog Form1, "WFS_Frame", "WINFILE.EXE", 103, "Associate", Ext$
  ExtPt% = GetProfileString("Extensions", Ext$, "DOG", Ret, 254)
End If
End Sub

Function CheckPrivate (E$) As Integer
```

```
'  *  *  *  *  *  *  *  *  *  *  *  *  *  *  *  *  *  *  *  *  *  *  *
'  * Look for extension in VBQ.INI
'  *  *  *  *  *  *  *  *  *  *  *  *  *  *  *  *  *  *  *  *  *  *  *
Dim x%
Dim Pvt As String * 255
CheckPrivate = True
x% = GetPrivateProfileString("Extensions", E$ + "_Print", "DOG", Pvt, 254, ⇔
    "VBQ.INI")
If Left$(Pvt, 3) = "DOG" Then CheckPrivate = False
End Function

Function CheckReg (Ext$) As Integer
'  *  *  *  *  *  *  *  *  *  *  *  *  *  *  *  *  *  *  *  *  *  *  *
'  * Look for print command in Registration Database
'  *  *  *  *  *  *  *  *  *  *  *  *  *  *  *  *  *  *  *  *  *  *  *
Dim x&, NewKey&, KeyName$, Y&, Result$
Const lRes& = 80
Result$ = String$(lRes&, 0)
KeyName$ = "." + Ext$
'  *  *  *  *  *  *  *  *  *  *  *  *  *  *  *  *  *  *  *  *  *  *  *
'  * Exit if Ext$ not listed in Registration Database
'  *  *  *  *  *  *  *  *  *  *  *  *  *  *  *  *  *  *  *  *  *  *  *
If RegOpenKey(HKEY_Classes_ROOT, KeyName$, NewKey&) <> Error_Success Then ⇔
    Exit Function
'  *  *  *  *  *  *  *  *  *  *  *  *  *  *  *  *  *  *  *  *  *  *  *
'  * get Identifier for this key
'  *  *  *  *  *  *  *  *  *  *  *  *  *  *  *  *  *  *  *  *  *  *  *
x& = RegQueryValue(NewKey&, 0&, Result$, lRes&)
Y& = RegCloseKey(NewKey&)
'  *  *  *  *  *  *  *  *  *  *  *  *  *  *  *  *  *  *  *  *  *  *  *
'  * exit if no identifier found
'  *  *  *  *  *  *  *  *  *  *  *  *  *  *  *  *  *  *  *  *  *  *  *
If x& <> Error_Success Then Exit Function
'  *  *  *  *  *  *  *  *  *  *  *  *  *  *  *  *  *  *  *  *  *  *  *
'  * get print command
'  *  *  *  *  *  *  *  *  *  *  *  *  *  *  *  *  *  *  *  *  *  *  *
Result$ = Left$(Result$, InStr(Result$, Chr$(0)) - 1) + "\shell\print"
'  *  *  *  *  *  *  *  *  *  *  *  *  *  *  *  *  *  *  *  *  *  *  *
'  * exit if no print command
'  *  *  *  *  *  *  *  *  *  *  *  *  *  *  *  *  *  *  *  *  *  *  *
If RegOpenKey(HKEY_Classes_ROOT, Result$, NewKey&) <> Error_Success Then ⇔
    Exit Function 'GoTo Fail
Y& = RegCloseKey(NewKey&)
CheckReg = True
End Function

Sub ClosePrintDialog ()
'  *  *  *  *  *  *  *  *  *  *  *  *  *  *  *  *  *  *  *  *  *  *  *
'  * Close print dialog left on screen
'  * by some apps after ShellExecute command
'  *  *  *  *  *  *  *  *  *  *  *  *  *  *  *  *  *  *  *  *  *  *  *
Dim t%, wTxt As String * 64
t% = GetWindowText(GetActiveWindow(), wTxt, 63)
If InStr(wTxt, Chr$(0)) = 6 Or InStr(wTxt, Chr$(160)) = 6 Then
    If Left$(wTxt, 5) = "Print" Then SendKeys ("~")
End If
End Sub

Sub CloseSaveChangesDialog ()
'  *  *  *  *  *  *  *  *  *  *  *  *  *  *  *  *  *  *  *  *  *  *  *
'  * Close "Save Changes Before Closing" dialogs
'  *  *  *  *  *  *  *  *  *  *  *  *  *  *  *  *  *  *  *  *  *  *  *
Dim cName As String * 80, Y%, C$
Y% = GetClassName(GetActiveWindow(), cName, 79)
```

```
'  *  *  *  *  *  *  *  *  *  *  *  *  *  *  *  *  *  *  *  *  *  *  *
'check for standard windows message box or BORDLG
'  *  *  *  *  *  *  *  *  *  *  *  *  *  *  *  *  *  *  *  *  *  *  *
Do While C$ = "#32" Or C$ = "BOR"
    SendKeys "n"
    Y% = DoEvents()
    Y% = GetClassName(GetActiveWindow(), cName, 79)
    C$ = Left$(cName, 3)
Loop

End Sub

Sub CountQFiles ()
Form1.Label2 = Form1.List1.ListCount & " files in queue"
End Sub

Sub DisplayTime ()
'  *  *  *  *  *  *  *  *  *  *  *  *  *  *  *  *  *  *  *  *  *  *  *
'  * Display scheduled print time
'  *  *  *  *  *  *  *  *  *  *  *  *  *  *  *  *  *  *  *  *  *  *  *
Dim AMPM$, t$, Sh%
t$ = Trim(Str$(StartTime.Minute))
If Len(t$) = 1 Then t$ = "0" + t$
Select Case StartTime.Hour
Case Is = 0
    Sh% = 12
    AMPM$ = " AM"
Case Is = 12
    Sh% = 12
    AMPM$ = " PM"
Case Is > 12
    Sh% = StartTime.Hour - 12
    AMPM$ = " PM"
Case Else
    Sh% = StartTime.Hour
    AMPM$ = " AM"
End Select
    Form1.Label3 = "Scheduled to print at: " & Sh% & ":" & t$ & AMPM$
End Sub

Sub DragDropEvent ()
'  *  *  *  *  *  *  *  *  *  *  *  *  *  *  *  *  *  *  *  *  *  *  *
'  * Handler for FM drag-drop events
'  *  *  *  *  *  *  *  *  *  *  *  *  *  *  *  *  *  *  *  *  *  *  *
Dim x%, ExtPt%, fCount%, Valid%
Dim Ret As String * 255
'  *  *  *  *  *  *  *  *  *  *  *  *  *  *  *  *  *  *  *  *  *  *  *
'  * Get drop file names
'  *  *  *  *  *  *  *  *  *  *  *  *  *  *  *  *  *  *  *  *  *  *  *
fCount% = Form1.DragDrop1.FileCount
ReDim dFile$(fCount%)
For x% = 1 To fCount%
    dFile(x%) = Form1.DragDrop1.FileName(x% - 1)
Next
'  *  *  *  *  *  *  *  *  *  *  *  *  *  *  *  *  *  *  *  *  *  *  *
'  * Disable control while files being checked
'  *  *  *  *  *  *  *  *  *  *  *  *  *  *  *  *  *  *  *  *  *  *  *
Form1.DragDrop1.Enabled = False
'  *  *  *  *  *  *  *  *  *  *  *  *  *  *  *  *  *  *  *  *  *  *  *
'  * Check files
'  *  *  *  *  *  *  *  *  *  *  *  *  *  *  *  *  *  *  *  *  *  *  *
For x% = 0 To fCount%
'  *  *  *  *  *  *  *  *  *  *  *  *  *  *  *  *  *  *  *  *  *  *  *
'  * get extension
```

```
'  * * * * * * * * * * * * * * * * * * * * * * * * * *
ExtPt% = InStr(dFile$(x%), ".")
    If ExtPt% Then
       Ext$ = Mid$(dFile$(x%), ExtPt% + 1)
'  * * * * * * * * * * * * * * * * * * * * * * * * * *
'    * check for reg db or vbq keys entry for ext$
'  * * * * * * * * * * * * * * * * * * * * * * * * * *
Valid% = ValidFile%(Ext$)
'  * * * * * * * * * * * * * * * * * * * * * * * * * *
'    * if not found, see if user wants to enter one
'  * * * * * * * * * * * * * * * * * * * * * * * * * *
If Not Valid% Then
    NoMethod.Show 1
    Form1.SetFocus
'  * * * * * * * * * * * * * * * * * * * * * * * * * *
'    * then check again
'  * * * * * * * * * * * * * * * * * * * * * * * * * *
Valid% = ValidFile%(Ext$)
    End If
    If Not Valid% Then
       MsgBox dFile$(x%) + " won't be printed", 48, "VB Q"
    Else
    Form1.List1.AddItem Ext$ + Chr$(9) + dFile$(x%)
    End If
    End If
Next
'  * * * * * * * * * * * * * * * * * * * * * * * * * *
'    * Enable drag-drop control
'  * * * * * * * * * * * * * * * * * * * * * * * * * *
Form1.DragDrop1.Enabled = True
'  * * * * * * * * * * * * * * * * * * * * * * * * * *
'    * Update counter label
'  * * * * * * * * * * * * * * * * * * * * * * * * * *
CountQFiles
End Sub

Sub DrawStatusBarLines (F As Form)
'  * * * * * * * * * * * * * * * * * * * * * * * * * *
'    * Draw 3D lines to separate status bar from main
'    * part of form
'  * * * * * * * * * * * * * * * * * * * * * * * * * *
Dim x%
For x% = 0 To 1
    F.Line1(x%).X1 = 0
    F.Line1(x%).X2 = F.Width
    F.Line1(x%).Y1 = x% * 20
    F.Line1(x%).Y2 = x% * 20
Next
End Sub

Sub EditMenuSelection (Index As Integer)
'  * * * * * * * * * * * * * * * * * * * * * * * * * *
'    * Edit menu item handler
'  * * * * * * * * * * * * * * * * * * * * * * * * * *
TargetApp$ = ""
Dim x%, A$, B$
Dim Ret As String * 255
Select Case Index
Case 0        'edit keys
    A$ = " VB Q Keys "
Case 1        'edit reg. database
    A$ = " Registration Database "
Case 2        'Remove Item
'  * * * * * * * * * * * * * * * * * * * * * * * * * *
```

```
'   * Handler for Remove File
'   * Start by
'   * identifying selected item
'   * * * * * * * * * * * * * * * * * * * * * * * * * *
x% = ActiveList.ListIndex
'   * * * * * * * * * * * * * * * * * * * * * * * * * *
'   * if the list isn't empty and an item is selected
'   * * * * * * * * * * * * * * * * * * * * * * * * * * *
If ActiveList.ListCount And x% > -1 Then
'   * * * * * * * * * * * * * * * * * * * * * * * * * *
'   * remove selected item
'   * * * * * * * * * * * * * * * * * * * * * * * * * *
ActiveList.RemoveItem x%
'   * * * * * * * * * * * * * * * * * * * * * * * * * *
'   * if it's not the bottom item in the list,
'   * select next item
'   * * * * * * * * * * * * * * * * * * * * * * * * * *
     If ActiveList.ListCount >= x% + 1 Then
     ActiveList.ListIndex = x%
'   * * * * * * * * * * * * * * * * * * * * * * * * * *
'   * otherwise, don't select item above x%
'   * * * * * * * * * * * * * * * * * * * * * * * * * *
ElseIf ActiveList.ListCount Then ActiveList.ListIndex = x% - 1
     End If
   End If
'   * * * * * * * * * * * * * * * * * * * * * * * * * *
'   * if report lists are empty, close the report
'   * * * * * * * * * * * * * * * * * * * * * * * * * *
If Form1.List2(0).ListCount = 0 And Form1.List2(1).ListCount = 0 And ⇔
   Form1.Command1.Visible Then
     Form1.Command5.Value = True
     ToggleReport False
     Form1.Command5.Enabled = False
   End If
   CountQFiles
'   * * * * * * * * * * * * * * * * * * * * * * * * * *
'   * Now exit the sub
'   * * * * * * * * * * * * * * * * * * * * * * * * * *
Exit Sub
End Select
'   * * * * * * * * * * * * * * * * * * * * * * * * * *
'   * if get to here,
'   * must be editing keys or reg database
'   * so first find out what file extension user wants to edit
'   * * * * * * * * * * * * * * * * * * * * * * * * * *
Ext$ = UCase$(InputBox$("Enter the file extension for which you wish to ⇔
   edit" + A$ + "data.", "Edit" + A$, ""))
If Ext$ = "" Then Exit Sub
If Len(Ext$) > 3 Then MsgBox "Three characters only!", 48, "Extension Too ⇔
   Long": Exit Sub
'   * * * * * * * * * * * * * * * * * * * * * * * * * *
'   * set up error string
'   * * * * * * * * * * * * * * * * * * * * * * * * * *
B$ = "There is no" + A$ + " entry for " + Ext$ + ". Do you wish to create ⇔
   one now?"

Select Case Index
Case 0    'edit vb q keys
'   * * * * * * * * * * * * * * * * * * * * * * * * * *
'   * look for extension in VBQ.INI
'   * * * * * * * * * * * * * * * * * * * * * * * * * *
   x% = CheckPrivate(Ext$)
   If x% = False Then
       x% = MsgBox(B$, 52, "VB Q")
```

```
          If x% <> 6 Then Exit Sub
          EditSpecial% = False
      Else
          EditSpecial% = True
      End If
'   * * * * * * * * * * * * * * * * * * * * * * * * * * * * *
'   * look for extension in WIN.INI
'   * * * * * * * * * * * * * * * * * * * * * * * * * * * * *
      CheckAssoc Ext$, Ret
      If Left$(Ret, 3) = "DOG" Then Exit Sub
'   * * * * * * * * * * * * * * * * * * * * * * * * * * * * *
'   * extract .EXE name
'   * * * * * * * * * * * * * * * * * * * * * * * * * * * * *
      TargetApp$ = BuildTarget(Ret)
      Screen.MousePointer = 1
'   * * * * * * * * * * * * * * * * * * * * * * * * * * * * *
'   * show VB Q Keys form
'   * * * * * * * * * * * * * * * * * * * * * * * * * * * * *
Special.Show 1
Case 1          'registration database
'   * * * * * * * * * * * * * * * * * * * * * * * * * * * * *
'   * look for extension in Reg Database
'   * * * * * * * * * * * * * * * * * * * * * * * * * * * * *
x% = CheckReg(Ext$)
      If x% = False Then 'ext not found
          x% = MsgBox(B$, 52, "VB Q")
          If x% <> 6 Then Exit Sub
'   * * * * * * * * * * * * * * * * * * * * * * * * * * * * *
'   * look for extension in WIN.INI
'   * * * * * * * * * * * * * * * * * * * * * * * * * * * * *
          CheckAssoc Ext$, Ret
          If Left$(Ret, 3) = "DOG" Then Exit Sub
          TargetApp$ = BuildTarget(Ret)
          NewRegEntry Ext$, TargetApp$, Ret
      Else
'   * * * * * * * * * * * * * * * * * * * * * * * * * * * * *
'   * info exists, so just run regedit and let user edit it
'   * * * * * * * * * * * * * * * * * * * * * * * * * * * * *
          x% = LockWindowUpdate(GetDesktopWindow())
          x% = Shell("REGEDIT.EXE", 1)
          CenterDialog "Registration Info Editor"
          x% = LockWindowUpdate(0)
      End If
End Select
End Sub

Function GetPvt (t$) As String
'   * * * * * * * * * * * * * * * * * * * * * * * * * * * * *
'   function to extract data from VBQ.INI
'   * * * * * * * * * * * * * * * * * * * * * * * * * * * * *
Dim x%
Dim Pvt As String * 255
GetPvt = ""
x% = GetPrivateProfileString("Extensions", t$, "DOG", Pvt, 254, "VBQ.INI")
If Left$(Pvt, 3) <> "DOG" Then GetPvt = Trim(Pvt)
End Function

Sub InitKeys ()
'   * * * * * * * * * * * * * * * * * * * * * * * * * * * * *
'   * Initialize VB Q Keys array
'   * * * * * * * * * * * * * * * * * * * * * * * * * * * * *
keys$(0, 0) = "{alt}"
keys$(0, 1) = "%"
keys$(1, 0) = "{control}"
```

```
keys$(1, 1) = "{^}"
keys$(2, 0) = "{tab}"
keys$(2, 1) = UCase$(keys$(2, 0))
keys$(3, 0) = "{enter}"
keys$(3, 1) = "~"
keys$(4, 0) = "{down}"
keys$(4, 1) = UCase$(keys$(4, 0))
keys$(5, 0) = "{up}"
keys$(5, 1) = UCase$(keys$(5, 0))
keys$(6, 0) = "{right}"
keys$(6, 1) = UCase$(keys$(6, 0))
keys$(7, 0) = "{left}"
keys$(7, 1) = UCase$(keys$(7, 0))
End Sub

Function KeysPrint (F$, Exe$, Ext$) As Integer
'  * * * * * * * * * * * * * * * * * * * * * * * * * *
'  * function returns either 33 for "went fine"
'  * or -5 for "vb q keys didn't work"
'  * * * * * * * * * * * * * * * * * * * * * * * * * *
Dim x%, Y%, wHand%, A%, B%, Ini$
On Error GoTo Failed
'  * * * * * * * * * * * * * * * * * * * * * * * * * *
'  * Find out if should run hidden
'  * * * * * * * * * * * * * * * * * * * * * * * * * *
Ini$ = GetPvt(Ext$ + "_Hidden")
Select Case Val(Ini$)
Case Is = 1  'True
    x% = WinExec(Exe$ + " " + F$, SW_HIDE)
Case Else    'False
    x% = Shell(Exe$ + " " + F$, 1)
End Select
On Error Resume Next
'  * * * * * * * * * * * * * * * * * * * * * * * * * *
'  * give app a chance to load
'  * * * * * * * * * * * * * * * * * * * * * * * * * *
Y% = DoEvents()
'  * * * * * * * * * * * * * * * * * * * * * * * * * *
'  * wait for its main window to become activated
'  * * * * * * * * * * * * * * * * * * * * * * * * * *
wHand% = 0
WaitForMsgBoxClose
Y% = Form1.hWnd
Y% = GetWindow(Y%, GW_HWndFirst)
Do While wHand% = 0
'  * * * * * * * * * * * * * * * * * * * * * * * * * *
'  * wait for a "loading" msgbox to close
'  * now loop, until you find a window associated with task
'  * * * * * * * * * * * * * * * * * * * * * * * * * *
If GetWindowWord(Y%, GWW_Hinstance) = x% Then
      wHand% = GetWindow(Y%, GW_OWNER)
      If wHand% = 0 Then wHand% = Y%
   End If
   A% = DoEvents()
   Y% = GetWindow(Y%, GW_HWNDNext)
   If Y% = 0 Then Y% = GetWindow(Form1.hWnd, GW_HWndFirst)
Loop
'  * * * * * * * * * * * * * * * * * * * * * * * * * *
'  * Get VB Q Keys print command
'  * * * * * * * * * * * * * * * * * * * * * * * * * *
Ini$ = GetPvt(Ext$ + "_Print")
A% = GetLastActivePopup(wHand%)
'  * * * * * * * * * * * * * * * * * * * * * * * * * *
'  * Send command to target window
```

```
' * * * * * * * * * * * * * * * * * * * * * * * * * * *
Y% = SetFocusAPI(wHand%)
SendCommandString Ini$, wHand%
x% = DoEvents()
' * * * * * * * * * * * * * * * * * * * * * * * * * * *
' * Check to see if need to repeat
' * * * * * * * * * * * * * * * * * * * * * * * * * * *
Ini$ = GetPvt(Ext$ + "_Repeat")
' * * * * * * * * * * * * * * * * * * * * * * * * * * *
' * If so, loop and repeat until target opens a pop-up menu
' * * * * * * * * * * * * * * * * * * * * * * * * * * *
If Val(Ini$) = 1 Then
    Dim l%
    Ini$ = GetPvt(Ext$ + "_Print")
    Do While GetLastActivePopup(wHand%) = A%
        l% = l% + 1
        Y% = DoEvents()
        If l% = 1000 Then
        SendCommandString Ini$, wHand%:
        Y% = DoEvents()
        l% = 1
        End If
    Loop
End If
' * * * * * * * * * * * * * * * * * * * * * * * * * * *
' * Wait for any message/pop-up to close
' * * * * * * * * * * * * * * * * * * * * * * * * * * *
WaitForMsgBoxClose
' * * * * * * * * * * * * * * * * * * * * * * * * * * *
' * Ask target window to close
' * * * * * * * * * * * * * * * * * * * * * * * * * * *
x% = PostMessage(wHand%, WM_CLOSE, 0, 0)
' * * * * * * * * * * * * * * * * * * * * * * * * * * *
' * Wait for it to close
' * * * * * * * * * * * * * * * * * * * * * * * * * * *
While IsWindow(wHand%)
    x% = DoEvents()
    CloseSaveChangesDialog
Wend
' * * * * * * * * * * * * * * * * * * * * * * * * * * *
' * Function succeeded/return val of 33
' * * * * * * * * * * * * * * * * * * * * * * * * * * *
KeysPrint = 33
kpRE:
Exit Function

Failed:
' * * * * * * * * * * * * * * * * * * * * * * * * * * *
' * Function failed/return val of 5
' * * * * * * * * * * * * * * * * * * * * * * * * * * *
    KeysPrint = -5
    Resume kpRE
End Function

Sub NewRegEntry (Ext$, TargetApp$, Ret As String)
' * * * * * * * * * * * * * * * * * * * * * * * * * * *
' * Trail Guide for Registration Editor dialog
' * * * * * * * * * * * * * * * * * * * * * * * * * * *
Dim Temp$, ExtPt%
Temp$ = "Registration Editor will run so you can add the command to print " ⇔
    + Ext$ + " files." + CRLF$ + CRLF$ + "Caution: do not change the value ⇔
    that VB Q enters into the 'Identifier' field on the Add File Type dialog
    box."
MsgBox Temp$, 64, "VB Q Trail Guide"
```

```
Temp$ = TargetApp$ + "_" + Ext$ + Chr$(9) + TargetApp$ + " " + Ext$ + " ⇔
    files{TAB}{RIGHT}{TAB}%U%B" + UCase$(Left$(Ret, InStr(Ret, " "))) + ⇔
    "~%C{RIGHT} "
BorrowDialog Form1, "Registration Editor", "REGEDIT.EXE", 1056, "AddFile ⇔
    Type", Temp$
ExtPt% = AddExtToReg(Ext$, TargetApp$)
End Sub

Sub PrintTopItem ()
' * * * * * * * * * * * * * * * * * * * * * * * * * * * * *
'   * Print top item in queue
' * * * * * * * * * * * * * * * * * * * * * * * * * * * * *
Dim A$, t%, ExtPt%, Exe$
A$ = Form1.List1.List(0)
t% = InStr(A$, Chr$(9))
A$ = Trim(Mid$(A$, t% + 1))
' * * * * * * * * * * * * * * * * * * * * * * * * * * * * *
'   * get extension
' * * * * * * * * * * * * * * * * * * * * * * * * * * * * *
ExtPt% = InStr(A$, ".")
If ExtPt% Then
    Ext$ = Mid$(A$, ExtPt% + 1)
End If
' * * * * * * * * * * * * * * * * * * * * * * * * * * * * *
'   * determine print method
'   * if print method is shell then
' * * * * * * * * * * * * * * * * * * * * * * * * * * * * *
If CheckReg(Ext$) = True Then
 ExtPt% = ShellExecute(Form1.hWnd, "print", A$, 0&, App.Path, SW_MINIMIZE)
' * * * * * * * * * * * * * * * * * * * * * * * * * * * * *
'   * if print method is vb q keys
' * * * * * * * * * * * * * * * * * * * * * * * * * * * * *
ElseIf CheckPrivate(Ext$) = True Then
    Dim Ret As String * 255
    CheckAssoc Ext$, Ret
    Exe$ = Left$(Ret, InStr(Ret, Chr$(32)) - 1)
    ExtPt% = KeysPrint(A$, Exe$, Ext$)
Else
' * * * * * * * * * * * * * * * * * * * * * * * * * * * * *
'   * shouldn't happen, but catch errors if neither print method applies
' * * * * * * * * * * * * * * * * * * * * * * * * * * * * *
ExtPt% = -10    ' No print method for this file type"
End If
If Not Form1.Command5.Enabled Then ToggleReport True
' * * * * * * * * * * * * * * * * * * * * * * * * * * * * *
'   * Check to see if print command returned error
' * * * * * * * * * * * * * * * * * * * * * * * * * * * * *
Select Case ExtPt%
    Case Is > 32
' * * * * * * * * * * * * * * * * * * * * * * * * * * * * *
'   * No error, add to Printed list
' * * * * * * * * * * * * * * * * * * * * * * * * * * * * *
        Form1.List2(1).AddItem Form1.List1.List(0)
    Case Else
' * * * * * * * * * * * * * * * * * * * * * * * * * * * * *
'   * Error, add to Not Printed list and add error-num
'   * to list item's ItemData property
' * * * * * * * * * * * * * * * * * * * * * * * * * * * * *
        Form1.List2(0).AddItem Form1.List1.List(0)
        Form1.List2(0).ItemData(Form1.List2(0).NewIndex) = ExtPt%
    End Select
On Error Resume Next
' * * * * * * * * * * * * * * * * * * * * * * * * * * * * *
'   * Remove file from queue
```

```
'  * * * * * * * * * * * * * * * * * * * * * * * * * * * *
Form1.List1.RemoveItem (0)
CountQFiles
End Sub

Sub ScheduleMenuSelection (Index As Integer)
'  * * * * * * * * * * * * * * * * * * * * * * * * * * * *
'  * Handler for Schedule menu selections
'  * * * * * * * * * * * * * * * * * * * * * * * * * * * *
Select Case Index
Case 0    'Set Print Time
    TimeForm.Show 1
    If StartTime.Hour > -1 Then
        Form1.sItem(3).Checked = False
        Form1.sItem(2).Checked = True
        Form1.Timer1.Enabled = True
        DisplayTime
    End If
Case 1    'Separator
Case 2    'Scheduled Print
'  * * * * * * * * * * * * * * * * * * * * * * * * * * * *
'  * If time not set, get it
'  * * * * * * * * * * * * * * * * * * * * * * * * * * * *
If StartTime.Hour = -1 Then
    TimeForm.Show 1
'  * * * * * * * * * * * * * * * * * * * * * * * * * * * *
'  * exit if user cancels TimeForm
'  * * * * * * * * * * * * * * * * * * * * * * * * * * * *
If StartTime.Hour = -1 Then Exit Sub
    End If
'  * * * * * * * * * * * * * * * * * * * * * * * * * * * *
'  * Toggle Scheduled Print check mark
'  * Toggle timer
'  * Turn off immediate mode
'  * * * * * * * * * * * * * * * * * * * * * * * * * * * *
    Form1.sItem(2).Checked = Not Form1.sItem(2).Checked
    Form1.Timer1.Enabled = Form1.sItem(2).Checked
    Form1.sItem(3).Checked = False
'  * * * * * * * * * * * * * * * * * * * * * * * * * * * *
'  * Update status label
'  * * * * * * * * * * * * * * * * * * * * * * * * * * * *
    If Form1.sItem(2).Checked Then
        DisplayTime
    Else
        Form1.Label3 = "Print mode not set"
    End If
Case 3    'Immediate Print
'  * * * * * * * * * * * * * * * * * * * * * * * * * * * *
'  * Toggle immediate mode
'  * * * * * * * * * * * * * * * * * * * * * * * * * * * *
    Form1.sItem(3).Checked = Not Form1.sItem(3).Checked
'  * * * * * * * * * * * * * * * * * * * * * * * * * * * *
'  * Turn off Scheduled Print
'  * * * * * * * * * * * * * * * * * * * * * * * * * * * *
    Form1.sItem(2).Checked = False
'  * * * * * * * * * * * * * * * * * * * * * * * * * * * *
'  * Update status label
'  * * * * * * * * * * * * * * * * * * * * * * * * * * * *
    Select Case Form1.sItem(3).Checked
    Case True
        Form1.Label3 = "Immediate Print"     'label it
        Form1.Timer1.Enabled = True       'turn timer on
    Case Else
        Form1.Label3 = "Print mode not set"
```

```
        Form1.Timer1.Enabled = False        'turn timer off
    End Select
End Select

End Sub

Sub SendCommandString (Key$, wHand%)
'   * * * * * * * * * * * * * * * * * * * * * * * * * * * * *
'   * Routine to send VBQ Keys command
'   * * * * * * * * * * * * * * * * * * * * * * * * * * * * *
Dim I%, x%
'   * * * * * * * * * * * * * * * * * * * * * * * * * * * * *
'   * strip null at end of string
'   * * * * * * * * * * * * * * * * * * * * * * * * * * * * *
I% = InStr(Key$, Chr$(0))
If I% > 1 Then Key$ = Left$(Key$, I% - 1)
'   * * * * * * * * * * * * * * * * * * * * * * * * * * * * *
'   * Filter out macros
'   * * * * * * * * * * * * * * * * * * * * * * * * * * * * *
Dim l%
For x% = 0 To 7
    l% = Len(keys$(x%, 0))
    I% = InStr(Key$, keys$(x%, 0))
    Do While I%
        Key$ = Left$(Key$, I% - 1) + keys$(x%, 1) + Mid$(Key$, I% + l%)
        I% = InStr(Key$, keys$(x%, 0))
    Loop
Next
'   * * * * * * * * * * * * * * * * * * * * * * * * * * * * *
'   * Send command string to target
'   * * * * * * * * * * * * * * * * * * * * * * * * * * * * *
I% = SetActiveWindow(wHand%)
SendKeys Key$
'   * * * * * * * * * * * * * * * * * * * * * * * * * * * * *
'   * close print dialog only if necessary
'   * * * * * * * * * * * * * * * * * * * * * * * * * * * * *
If Right$(Key$, 1) <> "~" Then ClosePrintDialog
End Sub




Sub ToggleReport (Flag%)
'   * * * * * * * * * * * * * * * * * * * * * * * * * * * * *
'   * disable/enable report controls to
'   * avoid tabbing/shortcutting to them
'   * when they're hidden
'   * * * * * * * * * * * * * * * * * * * * * * * * * * * * *
Dim x%
For x% = 0 To 1
    Form1.Label1(x% + 1).Enabled = Flag%
    Form1.List2(x%).Enabled = Flag%
Next x%
If Flag% Then Form1.Command5.Enabled = Flag%
End Sub

Function ValidFile% (Ext$)
'   * * * * * * * * * * * * * * * * * * * * * * * * * * * * *
'   * Determine if Ext$ listed in Reg.Database or
'   * VBQ.INI
'   * * * * * * * * * * * * * * * * * * * * * * * * * * * * *
Dim Valid%
Valid% = CheckReg(Ext$)
If Not Valid% Then Valid% = CheckPrivate(Ext$)
```

```
ValidFile% = Valid%
End Function

Sub WaitForMsgBoxClose ()
'   * * * * * * * * * * * * * * * * * * * * * * * * *
'   * Delay execution while standard windows message box
'   * or BORDLG is on screen
'   * * * * * * * * * * * * * * * * * * * * * * * * *
Dim cName As String * 80, Y%, x%, C$
Y% = GetActiveWindow()
x% = GetClassName(Y%, cName, 79)
C$ = Left$(cName, 3)
If C$ = "#32" Or C$ = "BOR" Then
    Do While IsWindow(Y%)
        x% = DoEvents()
    Loop
End If
End Sub
```

5

VB TYPOGRAPHER

VB Typographer puts you in control of Windows 3.1's font capabilities.

With every blessing comes a curse. The remarkable font-scaling capabilities of Windows-based type facilities such as Apple's TrueType and Adobe Type Manager (ATM) provide access to an almost unlimited selection of font choices. But, given the inadequacy of the font-preview capabilities of most font-selection dialog boxes, and the large difference in resolution between the typical screen display (72 dpi) and laser printer output (300 dpi or greater), font-scaling actually makes it more difficult to predict in advance how a printed document will look than it was when you didn't have a choice of fonts.

Windows provides no facilities for comparing the qualities of one typeface with another on screen or on paper, or for really seeing how a certain typeface will look when rendered in, for instance, 72-point bold italic. The Character Map utility included with Windows provides

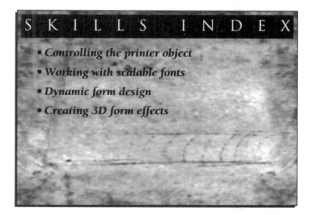

SKILLS INDEX

- *Controlling the printer object*
- *Working with scalable fonts*
- *Dynamic form design*
- *Creating 3D form effects*

you with the ability to see the entire character set for a font, but only at one small size, and only on screen.

VB Typographer addresses these shortcomings by allowing you to preview the entire character set of any font on screen at any size and in any style, and by allowing you to print out sample pages showing either a single font in various sizes and layouts, or complete characters sets of several fonts on a single page.

In designing VB Typographer, I took inspiration from several sources, including various shareware and commercial "type-book" programs that produce printed font sample pages, and a variety of on-screen font preview utilities. Perhaps the most innovative thing about VB Typographer is that it combines these closely related functions into a single application, rather than requiring the use of separate utilities to obtain on-screen font previews and printed font samples.

■ USING VB TYPOGRAPHER

The first thing you see when you launch VB Typographer is a small window with the text "Getting Printer Data." During the time that this window is visible, VB Typographer is using Windows API functions to obtain a variety of information about your printer, including the selected paper size and the printable area on the paper. When that window disappears, it is replaced by another window with the text "Loading font x of y" (where x is the font being loaded and y is the total number of printer fonts). This window's text is updated continually as VB Typographer reads the name of each font.

Once VB Typographer has read all the font names (the time this takes will vary according to the number of installed fonts), the Loading window disappears, and the program's main screen becomes visible. This is the program's primary user interface screen, and it supplies quite a bit of information to the user, as shown in Figure 5.1.

The most prominent features on the VB Typographer screen are a list box on the left side of the window that lists all available printer fonts, and a grid (without any grid lines) to its right that is used to display the character set for the selected font.

The font list box has its Sorted property set to True, so it presents the printer fonts in alphabetical order. In addition, the list box allows multiple selections (thus allowing the user to designate multiple fonts for VB Typographer's print operations).

A button located immediately above the font list box and labeled Select All is used to select all the fonts in the list box at once. To the button's right are three check boxes, labeled Bold, Italic, and Underline, which are used to set the characteristics of the typeface displayed in the character set grid, and a drop-down combo box that can be used to set the size of the grid text to any value between 7 and 128 points.

FIGURE 5.1

The main VB Typographer screen

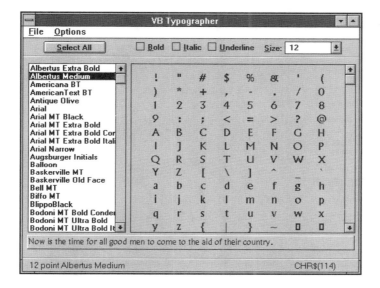

Meanwhile, immediately below the printer fonts list box and the display grid you'll find a panel that displays the phrase *Now is the time for all good men to come to the aid of their country.* in the selected font and style, and immediately beneath that is a status bar that identifies both the selected font, type size, and type style, and the ANSI standard code for the character that is active in the display grid.

By selecting a font and type size, and setting the style check boxes, you can view any printer font for which you have a matching screen font in any size or style, as shown in Figure 5.2. Thus, VB Typographer provides an on-screen font preview capability more flexible than that of the Character Map utility that accompanies Windows 3.1, which displays fonts only in a single type size.

VB Typographer's most important features, however, are its facilities for printing font sample sheets. These features are accessed through a pair of items on the program's File menu: Print Line Samples and Print Page Samples.

A Line Sample printout, such as the one shown in Figure 5.3, presents the entire character set of several fonts on a single page in 16-point type. Generally, six fonts fit on a page, but in some cases VB Typographer may fit fewer or more fonts on a page, depending upon the vertical space requirements of the characters produced by each font.

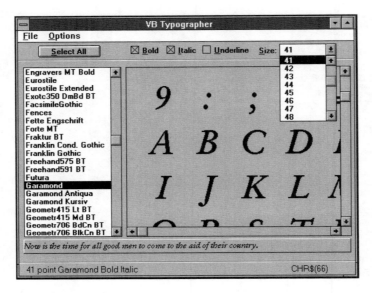

A Page Sample printout, on the other hand, presents a single font on a page. As shown in Figure 5.4, a Page Sample uses the selected font to present a sample text string in ten different point sizes, ranging from 6 points to 48 points. It also presents a paragraph of text in several different point-size and leading combinations. (Depending upon the characteristics of the font, up to six variations of the paragraph may be presented. In the case of unusually tall fonts, however, fewer iterations of the sample paragraph will be printed.)

When you select either the Print Line Samples or Print Page Samples menu items, VB Typographer counts the number of fonts that you've selected in the fonts list box. If you haven't selected any fonts, it asks if you want to print line samples or page samples for all the printer fonts accessible from your system. Otherwise, it uses the confirmation box shown in Figure 5.5 to confirm that you want to print samples for whatever number of fonts you've selected.

Once you have confirmed the request, VB Typographer begins to print out the sample page or pages. Be forewarned that this process, like any Windows print task that involves multiple fonts, can be quite time-consuming. In addition, if you're using Windows's Print Manager print spooler, and the fonts being printed aren't already resident in your printer (and so must be downloaded by a type manager such as TrueType or ATM), the temporary spool files that Windows creates for use by Print Manager will be quite large, averaging about 250K for a Page Samples page, and even more for a Line Samples page. Thus, Page Samples for 100 fonts might require about 25MB of disk space for temporary storage!

A Line Sample
printout
generated by
VB
Typographer.

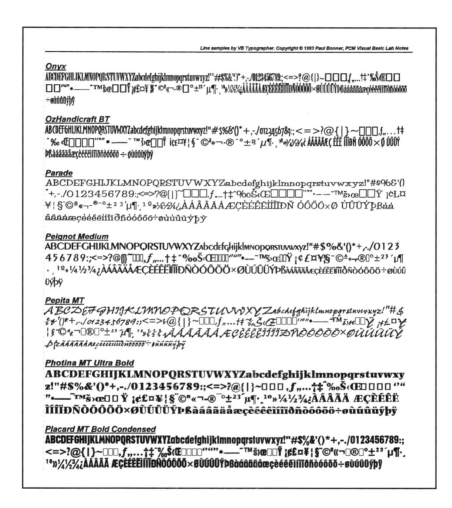

VB Typographer's remaining menu choices are used for a variety of utility functions, including accessing the standard Windows 3.1 Printer Setup dialog box, setting the font to be used for labels and template type on the Page Sample and Line Sample printouts, and viewing the program's About box.

FIGURE 5.4
A Page Samples sheet produced by VB Typographer

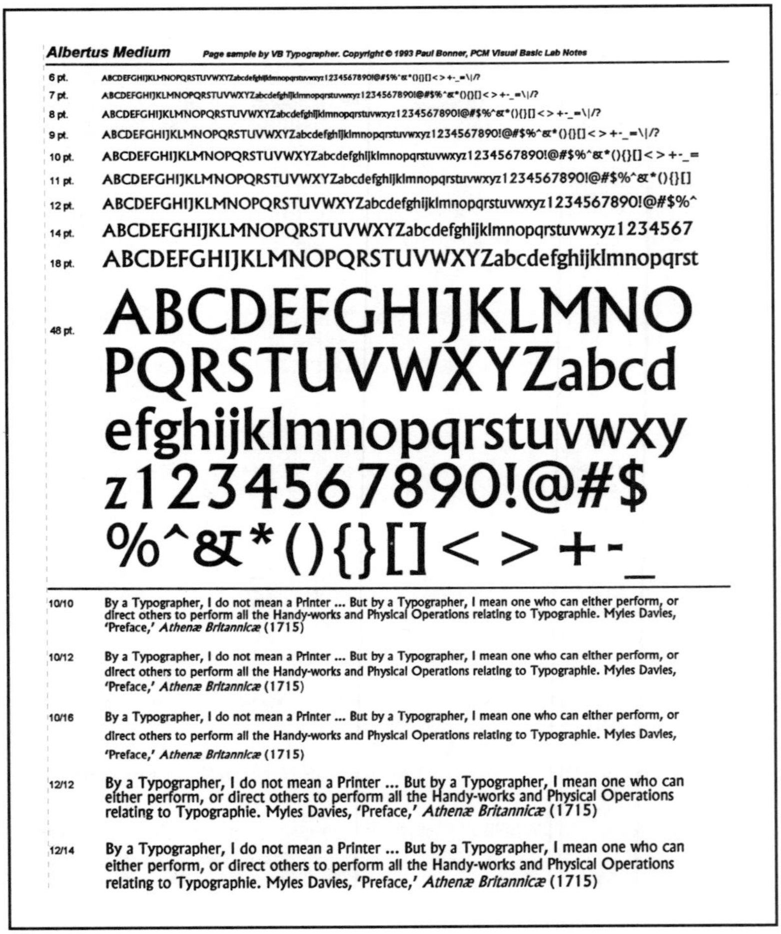

Albertus Medium *Page sample by VB Typographer. Copyright © 1993 Paul Bonner, PCM Visual Basic Lab Notes*

6 pt. ABCDEFGHIJKLMNOPQRSTUVWXYZabcdefghijklmnopqrstuvwxyz1234567890!@#$%^&*(){}[]<>+-_=\|/?
7 pt. ABCDEFGHIJKLMNOPQRSTUVWXYZabcdefghijklmnopqrstuvwxyz1234567890!@#$%^&*(){}[]<>+-_=\|/?
8 pt. ABCDEFGHIJKLMNOPQRSTUVWXYZabcdefghijklmnopqrstuvwxyz1234567890!@#$%^&*(){}[]<>+-_=\|/?
9 pt. ABCDEFGHIJKLMNOPQRSTUVWXYZabcdefghijklmnopqrstuvwxyz1234567890!@#$%^&*(){}[]<>+-_=\|/?
10 pt. ABCDEFGHIJKLMNOPQRSTUVWXYZabcdefghijklmnopqrstuvwxyz1234567890!@#$%^&*(){}[]<>+-_=
11 pt. ABCDEFGHIJKLMNOPQRSTUVWXYZabcdefghijklmnopqrstuvwxyz1234567890!@#$%^&*(){}[]
12 pt. ABCDEFGHIJKLMNOPQRSTUVWXYZabcdefghijklmnopqrstuvwxyz1234567890!@#$%^
14 pt. ABCDEFGHIJKLMNOPQRSTUVWXYZabcdefghijklmnopqrstuvwxyz1234567
18 pt. ABCDEFGHIJKLMNOPQRSTUVWXYZabcdefghijklmnopqrst
48 pt. ABCDEFGHIJKLMNO
PQRSTUVWXYZabcd
efghijklmnopqrstuvwxy
z1234567890!@#$
%^&*(){}[]<>+-_

10/10 By a Typographer, I do not mean a Printer ... But by a Typographer, I mean one who can either perform, or direct others to perform all the Handy-works and Physical Operations relating to Typographie. Myles Davies, 'Preface,' *Athenæ Britannicæ* (1715)

10/12 By a Typographer, I do not mean a Printer ... But by a Typographer, I mean one who can either perform, or direct others to perform all the Handy-works and Physical Operations relating to Typographie. Myles Davies, 'Preface,' *Athenæ Britannicæ* (1715)

10/16 By a Typographer, I do not mean a Printer ... But by a Typographer, I mean one who can either perform, or direct others to perform all the Handy-works and Physical Operations relating to Typographie. Myles Davies, 'Preface,' *Athenæ Britannicæ* (1715)

12/12 By a Typographer, I do not mean a Printer ... But by a Typographer, I mean one who can either perform, or direct others to perform all the Handy-works and Physical Operations relating to Typographie. Myles Davies, 'Preface,' *Athenæ Britannicæ* (1715)

12/14 By a Typographer, I do not mean a Printer ... But by a Typographer, I mean one who can either perform, or direct others to perform all the Handy-works and Physical Operations relating to Typographie. Myles Davies, 'Preface,' *Athenæ Britannicæ* (1715)

▪ INSIDE VB TYPOGRAPHER

Given the complexity of the tasks that it performs, most of VB Typographer's code is remarkably simple. Moreover, unlike most of the other applications presented in this book, VB Typographer is almost entirely composed of native Visual Basic code. With the exception of three Windows API calls used to obtain some font and printer information, VB Typographer relies entirely upon the Visual Basic command and function set.

FIGURE 5.5

VB Typographer uses this dialog box to confirm print requests.

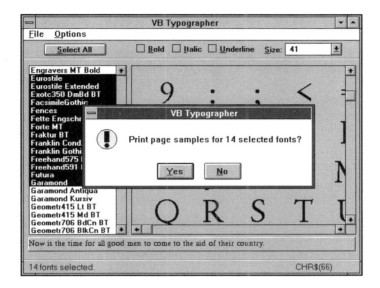

Despite that, this was not a particularly easy application to write. While VB Typographer's on-screen forms were reasonably simple to complete, fine-tuning its printed output required what seemed like endless tweaking and endless reams of printer paper. Once you get beyond printing an exact replica of a form, or printing a database report with the Crystal Reports custom control in Visual Basic 3.0, Visual Basic's print capabilities are primitive, and it can take a considerable amount of time to figure out how to make them do anything useful. While the pages that VB Typographer prints are not the most complex you'll ever see, they do require sufficient precision that producing them in Visual Basic was a chore. Fortunately, along the way I picked up a few tricks that should save me—and you—considerable effort on future projects that exercise the Visual Basic-printer connection.

▪ Getting Started

At the beginning of this project, I knew just enough about the difficulties of printing from within Visual Basic to want to avoid that part of the process of designing and coding VB Typographer as long as possible. Thus, at the beginning of the project I concentrated on VB Typographer's on-screen display of fonts.

This portion of the design process was driven entirely by user-interface considerations. I wanted to make the process of selecting fonts and specifying style characteristics absolutely transparent to the user. Thus, I decided to center VB Typographer's display around two elements: a long list of fonts and a large display area.

A list-box control was the obvious choice for presenting the font list, but the choice of a control to use as the font display element was slightly more difficult. I experimented with using both label and text controls in this capacity, but found both lacking. I wanted to present a nice, neat, columnar read-only display of the selected font's character set. Label controls didn't work because they lacked scroll bars, making it impossible to display fonts at large sizes when the width of the row of type exceeded the width of the control. With text controls, on the other hand, I discovered that columns of proportional text wouldn't line up correctly (because of the varying width of the characters in a proportional font).

Fortunately, my third choice, a grid control, proved to be the correct one. I hadn't thought of a grid control at first, because I had this vision of grid controls as spreadsheetlike things with nonscrollable border cells and horizontal and vertical grid lines between each cell—all of which seemed far too busy for the simple, orderly display that VB Typographer required. But Visual Basic's grid control is quite flexible. By settings its Gridlines property to False, I could eliminate the lines between cells, and by setting the background color of the rest of the grid to match the fixed rows at the top and left, I could use the fixed rows as borders to the remainder of the display. Finally, by setting the alignment property of each grid column to Centered, and adjusting each column's width to match that of the characters in the selected font, VB Typographer could display the neat columns I was after. It was even possible to get rid of the reversed-bar that highlighted the selected cell by setting the grid control's Highlight property to False.

I was able to set the grid background color, to disable gridlines, and to eliminate the highlight bar by setting design time properties, as shown in Figure 5.6. At this time, I also set the width of the grid to nine columns (one border column and eight columns for characters, a width that easily allowed display of 12-point text without scrolling) and its height to the minimum two rows (one border row and one additional row).

Most of the remaining work of preparing the grid is performed in a routine called SetUpTypographer. The SetUpTypographer routine is called by the Form_Load procedure for VB Typographer's main form:

```
T$ = Chr$(9)   'TAB character
F.DisplayGrid.RowHeight(0) = 150   'row & column 0 are
F.DisplayGrid.ColWidth(0) = 300    'fixed--so use as borders
F.DisplayGrid.Row = 1
For X% = 33 To 40 'first row of 8 characters
```

```
      F.DisplayGrid.Col = X% - 32   'select column
      F.DisplayGrid.Text = Chr$(X%)   'add character
      F.DisplayGrid.ColAlignment(X% - 32) = 2    'center column
   Next
   For X% = 41 To 255    'remaining characters
      i% = i% + 1   'increment counter
      T$ = T$ + Chr$(X%) + Chr$(9)  'add character and tab
      If i% = 8 Then  'if row is full
       F.DisplayGrid.AddItem Left$(T$, Len(T$) - 1) 'insert row
       T$ = Chr$(9)  'reinitialize string
       i% = 0           'reinitialize counter
      End If
   Next
   If T$ <> Chr$(9) Then F.DisplayGrid.AddItem T$ 'add last row
```

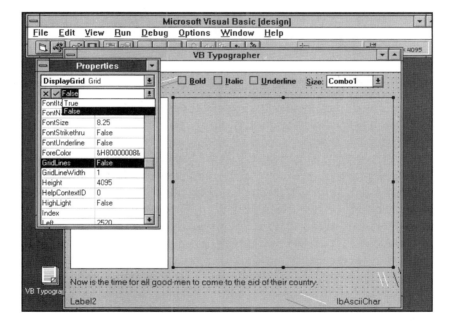

FIGURE 5.6

Much of the work of configuring the grid control was done at design time.

The routine starts by setting the width of column 0 and the height of row 0 (the grid's required fixed column and row, respectively) to values that I had determined, after a bit of experimentation, made for attractive border sizes.

Once the grid's borders have been established, the routine populates the first row of the grid with the first eight printable characters, CHR$(33) through CHR$(41). I planned on populating the remaining rows by building a string of characters separated by tabs and by using that string to insert an entire row at a time since it is faster than populating each cell individually; but that wasn't possible for the first row, which already existed on the control. Thus, the routine steps across the first row, selecting one cell at a time, inserting a character into the cells, and then setting the alignment property for the cell's column to Centered, until the first row is populated.

For the remaining characters, CHR$(41) through CHR$(255), the routine builds strings of eight characters separated by tabs, and issues the Grid.AddItem command as each string is built, thus inserting the string as a new row, with each character in a separate column.

The final part of setting up the grid was to adjust the width of each column to the width of the characters being displayed. Large characters set in 120-point type would require much wider cells than tiny characters in 8-point type, so I knew that this procedure would have to be performed whenever the style or size of the type displayed in the grid changed.

To adjust the width of the cells, VB Typographer needed to know the width of the characters that it was to display. While it is eminently visible to the naked eye when a character won't fit in a grid cell, or when the cell is much too wide for its contents, a program is sightless. Thus, VB Typographer needed a way to determine the width of the characters that it was to display, in order to adjust the width of the grid columns used to display them.

The closest Visual Basic comes to being capable of providing this information is its TextWidth property, which returns the width that a specified string will occupy for either a printer, a form, or a picture box. Undoubtedly I could have set the font characteristics of the form to those of the grid and then used the Form.TextWidth property to obtain the width of an "M" or "W" (typically the widest characters) for the specified font, but there was a better way to determine an optimum width for the grid columns: through the use of the Windows API GetTextMetrics function.

GetTextMetrics provides a wide variety of information about a font, returning it in the form of a TextMetric variable, which is defined as follows:

```
Type TextMetric
    tmHeight As Integer
    tmAscent As Integer
    tmDescent As Integer
    tmInternalLeading As Integer
    tmExternalLeading As Integer
    tmAveCharWidth As Integer
    tmMaxCharWidth As Integer
    tmWeight As Integer
    tmItalic As String * 1
    tmUnderlined As String * 1
    tmStruckOut As String * 1
```

```
    tmFirstChar As String * 1
    tmLastChar As String * 1
    tmDefaultChar As String * 1
    tmBreakChar As String * 1
    tmPitchAndFamily As String * 1
    tmCharSet As String * 1
    tmOverhang As Integer
    tmDigitizedAspectX As Integer
    tmDigitizedAspectY As Integer
End Type
```

To use the GetTextMetrics function, you first have to define a variable to be of type TextMetrics, and then call the TextMetrics function, passing it the handle of a device context in which the font about which you wish information is active, and the name of your TextMetric variable, as follows:

```
Dim TextStuff as TextMetric
X% = GetTextMetrics(Printer.hDC, TextStuff)
```

VB Typographer only needed one piece of the information returned by GetTextMetrics: the width of the widest character in the selected font. It uses that dimension, which is contained in the tmMaxCharWidth element of the TextStuff variable, to adjust the width of the columns on the display grid. The routine that carries out this process is called SizeRows.

```
Sub SizeRows ()
Dim X%, MinWidth%
On Error Resume Next
Typographer.FontName = F.DisplayGrid.FontName
Typographer.FontSize = F.DisplayGrid.FontSize
X% = GetTextMetrics(Typographer.hDC, TextStuff)
MinWidth% = (F.DisplayGrid.Width - 300) / 9
If TextStuff.tmMaxCharWidth * Screen.TwipsPerPixelX > MinWidth% Then
    MinWidth% = TextStuff.tmMaxCharWidth * Screen.TwipsPerPixelX
End If
For X% = 1 To 9
    F.DisplayGrid.ColWidth(X%) = MinWidth%
Next
End Sub
```

The SizeRows routine starts by setting the FontName and FontSize properties for the Typographer form to the active font name and size for the grid. Then it passes VB Typographer's device-context handle to the TextMetrics function to populate the Text-Stuff type variable. Next, after determining a minimum column width (based on 1/9 the width of the grid minus the width of the border column), the routine compares the width of the widest character in the font to the value that it has calculated for the minimum column width. If the widest character is wider than the minimum column width, the routine resets the value of the minimum column-width variable to match the width of the widest character, and then uses that new value to adjust the width of each column.

▪ Font Selection

As always, I'm getting a little ahead of myself here. I suppose that's what comes from trying to describe event-driven Windows applications in a linear fashion. In any case, before VB Typographer can adjust the width of a column to match the selected font, it has to present the user with a list of fonts to select. Accordingly, the SetUpTypographer procedure calls another procedure, GetFonts, which executes the following code to fill the FontList list box with a list of available printer fonts.

```
fc% = Printer.FontCount
If fc% = 0 Then Unload LoadForm: Exit Sub
For X% = 1 To fc%
    Y% = DoEvents()
    F.FontList.AddItem Printer.Fonts(X%)
    LoadForm.Label2 = Str$(X%)
Next
```

The list box's Visible property is set to False during this operation, because AddItem operations proceed much faster on invisible list boxes, and its Sorted property is set to True, so that by the time the routine is finished the list box contains a sorted list of all available printer fonts. Meanwhile, the DoEvents() call in the font-loading routine allows VB Typographer to load the font list without tying up your PC.

To allow the user to select multiple fonts for printed output, I set the FontList list box's MultiSelect property to Extended when I designed the form (thus allowing the selection of any number of contiguous or noncontiguous list-box entries). Since the display grid can only display one font at a time, if more than one font is selected, the FontList_Click procedure merely updates the status bar label at the bottom of the screen to read

```
lbStatBar = FontList.SelCount & " fonts selected."
```

Otherwise, if only a single font is selected in the list box, the FontList_Click procedure sets the FontName properties of both the font sample label (the label whose caption reads *Now is the time for all good men to come to the aid of their country.*) and the display grid to the selected font, and then calls the CheckAttributes routine, which updates other type characteristics, as described below.

```
On Error GoTo BadFont
lbTypeDemo.FontName=FontList.List(FontList.ListIndex)
On Error GoTo 0
DisplayGrid.FontName = lbTypeDemo.FontName
CheckAttributes
```

The On Error routine in this code segment catches errors that occur when there is no matching screen font for the selected printer font. This can occur when the user selects a resident printer font that doesn't have a screen equivalent, or if the screen font file is damaged. In either case, execution jumps to the BadFont routine, which posts an error message on the status bar label and hides the display grid.

```
BadFont:
DisplayGrid.Visible = False
lbStatBar="Noscreenfontavailablefor"+FontList.List(FontList.ListIndex)
Resume Re
```

■ Setting Other Type Characteristics

The job of updating all the other type characteristics, including size, or bold, italic, and underline attributes, is handled by the CheckAttributes routine. Whenever the user selects a new type size from the drop-down combo box or checks one of the style check boxes, VB Typographer calls the CheckAttributes routine.

CheckAttributes begins by hiding the display grid. Then it updates the grid and type sample to reflect the state of each of the three style check boxes, one by one. For example, the code that processes the state of Checkbox1(0), the Bold selector, is as follows:

```
c% = F.Check1(0)
F.DisplayGrid.FontBold = True * c%
F.lbTypeDemo.FontBold = True * c%
If c% = 1 Then l$ = l$ + "Bold "
```

First, CheckAttributes sets a temporary variable called c% equal to the value of the check box, then it sets the style characteristic of the display grid and the type sample label equal to c% * True. (This is the fastest way I've discovered to convert a check box value, which is equal to 1 if the box is checked and 0 if it isn't, to a True/False flag where True equals −1 and False = 0.) Finally, if the style attribute is active, it updates the status bar label which indicates the selected font's name and style to reflect that style.

Once CheckAttributes has processed all three check boxes in this manner, it sets the font size of the display grid to the value of the font-size combo box, calls the Size-

Rows function to adjust the width of the grid's columns, updates the status bar again, and then sets the display grid's Visible property to True to show off the results of its work.

```
F.DisplayGrid.FontSize = Val(F.Combo1)
SizeRows
F.lbStatBar = F.Combo1.List(F.Combo1.ListIndex) & " point " + ⇔
    F.DisplayGrid.FontName + " " + l$
If F.Visible Then F.DisplayGrid.Visible = True
```

That concludes the process of updating VB Typographer's font display. Considering the complexity of the task that it's performing—rendering any installed outline font in nearly any size or combination of styles—the code is remarkably straightforward, thanks in large part to Visual Basic's fine type-control capabilities.

The only additional code that needs discussion before we move on to VB Typographer's printing functions is the routine that handles resizing of VB Typographer's main form.

Resizing the VB Typographer Form

Unlike many Windows utilities, VB Typographer benefits greatly from running in a maximized, or at least large, state. While I designed the application to be a good citizen and to run in a moderately sized window, I also made sure that it takes advantage of any additional screen real estate that you give it. The bigger its window, the more characters you can see without scrolling the display grid, as shown in Figure 5.7.

The Form_Resize procedure for VB Typographer's main form is responsible for adjusting the size and position of the many elements on the form to fit a new window size. It begins by resetting the size of the FontList list box and of the display grid. First it sets the height of FontList to a value equal to the total height of the form minus 2120 (this value, and the others here, were arrived at the old fashioned way—endless experiments until I found ones that looked good in every resolution).

Then the routine sets the height of the display grid to equal the height of the list box. Notice that the routine specifies that DisplayGrid.Height should be equal to FontList.Height, rather than simply use the same value to which it just set FontList's height. That's because Visual Basic automatically adjusts the height of a list box downward to clean up the list box's appearance. Thus, if you set a list box to a height of 4,000 twips, and if at that height 12 1/4 items would be visible in the list, Visual Basic would adjust the height downward so that only 12 items were visible. One consequence of this is that *nearly everytime you change the font used to display the contents of a list box, the list box will get shorter.* Another consequence, more to the point here, is that if you want another control to be the exact same height as a list box, you should set its height equal to the list box's Height property, rather than to the value you used to set the list box's height.

FIGURE 5.7

*VB
Typographer
resizes its grid
when you
change the size
of its window.*

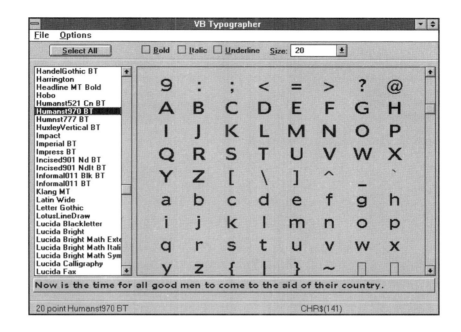

```
B% = Height - 2120
If B% < 400 Then B% = 400
FontList.Height = B%
'size displaygrid
DisplayGrid.Height = FontList.Height
B% = Width - (DisplayGrid.Left + 200)
If B% < 1500 Then B% = 1500
DisplayGrid.Width = B%
```

Next, the Form_Resize routine repositions the type demo label below the resized list box and grid, and redraws the three-dimensional border (which is composed of four Line controls) around the label.

```
lbTypeDemo.Top = FontList.Height + FontList.Top + 95
lbTypeDemo.Width = Width - 360
' Size lbTypeDemo 3D border
Dim X1%, X2%, Y1%, Y2%
X1% = lbTypeDemo.Left - 20
X2% = lbTypeDemo.Left + lbTypeDemo.Width + 20
Y1% = lbTypeDemo.Top - 40
Y2% = lbTypeDemo.Top + lbTypeDemo.Height + 40
DemoLine1(0).X1 = X1%
```

```
DemoLine1(0).X2 = X2%
DemoLine1(0).Y1 = Y1%
DemoLine1(0).Y2 = Y1%
DemoLine1(1).X1 = X1%
DemoLine1(1).X2 = X1%
DemoLine1(1).Y1 = Y1%
DemoLine1(1).Y2 = Y2%
DemoLine1(2).X1 = X1%
DemoLine1(2).X2 = X2%
DemoLine1(2).Y1 = Y2%
DemoLine1(2).Y2 = Y2%
DemoLine1(3).X1 = X2%
DemoLine1(3).X2 = X2%
DemoLine1(3).Y1 = Y1%
DemoLine1(3).Y2 = Y2%
```

Finally, the routine adjusts the width of the four line controls used to draw the three-dimensional lines at the top (separating the type style controls from the FontList list box and the display grid) and bottom (separating the status bar) of the screen.

```
'draw status bar line
BottomWhiteLine.X2 = Width
BottomGrayLine.X2 = Width
TopGrayLine.X2 = Width
TopWhiteLine.X2 = Width
```

The Resize routine concludes by calling SizeRows to adjust the width of the display grid's columns to the new width of the grid.

■ VB TYPOGRAPHER'S PRINTING ROUTINES

If I could have been content with having VB Typographer produce screen output, this project would have been a piece of cake. But instead, I had to get fancy, and by venturing into the world of printed output, I managed to open up several teeming cans of worms.

Actually, producing printed font samples didn't seem like it would be so difficult at the onset. I knew that I would have to devise a word wrap routine to fit the text that I wanted onto the page, and otherwise be careful about formatting, but I thought that Visual Basic's printer functions, while limited, would suffice to meet VB Typographer's needs.

The problem is that there are gaps in both the range of Visual Basic's printer support and in the documentation of that support, making it much more difficult to get the results you want from printed output.

For instance, Visual Basic's Printer object has properties called Width and Height, which you would suppose would be of some value in determining when a line is about to leave the printable width or height of a page. But those properties indicate the total width or total height of a page, not of its printable area (most laser printers, for instance, require at least ¾ inch margins on all sides of a page). If you base a word wraparound algorithm on those properties, your application will inevitably attempt to print in the nonprintable portion of the page, resulting in gaps in its printed output.

Clearly what VB Typographer needed was information about the printable area of the page. As it turns out, Visual Basic can supply that information too, through its Printer.ScaleWidth and Printer.ScaleHeight properties, which return the width and height, respectively, of the printable area of the page. But you'll be forgiven if, like me, you have difficulty finding any documentation for this use of the ScaleWidth and ScaleHeight properties. All the Visual Basic Reference Manual and on-line help system have to say about them is that they "determine the number of units for the internal horizontal…and vertical…measurement of an object…." Maybe that translates to printable area, but one could certainly say it more clearly than that.

To be fair, the Visual Basic Programmer's Guide does state specifically that "The ScaleHeight and ScaleWidth properties define the size of the printable area of the page." But if like most Visual Basic programmers, you put the Programmer's Guide away after the first week and rely exclusively upon the Reference Manual or Help system, you'll not find a mention of the words "printable area."

In any case, this confusion led me to some strange places, as I explored various Windows API commands attempting to determine the printable area of the page. To make a long story short, I eventually hit upon one that did the trick—a function called Escape—but then I finally figured out that the ScaleWidth and ScaleHeight properties would actually return the data I needed. So in the end I was able to get the information I needed from Visual Basic, but not without a few detours along the way.

VB Typographer stores the horizontal and vertical measurements of the physical size of the page, and of the printable area of the page, in a pair of PointAPI structures (consisting of x and y coordinates) called OffSet and Physize, using the following code:

```
Printer.ScaleMode = 1
OffSet.X = (Printer.Width - Printer.ScaleWidth) / 2
OffSet.y = (Printer.Height - Printer.ScaleHeight) / 2
```

```
Physize.X = Printer.Width
Physize.y = Printer.Height
```

■ Word Wraparound

Once VB Typographer had the information it needed about the printable area of the page, the next step was to take advantage of that information.

There are a lot of variables (no pun intended) associated with printing out multi-typeface output such as that of VB Typographer. The physical page size and the printable area of the page are both subject to change, depending upon the user's printer setup. In addition, the width and height of any given text string will vary considerably depending upon the typeface being printed. The same string printed in Helvetica Narrow and Wide Latin occupy considerably different amounts of space.

Despite these many variable elements, I wanted to achieve a consistent appearance in VB Typographer's printed output. For instance, I wanted to have equal right margins on each sample page, even though the width of the typefaces varied. This meant that VB Typographer had to be able to either wrap its output to a new line or truncate it when it reached the right edge of the page.

VB Typographer's WrapLine subroutine takes care of both requirements. WrapLine makes use of two properties of the Visual Basic printer object: Printer.TextWidth, which indicates how much horizontal space a string will occupy when printed, and Printer.CurrentX, which indicates the horizontal location at which the next item will start to print, and of the values of PhySize.X and OffSet.X.

WrapLine accepts three parameters: Sample$, the string to be printed; L1$, an empty string in which WrapLine will place that portion of Sample$ that can fit on the current line; and m%, an integer that WrapLine multiplies by the value of OffSet.X to determine the width of the right and left margins.

WrapLine uses a simple, brute-force method to determine how much of Sample$ will fit on the current line. Starting with a substring consisting of only the first character of Sample$, it adds the width of that substring to the value of Printer.CurrentX and checks to see if the result exceeds the sum of subtracting m% times OffSet.X from PhySize.X. If not, it adds the next character from Sample$ to the substring and checks again.

```
Sub WrapLine (Sample$, L1$, m%)
     Dim X%
     For X% = 1 To Len(Sample$)
      If Printer.TextWidth(Left$(Sample$, X%)) + Printer.CurrentX > ⇔
    PhySize.X - (m% * OffSet.X) Then
            L1$ = L1$ + Left$(Sample$, X% - 1)
            Sample$ = Mid$(Sample$, X%)
            Exit For
```

```
         End If
      Next X%
   If L1$ = "" Then L1$ = Sample$: Sample$ = ""     'none of Sample$ will fit
End Sub
```

WrapLine continues to loop through Sample$ until its width added to the current X location exceeds the printable width of the page. At that point, the routine ends, with L1$ containing the portion of the original contents of Sample$ that will fit on the current line, and Sample$ containing the remainder.

VB Typographer uses WrapLine in different ways depending upon whether it needs to print a string in its entirety, even if that means wrapping onto additional lines, or simply needs to print whatever portion of the string will fit on the current line. In the latter case, VB Typographer uses WrapLine to obtain a truncated version of the string, as follows:

```
WrapLine Sample$, L1$, 5
Printer.Print L1$
```

Here, Sample$ starts off containing the entire string that VB Typographer wants to print, while L1$ starts off empty. The 5 passed as the third parameter indicates that WrapLine should wrap Sample$ when its length added to the value of Printer.CurrentX exceeds the physical width of the page minus five times the value of Offset.X. But after WrapLine has done its work, L1$ will contain that portion of Sample$ that can fit in the specified area, so VB Typographer issues the Printer.Print command to print it.

Wrapping a string onto multiple lines is a just a bit more complex, due to two additional considerations. The first is that VB Typographer must keep track of the portion of the print string that won't fit on the current line and attempt to print it on the next line, and the second is that to break sentences properly, VB Typographer must modify WrapLine's results to break the line at a space, rather than in the middle of a word, if possible.

The portion of the code that carries out these responsibilities appears as follows:

```
Wrapper:
WrapLine Sample$, L1$, 5
If Sample$ <> "" Then
   If Left$(Sample$, 1) <> Chr$(32) Then      'try to break at a space
      For S% = Len(L1$) - 1 To 1 Step -1
         If Mid$(L1$, S%, 1) = Chr$(32) Then
            Sample$ = Mid$(L1$, S% + 1) + Sample$
            L1$ = Left$(L1$, S% - 1)
            Exit For
         End If
      Next
   End If
```

```
End If
Printer.Print L1$;
If Sample$ <> "" Then
    L1$ = ""
    Printer.Print
    GoTo Wrapper
End If
```

This fragment contains two important tests. The first, which attempts to break the output text at a space, starts by examining the leftmost character of the remainder string. If that character is a space, then the line was broken correctly. Otherwise, it loops backwards through the string to be printed looking for a space, and then moves the line break there if it finds one. Once this loop is complete, VB Typographer prints L1$.

The second important test is a check to see whether Sample$ is empty. If not, VB Typographer issues the Printer.Print statement to start a new line, and then jumps back to the Wrapper label to print more of Sample$.

Some readers might raise an eyebrow at my use of the GoTo command in this routine, given the near-universal contempt that most programmers have for GoTo. Certainly GoTo has been a cause of several million lines of spaghetti code in the past. But used judiciously in a tight, well-documented routine, it can be very valuable, and certainly makes for code no less lucid than, for instance, If-Then loops nested five levels deep.

That about wraps up (this time the pun was intended) VB Typographer's line-wrapping routines. While both the efficiency and sophistication of these routines could be improved, as they are they provide the capability for VB Typographer to output line-wrapped text in any typeface at any size on any printer or page. In fact, by substituting references to the Screen Object for those to the Printer object, they could also be modified to provide word-wrapped screen output on a picture control or form.

■ Vertical Sizing

In addition to wrapping lines of text horizontally, VB Typographer needed to be able to monitor and control the vertical location of output on the page. This capability was necessary both for VB Typographer to place items correctly on its output pages, and for it to know when to discontinue printing at the bottom of a page or start a new page.

VB Typographer uses the CurrentY of the Printer object both to determine and to control the vertical location of the printed output. By querying the value of Printer-.CurrentY, VB Typographer can determine the vertical location where the next item will be printed, while by setting Printer.CurrentY to a new value it can change that location.

For instance, VB Typographer makes use of frequent calls to a function called CheckYLoc() to determine if there is room to print another line of text on the page. CheckYLoc() simply adds the height of a capital J (one of the tallest characters in most typefaces) to Printer.CurrentY, and then determines if the result exceeds VB Typographer's vertical margin, which is defined as PhySize.Y minus four times OffSet.Y. If there is room for another line within that margin, CheckYLoc returns a value of True. Otherwise, it returns False.

```
Function CheckYLoc () As Integer
CheckYLoc = True
IfPrinter.TextHeight("J")+Printer.CurrentY>PhySize.Y-(4*OffSet.Y)Then
    CheckYLoc = False
End If
End Function
```

VB Typographer's PrintPageSamples routine uses CheckYLoc to determine whether it can fit another copy of the Myles Davies quote about the nature of a typographer's job onto the page. If it cannot, it ends the page. For instance, if it has just printed the quote in 12-point type with 14-point leading and CheckYLoc ends false, the routine exits without printing the quote at 12 points on 18-point leading. It would have been possible, of course, to start a new page at this point, but the point of Page Samples is to provide a one-page rendering of the font, and thus jumping to a second page would have made little sense.

■ Baseline Alignment

While it comes in very useful, the Printer.CurrentY property doesn't provide all the control that VB Typographer needs to print its output pages. For instance, on each of the Page Sample sheets, VB Typographer prints samples depicting as much of the upper- and lowercase character set for the selected font as it can fit on a line at 6-, 7-, 8-, 9-, 10-, 11-, 12-, 14-, and 18-point sizes, followed by up to five lines at 48 points. Before each of these sample lines, VB Typographer prints the point size of the sample that follows, using its default font—Arial unless changed by the user or not available on the selected printer—in 8-point type. And, if you examine the sample sheets closely, you'll notice that on each of the lines, the baseline of the 8-point Arial label lines up with that of the type that follows.

If you've ever tried to print type of different sizes and typefaces on a single line from within Visual Basic, you'll know that this isn't standard behavior. Instead, the default is to align the tops of the characters. To align the bottom edge of the characters, VB Typographer has to call the Windows API function SetTextAlign, passing it the hardware device-context handle of the printer and the parameter TA_BASELINE (the constant TA_BASELINE is defined as equal to 24), as follows:

```
z% = SetTextAlign(Printer.hDC, TA_BASELINE)
```

■ Line Spacing

VB Typographer's final bit of nonstandard vertical alignment wizardry is used to control line spacing on the Page Samples sheets.

When you issue a Printer.Print command, Visual Basic issues commands to the printer that move Current.X to the left edge of the page, and move Printer.CurrentY to the starting position of the next line. The latter isn't as simple as it seems. For example, how does the printer driver know where to begin the next line? The answer is that Visual Basic makes assumptions about line spacing. After a good deal of experimentation with a type ruler, for instance, I figured out that Visual Basic defaults to printing 10-point type on 12-point leading (meaning that there are 12 points of space between the baselines of successive lines), 12-point type on 14-point leading, and so on.

This default spacing improves readability at small sizes, but to demonstrate how the type will work in diverse situations, VB Typographer has to show it with various degrees of leading. Moreover, because Visual Basic produces larger text sizes with proportionally greater degrees of leading, at larger point sizes the default spacing leaves enough room to drive a truck between lines, which significantly degrades readability. For example, Visual Basic defaults to outputting 48-point type on 56-point leading, which is really far too much space for easy readability.

Unfortunately, Visual Basic doesn't provide a way to change the default leading. Nor is there a handy Windows API function to achieve it. Instead, VB Typographer has to manipulate the value of the Printer.CurrentY setting directly. Since VB Typographer sets Printer.ScaleMode to Points, it can direct the placement of the next line by issuing commands such as:

```
Printer.FontSize=12
Y%=Printer.CurrentY
Printer.Print A$
Printer.CurrentY=Y%+16
Printer.Print B$
```

This would print the two strings of 12-point type on 16-point leading.

VB Typographer uses this ability at several points, including the printing of the 48-point type sample on the Print Sample page, which it prints on 49-point leading rather than at the default of 56 points, and on the line spacing samples that follow, where a quote from the 18th-century writer Myles Davies is reproduced six times using varying type sizes and degrees of leading.

■ Utility Routines

That about concludes the major features and routines in VB Typographer. However, as you examine its listings you'll notice that the application makes heavy use of several utility routines for frequently accessed functions. For instance, most of VB Typographer's printed output passes through a routine called pOut which simply sets Printer.CurrentX equal to OffSet.X and then prints the specified string.

```
Sub pOut (P$)
Printer.CurrentX = OffSet.X
Printer.Print P$
End Sub
```

Among the other utility routines used by VB Typographer are several that are used to specify different type styles for various aspects of its formatted pages. For instance, a subroutine called SetHeaderFont is used to set the font to the style used to print the page header; SetPageSmallLabelFont is used to set the font to a style used to print small labels; and so on. Each of these routines in turn makes use of another utility routine called SetPrinterFont, which sets each of the printer font characteristics to the value specified by the calling routine, as follows:

```
Sub SetPrinterFont (fN$, fS%, fB%, fI%, fU%)
   Printer.FontName = fN$
   Printer.FontSize = fS%
   Printer.FontBold = fB%
   Printer.FontItalic = fI%
   Printer.FontUnderline = fU%
End Sub
```

Thus, the SetHeaderFont routine, which is used to activate the font specified by the variable DefFont$ in 16-point bold italic, consists of just one call to SetPrinterFont.

```
Sub SetHeaderFont ()
   'DefFont$--16 pt-- bold--italic--no underline
   SetPrinterFont DefFont$, 16, True, True, False
End Sub
```

With that, our discussion of VB Typographer comes to an end. It's a useful, albeit limited, utility, one which could be enhanced perhaps by giving the user the ability to print multiple styles (normal, bold, italic, bold italic, and so on) of any or all typefaces, rather than only the standard style. However, I hope that you find it of use, and moreover, that this report of my struggles with Visual Basic's printer functions ends up saving you some struggle in your own applications.

E N D N O T E

PERFORMANCE

I've never accepted the idea that Windows applications have to be big and slow. I've always felt they should be just as responsive as DOS applications, and that any additional time that they do take to get a job done should be more than offset by the additional capabilities they provide. As a result, I always strive to eliminate any performance bottlenecks from the Windows applications that I write.

Given that I haven't encountered many DOS applications that can print sample pages of any number of scalable fonts, I suppose VB Typographer's performance could be explained away under the "additional capabilities" category. Nevertheless, I am a little embarrassed by some aspects of it. As VB Typographer finishes printing each page, there is a lengthy delay, during which time your other Windows applications will be rather unresponsive. Moreover, VB Typographer sucks up temporary disk space like beer; it consumes 200K or more of space for each page that it prints. (Of course, this space is returned to your use as soon as the page is printed.)

I can't say that I'm very pleased about either of these items, but I'm also afraid that I have to pass the buck and blame these undesirable features on Windows and Visual Basic. As VB Typographer finishes printing a page, it issues a Printer.EndDoc command, at which point the page is transferred from memory to the disk for spooling to the printer. That process is slow under Windows, the resulting page eats up a lot of disk space, and there's no way that I've discovered to change it. So instead, I'll offer some advice. If you simply want to view fonts on screen, use VB Typographer anytime you want. But if you want to print out Line Samples or Page Samples for all your fonts, load up your printer with paper, make sure you've got plenty of free disk space, and run the process overnight rather than sitting in front of your PC waiting for the hourglass to go away.   ∎

ENDNOTE

ADDING 3D ELEMENTS TO FORMS

As you examine VB Typographer's .MAK file, you'll notice that it does not include THREED.VBX or any other custom control providing Visual Basic with three-dimensional user-interface controls. Nevertheless, the status bar at the bottom of VB Typographer's main form is separated from the remainder of the form by what appears to be a three-dimensional line, as is the type style selection area at the top of the form. And even the label that presents the sample text *Now is the time for all good men to come to the aid of their country.* appears to be located on a three-dimensional panel.

Rather than use custom controls to give VB Typographer a three-dimensional appearance, I created that appearance by using Line controls. For instance, dark gray lines along the bottom and right edges of the sample text label and white lines along the top and left edges combine to give it a three-dimensional appearance. VB Typographer adjusts the width and locations of these controls in the form's Form_Resize event, thus adjusting the apparent width of the label to the new size of the form.

I eschewed THREED.VBX and other custom controls for several reasons. First, I didn't want to require that the user install a 60K custom control just to have a few three-dimensional lines appear on the form. More importantly though, Line controls are essentially free in terms of system resource usage, while the three-dimensional panels and other elements in THREED.VBX consume considerable resources. Thus, the use of Line controls rather than three-dimensional panels makes VB Typographer a leaner, meaner little application, one that you can use without fear of running low on system resources.

For even greater efficiency, you can use the Line method to draw lines directly on a form during the Form_Paint event. This eliminates the tiny resource usage of Line controls. However, it also means that you must redraw the lines when the form needs to be repainted, or set the form's AutoRedraw property to True. ∎

VB TYPOGRAPHER

```
'   *  *  *  *  *  *  *  *  *  *  *  *  *  *  *  *  *  *  *  *  *  *  *  *
'   FONTVIEW.FRM
'   Copyright (c) 1993 by Paul Bonner
'   PC Magazine Visual Basic Utilities
'   *  *  *  *  *  *  *  *  *  *  *  *  *  *  *  *  *  *  *  *  *  *  *  *
VERSION 2.00
Begin Form Typographer
    BackColor        =    &H00C0C0C0&
    Caption          =    "VB Typographer"
    Height           =    6345
    Icon             =    FONTVIEW.FRX:0000
    Left             =    1905
    LinkTopic        =    "Form1"
    ScaleHeight      =    5655
    ScaleWidth       =    7860
    Top              =    1125
    Width            =    7980
    Begin CommandButton Command1
        Caption      =    "&Select All"
        Height       =    280
        Left         =    480
        TabIndex     =    2
        Top          =    80
        Width        =    1455
    End
    Begin CommonDialog CMDialog1
        Left         =    0
        Top          =    0
    End
    Begin CheckBox Check1
        BackColor    =    &H00C0C0C0&
        Caption      =    "&Bold"
        Height       =    375
        Index        =    0
        Left         =    2640
        TabIndex     =    3
        Top          =    0
        Width        =    735
    End
    Begin PictureBox Picture1
        Align        =    2    'Align Bottom
        BackColor    =    &H00C0C0C0&
        BorderStyle  =    0    'None
        Height       =    330
        Left         =    0
        ScaleHeight  =    330
        ScaleWidth   =    7860
        TabIndex     =    8
        TabStop      =    0    'False
        Top          =    5325
        Width        =    7860
        Begin Label lbAsciiChar
            BackStyle    =    0    'Transparent
            Caption      =    "lbAsciiChar"
```

```
            FontBold          =     0      'False
            FontItalic        =     0      'False
            FontName          =     "MS Sans Serif"
            FontSize          =     9.75
            FontStrikethru    =     0      'False
            FontUnderline     =     0      'False
            Height            =     495
            Left              =     6360
            TabIndex          =     10
            Top               =     60
            Width             =     1455
         End
         Begin Line BottomWhiteLine
            BorderColor       =     &H00FFFFFF&
            X1                =     4920
            X2                =     6120
            Y1                =     -240
            Y2                =     240
         End
         Begin Line BottomGrayLine
            BorderColor       =     &H00808080&
            X1                =     5160
            X2                =     6360
            Y1                =     120
            Y2                =     600
         End
         Begin Label lbStatBar
            BackColor         =     &H00C0C0C0&
            BackStyle         =     0      'Transparent
            Caption           =     "Label2"
            FontBold          =     0      'False
            FontItalic        =     0      'False
            FontName          =     "MS Sans Serif"
            FontSize          =     9.75
            FontStrikethru    =     0      'False
            FontUnderline     =     0      'False
            Height            =     255
            Left              =     120
            TabIndex          =     9
            Top               =     60
            Width             =     4455
         End
      End
      Begin Grid DisplayGrid
         BackColor            =     &H00C0C0C0&
         Cols                 =     9
         GridLines            =     0      'False
         Height               =     4095
         HighLight            =     0      'False
         Left                 =     2520
         TabIndex             =     1
         Top                  =     600
         Visible              =     0      'False
         Width                =     5175
      End
      Begin ComboBox Combo1
         Height               =     300
         Left                 =     6120
         Style                =     2      'Dropdown List
         TabIndex             =     7
         Top                  =     60
         Width                =     1335
      End
      Begin ListBox FontList
         Height               =     4125
```

```
        Left               =    120
        MultiSelect        =    2    'Extended
        Sorted             =    -1   'True
        TabIndex           =    0
        Top                =    600
        Width              =    2295
     End
     Begin CheckBox Check1
        BackColor          =    &H00C0C0C0&
        Caption            =    "&Underline"
        Height             =    375
        Index              =    2
        Left               =    4320
        TabIndex           =    5
        Top                =    0
        Width              =    1215
     End
     Begin CheckBox Check1
        BackColor          =    &H00C0C0C0&
        Caption            =    "&Italic"
        Height             =    375
        Index              =    1
        Left               =    3480
        TabIndex           =    4
        Top                =    0
        Width              =    735
     End
     Begin Line DemoLine1
        BorderColor        =    &H00404040&
        Index              =    3
        X1                 =    7800
        X2                 =    7920
        Y1                 =    4680
        Y2                 =    5040
     End
     Begin Line DemoLine1
        BorderColor        =    &H00404040&
        Index              =    2
        X1                 =    7680
        X2                 =    7800
        Y1                 =    4800
        Y2                 =    5160
     End
     Begin Line DemoLine1
        BorderColor        =    &H00FFFFFF&
        Index              =    1
        X1                 =    7440
        X2                 =    7560
        Y1                 =    4800
        Y2                 =    5160
     End
     Begin Line DemoLine1
        BorderColor        =    &H00FFFFFF&
        Index              =    0
        X1                 =    7320
        X2                 =    7440
        Y1                 =    4800
        Y2                 =    5160
     End
     Begin Label lbTypeDemo
        BackColor          =    &H00FFFFFF&
        BackStyle          =    0    'Transparent
      Caption           =    "Now is the time for all good men to come to the ⇔
    aid of their country."
```

```
        FontBold          =    0    'False
        FontItalic        =    0    'False
        FontName          =    "MS Sans Serif"
        FontSize          =    9.75
        FontStrikethru    =    0    'False
        FontUnderline     =    0    'False
        Height            =    255
        Left              =    120
        TabIndex          =    11
        Top               =    4920
        Width             =    7605
     End
     Begin Line TopWhiteLine
        BorderColor       =    &H00FFFFFF&
        X1                =    1800
        X2                =    3000
        Y1                =    360
        Y2                =    0
     End
     Begin Line TopGrayLine
        BorderColor       =    &H00808080&
        X1                =    2160
        X2                =    2880
        Y1                =    360
        Y2                =    120
     End
     Begin Label lbFontSize
        Alignment         =    1    'Right Justify
        AutoSize          =    -1   'True
        BackStyle         =    0    'Transparent
        Caption           =    "&Size: "
        Height            =    195
        Left              =    5640
        TabIndex          =    6
        Top               =    120
        Width             =    495
     End
     Begin Menu filemenu
        Caption           =    "&File"
        Begin Menu fItem
           Caption           =    "Print &Line Samples..."
           Index             =    0
        End
        Begin Menu fItem
           Caption           =    "Print &Page Samples..."
           Index             =    1
        End
        Begin Menu fItem
           Caption           =    "Printer Set&up..."
           Index             =    2
        End
        Begin Menu fItem
           Caption           =    "-"
           Index             =    3
        End
        Begin Menu fItem
           Caption           =    "&Exit"
           Index             =    4
        End
     End
     Begin Menu optMenu
        Caption           =    "&Options"
        Begin Menu optItem
           Caption           =    "&Set Label Font"
```

```
               Index              =     0
            End
            Begin Menu optItem
               Caption            =     "-"
               Index              =     1
            End
            Begin Menu optItem
               Caption            =     "&About VB Typographer..."
               Index              =     2
            End
         End
      End
End
DefInt A-Z
Option Explicit

Sub Check1_Click (Index As Integer)
' * * * * * * * * * * * * * * * * * * * * * * * * * * * * *
' * update Grid font attributes when user picks new font style
' * * * * * * * * * * * * * * * * * * * * * * * * * * * * *
CheckAttributes
End Sub

Sub Combo1_Click ()
' * * * * * * * * * * * * * * * * * * * * * * * * * * * * *
' * update Grid font attributes when user picks new font size
' * * * * * * * * * * * * * * * * * * * * * * * * * * * * *
CheckAttributes
End Sub

Sub Command1_Click ()
' * * * * * * * * * * * * * * * * * * * * * * * * * * * * *
' * select all type faces
' * * * * * * * * * * * * * * * * * * * * * * * * * * * * *
Dim X%
For X% = 0 To FontList.ListCount - 1
   FontList.Selected(X) = True
Next
End Sub

Sub DisplayGrid_RowColChange ()
' * * * * * * * * * * * * * * * * * * * * * * * * * * * * *
' * display ASCII code for newly selected character
' * * * * * * * * * * * * * * * * * * * * * * * * * * * * *
lbAsciiChar = ""
On Error Resume Next
lbAsciiChar = "CHR$(" & Asc(DisplayGrid.Text) & ")"
End Sub

Sub fItem_Click (Index As Integer)
' * * * * * * * * * * * * * * * * * * * * * * * * * * * * *
' * process file menu
' * * * * * * * * * * * * * * * * * * * * * * * * * * * * *
Dim X%
' * * * * * * * * * * * * * * * * * * * * * * * * * * * * *
' * if item 1 or 2 selected, verify that user wants to print
' * * * * * * * * * * * * * * * * * * * * * * * * * * * * *
If Index < 2 Then If Not VerifyPrintRequest%(Index) Then Exit Sub
' * * * * * * * * * * * * * * * * * * * * * * * * * * * * *
' * attempt to set printer font to DefFont$
' * jump to BadDefFontName routine if error occurs
' * * * * * * * * * * * * * * * * * * * * * * * * * * * * *
On Error GoTo BadDefFontName
If Index < 2 Then
DefFontTest:
```

```
      Printer.FontName = DefFont$
   End If
   On Error GoTo 0
   ' * * * * * * * * * * * * * * * * * * * * * * * * * *
   ' * switch based on menu selection
   ' * * * * * * * * * * * * * * * * * * * * * * * * * *
   Select Case Index
   Case Is = 0 'print line showings
      PrintLineSamples
      CheckAttributes
   Case Is = 1    ' print page samples
      PrintPageSamples
      CheckAttributes
   Case Is = 2      ' printer setup
        PrinterSetup
   Case Is = 4 '  exit
      End
   End Select
   Screen.MousePointer = 0
   Exit Sub

BadDefFontName:
   ' * * * * * * * * * * * * * * * * * * * * * * * * * *
   ' * DefFont$ not available--so tell the user
   ' * then load and display SetFontForm
   ' * * * * * * * * * * * * * * * * * * * * * * * * * *
      Beep
      MsgBox "You must select a label font!"
      SetFontForm.Show 1
      Resume DefFontTest
End Sub

Sub FontList_Click ()
Select Case FontList.SelCount
Case Is > 1
   ' * * * * * * * * * * * * * * * * * * * * * * * * * *
   ' * more than one font selected
   ' * so just update the status bar
   ' * * * * * * * * * * * * * * * * * * * * * * * * * *
      lbStatBar = FontList.SelCount & " fonts selected."
Case Else
   ' * * * * * * * * * * * * * * * * * * * * * * * * * *
   ' * single font selected
   ' * try to display it on type demo label and grid
   ' * * * * * * * * * * * * * * * * * * * * * * * * * *
      On Error GoTo BadFont
      lbTypeDemo.FontName = FontList.List(FontList.ListIndex)
      On Error GoTo 0
      DisplayGrid.FontName = lbTypeDemo.FontName
      CheckAttributes
End Select

Re:
Exit Sub

BadFont:
   ' * * * * * * * * * * * * * * * * * * * * * * * * * *
   ' * selected font not available
   ' * use status bar to tell user
   ' * * * * * * * * * * * * * * * * * * * * * * * * * *
      DisplayGrid.Visible = False
    lbStatBar = "No screen font available for " + FontList.List(FontList. ⇔
      ListIndex)
      Resume Re
```

```
End Sub

Sub Form_Load ()
Set F = Me
F.MousePointer = 11
' * * * * * * * * * * * * * * * * * * * * * * * * * *
' * call form setup routine
' * * * * * * * * * * * * * * * * * * * * * * * * * *
SetUpTypographer
' * * * * * * * * * * * * * * * * * * * * * * * * * *
' * show form
' * * * * * * * * * * * * * * * * * * * * * * * * * *
Me.Visible = True
' * * * * * * * * * * * * * * * * * * * * * * * * * *
' * trigger fontlist_click procedure
' * * * * * * * * * * * * * * * * * * * * * * * * * *
FontList_Click
F.MousePointer = 0
End Sub

Sub Form_Resize ()
If WindowState = 1 Then Exit Sub
' * * * * * * * * * * * * * * * * * * * * * * * * * *
' * hide form
' * then resize control elements
' * * * * * * * * * * * * * * * * * * * * * * * * * *
Me.Visible = False
' * * * * * * * * * * * * * * * * * * * * * * * * * *
' * size FontList
' * * * * * * * * * * * * * * * * * * * * * * * * * *
Dim B%
B% = Height - 2120
If B% < 400 Then B% = 400
FontList.Height = B%
' * * * * * * * * * * * * * * * * * * * * * * * * * *
' * size DisplayGrid
' * * * * * * * * * * * * * * * * * * * * * * * * * *
DisplayGrid.Height = FontList.Height
B% = Width - (DisplayGrid.Left + 200)
If B% < 1500 Then B% = 1500
DisplayGrid.Width = B%
' * * * * * * * * * * * * * * * * * * * * * * * * * *
' * size lbTypeDemo
' * * * * * * * * * * * * * * * * * * * * * * * * * *
lbTypeDemo.Top = FontList.Height + FontList.Top + 95     '105
lbTypeDemo.Width = Width - 360
' * * * * * * * * * * * * * * * * * * * * * * * * * *
' * size lbTypeDemo 3D border
' * * * * * * * * * * * * * * * * * * * * * * * * * *
Dim X1%, X2%, Y1%, Y2%
X1% = lbTypeDemo.Left - 20
X2% = lbTypeDemo.Left + lbTypeDemo.Width + 20
Y1% = lbTypeDemo.Top - 40
Y2% = lbTypeDemo.Top + lbTypeDemo.Height + 40
DemoLine1(0).X1 = X1%
DemoLine1(0).X2 = X2%
DemoLine1(0).Y1 = Y1%
DemoLine1(0).Y2 = Y1%
DemoLine1(1).X1 = X1%
DemoLine1(1).X2 = X1%
DemoLine1(1).Y1 = Y1%
DemoLine1(1).Y2 = Y2%
DemoLine1(2).X1 = X1%
DemoLine1(2).X2 = X2%
```

```
DemoLine1(2).Y1 = Y2%
DemoLine1(2).Y2 = Y2%
DemoLine1(3).X1 = X2%
DemoLine1(3).X2 = X2%
DemoLine1(3).Y1 = Y1%
DemoLine1(3).Y2 = Y2%
' * * * * * * * * * * * * * * * * * * * * * * * * *
' * size status bar 3D line
' * * * * * * * * * * * * * * * * * * * * * * * * *
BottomWhiteLine.X2 = Width
BottomGrayLine.X2 = Width
TopGrayLine.X2 = Width
TopWhiteLine.X2 = Width
' * * * * * * * * * * * * * * * * * * * * * * * * *
' * resize grid rows
' * * * * * * * * * * * * * * * * * * * * * * * * *
SizeRows
' * * * * * * * * * * * * * * * * * * * * * * * * *
' * show form
' * * * * * * * * * * * * * * * * * * * * * * * * *
Me.Visible = True
End Sub

Sub optItem_Click (Index As Integer)
' * * * * * * * * * * * * * * * * * * * * * * * * *
' * process Options menu
' * * * * * * * * * * * * * * * * * * * * * * * * *
Select Case Index
Case 0    'Select font
   SetFontForm.Show 1
Case 1    'separator
Case 2    'About
' * * * * * * * * * * * * * * * * * * * * * * * * *
'    * Display copyright notice
' * * * * * * * * * * * * * * * * * * * * * * * * *
  MsgBox "VB Typographer" + Chr$(13) + Chr$(10) + "Copyright (c) 1993, by ⇔
     Paul Bonner" + Chr$(13) + Chr$(10) + "PC Magazine Visual Basic ⇔
     Utilities", 64, "About VB Typographer"
End Select
End Sub
```

LISTING

LOADFORM

```
'    * * * * * * * * * * * * * * * * * * * * * * * * *
'    LOADFORM.FRM
'    Copyright (c) 1993 by Paul Bonner
'    PC Magazine Visual Basic Utilities
'    * * * * * * * * * * * * * * * * * * * * * * * * *
VERSION 2.00
Begin Form LoadForm
   BackColor        =    &H00C0C0C0&
   BorderStyle      =    3  'Fixed Double
   Caption          =    "VB Typographer"
```

```
        ControlBox       =    0      'False
        Height           =    1470
        Left             =    4575
        LinkTopic        =    "Form2"
        MaxButton        =    0      'False
        MinButton        =    0      'False
        ScaleHeight      =    1065
        ScaleWidth       =    2460
        Top              =    3720
        Width            =    2580
        Begin Label Label2
            BackStyle        =    0      'Transparent
            Caption          =    "1"
            FontBold         =    -1     'True
            FontItalic       =    0      'False
            FontName         =    "MS Sans Serif"
            FontSize         =    9.75
            FontStrikethru   =    0      'False
            FontUnderline    =    0      'False
            Height           =    255
            Left             =    1560
            TabIndex         =    1
            Top              =    360
            Width            =    1215
        End
        Begin Label Label1
            AutoSize         =    -1     'True
            BackStyle        =    0      'Transparent
            Caption          =    "Loading font:"
            FontBold         =    -1     'True
            FontItalic       =    0      'False
            FontName         =    "MS Sans Serif"
            FontSize         =    9.75
            FontStrikethru   =    0      'False
            FontUnderline    =    0      'False
            Height           =    240
            Left             =    120
            TabIndex         =    0
            Top              =    360
            Width            =    1350
        End
End
DefInt A-Z
Option Explicit

Sub Form_Load ()
Screen.MousePointer = 11
Left = (Screen.Width - Width) / 2
Top = (Screen.Height - Height) / 2
End Sub

Sub Form_Unload (Cancel As Integer)
Screen.MousePointer = 0
End Sub
```

LISTING

SETFONTFORM

```
'  * * * * * * * * * * * * * * * * * * * * * * * * *
'  SETFONTFORM.FRM
'  Copyright (c) 1993 by Paul Bonner
'  PC Magazine Visual Basic Utilities
'  * * * * * * * * * * * * * * * * * * * * * * * * *
VERSION 2.00
Begin Form SetFontForm
   BackColor       =    &H00C0C0C0&
   BorderStyle     =    3   'Fixed Double
   Caption         =    "Set Label Font"
   ControlBox      =    0   'False
   Height          =    3045
   Left            =    2610
   LinkTopic       =    "Form1"
   MaxButton       =    0   'False
   MinButton       =    0   'False
   ScaleHeight     =    2640
   ScaleWidth      =    5295
   Top             =    2925
   Width           =    5415
   Begin CommandButton Command1
      BackColor     =      &H00FFFFFF&
      Cancel        =      -1  'True
      Caption       =      "Cancel"
      Height        =      375
      Index         =      1
      Left          =      4200
      TabIndex      =      5
      Top           =      600
      Width         =      975
   End
   Begin CommandButton Command1
      BackColor     =      &H00FFFFFF&
      Caption       =      "OK"
      Height        =      375
      Index         =      0
      Left          =      4200
      TabIndex      =      4
      Top           =      120
      Width         =      975
   End
   Begin ComboBox Combo1
      BackColor     =      &H00FFFFFF&
      Height        =      300
      Left          =      720
      TabIndex      =      0
      Text          =      "Combo1"
      Top           =      1200
      Width         =      3375
   End
   Begin Label Label3
      BackColor     =      &H00C0C0C0&
      Caption       =      "&Fonts:"
      Height        =      255
```

```
            Left                =    120
            TabIndex            =    3
            Top                 =    1245
            Width               =    615
         End
         Begin Label Label2
            BackColor           =    &H00C0C0C0&
            Caption          =    "Select the font that VB Typographer should use ⇔
         to print headers and labels for the Page Samples and Line Samples ⇔
         sheets. (Helvetica or Arial would be a good choice if either is ⇔
         available on your system.)"
            Height              =    975
            Left                =    120
            TabIndex            =    2
            Top                 =    120
            Width               =    3855
         End
         Begin Label Label1
            BackColor           =    &H00FFFFFF&
            BorderStyle         =    1     'Fixed Single
            FontBold            =    -1    'True
            FontItalic          =    -1    'True
            FontName            =    "MS Sans Serif"
            FontSize            =    15
            FontStrikethru      =    0     'False
            FontUnderline       =    0     'False
            Height              =    855
            Left                =    120
            TabIndex            =    1
            Top                 =    1680
            Width               =    4935
         End
   End
Option Explicit
DefInt A-Z

Sub Combo1_Click ()
' * * * * * * * * * * * * * * * * * * * * * * * * * * * * * * *
' * display sample of selected font
' * * * * * * * * * * * * * * * * * * * * * * * * * * * * * * *
Label1 = "This is a sample of the current selection."
On Error GoTo BadFont
Label1.FontName = Combo1
On Error GoTo 0

Re:
    Exit Sub
BadFont:
' * * * * * * * * * * * * * * * * * * * * * * * * * * * * * * *
' * beep and display error message if font not available
' * * * * * * * * * * * * * * * * * * * * * * * * * * * * * * *
    Beep
    Label1 = "No screen font available!"
    Resume Re
End Sub

Sub Command1_Click (Index As Integer)
Select Case Index
Case 0     'ok
   DefFont$ = Combo1
Case 1     'cancel
End Select
Unload SetFontForm
```

```
End Sub

Sub Form_Load ()
'   *  *  *  *  *  *  *  *  *  *  *  *  *  *  *  *  *  *  *  *  *  *  *  *  *
'   * center form
'   *  *  *  *  *  *  *  *  *  *  *  *  *  *  *  *  *  *  *  *  *  *  *  *  *
Left = (Screen.Width - Width) / 2
Top = (Screen.Height - Height) / 2
Dim X%
'   *  *  *  *  *  *  *  *  *  *  *  *  *  *  *  *  *  *  *  *  *  *  *  *  *
'   * fill font list box from main form font list
'   *  *  *  *  *  *  *  *  *  *  *  *  *  *  *  *  *  *  *  *  *  *  *  *  *
For X% = 0 To F.FontList.ListCount - 1
    Combo1.AddItem F.FontList.List(X%)
Next X%
If Combo1.ListCount > 0 Then Combo1.ListIndex = 0
End Sub
```

LISTING

FONTVIEW

```
'   *  *  *  *  *  *  *  *  *  *  *  *  *  *  *  *  *  *  *  *  *  *  *  *  *
'   FONTVIEW.BAS
'   Copyright (c) 1993 by Paul Bonner
'   PC Magazine Visual Basic Utilities
'   *  *  *  *  *  *  *  *  *  *  *  *  *  *  *  *  *  *  *  *  *  *  *  *  *
DefInt A-Z
Option Explicit
Global F As Form
Global DefFont$
Dim PrintLine$(4)
Const CopyRight$ = "by VB Typographer. Copyright (c) 1993 Paul Bonner, PCM ⇔
    Visual Basic Utilities"
Type PointAPI
    X As Integer
    Y As Integer
End Type
Dim OffSet As PointAPI
Dim PhySize As PointAPI

Type TextMetric
    tmHeight As Integer
    tmAscent As Integer
    tmDescent As Integer
    tmInternalLeading As Integer
    tmExternalLeading As Integer
    tmAveCharWidth As Integer
    tmMaxCharWidth As Integer
    tmWeight As Integer
    tmItalic As String * 1
    tmUnderlined As String * 1
    tmStruckOut As String * 1
    tmFirstChar As String * 1
    tmLastChar As String * 1
```

```
      tmDefaultChar As String * 1
      tmBreakChar As String * 1
      tmPitchAndFamily As String * 1
      tmCharSet As String * 1
      tmOverhang As Integer
      tmDigitizedAspectX As Integer
      tmDigitizedAspectY As Integer
End Type
Dim TextStuff As TextMetric
Declare Function GetTextMetrics Lib "GDI" (ByVal hDC As Integer, lpMetrics ⇔
   As TextMetric) As Integer
Declare Function SetTextAlign Lib "GDI" (ByVal hDC%, ByVal wFlags%) As Integer
Const TA_BASELINE = 24

Function BuildLineSample$ ()
' * * * * * * * * * * * * * * * * * * * * * * * * * *
' * build output string for line samples
' * * * * * * * * * * * * * * * * * * * * * * * * * *
Dim X%, Sample$
For X% = 65 To 90 'upper case letter
    Sample$ = Sample$ + Chr$(X%)
Next
For X% = 97 To 122 'lower case letters
    Sample$ = Sample$ + Chr$(X%)
Next
For X% = 33 To 64 'remaining low bit chars
    Sample$ = Sample$ + Chr$(X%)
Next
For X% = 123 To 255   'high bit chars
    Sample$ = Sample$ + Chr$(X%)
Next
BuildLineSample$ = Sample$
End Function

Sub CheckAttributes ()
' * * * * * * * * * * * * * * * * * * * * * * * * * *
' * update display to reflect style and font size choices
' * * * * * * * * * * * * * * * * * * * * * * * * * *
F.MousePointer = 11
F.DisplayGrid.Visible = False
Dim X&, l$, c%
' * * * * * * * * * * * * * * * * * * * * * * * * * *
' * Set Bold
' * * * * * * * * * * * * * * * * * * * * * * * * * *
c% = F.Check1(0)
F.DisplayGrid.FontBold = True * c%
F.lbTypeDemo.FontBold = True * c%
If c% = 1 Then l$ = l$ + "Bold "
' * * * * * * * * * * * * * * * * * * * * * * * * * *
' * Set Italic
' * * * * * * * * * * * * * * * * * * * * * * * * * *
c% = F.Check1(1)
F.DisplayGrid.FontItalic = True * c%
F.lbTypeDemo.FontItalic = True * c%
If c% = 1 Then l$ = l$ + "Italic "
' * * * * * * * * * * * * * * * * * * * * * * * * * *
' * Set Underline
' * * * * * * * * * * * * * * * * * * * * * * * * * *
c% = F.Check1(2)
F.DisplayGrid.FontUnderline = True * c%
F.lbTypeDemo.FontUnderline = True * c%
If c% = 1 Then l$ = l$ + "Underline "
' * * * * * * * * * * * * * * * * * * * * * * * * * *
' * Set Size
```

```
'  * * * * * * * * * * * * * * * * * * * * * * * * * * *
F.DisplayGrid.FontSize = Val(F.Combo1)
'  * * * * * * * * * * * * * * * * * * * * * * * * * * *
' * resize grid rows
'  * * * * * * * * * * * * * * * * * * * * * * * * * * *
SizeRows
F.lbStatBar=F.Combo1.List(F.Combo1.ListIndex)&"point"+F.DisplayGrid.⇔
    FontName + " " + l$
If F.Visible Then F.DisplayGrid.Visible = True
F.MousePointer = 0
End Sub

Function CheckYLoc () As Integer
'  * * * * * * * * * * * * * * * * * * * * * * * * * * *
' * check if room for another line on page
'  * * * * * * * * * * * * * * * * * * * * * * * * * * *
CheckYLoc = True
IfPrinter.TextHeight("J")+Printer.CurrentY>PhySize.Y-(4*OffSet.Y)Then
    CheckYLoc = False
End If
End Function

Sub Draw3DSeparator (c As Control, Y%)
'  * * * * * * * * * * * * * * * * * * * * * * * * * * *
' * draw 3D line on form
'  * * * * * * * * * * * * * * * * * * * * * * * * * * *
c.X1 = 0
c.X2 = F.Width
c.Y1 = Y%
c.Y2 = Y%
End Sub

Sub DrawVertLine ()
'  * * * * * * * * * * * * * * * * * * * * * * * * * * *
' * draw line on printed page
'  * * * * * * * * * * * * * * * * * * * * * * * * * * *
Dim X1%, X2%, YL%
Printer.DrawWidth = 5
YL% = Printer.CurrentY - (Printer.TextHeight("A") / 4)
X1% = OffSet.X
X2% = Printer.ScaleWidth - (OffSet.X)
Printer.Line (X1%, YL%)-(X2%, YL%)
End Sub

Sub GetFonts ()
'  * * * * * * * * * * * * * * * * * * * * * * * * * * *
' * load printer fonts into font list
'  * * * * * * * * * * * * * * * * * * * * * * * * * * *
LoadForm.Show
Dim fc%, X%, Y%
fc% = Printer.FontCount
'  * * * * * * * * * * * * * * * * * * * * * * * * * * *
' * exit if no fonts to load
'  * * * * * * * * * * * * * * * * * * * * * * * * * * *
If fc% = 0 Then Unload LoadForm: Exit Sub
For X% = 1 To fc%
    Y% = DoEvents()
    F.FontList.AddItem Printer.Fonts(X%)
    LoadForm.Label2 = Str$(X%)   'show how many loaded
Next
'  * * * * * * * * * * * * * * * * * * * * * * * * * * *
' * Remove blank entries from list
'  * * * * * * * * * * * * * * * * * * * * * * * * * * *
Do While F.FontList.List(0) = ""
```

```
    F.FontList.RemoveItem (0)
Loop
F.FontList.ListIndex = 0
Unload LoadForm
End Sub

Sub GetPrinterInfo ()
Dim X%
'   * * * * * * * * * * * * * * * * * * * * * * * * *
'   * get printer characteristics
'   * * * * * * * * * * * * * * * * * * * * * * * * *
Printer.ScaleMode = 1
OffSet.X = (Printer.Width - Printer.ScaleWidth) / 2
OffSet.y = (Printer.Height - Printer.ScaleHeight) / 2
Physize.X = Printer.Width
Physize.y = Printer.Height
End Sub


Sub MultiWrap (Sample$, XPos%, LineSpacer%)
'   * * * * * * * * * * * * * * * * * * * * * * * * *
'   * wrap multiple lines of text
'   * * * * * * * * * * * * * * * * * * * * * * * * *
Dim S%, Sy%
Dim LC%, L1$
L1$ = ""
If LineSpacer% <> 0 Then
    Printer.ScaleMode = 2
    Sy% = Printer.CurrentY
    Printer.ScaleMode = 1
End If
Wrapper:
    LC% = LC% + 1
    Printer.CurrentX = XPos%
'   * * * * * * * * * * * * * * * * * * * * * * * * *
'   * get first line to print
'   * * * * * * * * * * * * * * * * * * * * * * * * *
    WrapLine Sample$, L1$, 5
'   * * * * * * * * * * * * * * * * * * * * * * * * *
'   * try to break at a space
'   * * * * * * * * * * * * * * * * * * * * * * * * *
    If Sample$ <> "" Then
        If Left$(Sample$, 1) <> Chr$(32) Then
            For S% = Len(L1$) - 1 To 1 Step -1
                If Mid$(L1$, S%, 1) = Chr$(32) Then
                    Sample$ = Mid$(L1$, S% + 1) + Sample$
                    L1$ = Left$(L1$, S% - 1)
                    Exit For
                End If
            Next
        End If
    End If
'   * * * * * * * * * * * * * * * * * * * * * * * * *
'   * print line
'   * * * * * * * * * * * * * * * * * * * * * * * * *
    Printer.Print L1$;
'   * * * * * * * * * * * * * * * * * * * * * * * * *
'   * if more text to print
'   * * * * * * * * * * * * * * * * * * * * * * * * *
    If Sample$ <> "" Then
        L1$ = ""
'   * * * * * * * * * * * * * * * * * * * * * * * * *
'   * exit if already printed five lines
'   * * * * * * * * * * * * * * * * * * * * * * * * *
        If LC% = 5 Then Exit Sub
```

```
'   * * * * * * * * * * * * * * * * * * * * * * * * * *
'   * start a new line
'   * * * * * * * * * * * * * * * * * * * * * * * * * *
      Printer.Print
      Printer.ScaleMode = 2
      If LineSpacer% <> 0 Then Printer.CurrentY = Sy% + LineSpacer%
      Sy% = Printer.CurrentY
      Printer.ScaleMode = 1
'   * * * * * * * * * * * * * * * * * * * * * * * * * *
'   * jump to Wrapper label
'   * * * * * * * * * * * * * * * * * * * * * * * * * *
      GoTo Wrapper
   End If
End Sub

Sub pOut (P$)
'   * * * * * * * * * * * * * * * * * * * * * * * * * *
'   * output string at OffSet.X
'   * * * * * * * * * * * * * * * * * * * * * * * * * *
Printer.CurrentX = OffSet.X
Printer.Print P$
End Sub

Sub PrinterSetup ()
'   * * * * * * * * * * * * * * * * * * * * * * * * * *
'   * run printer setup dialog
'   * * * * * * * * * * * * * * * * * * * * * * * * * *
      F.CMDialog1.Flags = &H40&
      F.CMDialog1.PrinterDefault = True
      F.CMDialog1.CancelError = True
      On Error Resume Next
      F.CMDialog1.Action = 5
      If Err = 32755 Then Exit Sub
      On Error GoTo 0
      Screen.MousePointer = 11
'   * * * * * * * * * * * * * * * * * * * * * * * * * *
'   * clear font list
'   * * * * * * * * * * * * * * * * * * * * * * * * * *
      F.FontList.Visible = False
      F.FontList.Clear
'   * * * * * * * * * * * * * * * * * * * * * * * * * *
'   * reload fonts
'   * * * * * * * * * * * * * * * * * * * * * * * * * *
      GetFonts
'   * * * * * * * * * * * * * * * * * * * * * * * * * *
'   * reload printer attributes
'   * * * * * * * * * * * * * * * * * * * * * * * * * *
      GetPrinterInfo
      F.FontList.Visible = True
      If F.FontList.ListCount Then F.FontList.ListIndex = 0
      Screen.MousePointer = 0
End Sub

Sub PrintLineSamples ()
'   * * * * * * * * * * * * * * * * * * * * * * * * * *
'   * print line sample pages
'   * * * * * * * * * * * * * * * * * * * * * * * * * *
Dim Test$, Y%, TotHeight%, Sample$, X%, l%, L1$, FontName$
Screen.MousePointer = 11
F.Enabled = False
'   * * * * * * * * * * * * * * * * * * * * * * * * * *
'   * get printer attributes
'   * * * * * * * * * * * * * * * * * * * * * * * * * *
Printer.ScaleMode=2
```

```
GetPrinterInfo
' * * * * * * * * * * * * * * * * * * * * * * * * * * *
' * print page header
' * * * * * * * * * * * * * * * * * * * * * * * * * * *
PrintLSHeader
For Y% = 0 To F.FontList.ListCount - 1
    If F.FontList.Selected(Y%) Then
        FontName$ = F.FontList.List(Y%)
        X% = DoEvents()
        If FontName$ <> "" Then
' * * * * * * * * * * * * * * * * * * * * * * * * * * *
' * print font name
' * * * * * * * * * * * * * * * * * * * * * * * * * * *
            SetSampleFont FontName$, 16
            F.lbStatBar = "Printing " + FontName$
            Sample$ = BuildLineSample$()
' * * * * * * * * * * * * * * * * * * * * * * * * * * *
' * wrap sample$ in this font
' * * * * * * * * * * * * * * * * * * * * * * * * * * *
            For l% = 0 To 4
                X% = DoEvents()
                L1$ = PrintLine$(l%)
                If Sample$ <> "" Then
                    WrapLine Sample$, L1$, 5
                    PrintLine$(l%) = L1$
                End If
            Next
' * * * * * * * * * * * * * * * * * * * * * * * * * * *
' * check to see if room for these lines
' * * * * * * * * * * * * * * * * * * * * * * * * * * *
            For l% = 0 To 4
                If PrintLine$(l%) <> "" Then
                TotHeight% = TotHeight% + Printer.TextHeight(PrintLine$(l%))
                End If
' * * * * * * * * * * * * * * * * * * * * * * * * * * *
' * start new page if not enough room
' * * * * * * * * * * * * * * * * * * * * * * * * * * *
            If TotHeight% + Printer.CurrentY > PhySize.Y - (4 * OffSet.Y) Then
                    Printer.NewPage
                    X% = DoEvents()
                    PrintLSHeader
                End If
            Next l%
            TotHeight% = 0
' * * * * * * * * * * * * * * * * * * * * * * * * * * *
' * print font name
' * * * * * * * * * * * * * * * * * * * * * * * * * * *
            SetFontLabelFont
            pOut ""
            pOut FontName$
' * * * * * * * * * * * * * * * * * * * * * * * * * * *
' * print sample lines
' * * * * * * * * * * * * * * * * * * * * * * * * * * *
            SetSampleFont FontName$, 16
            For l% = 0 To 4
                If PrintLine$(l%) <> "" Then pOut PrintLine$(l%)
                PrintLine$(l%) = ""
            Next l%
        End If
    End If
' * * * * * * * * * * * * * * * * * * * * * * * * * * *
' * loop back for next font
' * * * * * * * * * * * * * * * * * * * * * * * * * * *
Next Y%
```

```
Printer.EndDoc
F.lbStatBar = ""
Screen.MousePointer = 0
F.Enabled = True
End Sub

Sub PrintLSHeader ()
' * * * * * * * * * * * * * * * * * * * * * * * *
' * print header for line sample pages
' * * * * * * * * * * * * * * * * * * * * * * * *
SetHeaderFont
Printer.CurrentY = OffSet.Y
Dim H$
H$ = "Line samples " + CopyRight$
pOut ""
Printer.FontSize = 7
' * * * * * * * * * * * * * * * * * * * * * * * *
' * right justify string by padding left with spaces
' * * * * * * * * * * * * * * * * * * * * * * * *
Do While Printer.TextWidth(H$) + OffSet.X < PhySize.X - (4 * OffSet.X)
    H$ = Chr$(32) + H$
Loop
pOut H$
Printer.FontSize = 2
pOut ""
DrawVertLine
pOut ""
End Sub

Sub PrintPageSamples ()
' * * * * * * * * * * * * * * * * * * * * * * * *
' * print page samples
' * * * * * * * * * * * * * * * * * * * * * * * *
Const PS$ = "ABCDEFGHIJKLMNOPQRSTUVWXYZabcdefghijklmnopqrstuvwxyz1234567890
    !@#$%^&*(){}[] <>+-_=\|/?"
Dim FontName$, Y%, L1$, Sample$, z%, X%
Dim Lh&, oy%, Ask$, H$
Screen.MousePointer = 11
F.Enabled = False
For X% = 0 To F.FontList.ListCount - 1
    If F.FontList.Selected(X) Then
' * * * * * * * * * * * * * * * * * * * * * * * *
' *   move to top of page
' * * * * * * * * * * * * * * * * * * * * * * * *
        Printer.CurrentY = OffSet.Y
        z% = SetTextAlign(Printer.hDC, TA_BASELINE)
' * * * * * * * * * * * * * * * * * * * * * * * *
' *   initialize locals
' * * * * * * * * * * * * * * * * * * * * * * * *
        Lh& = 0: oy% = 0: Y% = 0: z% = 0: L1$ = ""
' * * * * * * * * * * * * * * * * * * * * * * * *
' * get font name
' *   print header
' * * * * * * * * * * * * * * * * * * * * * * * *
        FontName$ = F.FontList.List(X%)
        SetFontLabelFont
        Printer.FontUnderline = False
        F.lbStatBar = "Printing " + FontName$
        Printer.CurrentX = OffSet.X
        Printer.Print FontName$ + Chr$(9);
        Printer.FontSize = 7
        H$ = "Page sample " + CopyRight$
        Printer.Print H$
        DrawVertLine
```

```
        Printer.FontSize = 12
        pOut ""
'   *   *   *   *   *   *   *   *   *   *   *   *   *   *   *   *   *   *   *   *
'   *   loop from 6 pts to 48
'   *   *   *   *   *   *   *   *   *   *   *   *   *   *   *   *   *   *   *   *

        For Y% = 6 To 48
            z% = DoEvents()
'   *   *   *   *   *   *   *   *   *   *   *   *   *   *   *   *   *   *   *   *
'   *   skip sizes we don't want to print
'   *   *   *   *   *   *   *   *   *   *   *   *   *   *   *   *   *   *   *   *
            If Y% = 13 Then Y% = 14
            If Y% = 15 Then Y% = 18
            If Y% = 19 Then Y% = 48
'   *   *   *   *   *   *   *   *   *   *   *   *   *   *   *   *   *   *   *   *
'   *   print line label
'   *   *   *   *   *   *   *   *   *   *   *   *   *   *   *   *   *   *   *   *
            SetPageSmallLabelFont
            L1$ = ""
            Sample$ = PS$
'   *   *   *   *   *   *   *   *   *   *   *   *   *   *   *   *   *   *   *   *
'   *   print text at designated size
'   *   *   *   *   *   *   *   *   *   *   *   *   *   *   *   *   *   *   *   *
            Select Case Y%
                Case Is < 48
                    Printer.CurrentX = OffSet.X
                    Printer.Print Str$(Y%) + " pt." + Chr$(9);
                    SetSampleFont FontName$, Y%
                    Z%=Printer.CurrentX
                    WrapLine Sample$, L1$, 5
                    Printer.Print L1$
                    Printer.FontSize = 6
                    Printer.Print
                Case Is = 48
'   *   *   *   *   *   *   *   *   *   *   *   *   *   *   *   *   *   *   *   *
'   *   special case handling for 48 pt text
'   *   tightens up leading from default of 48/56
'   *   *   *   *   *   *   *   *   *   *   *   *   *   *   *   *   *   *   *   *
                    SetPageSmallLabelFont
                    Printer.CurrentX = OffSet.X
                    Printer.Print Str$(Y%) + " pt." + Chr$(9);
                    SetSampleFont FontName$, Y%
                    z% = Printer.CurrentX
                    MultiWrap Sample$, z%, 49
                    Printer.Print
            End Select
            z% = DoEvents()
            Sample$ = ""
            L1$ = ""
            If Y% = 18 Then Printer.FontSize = 20: Printer.Print
        Next Y%
'   *   *   *   *   *   *   *   *   *   *   *   *   *   *   *   *   *   *   *   *
'   *   now print vertical line
'   *   *   *   *   *   *   *   *   *   *   *   *   *   *   *   *   *   *   *   *
        Printer.CurrentY = Printer.CurrentY - 26
        DrawVertLine
        Printer.FontSize = 12
        Printer.Print
'   *   *   *   *   *   *   *   *   *   *   *   *   *   *   *   *   *   *   *   *
'   *   print "By a typographer" quotes
'   *   *   *   *   *   *   *   *   *   *   *   *   *   *   *   *   *   *   *   *
        SetUpQuote FontName$
'   *   *   *   *   *   *   *   *   *   *   *   *   *   *   *   *   *   *   *   *
'   *   end page
```

```
'   * * * * * * * * * * * * * * * * * * * * * * * * * *
        Printer.EndDoc
        z% = DoEvents()
     End If
Next X%
F.Enabled = True
End Sub

Sub PrintQuote (fSize%, Leading%, FontName$)
'   * * * * * * * * * * * * * * * * * * * * * * * *
'   *   routine called by SetUpQuote
'   * * * * * * * * * * * * * * * * * * * * * * * *
 If CheckYLoc() = False Then Exit Sub
 Dim L1$, z%
 z% = OffSet.X
'   * * * * * * * * * * * * * * * * * * * * * * * *
'   *   print font size/leading
'   * * * * * * * * * * * * * * * * * * * * * * * *
 SetPageSmallLabelFont
 Printer.CurrentX = z%
 Printer.Print Trim(Str$(fSize%)) + "/" + Trim$(Str$(Leading%)) + Chr$(9);
 SetSampleFont FontName$, fSize%
 Dim Q1$, Q2$, Q3$, Q4$, Q5$
 z% = Printer.CurrentX
'   * * * * * * * * * * * * * * * * * * * * * * * *
'   *   set up quote strings
'   * * * * * * * * * * * * * * * * * * * * * * * *
Q1$ = "By a Typographer, I do not mean a Printer ... But by a Typographer, I ⇔
     mean one who can either perform, or direct others to perform all the ⇔
     Handy works and Physical Operations relating to Typographie."
Q2$ = " Myles Davies,"
Q3$ = " " + Chr$(145) + "Preface," + Chr$(146)
Q4$ = " Athen" + Chr$(230) + " Britannic" + Chr$(230)
Q5$ = " (1715)"
L1$ = ""
'   * * * * * * * * * * * * * * * * * * * * * * * *
'   *   wrap strings and print
'   * * * * * * * * * * * * * * * * * * * * * * * *
If CheckYLoc() = True Then MultiWrap Q1$ + Q2$ + Q3$, z%, Leading%
Printer.FontItalic = True
WrapQuote Q4$, Leading%, z%
Printer.FontItalic = False
WrapQuote Q5$, Leading%, z%
z% = DoEvents()
If CheckYLoc() = True Then Printer.Print
End Sub

Sub SetFontLabelFont ()
'   * * * * * * * * * * * * * * * * * * * * * * * * * *
'   * set font to DefFont$--12 pt --bold--italic--underline
'   * * * * * * * * * * * * * * * * * * * * * * * * * *
    SetPrinterFont DefFont$, 12, True, True, True
End Sub

Sub SetHeaderFont ()
'   * * * * * * * * * * * * * * * * * * * * * * * * * *
'   * set font to DefFont$--16 pt --bold--italic--no underline
'   * * * * * * * * * * * * * * * * * * * * * * * * * *
    SetPrinterFont DefFont$, 16, True, True, False
End Sub

Sub SetPageSmallLabelFont ()
'   * * * * * * * * * * * * * * * * * * * * * * * * * *
'   * set font to DefFont$--8 pt --no bold--no italic--no underline
```

```
'  * * * * * * * * * * * * * * * * * * * * * * * *
   SetPrinterFont DefFont$, 8, False, False, False
End Sub

Sub SetPrinterFont (fN$, fS%, fB%, fI%, fU%)
'  * * * * * * * * * * * * * * * * * * * * * * * *
' * set printer font as specified in params
'  * * * * * * * * * * * * * * * * * * * * * * * *
   Printer.FontName = fN$
   Printer.FontSize = fS%
   Printer.FontBold = fB%
   Printer.FontItalic = fI%
   Printer.FontUnderline = fU%
End Sub

Sub SetSampleFont (fName$, fSize%)
'  * * * * * * * * * * * * * * * * * * * * * * * *
' * set font to fName$, no bold, no italic, no underline
'  * * * * * * * * * * * * * * * * * * * * * * * *
SetPrinterFont fName$, fSize%, False, False, False
End Sub

Sub SetUpQuote (FontName$)
'  * * * * * * * * * * * * * * * * * * * * * * * *
' * routine used to print Myles Davies quote
'  * * * * * * * * * * * * * * * * * * * * * * * *
Dim X%, z%, Lh&
For X% = 10 To 12 Step 2
   Printer.FontSize = X%
'  * * * * * * * * * * * * * * * * * * * * * * * *
' *   print quote three times in each point size,
' *  increasing leading each time
'  * * * * * * * * * * * * * * * * * * * * * * * *
   For z% = X% To X% + 6 Step 2  ' z%=leading
      If z% = X% + 4 Then z% = X% + 6  ' skip 10/14 and 12/16
      PrintQuote X%, z%, FontName$
      If CheckYLoc() = False Then Exit Sub
   If (X% <> 12) Or (z% <> X% + 6) Then Printer.Print ' print a blank line
   Next
   z% = DoEvents()
Next X%
End Sub

Sub SetUpTypographer ()
'  * * * * * * * * * * * * * * * * * * * * * * * *
' *   VB Typographer initialization routine
'  * * * * * * * * * * * * * * * * * * * * * * * *
DefFont$ = "Arial"
'  * * * * * * * * * * * * * * * * * * * * * * * *
' *   get printer data and fonts
' * display progress on LoadForm
'  * * * * * * * * * * * * * * * * * * * * * * * *
LoadForm.Label1 = "Getting Printer Data..."
LoadForm.Label2 = ""
LoadForm.Show
LoadForm.Refresh
GetPrinterInfo
Unload LoadForm
'  * * * * * * * * * * * * * * * * * * * * * * * *
' *   draw main form
'  * * * * * * * * * * * * * * * * * * * * * * * *
F.lbStatBar = ""
Draw3DSeparator F.TopGrayLine, 420
Draw3DSeparator F.TopWhiteLine, 440
```

```
Draw3DSeparator F.BottomGrayLine, 0
Draw3DSeparator F.BottomWhiteLine, 20
Dim i%, T$, X%
' * * * * * * * * * * * * * * * * * * * * * * * * *
' *   set up grid
' * * * * * * * * * * * * * * * * * * * * * * * * *
T$ = Chr$(9)
F.DisplayGrid.RowHeight(0) = 150
F.DisplayGrid.ColWidth(0) = 300
F.DisplayGrid.Row = 1
For X% = 33 To 40
    F.DisplayGrid.Col = X% - 32
    F.DisplayGrid.Text = Chr$(X%)
    F.DisplayGrid.ColAlignment(X% - 32) = 2    'centered
Next
' * * * * * * * * * * * * * * * * * * * * * * * * *
' *   add character set to grid
' * * * * * * * * * * * * * * * * * * * * * * * * *
For X% = 41 To 255
    i% = i% + 1
    T$ = T$ + Chr$(X%) + Chr$(9)
    If i% = 8 Then
        F.DisplayGrid.AddItem Left$(T$, Len(T$) - 1)
        T$ = Chr$(9)
        i% = 0
    End If
Next
If T$ <> Chr$(9) Then F.DisplayGrid.AddItem T$
F.DisplayGrid.Col = 1
F.DisplayGrid.SelEndCol = 1
F.lbAsciiChar = "CHR$(" & Asc(F.DisplayGrid.Clip) & ")"
' * * * * * * * * * * * * * * * * * * * * * * * * *
' *   load font sizes into combo box
' * * * * * * * * * * * * * * * * * * * * * * * * *
For X% = 7 To 128
    F.Combo1.AddItem Str$(X%)
Next
' * * * * * * * * * * * * * * * * * * * * * * * * *
' *   select 12 pt type as default
' * * * * * * * * * * * * * * * * * * * * * * * * *
F.Combo1.ListIndex = 5
' * * * * * * * * * * * * * * * * * * * * * * * * *
' *   load font names
' * * * * * * * * * * * * * * * * * * * * * * * * *
GetFonts
End Sub

Sub SizeRows ()
' * * * * * * * * * * * * * * * * * * * * * * * * *
' *   adjust grid columns to fit newly selected font
' * * * * * * * * * * * * * * * * * * * * * * * * *
Dim X%, MinWidth%
On Error Resume Next
Typographer.FontName = F.DisplayGrid.FontName
Typographer.FontSize = F.DisplayGrid.FontSize
X% = GetTextMetrics(Typographer.hDC, TextStuff)
MinWidth% = (F.DisplayGrid.Width - 300) / 9
If TextStuff.tmMaxCharWidth * Screen.TwipsPerPixelX > MinWidth% Then
    MinWidth% = TextStuff.tmMaxCharWidth * Screen.TwipsPerPixelX
End If
For X% = 1 To 9
    F.DisplayGrid.ColWidth(X%) = MinWidth%
Next
End Sub
```

```
Function VerifyPrintRequest% (i%)
' * * * * * * * * * * * * * * * * * * * * * * * * *
' *   verify user's print request
' * * * * * * * * * * * * * * * * * * * * * * * * *
VerifyPrintRequest% = True
Dim Ask$, fCount$, l%
fCount$ = " fonts?"
If F.FontList.SelCount > 0 Then
    If F.FontList.SelCount = 1 Then fCount$ = " font?"
    Ask$ = F.FontList.SelCount & " selected"
Else
    Ask$ = "all " & F.FontList.ListCount
End If
If i% = 0 Then
    Ask$ = "Print line samples for " + Ask$
Else
    Ask$ = "Print page samples for " + Ask$
End If
l% = MsgBox(Ask$ + fCount$, 52, "VB Typographer")    ' y/n
If l% <> 6 Then VerifyPrintRequest% = False: Exit Function ' No button selected
' * * * * * * * * * * * * * * * * * * * * * * * * *
' *   select all fonts if user says yes
' * * * * * * * * * * * * * * * * * * * * * * * * *
If Not F.FontList.SelCount > 0 Then
    For l% = 0 To F.FontList.ListCount - 1
        F.FontList.Selected(l%) = True
    Next
End If
End Function

Sub WrapLine (Sample$, L1$, m%)
Dim X%
' * * * * * * * * * * * * * * * * * * * * * * * * *
' *   break specified line at right margin
' *   put line to print into L1$
' *   leave remainder in Sample$
' * * * * * * * * * * * * * * * * * * * * * * * * *
For X% = 1 To Len(Sample$)
 If Printer.TextWidth(Left$(Sample$, X%)) + Printer.CurrentX > PhySize.X - ⇔
    (m% * OffSet.X) Then
        L1$ = L1$ + Left$(Sample$, X% - 1)
        Sample$ = Mid$(Sample$, X%)
        Exit For
    End If
Next X%
If L1$ = "" Then L1$ = Sample$: Sample$ = ""
End Sub

Sub WrapQuote (Sample$, SpaceBetweenLines%, ofX%)
' * * * * * * * * * * * * * * * * * * * * * * * * *
' *   Wrap Myles Davies quote
' * * * * * * * * * * * * * * * * * * * * * * * * *
If Printer.CurrentX = ofX% And CheckYLoc() = False Then Exit Sub
Dim L1$, S%, Sy%, Broke%
Sy% = Printer.CurrentY
' * * * * * * * * * * * * * * * * * * * * * * * * *
' *   get line wrap
' * * * * * * * * * * * * * * * * * * * * * * * * *
WrapLine Sample$, L1$, 5
' * * * * * * * * * * * * * * * * * * * * * * * * *
' *   adjust to break at space
' * * * * * * * * * * * * * * * * * * * * * * * * *
If Sample$ <> "" Then
```

```
    If Left$(Sample$, 1) <> Chr$(32) Then
        For S% = Len(L1$) - 1 To 1 Step -1
            If Mid$(L1$, S%, 1) = Chr$(32) Then
                Sample$ = Mid$(L1$, S% + 1) + Sample$
                L1$ = Left$(L1$, S% - 1)
                Exit For
            End If
        Next
    End If
End If
' * * * * * * * * * * * * * * * * * * * * * * * * *
' *   print first line
' * * * * * * * * * * * * * * * * * * * * * * * * *
Printer.Print L1$;
L1$ = ""
' * * * * * * * * * * * * * * * * * * * * * * * * *
' *   if more to print...print remainder
' * * * * * * * * * * * * * * * * * * * * * * * * *
If Sample$ <> "" Then
    Printer.Print
    Printer.CurrentY = Sy% + SpaceBetweenLines%
    Sy% = Printer.CurrentY
    Printer.CurrentX = ofX%
    WrapLine Sample$, L1$, 5
    If CheckYLoc() = True Then Printer.Print LTrim$(L1$);
End If
End Sub
```

C H A P T E R

6

CLIPS

Clips retains the text from a nearly unlimited number of clipboard operations, and allows you to freely edit or combine clipboard text.

Windows's clipboard has a lot going for it. It employs simple concepts—Cut, Copy, and Paste—to provide ways for you to move, duplicate, or delete data within an application or between applications. And since any Windows application worth its salt supports these standard clipboard functions, the clipboard facility and its basic methods are nearly universal throughout the Windows environment.

For all its good points, however, Windows's clipboard has one big problem: There's only one clipboard. So every time you copy or cut something, the previous contents of the clipboard are lost. That's fine if you're simply moving text around in a document or rearranging a spreadsheet, because in those cases each cut or copy then paste action is a discrete operation. But what if you want to build a new document using a series of discontiguous selections from an existing document? Or to copy some, but

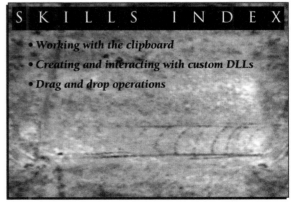

S K I L L S   I N D E X

• *Working with the clipboard*

• *Creating and interacting with custom DLLs*

• *Drag and drop operations*

not all, messages about Visual Basic from the Microsoft BASIC forum on CompuServe? Or to perform any other task where you need to make multiple cuts or copies and then a single paste operation to move the data to a new location?

In those cases, what you need is a clipboard that retains the text from an unlimited
number of cut and copy operations, rather than just one. That's just what Clips, the
subject of this chapter, is designed to do. Clips constantly monitors the status of Windows's clipboard; whenever new text appears there, Clips captures and stores it so
that you can later edit it, combine it with other captured cuts or copies, or make
other use of it.

Clips captures and works with data in text only format. If you cut or copy a
graphic image to the clipboard, Clips will ignore the operation. Similarly, if you cut
or copy rich text (text with font and style attributes) in a word processor or other application that supports rich text, Clips will capture and store only the ASCII text, not
the additional formatting information. Of course, it doesn't interfere with the capability of other applications that *do* support rich text to use the clipboard; Clips simply
ignores the additional formatting information.

■ USING CLIPS

Clips's main screen is dominated by two large controls: a list box at the top of the
window, and then immediately beneath it, a text box. As shown in Figure 6.1, the list
box is contained in a frame labeled Clip Titles, while the text box is contained in a
frame labeled Clip Text.

The first time you load Clips in the current Windows session, both the Clip Titles
list box and the Clip Text text box are empty. If you've previously created and saved a
Clips file, you can open it at this time by using the Open item on Clips's File menu.
Clips makes use of the Windows 3.1 common dialog boxes for selecting a file to open
and for specifying the name and path of a file being saved, as shown in Figure 6.2.

Generally, however, you'll populate the Clip Titles and Clip Text boxes not by
opening a file in Clips, but by switching to another application and copying or cut-
ting text there. Clips monitors any changes in the contents of the clipboard that take
place while another application is active, and captures all new text that you place on
the clipboard. Each time it captures a new clip, Clips beeps your PC's speaker. (For
those who hate noisy PCs, the beep can be disabled by removing the check mark
from the Beep item on Clips's Settings menu.)

FIGURE 6.1

*Clips's main
screen*

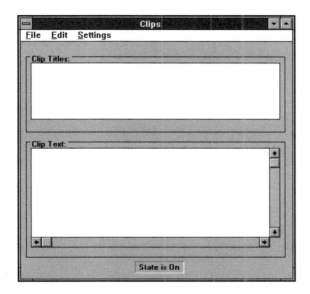

FIGURE 6.2

*Clips makes
use of Win-
dows 3.1's
common dialog
boxes; the
Open File
dialog box is
shown here.*

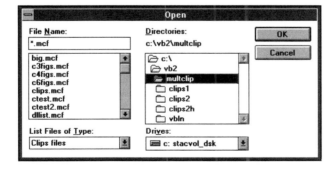

When you switch back to Clips, you'll notice that it has added a title to the Clip
Titles list box for each piece of clipboard text that it has captured. The title can be up
to 60 characters long. Clips assigns it automatically by taking the first 60 characters

of text from the clipboard, stripping off any leading control characters, and then trun-
cating the string at the first carriage return. So if you capture a block of text that reads

```
Mr. Jones was pleased to see what a lovely day it was.
"Why, I think I'll go out for a stroll," he said, and with that he picked up
his hat and his umbrella (because you can never be too careful; a shower might
spoil even the loveliest day) and out the door he went.
```

Clips would assign it the title *Mr. Jones was pleased to see what a lovely day it was.*
Whereas, if you captured this text:

```
Mr. Orlando Jones
12345 Kale Vista Drive,
Mustard Greens, CA 12345
```

Clips would assign it the title *Mr. Orlando Jones.*

Clearly, Clips's automatic assignment of titles makes more sense in some cases than
in others. But rest assured, you can change the title of any clip at any time, by using
the Change Title item on Clips's Edit menu.

The Clip Text box, located beneath the Clip Titles list box, displays the full text of
the active clip whose title is displayed in the Clip Titles list. So if you selected the
first title above (Mr. Jones was…), the text box would display the full two paragraphs
of text that you copied about Mr. Jones's plans to saunter, while if you selected the
second title (Mr. Orlando Jones), the text box would display the address of Mr. Jones's
manse on Kale Vista Drive.

Each time you capture or cut text in an application, another title is added to the
Clip Titles list box. Clips stores the full text that you've placed on the clipboard so
that it can display that text when you select the corresponding title.

If, after you've copied or cut chunks of text, you switch back to Clips, its display
will resemble that shown in Figure 6.3. The Clip Titles list box will display a title for
each item that you've copied or cut since Clips was launched, and the Clip Text box
will display the text of the most recently captured item.

The Clip Text text box is linked to the Clip Titles list box. So each time you select
a new item in the Clip Titles list box, the full text of the clip associated with that title
will be displayed in the Clip Text box.

■ Working with Captured Text

So far, so good. Clips has proven that it can capture any text that's placed on the clipboard. But what can you do with the text that it captures?

Quite a lot, really.

FIGURE 6.3

*Clips's main
screen after it
has captured
several clips*

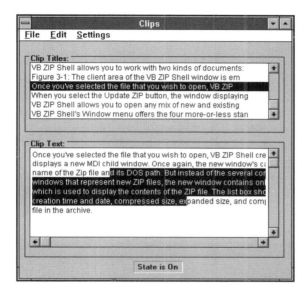

For starters, the text that Clips captures is fully editable. You can add more text to any clip simply by typing it into the Clip Text box, or you can delete text. You can even use the standard cut, copy, and paste commands, either by selecting them from Clips's Edit menu or by pressing the appropriate shortcut keys. Clips is smart enough to know the difference between a copy or cut that takes place in another application, which creates a new clip, and one that takes place inside Clips itself. So don't worry, you can safely copy text in existing clips to your heart's content without having a new clip created each time.

You can also combine text from two or more clips by using one of two different methods. If you want to combine the text from all the clips in the active file, you can simply select Combine All from Clips's Edit menu. Clips will then post the message box shown in Figure 6.4, to confirm that you want to combine all the clips into a single clip.

If you click the Yes button, Clips will combine all the clips in the active file into a single clip, and give that clip a title indicating how many clips were combined. For instance, if there were eleven clips in the file prior to the Combine All procedure, afterwards the text from all eleven clips will have been combined into a single clip with the title "Combined 11 clips." As always, this title can be changed.

FIGURE 6.4
Clips uses this
message box to
confirm
Combine All
requests.

The Combine All operation combines clips in the order in which they appear in the Clip Titles list box, which itself reflects the order in which they were captured. Thus, the first clip in the list box will appear first in the combined clip, followed by the second, followed by the third, and so on. Once all the clips have been combined, all but the combined clip are removed from the list box, as shown in Figure 6.5.

FIGURE 6.5
Following a
Combine All
operation,
Clips presents
a single clip
that contains
all the text
from the
combined clips.

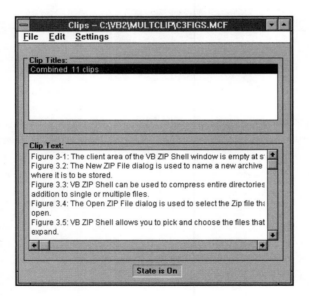

If, on the other hand, you only want to combine some of the clips in the active file, or you want more control over the order in which they are combined, you can use Clips's manual Combine mode by selecting Combine from the Settings menu. When you do so, Clips enters a special mode in which you can drag the text from any number of clips one by one into the clip that was selected at the time you activated Combine Mode.

When Combine mode is active, Clips does not update the Clip Text text box in response to mouse clicks in the Clip Titles list box. Instead, it allows you to drag down an icon representing the newly selected title from the list box and place it into the text box, as shown in Figure 6.6, at which point the clip text associated with that title is inserted into the clip whose text is visible at the current insertion point. Clips remains in Combine mode until you signal that it should end by selecting On or Off from the Settings menu.

FIGURE 6.6

Clips lets you drag the text from one clip into another while Combine mode is active.

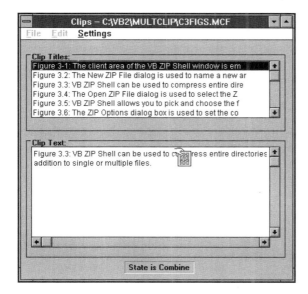

Clips's manual Combine mode capability is quite useful for tasks such as assembling boilerplate documents from a series of captured blocks of text. You can simply drag sentences, paragraphs, or even whole pages of text down into the target clip, assembling them in any order you like. The automatic Combine All facility, meanwhile, is most useful for assembling lists of items for which the sequence doesn't matter. For instance, while browsing an electronic bulletin board's file lists off line, you could highlight and copy the names of the files that you want to download, and then combine them all into a single clip. Then when you go on line and get to a prompt asking you to enter the names of the files you wish to download, you can paste that single clip into the your terminal program, supplying all the file names in one fell swoop.

To copy the text from a clip back onto the clipboard so that you can paste it into another application, you can either highlight the text that you want to copy, or choose the Select All item on the Edit menu to highlight all of the text in the active clip. Then you just select the Copy item from the Edit menu to copy that text back onto the clipboard.

Clips also allows you to save all the current clips into a file, or to reload previously saved clips, using the Open and Save items from its File menu. This capability allows you to use Clips as a storage facility for text that you use frequently. You might save boilerplate paragraphs for standard business letters in a Clips file, or fill-in-the-blank memos, or business forms.

You can change the title of the active selected clip at any time by selecting the Change Title item from the Edit menu. When you do so, Clips opens an input box containing the current title and giving you the opportunity to change it, as shown in Figure 6.7.

FIGURE 6.7

This input box allows you to change the title of a clip.

You also can delete the active clip by selecting the Delete Clip item from Clips's Edit menu. When you do so, Clips posts a standard message box to confirm your choice.

Finally, you can configure several aspects of Clips's operation. You can deactivate Clips so that it doesn't capture text that you copy or cut in other applications by selecting the Off item from Clips's Settings menu. And you can turn off the beep that Clips emits when it captures data by removing the check mark from the Beep item on the Settings menu.

You can also toggle through Clips's three possible states (On, Off, and Combine) by double-clicking on the state indicator label at the bottom of Clips's main screen.

■ INSIDE CLIPS

Clips largely defined itself, designwise. Its most important functional requirements were obvious once I set out to overcome the limitations of Windows's one-chunk-of-text-at-a-time clipboard: Clips had to be able to monitor the Windows clipboard, capture any text that appeared there, and allow the user to access, store, and manipulate that text at will.

As I set out to design Clips, I couldn't help but notice that its data storage and access requirements were not unlike those of VB Code Librarian, the utility presented in Chapter 1 of this book. As was the case with VB Code Librarian, Clips had to store and present to the user a series of text blocks of varying size and content, and to provide the user with a way to quickly select the text block of particular interest at that moment.

I'm not a believer in reinventing the wheel—especially when you've already got one that works well—so you'll notice that structurally and visually, Clips bears a strong resemblance to VB Code Librarian. Both present lists of items (captured clips in Clips's case and stored library routines in VB Code Librarian's case) in a list box, with each item linked to an editable block of text presented in a nearby text box.

The resemblance is more than skin deep. The similarities between the way Clips and VB Code Librarian organize and present data allowed me to base Clips's file-access routines on those used in VB Code Librarian—although with some significant enhancements, as detailed later in this chapter.

The key difference between the two applications, and thus the key design problem I faced in creating Clips, was the need to have Clips monitor the Windows clipboard. It was one thing to say that Clips would capture any text placed on the clipboard, it was another thing to make it happen.

■ Monitoring the Clipboard

Windows provides a very simple way for an application to monitor changes to the clipboard. All the application has to do is use the Windows API function SetClipboardViewer to inform Windows that the application wants to be signaled when the clipboard's contents change.

While Windows has only one clipboard, it can support multiple clipboard viewer applications. One such application is CLIPBRD.EXE, also known as the Clipboard accessory, but any number of other applications can also act as clipboard viewers. When the contents of the clipboard change, Windows sends a special message to the first viewer in the chain. It, in turn, is required to pass the message on to the next viewer in the chain, which in turn passes it to the next, and so on, so that at any one time several applications can process these "the clipboard has changed" messages.

Sounds like a simple solution, doesn't it? There was just one problem. Visual Basic's default message handling procedure discards "the clipboard has changed" messages without blinking an eye, so there was no way for Clips to receive and process them without the help of a dynamic link library (DLL) or custom control that could grab the message before it got to Visual Basic's default message processing routine.

If it was at all possible, I wanted to avoid using a custom control or DLL to help Clips monitor the clipboard. One less file to distribute with an application is one less file to lose, so I explored a variety of ways of monitoring changes to the clipboard without using SetClipboardViewer.

The most obvious solution was to have Clips store the clipboard text that it had most recently captured in a string, and then periodically to compare that with the results of a Clipboard.GetText() function to see if the clipboard's contents had changed. The code would look something like this:

```
B$ = Clipboard.GetText()
If B$ = OldClipText$ Then Exit Sub
' otherwise...
OldClipText$=B$
```

Of course, that meant that Clips would always have to maintain a copy of the old clipboard text in memory, which would be wasteful, and also that it would have to both grab the clipboard text and perform a string comparison every time it called the routine. Both of those processes are time-consuming, and given the fact that Clips would have to call the routine at least once every couple of seconds to make sure that it captured all the clipboard changes, this approach threatened to be a significant drain on system performance.

I looked further, searching the Windows API for anything that would give me a clue as to when the contents of the clipboard had changed.

I thought I had hit pay dirt with the Windows API GetClipboardData() function, which returns not the data itself but rather the handle to the data. As I experimented with GetClipboardData, it seemed to return a different handle whenever the contents of the clipboard changed. That was great news, because it meant that Clips could simply monitor the integer value returned by GetClipboardData, rather than having to indulge in time-consuming string comparisons. But further experimentation revealed that the handle returned by GetClipboardData only changed regularly with applications that use standard, plain-text clipboard formats. For instance, if you copied five things in a row in Notepad, GetClipboardData would return five different handles. But with applications that use private formats to store extended text characteristics— for instance, Windows's Write—the clipboard handle was the same for every clipboard operation. Thus, GetClipboardData proved to be an unreliable indicator of clipboard changes.

In the end, it appeared that I was stuck with comparing the results of successive Clipboard.GetText( ) functions. So I added a timer control with an interval of 1,000 milliseconds to Clips's main form (MClipForm) to manage this process. Every time the timer fired, Clips would use Clipboard.GetText to grab the current contents of the clipboard, then compare them to the value of a variable called OldText$. If the strings were the same, Clips would exit the timer routine. Otherwise, it would assign the contents of the clipboard to OldText$ and carry out the process of adding that text to its data files.

It worked, but as predicted, the performance stunk. While I could have attempted to optimize it a bit, its performance was going to continue to stink as long as Clips had to make incessant string comparisons. Thus, it appeared that I would have to consign Clips to the "nice try, but not good enough" bin.

■ Fate Lends a Hand

That's when I got lucky. Work on another project had given me some experience with GFA-BASIC, a complex but powerful implementation of BASIC from GFA Software. Just about the time I was ready to give up on Clips, GFA Software released GFA-BASIC Professional for Windows, which included the first true BASIC compiler for Windows. Unlike Visual Basic or other pseudo-compilers that require a runtime DLL, the GFA-BASIC compiler can create true .EXEs and dynamic link libraries, thus allowing you to use BASIC syntax to perform all sorts of tricks, including callback functions and subclassing windows, which previously could be done only through C or Pascal.

Given GFA-BASIC's impressive list of capabilities, you might wonder "Why use Visual Basic at all? Why not just work in GFA-BASIC?" But, in my opinion, GFA-BASIC is much more useful as a complement to Visual Basic than as a soup-to-nuts programming tool. The GFA program editor is very weak, the language is much more low-level than Visual Basic, requiring much more work on the part of the programmer, and its visual design tools are primitive in comparison to those of Visual Basic. While it is certainly possible to write complete applications in GFA-BASIC, I find that it is much more efficient as an adjunct to Visual Basic than as a stand-alone programming tool.

To make a long story short, within a week or so of getting my hands on the GFA compiler, I had used it to create a small dynamic link library called CLPWATCH.DLL that enables Clips to make use of the SetClipboardViewer function. The process was so simple that every Visual Basic user should know about it.

■ BUILDING CLPWATCH.DLL

GFA-BASIC is more of a BASIC wrapper for the Windows API, in the same way that the Windows SDK is a C language wrapper for it, than a true visual-programming environment. It is difficult to learn and to work with, and I don't intend to use it for the bulk of my applications development work. But because it is rooted in the same BASIC language as Visual Basic, and offers significant capabilities in an area that Visual Basic ignores, it provides a wonderful alternative to C for Visual Basic programmers who need to be able to create DLLs.

Dynamic link libraries are files that contain one or more compiled functions. Theoretically, at least, the functions in a DLL can be called from any other Windows application. This allows several applications to share a single DLL, saving both memory and disk space, and, in the case of Visual Basic, providing access to features not found in the core language.

The CLPWATCH.DLL contains only one function that can be called from an external program: RegClipViewer. This function accepts two parameters: the handle of the window that it is to subclass, and a True/False flag indicating whether it should turn subclassing On or Off. Also, the DLL contains three additional routines that aren't designed to be directly called by another program: LibMain(), CC(), and Pass().

The LibMain() routine is used to initialize three global variables (MyWin&, Old-Proc%, and OldViewer%) and to identify the callback function used by the DLL. (Just to make things interesting, the meaning of the suffixes "%" and "&" is reversed in GFA-BASIC. The "%" suffix signifies a Long value, while the "&" suffix signifies an integer, not the other way around as in Visual Basic.)

GFA-BASIC includes a special command called _CB() that is used to identify a callback procedure. For anyone who is approaching this with an understanding of programming callbacks in C, _CB() essentially takes the place of MakeProcInstance().

The RegClipViewer procedure is the DLL's interface to the outside world. The actions it performs depend upon the value of the OnOff& parameter passed to it by Clips. If Clips passes a value of −1 (True), RegClipViewer calls the Windows SetClipboardViewer() function to identify Clips's main window as a clipboard viewer. This instructs Windows to inform the window when the contents of the clipboard change. The SetClipboardViewer function returns the handle of the next viewer, if any, in the clipboard viewer chain. RegClipViewer stores this handle in the variable called OldViewer&.

Next, RegClipViewer subclasses Clips's main window, by using the SetWindowLong function to tell Windows that all messages for that window should be sent to the procedure identified by _cb(1), rather than to the window's default message-handling procedure. Finally, RegClipViewer returns a pointer that identifies the window's default message-handling procedure to Clips.

If, on the other hand, Clips passes a value of 0 (False) to RegClipViewer, instructing it to turn off the subclassing, the process is reversed. First, RegClipViewer calls the ChangeClipboardChain function, instructing Windows to remove Clips's window from the chain and to allow the window identified by OldViewer& to take its place. Next, it calls SetWindowLong to tell Windows to send messages for Clip's window to its default handling procedure, as identified by OldProc%.

Once RegClipViewer has replaced the default message-handling procedure for Clips's window with the DLL's CC() procedure, Windows sends all messages that would have gone to the Clips window directly to the CC() procedure. As it happens, however, the DLL is only interested in two of those messages: WM_DRAWCLIPBOARD, which tells it that the clipboard's contents have changed, and WM_CHANGECBCHAIN, which tells it that the clipboard chain has been modified. As a clipboard viewer, the DLL is required to pass both those messages on to the next clipboard viewer, which it does by using the Pass procedure. In addition, when it receives a WM_DRAWCLIPBOARD function, it notifies Clips that the clipboard has changed by sending its main window an &H7F key-down code (the equivalent of pressing the F16 key, if your keyboard is so equipped).

Any other messages received by the function are simply passed on to the default message-handling procedure for the window by sending them to OldProc% using the CallWindowProc function.

The complete listing for CLPWATCH.DLL follows.

```
' CB6.GFW
' Source listing for CLPWATCH.DLL
' Created using the GFA-BASIC 4.2 Compiler
' Copyright 1993 by Paul Bonner
' All Rights Reserved
$Library CLPWATCH
$LNK EXE CLPWATCH.DLL

Procedure LibMain(inst&,dseg&,hpsz&,lpcmd%)
' ********************************
' Initialize global variables
'   and callback function
' ********************************
  MyWin&=0
  OldClipProc%=0
  OldClipViewer&=0
  _cb (1)=CC(W,W,W,L)
Return
```

```
Procedure RegClipViewer(h&, OnOff&)
   ' **********************************
   ' Call this from VB --passing handle of Window
   ' to receive clipboard-change notifications, and
   ' true/false flag to start/stop monitoring of
   ' clipboard
   ' **********************************
   $Export RegClipViewer
   MyWin&=h&
   Switch OnOff&
   Case -1           'Turn on
      ' **********************************
      ' Identify MyWin& as clipboard viewer
      ' then set callback function as window procedure for MyWin&
      ' **********************************
      OldClipViewer&=SetClipboardViewer(MyWin&)
      OldClipProc%=SetWindowLong(MyWin&,GWL_WNDPROC,_cb(1))
      Retval OldClipProc%
   Case 0         'Turn off
      ' **********************************
      ' remove MyWin& from clipboard viewer chain
      ' then restore default window procedure for MyWin&
      ' **********************************
      If IsWindow(OldClipViewer&) Then
         ~ChangeClipboardChain(MyWin&,OldClipViewer&)
      EndIf
      If IsWindow(MyWin&) Then
         Retval SetWindowLong(MyWin&,GWL_WNDPROC,OldClipProc%)
      Else
         Retval 0
      EndIf
   EndSwitch
Return

Procedure CC(wHand&,Mess&,w&,1%)
   ' **********************************
   ' callback procedure used to process
   ' clipboard change messages
   ' monitors all messages for the VB app's window
   ' **********************************
   $Export CC
   Switch Mess&
   Case  WM_DRAWCLIPBOARD
      ' **********************************
      ' if the clipboard changes, tell the vb app about it
      ' then pass the message on to the next clipboard viewer
      ' **********************************
      ~PostMessage(wHand&, WM_KEYDOWN,&H7F,0)
      Pass(OldClipViewer&,Mess&,w&,1%)
      Retval 0
   Case  WM_CHANGECBCHAIN
      ' **********************************
      ' if the clipboard chain changes,
      ' pass the message on to the next clipboard viewer
      ' **********************************
      Pass(OldClipViewer&,Mess&,w&,1%)
      Retval 0
   Default
      ' **********************************
      ' otherwise, just pass the message on to your vb app
      ' **********************************
      Retval CallWindowProc(OldClipProc%,wHand&,Mess&,w&,1%)
   EndSelect
```

```
Return

Procedure Pass(wHand&,Mess&,w&,l%)
  ' *************************************
  ' handles passing of messages to next clipboard viewer
  ' does a little error checking first
  ' *************************************
  If wHand&<>0 And wHand&<>MyWin& And IsWindow(wHand&) Then
    ~PostMessage(wHand&,Mess&,w&,l%)
  EndIf
Return
```

That's it. No include files. No need to define API functions such as PostMessage or CallWindowProc. The GFA compiler handles all that for you, making it a powerful tool for creating DLLs quickly and easily. The result is a little 10K DLL, which can be used from within Visual Basic by declaring the RegClipViewer function as follows:

```
Declare Function RegClipViewer Lib "CLPWATCH.DLL" (ByVal wHand%, ByVal ⇔
    OnOff%) As Long
```

Both the source and compiled code for the CLPWATCH.DLL are included on the companion disk. I don't intend to go into a detailed explanation of the code here, since doing so would require extensive discussion of callbacks, windows procedures, and message-handling procedures; however, I do want to point out the two road-blocks I faced in writing the DLL, and how I managed to overcome them.

The first roadblock was simply figuring out how you subclass a window. This procedure isn't wonderfully documented, even for C programmers, and there was no documentation of how you do it in GFA-BASIC. So I searched on CompuServe until I found some simple examples of subclassing that included C-language source code, downloaded them, and studied them until I figured out what they were doing. I'm no C programmer—I would struggle to write a "Hello, world" program—but at least I recognize an API call when I see one, and was able to determine more or less what the C programs were doing. Then all I had to do was figure out how to do the same thing in GFA-BASIC. That was anything but easy since, as you can see, GFA-BASIC's syntax differs greatly from Visual Basic's, but it's still BASIC and, in my view, nearly any effort is justified if it lets you avoid C language.

The other big roadblock was figuring out how to let Clips know that the CLP-WATCH.DLL had received notification that the clipboard had changed.

It seemed I had two options. The first was to have Clips poll the DLL constantly to check the value of an integer flag that would indicate if the DLL had received a WM_-DRAWCLIPBOARD message. That would have been much more efficient than captur-ing the clipboard's contents and performing a string comparison, but it still was likely that 99.9 percent of the calls to the DLL would have a negative result, which would mean that Clips wasted a lot of time calling the DLL for no good reason.

The other option, and the obviously more efficient one, was to have the DLL notify Clips when it received the WM_DRAWCLIPBOARD message—in other words, to implement a callback mechanism in Visual Basic! Now, if the CLPWATCH.DLL were going to be used with an application written in C, that would be simple—I would have it send a user-defined message to the application. But of course, the reason I was fooling around with writing DLLs in the first place was that Visual Basic doesn't provide access to the message queue, so that option was right out. Instead, I had to have the DLL post a message that Visual Basic would pass through to an event procedure in Clips, and that meant that the message would have to be in the form of a standard Visual Basic event, such as a mouse click, a form resize, or a key-up message.

The only problem was that Clips would have no way of distinguishing between a mouse-down message sent from my DLL and a real mouse-down event, so I had to come up with an event that wouldn't be triggered in any manner other than by my DLL. The obvious first choice was the form key-down event for Clips's main form, because unless you set a form's KeyPreview property to True (which I hadn't), a form with any visible and enabled controls on it never receives a key-down message—the event always goes to the control with the input focus. Plus, the key-down event allowed the DLL to attach parameters to the message, in the form of a keycode and a shift state. This means that a DLL could send a range of messages to the same event handler, modifying the keycode or shift parameter for each, and that the event handler could examine those parameters to determine exactly what message the DLL was sending it. That wasn't necessary with the CLPWATCH.DLL, since it posts only one message to Clips, but it could certainly come in handy in other applications that place more rigorous demands on DLLs.

The Form_KeyDown handler for Clips's main form, which processes these messages from the CLPWATCH.DLL, looks like this:

```
Sub Form_KeyDown (KeyCode As Integer, Shift As Integer)
If (State% <> sOn) Or (GetActiveWindow() = hWnd) Then Exit Sub
If KeyCode = &H7F Then GetClip
End Sub
```

The first line of the subroutine stops the routine if Clips has been turned off or if Clips is the active window (meaning that the clipboard operation occurred while the user was editing the text of an existing Clip or placing that text on the clipboard.) Otherwise, it checks to make sure that the keycode parameter matches the one it expects the DLL to send it (again, this isn't really necessary here, but it doesn't hurt to be careful), and, if so, calls a routine called GetClip that handles the task of capturing the contents of the clipboard.

Thanks to the CLPWATCH.DLL, Clips spends most of its time sitting quietly in the background doing nothing and, more importantly, consuming very little processing time. It springs to action only when you activate it, or when it receives a message from the CLPWATCH.DLL that the clipboard's contents have changed.

■ CAPTURING THE CLIPBOARD

Once Clips had a mechanism for determining when the clipboard's contents changed, capturing the text from the clipboard each time that it changed was fairly easy. The Form_Keydown event for Clips's main form calls the GetClip routine when it receives notification from the DLL that the clipboard's contents have changed.

While testing this routine, I discovered one unexpected complication that could result in unwanted duplicate copies of the last text added to the clipboard. When an application that has registered a private clipboard format—for instance, Windows Write—shuts down, Windows broadcasts one or more WM_DRAWCLIPBOARD messages to all registered clipboard viewers. CLPWATCH.DLL has no way to distinguish those messages from those that it receives when new text is placed on the clipboard, so it sends its notification message to Clips, which proceeds to capture additional copies of the last text placed on the clipboard.

In order to eliminate these duplicates, I inserted some code at the beginning of the GetClip routine which calls DoEvents() ten times in order to allow Windows time to finish closing the application that's in the process of shutting down, and then calls GetClipboardOwner. If the application that owns the clipboard text has shut down, that call will return either a value of 0 (indicating that no window owns the clipboard) or a handle to a window which no longer exists. The next line of GetClip checks for either of those conditions and exits if either evaluates to True, thus eliminating spurious duplication of clipboard text when an application shuts down.

```
For Y% = 1 To 10
  X% = DoEvents()
Next
Y% = GetClipboardOwner%()
If (Y% = 0) Or (IsWindow%(Y%) = 0) Then Exit Sub
```

If it makes it past these tests, GetClip assigns the contents of the clipboard to a variable called B$. Then it checks to see if B$ trimmed of all leading spaces is an empty string, in which case it exits. Otherwise, it passes the leftmost 60 characters of

B$ to a function called CleanString, which is used to tailor the title for the clip. Clean-String trims off any non-printing characters (control characters or spaces) at the beginning of the string, and terminates the string at the first carriage return/line feed juncture, then returns the remnant to GetClip for use as the clip's title.

```
B$ = Clipboard.GetText()
If LTrim(B$) = "" Then Exit Sub
T$ = Left$(B$, 60)
T$ = CleanString(T$)
```

At this point, Clips has both the full text of the clip, and a title for it. Now it has to do something with them.

Clearly, Clips needs some sort of data structure or structures in which to store the titles and text of all the clips that it captures. Here again, this was reminiscent of the VB Code Librarian project, where VB Code Librarian needed to track the titles and text of all the library routines. In the case of VB Code Librarian, I chose to keep track of the titles in memory and store the code text on disk, but in Clips's case I decided to keep both the titles and text of all the clips in the current file in memory.

I didn't have any great reason for making this choice. Although on very large files, this implementation would certainly be faster than keeping the clip text on disk, it also would consume more memory, so the trade-off was about even. Mostly, I thought it would be interesting to try a different approach in this project.

To that end, Clips maintains two global arrays, which are defined in MCLIP.BAS as follows:

```
Global Title() As String      'Clip Titles array
Global Clip() As Variant      'Clip Text array
```

You'll notice that Clips uses the Variant data format, rather than the String format, for the Clip() array. This enables Clips to circumvent the normal 64K limit on variable-length string arrays, which seemed far too restricting. While the Variant data type does use a little extra memory, it enables the Clip() array to keep track of up to 64MB of clipboard text (theoretically, at least).

Clips uses a global integer variable called ClipCount% to keep track of the number of elements in both the Title() and Clip() arrays. Thus, once the GetClip routine has obtained the new clip's title, it increments ClipCount% and redimensions the Clip() and Title() arrays.

```
ClipCount% = ClipCount% + 1
ReDim Preserve Title(ClipCount%)
ReDim Preserve Clip(ClipCount%)
```

Next, GetClip adds the title of the new clip to the Titles list box and to the Title()
array, selects the new list-box item, and adds the clip's text to the ClipText text box.

```
MClipForm.Titles.AddItem T$
Title(ClipCount% - 1) = T$
MClipForm.Titles.ListIndex = MClipForm.Titles.NewIndex
MClipForm.ClipText = B$
```

Modifying MClipForm.ClipText triggers that text box's Change event, where an integer flag called OldChoiceChanged% is set to True. OldChoiceChanged% is used by
a function called CheckChanges to determine if it needs to update the Clip() array
element corresponding to the active clip prior to saving the file or displaying another
clip in the ClipText box.

■ FILE SYSTEM

I followed VB Code Librarian's example much more closely when it came to Clips's
file-handling routines. Clips uses the same indexed, structured sequential-access file
format as VB Code Librarian: Clip titles are stored in one file, while the corresponding clip text is stored in a separate file. Each entry in the clip text file is preceded by
an index number in brackets, and followed by the word STOP in brackets (which is
identified by the constant ClipEnd$). Thus, Clips's GetFiles routine (which is nearly
identical to that of VB Code Librarian's) can read through the file quickly to locate a
clip's text, by using this code:

```
Line Input #F, C$
Do While C$ <> ClipEnd$
   D$ = D$ + C$ + CRLF$
   Line Input #F, C$
Loop
Clip(X - 1) = D$
Next X
```

In Clips's case, this routine is even more efficient than in VB Code Librarian. Because Clips is designed to keep all the text for the open file in memory, it reads in the
entire file at once, and thus starts looking for a record's data immediately after the previous record's data. In contrast, VB Code Librarian reads in only one routine at a
time, and must read from the beginning of the file each time.

That might not sound like a big deal, but it makes a significant difference in how
much work the application's file routines have to do. Let's say you have 25 record
files in both programs. How many records would each program have to read if you

clicked first on the first item in the list box, then on the tenth, then on the 20th and finally on the 25th?

VB Code Librarian would read 1 record for the first click, 10 for the second click, 20 for the third click, and 25 for the fourth click, for a total of 56 records read.

In contrast, Clips would have read the entire 25-record file prior to your clicking on any item, and stored all 25 records in memory, so it would not have to conduct any additional disk read operations until you opened another file.

Similarly, VB Code Librarian saves any changes that you've made to a library routine to disk as soon as you select another routine or add another routine to the library. Each time that the application does so, it must save the entire library file. Thus, if you made changes to records 1, 10, 20 and 25, VB Code Librarian would have to write all 25 records to disk on four separate occasions, for a total of 100 records written. In contrast, Clips saves the file to disk only when you issue a File Save command, so it would probably end up having to write significantly fewer records to disk.

■ Common Dialogs

Another significant difference between Clips's file-handling requirements and those of VB Code Librarian is that while VB Code Librarian works with only a single library file, Clips can work with many different files, and allows the user to name, save, and load those files at will.

Once you give the user the power to name files, specify their locations, and otherwise control an application's file usage, you've got to beef up its error-checking facilities. Otherwise, the user might direct your application to open a nonexistent file, or to store a file on a disk that isn't ready, or otherwise force an error that would crash your application if it wasn't caught.

VB ZIP Shell, presented in Chapter 3, showed one way to perform this error checking: Write error-checking routines yourself. Clips takes another, much easier path, by using the error-checking routines built into the Windows 3.1 common dialog boxes.

To access those dialog boxes, Clips makes use of the CMDIALOG.VBX custom control included in the Professional Edition of Visual Basic 2.0 and both the Standard and Professional Editions of Visual Basic 3.0.

The common dialog boxes offer several advantages compared to custom dialog boxes. From the user's point of view, they act as standardized interfaces to common functions. The user who learns how to open a file with one application that uses the common File Open dialog box will be at home with any application that uses it.

Meanwhile, the common dialog boxes obviously save developers a lot of time that would be spent designing new dialog boxes. But more importantly, they offer a wide

range of built-in error-checking facilities. By setting a few simple flags, one can instruct the common File dialog box to ensure that the path specified by the user is
valid, that the file specified by the user really exists, that the file specified by the user
has a particular extension, to warn the user that a file is about to be overwritten, to
determine if the user wants to create a new file, and so on. Clips's File Open routine,
for instance, uses the following statement to ensure that its File Open dialog box
hides read-only files, and only allows the user to select an existing file.

CMDialog1.Flags = OFN_HIDEREADONLY Or OFN_FILEMUSTEXIST

The next line in the routine identifies a default file extension. Once a default extension has been identified, the common dialog box will set a flag if the user selects a file
with any other extension.

CMDialog1.DefaultExt = "MCF"

Error-checking facilities such as these—and the common dialog box's automatic
screening of illegal file names, drive-not-ready errors, and other common errors—undoubtedly saved me several hundred lines of code in writing Clips.

Of course, using the common dialog boxes doesn't entirely eliminate the need to
write error-trapping code for one's file-access routines. With Clips's File Open routine, for instance, I needed to provide error-trapping code for two possible errors: the
user selecting the Cancel button on the File Open dialog box, and the user entering a
file with an extension other than the default. In both cases, however, the common dialog boxes made that process simple.

By setting the common dialog box's CancelError property to True, I instructed the
dialog box to set the error flag equal to a global constant called CancelButton (32755) if
the user closed the dialog box by clicking the Cancel button. Meanwhile, because I
had set a default file extension for the dialog, Clips could check the OFN_EXTEN-
TIONDIFFERENT flag to determine if the user had selected a file with an extension
other than the default.

Thus, the sum total of Clips's error-checking code for its File Open dialog box appears as follows:

```
CMDialog1.CancelError = True
On Error Resume Next
ExtenErrorLoop:
CMDialog1.Filter = "Clips files|*.MCF"
CMDialog1.Action = 1
If Err = CancelButton Then Exit Sub
If CMDialog1.Flags And OFN_EXTENTIONDIFFERENT Then
```

```
    MsgBox "File must have an MCF extension!"
    GoTo ExtenErrorLoop
End If
On Error GoTo 0
```

If the user selects the Cancel button, the procedure exits, while if the user selects a file with a different extension, the procedure creates a message box saying that that isn't allowed, then jumps back to the ExtenErrorLoop label and calls the File Open dialog box again.

Clips file-saving routines make use of the same common dialog box error-checking facilities.

■ **COMMAND LINE PARAMETERS**

If I had been content to have Clips open files only in response to the user selecting a file from a file open dialog box, I would have been off the hook at that point. But I decided that, like any good Windows application, Clips should also open files in response to the user "running" the file by double-clicking on it in the File Manager. That meant that Clips had to be able to process file names passed to it through the Command$ parameter.

The form-load procedure for MClipForm contains the following code to process command line parameters:

```
If Command$ <> "" Then
    tFile$ = UCase$(Command$)
    If InStr(tFile$, ".MCF") = 0 Then Exit Sub
    LoadFile tFile$
End If
```

Thus, Clips calls its LoadFile routine at start-up if the Command$ variable contains a file with an .MCF extension. The .MCF file is the index file in which Clips lists the titles of a group of clips. An .MCF file must be accompanied by a file with a .CLP extension in the same directory. The .CLP file contains the text for all the clips listed in the .MCF file.

LoadFile contains the following line, which assigns the name of the CLP file that accompanies the specified .MCF file to the variable cFile$:

```
cFile$ = Left$(tFile$, InStr(tFile$, ".")) + "CLP"
```

The next line in the LoadFile routine makes two calls to a function called Exists() to ensure that both the .CLP and .MCF files are valid.

```
If Not Exists(tFile$) Or Not Exists(cFile$) Then Exit Sub
```

The Exists routine uses the Visual Basic Dir$ function, which takes a file specification and returns a string listing the files that match that specification. If the returned string has a length of zero, no file matches the specification. If you pass Dir$ a fully qualified file name, you can use it to determine if that file exists. However, passing Dir$ an invalid path will cause an error, so the function traps the error using an On Error Resume Next statement.

```
Function Exists% (F$)
On Error Resume Next
Exists% = True
If Len(Dir$(F$)) = 0 Then Exists% = False
On Error GoTo 0
End Function
```

The Exists() function returns a value of True if the file exists, or False if it does not exist, or if the specified drive or path is invalid.

Having ensured that the files it intends to open do in fact exist, LoadFiles continues with the process of opening the files, using much the same methods described in Chapter 1 for VB Code Librarian.

Once Clips has loaded a file, no matter whether it was specified through the File Open dialog box or through Command$, it sets the listindex property for the Titles list box to 0, thus selecting the first item in the list. That, in turn, triggers the Titles_Click procedure, which first determines if the text in the ClipText text box has changed and needs to be saved, and then executes the following statement:

```
LI = Titles.ListIndex: ClipText = Clip(LI)
```

This replaces the current contents of the ClipText text box with the text of the selected clip.

■ TRACKING MODIFICATIONS TO CLIPS

Because the contents of the ClipText text box are fully editable, Clips needed a way to track modifications to them and to save those modifications. To do so, it employs a global integer variable called OldChoiceChanged%. The ClipText_Change event sets OldChoiceChanged% equal to True when the user modifies the text box's contents.

To make the OldChoiceChanged% flag useful, Clips needed to be capable of distinguishing between changes made by the user, and changes made under programmatic control. For instance, every time the user clicks on an item in the Titles list box, the contents of the text box are changed; however, there is no need for Clips to note that change and save the new text in the Clip() array because the text was read directly from that array. So Clips uses another integer flag, IgnoreChange%, to determine if it should take note of changes to the contents of ClipText.

Thus, the Titles_Click procedure wraps the statement in which it modifies Clip-Text between two statements that toggle the value of IgnoreChange%, as follows:

```
IgnoreChange% = True
LI = Titles.ListIndex: ClipText = Clip(LI)
IgnoreChange% = False
```

The ClipText_Change routine checks the value of IgnoreChange%, and only sets the value of OldChoiceChanged% to True if IgnoreChange% equals False.

```
Sub ClipText_Change ()
If IgnoreChange% = False Then OldChoiceChanged% = True: FileDirty% = True
End Sub
```

At the same time that it sets OldChoiceChanged%, the ClipText_Change procedure sets the value of the FileDirty% flag—used to indicate that the contents of the active file have changed—to True.

■ **The CheckChanges() Function**

Once the OldChoiceChanged% flag has been set to True, Clips knows that the user has modified the contents of the ClipText box, and that those contents should be saved to the Clip() array before another clip's text is displayed in the box. The CheckChanges() function, which is called by both the Titles_Click procedure and the fItem_Click procedure (which handles item choices from the File menu), handles the job of saving the modified data to the Clip() array.

CheckChanges() checks the value of the OldChoiceChanged% flag. If it is not equal to False, CheckChanges() sets up an On Error routine, then assigns the current contents of the active member of the Clip() array to a string variable called OC$, places the contents of ClipText into that array member, then resets the values of Old-Choice% and OldChoiceChanged%, and returns a value of True. The function also returns a value of True if OldChoiceChanged% is False.

```
Function CheckChanges () As Integer
Dim OC$
CheckChanges = True
If OldChoiceChanged% Then
    On Error GoTo TCMemError
    OC$ = Clip(OldChoice%)
    Clip(OldChoice%) = ClipText
```

```
    On Error GoTo 0
End If
OldChoice% = Titles.ListIndex
OldChoiceChanged% = False
BD1:
Exit Function
```

The On Error routine in CheckChanges() is designed to catch any out-of-memory or out-of-string-space errors that might occur. The error routine jumps to the label TCMemError where the current member of the Clip() array's original contents are restored from OC$ and the function result is set to False. Then a routine called DispErrorMsg, which serves only to display error messages, is called with a string parameter describing the error, and finally the routine exits.

```
TCMemError:
    Screen.MousePointer = 0
    Clip(OldChoice%) = OC$
    CheckChanges% = False
    DispErrorMsg "Ran out of memory trying to modify " + Title(OldChoice%)
    Resume BD1
End Function
```

Memory or string space errors occur rarely in this routine, thanks to Clips's use of the Variant data type for the Clip() array, but they are possible, and proved quite difficult to predict in my testing of Clips. Given their unpredictability, writing an On Error routine to handle them was the prudent course.

■ COMBINING CLIP TEXT

Sometimes the hardest thing about adding a new feature to an application is defining the behavior that you want it to exhibit. That was true of Clips's Combine mode. I knew that I wanted to enable the user to be able to selectively combine clips, but I had to figure out what that meant and how it could be accomplished most efficiently. Once I had done so, writing the code to implement the Combine mode was a snap.

My starting premise was that the Combine mode would primarily be used after the user had copied a series of discontiguous selections or data to Clips. At that point, the user might need a way to combine and reorder those selections. In other words, a Combine mode.

That premise allowed me to make several decisions about how the Combine mode should be implemented. Clearly, the user needed to be able to select source clips in any order for combination with a target clip, and to be able to specify the location in the target at which the source clip's text would be inserted.

At this point, I had at least two options for implementing the Combine mode. I could have designed a new screen form, one that provided side-by-side list and edit boxes showing the source and target text, as well as a list box for selecting source clips. That solution would have had some advantages compared to the solution that I ultimately chose: It would have allowed the user to see the full text of the source clip, rather than just its title, and it would have avoided imposing a new mode of operation onto Clips. Modal states, in which the same controls act in different manners, are generally considered poor programming practice in a graphical environment, and with good reason.

On the other hand, the single-screen solution that I ultimately chose had several benefits of its own. One was simplicity. Not only did selecting this option mean that I didn't have to design a new screen form, but also that the user didn't have to learn the operation of a new form—a significant consideration, especially in a utility where convenience and simplicity are of overriding importance. Moreover, in this case a modal state didn't seem like such a bad idea. By making the combining of clips a separate and distinct activity from any other, the Combine mode prevents the user from combining them accidentally and, more importantly, signals that the user needs to think in a different way about what he or she is doing.

■ How Combine Mode Works

When the user activates Combine mode, Clips calls its SetCombineMode routine, which sets the two global flags, updates the status label, and disables the File and Edit menus. IgnoreChange% is set to True, thus disabling the ClipText_Change event, and State% is set to sCombine%, thus signaling that Combine mode has been activated.

The sCombine% flag for the State% variable is of interest to two event procedures for the Titles list box. The Titles_Click procedure exits immediately if State%=sCombine%, thus skipping the code that would normally update the ClipText text box to display the text of the selected title. Meanwhile, the Titles_MouseDown procedure issues the command

```
Titles.Drag 1
```

if State%=sCombine%, thus activating the list box's drag method.

When the user drops the selected title over the ClipText text box, the ClipText_Drag-Drop event is triggered. The handler for this event inserts the full text of the source clip at the position indicated by the SelStart property of the ClipText text box. Thus, if the user has placed the insertion point at the end of the ClipText text box, the source clip will be inserted there. But if the user has highlighted a range of text in the ClipText box, the source clip will replace that text.

```
S% = ClipText.SelStart + ClipText.SelLength
ClipText.Text=Left$(Drop$,S%)+Clip(Titles.ListIndex)+Mid$(Drop$,S%+1)
ClipText.SelStart = S% + Len(Clip(Titles.ListIndex))
Clip(CombineIndex%) = ClipText
```

The last line of this code fragment updates the contents of the Clip() array member associated with the target clip.

■ COMBINING ALL CLIPS

Designing the Combine All function was more straightforward than designing the Combine mode. It seemed obvious that the function should combine the text of all the clips in the order in which they appear in the Titles list box, starting each on a new line and eliminating any trailing spaces or empty lines, and then delete all the clips from the file except for the target clip.

When the user selects Combine All from the Edit menu, Clips posts a message box to confirm that instruction, then selects the first title in the Titles list box and sets about the task of combining the text of all the other clips in the file with the text for that clip. It begins by assigning the text of the first item to a temporary string. Next, it strips any trailing carriage return/line feed combinations from that string (to eliminate big gaps in the text of the combined clip), then it adds the target clip's text to the string, preceded by one carriage return/line feed. It repeats the process until it has combined the text of all the clips in the Clip() array, at which point it assigns the temporary string to the ClipText text box.

```
temp$ = MClipForm.ClipText
For X% = 1 To Ubound(Clip,1)
    ' first strip off trailing CRLF$'s
    Do While Right$(temp$, 2) = CRLF$
        temp$ = Left$(temp$, Len(temp$) - 2)
    Loop
    'now add new string, separated by 1 CRLF$
    temp$ = temp$ + CRLF$ + Clip(X%)
    If Len(temp$) > 32567 Then Err = 14
Next
MClipForm.ClipText = temp$
```

Next, Clips redimensions the Title() and Clip() arrays, assigns the contents of Clip-Text to the zero element of the Clip() array, assigns a new title to the combined clip, adds that title to the Title() array, and resets ClipCount% to 1.

```
ReDim Title(0)
ReDim Clip(0)
Clip(0) = MClipForm.ClipText
MClipForm.Titles.List(0)="Combined"+Str$(MClipForm.Titles.ListCount)+⇔
    " clips"
Title(0) = MClipForm.Titles.List(0)
ClipCount% = 1
```

Finally, Clips removes the titles of the old, now-combined items from the Titles list box.

```
For X% = MClipForm.Titles.ListCount - 1 To 1 Step -1
    MClipForm.Titles.RemoveItem X%
Next
```

That's all there is to combining the text of all the clips in a file into a single clip.

■ TRACKING CLIPS'S STATUS

Clips makes use of both a status label on its main form and Settings menu check marks to indicate its state (On, Off, or Combine mode). In addition, it enables or disables various menus and menu items depending on a variety of factors relating to its status. For instance, if the Titles list box contains less than two items, both the Combine All item on the Edit menu and the Combine Mode item on the Settings menu are disabled.

This sort of constant updating of controls and menu items simplifies things for the user by making it apparent at each moment what Clips can and cannot do, and also prevents errors that might occur if the user asked Clips to do the temporarily impossible. It also means that you've got to make sure that the status indicators are correct at all times, which can require a lot of effort.

The best way to minimize that effort is to develop utility routines to toggle your settings or status indicators on or off. This ensures that groups of related indicators will remain in sync.

Clips relies upon three such routines: ToggleMenu, ToggleSettings, and LabelIt.

■ The ToggleMenu Routine

ToggleMenu is used to enable or disable the Save and Save As items on the File menu and all the items on the Edit menu, except the Combine All item, and to enable or disable the Combine All and the Combine Mode items.

Clips calls the ToggleMenu routine whenever the number of items in the Titles list box changes. The routine takes one parameter, a True or False flag called E%. If the Titles list box is empty (for instance, after a File New operation or after the sole item in the list box has been deleted), the ToggleMenu routine is called with a False parameter. Otherwise, it is called with a parameter equal to True.

ToggleMenu starts by enabling or disabling the File and Edit menu items (except Combine All) according to the value of E%.

```
For X% = 0 To 7
   If X% <> 5 Then MClipForm.eItem(X%).Enabled = E%
Next
MClipForm.fItem(3).Enabled = E%
MClipForm.fItem(4).Enabled = E%
```

Next, the routine enables or disables the two Combine items based on a Boolean evaluation of the statement ClipCount% > 1. That statement evaluates to True if there is more than one clip in the file, meaning that there are enough items for a combine operation, or to False if there are fewer than two clips in the file.

```
MClipForm.sItem(3).Enabled = ClipCount% > 1
MClipForm.eItem(9).Enabled = ClipCount% > 1
```

■ The ToggleSettings Routine

Clips uses the ToggleSettings routine to ensure that the correct Settings menu item is checked, and that the File and Edit menus are disabled when Combine mode is active.

ToggleSettings takes one parameter, called CheckMe%. The sItem_Click procedure, which processes Settings menu choices, calls ToggleSettings whenever the user selects a Settings menu item, passing the Index number of the selected menu item as the CheckMe% parameter.

```
Sub ToggleSettings (CheckMe%)
Dim X%
For X%= 1 To 3
    If X% = CheckMe% Then
        MClipForm.sItem(X%).Checked = True
    Else
        MClipForm.sItem(X%).Checked = False
    End If
Next
```

Once the check mark has been placed correctly, ToggleSettings enables or disables the File and Edit menus depending upon the results of a Boolean evaluation of the expression CheckMe% < 3.

```
MClipForm.fMenu.Enabled = CheckMe% < 3
MClipForm.eMenu.Enabled = CheckMe% < 3
```

This raises an interesting point about Boolean expressions. Generally, I'm not fond of them. They tend to be difficult to understand when you read someone else's code or go back to your own code after some weeks or months of working on other projects. Moreover, I think you can probably go your entire programming life without ever *needing* to use a Boolean expression. There is always another way to express the thought. Nevertheless, I learned to make an exception for the case of toggle-switch items such as enabling or disabling a control, hiding or showing a control, and adding or removing a check mark, because a little Boolean expression such as CheckMe% < 3 can save you many, many lines of code sometimes, and because, in some odd way, Booleans seem to make more sense and to be more understandable when used this way.

■ The LabelIt Routine

LabelIt, the last of Clips's status-tracking routines, is used to update the text and appearance of lblStatus, the status label on Clips's main form that displays the current state and acts as a toggle switch for selecting another state. The routine sets the text of lblStatus based on the value of the State% variable, and then calls another routine called FrameControl to draw the box that gives the label its 3D appearance.

```
MClipForm.lblStatus.Visible = False
If State% = sOn Then
     MClipForm.lblStatus = "State is On"
Else
     MClipForm.lblStatus = "State is Off"
End If
FrameControl MClipForm, MClipForm.lblStatus
MClipForm.lblStatus.Visible = True
```

Through frequent calls to its three status-tracking routines, Clips ensures that its status indicators and menus always reflect the current state of the application and all the options available to the user.

■ LIMITS AND ERROR-TRAPPING

As described previously, Clips's use of a variant, rather than a string, array to hold clipboard text allows it to circumvent Visual Basic's 64K limit on the length of a variable-length string array. Nevertheless, Clips is subject to a few significant limits. The sum of the lengths of the titles of all the clips in a file cannot exceed 64,536 characters (leaving room for approximately 1,092 clips in a file if each title is the full 60 characters in length), and no single clip can exceed 32K in length (the capacity limit of the text box control). In addition, under some conditions Clips can experience an out-of-string-space error while grabbing large clips from the clipboard.

Clips includes several simple error-trapping routines to prevent errors caused by exceeding these limits from interrupting its operation. For instance, prior to assigning the text of the clipboard to a string, the GetClip routine executes the statement:

```
On Error GoTo MemError
```

Thus, if there is too much text on the clipboard for Clips to handle, or if it encounters any other error in the process of assigning the clipboard text to a string or in subsequently manipulating that string, execution jumps to the MemError routine. There, Clips is instructed to simply beep the speaker several times in succession to alert the user that the clip *was not* captured, and then to exit the GetClip routine.

```
MemError:
   For X% = 1 To 8
      Beep
   Next
Resume BackDoor1
```

Similarly, CombineAll includes an On Error routine designed to catch errors that occur while Clips is combining all the clips in the current file into a single clip. The most likely error here would be that the total length of the text of all the clips in the file exceeds 32K, and thus exceeds the capacity of the ClipText text box.

When an error occurs in the CombineAll routine, execution jumps to the CAMemError label

```
CAMemError:
   MClipForm.ClipText = Original$
   Clip(0) = Original$
   IgnoreChange% = False
   DispErrorMsg "Too much data to combine into a single Clip!"
Resume CABackDoor
```

The error routine starts by restoring the original text of the ClipText text box and of the zero element of the Clip() array, resets IgnoreChange%, and then finally displays an error message before exiting.

EXTENDING VISUAL BASIC'S REACH

All in all, Clips is a remarkably straightforward Visual Basic application, consisting for the most part of simple and easily understood code. The key to the application, however, was Clips's ability to extend its reach beyond the limits of Visual Basic through use of the CLPWATCH.DLL.

DLLS in general are not simple, and ones that implement subclassing or callback functions, like CLPWATCH.DLL and DMENU.DLL (which will be presented in Chapter 7) are especially complex. While both of these DLLs work well with the specific utilities for which they were designed, neither is intended for general-purpose use. For instance, while they work well together, both CLPWATCH.DLL and DMENU.DLL could cause conflicts with other subclassing utilities.

Anyone interested in producing more bullet-proof subclassing DLLs would be well-advised to study Daniel Appleman's excellent article, "Rules of the Road," in the August, 1993 issue of *Windows Tech Journal*. Alternately, you might consider using a commercial custom control that provides generic access to callbacks, subclassing functions, and the Windows message loop, such as DesaWare's SpyWorks/VB, in lieu of a custom DLL. Finally, you might look for a custom control that specifically addresses the requirements of your application. For instance, Clips might well have made use of Crescent Software's CSForm control (part of Crescent's QuickPak Professional for Windows), which adds a custom event called ClipBoardChange to Visual Basic forms, through which the form is notified of any change in the contents of the clipboard.

MCLIP.FRM

```
'   * * * * * * * * * * * * * * * * * * * * * * * * * * * * *
'   MULTCLIP.FRM
'   Copyright (c) 1993 by Paul Bonner
'   PC Magazine Visual Basic Utilities
'   * * * * * * * * * * * * * * * * * * * * * * * * * * * * *
VERSION 2.00
Begin Form MClipForm
    BackColor       =    &H00C0C0C0&
    Caption         =    "Clips"
    Height          =    6000
    Icon            =    MULTCLIP.FRX:0000
    KeyPreview      =    -1   'True
    Left            =    1770
    LinkTopic       =    "Form1"
    ScaleHeight     =    5310
    ScaleWidth      =    6360
    Top             =    1470
    Width           =    6480
    Begin Frame Frame2
        BackColor       =    &H00C0C0C0&
        Caption         =    "Clip Text:"
        Height          =    2535
        Left            =    120
        TabIndex        =    4
        Top             =    2040
        Width           =    6135
        Begin TextBox ClipText
            FontBold        =    0     'False
            FontItalic      =    0     'False
            FontName        =    "Arial"
            FontSize        =    9
            FontStrikethru  =    0     'False
            FontUnderline   =    0     'False
            Height          =    1935
            Left            =    120
            MultiLine       =    -1    'True
            ScrollBars      =    3     'Both
            TabIndex        =    1
            Top             =    360
            Width           =    5775
        End
    End
    Begin Frame Frame1
        BackColor       =    &H00C0C0C0&
        Caption         =    "Clip Titles:"
        Height          =    1695
        Left            =    120
        TabIndex        =    3
        Top             =    240
        Width           =    6135
        Begin ListBox Titles
            DragIcon        =    MULTCLIP.FRX:0302
            FontBold        =    0     'False
            FontItalic      =    0     'False
```

```
            FontName          =     "Arial"
            FontSize          =     9
            FontStrikethru    =     0      'False
            FontUnderline     =     0      'False
            Height            =     1155
            Left              =     120
            TabIndex          =     0
            Top               =     360
            Width             =     5775
        End
    End
    Begin CommonDialog CMDialog1
        Left              =     600
        Top               =     4680
    End
    Begin Label lblStatus
        AutoSize          =     -1     'True
        BackColor         =     &H00C0C0C0&
        Caption           =     "lblStatus"
        Height            =     195
        Left              =     1920
        TabIndex          =     2
        Top               =     4800
        Width             =     750
    End
    Begin Menu fMenu
        Caption           =     "&File"
        Begin Menu fItem
            Caption           =     "&New"
            Index             =     1
        End
        Begin Menu fItem
            Caption           =     "&Open"
            Index             =     2
        End
        Begin Menu fItem
            Caption           =     "&Save"
            Enabled           =     0      'False
            Index             =     3
        End
        Begin Menu fItem
            Caption           =     "Save &As..."
            Enabled           =     0      'False
            Index             =     4
        End
        Begin Menu fItem
            Caption           =     "E&xit"
            Index             =     5
        End
        Begin Menu fsep
            Caption           =     "-"
        End
        Begin Menu aboutItem
            Caption           =     "&About..."
        End
    End
    Begin Menu eMenu
        Caption           =     "&Edit"
        Begin Menu eItem
            Caption           =     "Cu&t"
            Enabled           =     0      'False
            Index             =     0
            Shortcut          =     ^X
        End
```

```
    Begin Menu eItem
       Caption          =    "&Copy"
       Enabled          =    0     'False
       Index            =    1
       Shortcut         =    ^C
    End
    Begin Menu eItem
       Caption          =    "&Paste"
       Enabled          =    0     'False
       Index            =    2
       Shortcut         =    ^V
    End
    Begin Menu eItem
       Caption          =    "Select &All"
       Enabled          =    0     'False
       Index            =    3
    End
    Begin Menu eItem
       Caption          =    "Clea&r"
       Enabled          =    0     'False
       Index            =    4
    End
    Begin Menu eItem
       Caption          =    "-"
       Index            =    5
    End
    Begin Menu eItem
       Caption          =    "Change &Title"
       Enabled          =    0     'False
       Index            =    6
    End
    Begin Menu eItem
       Caption          =    "De&lete Clip"
       Enabled          =    0     'False
       Index            =    7
    End
    Begin Menu eItem
       Caption          =    "-"
       Index            =    8
    End
    Begin Menu eItem
       Caption          =    "Co&mbine All"
       Enabled          =    0     'False
       Index            =    9
    End
 End
 Begin Menu setMenu
    Caption          =    "&Settings"
    Begin Menu sItem
       Caption          =    "&On"
       Checked          =    -1    'True
       Index            =    1
    End
    Begin Menu sItem
       Caption          =    "O&ff"
       Index            =    2
    End
    Begin Menu sItem
       Caption          =    "&Combine"
       Index            =    3
    End
    Begin Menu sItem
       Caption          =    "-"
       Index            =    4
```

```
            End
        Begin Menu sItem
            Caption            =      "&Beep"
            Checked            =      -1   'True
            Index              =      5
        End
    End
End
DefInt A-Z
Option Explicit
Dim OldChoiceChanged%
Dim OldChoice%

Sub aboutItem_Click ()
'  * * * * * * * * * * * * * * * * * * * * * * * * * * * * *
'  display About box
'  * * * * * * * * * * * * * * * * * * * * * * * * * * * * *
MsgBox "Clips 2.1" + CRLF$ + "Copyright (c) 1993 by Paul Bonner," + CRLF$ + ⇔
    "PC Magazine Visual Basic Utilities." + CRLF + "All Rights Reserved.", ⇔
        64, "About Clips 2.1"
End Sub

Function CheckChanges () As Integer
'  * * * * * * * * * * * * * * * * * * * * * * * * * * * * *
'  * determines whether ClipText has changed,
'  * saves contents to Clip() array if necessary
'  * * * * * * * * * * * * * * * * * * * * * * * * * * * * *
Dim OC$
CheckChanges = True
If OldChoiceChanged% Then
    On Error GoTo TCMemError
    OC$ = Clip(OldChoice%)
    Clip(OldChoice%) = ClipText
    On Error GoTo 0
End If
OldChoice% = Titles.ListIndex
OldChoiceChanged% = False
BD1:
Exit Function

TCMemError:
'  * * * * * * * * * * * * * * * * * * * * * * * * * * * * *
'  restore original contents of Clip() array member
'  * * * * * * * * * * * * * * * * * * * * * * * * * * * * *
    Screen.MousePointer = 0
    Clip(OldChoice%) = OC$
    CheckChanges = False
    DispErrorMsg "Ran out of memory trying to modify " + Title(OldChoice%)
    Resume BD1
End Function

Sub ClipText_Change ()
'  * * * * * * * * * * * * * * * * * * * * * * * * * * * * *
'  set OldChoiceChanged% flag
'  * * * * * * * * * * * * * * * * * * * * * * * * * * * * *
If IgnoreChange% = False Then OldChoiceChanged% = True: FileDirty% = True
End Sub

Sub ClipText_DragDrop (Source As Control, X As Single, Y As Single)
'  * * * * * * * * * * * * * * * * * * * * * * * * * * * * *
'  called when title dropped on ClipText in combine mode
'  * * * * * * * * * * * * * * * * * * * * * * * * * * * * *
Dim Drop$, S%, ddOriginal$
ddOriginal$ = ClipText
```

```
Drop$ = ddOriginal$
On Error GoTo DropError
' * * * * * * * * * * * * * * * * * * * * * * * * * * *
'   dropped text inserted at selstart
'   replaces any selected text in target
' * * * * * * * * * * * * * * * * * * * * * * * * * * *
S% = ClipText.SelStart + ClipText.SelLength
ClipText.Text=Left$(Drop$,S%)+Clip(Titles.ListIndex)+Mid$(Drop$,S%+1)
ClipText.SelStart = S% + Len(Clip(Titles.ListIndex))
Clip(CombineIndex%) = ClipText
FileDirty% = True
On Error GoTo 0
ddBD:
Exit Sub

DropError:
ClipText = ddOriginal$
Clip(CombineIndex%) = ddOriginal$
DispErrorMsg "These clips are too big to combine."
Resume ddBD
End Sub

Sub ClipText_GotFocus ()
' * * * * * * * * * * * * * * * * * * * * * * * * * * *
'   don't accept focus if no clips in file
' * * * * * * * * * * * * * * * * * * * * * * * * * * *
If Titles.ListCount < 1 Then Titles.SetFocus
End Sub

Sub ClipText_KeyDown (KeyCode As Integer, Shift As Integer)
' * * * * * * * * * * * * * * * * * * * * * * * * * * *
'   don't accept focus if no clips in file
' * * * * * * * * * * * * * * * * * * * * * * * * * * *
If Titles.ListCount < 1 Then Titles.SetFocus : Exit Sub
End Sub

Sub eItem_Click (Index As Integer)
' * * * * * * * * * * * * * * * * * * * * * * * * * * *
'   processes Edit menu selections
'
'   starts by making sure ClipText has focus for most operations
' * * * * * * * * * * * * * * * * * * * * * * * * * * *
If ActiveControl <> ClipText And Index < 6 Then ClipText.SetFocus

Select Case Index
Case 0     'Cut
   SendKeys "+{DEL}"
Case 1     'Copy
   SendKeys "^{INSERT}"
Case 2     'Paste
   SendKeys "+{INSERT}"
Case 3     'Select All
   ClipText.SelStart = 0
   ClipText.SelLength = Len(ClipText)
Case 4     'Clear
   ClipText = ""
Case 6     'Retitle
   Dim LI, DefVal$, Answer$
   LI = Titles.ListIndex
   If LI < 0 Then Exit Sub
   DefVal$ = Titles.List(LI)
  Answer$ = InputBox("Enter a new title for this item:", "Change Title",⇔
     DefVal$)
   If Answer$ <> "" Then Titles.List(LI) = Answer$
```

```
      FileDirty% = True
Case 7    'Delete
   DeleteClip
Case 8    'separator
Case 9    'Combine All
   CombineAll
End Select
End Sub

Sub fItem_Click (Index As Integer)
' * * * * * * * * * * * * * * * * * * * * * * * * * * *
'  processes File item selections
'
'  start by calling CheckChanges() to
'  save ClipText changes to Clip() array
' * * * * * * * * * * * * * * * * * * * * * * * * * * *
Dim X%
X% = CheckChanges()
Select Case Index
Case 1    'New
' * * * * * * * * * * * * * * * * * * * * * * * * * * *
'  exit if file needs to be saved and user cancels
' * * * * * * * * * * * * * * * * * * * * * * * * * * *
   If CheckDirty() = True Then Exit Sub
' * * * * * * * * * * * * * * * * * * * * * * * * * * *
'  reset state to On
' * * * * * * * * * * * * * * * * * * * * * * * * * * *
   OldState% = sOn
   State% = sOn
' * * * * * * * * * * * * * * * * * * * * * * * * * * *
'  reinitialize globals
' * * * * * * * * * * * * * * * * * * * * * * * * * * *
   cFile$ = ""
   tFile$ = ""
   IgnoreChange% = True
   LabelIt
   ReDim Clip(0)
   ReDim Title(0)
   ClipCount% = 0
   CombineIndex% = 0
' * * * * * * * * * * * * * * * * * * * * * * * * * * *
'  clear Titles list box and ClipText edit box
' * * * * * * * * * * * * * * * * * * * * * * * * * * *
   Titles.Clear
   ClipText = ""
   IgnoreChange% = False
   FileDirty% = False
' * * * * * * * * * * * * * * * * * * * * * * * * * * *
'  reset menus and caption
' * * * * * * * * * * * * * * * * * * * * * * * * * * *
   MClipForm.Caption = "Clips"
   ToggleMenu False
Case 2    'Open
   If CheckDirty() = True Then Exit Sub
' * * * * * * * * * * * * * * * * * * * * * * * * * * *
'  set up common dialog
' * * * * * * * * * * * * * * * * * * * * * * * * * * *
   CMDialog1.Flags = OFN_HIDEREADONLY Or OFN_FILEMUSTEXIST
   CMDialog1.DefaultExt = "MCF"
   CMDialog1.CancelError = True
   On Error Resume Next
ExtenErrorLoop:
   CMDialog1.Filter = "Clips files|*.MCF"
' * * * * * * * * * * * * * * * * * * * * * * * * * * *
```

```
'   call common dialog
'   exit if user cancels
'   * * * * * * * * * * * * * * * * * * * * * * * * *
    CMDialog1.Action = 1
    If Err = CancelButton Then Exit Sub
'   * * * * * * * * * * * * * * * * * * * * * * * * *
'   don't accept extension other than default (MCF)
'   * * * * * * * * * * * * * * * * * * * * * * * * *
    If CMDialog1.Flags And OFN_EXTENTIONDIFFERENT Then
        MsgBox "File must have an MCF extension!"
        GoTo ExtenErrorLoop
    End If
    On Error GoTo 0
    tFile$ = CMDialog1.Filename
    If tFile$ = "" Then Exit Sub
    OldChoiceChanged% = False
'   * * * * * * * * * * * * * * * * * * * * * * * * *
'   load file
'   * * * * * * * * * * * * * * * * * * * * * * * * *
    LoadFile tFile$
Case 3    'Save
'   * * * * * * * * * * * * * * * * * * * * * * * * *
'   call file naming routine if not yet named
'   otherwise just save it
'   * * * * * * * * * * * * * * * * * * * * * * * * *
    If cFile$ = "" Then
        SaveWithNewName
    Else
        SaveClipsFile
    End If
Case 4      'Save As
    SaveWithNewName
Case 5    'Exit
    Unload MClipForm
End Select
End Sub

Sub Form_KeyDown (KeyCode As Integer, Shift As Integer)
'   * * * * * * * * * * * * * * * * * * * * * * * * *
'   calls GetClip when DLL notifies form that clipboard has changed
'   * * * * * * * * * * * * * * * * * * * * * * * * *
If (State% <> sOn) Or (GetActiveWindow() = hWnd) Then Exit Sub
If KeyCode = &H7F Then GetClip
End Sub

Sub Form_Load ()
'   * * * * * * * * * * * * * * * * * * * * * * * * *
'   exit if another instance of Clips already loaded
'   * * * * * * * * * * * * * * * * * * * * * * * * *
If App.PrevInstance Then End
'   * * * * * * * * * * * * * * * * * * * * * * * * *
'   register this window as a clipboard viewer
'   * * * * * * * * * * * * * * * * * * * * * * * * *
Dim OldViewer&
OldViewer& = RegClipViewer(hWnd, True)
'   * * * * * * * * * * * * * * * * * * * * * * * * *
'   initialize some globals
CRLF$ = Chr$(13) + Chr$(10)
Path$ = App.Path
If Right$(Path$, 1) <> "\" Then Path$ = Path$ + "\"
OldState% = sOn
State% = sOn
Beeper% = True
'   * * * * * * * * * * * * * * * * * * * * * * * * *
```

```
'   update status label and menus
'   * * * * * * * * * * * * * * * * * * * * * * * * *
LabelIt
ToggleMenu False
'   * * * * * * * * * * * * * * * * * * * * * * * * *
'   process command line file spec, if any
'   * * * * * * * * * * * * * * * * * * * * * * * * *
If Command$ <> "" Then
    tFile$ = UCase$(Command$)
    If InStr(tFile$, ".MCF") = 0 Then Exit Sub
    LoadFile tFile$
End If
End Sub


Sub Form_Paint ()
'   * * * * * * * * * * * * * * * * * * * * * * * * *
'   draw 3d box around status label
'   * * * * * * * * * * * * * * * * * * * * * * * * *
FrameControl Me, lblStatus
End Sub


Sub Form_QueryUnload (Cancel As Integer, UnloadMode As Integer)
'   * * * * * * * * * * * * * * * * * * * * * * * * *
'   give user a chance to save file or to cancel operation
'   * * * * * * * * * * * * * * * * * * * * * * * * *
Select Case CheckDirty()
Case True
    Cancel = True
Case False
'   * * * * * * * * * * * * * * * * * * * * * * * * *
'   cancel clipboard viewer status
'   * * * * * * * * * * * * * * * * * * * * * * * * *
    Dim OldViewer&
    OldViewer& = RegClipViewer(MClipForm.hWnd, False)
End Select
End Sub


Sub Form_Resize ()
'   * * * * * * * * * * * * * * * * * * * * * * * * *
'   if form isn't minimized
'   resize everything
'   * * * * * * * * * * * * * * * * * * * * * * * * *
If Windowstate = 1 Then Exit Sub
Dim fHeight%, X%
fHeight% = MClipForm.Height
X% = MClipForm.Width - 400
If X% > 400 Then
    Frame1.Width = X%
    Frame2.Width = X%
End If
X% = Frame1.Width - 240
If X% > 240 Then
    Titles.Width = X%
    ClipText.Width = X%
End If
Frame1.Top = .0425 * fHeight%
Titles.Top = 240
Frame1.Height = .3 * fHeight%
X% = Frame1.Height - 480
If X% > 480 Then Titles.Height = X%
Frame2.Top = .363 * fHeight%
Frame2.Height = .449 * fHeight%
ClipText.Top = 240
X% = Frame2.Height - 480
```

```
If X% > 480 Then ClipText.Height = X%
lblStatus.Top = fHeight% * .832
FrameControl Me, lblStatus
End Sub

Sub lblStatus_DblClick ()
' * * * * * * * * * * * * * * * * * * * * * * * * * *
'   increment state when user double clicks label
'   skipping sCombine if fewer than 2 clips in file,
'   and dropping back to sOn after sCombine
' * * * * * * * * * * * * * * * * * * * * * * * * * *
Dim Y%
Y% = State% + 1
If Y% = 3 And Titles.ListCount < 2 Then Y% = 1
If Y% = 4 Then Y% = 1
sItem_Click Y%
End Sub

Sub sItem_Click (Index As Integer)
' * * * * * * * * * * * * * * * * * * * * * * * * * *
'   process Settings menu choices
' * * * * * * * * * * * * * * * * * * * * * * * * * *
Select Case Index
Case Is < 3 'turn On or Off
    If State% = sCombine Then SetCombineMode False
    ToggleSettings Index
    State% = Index
    LabelIt
Case Is = 3
    If State% <> sCombine Then SetCombineMode True
    ToggleSettings 3
Case Is = 5
    Beeper% = Not Beeper%
    sItem(5).Checked = Beeper%
End Select
End Sub

Sub Titles_Click ()
' * * * * * * * * * * * * * * * * * * * * * * * * * *
'   exit if Combine Mode active, else if list isn't empty
'   save any changes in ClipText to Clip() array,
'   then update ClipText
' * * * * * * * * * * * * * * * * * * * * * * * * * *
Dim LI
If State% = sCombine Then Exit Sub
If Titles.ListCount Then
    Screen.MousePointer = 11
    If CheckChanges() = False Then Exit Sub
    OldChoice% = Titles.ListIndex
    OldChoiceChanged% = False
    IgnoreChange% = True
    LI = Titles.ListIndex: ClipText = Clip(LI)
    IgnoreChange% = False
End If
Screen.MousePointer = 0
End Sub

Sub Titles_MouseDown (Button As Integer, Shift As Integer, X As Single, Y As↩
    Single)
' * * * * * * * * * * * * * * * * * * * * * * * * * *
'   if Combine Mode is active activate drag/drop
' * * * * * * * * * * * * * * * * * * * * * * * * * *
If Not State% = sCombine Then Exit Sub
Titles.Drag 1
End Sub
```

LISTING

MC_FILE.BAS

```
'  * * * * * * * * * * * * * * * * * * * * * * * * * * *
'  MC_FILE.BAS
'  Copyright (c) 1993 by Paul Bonner
'  PC Magazine Visual Basic Utilities
'  * * * * * * * * * * * * * * * * * * * * * * * * * * *
DefInt A-Z
Option Explicit
Global Path$                          'application path
Const ClipEnd$ = "[Stop]"            'end of Clip marker for cFile$
Dim F As Integer                     'file handle
Dim J As Integer                     'file handle
Dim RecordNum As Integer             'identifies current record
'  * * * * * * * * * * * * * * * * * * * * * * * * * * *
'  Common Dialog constants
'  * * * * * * * * * * * * * * * * * * * * * * * * * * *
Global Const OFN_HIDEREADONLY = &H4&
Global Const OFN_OVERWRITEPROMPT = &H2&
Global Const OFN_EXTENTIONDIFFERENT = &H400&
Global Const OFN_FILEMUSTEXIST = &H1000&
Global Const CancelButton = 32755


Sub CleanUpFiles ()
Dim X%
'  * * * * * * * * * * * * * * * * * * * * * * * * * * *
'  Kill old backups
'  Backup current files
'  Make temp files current
'  * * * * * * * * * * * * * * * * * * * * * * * * * * *
On Error Resume Next
Kill Path$ + "Titles.Bak"
Kill Path$ + "ClipText.Bak"
Name tFile$ As Path$ + "Titles.Bak"
Name cFile$ As Path$ + "ClipText.Bak"
'  * * * * * * * * * * * * * * * * * * * * * * * * * * *
'  if temp files and dest file on same drive
'  just rename temp to dest
'  * * * * * * * * * * * * * * * * * * * * * * * * * * *
If Left$(tFile$, 1) = Left$(Path$, 1) Then
    Name Path$ + "tTmp.Asc" As tFile$
    Name Path$ + "ClipTmp.Asc" As cFile$
Else
'  * * * * * * * * * * * * * * * * * * * * * * * * * * *
'  otherwise copy temp files to dest
'  then delete temp files
'  * * * * * * * * * * * * * * * * * * * * * * * * * * *
    On Error Resume Next
    FileCopy Path$ + "tTmp.Asc", tFile$
    X% = DoEvents()
    FileCopy Path$ + "ClipTmp.Asc", cFile$
    X% = DoEvents()
    Kill Path$ + "tTmp.Asc"
    Kill Path$ + "ClipTmp.Asc"
End If
```

```
X% = DoEvents()
End Sub

Function Exists% (F$)
'  * * * * * * * * * * * * * * * * * * * * * * * * * *
'  returns 0 if file not found, or if error in file spec,
'  otherwise returns -1
'  * * * * * * * * * * * * * * * * * * * * * * * * * *
On Error Resume Next
Exists% = True
If Len(Dir$(F$)) = 0 Then Exists% = False
On Error GoTo 0
End Function

Sub GetFiles ()
Dim C$, X, Y, Look$, D$
'  * * * * * * * * * * * * * * * * * * * * * * * * * *
'  Open Titles file
'  * * * * * * * * * * * * * * * * * * * * * * * * * *
On Error GoTo IDXNotFound
F = FreeFile
Open tFile$ For Input As F
'  * * * * * * * * * * * * * * * * * * * * * * * * * *
'  Input total records
'  * * * * * * * * * * * * * * * * * * * * * * * * * *
Input #F, C$
ClipCount% = Val(C$)
If ClipCount% = 0 Then
    ToggleMenu False
    Close F
    IgnoreChange% = True
    MClipForm.ClipText = ""
    IgnoreChange% = False
    Exit Sub
End If
'  * * * * * * * * * * * * * * * * * * * * * * * * * *
'  Redimension Title and Clip arrays to hold
'  all clips
'  * * * * * * * * * * * * * * * * * * * * * * * * * *
ReDim Title(ClipCount% - 1)
ReDim Clip(ClipCount% - 1)
'  * * * * * * * * * * * * * * * * * * * * * * * * * *
'  Read  clip titles
'  * * * * * * * * * * * * * * * * * * * * * * * * * *
For X = 1 To ClipCount%
    Input #F, Title(X - 1)
    MClipForm.Titles.AddItem Title(X - 1)
Next
Close F
'  * * * * * * * * * * * * * * * * * * * * * * * * * *
'  Get Clip Text for each item
'  * * * * * * * * * * * * * * * * * * * * * * * * * *
F = FreeFile
Open cFile$ For Input As F
For X = 1 To ClipCount%
'  * * * * * * * * * * * * * * * * * * * * * * * * * *
'  Set Look$ to select item's index tag
'  * * * * * * * * * * * * * * * * * * * * * * * * * *
Look$ = "[" & X & "]"
'  * * * * * * * * * * * * * * * * * * * * * * * * * *
'  Find item's header
'  * * * * * * * * * * * * * * * * * * * * * * * * * *
Do While C$ <> Look$
    Line Input #F, C$
```

```
Loop
'   *  *  *  *  *  *  *  *  *  *  *  *  *  *  *  *  *  *  *  *  *  *  *
'   Read Text
'   *  *  *  *  *  *  *  *  *  *  *  *  *  *  *  *  *  *  *  *  *  *  *
D$ = ""
C$ = ""
Line Input #F, C$
Do While C$ <> ClipEnd$
    D$ = D$ + C$ + CRLF$
    Line Input #F, C$
Loop
Clip(X - 1) = D$
Next X
Close F
'   *  *  *  *  *  *  *  *  *  *  *  *  *  *  *  *  *  *  *  *  *  *  *
'   Fix Menus and Restore standard pointer
'   *  *  *  *  *  *  *  *  *  *  *  *  *  *  *  *  *  *  *  *  *  *  *
BackDoor:
ToggleMenu True
MClipForm.Caption = "Clips -- " + tFile$
Screen.MousePointer = 1

Exit Sub
'   *  *  *  *  *  *  *  *  *  *  *  *  *  *  *  *  *  *  *  *  *  *  *
'   Error handling routine
'   *  *  *  *  *  *  *  *  *  *  *  *  *  *  *  *  *  *  *  *  *  *  *
IDXNotFound:
    MsgBox "Error loading " + tFile$ + ". File truncated."
    Close #F
    ClipCount% = X%
    Dim Z%
    Resume BackDoor
End Sub

Sub LoadFile (tFile$)
'   *  *  *  *  *  *  *  *  *  *  *  *  *  *  *  *  *  *  *  *  *  *  *
'   check for existence of MCF and CLP files before proceeding
'   exit if either can't be found
'   *  *  *  *  *  *  *  *  *  *  *  *  *  *  *  *  *  *  *  *  *  *  *
cFile$ = Left$(tFile$, InStr(tFile$, ".")) + "CLP"
If Not Exists(tFile$) Or Not Exists(cFile$) Then Exit Sub
'   *  *  *  *  *  *  *  *  *  *  *  *  *  *  *  *  *  *  *  *  *  *  *
'   disable titles list (to speed update process)
'   set hourglass cursor
'   clear list box
'   call getfiles routine
'   *  *  *  *  *  *  *  *  *  *  *  *  *  *  *  *  *  *  *  *  *  *  *
MClipForm.Titles.Enabled = False
Screen.MousePointer = 11
MClipForm.Titles.Clear
GetFiles
'   *  *  *  *  *  *  *  *  *  *  *  *  *  *  *  *  *  *  *  *  *  *  *
'   re-enable list box
'   select first item
'   reset cursor and FileDirty% variable
'   *  *  *  *  *  *  *  *  *  *  *  *  *  *  *  *  *  *  *  *  *  *  *
MClipForm.Titles.Enabled = True
If MClipForm.Titles.ListCount Then MClipForm.Titles.ListIndex = 0
Screen.MousePointer = 1
FileDirty% = False
End Sub

Sub SaveClipsFile ()
Screen.MousePointer = 11
```

```
Dim Index, Header$, C$
' * * * * * * * * * * * * * * * * * * * * * * * *
' Create tTmp.Asc so that CleanUpFiles doesn't clobber index
' * * * * * * * * * * * * * * * * * * * * * * * *
On Error Resume Next
    Name cFile$ As Path$ + "tTmp.Asc"
On Error GoTo 0
' * * * * * * * * * * * * * * * * * * * * * * * *
'   Save Title of each item
' * * * * * * * * * * * * * * * * * * * * * * * *
F = FreeFile
Open Path$ + "tTmp.Asc" For Output Access Write As #F
C$ = Trim(Str$(ClipCount%))
Print #F, C$
For RecordNum = 1 To ClipCount%
        Print #F, Title(RecordNum - 1)
Next
Close F
' * * * * * * * * * * * * * * * * * * * * * * * *
'   Save Text for each item
' * * * * * * * * * * * * * * * * * * * * * * * *
F = FreeFile
Open Path$ + "ClipTmp.Asc" For Output Access Write As #F Len = 4096
For RecordNum = 1 To ClipCount%
    Header$ = "[" & RecordNum & "]"
    Print #F, Header$
    Print #F, Clip(RecordNum - 1)
    Print #F, ClipEnd$
Next RecordNum
Close F
' * * * * * * * * * * * * * * * * * * * * * * * *
'   Now clean up files
' * * * * * * * * * * * * * * * * * * * * * * * *
CleanUpFiles
FileDirty% = False
Screen.MousePointer = 1
End Sub


Sub SaveWithNewName ()
' * * * * * * * * * * * * * * * * * * * * * * * *
'   set Common Dialog flags
' * * * * * * * * * * * * * * * * * * * * * * * *
MClipForm.CMDialog1.Flags = OFN_HIDEREADONLY Or OFN_OVERWRITEPROMPT
MClipForm.CMDialog1.DefaultExt = "MCF"
MClipForm.CMDialog1.Filter = "Clips files|*.MCF"
On Error Resume Next
' * * * * * * * * * * * * * * * * * * * * * * * *
'   call Save dialog
' * * * * * * * * * * * * * * * * * * * * * * * *
MClipForm.CMDialog1.Action = 2
' * * * * * * * * * * * * * * * * * * * * * * * *
'   exit if user pressed cancel button
'   otherwise, force an MCF extension
' * * * * * * * * * * * * * * * * * * * * * * * *
If Err = CancelButton Then Exit Sub
If MClipForm.CMDialog1.Flags And OFN_EXTENTIONDIFFERENT Then
    MsgBox "File must have an MCF extension!"
    Exit Sub
End If
' * * * * * * * * * * * * * * * * * * * * * * * *
'   set file name and path variables
'   call SaveClipsFile routine to save data
' * * * * * * * * * * * * * * * * * * * * * * * *
tFile$ = MClipForm.CMDialog1.Filename
```

```
If tFile$ = "" Then Exit Sub
cFile$ = Left$(tFile$, InStr(tFile$, ".")) + "CLP"
Dim X
For X = Len(tFile$) To 1 Step -1
    If Mid$(tFile$, X) = "\" Then
        Path$ = Left$(tFile$, X)
        Exit For
    End If
Next
SaveClipsFile
'  * * * * * * * * * * * * * * * * * * * * * * * *
'   update caption to display file name
'  * * * * * * * * * * * * * * * * * * * * * * * *
MClipForm.Caption = "Clips -- " + tFile$
End Sub
```

LISTING

MCLIP.BAS

```
'  * * * * * * * * * * * * * * * * * * * * * * * * * *
'   MCLIP.BAS
'   Copyright (c) 1993 by Paul Bonner
'   PC Magazine Visual Basic Utilities
'  * * * * * * * * * * * * * * * * * * * * * * * * * *
DefInt A-Z
Option Explicit
'  * * * * * * * * * * * * * * * * * * * * * * * * * *
'   CLPWATCH.DLL declaration
'  * * * * * * * * * * * * * * * * * * * * * * * * * *
DeclareFunctionRegClipViewerLib"clpwatch.dll"(ByValwHand%,ByValOnOff%)⇔
    As Long
'  * * * * * * * * * * * * * * * * * * * * * * * * * *
'   global State variables and flags
'  * * * * * * * * * * * * * * * * * * * * * * * * * *
Global State%
Global OldState%
Global Const sOn = 1
Global Const sOff = 2
Global Const sCombine = 3
Global IgnoreChange%
'  * * * * * * * * * * * * * * * * * * * * * * * * * *
'   Other globals
'  * * * * * * * * * * * * * * * * * * * * * * * * * *
Global CRLF$      'Carriage Return
Global FileDirty%    'True if changes not yet saved
Global Beeper% 'Beep after adding new item
Global Title() As String      'Titles array
Global Clip() As Variant       'Text array
Global ClipCount%    'Array elements counter
Global CombineIndex%       'Item being combined
'  * * * * * * * * * * * * * * * * * * * * * * * * * *
'   fileName holders
'  * * * * * * * * * * * * * * * * * * * * * * * * * *
Global cFile$
```

```
Global tFile$
' * * * * * * * * * * * * * * * * * * * * * * * * * * *
'   API function declaration
' * * * * * * * * * * * * * * * * * * * * * * * * * * *
Declare Function GetActiveWindow Lib "User" () As Integer
' * * * * * * * * * * * * * * * * * * * * * * * * * * *
'   * clipboard owner test declarations
' * * * * * * * * * * * * * * * * * * * * * * * * * * *
Declare Function GetClipboardOwner% Lib "User" ()
Declare Function IsWindow% Lib "User" (ByVal hWnd As Integer)
Function CheckDirty () As Integer
' * * * * * * * * * * * * * * * * * * * * * * * * * * *
'   if FileDirty% flag set, check if user wants to abandon
'   changes. if user says no, return True, otherwise false
' * * * * * * * * * * * * * * * * * * * * * * * * * * *
If FileDirty% = True Then
    Dim C%
    C% = MsgBox("Abandon changes to this file?", 49, "Clips")
    If C% <> 1 Then CheckDirty = True: Exit Function
End If
CheckDirty = False
End Function

Function CleanString (Test$) As String
' * * * * * * * * * * * * * * * * * * * * * * * * * * *
'   used to build title from first 60 chars of new clip
' * * * * * * * * * * * * * * * * * * * * * * * * * * *
Dim I%
Test$ = Trim(Test$)
' * * * * * * * * * * * * * * * * * * * * * * * * * * *
'   first strip off leading control chars
' * * * * * * * * * * * * * * * * * * * * * * * * * * *
Do While Len(Test$) > 2
    If Asc(Left$(Test$, 1)) < 33 Then
        Test$ = Mid$(Test$, 2)
    Else
        Exit Do
    End If
Loop
' * * * * * * * * * * * * * * * * * * * * * * * * * * *
'   now chop at 1st return
' * * * * * * * * * * * * * * * * * * * * * * * * * * *
I% = InStr(Test$, CRLF$)
If I% Then Test$ = Left$(Test$, I% - 1)
CleanString = Test$
End Function

Sub CombineAll ()
' * * * * * * * * * * * * * * * * * * * * * * * * * * *
'   combine all clips into a single clip
' * * * * * * * * * * * * * * * * * * * * * * * * * * *
Dim X%, Original$, temp$
X% = MsgBox("Combine all entries into a single Clip?", 52, "Clips")
If X% <> 6 Then Exit Sub
' * * * * * * * * * * * * * * * * * * * * * * * * * * *
'   select first clip
' * * * * * * * * * * * * * * * * * * * * * * * * * * *
MClipForm.Titles.ListIndex = 0
Original$ = MClipForm.ClipText
On Error GoTo CAMemError
IgnoreChange% = True
' * * * * * * * * * * * * * * * * * * * * * * * * * * *
'   assign ClipText.Text to temp$
temp$ = MClipForm.ClipText
```

```
'    * * * * * * * * * * * * * * * * * * * * * * * * * * *
'    loop through Clip()
'    * * * * * * * * * * * * * * * * * * * * * * * * * * *
For X% = 1 To UBound(Clip, 1)
'       * * * * * * * * * * * * * * * * * * * * * * * * * * *
'       first strip off trailing CRLF$'s
'       * * * * * * * * * * * * * * * * * * * * * * * * * * *
    Do While Right$(temp$, 2) = CRLF$
        temp$ = Left$(temp$, Len(temp$) - 2)
    Loop
'       * * * * * * * * * * * * * * * * * * * * * * * * * * *
'       now add new string, separated by a CRLF$
'       * * * * * * * * * * * * * * * * * * * * * * * * * * *
    temp$ = temp$ + CRLF$ + Clip(X%)
'       * * * * * * * * * * * * * * * * * * * * * * * * * * *
'       error if string too long to fit into ClipText
'       * * * * * * * * * * * * * * * * * * * * * * * * * * *
    If Len(temp$) > 32567 Then Err = 14
Next
'    * * * * * * * * * * * * * * * * * * * * * * * * * * *
'    assign temp$ to ClipText
'    * * * * * * * * * * * * * * * * * * * * * * * * * * *
MClipForm.ClipText = temp$
'    * * * * * * * * * * * * * * * * * * * * * * * * * * *
'    reset arrays
'    * * * * * * * * * * * * * * * * * * * * * * * * * * *
ReDim Title(0)
ReDim Clip(0)
'    * * * * * * * * * * * * * * * * * * * * * * * * * * *
'    reset zero elements & title of combined clip
'    * * * * * * * * * * * * * * * * * * * * * * * * * * *
Clip(0) = MClipForm.ClipText
MClipForm.Titles.List(0)="Combined"+Str$(MClipForm.Titles.ListCount)+⇔
    " clips"
Title(0) = MClipForm.Titles.List(0)
FileDirty% = True
IgnoreChange% = False
On Error GoTo 0
ClipCount% = 1
'    * * * * * * * * * * * * * * * * * * * * * * * * * * *
'    remove all but first item from Titles list box
'    * * * * * * * * * * * * * * * * * * * * * * * * * * *
For X% = MClipForm.Titles.ListCount - 1 To 1 Step -1
    MClipForm.Titles.RemoveItem X%
Next
ToggleMenu True

CABackDoor:
Exit Sub

CAMemError:
    MClipForm.ClipText = Original$
    Clip(0) = Original$
    IgnoreChange% = False
    DispErrorMsg "Too much data to combine into a single Clip!"
Resume CABackDoor
End Sub

Sub DeleteClip ()
Dim X, Index
'    * * * * * * * * * * * * * * * * * * * * * * * * * * *
'    exit if Titles list box is empty
'    * * * * * * * * * * * * * * * * * * * * * * * * * * *
If MClipForm.Titles.ListCount = 0 Then Exit Sub
```

```
'   * * * * * * * * * * * * * * * * * * * * * * * * * * * *
'   confirm user wants to delete
'   * * * * * * * * * * * * * * * * * * * * * * * * * * * *
X = MsgBox("Are you sure that you want to delete the selected clip?", 68,⇔
    "Clips")
If X <> 6 Then Exit Sub
MClipForm.Titles.Enabled = False
'   * * * * * * * * * * * * * * * * * * * * * * * * * * * *
'   identify record to delete
'   * * * * * * * * * * * * * * * * * * * * * * * * * * * *
Index = MClipForm.Titles.ListIndex
'   * * * * * * * * * * * * * * * * * * * * * * * * * * * *
'   delete it
'   * * * * * * * * * * * * * * * * * * * * * * * * * * * *
MClipForm.Titles.RemoveItem Index
'   * * * * * * * * * * * * * * * * * * * * * * * * * * * *
'   renumber array elements
'   * * * * * * * * * * * * * * * * * * * * * * * * * * * *
For X = Index To ClipCount% - 2
    Title(X) = Title(X + 1)
    Clip(X) = Clip(X + 1)
Next
'   * * * * * * * * * * * * * * * * * * * * * * * * * * * *
'   clear last element
'   * * * * * * * * * * * * * * * * * * * * * * * * * * * *
Clip(X) = ""
Title(X) = ""
'   * * * * * * * * * * * * * * * * * * * * * * * * * * * *
'   decrement record count
'   * * * * * * * * * * * * * * * * * * * * * * * * * * * *
ClipCount% = ClipCount% - 1
'   * * * * * * * * * * * * * * * * * * * * * * * * * * * *
'   redim arrays
'   * * * * * * * * * * * * * * * * * * * * * * * * * * * *
ReDim Preserve Title(ClipCount%)
ReDim Preserve Clip(ClipCount%)
'   * * * * * * * * * * * * * * * * * * * * * * * * * * * *
'   toggle menus based on Titles list count
'   * * * * * * * * * * * * * * * * * * * * * * * * * * * *
Select Case ClipCount%
Case Is = 0
    ToggleMenu False
    FileDirty% = True
    IgnoreChange% = True
    MClipForm.ClipText = ""
    IgnoreChange% = False
Case Else
    FileDirty% = True
    MClipForm.Titles.ListIndex = 0
    ToggleMenu True
End Select
MClipForm.Titles.Enabled = True
End Sub

Sub DispErrorMsg (M$)
'   * * * * * * * * * * * * * * * * * * * * * * * * * * * *
'   utility routine to display error message
'   * * * * * * * * * * * * * * * * * * * * * * * * * * * *
On Error GoTo 0
Dim X%
MClipForm.WindowState = 0
X% = MsgBox(M$, 48, "Clips")
End Sub
```

```
Sub FrameControl (F As Form, C As Control)
'   * * * * * * * * * * * * * * * * * * * * * * * * * *
'   centers control on form and
'   draws 3D frame around control
'   * * * * * * * * * * * * * * * * * * * * * * * * * *
Dim Cl%, ct%, ch%, cw%
Const White = &HFFFFFF
Const DarkGray = &H808080
Const hOffSet% = 90
Const vOffSet% = 45
Const dw% = 1
F.DrawWidth = dw%
'   * * * * * * * * * * * * * * * * * * * * * * * * * *
'   center control on form
'   * * * * * * * * * * * * * * * * * * * * * * * * * *
Cl% = (F.Width / 2) - (C.Width / 2)
C.Left = Cl%
ct% = C.Top
cw% = C.Width
ch% = C.Height
'   * * * * * * * * * * * * * * * * * * * * * * * * * *
'   clear form
'   * * * * * * * * * * * * * * * * * * * * * * * * * *
F.Cls
'   * * * * * * * * * * * * * * * * * * * * * * * * * *
'   draw box
'   * * * * * * * * * * * * * * * * * * * * * * * * * *
F.ForeColor = DarkGray
F.Line (Cl% - hOffSet%, ct% - vOffSet%)-(Cl% - hOffSet%, ct% + ch% + vOffSet%)
F.ForeColor = White
F.Line -(Cl% + cw% + hOffSet%, ct% + ch% + vOffSet%)
F.Line -(Cl% + cw% + hOffSet%, ct% - vOffSet%)
F.ForeColor = DarkGray
F.Line -(Cl% - hOffSet%, ct% - vOffSet%)
End Sub

Sub GetClip ()
Dim B$, T$, ec%, X%, Y%, Z&
On Error GoTo MemError
'   * * * * * * * * * * * * * * * * * * * * * * * * * *
'   check to ensure that clipboard change wasn't spurred by
'   clipboard owner shutting down
'   * * * * * * * * * * * * * * * * * * * * * * * * * *
For Y% = 1 To 10
  X% = DoEvents()
Next
Y% = GetClipboardOwner%()
If (Y% = 0) Or (IsWindow%(Y%) = 0) Then Exit Sub
'   * * * * * * * * * * * * * * * * * * * * * * * * * *
'   grab clipboard text
'   * * * * * * * * * * * * * * * * * * * * * * * * * *
B$ = Clipboard.GetText()
If LTrim(B$) = "" Then Exit Sub
'   * * * * * * * * * * * * * * * * * * * * * * * * * *
'   generate title for new clip
'   * * * * * * * * * * * * * * * * * * * * * * * * * *
T$ = Left$(B$, 60)
On Error GoTo 0
T$ = CleanString(T$)
'   * * * * * * * * * * * * * * * * * * * * * * * * * *
'   increment record counter,
'   redim arrays
'   * * * * * * * * * * * * * * * * * * * * * * * * * *
ClipCount% = ClipCount% + 1
```

```
ReDim Preserve Title(ClipCount%)
ReDim Preserve Clip(ClipCount%)
' * * * * * * * * * * * * * * * * * * * * * * * * *
'   add title to list box, then select it
MClipForm.Titles.AddItem T$
MClipForm.Titles.ListIndex = MClipForm.Titles.NewIndex
' * * * * * * * * * * * * * * * * * * * * * * * * *
'   add title to Title() array
' * * * * * * * * * * * * * * * * * * * * * * * * *
Title(ClipCount% - 1) = T$
' * * * * * * * * * * * * * * * * * * * * * * * * *
'   add clipboard text to ClipText
' * * * * * * * * * * * * * * * * * * * * * * * * *
MClipForm.ClipText = B$
ToggleMenu True
If Beeper% Then Beep

BackDoor1:
    Exit Sub
MemError:
    ' * * * * * * * * * * * * * * * * * * * * * * * * *
    '   emit extended beep on memory error
    ' * * * * * * * * * * * * * * * * * * * * * * * * *
    For X% = 1 To 8
        Beep
    Next
Resume BackDoor1
End Sub

Sub LabelIt ()
' * * * * * * * * * * * * * * * * * * * * * * * * *
'   update status label based on value of State%,
'   then redraw 3d box around label
' * * * * * * * * * * * * * * * * * * * * * * * * *
MClipForm.lblStatus.Visible = False
If State% = sOn Then
    MClipForm.lblStatus = "State is On"
Else
    MClipForm.lblStatus = "State is Off"
End If
FrameControl MClipForm, MClipForm.lblStatus
MClipForm.lblStatus.Visible = True
End Sub

Sub SetCombineMode (CombineModeSwitch%)
' * * * * * * * * * * * * * * * * * * * * * * * * *
'   activate/deactivate Combine Mode
' * * * * * * * * * * * * * * * * * * * * * * * * *
Select Case CombineModeSwitch%
Case Is = True    ' activate
    IgnoreChange% = True
    State% = sCombine%
    MClipForm.lblStatus.Visible = False
    MClipForm.lblStatus = "State is Combine"
    FrameControl MClipForm, MClipForm.lblStatus
    MClipForm.lblStatus.Visible = True
    CombineIndex% = MClipForm.Titles.ListIndex
    MClipForm.ClipText.SetFocus
Case Is = False   ' deactivate
    MClipForm.Titles.ListIndex = CombineIndex%
    IgnoreChange% = False
End Select
End Sub
```

```
Sub ToggleMenu (E%)
'  * * * * * * * * * * * * * * * * * * * * * * * * * *
'  enable/disable all Edit Menu items except Combine All
'  * * * * * * * * * * * * * * * * * * * * * * * * * *
Dim X%
For X% = 0 To 7
    If X% <> 5 Then MClipForm.eItem(X%).Enabled = E%
Next
MClipForm.fItem(3).Enabled = E%
MClipForm.fItem(4).Enabled = E%
'  * * * * * * * * * * * * * * * * * * * * * * * * * *
'  enable/disable 2 Combine items based on Titles list count
'  * * * * * * * * * * * * * * * * * * * * * * * * * *
MClipForm.sItem(3).Enabled = ClipCount% > 1
MClipForm.eItem(9).Enabled = ClipCount% > 1
End Sub

Sub ToggleSettings (CheckMe%)
Dim X%
'  * * * * * * * * * * * * * * * * * * * * * * * * * *
'  move check mark to specified settings menu item
'  * * * * * * * * * * * * * * * * * * * * * * * * * *
For X% = 1 To 3
    If X% = CheckMe% Then
        MClipForm.sItem(X%).Checked = True
    Else
        MClipForm.sItem(X%).Checked = False
    End If
Next
'  * * * * * * * * * * * * * * * * * * * * * * * * * *
'  disable File and Edit menus if Combine Mode selected
'  * * * * * * * * * * * * * * * * * * * * * * * * * *
MClipForm.fMenu.Enabled = CheckMe% < 3
MClipForm.eMenu.Enabled = CheckMe% < 3
End Sub
```

C H A P T E R

7

DESKMENU

DeskMenu provides pop-up menu access to all of your Program Manager group items.

Most useful utilities are born out of need. You've got a problem; you want to be able to de-compress ZIP archives from within Windows, or you want to see what a particular font will look like at 48 points, and you figure out how to solve it. That's been the case with the first six projects in this book, and certainly should be the case with most utilities.

Sometimes things work a bit differently, though. Sometimes you stumble upon a great solution, and then have to figure out what problem it solves.

That was the case with DeskMenu, the utility featured in this chapter. I could pretend that I set out to build the finest and most convenient application launcher that Windows has ever seen, and that I studied the problem carefully to arrive at my solution, but that's not what happened. I simply happened upon the key piece—the unique nugget of programming technique—

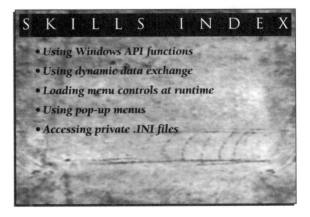

SKILLS INDEX

- *Using Windows API functions*
- *Using dynamic data exchange*
- *Loading menu controls at runtime*
- *Using pop-up menus*
- *Accessing private .INI files*

that makes DeskMenu sing, and got so excited by it that I started wracking my brain for a way to use it. Now, in retrospect, DeskMenu might seem like such an ideal application of that technique that it must have been destined for it from the start, but the truth is that it was just a happy accident.

Of course, once the initial idea of creating DeskMenu struck, there was a lot of work to be done in figuring out exactly how it should look and how it should work, and then writing the code to make it all happen. It all started with me asking one day, "I wonder if this will work…[tinker, tinker, sound of code being written]…Wow, it does…Now, what am I going to do with it?"

■ USING DESKMENU

DeskMenu, as you've probably guessed by now, is an application launcher. Specifically, it pops up a menu of all your Program Manager groups, and all the items that they contain, whenever you press the right mouse button while the mouse pointer is positioned over Windows's desktop window. (The desktop window is the background window behind all other windows, the window upon which desktop patterns or wallpaper is displayed. Anytime the mouse isn't pointing at an application's window, it's pointing at the desktop window.)

When you press down the right mouse button over the desktop window, DeskMenu pops up its menu, which contains a series of hierarchical submenus. The first two submenus are labeled DeskMenu and Windows, and offer a series of menu items related to DeskMenu's operation (in the former case) and for exiting or restarting Windows (in the latter case). Immediately below the Windows item is a separator bar, and then a hierarchical submenu for each of your Program Manager groups, presented in alphabetical order, as shown in Figure 7.1.

When you select any of the Program Manager group submenus using either mouse button, DeskMenu unveils another menu presenting the titles of all the applications in the selected program group, as shown in Figure 7.2.

Selecting any item's title with the mouse launches the associated application or document almost exactly as if it were being launched from within the Program Manager. The application's working directory is set to the directory specified on the item's Properties dialog box in the Program Manager (Figure 7.3) and the application is run in a minimized state if that option is selected.

The only Program Manager property that DeskMenu does not support is the little-used hotkey facility for switching back and forth between applications launched by the Program Manager.

DeskMenu's main menu provides access to each of your Program Manager groups.

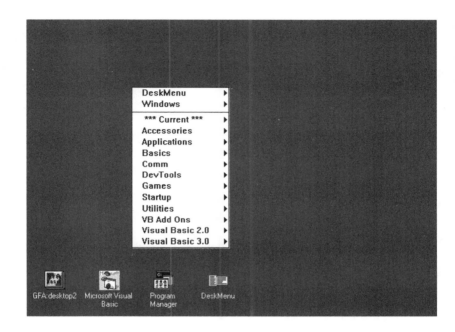

DeskMenu's hierarchical menus provide access to all the applications in a program group.

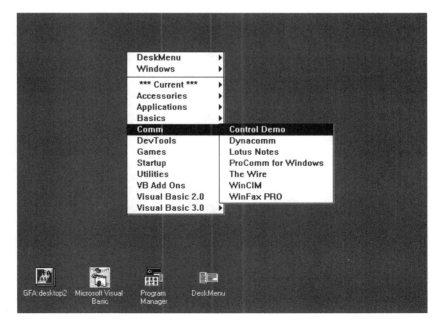

*DeskMenu sets
the working
directory for
an application
according to
the directory
specified in the
Program
Manager's
Properties
dialog box.*

The DeskMenu hierarchical menu item, which appears first on DeskMenu's main menu, opens up to reveal several items related to DeskMenu's operation, as shown in Figure 7.4. The first, About DeskMenu, is used to reveal DeskMenu's About Box.

*The DeskMenu
submenu
presents
several options
relating to
DeskMenu's
operation.*

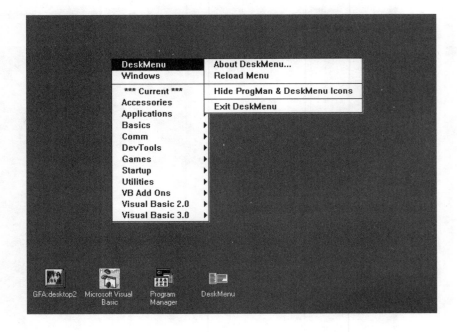

The next item on the DeskMenu submenu, Reload Menu, is used to force Desk-Menu to reload the Program Manager groups and the items in each group. DeskMenu normally loads these just once as it is loaded into memory, using the Program Manager DDE interface to obtain the names of all your Program Manager groups and the names of the items in each group. Thus, if you install a new application that creates a new Program Manager group, or otherwise edit the Program Manager's contents, DeskMenu's menu will no longer perfectly reflect the contents of the Program Manager, and you won't be able to use it to launch the programs that you've just added to the Program Manager. The Reload Menu item tells DeskMenu to reestablish its DDE link with the Program Manager and obtain a new list of Program Groups and Program Items, thus bringing the application-launching capabilities of the two programs back into sync.

You may be wondering why I didn't simply have DeskMenu act as a replacement shell, and forgo the use of Program Manager altogether, since it is fairly simple to make a program perform the basic tasks expected of a shell: for example, shutting down Windows when the shell program is shut down, and notifying other applications that it is about to do so, giving them the opportunity to cancel the operation. Those basics are simple to achieve; however, it is considerably more difficult to make a shell function exactly like the Program Manager in all respects, which is an important concern when you're using other programs that expect the Program Manager to be present at all times. In particular, most replacement shells that I've encountered have difficulty duplicating the Program Manager's DDE interface, which has resulted at least one time too many for my liking in application installation programs crashing at the very end just as they try to establish DDE contact with the Program Manager.

DeskMenu, I think, provides a better solution than replacing the Program Manager altogether. Instead, use DeskMenu, with its very light system resource consumption, as your chief application launching pad, but leave the Program Manager in place to do the things that it can do best. You escape the worst part of the Program Manager—having to open up Program Group icon after Program Group icon while you hunt for the application or document you want to launch—while retaining its benefits.

The next item on the DeskMenu submenu, Hide ProgMan & DeskMenu Icons, makes that prospect even more palatable. This is a check-mark item which, when selected, instructs DeskMenu to hide both its own icon and that of the Program Manager. Both applications remain active, but they don't clutter the bottom of your screen with useless icons. Instead, DeskMenu's pop-up menu becomes your Windows control center.

The final item on the DeskMenu submenu, Exit DeskMenu, is used to close down DeskMenu. When you do, the Program Manager's icon is immediately made visible if it was hidden. Meanwhile, the two items on the Windows submenu, Exit Windows and Restart Windows, provide a quick exit from Windows, or a quick way to restart Windows. Both notify other applications before shutting down Windows, so there is no danger of losing data from other applications when using these items.

That about sums up DeskMenu's capabilities. There's nothing too fancy here, just a simple, fast, and—in my view—downright habit-forming method for launching applications in Windows.

■ THE ORIGIN OF DESKMENU

The seed from which DeskMenu sprung was planted one day shortly after I had completed work on the Clips project described in Chapter 6. Flush with the success of my first effort at subclassing a window, I started to ponder the fact that from Windows's perspective, the desktop was apparently just another window. (Rereading that last sentence makes me think I should spend more time digging in my garden and less time digging through Windows's innards.) Indeed, Windows has a special function, GetDesktopWindow(), which returns the handle of the desktop window.

A special function like that almost begs you to do something with it. So I began to wonder just how windowlike the desktop really is, whether it receives standard messages from Windows when the time comes to redraw itself, or when the user interacts with it in some way, such as by moving the mouse over the desktop or by clicking the mouse on it. If so, would it be possible to subclass the desktop window, so that a program might intercept some of the messages that Windows sends to it and act on them?

If the desktop was indeed just another window, I knew that I should be able to create a dynamic link library and use SetWindowLong to replace the desktop's default window procedure with a callback function in my DLL, just as I had in CLPWATCH-.DLL. Once I had rerouted those messages to the callback function, I could do anything I wanted with them. Still, I wondered if it would work. One function that returns a handle does not a window make.

To test my theory, I loaded up the GFA-BASIC editor and made some modifications to the source code for CLPWATCH.DLL, so that the call to SetWindowLong now pointed at the handle returned by GetDesktopWindow(). Then I modified the callback procedure so that it emitted a beep whenever it received a WM_RBUTTON-DOWN (right mouse button down) message, and otherwise called the desktop window's original window procedure to handle any other messages. Then I compiled the new DLL, wrote a little Visual Basic application that activated it, and tried clicking a couple of times on the desktop with the righthand mouse button.

Beep. Beep.

It worked! And, since I had already figured out with CLPWATCH.DLL how to have a DLL notify my Visual Basic application when a specified message was received for a subclassed window, that meant I could have my application respond to any desktop window event that I chose. (It would be immodest to pretend here that I was anywhere near the first person to think of subclassing the desktop window. In retrospect, it seems clear that other applications work the same magic. But it's not a practice you'll find documented in the Windows SDK manuals, and I feel confident that I was probably the first person to ever make it happen entirely with BASIC code.)

Once I knew that it would work, I had only one problem: What should I do with this fantastic new capability? I could have intercepted nearly any message that Windows sent to the desktop window. But early on the idea of capturing righthand mouse-button clicks stuck in my mind, and I began to find the notion of a pop-up menu appearing on the desktop, like the right-button pop-up menus that are starting to appear in many new Windows applications, very appealing.

That led to another question. What to put on the menu? I could have duplicated or expanded upon the capabilities of the Windows Task Manager, but you don't have to subclass the desktop window to create a replacement Task Manager. You can do that by simply specifying your application using the TASKMAN.EXE= line in SYSTEM.INI, at which point it will appear in all those instances where the Task Manager would normally appear.

Instead, I decided to try to make the process of launching applications a little bit easier by popping up a menu of Program Manager groups and program items. I already knew that the Program Manager had a dynamic data exchange interface that could be used to obtain a list of all its groups and program items. I also knew how to use either the Visual Basic 3.0 PopupMenu command or the Windows API function TrackPopupMenu to pop up a menu anywhere on the screen, so now that I could capture mouse clicks in the desktop window, all the pieces were in place that I would need to build DeskMenu.

Of course, as the project progressed, I needed to polish those pieces. I added a few more key elements, such as the capability to hide the Program Manager's and DeskMenu's icons, or to exit or restart Windows.

■ INSIDE DESKMENU

DeskMenu is a fairly small application, but it uses several interesting, if rather complex, techniques that might be of use in many applications.

The first of these, in the sense that DeskMenu could do nothing without it, is subclassing the desktop window.

■ Subclassing the Desktop Window

Like Clips, DeskMenu takes advantage of the Windows SetWindowLong function to redirect messages for a specified window from the window's default window-handling procedure to a callback routine in a dynamic link library. This enables the callback routine to examine those messages and, when appropriate, to react to them. The callback procedure then passes each message on to the window's default window-handling procedure, to allow that procedure to respond to the message.

Visual Basic didn't gain the capability to handle callbacks between Chapters 6 and 7 so, once again, I turned to GFA-BASIC to create the DLL that calls SetWindowLong and contains the callback function. The DLL used by DeskMenu, called DMENU.DLL, is modeled closely after the CLPWATCH.DLL presented in the previous chapter. It begins with a copyright notice and some compiler directive statements which tell the GFA Compiler that it is to create a dynamic link library rather than an executable file, and that the library should be named DMENU.DLL.

```
' DESKMEN3.GFW
' Copyright 1993 by Paul Bonner
' All Rights Reserved
$LIBRARY DMENUDLL
$LNK EXE DMENU.DLL
```

Next, the LibMain procedure, which is executed as the library is loaded into memory, simply initializes the value of two global variables and identifies the callback procedure using the _cb function. (In examining this code, remember that GFA-BASIC reverses Visual Basic's use of suffixes for integer and long variables. Thus, Watcher& represents an integer, while Watcher% would represent a long).

```
Procedure LibMain(inst&,dseg&,hpsz&,lpcmd%)
  OldDeskProc%=0
  Watcher&=0
  _cb (1)=CC(W,W,W,L)
Return
```

The WatchDesk procedure is the library's window to the outside world because this is the function that the Visual Basic application will call to activate or deactivate the library's subclassing of the desktop window. The procedure takes two parameters: W& (the window handle of the calling application's main window), and OnOff! (a True/False switch indicating whether the library should initiate or terminate its subclassing efforts.) If the OnOff! switch has a value of –1 (True), the WatchDesk procedure calls the Windows API function GetDesktopWindow to obtain the desktop window's handle, and then passes that value and the address of the library's callback function to SetWindowLong.

SetWindowLong returns the address of the subclassed window's standard window procedure. WatchDesk stores this value in the variable OldDeskProc%, and uses it when the Visual Basic application calls WatchDesk with a value of 0 (False) for the OnOff! parameter to restore the desktop window's default window-handling procedure:

```
Procedure WatchDesk(W&, OnOff!)
  $Export WatchDesk
  Watcher&=W&
  Switch OnOff!
  Case -1          'Turn on
    X&= GetDesktopWindow()
   OldDeskProc%=SetWindowLong(X&,GWL_WNDPROC,_cb(1))
  Case 0        'Turn off
    X&= GetDesktopWindow()
    ~SetWindowLong(X&,GWL_WNDPROC,OldDeskProc%)
  EndSwitch
  Retval 0
Return
```

The final procedure in DMENU.DLL, called CC, is the callback procedure to which all messages for the desktop window are routed.

Although CC receives all messages for the desktop window, it only cares about one of them, WM_RBUTTONDOWN, which Windows sends to the desktop window whenever the user clicks the righthand mouse button over the window.

When CC receives a WM_RBUTTONDOWN message, it posts a WM_KEYDOWN message to the window identified by the variable Watcher& (DeskMenu's main window), with a value of 127 as the first parameter to the message.

Next, no matter what message was received, CC calls the desktop window's default window-handling procedure (as identified by OldProc%), and returns the value returned by that procedure to Windows.

```
Procedure CC(wHand&,Mess&,W&,L%)
  $Export CC
  Switch Mess&
  Case WM_RBUTTONDOWN
```

```
   ~PostMessage(Watcher&, WM_KEYDOWN,127,0)
 EndSelect
RetvalCallWindowProc(OldDeskProc%,wHand&,Mess&,W&,L%)
 Return
```

That's the sum total of DMENU.DLL's code. Visual Basic users might be wondering where the declarations are for all those Windows API functions, while C programmers might wonder where the include files and definition files are hiding. To its credit, GFA-BASIC doesn't require either. This makes it a good tool for building special-purpose DLLs like DMENU.DLL.

DMENU.DLL does its job well in the context of the DeskMenu application. However, if you're thinking about adopting it for other purposes, there are a couple of limitations that you should think about. The first is that only one application at a time can use DMENU.DLL: It isn't robust enough to support multiple applications at once. Moreover, DMENU.DLL might cause problems in the presence of other applications that subclass the Windows desktop. Thus, you might want to do some additional work to fortify DMENU.DLL's error-checking capabilities before applying it to other applications.

■ Calling DMENU.DLL

DeskMenu's DMENU.BAS module contains a one-line declaration that enables it to interact with DMENU.DLL:

```
Declare Function WatchDesk% Lib "DMENU.DLL" (ByVal MyWin%, ByVal OnOff%)
```

As defined here, the WatchDesk() function requires two integer parameters: the handle of the window which is to be notified when the DLL receives a WM_RBUT-TONDOWN message, and a True/False flag indicating whether the DLL is being activated or deactivated. Thus, DeskMenu can instruct the DLL to subclass the desktop window with this call:

```
X% = WatchDesk(MainFrm.hWnd, True)
```

■ Processing Messages from DMENU.DLL

DMENU.DLL communicates with DeskMenu by posting a WM_KEYDOWN message to DeskMenu's main form. This triggers the Form_Keydown event, where the first parameter attached to the message (with a value of 127) is treated as the keycode of the pressed key and the second parameter (which has a value of 0) is treated as the shift state.

Once DeskMenu has received the WM_KEYDOWN message from the DLL, its job is to pop up its menu on screen at the current location of the mouse pointer. If all DeskMenu had to do was wait for that message, I could have had the Form_Keydown event call the procedure which pops up the menu directly once the message came in. However, DeskMenu's option to hide the Program Manager's and DeskMenu's icons meant that in addition to waiting for a notification message from the DLL, DeskMenu also had to constantly monitor the window state and position of both the Program Manager and DeskMenu. Thus, I elected to build DeskMenu around the Visual Basic construct best suited for this kind of monitoring chore: the DoEvents() loop.

■ DOEVENTS() LOOPS

Most Visual Basic programmers know DoEvents() only as a means to force Visual Basic to yield to Windows in the midst of extended processes so that other applications can process events. However, the DoEvents() function has at least two other interesting uses. First, it returns the number of your applications forms that are visible at the time that it is called (there must be a use for this, although I've never found one.) Far more importantly, it can be used to safely build endless loops for purposes such as DeskMenu's monitoring chores.

To build an endless loop with DoEvents(), you must first create a subroutine called Main() in a module file and use Visual Basic's Project Options dialog box to identify Sub Main() as your application's start-up form. Then you simply put any steps that you want your application to execute continually from the time it loads until it is unloaded into a Do While DoEvents() loop, as follows:

```
Sub Main()
'REM put startup code here
Dim I%
Form1.Show
'REM now enter the loop
Do While DoEvents()
   I%=I%+1
   Form1.Label1=Str$(I%)
Loop
End Sub
```

The beauty of a DoEvents() loop is that your application will complete one trip through the loop every time Windows, in its context-switching wisdom, affords DeskMenu a little processing time, which usually means several times per second. This makes DoEvents() loops quite useful for jobs where you want to constantly monitor user activity or the value returned by a Windows API call. For instance, if you wanted to create a system resource monitor you might put a call to the API function GetFreeSystemReources in a DoEvents() loop.

On the other hand, DoEvents() loops also have the potential to eat up huge amounts of processor time, because they get called so frequently. This means that you must make the code within your DoEvents() loop as tight as possible, and avoid calling any extended procedures from within it.

There is another danger to be avoided with DoEvents() loops. You should not call the DoEvents() from within a DoEvents() loop. Although doing so might seem like a good way to lessen the processor-hogging danger of this sort of loop, it inevitably leads to Out of Stack Space errors as your application starts another iteration of the loop prior to the first one ending.

Still, despite these hazards, DoEvents() loops are a valuable tool. You just have to use them wisely. For instance, consider the DoEvents() loop in DeskMenu's Sub Main().

■ **Sub Main( ) Procedure**

The DoEvents() loop in DeskMenu is intended to carry out two tasks: to make Desk-Menu's menu appear when the user clicks the righthand mouse button on the desktop window and to ensure that the icons for the Program Manager and DeskMenu remain hidden if the user has selected that option.

To carry out its first responsibility, DeskMenu examines the value of a global variable called DLLCommand%, which will be equal to 127 if DeskMenu has received notification of a righthand mouse-button click from DMENU.DLL. Why will it have this value? Because the Form_KeyDown event responds to messages from the DLL by executing this code:

```
Sub Form_KeyDown (KeyCode As Integer, Shift As Integer)
DLLCommand% = KeyCode
End Sub
```

Thus, the KeyDown event merely sets the value of DLLCommand% to the KeyCode passed to it by the DLL (which will always be equal to 127), and then exits. Then, the next time the DoEvents() loop is called, DLLCommand% is found to have a value of 127.

```
Do While DoEvents()
   If DLLCommand% = 127 Then
      TrackPopUp 0, MainFrm
      DLLCommand% = False
   End If
```

DeskMenu responds to the command by calling a function called TrackPopUp (which will be discussed below) to display its menu, and then resetting DLLCommand% to False (0).

This approach, having the Form_KeyDown event set the value of a variable and then leave it for the DoEvents() loop to process, has the advantage of being easily expanded. If DMENU.DLL tracked several messages instead of just one, it could assign a value to the KeyCode parameter of the WM_KEYDOWN message that it sends to MainFrm for each message. The Form_KeyDown handler would relay those codes to the DoEvents() loop through DLLCommand%, and the DoEvents() loop could easily be rewritten to select between them.

```
Do While DoEvents()
Select Case DLLCommand%
Case Is = 127
    TrackPopUp 0, MainFrm
    DLLCommand% = False
Case Is = 128
    'Do something else
Case Else
    'Do something Else
End Select
DLLCommand%=0
```

The use of DoEvents() loops is a bit controversial. Some authorities would suggest that their use should be avoided whenever possible, due to both their processor overhead and stylistic issues. In DeskMenu's case, for instance, it could be argued that a time control should be used in place of the DoEvents() loop. But the fact remains that the DoEvents() loop in DeskMenu does its job well without any noticeable impact on performance, and that DoEvents() loops are an important technique that every Visual Basic programmer should know, even if they are to be used only in rare cases.

■ Hiding Icons

The further I went with the DeskMenu project, the more it appealed to my minimalist side. The whole thing seemed so clean and uncluttered—a single menu that popped up in response to a single mouse click—and so much more direct than hunting through Program Manager group windows for icons.

In fact, the only thing that wasn't clean and uncluttered was the bottom of the screen. There, the Program Manager icon, which I never touched once I started using DeskMenu, was joined by DeskMenu's icon, which was also unnecessary since all of

DeskMenu's functions could be accessed through its pop-up menu. So I decided to offer the user the option to hide the icons from both applications.

That seemed like it would be simple enough to do. I figured I could simply use the Windows API function ShowWindow to Program Manager and then set Main-Frm's Visible property to False to hide DeskMenu. I thought something like this would do the trick:

```
X% = ShowWindow(DeskMenuHandle%, SW_HIDE)
MainFrm.Visible=False
```

As it turned out, hiding the icons wasn't quite that simple. For one thing, hidden windows—or at least hidden Visual Basic windows—don't receive keydown messages, no matter whether you hide the window by setting its Visible property to False or by using ShowWindow. If DeskMenu couldn't receive keydown messages, it couldn't pop up its menu in response to a mouse click on the desktop, so I had to find another method to make its icon disappear.

The obvious answer was to move MainFrm off screen when it was minimized. So I tried adding code such as the following to MainFrm's Form_Resize handler.

```
If WindowState=1 Then
    Left=-50
    Top=-50
End If
```

That didn't work either. Visual Basic refuses to move a minimized form. Fortunately, however, the Windows API function SetWindowPlacement isn't so picky. In fact, it provides an option specifically intended to change the position of a minimized window.

The SetWindowPlacement function serves many purposes. It can be used to modify the show state (hidden, visible, minimized, maximized, normal, or restored) of the specified window, or to modify the coordinates at which the window or its icon will appear. The function takes two parameters, the handle of the window whose placement is being adjusted, and a pointer to a WindowPlacement structure, which is used to retrieve or set the position and visibility of a window.

You'll need a guide to the Windows API to understand the full use of the Window-Placement structure and the GetWindowPlacement and SetWindowPlacement functions, but suffice it to say that by setting the Flags element of the WindowPlacement structure to WPF_SETMINPOSITION (&H1) and specifying the desired location for the window's icon in the x and y elements of a PointAPI structure, you can use SetWindowPlacement to reposition a window's icon. That is exactly what DeskMenu's MoveIconOffScreen routine, which it calls to hide its own icon, does.

```
Dim WinPlace As WindowPlacement
WinPlace.Length = 22
X% = GetWindowPlacement%(F.hWnd, WinPlace)
WinPlace.PtMinPosition.Y = -50
WinPlace.PtMinPosition.X = -50
WinPlace.Flags = WPF_SETMINPOSITION
WinPlace.ShowCmd = SW_MINIMIZE
X% = SetWindowPlacement%(F.hWnd, WinPlace)
```

Hiding the Program Manager's icon was considerably simpler. Since there was no need for Program Manager to be able to receive keystrokes while hidden, DeskMenu could really hide it, as opposed to simply moving it off screen. Thus, DeskMenu makes use of a routine called HideIconicApp. HideIconicApp% takes one parameter, the handle of the window to be hidden.

```
Sub HideIconicApp (Handle%)
If IsIconic(Handle%) <> 0 And IsWindowVisible(Handle%) <> 0 Then
   Handle% = ShowWindow(Handle%, SW_HIDE)
End If
End Sub
```

As you can see, HideIconicApp checks first to make sure that the specified window is both iconized and visible prior to setting ShowWindow to hide it. This checking allows DeskMenu to call this function at any time, no matter whether the Program Manager is iconized or not, without fear of hiding a window that the user is trying to work with. The Program Manager is hidden only if it is in an iconic state.

The reason that HideIconicApp has to perform all this checking is that, as I soon discovered in testing DeskMenu, it doesn't suffice to simply hide the Program Manager's icon and to move DeskMenu's icon when the user selects that menu item. The Program Manager might not even be iconized at the time the user does so, or if it is, it might later be restored and thus require hiding again when the user again iconizes it. (While the standard Windows Task Manager can't be used to switch to a hidden application, many replacement task managers have that capability, and thus the Program Manager might easily be restored from its hidden state.) Similarly, since Desk-Menu's icon is not actually hidden, but simply positioned off screen, an Arrange Icons command from the Task Manager will make the DeskMenu icon reappear.

What this adds up to is that DeskMenu not only has to hide the two icons, but it also has to keep checking to make sure that they stay hidden. Its mechanism to do so is a series of commands in the DoEvents loop in Sub Main().

```
If HidePM% = True Then
    loopCounter% = loopCounter% + 1
    If loopCounter% = 100 Then
        HideIconicApp FindWindow("ProgMan", 0&)
        If MeIconic% Then
            If MainFrm.Left > 0 Then MoveIconOffScreen MainFrm
        End If
        loopCounter% = 0
    End If
End If
```

A routine like this has the potential to be a heavy consumer of processor time. Thus, I took several steps to minimize that consumption. First, I used the global variables HidePM% and MeIconic%—the former to indicate whether icons are to be hidden and the later to indicate whether DeskMenu's form is iconized. HidePM% is set to True when the user checks the Hide PM & DeskMenu Icons item, while MeIconic% is set to True whenever DeskMenu is iconized. Obviously, DeskMenu could have determined the same information by examining the values of either the MainFrm.DeskMenu(4).Checked property or the MainFrm.WindowState property, but checking the values of object properties takes much longer than examining an integer variable, so I elected to use variable flags to represent these properties.

In addition, this command sequence maintains an integer counter called loop-Counter% and actually only proceeds with further checks if loopCounter% is equal to 100. Thus 99 times out of 100 the loop never even checks the value of MeIconic% or HidePM%, speeding its processing in those 99 instances. The 100th time through, it checks them and, if need be, hides the icons before resetting loopCounter% to 0. This imposes only a slight delay upon the actual hiding of DeskMenu's or the Program Manager's icon, amounting to perhaps a half second or so in most cases, while significantly reducing the number of instructions that DeskMenu must perform on each trip through the loop, and thus the amount of processing time it consumes.

■ THE HIDEICONS ROUTINE

There was just one more hurdle to cross in the process of hiding the icons. Doing so left unsightly gaps in the line up of icons across the bottom of the screen. There would be a gap at the location that the Program Manager's icon had occupied, and another at the spot where DeskMenu's icon had last been seen. In an application as minimalist as DeskMenu, aesthetics are everything, so I wanted to have DeskMenu arrange the remaining visible icons automatically when it first hid the Program Manager's and DeskMenu's icons.

Fortunately, Windows has an API function designed to do just that: ArrangeIconic-Windows, which accepts just one parameter, the handle of the window whose iconic children are to be arranged. If you pass ArrangeIconicWindows the handle of the desktop window, it responds by tidying up all the minimized icons on the desktop.

The HideIcons subroutine is called whenever the user checks or removes the check mark from the Hide Icons menu item. It starts by examining the value of the menu item's Checked property, to determine if the item is checked or not.

If the menu item is checked, indicating that the icons should be hidden, Hide-Icons calls HideIconicApp to hide the Program Manager's icon, then uses the IsIconic function to determine if DeskMenu's main window is in a minimized state. If so, it calls MoveIconOffScreen to move the icon to an invisible location. Finally, it calls ArrangeIconicWindows to tidy up the remaining icons at the bottom of the screen.

```
If MainFrm.deskMenu(3).Checked Then
    X% = FindWindow("ProgMan", 0&)
    HideIconicApp X%          'hide pm
    HidePM% = True            'flag to hide whenever minimized
    If IsIconic(MainFrm.hWnd) Then MoveIconOffScreen MainFrm
    X% = ArrangeIconicWindows(GetDesktopWindow())
```

If the menu item is not checked, then the user wants to reveal the hidden icons. So HideIcons sets the HidePM% flag to False, then uses the ShowWindow function to make the Program Manager's icon visible and ArrangeIconicWindows to tidy up the on-screen icons. Since DeskMenu's icon is located just off-screen, rather than being truly hidden, the ArrangeIconicWindows command includes it in its tidying, and DeskMenu's icon reappears at the bottom of the screen. Also, since HidePM% is False, DeskMenu won't attempt to move the icon back off screen again, so both the Program Manager and DeskMenu icons are visible after the completion of this sequence:

```
Else
    HidePM% = False
    X% = FindWindow("ProgMan", 0&)
    X% = ShowWindow(X%, SW_SHOW)
    X% = ArrangeIconicWindows(GetDesktopWindow())
End If
```

■ Exiting Windows

While for the most part hiding the DeskMenu and the Program Manager icons was beneficial, it did have one inconvenient side effect. If Program Manager's icon was hidden when I wanted to exit Windows, I had to first remove the check mark from the Hide…Icons menu item, and then shut down the Program Manager.

That wasn't a lot of extra steps, but it seemed silly to require any extra steps for such a simple task. So I decided to turn an inconvenience into a convenience by adding Exit Windows and Restart Windows items to DeskMenu's pop-up menu.

Both items make use of the Windows API function ExitWindows, which either terminates Windows, reboots the system, or restarts Windows, depending on the value of the first of its two integer parameters. (The second parameter is always a zero.)

When either of the two items is selected, DeskMenu calls the ProcessSpecialMenu routine, where it first posts a yes/no message box asking you to confirm your choice and, if you click the Yes button, issues the ExitWindows command with the appropriate parameters.

```
Sub ProcessSpecialMenu (Ind%)
Dim X%, Reboot%
Select Case Ind%
Case 0
   X% = MsgBox("Restart Windows now?", 49, "DeskMenu")
   If X% <> 1 Then Exit Sub
   Reboot% = &H42
Case 1
   X% = MsgBox("Exit Windows now?", 49, "DeskMenu")
   If X% <> 1 Then Exit Sub
   Reboot% = &H0
End Select
X% = ExitWindows(Reboot%, 0)
End Sub
```

When ExitWindows is called, it notifies every application running in windows *except* for the application that called the function, that Windows is about to shut down. Each application is given the opportunity to cancel the operation. This gives you the opportunity to cancel an ExitWindows operation if, for instance, you have unsaved files in another application. However, you should remember while working with this function that it does not extend the notification to the application that called it. Thus, if you're working with an uncompiled version of your application in the Visual Basic development environment, make sure you save your work before testing this function, because Visual Basic won't be given the chance to post its "Save Files Before Closing" message box before Windows shuts down.

■ LOADING THE PROGRAM MANAGER MENUS

You'll recall that DeskMenu's primary job is to present the user with a pop-up menu of the Program Manager program items in response to a righthand mouse-button click on the desktop. To do so, DeskMenu must complete a series of closely related tasks:

- Obtain a list of Program Manager groups

- Create a hierarchical menu for each group

- Obtain a list of the program items in each group

- Create a menu item for each program item

- Pop up the resulting menu when the user clicks the righthand mouse button on the desktop window

- Respond to the selection of any program item by executing the program it represents

As always when you're programming for Windows, the key to making each of these steps work is knowing what Visual Basic can do for you, what the Windows API can do, and what you've got to do for yourself.

In this case, the key thing you've got to know about is the Program Manager's dynamic data exchange interface which, among other things, allows other applications to query the Program Manager to determine the names of its program groups and the names and other data of the items in each group.

To obtain a list of program groups from the Program Manager, an application must establish a DDE link with the LinkTopic "PROGMAN|PROGMAN" and then issue a request for a LinkItem called "PROGMAN" (whoever designed this was clearly very inventive). The Program Manager will respond to the request by supplying a carriage return-delimited list of program groups.

Once the list of program groups has been obtained, an application can access the contents of any group by issuing another link request using the group's name as the LinkItem. The Program Manager responds with a long series of comma-delimited data. The first line of data includes the group name (in quotation marks), the path of the group file, and the number of items in the group. Each subsequent line contains information about an item in the group, including the command line (in quotation marks), the default directory, the icon path, the position in the group, the icon index, the shortcut key (in numeric form), and the minimize flag (indicating whether the application should be launched in a minimized state).

As I designed DeskMenu, I knew that it would be able to make use of this DDE interface to populate its menus. Furthermore, I knew DeskMenu would present each program item as a menu item under a hierarchical submenu representing the program item's program group. What I wasn't sure of was how to map the information DeskMenu obtained from the Program Manager onto custom menus.

On the surface, this would seem like a perfect job for a menu array. All DeskMenu would have to do is provide a single hierarchical submenu, with a single menu item underneath it, and clone both as needed to provide enough hierarchical submenus to represent all the program groups and enough menu items beneath each one to hold all the program items in the group.

Unfortunately, Visual Basic control arrays don't work that way. While you can load new instances of a control that is contained in another control (for example, as a command button might be contained in a picture control or, in this case, a submenu item is contained in a higher-level menu item) and you can load new instances of a container control, you can't do both at once. That is, if you load a second instance of a control which contains another control, the new instance of the container will be empty; the control(s) it contains will not be loaded along with it.

What this meant to DeskMenu was simple: I had to provide it in advance with all the hierarchical submenus (program group menus) that it would ever need, and include one menu item (program-item menu item) below each hierarchical submenu. This would allow DeskMenu to load additional menu items as needed to hold all the program items in a program group.

I don't know whether there is a limit to the number of program groups that the Program Manager can contain—I couldn't find it documented anywhere—so I elected to go with a practical estimate, and provide DeskMenu with the capability to work with up to 25 program groups. This led to a few boring minutes working in the Visual Basic Menu Design Window to create the raw menu (shown in Figure 7.5) with its 25 submenu control arrays, but also raised the question of how DeskMenu could most efficiently distinguish between menu items. While doing so would have been simple if DeskMenu had only had to work with the elements of one array of menu items, this solution meant that it had to work with the elements of 25 arrays of program-item menu items, plus an array of program group submenus—a considerably more complex problem, the solution to which I'll present a little further on in this chapter.

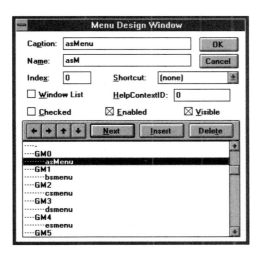

FIGURE 7.5

DeskMenu's
Menu Design
Window
reveals the
menu template
for its pop-up
menu of the
Program
Manager
groups and
icons.

■ Obtaining Program Group Data

DeskMenu uses a routine called GetGroups, which is initially called as the program loads and then again whenever the user instructs DeskMenu to reload its menus, to obtain the names of each program group and assign them to hierarchical submenus.

The GetGroups routine calls a little utility subroutine called GetLinkData, instructing it to obtain data for the LinkItem "PROGMAN".

```
Sub GetLinkData (Item$)
MainFrm.Text1.LinkTopic = "ProgMan|Progman"
MainFrm.Text1.LinkItem = Item$
MainFrm.Text1.LinkMode = 2      ' Establish cold link.
MainFrm.Text1.LinkRequest    ' Get a list of the groups.
On Error Resume Next
MainFrm.Text1.LinkMode = 0          'Disconnect link
On Error GoTo 0
End Sub
```

The On Error statements surrounding the statement which disconnects the link compensate for a bug in Windows 3.0 whereby disconnecting a link to the Program Manager causes an error.

The GetLinkData routine uses a text box called Text1 on DeskMenu's main form to establish the link, so that once the link request has been made, MainFrm.Text1 contains the carriage return-delimited list of program-group names. At this point, all DeskMenu has to do is assign each line of text it finds in MainFrm.Text1 to a submenu caption. However, in early testing of DeskMenu I realized that its menus would be much more usable if the program groups, and the program items in each group, were presented in alphabetical order.

Doing so meant that DeskMenu had the list of groups, and the list of items in each group. Here, depending on your perspective, I either got a little lazy or a little smart. Rather than writing a sort routine to do this job, I simply added an invisible list box to DeskMenu's HelloFrm (a form displayed while DeskMenu is being loaded). This form is unloaded as soon as DeskMenu has completed loading its menu, so the list box—called HelloFrm.Sorter—doesn't consume any system resources once Desk-Menu has loaded, and by setting its Sorted property to True, DeskMenu is able to use it to sort the lists of group names and program items.

Once GetLinkData has inserted the list of group names into MainFrm.Text1, Get-Groups assigns that list to a string, then loops through the string, adding each line of text in it to HelloFrm.Sorter. The list is automatically sorted as each item is added to the list box, so GetGroups can then go through the list box from top to bottom, assigning each list box item to a member of its submenu array, in order to create its alphabetized list of submenus.

```
Temp$ = MainFrm.Text1
i% = InStr(Temp$, CRLF$)
Do While i%
  HelloFrm.sorter.AddItem Left$(Temp$, i% - 1)
  Temp$ = Mid$(Temp$, i% + 2)
    i% = InStr(Temp$, CRLF$)
    CT% = CT% + 1
Loop
For X% = 0 To CT% - 1
MainFrm.GroupMenu(X%).Caption=HelloFrm.sorter.List(X%)
  Next
```

Next, GetGroups redimensions a global integer array called Groups%() to reflect the number of program groups, sets the visible property of the remaining submenus to False, and finally clears the Sorter list box.

```
ReDim Groups%(CT% - 1)
For i% = CT% To 24
    MainFrm.GroupMenu(i%).Visible = False
Next
HelloFrm.sorter.Clear
End Sub
```

Using a list box to sort a list isn't as fast as sorting an array in memory, but it does save you the effort of writing some code, and with lists as small as those being handled by DeskMenu, it adds only a second or two to the time it takes the application to load its menus. Using a list box to sort is not a solution I recommend for all occasions, but it's worth keeping in your bag of tricks and using when appropriate. In this case, I originally thought of this trick as a place holder that I would eventually replace with a coded sort routine. As it turned out, though, the routine was fast enough that I never felt the need to improve upon it.

■ Obtaining Program Item Data

Once DeskMenu has obtained a list of program groups, and assigned each element of that list to a menu caption, it has to obtain the program items belonging to each group and create a menu item for each item. Several factors make this process considerably more involved than that of obtaining program groups, including the need to parse each line of data to extract relevant information from it, and the need to load new menu array elements and carefully track the data assigned to each.

The greatest complicating factor, however, is the fact that DeskMenu is expected to do something when the user selects one of the program-item menu items. Opening up a hierarchical menu occurs automatically in Visual Basic, but when the user selects "Calculator" under the "Accessories" menu, he or she expects DeskMenu to launch the Calculator accessory. That means that DeskMenu has to do more than simply display the item's name in the proper submenu; it also has to be able to launch the correct application or document when that item is selected, set the application's working directory, and even run the application in an iconic state if so indicated.

The Program Manager's DDE interface provides all the information DeskMenu needs to carry out these tasks: the name of the application or document to be launched, the path of its working directory, and a flag indicating whether it should be run minimized or not. DeskMenu simply had to keep track of this information and apply it at the appropriate moment.

As described above, I was forced to create a separate control array for each submenu—for a total of 25 menu arrays. That was okay, but I didn't want to also have to maintain 25 arrays of program names, and 25 arrays of working directories, and so on. Instead, I created a global integer array called Groups%(), and a pair of global string arrays called Progs() and WorkDirs(), respectively.

Progs() and WorkDirs() are simply flat string arrays to which DeskMenu adds the application and working directory for each menu item as it is created. Groups%(), meanwhile, acts as a kind of index that allows DeskMenu to determine, based on a menu selection from one of the 25 submenus, which program to run and which working directory to use.

As the program items for each new group are added to its menu, DeskMenu assigns to the Groups%() array element of the current group the cumulative total of program items in the groups that have already been added to DeskMenu's menu. For instance, if the alphabetically first program group contains six program items, the second program group contains eight program items, and the third program group contains nine program items; Groups%(0), the Groups%() array element for the first group, will have a value of 0 (as it always will); Groups%(1), the element for the second group, will have a value of 6 (reflecting the six elements in the first group); and Groups%(2) will have a value of 14 (reflecting the six elements in the first group and the eight elements in the second group).

When the user selects a menu item—say the fourth item on the fourth submenu—DeskMenu takes the value of the Groups%() array element associated with that submenu (let's say it equals 18) and adds to that the index number of the selected menu item (3) to determine that it needs to execute the program specified in Progs(21) and to set the working directory to the path specified in WorkDir(21).

■ The GetItems Routine

The routine that DeskMenu uses to obtain program items is called GetItems. DeskMenu always calls GetItems immediately after GetGroups, since there would be no point in its loading a new list of groups without also loading a new list of the program items in each group.

GetItems loops through the 25 elements of the GroupMenu() menu array, examining the Visible property of each. If the menu element is visible, then GetItems calls the GetLinkData subroutine, passing it the menu item's caption to use as the LinkTopic.

Once GetLinkData has made its link request, MainFrm.Text1 contains the complete data for all the program items in the current group. GetItems assigns that data to a string variable called Temp$, then proceeds to parse it into individual items.

The first line of data, which GetItem assigns to Cap$, includes the name of the program group, and the number of program items that it contains. GetItems extracts that number and uses it to redimension the Progs() and WorkDirs() arrays.

```
Groups%(X%) = AccumGroup%
AccumGroup% = AccumGroup% + Val(Cap$)
ReDim Preserve Progs(AccumGroup%)
ReDim Preserve WorkDirs(AccumGroup%)
```

Next, GetItems looks at the remaining lines of data. It starts by calling the cChecker routine, which sets the object variable C, defined locally as a control, equal to the existing zero element of the active menu array. Then GetItems sets that menu item's Visible property to True, adds the next line of Temp$ to the Sorter list box, chops that line off of Temp$, and then checks to see if there is another line to process. If so, it calls a routine called cLoader to load a new element in the active menu array.

```
CT% = 0
cChecker X%, 0 'set value of C to first menu item
Do While i%
    C.Visible = True        'set menu item visible
    HelloFrm.Sorter.AddItem Left$(Temp$, InStr(Temp$, CRLF$) - 1)
    Temp$ = Mid$(Temp$, i% + 2)    'chop off current line
    i% = InStr(Temp$, CRLF$)           'is there another line
    CT% = CT% + 1                         'if so, then
    If i% Then cLoader X%, CT%        'load new menu item
Loop
```

■ **THE CCHECKER AND CLOADER ROUTINES**

The cChecker routine that GetItem calls is responsible for setting the value of the object variable C. It takes two parameters, the submenu to which the desired menu item belongs and the index number of that menu item, and uses a Select Case routine to assign the variable to the correct submenu.

```
Sub cChecker (X%, tCt%)
Select Case X%
Case 0
    Set C = MainFrm.asM(tCt%)
Case 1
    Set C = MainFrm.bsM(tCt%)
Case 2
  Set C = MainFrm.csM(tCt%)
'   and so on...
```

The cLoader routine takes the same two parameters, but it is responsible for loading the specified submenu. Then, once it has done so, it calls cChecker to make the variable C point to the newly loaded menu item.

```
Sub cLoader (X%, CT%)
Select Case X%
Case 0
    Load MainFrm.asM(CT%)
Case 1
    Load MainFrm.bsM(CT%)
Case 2
    Load MainFrm.csM(CT%)
'   and so on...
End Select
cChecker X%, CT%
End Sub
```

The reason for all these machinations to set the value of C is simple: I wanted Get-Items and other routines to be able to refer to a menu control by means of a variable, thus allowing simple statements like:

```
C.Caption="Dog"
```

Since there is no equivalent for the Me variable (which always identifies the active form) for a control, DeskMenu needed a way to determine under programmatic control what menu item it was dealing with. The cChecker and cLoader routines are the best solution I could come up with.

■ **ASSIGNING MENU CAPTIONS**

Once all the menu items needed for the current submenu have been loaded, and the data for each added to the Sorter list box, GetItems has to extract each item's menu caption from that data, as well as the data for the Progs() and WorkDirs() arrays. It does this by looping through the Sorter list box, calling a subroutine called GetExe for each item in order to obtain the Progs() and WorkDirs() data for the item, and by extracting the menu caption from the text in the list box. The list box, of course, contains the full line of data sent by the Program Manager, which includes quotation marks and spaces around the item's description, so GetItem uses the Mid$ function to strip off those extraneous characters.

```
For Y% = 0 To HelloFrm.Sorter.ListCount - 1
    Cap$ = HelloFrm.Sorter.List(Y%)
    GetExe Cap$, Groups%(X) + Y%
    Cap$ = Left$(Cap$, InStr(Cap$, ",") - 1)
   Cap$ = Mid$(Cap$, 2, Len(Cap$) - 2) 'trim off spaces & quotation marks
    cChecker X%, CT%
    C.Caption = Cap$
    CT% = CT% + 1
  Next Y%
```

■ **THE GETEXE ROUTINE**

GetExe's job is to extract the program name, working directory, and run minimized flag from the data sent by the Program Manager for a menu item, and to apply the extracted information to a specified element of the Progs() and the WorkDirs() arrays. It accepts two parameters: Temp$, the full text of the data sent by the Program Manager for the active item, and ProgCt%, the element in the Progs() and WorkDirs() arrays to which the extracted data is to be added. (GetItems determines the proper element number by adding the values of the current member of the Groups%() array to the active menu item's index number).

GetExe starts by checking whether the application is to be run in a minimized state, which would be indicated by a numeral 1 immediately following the last comma in Temp$. If it finds the flag, it sets the value of Min% to True.

```
For Min% = Len(Temp$) To 1 Step -1
    If Mid$(Temp$, Min%, 1) = "," Then Exit For
Next
If Mid$(Temp$, Min% + 1, 1) = "1" Then
    Min% = True
Else
    Min% = False
End If
```

Next, GetExe looks for the name of the program or document to be launched when this menu item is selected, which is located between the first two commas in Temp$. It extracts that data, appends the string "DTMRunMin" to it if Min% equals True, and assigns it to the current element of the Progs() array. Then it looks for the program's working directory, which is located between the second and third commas in Temp$, and assigns that to the current element in WorkDirs().

```
Dim i%, C1%, C2%, AppExe$, AppPath$
C1% = InStr(Temp$, ",")
If C1% Then
    C2% = InStr(C1% + 1, Temp$, ",")
    AppExe$ = Left$(Temp$, C2% - 2)
    AppExe$ = Mid$(AppExe$, C1% + 2)
    If Min% = True Then AppExe$ = AppExe$ + "DTMRunMin"
    Progs(Prog(t%) = AppExe$
    C1% = InStr(C2% + 1, Temp$, ",")
    AppPath$ = Left$(Temp$, C1% - 1)
    AppPath$ = Mid$(AppPath$, C2% + 1)
    WorkDirs(ProgCt%) = AppPath$
End If
```

Once it has assigned the extracted data to the current elements of the Progs() and WorkDirs() directory, GetExe exits, and GetItems proceeds to load additional menu items, calling GetExe each time, until it has loaded a menu item for each program item in every Program Manager group.

- **Reloading the Menu**

If the user creates a new program item or group in the Program Manager, or deletes one or more program items or groups, or installs an application that does so, Desk-Menu's menus no longer are an accurate reflection of the Program Manager's contents. DeskMenu's Reload Menus menu item provides a way to correct this problem and once again synchronize DeskMenu's menus with the Program Manager by forcing DeskMenu to reload its menus.

The process is handled by a routine called ReloadMenus. The routine begins by setting a global flag called Reloading% to True. Then it stores the value of MainFrm.-deskMenu(3)'s Checked quality (the Hide...Icons menu item), and unloads Main-Frm. This effectively wipes out all of DeskMenu's custom menus.

```
Dim OldCheck%
Reloading% = True
OldCheck%= MainFrm.deskMenu(3).Checked
Unload MainFrm
```

The Reloading% flag, incidentally, tells MainFrm's QueryUnload procedure that it needn't make the Program Manager's icon visible if it happens to be hidden, as it would if MainFrm were being unloaded because DeskMenu was shutting down.

The QueryUnload procedure still issues a call to the DMENU.DLL, however, canceling its subclassing efforts, prior to allowing MainFrm to unload.

Next, ReloadMenus reinitializes the Groups%(), Progs(), and WorkDirs() arrays, and then issues a MainFrm.Show command to both load and show DeskMenu's main form. Then it calls GetGroups and GetIcons to reload DeskMenu's custom menus.

```
ReDim Groups%(0)
ReDim Progs(0)
ReDim WorkDirs(0)
MainFrm.Show
GetGroups
GetItems
Unload HelloFrm
```

Because GetGroups and GetIcons make use of the Sorter list box on HelloFrm, calling those routines loads HelloFrm into memory, even though it remains invisible throughout the process of reloading menus. Thus, ReloadMenus issues the command Unload HelloFrm immediately after its call to GetItems, in order to remove that form from memory.

Finally, ReloadMenus switches DMENU.DLL's subclassing efforts back on with a call to WatchDesk, restores the value of MainFrm.deskMenu(3)'s Checked property, and issues a call to HideIcons if that property has a value of True.

```
X% = WatchDesk(MainFrm.hWnd, True)
MainFrm.deskMenu(3).Checked = OldCheck%
If OldCheck% Then HideIcons
```

That's all there is to reloading DeskMenu's menus.

▪ TRACKING POP-UP MENUS

Sometimes it is easier to do things the hard way. At least, that's what my experience with tracking DeskMenu's pop-up menus would seem to indicate.

As you probably know, until Visual Basic 3.0 was released, the only way to use a pop-up menu with Visual Basic was to call the Windows TrackPopupMenu API function. That wasn't difficult, but since API functions in general tend to be more complex than the functions built into Visual Basic, once Visual Basic 3.0 with its PopupMenu method came out, I didn't think I would ever have reason to use Track-PopupMenu again.

DeskMenu proved me wrong. You see, I wanted to have DeskMenu's menu appear under the mouse cursor which, by definition, would be located somewhere over the desktop window, rather than over DeskMenu's window. That made using the Popup-Menu method a bit tricky, since it requires that you specify coordinates relative to the upper lefthand corner of DeskMenu's window. Thus, to use Visual Basic's PopupMenu method for DeskMenu, I would have had to first determine the absolute screen coordinates of the mouse, then transform them to make them relative to DeskMenu's window.

That seemed like a lot of unnecessary work, especially since the Windows API TrackPopupMenu function accepts absolute coordinates, rather than coordinates relative to the position of a window. So in response to a right mouse-button click on the desktop, DeskMenu calls a subroutine called TrackPopUp, which in turn calls the Windows API function TrackPopupMenu, not Visual Basic's PopupMenu method.

TrackPopupMenu requires six parameters: the handle of the menu it is to pop up; a flag indicating which menu alignment and which mouse button will be used to signal menu choices; the x and y coordinates at which the menu is to appear, a reserved value that must equal 0; the handle of the window which owns the menu, and finally, the address of a rectangular structure within which the user can click without closing the menu. (If the last parameter is null, the menu is dismissed whenever the user clicks outside of the menu's borders).

Thus, TrackPopUp must determine the location of the cursor before it can call TrackPopupMenu. It does so by using the Windows API routine GetCursorPos, which populates a PointAPI structure with the horizontal and vertical coordinates of the mouse. Once that's done, DeskMenu uses the Windows API function GetMenu to obtain the handle of MainFrm's menu bar, and GetSubMenu to obtain the handle of its first pop-up menu. Finally, it calls TrackPopupMenu.

```
Dim MD As POINTAPI
GetCursorPos MD
Dim hMenu%, hSubMenu%, r As Integer
```

```
hMenu% = GetMenu(F.hWnd)
hSubMenu% = GetSubMenu(hMenu%, Menu)
r=TrackPopupMenu(hSubMenu%,2,MD.X,MD.Y,0,F.hWnd,0&)
```

Once TrackPopUp calls TrackPopupMenu, DeskMenu's menu appears at the current mouse location, and remains visible until the user selects a menu item or—since the final parameter passed to TrackPopupMenu is hexadecimal zero, or null—clicks anywhere outside the menu. Once the user selects a menu item, DeskMenu calls the event handler for the selected menu item, just as if the user had pulled down the menu from within DeskMenu's window and selected the same menu item.

■ LAUNCHING APPLICATIONS

Here's where DeskMenu puts those 25 menu arrays, and all the work it does maintaining the Progs(), WorkDirs(), and Groups%() arrays to work.

The 25 menu arrays start with a menu and are called MainFrm.asM(), MainFrm.bsM(), MainFrm.csM(), and so on, right on through to MainFrm.ysM(). Each has a slightly different Click event procedure, which uses the Groups%() array to point DeskMenu toward the correct program and working directory.

Actually, the asM_Click procedure doesn't make any reference to Groups%(). Since it is the first submenu, the index number of the selected menu item points directly to the correct elements in the Progs() and WorkingDirs() arrays.

```
Sub asM_Click (Index As Integer)
RunProg Index
End Sub
```

With the remaining submenus, the value of the appropriate Groups%() array element is added to the selected menu item's index number. Thus, the bsM_Click looks like this:

```
Sub bsM_Click (Index As Integer)
RunProg Index + Groups%(1)
End Sub
```

The sole statement in the csM_Click procedure, meanwhile, reads

```
RunProg Index + Groups%(2)
```

As you might expect, the procedures for subsequent submenus follow the same pattern, with the element indicator for the Groups%() array increasing with each subsequent submenu, so that the ysM_Click procedure instructs DeskMenu to

```
RunProg Index + Groups%(24)
```

■ The RunProg Routine

Now we're getting to the good stuff. The RunProg routine is where DeskMenu earns its keep, by launching applications or documents exactly as if you had double-clicked on them in the Program Manager.

As I wrote this routine, I discovered that making DeskMenu do this was just a little bit trickier than it might at first appear. The Program Manager does more than simply launch an application; it also sets the application's working directory so that when, for instance, you issue a File Open command in the newly launched application, the files in the working directory will be displayed (unless the application specifically calls another directory while opening its File Open dialog box.)

Normally, this is a matter of convenience only—if you mess up in setting the working directory, all it means is that you've got to go up or down the directory tree a bit to get to the files that you want. But a few applications rely upon their working directory being set correctly, and won't run if it is not set correctly.

This was a problem because neither of the two standard means for launching an application from within Visual Basic, the internal Shell command or the Windows API function WinExec, provide a means to set the launch application's working directory. You can issue a CHDIR command to the specified directory prior to launching the application, but that doesn't accomplish the same thing, and usually doesn't solve the problem of applications that expect their working directory to be set properly. This problem becomes apparent only with applications whose working directory is different from the directory in which their .EXE file is found.

Fortunately, the VB Q project had given me a good deal of exposure to the Shell-Execute function, from SHELL.DLL, and one of the parameters that ShellExecute expects is the application's default directory. It turns out that passing the working directory specified in the Program Manager as that parameter sets the working directory correctly for even the most fickle programs. (This doesn't solve the mystery of how the Program Manager sets an application's working directory, since it was doing so long before the appearance of SHELL.DLL in the 3.1 release of Windows.)

Once that problem was solved, the RunProg routine was a breeze.

The routine begins by looking for the string "DTMRunMin" in the ProgtoRun% element of the Progs() array. You'll recall that DeskMenu appends that string to the command lines of applications that are to be run in a minimized state. RunProg assigns the location of "DTMRunMin" in the command-line string to a variable called Min%. If Min% is greater than zero, indicating that "DTMRunMin" was found, RunProg strips it from the end of the command line.

```
Dim X%, Temp$, Min%
Min% = InStr(Progs(ProgtoRun%), "DTMRunMin")
If Min% > 0 Then Progs(ProgtoRun%) = Left$(Progs(ProgtoRun%), Min% - 1)
```

Next, RunProg checks for the presence of a decimal point in the run command, and posts an error message if it does not find one, indicating that the specified application or file has no extension.

```
X% = InStr(Progs(ProgtoRun%), ".")
If X% < 2 Then MsgBox "Can't run " & Progs(ProgtoRun%): Exit Sub
```

Having performed at least a cursory check for illegal file names, RunProg next sets up an On Error Resume Next error handler so that any other error that occurs won't stop the routine, and then attempts to ShellExecute the specified application, passing ShellExecute a show command of either SW_MINIMIZE or SW_SHOW depending on the value of Min%.

```
On Error Resume Next
   If Min% > 0 Then
     X% = ShellExecute(MainFrm.hWnd, "open", Progs(ProgtoRun%), 0&, ⇔
   WorkDirs(ProgtoRun%), SW_MINIMIZE)
   Else
     X% = ShellExecute(MainFrm.hWnd, "open", Progs(ProgtoRun%), 0&, ⇔
   WorkDirs(ProgtoRun%), SW_SHOW)
   End If
```

ShellExecute returns a value of 32 or greater if it was successful in launching the specified application. If ShellExecute fails, DeskMenu makes one more attempt to launch the application, calling the Visual Basic Shell command.

```
If X% < 32 Then
   If Min% > 0 Then
      X% = Shell(Progs(ProgtoRun%), 2)
   Else
      X% = Shell(Progs(ProgtoRun%), 1)
   End If
End If
```

If Shell also fails, RunProg posts a message box stating that it can't run the application. Otherwise, it exits.

```
On Error GoTo 0
If X% = 0 Then
   MsgBox "Can't run " & Progs(ProgtoRun%)
End If
```

These last few steps, starting with "If X% < 32," are probably unnecessary. Desk-Menu's ShellExecute command seems to work with any application that will launch correctly from the Program Manager.

■ USING PRIVATE .INI FILES

DeskMenu uses a private .INI file to save the Checked status of the Hide...Icons menu item from one session to the next.

As DeskMenu loads, it calls a routine called GetConfig to determine if it should place a check mark next to the menu item and hide Program Manager and Desk-Menu's icons. GetConfig uses the Windows API function GetPrivateProfileString to read the contents of DESKMENU.INI. As always, when you're dealing with an external function that will modify a string that you pass to it, you must first create a fixed-length string, and then tell the external function how long that string is.

Here, DeskMenu instructs GetPrivateProfileString to copy the contents of the Hide-Icons key of the Settings area of DESKMENU.INI into a fixed-length string called Ini-String. The "0" in the function call supplies a default value if GetPrivateProfileString can't find the specified key, while the 255 indicates IniString's length.

```
Sub GetConfig (ShowIcons%)
Dim IniString As String * 255, X%
X% = GetPrivateProfileString("Settings", "HideIcons", "0", IniString, ⇔
   255, "DESKMENU.INI")
ShowIcons% = Val(Left$(IniString, InStr(IniString, Chr$(0)) - 1))
End Sub
```

DeskMenu saves the setting for this menu item through a routine called SaveConfig, which it calls during the MainFrm_Unload event.

```
Sub SaveConfig ()
Dim X%
X% = WritePrivateProfileString("Settings", "HideIcons", Str$ ⇔
   (MainFrm.deskMenu(3).Checked), "DESKMENU.INI")
End Sub
```

The SaveConfig and GetConfig routines could easily be expanded to handle any number of additional settings that were to be saved from session to session.

■ ANIMATED LOADING SEQUENCE

DeskMenu's minimalist nature pretty much eliminated the form-design question from
the design process. However, since the application takes five to ten seconds to load as
it makes repeated DDE requests to the Program Manager, sorts menu items, loads
menu controls, and so on, I wanted to give the user an indication of its progress.
Thus, I designed a greetings screen and a slightly animated opening display, as shown
in Figure 7.6.

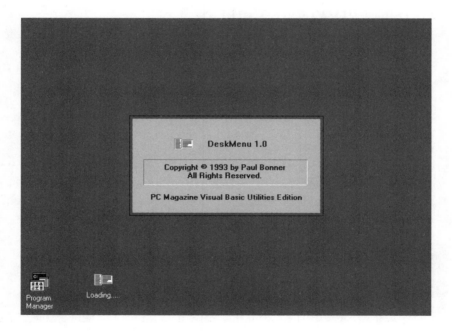

As DeskMenu loads, it displays a copyright form at the center of the screen. (The
same form is used as an About DeskMenu… dialog box, except that on the About
DeskMenu… dialog box an OK button is visible that is hidden on the opening
screen.) In addition, DeskMenu's main form appears iconized at the bottom of the
screen, with the caption "Loading." Then, as the GetItems routine builds DeskMenu's
custom menus, it adds a single period to the end of the caption for every second
group that it processes, thus animating the display of the caption.

The code which does so looks like this:

```
For X% = 0 To 24
   If X% / 2 = Int(X% / 2) Then
     MainFrm.Caption = MainFrm.Caption + "."
   End If
   i% = DoEvents()
```

The call to DoEvents() pauses the GetItems loop long enough for Windows to update the caption, thus turning the caption into a progress meter of sorts that indicates how many program groups GetItems has processed.

LISTING

DMENU.FRM

```
'  * * * * * * * * * * * * * * * * * * * * * * * * * * * * *
'  DMENU.FRM
'  Copyright (c) 1993 by Paul Bonner
'  PC Magazine Visual Basic Utilities
'  * * * * * * * * * * * * * * * * * * * * * * * * * * * * *
VERSION 2.00
Begin Form MainFrm
   BackColor       =    &H00C0C0C0&
   BorderStyle     =    1  'Fixed Single
   Caption         =    "DeskMenu"
   Height          =    3360
   Icon            =    DMENU.FRX:0000
   Left            =    915
   LinkTopic       =    "Form1"
   MaxButton       =    0  'False
   ScaleHeight     =    2670
   ScaleWidth      =    4275
   Top             =    1365
   Width           =    4395
   WindowState     =    1  'Minimized
   Begin TextBox Text1
      Height       =    285
      Left         =    360
      TabIndex     =    3
      Text         =    "Text1"
      Top          =    1920
      Visible      =    0   'False
      Width        =    1095
   End
   Begin Label Label3
      BackStyle    =    0   'Transparent
      Caption      =    "reg"
      Height       =    975
      Left         =    240
      TabIndex     =    2
      Top          =    1440
      Width        =    3735
      WordWrap     =    -1  'True
   End
   Begin Label Label2
      Alignment    =    2   'Center
      BackStyle    =    0   'Transparent
      Caption      =    "copyright"
      Height       =    555
      Left         =    240
      TabIndex     =    1
      Top          =    840
      Width        =    3735
      WordWrap     =    -1  'True
   End
   Begin Image Image1
      Height       =    480
      Left         =    840
      Picture      =    DMENU.FRX:0302
```

```
      Top             =     120
      Width           =     480
   End
   Begin Label Label1
      Alignment       =     1      'Right Justify
      AutoSize        =     -1     'True
      BackColor       =     &H00C0C0C0&
      BackStyle       =     0      'Transparent
      Caption         =     "DeskMenu 1.0"
      FontBold        =     -1     'True
      FontItalic      =     0      'False
      FontName        =     "Arial"
      FontSize        =     9.75
      FontStrikethru  =     0      'False
      FontUnderline   =     0      'False
      Height          =     240
      Left            =     1695
      LinkTopic       =     """PROGMAN|PROGMAN"""
      TabIndex        =     0
      Top             =     240
      Width           =     1305
   End
   Begin Menu MyMenu
      Caption         =     "&DeskMenu"
      Begin Menu mDeskMenu
         Caption         =     "DeskMenu"
         Begin Menu deskMenu
            Caption         =     "About DeskMenu..."
            Index           =     0
         End
         Begin Menu deskMenu
            Caption         =     "Reload Menu"
            Index           =     1
         End
         Begin Menu deskMenu
            Caption         =     "-"
            Index           =     2
         End
         Begin Menu deskMenu
            Caption         =     "Hide ProgMan && DeskMenu Icons"
            Index           =     3
         End
         Begin Menu deskMenu
            Caption         =     "-"
            Index           =     4
         End
         Begin Menu deskMenu
            Caption         =     "Exit DeskMenu"
            Index           =     5
         End
      End
      Begin Menu specialMenu
         Caption         =     "Windows"
         Begin Menu sMenu
            Caption         =     "Restart Windows"
            Index           =     0
         End
         Begin Menu sMenu
            Caption         =     "Exit Windows"
            Index           =     1
         End
      End
      Begin Menu sep
         Caption                =     "-"
```

```
End
Begin Menu GroupMenu
    Caption         =      "GM0"
    Index           =      0
    Begin Menu asM
        Caption             =      "asMenu"
        Index               =      0
    End
End
Begin Menu GroupMenu
    Caption         =      "GM1"
    Index           =      1
    Begin Menu bsM
        Caption             =      "bsmenu"
        Index               =      0
    End
End
Begin Menu GroupMenu
    Caption         =      "GM2"
    Index           =      2
    Begin Menu csM
        Caption             =      "csmenu"
        Index               =      0
    End
End
Begin Menu GroupMenu
    Caption         =      "GM3"
    Index           =      3
    Begin Menu dsM
        Caption             =      "dsmenu"
        Index               =      0
    End
End
Begin Menu GroupMenu
    Caption         =      "GM4"
    Index           =      4
    Begin Menu esM
        Caption             =      "esmenu"
        Index               =      0
    End
End
Begin Menu GroupMenu
    Caption         =      "GM5"
    Index           =      5
    Begin Menu fsM
        Caption             =      "fsmenu"
        Index               =      0
    End
End
Begin Menu GroupMenu
    Caption         =      "GM6"
    Index           =      6
    Begin Menu gsM
        Caption             =      "gsmenu"
        Index               =      0
    End
End
Begin Menu GroupMenu
    Caption         =      "GM7"
    Index           =      7
    Begin Menu hsM
        Caption             =      "hsmenu"
        Index               =      0
    End
```

```
End
Begin Menu GroupMenu
   Caption        =      "GM8"
   Index          =      8
   Begin Menu isM
      Caption     =         "ismenu"
      Index       =         0
   End
End
Begin Menu GroupMenu
   Caption        =      "GM9"
   Index          =      9
   Begin Menu jsM
      Caption     =         "jsmenu"
      Index       =         0
   End
End
Begin Menu GroupMenu
   Caption        =      "GM10"
   Index          =      10
   Begin Menu ksM
      Caption     =         "ksmenu"
      Index       =         0
   End
End
Begin Menu GroupMenu
   Caption        =      "GM11"
   Index          =      11
   Begin Menu lsM
      Caption     =         "lsmenu"
      Index       =         0
   End
End
Begin Menu GroupMenu
   Caption        =      "GM12"
   Index          =      12
   Begin Menu msM
      Caption     =         "msmenu"
      Index       =         0
   End
End
Begin Menu GroupMenu
   Caption        =      "GM13"
   Index          =      13
   Begin Menu nsM
      Caption     =         "nsmenu"
      Index       =         0
   End
End
Begin Menu GroupMenu
   Caption        =      "GM14"
   Index          =      14
   Begin Menu osM
      Caption     =         "osmenu"
      Index       =         0
   End
End
Begin Menu GroupMenu
   Caption        =      "GM15"
   Index          =      15
   Begin Menu psM
      Caption     =         "psmenu"
      Index       =         0
   End
```

```
            End
            Begin Menu GroupMenu
                Caption              =      "GM16"
                Index                =      16
                Begin Menu qsM
                    Caption          =        "qsmenu"
                    Index            =        0
                End
            End
            Begin Menu GroupMenu
                Caption              =      "GM17"
                Index                =      17
                Begin Menu rsM
                    Caption          =        "rsmenu"
                    Index            =        0
                End
            End
            Begin Menu GroupMenu
                Caption              =      "GM18"
                Index                =      18
                Begin Menu ssM
                    Caption          =        "ssmenu"
                    Index            =        0
                End
            End
            Begin Menu GroupMenu
                Caption              =      "GM19"
                Index                =      19
                Begin Menu tsM
                    Caption          =        "tsmenu"
                    Index            =        0
                End
            End
            Begin Menu GroupMenu
                Caption              =      "GM20"
                Index                =      20
                Begin Menu usM
                    Caption          =        "usmenu"
                    Index            =        0
                End
            End
            Begin Menu GroupMenu
                Caption              =      "GM21"
                Index                =      21
                Begin Menu vsM
                    Caption          =        "vsmenu"
                    Index            =        0
                End
            End
            Begin Menu GroupMenu
                Caption              =      "GM22"
                Index                =      22
                Begin Menu wsM
                    Caption          =        "wsmenu"
                    Index            =        0
                End
            End
            Begin Menu GroupMenu
                Caption              =      "GM23"
                Index                =      23
                Begin Menu xsM
                    Caption          =        "xsmenu"
                    Index            =        0
                End
```

```
        End
        Begin Menu GroupMenu
            Caption          =    "GM24"
            Index            =    24
            Begin Menu ysM
                Caption          =    "ysmenu"
                Index            =    0
            End
        End
    End
End
Option Explicit
DefInt A-Z

Sub asM_Click (Index As Integer)
RunProg Index
End Sub

Sub bsM_Click (Index As Integer)
RunProg Index + Groups%(1)
End Sub

Sub csM_Click (Index As Integer)
RunProg Index + Groups%(2)
End Sub

Sub DeskMenu_Click (Index As Integer)
ProcessDeskMenuItem Index
End Sub

Sub dsM_Click (Index As Integer)
RunProg Index + Groups%(3)
End Sub

Sub esM_Click (Index As Integer)
RunProg Index + Groups%(4)
End Sub

Sub Form_KeyDown (KeyCode As Integer, Shift As Integer)
' * * * * * * * * * * * * * * * * * * * * * * * * * *
' * pass keycode from DLL onto Main() routine
' * * * * * * * * * * * * * * * * * * * * * * * * * *
DLLCommand% = KeyCode
End Sub

Sub Form_Load ()
WindowState = 1
Label1.FontName = "MS Sans Serif"
Copyright$ = "Copyright (c) 1993 by Paul Bonner" + ⇔
    CRLF$ + "All Rights Reserved."
Label2 = Copyright$
Label3 = "PC Magazine Visual Basic Utilities Edition"
Label3.Left = (Width - Label3.Width) / 2
Label3.Top = Label3.Top + 120
Height = Label3.Top + Label3.Height + 120
End Sub

Sub Form_Paint ()
Me.AutoRedraw = True
' * * * * * * * * * * * * * * * * * * * * * * * * * *
' * draw 3D box
' * * * * * * * * * * * * * * * * * * * * * * * * * *
Frame Me, 130, Label2.Top - 80, Label2.Height - 20, Me.Width - 320, 1
End Sub
```

```
Sub Form_Resize ()
Select Case WindowState
'  * * * * * * * * * * * * * * * * * * * * * * * * *
'  * set global flag used in Main() to monitor icon's status
'  * * * * * * * * * * * * * * * * * * * * * * * * *
Case 0
    MeIconic% = False
Case 1
    MeIconic% = True
End Select
If MeIconic% And DeskMenu(3).Checked = True Then HideIcons
End Sub

Sub Form_Unload (Cancel As Integer)
Dim X%
'  * * * * * * * * * * * * * * * * * * * * * * * * *
'  * turn off subclassing of desktop window
'  * * * * * * * * * * * * * * * * * * * * * * * * *
X% = WatchDesk(MainFrm.hWnd, False)
'  * * * * * * * * * * * * * * * * * * * * * * * * *
'  * save Hide...Icons setting
'  * * * * * * * * * * * * * * * * * * * * * * * * *
SaveConfig
'  * * * * * * * * * * * * * * * * * * * * * * * * *
'  * if not reloading, make sure ProgMan icon is visible
'  * * * * * * * * * * * * * * * * * * * * * * * * *
If Not Reloading% Then
    CheckProgMan
    End
End If
End Sub

Sub fsM_Click (Index As Integer)
RunProg Index + Groups%(5)
End Sub

Sub gsM_Click (Index As Integer)
RunProg Index + Groups%(6)
End Sub

Sub hsM_Click (Index As Integer)
RunProg Index + Groups%(7)
End Sub

Sub isM_Click (Index As Integer)
RunProg Index + Groups%(8)
End Sub

Sub jsM_Click (Index As Integer)
RunProg Index + Groups%(9)
End Sub

Sub ksM_Click (Index As Integer)
RunProg Index + Groups%(10)
End Sub

Sub lsM_Click (Index As Integer)
RunProg Index + Groups%(11)
End Sub

Sub msM_Click (Index As Integer)
RunProg Index + Groups%(12)
End Sub
```

```
Sub nsM_Click (Index As Integer)
RunProg Index + Groups%(13)
End Sub

Sub osM_Click (Index As Integer)
RunProg Index + Groups%(14)
End Sub

Sub psM_Click (Index As Integer)
RunProg Index + Groups%(15)
End Sub

Sub qsM_Click (Index As Integer)
RunProg Index + Groups%(16)
End Sub

Sub rsM_Click (Index As Integer)
RunProg Index + Groups%(17)
End Sub

Sub sMenu_Click (Index As Integer)
ProcessSpecialMenu Index
End Sub

Sub ssM_Click (Index As Integer)
RunProg Index + Groups%(18)
End Sub

Sub tsM_Click (Index As Integer)
RunProg Index + Groups%(19)
End Sub

Sub usM_Click (Index As Integer)
RunProg Index + Groups%(20)
End Sub

Sub vsM_Click (Index As Integer)
RunProg Index + Groups%(21)
End Sub

Sub wsM_Click (Index As Integer)
RunProg Index + Groups%(22)
End Sub

Sub xsM_Click (Index As Integer)
RunProg Index + Groups%(23)
End Sub

Sub ysM_Click (Index As Integer)
RunProg Index + Groups%(24)
End Sub
```

LISTING

GREET.FRM

```
'  * * * * * * * * * * * * * * * * * * * * * * * * * * *
'  GREET.FRM
'  Copyright (c) 1993 by Paul Bonner
'  PC Magazine Visual Basic Utilities
'  * * * * * * * * * * * * * * * * * * * * * * * * * * *
VERSION 2.00
Begin Form HelloFrm
   BackColor       =   &H00C0C0C0&
   BorderStyle     =   3  'Fixed Double
   ControlBox      =   0    'False
   Height          =   4185
   Left            =   2370
   LinkTopic       =   "Form3"
   MaxButton       =   0    'False
   MinButton       =   0    'False
   ScaleHeight     =   3780
   ScaleWidth      =   4395
   Top             =   1905
   Width           =   4515
   Begin ListBox sorter
      Height       =   225
      Left         =   2280
      Sorted       =   -1  'True
      TabIndex     =   4
      Top          =   1920
      Visible      =   0    'False
      Width        =   1815
   End
   Begin CommandButton Command1
      Caption      =   "OK"
      Height       =   285
      Left         =   1560
      TabIndex     =   3
      Top          =   3000
      Visible      =   0    'False
      Width        =   735
   End
   Begin Label Label3
      AutoSize     =   -1  'True
      BackStyle    =   0  'Transparent
      Caption      =   "reg"
      Height       =   195
      Left         =   420
      TabIndex     =   2
      Top          =   1800
      Width        =   285
   End
   Begin Label Label2
      Alignment    =   2  'Center
      BackStyle    =   0  'Transparent
      Caption      =   "copyright"
      Height       =   615
      Left         =   360
      TabIndex     =   1
```

```
        Top             =    1080
        Width           =    3615
        WordWrap        =    -1    'True
    End
    Begin Label Label1
        Alignment       =    1    'Right Justify
        AutoSize        =    -1    'True
        BackColor       =    &H00C0C0C0&
        BackStyle       =    0    'Transparent
        Caption         =    "DeskMenu 1.0"
        FontBold        =    -1    'True
        FontItalic      =    0    'False
        FontName        =    "MS Sans Serif"
        FontSize        =    9.75
        FontStrikethru  =    0    'False
        FontUnderline   =    0    'False
        Height          =    240
        Left            =    1680
        LinkTopic       =    """PROGMAN|PROGMAN"""
        TabIndex        =    0
        Top             =    480
        Width           =    1470
    End
    Begin Image Image1
        Height          =    480
        Left            =    960
        Top             =    360
        Width           =    480
    End
End
Option Explicit
DefInt A-Z

Sub Command1_Click ()
Unload Me
End Sub

Sub Form_Load ()
'  * * * * * * * * * * * * * * * * * * * * * * * * * *
'  * set up copyright notice
'  * * * * * * * * * * * * * * * * * * * * * * * * * *
Label1.FontName = "System"
Label1.FontBold = False
Label1.FontSize = 10
Image1.Picture = MainFrm.Image1.Picture
Label2 = Copyright$
Label3 = "PC Magazine Visual Basic Utilities Edition"
Label3.Height = 600
Height = Label3.Top + Label3.Height + 30
If AboutButtonVis% Then
    Command1.Visible = True
    Command1.Top = Label3.Top + Label3.Height + 40
    Height = Command1.Top + Command1.Height + 310
    Command1.Left = (Width - Command1.Width) / 2
End If
CenterForm Me
End Sub

Sub Form_Paint ()
'  * * * * * * * * * * * * * * * * * * * * * * * * * *
'  * paint 3D frame
'  * * * * * * * * * * * * * * * * * * * * * * * * * *
Frame Me, 260, Label2.Top - 80, Label2.Height - 20, Me.Width - 720, 1
End Sub
```

LISTING

DMENU.BAS

```
'  * * * * * * * * * * * * * * * * * * * * * * * * * *
'   DMENU.BAS
'   Copyright (c) 1993 by Paul Bonner
'   PC Magazine Visual Basic Utilities
'  * * * * * * * * * * * * * * * * * * * * * * * * * *
Option Explicit
DefInt A-Z
'  * * * * * * * * * * * * * * * * * * * * * * * * * *
'   global vars
'  * * * * * * * * * * * * * * * * * * * * * * * * * *
Global DLLCommand%
Global loopCounter%
Global HidePM%
Global AboutButtonVis%
Global Copyright$
Dim C As Control
Global CRLF$
Global Groups%()
Global MeIconic%
Global Reloading% 'flag used when reloading menus to skip form/unload proc.
'  * * * * * * * * * * * * * * * * * * * * * * * * * *
'   module-level vars
'  * * * * * * * * * * * * * * * * * * * * * * * * * *
Dim Progs() As String
Dim WorkDirs() As String
Dim Registered%
'  * * * * * * * * * * * * * * * * * * * * * * * * * *
'   * DMENU.DLL declare
'  * * * * * * * * * * * * * * * * * * * * * * * * * *
Declare Function WatchDesk% Lib "DMENU.DLL" (ByVal MyWin%, ByVal OnOff%)
'  * * * * * * * * * * * * * * * * * * * * * * * * * *
'   * TrackPopupMenu declares
'  * * * * * * * * * * * * * * * * * * * * * * * * * *
Declare Function TrackPopupMenu% Lib "user" (ByVal hMenu%, ByVal wFlags%, ⇔
    ByVal X%, ByVal Y%, ByVal r2%, ByVal hWnd%, ByVal r1&)
Declare Function GetMenu% Lib "user" (ByVal hWnd%)
Declare Function GetSubMenu% Lib "user" (ByVal hMenu%, ByVal nPos%)
'  * * * * * * * * * * * * * * * * * * * * * * * * * *
'   * cursor positioning declares
'  * * * * * * * * * * * * * * * * * * * * * * * * * *
Type POINTAPI
    X As Integer
    Y As Integer
End Type
Declare Sub GetCursorPos Lib "User" (lpPoint As POINTAPI)
'  * * * * * * * * * * * * * * * * * * * * * * * * * *
'   * shell declares
'  * * * * * * * * * * * * * * * * * * * * * * * * * *
Declare Function ShellExecute Lib "Shell.dll" (ByVal hWnd%, ByVal lpszOp$, ⇔
    ByVal lpszFile$, ByVal lpszParams As Any, ByVal lpszDir$, ByVal ⇔
    fsShowCnd%) As Integer
Global Const SW_SHOW = 5
Const SW_MINIMIZE = 6
'  * * * * * * * * * * * * * * * * * * * * * * * * * *
```

```
'   * ExitWindows declare
'   * * * * * * * * * * * * * * * * * * * * * * * * * * * * *
Declare Function ExitWindows Lib "User" (ByVal dwReserved As Long, ⇔
    ByVal wReturnCode As Integer) As Integer
'   * * * * * * * * * * * * * * * * * * * * * * * * * * * * *
'   * hide progman declares
'   * * * * * * * * * * * * * * * * * * * * * * * * * * * * *
Declare Function FindWindow Lib "User" (ByVal lpClassName As Any, ⇔
    ByVal lpWindowName As Any) As Integer
Declare Function ShowWindow Lib "User" (ByVal hWnd As Integer, ByVal ⇔
    nCmdShow As Integer) As Integer
Const SW_HIDE = 0
Global Const SW_SHOWNORMAL = 1
Declare Function IsWindowVisible Lib "User" (ByVal hWnd As Integer) As Integer
Declare Function IsIconic Lib "User" (ByVal hWnd As Integer) As Integer
'   * * * * * * * * * * * * * * * * * * * * * * * * * * * * *
'   arrange icons declares
'   * * * * * * * * * * * * * * * * * * * * * * * * * * * * *
Declare Function GetDesktopWindow Lib "User" () As Integer
Declare Function ArrangeIconicWindows Lib "User" (ByVal hWnd As Integer) As ⇔
    Integer
'   * * * * * * * * * * * * * * * * * * * * * * * * * * * * *
'   * window placement declares
'   * * * * * * * * * * * * * * * * * * * * * * * * * * * * *
Type RECT
    Left As Integer
    Top As Integer
    Right As Integer
    Bottom As Integer
End Type
Type WindowPlacement
    Length As Integer
    Flags As Integer
    ShowCmd As Integer
    PtMinPosition As POINTAPI
    ptMaxPosition As POINTAPI
    rcNormalPosition As RECT
End Type
Declare Function SetWindowPlacement% Lib "USER" (ByVal hWnd%, lpwndpl As ⇔
    WindowPlacement)
Declare Function GetWindowPlacement% Lib "USER" (ByVal hWnd%, lpwndpl As ⇔
    WindowPlacement)
'   * * * * * * * * * * * * * * * * * * * * * * * * * * * * *
'   * private INI declares
'   * * * * * * * * * * * * * * * * * * * * * * * * * * * * *
Declare Function WritePrivateProfileString Lib "Kernel" (ByVal ⇔
    lpApplicationName As String, ByVal lpKeyName As String, ByVal lpString ⇔
    As String, ByVal lplFileName As String) As Integer
Declare Function GetPrivateProfileString Lib "Kernel" (ByVal ⇔
    lpApplicationName As String, ByVal lpKeyName As String, ByVal lpDefault ⇔
    As String, ByVal lpReturnedString As String, ByVal nSize As Integer, ⇔
    ByVal lpFileName As String) As Integer

Sub cChecker (X%, tCt%)
'   * * * * * * * * * * * * * * * * * * * * * * * * * * * * *
'   * sets object var C to specified menu item
'   * X%=subMenu
'   * tCt%=counter indicates which item on submenu
'   * * * * * * * * * * * * * * * * * * * * * * * * * * * * *
Select Case X%
Case 0
    Set C = MainFrm.asM(tCt%)
Case 1
    Set C = MainFrm.bsM(tCt%)
```

```
    Case 2
      Set C = MainFrm.csM(tCt%)
    Case 3
      Set C = MainFrm.dsM(tCt%)
    Case 4
      Set C = MainFrm.esM(tCt%)
    Case 5
      Set C = MainFrm.fsM(tCt%)
    Case 6
      Set C = MainFrm.gsM(tCt%)
    Case 7
      Set C = MainFrm.hsM(tCt%)
    Case 8
      Set C = MainFrm.isM(tCt%)
    Case 9
      Set C = MainFrm.jsM(tCt%)
    Case 10
      Set C = MainFrm.ksM(tCt%)
    Case 11
      Set C = MainFrm.lsM(tCt%)
    Case 12
      Set C = MainFrm.msM(tCt%)
    Case 13
      Set C = MainFrm.nsM(tCt%)
    Case 14
      Set C = MainFrm.osM(tCt%)
    Case 15
      Set C = MainFrm.psM(tCt%)
    Case 16
      Set C = MainFrm.qsM(tCt%)
    Case 17
      Set C = MainFrm.rsM(tCt%)
    Case 18
      Set C = MainFrm.ssM(tCt%)
    Case 19
      Set C = MainFrm.tsM(tCt%)
    Case 20
      Set C = MainFrm.usM(tCt%)
    Case 21
      Set C = MainFrm.vsM(tCt%)
    Case 22
      Set C = MainFrm.wsM(tCt%)
    Case 23
      Set C = MainFrm.xsM(tCt%)
    Case 24
      Set C = MainFrm.ysM(tCt%)
    End Select

    End Sub

    Sub CenterForm (F As Form)
    ' * * * * * * * * * * * * * * * * * * * * * * * * * * * *
    ' * center specified form on screen
    ' * * * * * * * * * * * * * * * * * * * * * * * * * * * *
    F.Left = (Screen.Width - F.Width) / 2
    F.Top = (Screen.Height - F.Height) / 2
    End Sub

    Sub CheckProgMan ()
    ' * * * * * * * * * * * * * * * * * * * * * * * * * * * *
    ' * make PM visible
    ' * * * * * * * * * * * * * * * * * * * * * * * * * * * *
    Dim X%
    X% = FindWindow("ProgMan", 0&)
```

```
If IsWindowVisible(X%) = False Then
    X% = ShowWindow(X%, SW_SHOW)
    X% = ArrangeIconicWindows(GetDesktopWindow())
End If
End Sub

Sub cLoader (X%, CT%)
'  * * * * * * * * * * * * * * * * * * * * * * * * *
'  * loads specified menu control
'  * then calls cChecker
'  * X%=SubMenu
'  * Ct%=counter indicating which item on submenu
'  * * * * * * * * * * * * * * * * * * * * * * * * *
Select Case X%
Case 0
    Load MainFrm.asM(CT%)
Case 1
    Load MainFrm.bsM(CT%)
Case 2
    Load MainFrm.csM(CT%)
Case 3
    Load MainFrm.dsM(CT%)
Case 4
    Load MainFrm.esM(CT%)
Case 5
    Load MainFrm.fsM(CT%)
Case 6
    Load MainFrm.gsM(CT%)
Case 7
    Load MainFrm.hsM(CT%)
Case 8
    Load MainFrm.isM(CT%)
Case 9
    Load MainFrm.jsM(CT%)
Case 10
    Load MainFrm.ksM(CT%)
Case 11
    Load MainFrm.lsM(CT%)
Case 12
    Load MainFrm.msM(CT%)
Case 13
    Load MainFrm.nsM(CT%)
Case 14
    Load MainFrm.osM(CT%)
Case 15
    Load MainFrm.psM(CT%)
Case 16
    Load MainFrm.qsM(CT%)
Case 17
    Load MainFrm.rsM(CT%)
Case 18
    Load MainFrm.ssM(CT%)
Case 19
    Load MainFrm.tsM(CT%)
Case 20
    Load MainFrm.usM(CT%)
Case 21
    Load MainFrm.vsM(CT%)
Case 22
    Load MainFrm.wsM(CT%)
Case 23
    Load MainFrm.xsM(CT%)
Case 24
    Load MainFrm.ysM(CT%)
```

```
End Select
cChecker X%, CT%
End Sub

Sub Frame (F As Form, L, t, h, W, Style)
'  * * * * * * * * * * * * * * * * * * * * * * * *
'  * draws 3D frame on control at specified
'  * left, top, height, width
'  * concave or convex depending upon Style param
'  * * * * * * * * * * * * * * * * * * * * * * * *
Const HiColor = &HFFFFFF
Const LoColor = &H808080
Dim BigOffSet
BigOffSet = 10
F.DrawWidth = 1
F.ForeColor = HiColor:  If Style = 2 Then F.ForeColor = LoColor
'bottom:
F.Line (L + F.DrawWidth, t + h)-(L + W - F.DrawWidth, t + h)
'right:
F.Line (L + W, t + F.DrawWidth)-(L + W, t + h - F.DrawWidth)
F.ForeColor = LoColor: If Style = 2 Then F.ForeColor = HiColor
'top:
F.Line (L - BigOffSet + F.DrawWidth, t - BigOffSet)-(L + W + BigOffSet - ⇔
    F.DrawWidth, t - BigOffSet)
'left:
F.Line (L - BigOffSet, t + F.DrawWidth - BigOffSet)-(L - BigOffSet, t + h + ⇔
    BigOffSet - F.DrawWidth)
End Sub

Sub GetConfig (ShowIcons%)
'  * * * * * * * * * * * * * * * * * * * * * * * *
'  * read string from private INI file
'  * * * * * * * * * * * * * * * * * * * * * * * *
Dim IniString As String * 255, X%
X%=GetPrivateProfileString("Settings","HideIcons","0",IniString,255,⇔
    "DESKMENU.INI")
ShowIcons% = Val(Left$(IniString, InStr(IniString, Chr$(0)) - 1))
End Sub

Sub GetExe (Temp$, ProgCt%)
'  * * * * * * * * * * * * * * * * * * * * * * * *
'  * examine progman data string for Run Minimized flag
'  * * * * * * * * * * * * * * * * * * * * * * * *
Dim Min%
For Min% = Len(Temp$) To 1 Step -1
    If Mid$(Temp$, Min%, 1) = "," Then Exit For
Next
If Mid$(Temp$, Min% + 1, 1) = "1" Then
    Min% = True
Else
    Min% = False
End If
Dim i%, C1%, C2%, AppExe$, AppPath$
'  * * * * * * * * * * * * * * * * * * * * * * * *
'  * extract command line and working dir from progman data
'  * * * * * * * * * * * * * * * * * * * * * * * *
C1% = InStr(Temp$, ",")
If C1% Then
    C2% = InStr(C1% + 1, Temp$, ",")
    AppExe$ = Left$(Temp$, C2% - 2)
    AppExe$ = Mid$(AppExe$, C1% + 2)
'  * * * * * * * * * * * * * * * * * * * * * * * *
'  * append flag if to run minimized
'  * * * * * * * * * * * * * * * * * * * * * * * *
```

```
      If Min% = True Then AppExe$ = AppExe$ + "DTMRunMin"
      Progs(ProgCt%) = AppExe$
      C1% = InStr(C2% + 1, Temp$, ",")
      AppPath$ = Left$(Temp$, C1% - 1)
      AppPath$ = Mid$(AppPath$, C2% + 1)
      WorkDirs(ProgCt%) = AppPath$
End If
End Sub

Sub GetGroups ()
' * * * * * * * * * * * * * * * * * * * * * * * * * * * * *
'  * load program group names from ProgMan
' * * * * * * * * * * * * * * * * * * * * * * * * * * * * *
MainFrm.Caption = "Loading."
GetLinkData "PROGMAN"
Dim i%, X%, Temp$, CT%
CRLF$ = Chr$(13) + Chr$(10)
Temp$ = MainFrm.Text1
i% = InStr(Temp$, CRLF$)
' * * * * * * * * * * * * * * * * * * * * * * * * * * * * *
'  * add each name to sorter list box
' * * * * * * * * * * * * * * * * * * * * * * * * * * * * *
Do While i%
   HelloFrm.sorter.AddItem Left$(Temp$, i% - 1)
   Temp$ = Mid$(Temp$, i% + 2)
   i% = InStr(Temp$, CRLF$)
   CT% = CT% + 1
Loop
' * * * * * * * * * * * * * * * * * * * * * * * * * * * * *
'  * now take from list box and assign to menu captions
' * * * * * * * * * * * * * * * * * * * * * * * * * * * * *
For X% = 0 To CT% - 1
   MainFrm.GroupMenu(X%).Caption = HelloFrm.sorter.List(X%)
Next
ReDim Groups%(CT% - 1)
' * * * * * * * * * * * * * * * * * * * * * * * * * * * * *
'  * now hide unused menus
' * * * * * * * * * * * * * * * * * * * * * * * * * * * * *
For i% = CT% To 24
   MainFrm.GroupMenu(i%).Visible = False
Next
HelloFrm.sorter.Clear
End Sub

Sub GetItems ()
' * * * * * * * * * * * * * * * * * * * * * * * * * * * * *
'  * get menu items for each program group
' * * * * * * * * * * * * * * * * * * * * * * * * * * * * *
Dim i%, X%, CT%, Cap$, Temp$, Y%
Dim AccumGroup%
' * * * * * * * * * * * * * * * * * * * * * * * * * * * * *
'  * loop through all groups
' * * * * * * * * * * * * * * * * * * * * * * * * * * * * *
For X% = 0 To 24
' * * * * * * * * * * * * * * * * * * * * * * * * * * * * *
'  * animate DeskMenu icon caption
' * * * * * * * * * * * * * * * * * * * * * * * * * * * * *
   If X% / 2 = Int(X% / 2) Then
     MainFrm.Caption = MainFrm.Caption + "."
   End If
   i% = DoEvents()
' * * * * * * * * * * * * * * * * * * * * * * * * * * * * *
'  get all program items for current group
' * * * * * * * * * * * * * * * * * * * * * * * * * * * * *
```

```
        If MainFrm.GroupMenu(X%).Visible = True Then
            Temp$ = MainFrm.GroupMenu(X%).Caption
            GetLinkData Temp$
            Temp$ = MainFrm.Text1
            i% = InStr(Temp$, CRLF$)
            Cap$ = Left$(Temp$, i% - 1)
            Cap$ = Trim(Cap$)
            i% = InStr(Cap$, ",")
            i% = InStr(i% + 1, Cap$, ",")
            Cap$ = Mid$(Cap$, i% + 1)
' * * * * * * * * * * * * * * * * * * * * * * * * * * * *
' * redim arrays to hold items in this group
' * * * * * * * * * * * * * * * * * * * * * * * * * * * *
            Groups%(X%) = AccumGroup%
            AccumGroup% = AccumGroup% + Val(Cap$)
            ReDim Preserve Progs(AccumGroup%)
            ReDim Preserve WorkDirs(AccumGroup%)
' * * * * * * * * * * * * * * * * * * * * * * * * * * * *
' * strip off 1st line of label
' * * * * * * * * * * * * * * * * * * * * * * * * * * * *
            i% = InStr(Temp$, CRLF$)
            If i% Then
                    Temp$ = Mid$(Temp$, i% + 2)
                    i% = InStr(Temp$, CRLF$)
            End If
            CT% = 0
' * * * * * * * * * * * * * * * * * * * * * * * * * * * *
' * set initial value of C to existing menu item
' * * * * * * * * * * * * * * * * * * * * * * * * * * * *
            cChecker X%, 0
            Do While i%
                    C.Visible = True
' * * * * * * * * * * * * * * * * * * * * * * * * * * * *
' * add item's data to sorter
' * * * * * * * * * * * * * * * * * * * * * * * * * * * *
            HelloFrm.sorter.AddItem Left$(Temp$, InStr(Temp$, CRLF$) - 1)
            Temp$ = Mid$(Temp$, i% + 2)
            i% = InStr(Temp$, CRLF$)
            CT% = CT% + 1
' * * * * * * * * * * * * * * * * * * * * * * * * * * * *
' * if there's another item, load another menu item
' * * * * * * * * * * * * * * * * * * * * * * * * * * * *
            If i% Then cLoader X%, CT%
            Loop
            CT% = 0
' * * * * * * * * * * * * * * * * * * * * * * * * * * * *
' * loop through sorter list box
' * * * * * * * * * * * * * * * * * * * * * * * * * * * *
            For Y% = 0 To HelloFrm.sorter.ListCount - 1
' * * * * * * * * * * * * * * * * * * * * * * * * * * * *
' * extract command line/work dir
' * * * * * * * * * * * * * * * * * * * * * * * * * * * *
                    Cap$ = HelloFrm.sorter.List(Y%)
                    GetExe Cap$, Groups%(X) + Y%
' * * * * * * * * * * * * * * * * * * * * * * * * * * * *
' * now trim caption
' * * * * * * * * * * * * * * * * * * * * * * * * * * * *
                    Cap$ = Left$(Cap$, InStr(Cap$, ",") - 1)
                    Cap$ = Mid$(Cap$, 2, Len(Cap$) - 2)
' * * * * * * * * * * * * * * * * * * * * * * * * * * * *
' * select object variable
' * * * * * * * * * * * * * * * * * * * * * * * * * * * *
                    cChecker X%, CT%
' * * * * * * * * * * * * * * * * * * * * * * * * * * * *
```

```
'   * set menu caption
'   * * * * * * * * * * * * * * * * * * * * * * * * * * * * * *
                 C.Caption = Cap$
                 CT% = CT% + 1
         Next Y%
     End If
     HelloFrm.sorter.Clear
 Next X%
 End Sub

 Sub GetLinkData (Item$)
 '   * * * * * * * * * * * * * * * * * * * * * * * * * * * * * *
 '   * establish DDE link with ProgMan
 '   * request Item$
 '   * * * * * * * * * * * * * * * * * * * * * * * * * * * * * *
 MainFrm.Text1.LinkTopic = "ProgMan|Progman"
 MainFrm.Text1.LinkItem = Item$
 MainFrm.Text1.LinkMode = 2
 MainFrm.Text1.LinkRequest
 On Error Resume Next
 MainFrm.Text1.LinkMode = 0
 On Error GoTo 0
 End Sub

 Sub HideIconicApp (Handle%)
 '   * * * * * * * * * * * * * * * * * * * * * * * * * * * * * *
 '   * if specified window is iconic and visible, hide it
 '   * * * * * * * * * * * * * * * * * * * * * * * * * * * * * *
 If IsIconic(Handle%) <> 0 And IsWindowVisible(Handle%) <> 0 Then
     Handle% = ShowWindow(Handle%, SW_HIDE)
 End If
 End Sub

 Sub HideIcons ()
 '   * * * * * * * * * * * * * * * * * * * * * * * * * * * * * *
 '   hide or display pm and deskmenu icons
 '   * * * * * * * * * * * * * * * * * * * * * * * * * * * * * *
 Dim X%, Y%
 If MainFrm.deskMenu(3).Checked Then
     X% = FindWindow("ProgMan", 0&)
     HideIconicApp X%
     HidePM% = True
     If IsIconic(MainFrm.hWnd) Then MoveIconOffScreen MainFrm
     X% = ArrangeIconicWindows(GetDesktopWindow())
 Else
     HidePM% = False
     X% = FindWindow("ProgMan", 0&)
     X% = ShowWindow(X%, SW_SHOW)
     X% = ArrangeIconicWindows(GetDesktopWindow())
 End If
 loopCounter% = False
 End Sub

 Sub Main ()
 '   * * * * * * * * * * * * * * * * * * * * * * * * * * * * * *
 '   * sub main() is startup routine for DeskMenu
 '   * prevent multiple instances
 '   * * * * * * * * * * * * * * * * * * * * * * * * * * * * * *
 If App.PrevInstance Then AppActivate "DeskMenu": End
 CRLF$ = Chr$(13) + Chr$(10)
 Dim X%
 MainFrm.Show
 '   * * * * * * * * * * * * * * * * * * * * * * * * * * * * * *
 '   * disable menu until fully customized
```

```
' * * * * * * * * * * * * * * * * * * * * * * * * * * *
MainFrm.MyMenu.Enabled = False
HelloFrm.Show
X% = DoEvents()
Screen.MousePointer = 11
' * * * * * * * * * * * * * * * * * * * * * * * * * * *
' * get progman data
' * * * * * * * * * * * * * * * * * * * * * * * * * * *
GetGroups
GetItems
MainFrm.Caption = "DeskMenu"
Screen.MousePointer = 0
Unload HelloFrm
' * * * * * * * * * * * * * * * * * * * * * * * * * * *
' * enable menu, minimize main form
' * * * * * * * * * * * * * * * * * * * * * * * * * * *
MainFrm.MyMenu.Enabled = True
MainFrm.WindowState = 1
MeIconic% = True
' * * * * * * * * * * * * * * * * * * * * * * * * * * *
' * hide deskmenu and progman icons if indicated by INI
' * * * * * * * * * * * * * * * * * * * * * * * * * * *
Dim ShowIcons%
GetConfig ShowIcons%
If ShowIcons% = True Then ProcessDeskMenuItem 3
' * * * * * * * * * * * * * * * * * * * * * * * * * * *
' * subclass desktop window
' * * * * * * * * * * * * * * * * * * * * * * * * * * *
On Error GoTo DLlError
X% = WatchDesk(MainFrm.hWnd, True)
On Error GoTo 0
' * * * * * * * * * * * * * * * * * * * * * * * * * * *
' * enter endless loop
' * * * * * * * * * * * * * * * * * * * * * * * * * * *
Do While DoEvents()
' * * * * * * * * * * * * * * * * * * * * * * * * * *
' * pop up menu if command received from dll
' * * * * * * * * * * * * * * * * * * * * * * * * * *
    If DLLCommand% = 127 Then TrackPopUp 0, MainFrm: DLLCommand% = False
' * * * * * * * * * * * * * * * * * * * * * * * * * *
' if supposed to hide icons
' look for them every 100 trips through loop
' * * * * * * * * * * * * * * * * * * * * * * * * * *
    If HidePM% = True Then
        loopCounter% = loopCounter% + 1
        If loopCounter% = 100 Then
                HideIconicApp FindWindow("ProgMan", 0&)
            If MeIconic% Then
                    If MainFrm.Left > 0 Then MoveIconOffScreen MainFrm
            End If
                loopCounter% = 0
        End If
    End If
Loop
Exit Sub
' * * * * * * * * * * * * * * * * * * * * * * * * * * *
' * end if can't access DLL
' * * * * * * * * * * * * * * * * * * * * * * * * * * *
DLlError:
    If Err = 48 Then MsgBox "Can't load DESKMENU.DLL"
    End
End Sub

Sub MoveIconOffScreen (F As Form)
```

```
'   * * * * * * * * * * * * * * * * * * * * * * * * * * * *
'   * move DeskMenu icon off screen
'   * * * * * * * * * * * * * * * * * * * * * * * * * * * *
Const WPF_SETMINPOSITION = &H1
Dim WinPlace As WindowPlacement, X%
WinPlace.Length = 22
X% = GetWindowPlacement%(F.hWnd, WinPlace)
WinPlace.PtMinPosition.Y = -50
WinPlace.PtMinPosition.X = -50
WinPlace.Flags = WPF_SETMINPOSITION
WinPlace.ShowCmd = SW_MINIMIZE
X% = SetWindowPlacement%(F.hWnd, WinPlace)
End Sub

Sub ProcessDeskMenuItem (Index As Integer)
'   * * * * * * * * * * * * * * * * * * * * * * * * * * * *
'   * process DeskMenu menu selections
'   * * * * * * * * * * * * * * * * * * * * * * * * * * * *
Select Case Index
Case 0
'   * * * * * * * * * * * * * * * * * * * * * * * * * * * *
'   * load about form
'   * * * * * * * * * * * * * * * * * * * * * * * * * * * *
    AboutButtonVis% = True
    Load HelloFrm
    HelloFrm.Show 1
Case 1
    ReloadMenus
Case 2
Case 3
    MainFrm.deskMenu(3).Checked = Not MainFrm.deskMenu(3).Checked
    HideIcons
Case 4
Case 5
    Unload MainFrm
End Select
End Sub

Sub ProcessSpecialMenu (Ind%)
'   * * * * * * * * * * * * * * * * * * * * * * * * * * * *
'   * process Windows menu selections
'   * * * * * * * * * * * * * * * * * * * * * * * * * * * *
Dim X%, Reboot%
Select Case Ind%
Case 0
    X% = MsgBox("Restart Windows now?", 49, "DeskMenu")
    If X% <> 1 Then Exit Sub
    Reboot% = &H42
Case 1
    X% = MsgBox("Exit Windows now?", 49, "DeskMenu")
    If X% <> 1 Then Exit Sub
    Reboot% = &H0
End Select
X% = ExitWindows(Reboot%, 0)
End Sub

Sub ReloadMenus ()
'   * * * * * * * * * * * * * * * * * * * * * * * * * * * *
'   * unload MainFrm, then reload to reinitialize custom menus
'   * * * * * * * * * * * * * * * * * * * * * * * * * * * *
Dim OldCheck%
Reloading% = True
OldCheck% = MainFrm.deskMenu(3).Checked
Unload MainFrm
```

```
ReDim Groups%(0)
ReDim Progs(0)
ReDim WorkDirs(0)
MainFrm.Show
Reloading% = False
GetGroups
GetItems
Unload HelloFrm
MainFrm.Caption = "DeskMenu"
Dim X%
X% = WatchDesk(MainFrm.hWnd, True)
MainFrm.deskMenu(3).Checked = OldCheck%
If OldCheck% Then HideIcons
End Sub

Sub RunProg (ProgtoRun%)
Dim X%, Temp$, Min%
' * * * * * * * * * * * * * * * * * * * * * * * * *
' * look for run minimized flag
' * * * * * * * * * * * * * * * * * * * * * * * * *
Min% = InStr(Progs(ProgtoRun%), "DTMRunMin")
If Min% > 0 Then Progs(ProgtoRun%) = Left$(Progs(ProgtoRun%), Min% - 1)
X% = InStr(Progs(ProgtoRun%), ".")
If X% < 2 Then MsgBox "Can't run " & Progs(ProgtoRun%): Exit Sub
' * * * * * * * * * * * * * * * * * * * * * * * * *
' * use ShellExecute to launch
' * * * * * * * * * * * * * * * * * * * * * * * * *
On Error Resume Next
   If Min% > 0 Then
      X% = ShellExecute(MainFrm.hWnd, "open", Progs(ProgtoRun%), 0&, ⇔
      WorkDirs(ProgtoRun%), SW_MINIMIZE)
   Else
      X% = ShellExecute(MainFrm.hWnd, "open", Progs(ProgtoRun%), 0&, ⇔
      WorkDirs(ProgtoRun%), SW_SHOW)
   End If
' * * * * * * * * * * * * * * * * * * * * * * * * *
' * if ShellExecute fails, try Shell
' * * * * * * * * * * * * * * * * * * * * * * * * *
If X% < 32 Then
   If Min% > 0 Then
      X% = Shell(Progs(ProgtoRun%), 2)
   Else
      X% = Shell(Progs(ProgtoRun%), 1)
   End If
End If
On Error GoTo 0
' * * * * * * * * * * * * * * * * * * * * * * * * *
' * if still no success, announce failure
' * * * * * * * * * * * * * * * * * * * * * * * * *
If X% = 0 Then
   MsgBox "Can't run " & Progs(ProgtoRun%)
End If
End Sub

Sub SaveConfig ()
' * * * * * * * * * * * * * * * * * * * * * * * * *
' * save data to private INI file
' * * * * * * * * * * * * * * * * * * * * * * * * *
Dim X%
X% = WritePrivateProfileString("Settings", "HideIcons", ⇔
   Str$(MainFrm.deskMenu(3).Checked), "DESKMENU.INI")
End Sub

Sub TrackPopUp (Menu As Integer, F As Form)
```

```
'   * * * * * * * * * * * * * * * * * * * * * * * * * * * *
'   API routine to track popup menu, with right mouse button
'   * * * * * * * * * * * * * * * * * * * * * * * * * * * *
Dim MD As POINTAPI
GetCursorPos MD
Dim hMenu%, hSubMenu%, r As Integer
hMenu% = GetMenu(F.hWnd)
hSubMenu% = GetSubMenu(hMenu%, Menu)
r = TrackPopupMenu(hSubMenu%, 2, MD.X, MD.Y, 0, F.hWnd, 0&)
End Sub
```

C H A P T E R

8

VB MAKER

VB MAKer keeps track of Visual Basic custom controls and makes it easier to add them to projects.

When you think about it, Visual Basic custom controls are about as annoying as a good thing can get. Oh, the good ones are worth their weight in gold once you've got them in place, but adding them to your project, or removing unwanted ones from a project, can be a royal pain in the posterior. VB MAKer takes the pain out of managing the custom controls in a Visual Basic project.

The problem is that, to get custom controls into your application, you've got to add the files that contain them one by one to the application's project file. This means that you've got to locate each custom control's .VBX file, which is usually stored in either your WINDOWS or SYSTEM directory, or some other directory other than the one in which your project will be stored. I just counted 37 .VBX files in my WINDOWS and SYSTEM directories, for instance, and I've got several others scattered around in

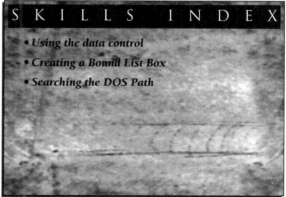

SKILLS INDEX

- *Using the data control*
- *Creating a Bound List Box*
- *Searching the DOS Path*

other directories. And the problem doesn't stop with sheer numbers. You've got to be able to remember which of the often cryptically named .VBX files you find contains the custom control or controls that you want to add to your project.

Microsoft's solution to this problem is the AUTOLOAD.MAK file, which specifies the custom controls that are to be added to all new projects as they are created. When you install Visual Basic 3.0 Professional Edition, for instance, the installation program automatically creates an AUTOLOAD.MAK file that adds 14 of the custom controls included with the Professional Edition to every new project you create. Unfortunately, that means that you have to wait for all 14 controls to load every time you launch Visual Basic 3.0.

I don't know about you, but as evidenced by the projects in this book, I don't use the MSCOMM.VBX control in every application I write. Nor GRAPH.VBX, nor THREED.VBX, nor MSOLE2.VBX. In fact, I have my doubts as to whether any Visual Basic programmer uses all 14 of those controls in even one project, let alone in every one that he or she creates.

Since unused controls take up memory and resources and slow down project loading, you want to get rid of them. If you're not using any of those controls in your project, you've got to select a .VBX file in the Project window, and then pull down Visual Basic's File menu and select the Remove File item, 14 times; once for each of the 14 custom controls that AUTOLOAD.MAK has so thoughtfully loaded for you. Yech. There has to be a better way to manage custom controls than that.

There is. It's VB MAKer, the project presented in this chapter.

VB MAKer uses Visual Basic 3.0's data control and an Access database to keep track of all the custom controls that you've installed. It allows you to create new projects with the custom controls you specify, or to add or remove custom controls from any existing project. It will even launch Visual Basic for you, or instruct an already-running instance of Visual Basic to load the new or modified project.

■ USING VB MAKER

The first time you run VB MAKer, it presents you with the form shown in Figure 8.1. Because you have not yet added any .VBX files to its database, both the "Available controls" and "Current MAK file" list boxes are empty, and the Path and Description fields are blank.

FIGURE 8.1

VB MAKer's
opening screen,
before any
custom controls
have been
added to its
.VBX database

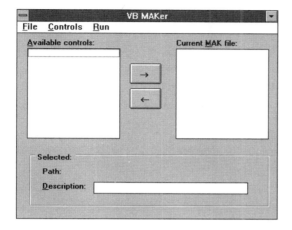

The first step to using VB MAKer, then, is to add the custom controls that are installed on your system to its .VBX database. To do so, you can select the Add Controls to Database… item on the form's Control menu, or press Control+A, the shortcut key for that menu item.

When you do so, VB MAKer presents you with the dialog box shown in Figure 8.2, which offers you the choice of finding all .VBX files on the DOS path, locating individual .VBX files, or canceling the Add Controls operation.

FIGURE 8.2

The Add
Controls dialog
box offers two
methods for
adding controls
to the .VBX
database.

I recommend that you start the process of building your .VBX database by selecting the option to find all .VBXs on the DOS path. When you do so, VB MAKer searches through every directory on the DOS path, plus your WINDOWS and SYSTEM directories, to identify any .VBXs stored in those directories that aren't currently listed in the database. It then creates a message box to tell you how many .VBXs it found, as shown in Figure 8.3.

VB MAKer
reports its
findings after
searching the
DOS path for
custom controls
that aren't
already listed in
its database.

Once you've closed the message box, you can select any or all of the controls found during the search from the list box on the Find All VBXs dialog box, as shown in Figure 8.4. Then you simply press the "Add to VBX database" button to add all the controls that you've selected to the database.

The selected
controls will be
added to VB
MAKer's
database when
you press the
"Add to VBX
database"
button.

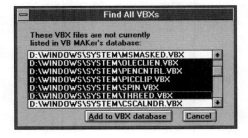

If, after using the Find All VBXs option, you realize that VB MAKer has missed some of the .VBXs on your system because they're installed in a directory that is not on your DOS path, you can use the Locate Individual VBX Files option to add them to the database. When you do so, VB MAKer presents you with the dialog box shown in Figure 8.5, which lists any .VBXs that are not currently listed in VB MAKer's database for any drive and directory you select.

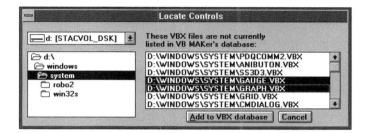

The Locate Controls dialog box displays any .VBX files in the selected directory that are not currently listed in VB MAKer's database.

■ Duplicate .VBXs

If a custom control is already listed in VB MAKer's database, it won't appear in this list box, nor in the list box presented by the Find All VBXs option. Note, however, that since VB MAKer uses a control's fully qualified path name (consisting of its DOS path and file name) to determine its uniqueness, if you have copies of the same control in five directories on your DOS path, you'll have five entries for it in the Find All VBXs list box, and will be able to add five entries for it to your database.

Thus, VB MAKer makes it easy to identify duplicate copies of a .VBX file. Fortunately, it also makes it easy to get rid of them, using the Delete Selected Control... item on its Controls menu.

Selecting that item produces the dialog box shown in Figure 8.6, which identifies the selected control, and offers you the option of either removing it from VB MAKer's database, or of removing it from the database *and* deleting it from disk.

The Delete Control dialog box allows you to remove a custom control from VB MAKer's database or from your hard disk.

If you select either deletion option, VB MAKer posts a standard Yes/No message box to confirm your choice, as shown in Figure 8.7.

VB MAKer
uses this
message box to
confirm that
you wish to
remove a
custom control
from its
database.

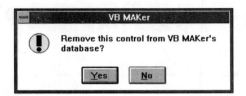

VB MAKer's Controls menu also offers you the option to clear the entire database. Because this action is so destructive, the program requires you to click the Yes button on not one, but two confirmation message boxes before it carries out your instruction.

■ Describing Controls

Every time you select a control in VB MAKer's Available Controls list box, VB MAKer displays the full path of the selected control in the Path field, and whatever description you've given the control in the Description field. Of course, no control has a description when you initially add it to the database, but you can provide a description for any control, or edit an existing description, simply by selecting the control in either list box and typing the description that you want to give it into the Description field. The description will be saved to the database automatically.

There are two reasons for adding a description to the database entry for a custom control. One is to increase the comprehensibility of the list of controls. "MicroHelp Graphics Controls" is certainly easier to understand than MHGR200.VBX. In addition, however, filling out the description field for a control enables you to locate that control with VB MAKer's Find facility.

VB MAKer's Controls menu offers two choices for searching the database: Find by Description and Find Next. When you select the first of these, either by selecting it from the menu or entering its shortcut key, Control+F, VB MAKer presents the input box shown in Figure 8.8, allowing you to enter a word or phrase for which you wish it to search.

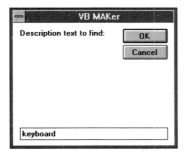

FIGURE 8.8

VB MAKer will search the Description field of each item in either list box to locate the word or phrase you specify in this input box.

If, for instance, you enter the word "Graphics" in the input box, VB MAKer will search through the Available Controls list starting with the list box item that follows the current item until it finds the first item whose description contains the word "graphics" or "GRAPHICS" or "GrapHIcS" (the search is not case-sensitive). When it locates a control, it highlights it in the list box, and enables the Find Next item (shortcut key F3) in the Controls menu. Pressing F3 or selecting the Find Next item continues the search, which will continue until another match is found or until every record has been examined.

▪ Working with .MAK files

So far you've got a database of .VBX files, to which you can add or delete entries, and which you can search via a description field. But what practical purpose does it solve?

The answer is that it lets you create or edit .MAK files. VB MAKer starts off presenting a new, empty .MAK file in its right-hand list box. To add a custom control to this .MAK file, you simply select the control that you want to add, and then either click the right arrow button, or double-click on the control. Performing either action will move the control to the Current MAK file list box, as shown in Figure 8.9. The control is, of course, still present in VB MAKer's database, but VB MAKer removes it from the Available Controls list because, since it is now part of the current .MAK file, there would be no sense in adding it to the .MAK file again.

When you've added all the controls that you want to the new .MAK file, you can select the Save or Save As... items from VB MAKer's File menu. Doing so will first generate a standard Save As... dialog box in which you can specify the name and path of the new .MAK file, and then save the file as specified.

FIGURE 8.9

All controls in the current .MAK file are listed in the right-hand list box on VB MAKer's main form.

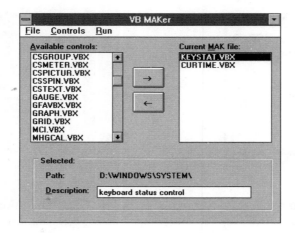

More interesting, perhaps, is VB MAKer's capability to edit existing .MAK files. A .MAK file is a standard ASCII file that contains a variety of data about a project, including a list of all the .BAS and .FRM files in the project, a list of all the .VBX files in the project, and information about the project's design-time window layout, its title, the name of its executable file, and the form which serves as the source for the .EXE file's icon.

The only part of this information that VB MAKer cares about is the list of .VBX files in the project. It stores the other data so that it can write it back to the .MAK file later if you first instruct it to save the file.

As VB MAKer loads the .MAK file, it adds each custom control listed in the file to the Current MAK file list box, and removes it from the Available Controls list box.

If VB MAKer can't find a control listed in the .MAK file in its database, it posts a message telling you that you must add the control to the database before you can edit the .MAK file, and then aborts the file-loading procedure.

Once you've opened an existing .MAK file, you can add new custom controls to it or remove existing custom controls from it, by simply selecting the custom control that you wish to move and clicking on the appropriate arrow button or by double-clicking on the control's name. Then you can save the edited .MAK file, using either its current name or a new name.

■ **Launching the .MAK File**

Once you've finished editing a .MAK file and have saved your edits, you can ask VB MAKer to launch Visual Basic and instruct it to open the edited .MAK file, by selecting the Launch Current MAK item on VB MAKer's Run menu. If Visual Basic is already running and is in Design (as opposed to Run) mode, VB MAKer will instruct it to open the current project when you select the Launch Current MAK menu item. (If Visual Basic is in Run mode, VB MAKer will use a message box to inform you that it cannot launch the current project.) In either case, as soon as Visual Basic is launched or has been instructed to open the .MAK file, VB MAKer minimizes its own window, so as to be as unobtrusive as possible while you work in Visual Basic.

Finally, everytime you open a .MAK file, or create a new one, VB MAKer reinitializes its list of available controls by reloading its .VBX database.

That's about all there is to VB MAKer's operation. As far as the user is concerned, it provides a simple solution to a vexing problem. From the developer's viewpoint, on the other hand, using an Access database to track .VBXs might seem like killing ants with a hammer. Still, Visual Basic 3.0 makes the use of database technology so simple that in many ways it is easier to implement a full-scale database for a task like this than to use supposedly simpler, random-access or sequential text files to keep track of data.

■ INSIDE VB MAKER

More than anything, VB MAKer demonstrates the power of high-level objects such as Visual Basic 3.0's data control. Nearly everything that happens in VB MAKer revolves around the invisible data control on MAKerMain.Frm and the Access database table to which it is linked, and yet only a tiny fraction of VB MAKer's code makes any reference to the data control or its linked table. Instead, VB MAKer takes advantage of the capability of data-aware controls to almost completely automate the process of maintaining a database.

In designing VB MAKer, I set out to take advantage of this capability as often as possible. I didn't see any advantage to writing database code when a bound control would do the job just as well. So, for instance, there is absolutely no code in VB MAKer for the task of adding the description that a user has assigned to a control to the controls database. Instead, the database table's description field is automatically updated whenever the user modifies the description, because the text box in which the description is displayed is bound to the description field in the database table.

Similarly, I didn't see any purpose for including code to create the database table that VB MAKer uses within VB MAKer. That would have made sense if VB MAKer made use of multiple databases. Since it only requires one database, however, and one with very simple data-tracking needs at that, there didn't seem to be any justification for adding the necessary code to create a database for the project. Instead, I used the Data Manager application that accompanies Visual Basic 3.0 to create an Access database, called CONTROLS.MDB, consisting of one table, called Custom Controls. The Custom Controls table includes three text fields, called Filename, Path, and Description, respectively.

Creating the empty database using the Data Manager took only a few moments. I left the job of adding data to it to VB MAKer.

My plan to use bound controls in lieu of code ran into a large roadblock early on: the lack of a bound, or data-aware, list-box control. A list box is, of course, the preferred control for presenting lists of data to the user, and I intended to use two of them on VB MAKer's main form: one to present the list of available controls and the other to present the list of controls in the current project. Unfortunately, the data control is oriented toward presenting one record at a time; there is no automatic way to have it populate a list box with data from all the records in a table. Because of that, I was forced to experiment a bit to create a semi-bound list box.

This is what I mean by semi-bound: When the user selects an item in either list box, VB MAKer moves the data control's record pointer to point to the corresponding record in the data table, updating the contents of the bound Description and Path fields to reflect the values for that record in the process. In addition, I added supplemental code to ensure that whenever a record is added to the database, a corresponding item is added to one of the list boxes, while whenever a record is deleted from the database table, its corresponding item is also removed the list box in which it appears.

VB MAKer's list boxes reflect the file names of custom controls, and since VB MAKer doesn't provide a facility to rename files, there was no need to link edits to database records to the list boxes. Aside from that, however, VB MAKer's list box acts like a true bound control. Unlike a true bound control, however, it took a good deal of code to make it do so.

It's worth noting that while the methods I devised for VB MAKer—using a list box to view the entire contents of one field of the table—should work well with small- to medium-sized tables, they would not be suitable for large tables. With large tables, you would have to expect some performance slowdowns with these methods, and would be in danger of exceeding the capacity limits of a list box.

■ Creating a Semi-Bound List Box

Visual Basic's data control greatly simplifies database access, but because it is primarily intended for browsing database tables one record at a time, some additional effort is required to use it effectively in an application that needs to be capable of viewing the entire contents of a database table at once.

VB MAKer's bound list box is my attempt to solve that deficiency. It allows the user to view the entire contents of one field of the database table—in VB MAKer's case the filename field—and to navigate through the database by means of selecting items from the list box. The list box sorts the file names into alphabetical order, thus presenting them in a more coherent manner than would the data control alone, which displays records one by one in the order in which they were created.

VB MAKer uses a routine called InitializeDatabase to generate this link between its Available Controls list box and the data control. This routine is called by the form-load procedure for VB MAKer's main form, and again later whenever VB MAKer needs to ensure that the contents of the data control and list box are in sync.

The routine begins by selecting the first record in the database table, and adding the contents of the filename field for that record to the Available Controls list box. Then Initialize Database enters a Do Loop in which it reads through the entire database table until it reaches the end-of-file marker, selecting each record one by one and adding the contents of its filename field to the Available Controls list box.

At the same time as it is doing this, VB MAKer populates two global string arrays. The first, called rsBookMark(), is used to store the bookmark property of each record in the table. A record's bookmark is a unique string of binary data that can be used to select that record. If, for instance, you have previously set A$ equal to the bookmark for a record in Data1's recordset, you can jump to that record by issuing this command:

`Data1.RecordSet.Bookmark=A$.`

The second string array, called cFullPath(), stores the fully qualified pathname (consisting of the path and file name) for each record in the database. Thus, this array duplicates the information from the Pathname and Filename fields of each database record. The primary reason for duplicating this information in an array is to speed searches of the database. For instance, when VB MAKer needs to determine if a control is already listed in the database, it can do so by looping quickly through the cFullpath() array, comparing the control in question's fully qualified path name to the value of each array element, rather than by using the data control to examine the values of the Pathname and Filename fields of each record in the database table.

Finally, the InitializeDatabase routine uses an integer variable called Counter% to assign a record number to each record in the table, and stores the value of Counter% for each record in the ItemData property of its associated list-box entry. The program needs to store this data to link the list box to the data control because since the list box's Sort property is set to True, the list box's ListIndex property does not provide a reliable indicator of where a selected item appears in the database.

What I would really like to have done in building VB MAKer was to store the bookmark for each database record in the ItemData property of its associated list-box item. However, the ItemData property can only be used to store integers. Instead, I elected to create the rsBookMark() array to hold the bookmarks and simply use the ItemData property of each list-box entry to point to the element of the rsBookMark() array with which the item is associated. This solution involves a little more overhead, but works well and quickly.

Whenever you select an item in the list box, VB MAKer sets Data1.Recordset.Bookmark equal to

```
rsBookMark((MAKerMain.List1(Index).ItemData(MAKerMain.List1(Index).ListIndex)))
```

This causes the data control to select the database record associated with the selected list-box item. Since the Path and Description fields on VB MAKer's main form are bound to the data control, their values are automatically updated to reflect those of the selected record.

Let's look at the complete InitializeDatabase routine to see how this works in practice: First, the routine begins by moving to the first record in the database. In the event that the database is empty, there won't be a first record, so the routine simply continues with the next statement:

```
Sub InitializeDatabase ()
On Error Resume Next
MAKerMain.Data1.Recordset.MoveFirst
On Error GoTo 0
```

Next, the routine dimensions a set of three local variables: ArraySize%, which is used to dynamically dimension the cFullPath() and rsBookMark() arrays; Counter%, which is used to keep track of record numbers; and P$, a temporary variable used to hold the current record's path. It then assigns a starting value of 24 to ArraySize%, and redimensions cFullPath() and rsBookMark to that size.

```
Dim ArraySize%, Counter%, P$
ArraySize% = 24
ReDim cFullPath(ArraySize%)
ReDim rsBookMark(ArraySize%)
```

The routine then begins to loop through the database, incrementing Counter% for each record that it reads, and redimensioning the cFullPath() and rsBookMark(), while preserving their contents, by adding another 12 elements to ArraySize% when Counter% equals ArraySize%.

```
Do While Not MAKerMain.Data1.Recordset.EOF
     Counter% = Counter% + 1
     If Counter% = ArraySize% Then
        ArraySize% = ArraySize + 12
        ReDim Preserve cFullPath(ArraySize%)
        ReDim Preserve rsBookMark(ArraySize%)
     End If
```

The idea behind seeding ArraySize% with a value of 24 and incrementing it in groups of 12 is to reduce the number of times that VB MAKer needs to execute the relatively time-consuming process of redimensioning the two string arrays. This means that unless the number of records in the database equals 24 or a multiple of 12 greater than 24, there will be empty elements in both arrays, but the initial speed gain would seem to justify the relatively minor memory cost of maintaining those empty elements.

Once VB MAKer has ensured that the two string arrays are large enough to hold the data for the current record, it examines the value of the record's FileName field. If it is not equal to Null, VB MAKer adds the file name to the list box. Then it sets the value of the Counter% element of rsBookMark() equal to the Bookmark for the current record, and the value of the list box's ItemData property for the newly added item equal to Counter%. Next, VB MAKer assigns the value of the Path field for the current record to P$, uses a function called FixPath$ to ensure that P$ ends in a backslash, combines the contents of P$ and the current record's file name, and then assigns those to the Counter% element of the cFullPath() array. Finally, it selects the next record in the database:

```
If Not IsNull(MAKerMain.Data1.Recordset("FileName")) Then
    MAKerMain.List1(0).AddItem MAKerMain.Data1.Recordset("FileName")
    rsBookMark(Counter%) = MAKerMain.Data1.Recordset.Bookmark
    MAKerMain.List1(0).ItemData(MAKerMain.List1(0).NewIndex) = Counter%
    P$ = MAKerMain.Data1.Recordset("Path")
    P$ = FixPath$(Trim(P$))
    cFullPath(Counter%) = P$ + MAKerMain.Data1.Recordset("FileName")
End If
MAKerMain.Data1.Recordset.MoveNext
```

When the last record in the database table has been read, InitializeDatabase exits the Do Loop and executes one final statement to highlight the first item in the Available Controls list box before returning to the routine that called it:

```
If MAKerMain.List1(0).ListCount Then MAKerMain.List1(0).ListIndex = 0
```

■ **SELECTING A LIST-BOX ITEM**

When the user selects an item in either the Available Controls or Current MAK File list boxes, VB MAKer calls a routine called ControlListClick, which is designed to select the corresponding record in Data1's recordset, and perform a few housekeeping duties. The routine starts by setting a global variable called ActiveList%, which stores the index number of the most-recently selected of the two list boxes. Then it sets the recordset's Bookmark property equal to the element of the rsBookMark array which corresponds to the listindex property of the selected list-box item. Finally, it sets the listindex of the other list box (whose index number it obtains by calling a function known as OtherC) to −1, to remove the highlight bar from that list box:

```
If MAKerMain.List1(Index).ListIndex > -1 Then
    ActiveList% = Index
    MAKerMain.Data1.Recordset.Bookmark = ⇔
     rsBookMark((MAKerMain.List1(Index).ItemData ⇔
     (MAKerMain.List1(Index).ListIndex)))
     ' deselect other list
    MAKerMain.List1(OtherC%(Index)).ListIndex = -1
End If
```

The OtherC%() function used above accepts one parameter—the index of the selected control in a two-member control index consisting of elements 0 and 1, and returns the index of the other control. That's a trivial function, of course, but one that was frequently necessary to VB MAKer's operation, given its use of control indexes matching that description for both the two list boxes on its main form and the two buttons. Creating a function to produce the required index number saved a lot of typing.

```
Function OtherC% (I%)
If I% = 0 Then
    OtherC% = 1
Else
    OtherC% = 0
End If
End Function
```

■ **MOVING ITEMS BETWEEN LIST BOXES**

When the user clicks one of the arrow buttons on VB MAKer's main form to move an item from one list box to another (or when VB MAKer itself moves an item from the Available Controls list to the Current MAK File list as it reads an existing .MAK file), VB MAKer obviously needs to move the text of the selected list item to the other list box. In addition, it has to move the ItemData associated with the source item to the newly created item in the destination list box. As noted above, the ItemData property

of the .VBX files that appear as items in VB MAKer's list boxes is used to store a
pointer to an element of the rsBookMark() array, which in turn points to the database
record associated with that item. There is no need for VB MAKer to modify the contents of the rsBookMark() array itself when an item moves, as long as it makes sure
that the item's ItemData property moves with it.

To manage this process, VB MAKer calls a routine named MoveControl whenever it
needs to move an item from the Available Controls list box to the Current MAK File list
box or vice versa. The MoveControls routine takes one parameter: the Index number of
the source list box. It begins by setting a global integer called FileDirty% to True, indicating that the current .MAK file has changed since it was loaded or created, and then
obtains the index of the destination control using the OtherC%() function:

```
Sub MoveControl (Index As Integer)
Dim Dest%, rSource%
FileDirty% = True
Dest% = OtherC%(Index)
```

Next, the routine assigns the listindex of the item to be moved to a variable called
rSource% and then, after checking to make sure that rSource% reflects a valid listindex, it adds the text of the selected item to the destination list box:

```
rSource% = MAKerMain.List1(Index).ListIndex
If rSource% = -1 Then Exit Sub
MAKerMain.List1(Dest%).AddItemMAKerMain.List1(Index)
```

Once the item has been added to the destination list box, MoveControl copies the
source item's ItemData property to that of the newly created item, and then removes
the source item from the source list box:

```
MAKerMain.List1(Dest%).ItemData(MAKerMain.List1(Dest%).⇔
   NewIndex) = MAKerMain.List1(Index).ItemData(rSource%)
MAKerMain.List1(Index).RemoveItem rSource%
```

The final step that MoveControl takes depends upon whether the control that was
just moved was the sole remaining control in the source list box. If not, MoveControl
calls a subroutine called SelectNextVBXInList to highlight the next item in the source
list box. Otherwise, it moves the highlight bar to the newly created item in the destination list box, and then calls ControlListClick to simulate a click event on that item,
which moves the recordset pointer to the newly selected item:

```
If MAKerMain.List1(Index).ListCount > 0 Then
   SelectNextVBXInList Index, rSource%
Else
```

```
    MAKerMain.List1(Dest%).ListIndex = MAKerMain.List1(Dest%).NewIndex
       ControlListClick Dest%
End If
End Sub
```

The SelectNextVBXInList routine takes care of answering the question: What do you do with the highlight bar when you remove an item from a list box? If the item being removed was the bottom item in the list box, the routine selects the item above it. Otherwise, it selects the item that appears immediately below the item being removed from the list box.

■ Adding Controls to the Database

VB MAKer offers the user two ways to locate .VBX files that are not already listed in its database. The first is its automatic search mode, which identifies any file with a .VBX extension on the DOS path or in the WINDOWS or SYSTEM directories. The second option is a browse mode that allows the user to identify files one by one in any directory.

In designing VB MAKer, I went on the assumption that most users would start with the automatic search mode, using that to locate most of their .VBX files, and then use the browser to locate any additional .VBX files that aren't located on the DOS path.

Both functions can be accessed by selecting the Add Controls to Database… item from the Controls menu on VB MAKer's main form. When the user does so, the Add Controls dialog box appears, offering the user a choice of search methods.

The three buttons on the Add Controls form make up a control array. The first button, Find All…, has an index number of 0, the second, Locate Individual…, has an index number of 1, and the Cancel button has an index number of 2. The Click procedure for the array simply examines the clicked button's Index property to determine which steps it should take:

```
Select Case Index
Case 0 To 1   'find all/individual
   AutoSearch% = (Index = 0)
   NewCFrm.Show 1
Case 2    'Cancel
   Unload Me
End Select
```

Selecting either search method causes VB MAKer to load another form called NewCFrm. First, however, the Click event sets the value of the global integer flag AutoSearch% to the result of the Boolean expression (Index=0). So if the user clicked the Find All… button, AutoSearch% will be True. Otherwise, it will be assigned a value of False.

Setting the AutoSearch% variable in this manner allowed me to use a single form to perform two quite different types of searches. When NewCFrm is loaded, its Form_Load procedure checks the value of AutoSearch% to determine how the form should be laid out.

NewCFrm contains standard Visual Basic directory and drive controls; a standard list box called VBXLister; a label control called Label1; two buttons: bAdd which is used to add selected .VBX files to the database, and bCancel, which is used to close the form; and a timer control, which is used to launch the automatic search routine.

If AutoSearch% is False, indicating that the user wishes to browse for files, the routine disables the form's timer control and sets the form's label control to read "These .VBX files are not currently listed in VB MAKer's database:". The form's default caption of "Locate Controls" is unchanged in this case.

Once the form is visible, the user can navigate through any disk's directory tree by making selections from the drive and directory controls. Whenever the user changes the search directory, VB MAKer executes the Dir1_Change event, which clears the contents of VBXLister, calls a subroutine called FixPath$ to ensure that the directory ends in a backslash, and then calls a routine called FindEm which adds the full path of any .VBXs not currently listed in VB MAKer's database to the VBXLister list box:

```
VBXLister.Clear
Dim CurrentDir$
CurrentDir$ = FixPath$(UCase$(Dir1))
Findem CurrentDir$
```

- **THE FINDEM SUBROUTINE**

FindEm accepts one parameter: the directory that it is to search, and it makes use of Visual Basic's Dir$ function to identify any .VBX files in that directory. Dir$ is designed to be used repeatedly. The first time that it is called you should pass it a full path and file name (wildcards are acceptable), to which it responds by returning the name of the first file matching that criteria. Subsequent calls which have no parameters to Dir$ return any additional files matching that criteria, one by one. When no more files match the criteria, Dir$ returns an empty string.

When Dir$ returns a file name, FindEm invokes a function called CntrlAlreadyListed%() to determine if that file is already present in VB MAKer's database. If

CntrlAlreadyListed%() returns a value of False, FindEm adds the file's fully qualified file name to the VBXLister list box:

```
Sub Findem (CurrentDir As String)
Dim x%, Found$
If AutoSearch% Then NewCFrm.Label1 = "Searching " + CurrentDir
CurrentDir$ = FixPath$(CurrentDir$)
Found$ = Dir$(CurrentDir + "*.VBX")
x% = DoEvents()
Do While Len(Found$) <> 0
    If Not CntrlAlreadyListed%(CurrentDir + Found$) Then
        NewCFrm.VBXLister.AddItem CurrentDir + Found$
    End If
    Found$ = Dir$
Loop
End Sub
```

The CntrlAlreadyListed%() function performs a vital duty, determining whether a control is already listed in VB MAKer's database. It does so by looping through the cFullPath() array, comparing the file name that is passed to it to each element in the array, and returning a value of True if the test string matches any element in the array:

```
Function CntrlAlreadyListed% (Test$)
CntrlAlreadyListed% = False
Dim x%, ac%
ac% = UBound(cFullPath)
For x% = 0 To ac%
    If cFullPath(x%) = Test$ Then
        CntrlAlreadyListed% = True
        Exit For
    End If
Next
End Function
```

This function prevents VB MAKer from listing the same .VBX file more than once in its database. It does not, however, prevent VB MAKer from listing multiple instances of the same control which are located in different directories. There are two reasons for this. First, you might want to have multiple versions of a custom control, stored in different directories but with the same file name. Second, allowing you to add multiple copies of a control from different directories to VB MAKer's database is a good way of flagging the fact that you have multiple copies of the control and may wish to delete one or more of them, using VB MAKer's Delete Control command.

Once VB MAKer has listed the .VBX files which appear in the directory you've chosen, you can add them to its database by highlighting them in the VBXLister list box and then clicking the Add to VBX Database button.

■ **THE AUTOMATIC DIRECTORY SEARCH ROUTINE**

VB MAKer's automatic directory search routine also uses CNewFrm. However, rather than having you locate the directory in which you wish to look for unlisted controls, it automatically searches the full DOS path, and your WINDOWS and SYSTEM directories for any .VBX files that do not appear in its database.

The Form_Load process for CNewFrm initiates this process when AutoSearch% is True. It begins by changing the form's caption, then sets the visible properties of the directory, drive, and bAdd controls to False, then rearranges the remaining controls on the form and enables the timer control:

```
Caption = "Find All VBXs"
Drive1.Visible = False
Dir1.Visible = False
bAdd.Visible = False
Label1.Left = 300
VBXLister.Left = 240
Width = VBXLister.Width + 640
bAdd.Left = (Width - bAdd.Width) / 2
bCancel.Left = bAdd.Left + bAdd.Width + 240
Timer1.Enabled = True
```

The timer control has an interval of ten, so it fires almost immediately after being enabled, initiating the automatic search routine. I wanted this routine to start immediately after the form appeared, but not before Visual Basic had a chance to paint the form. If I had placed the routine at the end of the Form_Load event, it would launch before the form had been painted. Placing it in the timer event allowed Visual Basic a chance to finish loading and painting the form prior to the automatic search routine being launched.

The timer event's code starts by calling a function called SearchPath%(), which performs the actual directory search. It then disables the timer, updates the form's label, and, if at least one unlisted control is found, sets the Visible property of the bAdd button control to True:

```
Dim X%
X% = SearchPath%()
Timer1.Enabled = False
Label1 = "These VBX files are not currently listed in VB MAKer's database:"
If VBXLister.ListCount > 0 Then bAdd.Visible = True
```

■ **SEARCHING THE DISK FOR .VBX FILES**

The SearchPath%() function automates the process of supplying directory names to the FindEm routine. It feeds directories to FindEm in this order: the active application's App.Dir, the SYSTEM directory, then the WINDOWS directory, and finally each

directory on the DOS path which is not equal to any of the three directories that have
already been searched.

The function starts by dimensioning several local variables, including a fixed-
length string called sBuffer, which it will use to interact with the Windows API functions that supply the names of the WINDOWS and SYSTEM directories.

```
Dim Path As String, CurrentDir As String, Found$
Dim Y%, WinDir$, SystemDir$, SemiColon
Dim sBuffer As String * 254
```

Next, the function disables the Cancel button on cNewFrm (preventing the user
from interupting the search process), and instructs FindEm to search the current
App.Dir directory:

```
NewCFrm.bCancel.Enabled = False
CurrentDir = App.Path
FindEm UCase$(CurrentDir)
```

The function then searches the SYSTEM and WINDOWS directories in succession,
obtaining their paths using the GetSystemDirectory and GetWindowsDirectory API
calls. In doing so, it makes use of a little utility function called FixAPIString$ which
trims leading and trailing spaces and trailing CHR$(0)'s from strings returned by API
functions:

```
Y% = GetSystemDirectory(sBuffer, 254)
SystemDir$ = FixAPIString$(sBuffer)
FindEm UCase$(SystemDir$)
Y% = GetWindowsDirectory(sBuffer, 254)
WinDir$ = FixAPIString$(sBuffer)
FindEm UCase$(WinDir$)
```

Next, the SearchPath%() function uses the Visual Basic Environ$ function to ob-
tain a semicolon-delimited list of directories on the DOS path. Then it loops through
the list, assigning the name of each directory it finds to the string CurrentDir, and, if
CurrentDir is not in the WINDOWS directory, the SYSTEM directory, or App.Dir,
SearchPath$() passes it to FindEm:

```
'Search path
Path = Environ$("PATH")
If Path <> "" Then
   If Right$(Path, 1) <> ";" Then Path = Path + ";"
   SemiColon = InStr(Path, ";")
   Do
      CurrentDir = Left$(Path, SemiColon - 1)
      If CurrentDir <> App.Path And CurrentDir <> SystemDir$ And ⇔
   CurrentDir <> WinDir$ Then
```

```
        FindEm UCase$(CurrentDir)
     End If
     Path = Right$(Path, Len(Path) - SemiColon)
     SemiColon = InStr(Path, ";")
  Loop While SemiColon <> 0
End If
```

Finally, SearchPath% concludes by examining the value of the VBXLister list box's ListCount property. If the list is empty (indicating that not even one unlisted .VBX was found in all those calls to FindEm), SearchPath% calls the Alert utility routine, which creates a message box informing the user that all .VBX files on the path already appear in the database. Otherwise, it uses Alert to tell the user how many unlisted files were found. The routine then concludes by enabling the NewCFrm's Cancel button:

```
On Error GoTo 0
Y% = NewCFrm.VBXLister.ListCount
Select Case Y%
Case 0
   Alert "All VBXs on path are already listed in the database."
   SearchPath% = False
Case Else
 Alert "Found " + Str$(NewCFrm.VBXLister.ListCount) + " unlisted VBX files."
   SearchPath% = True
End Select
NewCFrm.bCancel.Enabled = True
```

■ **Adding New Records to the .VBX Database**

So far, both of the methods for adding controls to the database have gotten us to the point of having VBXLister list the controls that aren't already present in the database, and of enabling the bAdd button. However, the controls aren't actually added to the database until the user selects them in the VBXLister list box and clicks the Add to VBX Database button, which invokes the bAdd_Click procedure.

bAdd_Click starts by checking that the user has selected at least one .VBX file item in VBXLister. If not, it tells the user that he or she must select a control to add, and then exits. Otherwise, it steps backwards through the list, examining the Selected property of each list-box item. If the item is selected, the procedure adds a new record to the database. It then breaks the text of the selected item from VBXLister into two strings: cFile$ to hold the file's name, and cPath$ to hold the file's path:

```
MAKerMain.Data1.Recordset.AddNew
cFile$ = VBXLister.List(LI%)
For X% = Len(cFile$) To 1 Step -1
   If Mid$(cFile$, X%, 1) = "\" Then
       cPath$ = Left$(cFile$, X%)
       cFile$ = Mid$(cFile$, X% + 1)
       Exit For
```

```
    End If
Next
```

Next, the routine assigns cFile$ to the FileName field of the new record, and cPath$ to the Path field. It leaves the Description field blank for the user to fill in later. Then it issues an UpdateRecord command to save the changes to the active record.

```
MAKerMain.Data1.Recordset("FileName") = cFile$
cPath$ = FixPath$(cPath$)
MAKerMain.Data1.Recordset("Path") = cPath$
MAKerMain.Data1.Recordset("Description") = ""
MAKerMain.Data1.UpdateRecord
```

The routine then removes the selected item from the VBXLister list box, and loops back to check the next item's Selected status.

Once all the selected records have been added to the database, the routine clears the Available Controls list, and then calls the InitializeDatabase routine to reload the database. This ensures that the cFullPath() and rsBookMark() arrays will include the newly added records.

```
MAKerMain.List1(0).Clear
InitializeDatabase
```

The above routine would seem to complete the task of adding controls to the database, but there is in fact one final step that it must complete. Because VB MAKer allows you to add new controls to a database at any time, the Current MAK File list box on MAKerMain might contain a list of .VBX files when you do so. Thus, the bAdd_Click routine has to loop through that list box, and for each item that it contains, find the corresponding .VBX file in the Available Controls box, copy its ItemData property to the selected item in the Current MAK File list box, and then remove the file from the Available Controls list box:

```
Dim cPat1$
For X% = 0 To MAKerMain.List1(1).ListCount - 1
   cPat1$ = cFullPath(MAKerMain.List1(1).ItemData(X%))
   For Y% = 0 To MAKerMain.List1(0).ListCount - 1
      If cFullPath(MAKerMain.List1(0).ItemData(Y%)) = cPat1$ Then
         MAKerMain.List1(0).RemoveItem Y%
         Exit For
      End If
   Next Y%
Next X%
```

The bAdd_Click routine concludes by moving the highlight bar to the next item, if any, in the VBXLister list box, and disabling the bAdd button if the VBXLister box is empty:

```
X% = VBXLister.ListCount
If LI% < X% Then
    VBXLister.ListIndex = LI%
Else
    VBXLister.ListIndex = LI% - 1
End If
If X% = 0 Then bAdd.Enabled = False
Screen.MousePointer = 0
```

Thus, by the time the routine concludes, all the selected .VBX files have been added to VB MAKer's database and to one or the other of the list boxes on MAKerMain.

■ **Deleting Database Items**

VB MAKer also provides facilities for deleting items from its database, and for deleting .VBX files from disk.

When you indicate on the Delete Control dialog box that you wish to remove a control from VB MAKer's database, it invokes the RemoveControlFromDatabase routine. Prior to getting to this routine, you must have first selected the control in one of the list boxes on MAKerMain, which triggers the List_Click event which in turn selects that control in Data1's RecordSet. So the RemoveControlFromDatabase routine begins by deleting the current record in Data1.Recordset, removes the selected item from the active list box on MAKerMain, and finally sets the element of the cFullPath() array that was associated with that record to an empty string. There is no need to delete the element—setting it to an empty string is sufficient to ensure that VB MAKer won't end up finding a control that no longer exists in its database when it searches the array. Finally, the routine moves the highlight bar to the next item in the active list box on MAKerMain:

```
MAKerMain.Data1.Recordset.Delete
A% = MAKerMain.List1(ActiveList%).ListIndex
MAKerMain.List1(ActiveList%).RemoveItem A%
cFullPath(cdel%) = ""
SelectNextVBXInList ActiveList%, A%
```

The process of deleting a control from a disk is similar. It begins by issuing the Kill command to delete the disk file, and then calls RemoveControlFromDatabase to remove the entry for that file from VB MAKer's database:

```
On Error Resume Next
Kill cFullPath(cdel%)
On Error GoTo 0
RemoveControlFromDatabase
```

Prior to carrying out either of the Delete commands, of course, VB MAKer posts a confirmation dialog box to ensure that the user really wants to do so.

■ Finding Controls by Description

The Find by Description and Find Next items on VB MAKer's Controls menu allow you to search for any control in the database by specifying a word or phrase that occurs in its description. The Find Next item, which is initially disabled, is enabled after a successful Find by Description search, and disabled after an unsuccessful search.

When you select the Find by Description item, VB MAKer creates an input box in which you are asked to enter the description text that you wish to locate. For instance, if you were searching for any control whose description included the word "bound," you would enter "bound". The cItem_Click procedure, which processes Controls menu selections, stores the text you specify in a static variable called Find-Des$, and then invokes the ItemFinder routine.

ItemFinder begins by hiding the Description and Path fields on MAKerMain. Then it selects each item after the current selection in the active list box on MAKerMain in turn. After selecting each item, it examines the contents of the Description field (MAKerMain.Text1) to see if they contain the specified text. If so, it enables the Find Next item, sets the visible property of the two fields to True, and returns. Otherwise, it disables the Find Next item, sets the visible property of the two fields to True, and informs the user that it couldn't find the specified text:

```
Sub ItemFinder (ByVal FindMe$)
Dim LI%, iFound%
ShowFields False
FindMe$ = UCase$(FindMe$)
LI% = MAKerMain.List1(ActiveList%).ListIndex + 1
Do While LI% < MAKerMain.List1(ActiveList%).ListCount
    MAKerMain.List1(ActiveList%).ListIndex = LI%
    If InStr(UCase$(MAKerMain.Text1), FindMe$) Then
        iFound% = True
        Exit Do
    End If
    LI% = LI% + 1
Loop
If iFound% Then
    MAKerMain.cItem(4).Enabled = True
```

```
Else
    MAKerMain.cItem(4).Enabled = False
    Alert "Couldn't find that text."
End If
ShowFields True
End Sub
```

Thus, if ItemFinder is successful, the routine ends with the first matching record selected in the active list box. Otherwise, the last item in the list box is selected.

The Find Next item, when enabled, simply calls ItemFinder passing it the current value of the FindDes$ static variable, thus bypassing the input box used for Find by Description.

■ Opening Existing Projects

One of VB MAKer's most useful features is its capability to open existing .MAK files so that you can add new custom controls to the projects they represent or remove custom controls that are no longer needed.

VB MAKer is capable of doing this because Visual Basic .MAK files are simply ASCII files. While the order of the elements within the file varies somewhat, the typical .MAK file includes a list of the .BAS and .FRM files in the project, a list of the .VBX files that the project makes use of, and a few lines of data providing the project's title, the layout of its design-time windows, and other data needed by the Visual Basic development environment.

Since VB MAKer is designed only to assist in adding or removing custom controls from .MAK files, it isn't concerned with any of the data in the .MAK file other than the list of .VBX files. Nevertheless, it needs to keep track of the other data as it loads an existing .MAK file, so that it can include that data later when it saves the .MAK file. To do so, it makes use of two global string variables, NonVBXData1$ and Non-VBXData2$. VB MAKer uses the former to store a list of all the files with an extension other than .VBX in the .MAK file, and the latter to store all other kinds of data from the file.

When you select the Open command from VB MAKer's File menu, VB MAKer uses Visual Basic's Common Dialogs control to obtain the name of the .MAK file that you want to open. Then it jumps to a subroutine called GetMAKFile which performs the work of actually loading the file.

GetMAKFile opens the specified .MAK file for input and reads through the file sequentially until it encounters the end of file marker. As it reads the file, the subroutine also examines the contents of each line to determine if it includes the characters ".VBX," and thus whether it represents a custom control.

If the line represents a custom control, VB MAKer checks to see whether the specified control already appears in its database, using a function called FindCntrlIndex%.

My original intent was to have FindCntrlIndex% determine if the specified control is listed in VB MAKer's database by comparing the contents of the current line in the .MAK file with each element of the cFullPath() array until it arrived at a match. Visual Basic, however, doesn't always include a path designation before a custom control's file name if the control was loaded from the SYSTEM directory, which Visual Basic considers the default location for custom controls. In many cases the .MAK file data will consist of just a file name. FindCntrlIndex% compensates for this by checking for the presence of a backslash in the .MAK file data. If none is found, FindCntrlIndex% strips the path from each member of the cFullPath array prior to conducting the test:

```
FindCntrlIndex = -1
ac% = UBound(cFullPath)
If InStr(test$, "\") > 0 Then fp% = True
For x% = 0 To ac%
    If fp% = True Then
        temp$ = cFullPath(x%)
    Else
        temp$ = StripPath$(cFullPath(x%))
    End If
    If temp$ = test$ Then
        FindCntrlIndex% = x%
        Exit For
    End If
Next
```

If FindCntrlIndex% finds a match with a member of the cFullPath() array, it returns the index number of the matching array element. Otherwise, it returns a value of –1.

Although this routine works reliably in the vast majority of cases, it is not foolproof. If you have more than one control with the same file name (albeit different paths) in the .VBX database, and the .MAK file doesn't specify a path, FindCntrlIndex% could return a pointer to the wrong version of the .VBX file if that version was added to the database prior to the correct version. VB MAKer attempts to minimize this problem by including a full path specification with every .MAK file that it saves. The only way to ensure that this problem never occurs, however, is for you to eliminate duplicate .MAK files from the .VBX database.

If FindCntrlIndex% returns a value of –1, indicating that the control is not listed in its database, VB MAKer closes the .MAK file, posts a message box indicating so, and aborts the file-loading procedure. I considered having it offer the user the chance

to add the file to the .VBX database and then continue with the file-opening procedure, but doing so was impractical because in all likelihood the file specification in
the .MAK file would not include a full path. Since VB MAKer's database relies upon
full paths to identify files, there would be no reliable way to add the custom control
to the database from its file name alone. Instead, VB MAKer simply requests that the
user locate the specified custom control on his or her disk and add it to the database
prior to attempting to open the .MAK file.

If, on the other hand, FindCntrlIndex% indicates that the file is already listed in
the database, VB MAKer needs to move the specified file from the Available Controls
list box to the Current .MAK File list box. It does so by examining the ItemData property of each item in the former list box until it obtains a match with the index number returned by FindCntrlIndex%. Once it has a match, it selects the matching list
box item and then calls the ArrowButtonHandler procedure to move it to the other
list box:

```
For x% = 0 To MAKerMain.List1(0).ListCount - 1
   If MAKerMain.List1(0).ItemData(x%) = indx% Then
      MAKerMain.List1(0).ListIndex = x%
      Exit For
   End If
Next
ArrowButtonHandler 0
```

- **HANDLING NONVBX DATA**

As noted above, the order of data within a .MAK file varies somewhat. Specifically,
.VBX, .BAS, and .FRM files may be specified in any order. However, one thing that Visual Basic does insist upon is that the remaining data concerning the layout of project
windows, the project title, the name of the project's .EXE file, and so forth, appear at
the end of the file. VB MAKer separates this data from the data about non-.VBX files
by storing the two kinds of information in separate strings.

Thus, if the current line from the MAK file does not represent a .VBX file, VB
MAKer checks to see if it represents any other sort of file. It does so by checking to
see whether the current line includes a period ("."), which a file name in a .MAK file
must include, and that it does not include a quotation mark (a CHR$(34)), such as
the two found in:

EXENAME="LOAN.EXE"

If the line includes a period and doesn't include a quotation mark, VB MAKer decides
that it represents a file and adds it to NonVBXData1$, followed by a carriage-return

and line-feed combination. Otherwise, VB MAKer adds the line, again followed by a carriage-return and line-feed, to NonVBXData2$:

```
If InStr(I$, ".") And (InStr(I$, Chr$(34)) = 0) Then
   NonVBXData1$ = NonVBXData1$ + I$ + CRLF$
Else
   NonVBXData2$ = NonVBXData2$ + I$ + CRLF$
End If
```

The GetMAKFile routine concludes by setting the FileDirty% flag to False, selecting the first item in the Available Controls list box if the list isn't empty after the .MAK file has been read, and then adding the name of the .MAK file to VB MAKer's caption:

```
FileDirty% = False
If MAKerMain.List1(0).ListCount Then MAKerMain.List1(0).ListIndex = 0
MAKerMain.Caption = "VB MAKer -- " + MAKfile$
```

At the conclusion of the GetMAKFile routine, the Current MAK File list box contains a list of all the .VBX files in the project, the Available Controls list box lists all the remaining custom controls in the .VBX database, NonVBXData1$ lists all the non-.VBX files in the project, and NonVBXData2$ lists all the other project data.

■ Creating a New .MAK File

Of course, VB MAKer is intended to allow you to create new .MAK files as well as edit existing ones. When you select the New option from VB MAKer's File menu, VB MAKer invokes its NewFile routine.

NewFile begins by storing the current value of the MAKerMain.fileMenu.Enabled property, and then disables the File menu. This allows VB MAKer to restore the menu's previous Enabled status at the end of the routine. This is necessary because NewFile also gets called at various other times when VB MAKer wants to start with a clean, freshly initialized database (the start of the File Open process is one of those instances), and the menu may already be disabled at that point:

```
Dim fe%
fe% = MAKerMain.fileMenu.Enabled
MAKerMain.fileMenu.Enabled = False
```

Next, NewFile sets both NonVBXData1$ and NonVBXData2$ to empty strings, instructs a subroutine called ShowFields to hide the Description and Path database fields in MAKerMain, sets FileDirty% to False, clears MAKerMain's two list boxes, and then calls the InitializeDatabase routine to reload the database. Hiding the two database fields speeds the InitializeDatabase process, since it means that Visual Basic doesn't need to update those fields as it reads through the entire database:

```
NonVBXData1$ = ""
NonVBXData2$ = ""
ShowFields False
FileDirty% = False
MAKerMain.List1(0).Clear
MAKerMain.List1(1).Clear
MAKerMain.Caption = "VB MAKer"
InitializeDatabase
```

Finally, NewFile calls ShowFields again to set the Visible property of the Description and Path fields to True, and then restores the Enabled property of the File menu to its previous value:

```
ShowFields True
MAKerMain.fileMenu.Enabled = fe%
```

When NewFile is finished, the Current MAK File list box is empty, and the Available Controls list box lists all the controls in VB MAKer's .VBX database.

■ Saving Project Files

VB MAKer saves new or modified .MAK files to disk using a routine called SaveFile. It saves the current .MAK file to a file name specified in the global variable MAKfile$, the value having been set either during the File Open process or through the use of the common Save As… dialog box. The routine first disables the File menu on MAKerMain, then opens MAKfile$ for output:

```
MAKerMain.fileMenu.Enabled = False
Dim x, ff%
ff% = FreeFile
Open MAKfile$ For Output As ff%
```

SaveFile next saves the contents of NonVBXData1$, which lists all non-.VBX files in the project, to MAKfile$. Because the GetMAKFile routine appends a carriage-return and line-feed combination to the end of every line that it adds to NonVBXData1$, SaveFile follows its Print # command with a semicolon to prevent the Print # command from appending a blank line to the file:

```
If NonVBXData1$ <> "" Then Print #ff%, NonVBXData1$;
```

VB MAKer then saves the full path of each VBX file specified in the Current MAK File list box to the .MAK file. It accomplishes this by selecting each item in the list box and then saving the element of the cFullPath() array corresponding to the selected item's ListIndex:

```
For x% = 0 To MAKerMain.List1(1).ListCount - 1
   MAKerMain.List1(1).ListIndex = X%
Print#ff%,cFullPath(MAKerMain.List1(1).ItemData(X%))
Next
```

Finally, the SaveFile routine stores the remaining project data stored in NonVBX-Data2$ to the .MAK file, closes the output file, sets the FileDirty% flag to False, and appends the .MAK file's name to MAKerMain's caption:

```
If NonVBXData2$ <> "" Then Print #ff%, NonVBXData2$
Close #ff%
FileDirty% = False
MAKerMain.Caption = "VB MAKer -- " + MAKfile$
```

By saving the full path of each .VBX file in the project, VB MAKer ensures that Visual Basic will be able to find files that don't appear on the DOS path, or that use alternate versions of custom control files. Of course, doing so also makes the resulting .MAK file somewhat dependent upon the directory structure of the user's hard disk, and if another user attempts to use that .MAK file, he or she may have a different path structure, and thus Visual Basic may not be able to find all the .VBX files specified in the .MAK file. Fortunately, however, Visual Basic is fairly smart about loading .MAK files; if it cannot locate a control on the path specified in the .MAK file, it automatically looks for it in the SYSTEM directory. Thus, as long as the specified control can be found in the user's SYSTEM directory, Visual Basic will find it even if the path specified in the .MAK file doesn't exist.

■ Launching Visual Basic

Once the current .MAK file has been saved, VB MAKer can instruct Visual Basic to open the .MAK file, even if Visual Basic is not currently running. If Visual Basic is already running, it must be in design mode for VB MAKer to do so—VB MAKer can't interrupt Visual Basic when it is running a project. Thus, VB MAKer itself must be running as a compiled .EXE, rather than within the development environment, to put this capability to use.

The code for launching the current .MAK file is attached to the RunItem_Click procedure in MAKerMain. It begins by examining the contents of the two list boxes on MAKerMain. If both are empty, it calls a routine named AlertNoDB to let you know that you must add controls to VB MAKer's database before this function can be used:

```
If List1(0).ListCount + List1(1).ListCount = 0 Then AlertNoDB: Exit Sub
```

The RunItem_Click routine next conducts a pair of checks to ensure that there is an open .MAK file and that its FileDirty% flag is set to False. If either test fails, the routine asks you to save the file before attempting to launch it:

```
If Not InStr(MAKerMain.Caption, ".MAK") > 0 Then
    Alert "You must save this MAK file before you can launch it."
    Exit Sub
End If
  If FileDirty% = True Then
    Alert "Please save changes in this MAK file first."
    Exit Sub
End If
```

Next, VB MAKer calls a subroutine named SearchWindowList, which identifies the first window with a caption that begins "Microsoft Visual Basic" to determine if the Visual Basic development environment is already running. If SearchWindowList returns a window handle, VB MAKer uses the Windows API GetWindowText function to obtain the window's full caption, and checks to see whether it includes the text "[run]," which would indicate that the Visual Basic development project is currently running a project. If that text is found, VB MAKer alerts the user that it cannot launch the current project while Visual Basic is in run mode:

```
Dim vbwin%
vbwin% = SearchWindowList("Microsoft Visual Basic")
If vbwin% > 0 Then
    Dim winText As String * 255
    Dim y%
    y% = GetWindowText(vbwin%, winText, 255)
    If InStr(winText, "[run]") Then
        Alert "Can't launch project while VB is in [run] mode."
        Exit Sub
    End If
End If
```

If Visual Basic is not in run mode, VB MAKer sends it the keystrokes necessary to open MAKfile$. If NonVBXData1$ is empty, indicating that there are currently no form files attached to the project, VB MAKer follows that command with another SendKeys command that instructs Visual Basic to create a new form:

```
vbwin% = SetFocusAPI(vbwin%)
SendKeys "%FO" + MAKfile$ + Chr$(13)
y% = DoEvents()
If NonVBXData1$ = "" Then SendKeys "%FF"
```

Meanwhile, if SearchWindowList% failed to locate the Visual Basic development environment, VB MAKer uses the ShellExecute function to launch Visual Basic and load the current .MAK file. ShellExecute returns a value of less than 32 if it is unable to launch an application. The most likely cause of this is that no association exists between .MAK files and VB.EXE, so if ShellExecute fails, VB MAKer asks the user to use File Manager to create the association. Otherwise, VB MAker checks the contents of NonVBXData1$ and, if it is empty, instructs the newly launched Visual Basic development environment to add a new form to the project:

```
vbwin% = ShellExecute(MAKerMain.hWnd, "Open", MAKfile$, "", "", SW_SHOW)
If vbwin% < 32 Then Alert "Can't launch Visual Basic. ⇔
    Please use File Manager to Associate MAK files with VB.EXE": Exit Sub
y% = DoEvents()
If NonVBXData1$ = "" Then SendKeys "%FF"
```

Finally, VB MAKer minimizes its own window, leaving it ready for later use.

■ **SEARCHING THE WINDOW LIST**
Visual Basic's AppActivate command suffers from one great liability: It depends upon your application supplying a complete caption for the window which is to be activated. Unfortunately, window captions change frequently, and there are many times when you want to find, for instance, Visual Basic's window no matter whether its caption reads "Microsoft Visual Basic [design]" or "Microsoft Visual Basic [run]."

VB MAKer's SearchWindowList%() function is designed to overcome AppActivate's limitation by identifying the first window whose caption begins with the same text as a test caption (Cap$) supplied by your application.

SearchWindowList%() works by using the Windows API function GetWindow%() to step through the list of top-level windows. Once it obtains a window's handle, it calls the GetWindowText() function to obtain that window's caption, which it stores in a variable called winCap. Then the function checks to see whether Left$(winCap, Len(Cap$)) = Cap$. If so, it has found a match, and returns the matching window's handle. If not, it proceeds to the next window. If SearchWindowList%() reaches the end of the window list without obtaining a match, it returns a value of zero:

```
Function SearchWindowList% (Cap$)
SearchWindowList% = 0
Dim w%, Y%, winCap As String * 255
w% = GetWindow%(MAKerMain.hWnd, GW_HWNDFIRST)
Do While w% <> 0
    Y% = GetWindowText(w%, winCap, 254)
    If Left$(winCap, Len(Cap$)) = Cap$ Then
        SearchWindowList% = w%
```

```
     Exit Do
   End If
   w% = GetWindow%(w%, GW_HWNDNEXT)
Loop
End Function
```

Because SearchWindowList%() returns the handle of the first matching window, you must supply it with enough of a caption to guarantee a unique match. Passing it a caption of "M" or a caption of "Microsoft" could result in any number of matches, but passing it a caption of "Microsoft Visual Basic" is pretty much guaranteed to return the window handle of the Visual Basic development environment.

■ Clearing VB MAKer's Database

The final command on VB MAKer's menu that requires discussion is the Clear Database item under the Controls menu, which deletes all records in VB MAKer's .VBX database. I wrote the ClearDatabase routine which the menu item invokes while testing VB MAKer, and I considered removing it from the final project, since it is unlikely to be of great value in the day-to-day use of VB MAKer. I left it in the project only because it offers a quick way to clear the contents of the database being accessed through the data control.

The routine begins by selecting the first record in the database. It then issues the BeginTrans command to initiate a series of changes to the database that will be treated as a single unit. Next, it loops through the database, issuing the Delete command for each record, followed by a MoveNext command, and then issues the CommitTrans command to accept all the changes made since the BeginTrans command. Finally, it updates Data1.RecordSet, and adds a new, empty record to the database:

```
MAKerMain.Data1.Recordset.MoveFirst
BeginTrans
Do While Not MAKerMain.Data1.Recordset.EOF
   MAKerMain.Data1.Recordset.Delete
   MAKerMain.Data1.Recordset.MoveNext
Loop
CommitTrans
MAKerMain.Data1.Recordset.Update
MAKerMain.Data1.Recordset.AddNew
```

■ CREATING 3D PANELS

VB MAKer's main form contains what appears to be a 3D Panel control from the THREED.VBX custom control. I wanted to use a panel to separate the Description and Path fields from the two list boxes on the form. However, in designing the form I couldn't bring myself to include the large THREED.VBX file just for the sake of one 3D panel, so I looked around for another method.

The solution I came up with is a subroutine called Draw3DFrame, which draws a 3D panel around the outer limits of a label control, using Visual Basic's Line method. To use this routine, you have to first draw the label control to the full size of the panel that you want to create and make sure that the label control's AutoSize property is set to False. You'll also want to set the BorderStyle property to 0 (none), so that the label's border line doesn't interfere with the lines drawn by the routine. The label's backstyle property should be set to 0 (transparent) and the form should have a light-gray background.

In positioning the label, you should be aware that the left edge of the frame will be 180 twips to the left of the label's left edge and that its width will be 180 twips less than that of the label.

Once that's done, you can create the 3D panel by calling Draw3DFrame and passing it the names of the form and label control on which the frame is to be drawn.

The routine simply draws white and dark-gray lines around the left, bottom, and right edges of the label, and to the left and right of the label's text on the top edge, as follows:

```
Sub Draw3dFrame (f As Form, C As Label)
Const White = &HFFFFFF
Const DarkGray = &H808080
Dim X1%, X2%, Y1%, Y2%, FrameHeight%, FrameWidth%, FrameLeft%, FrameTop%
f.DrawWidth = 1
FrameLeft% = C.Left
FrameTop% = C.Top
FrameHeight% = C.Height
FrameWidth% = C.Width
'       Draw top line to left of label text
X1% = FrameLeft% - 60
X2% = FrameLeft% - 180
Y1% = FrameTop% + (f.TextHeight(C.Caption) / 2) - 60
f.ForeColor = DarkGray
f.Line (X1%, Y1%)-(X2, Y1%)
Y1% = Y1% + 20
f.ForeColor = White
f.Line (X1%, Y1%)-(X2, Y1%)
'       Draw left side
Y2% = Y1% + FrameHeight%
f.ForeColor = DarkGray
f.Line (X2%, Y1%)-(X2%, Y2%)
X2% = X2% + 20
f.ForeColor = White
f.Line (X2%, Y1%)-(X2%, Y2%)
' Draw bottom
X1% = X2%
X2% = FrameLeft% + FrameWidth%
f.ForeColor = DarkGray
f.Line (X1%, Y2)-(X2%, Y2%)
Y2% = Y2% + 15
```

```
f.ForeColor = White
f.Line (X1%, Y2)-(X2%, Y2%)
'    Draw right
Y1% = FrameTop% + (f.TextHeight(C.Caption) / 2) - 60
f.Line -(X2%, Y1%)
f.ForeColor = DarkGray
X1% = X2% - 20
f.Line (X1%, Y2% - 20)-(X1%, Y1% + 20)
'   Draw top line to right edge of label text
X2% = FrameLeft% + f.TextWidth(C.Caption) + 60
f.Line (X1%, Y1% - 15)-(X2%, Y1% - 15)
f.ForeColor = White
f.Line (X1%, Y1%)-(X2%, Y1%)
End Sub
```

Similar techniques can be used to draw nearly any kind of three-dimensional effect upon a form. In addition to eliminating the use of THREED.VBX, routines like this cut down on your application's system resource use, since both the label control and the line method use almost no system resources. Speed might be a concern, but in my testing this routine proved to be so fast as to be unnoticeable, so I was able to leave MAKerMain's AutoRedraw property set to False and, instead, simply include the following statement in MAKerMain's Form_Paint routine, thus ensuring that the 3D Panel would be redrawn whenever the form was repainted.

```
Draw3dFrame Me, SelRecord
```

■ **STANDARD MESSAGE BOXES**
When I think back on it, I've probably had to look up the proper parameters for the MsgBox functions at least twice in every application I've written in Visual Basic. Finally, though, I got smart in the course of writing VB MAKer's code, and realized that I almost always end up looking up the same parameters. Thus, I've started to build a library of standard message boxes, of which VB MAKer uses two. The first, embedded in a function called Confirm%, displays a string that you pass to it in a message box with Yes and No buttons and an exclamation-point icon, and returns True if the user selects the Yes button or False if the user selects the No button. The function uses the contents of App.Title to title the message box:

```
Function Confirm% (Ask$)
If MsgBox(Ask$, 52, App.Title) = 6 Then Confirm% = True
End Function
```

This allows the use of statements such as:

```
If Confirm%("Abandon changes?") Then
```

To me, that's a lot simpler than having to look up the proper parameters for creating a Yes/No message box, and then having to look up again how one is supposed to interpret the value returned by the MsgBox function.

The other standard message box used by VB MAKer is embedded in a subroutine called Alert. It simply creates a message box with an exclamation-point icon and a single OK button, displaying the message you pass to it:

```
Sub Alert (Mess$)
MsgBox Mess$, 48, App.Title
End Sub
```

There are other ways to simplify message-box use, of course. You can include the standard constants for message boxes in module-definition statements and then specify your message box like this:

```
Msgbox Mess$,MB_OK or MB_ICONEXCLAMATION,App.Title
```

But from my perspective, those methods aren't as simple or as straightforward as designing standard message boxes and embedding them in functions or subroutines with easy-to-remember names.

LISTING

ADDCONTR.FRM

```
'  *  *  *  *  *  *  *  *  *  *  *  *  *  *  *  *  *  *  *  *  *  *  *  *  *
'  ADDCONTR.FRM
'  Copyright (c) 1993 by Paul Bonner
'  PC Magazine Visual Basic Utilities
'  *  *  *  *  *  *  *  *  *  *  *  *  *  *  *  *  *  *  *  *  *  *  *  *  *
VERSION 2.00
Begin Form AddControlFrm
    BackColor        =   &H00C0C0C0&
    BorderStyle      =   3   'Fixed Double
    Caption          =   "Add Controls"
    ClientHeight     =   2010
    ClientLeft       =   4680
    ClientTop        =   3885
    ClientWidth      =   4050
    ControlBox       =   0   'False
    Height           =   2415
    Left             =   4620
    LinkTopic        =   "Form3"
    MaxButton        =   0   'False
    MinButton        =   0   'False
    ScaleHeight      =   2010
    ScaleWidth       =   4050
    Top              =   3540
    Width            =   4170
    Begin CommandButton Command5
        Cancel           =   -1   'True
        Caption          =   "Cancel"
        Height           =   375
        Index            =   2
        Left             =   720
        TabIndex         =   2
        Top              =   1440
        Width            =   2535
    End
    Begin CommandButton Command5
        Caption          =   "&Find All VBXs on DOS Path"
        Height           =   375
        Index            =   0
        Left             =   720
        TabIndex         =   0
        Top              =   240
        Width            =   2535
    End
    Begin CommandButton Command5
        Caption          =   "&Locate Individual VBX Files"
        Height           =   375
        Index            =   1
        Left             =   720
        TabIndex         =   1
        Top              =   840
        Width            =   2535
    End
End
Option Explicit
```

```
DefInt A-Z

Sub Command5_Click (Index As Integer)
Select Case Index
'    * * * * * * * * * * * * * * * * * * * * * * * * * * * *
'    * set AutoSearch% global var. based on value of
'    * command button index
'    * * * * * * * * * * * * * * * * * * * * * * * * * * * *
Case 0 To 1 'find all / locate individual
    AutoSearch% = (Index = 0)
    NewCFrm.Show 1
Case 2    'cancel
    Unload Me
End Select
End Sub

Sub Form_Load ()
CenterForm Me
End Sub
```

LISTING

DELCONTR.FRM

```
'    * * * * * * * * * * * * * * * * * * * * * * * * * * * *
'    DELCONTR.FRM
'    Copyright (c) 1993 by Paul Bonner
'    PC Magazine Visual Basic Utilities
'    * * * * * * * * * * * * * * * * * * * * * * * * * * * *
VERSION 2.00
Begin Form DelControl
    BackColor       =    &H00C0C0C0&
    BorderStyle     =    3    'Fixed Double
    Caption         =    "Delete Control"
    ClientHeight    =    2595
    ClientLeft      =    3255
    ClientTop       =    3780
    ClientWidth     =    4860
    ControlBox      =    0    'False
    Height          =    3000
    Left            =    3195
    LinkTopic       =    "Form3"
    MaxButton       =    0    'False
    MinButton       =    0    'False
    ScaleHeight     =    2595
    ScaleWidth      =    4860
    Top             =    3435
    Width           =    4980
    Begin CommandButton Command1
        Cancel      =    -1    'True
        Caption     =    "Cancel"
        Height      =    375
        Index       =    2
        Left        =    1080
        TabIndex    =    2
```

```
            Top             =    2040
            Width           =    2655
        End
        Begin CommandButton Command1
            Caption         =    "&Delete from disk"
            Height          =    375
            Index           =    1
            Left            =    1080
            TabIndex        =    1
            Top             =    1440
            Width           =    2655
        End
        Begin CommandButton Command1
            Caption         =    "&Remove from database"
            Height          =    375
            Index           =    0
            Left            =    1080
            TabIndex        =    0
            Top             =    840
            Width           =    2655
        End
        Begin Label Label1
            AutoSize        =    -1    'True
            BackStyle       =    0     'Transparent
            Caption         =    "Label1"
            Height          =    195
            Left            =    240
            TabIndex        =    3
            Top             =    240
            Width           =    585
        End
    End
End
Option Explicit
DefInt A-Z
Dim cdel%    'listindex of record being deleted

Sub Command1_Click (Index As Integer)
Select Case Index
Case 0
'   * * * * * * * * * * * * * * * * * * * * * * * * * *
'   * delete control from database
'   * * * * * * * * * * * * * * * * * * * * * * * * * *
    If Confirm%("Remove this control from VB MAKer's database?") Then
        RemoveControlFromDatabase
    End If
Case 1
    '   * * * * * * * * * * * * * * * * * * * * * * * * * *
    '   * remove control from disk
    '   * * * * * * * * * * * * * * * * * * * * * * * * * *
    If Confirm%("Permanently delete this control from your disk?") Then
        On Error Resume Next
        Kill cFullPath(cdel%)
        On Error GoTo 0
        RemoveControlFromDatabase
    End If
Case 2    'Cancel
End Select
Unload Me
End Sub

Sub Form_Load ()
CenterForm Me
'   * * * * * * * * * * * * * * * * * * * * * * * * * *
'   * identify control to be deleted
```

```
'  * * * * * * * * * * * * * * * * * * * * * * * * * * * * * *
cdel%=MAKerMain.List1(ActiveList%).ItemData(MAKerMain.List1(ActiveList%)⇔
    ListIndex)
Label1 = cFullPath(cdel%)
End Sub

Sub RemoveControlFromDatabase ()
Dim A%
'  * * * * * * * * * * * * * * * * * * * * * * * * * * * * * *
'   * delete current record in database
'  * * * * * * * * * * * * * * * * * * * * * * * * * * * * * *
MAKerMain.Data1.Recordset.Delete
'  * * * * * * * * * * * * * * * * * * * * * * * * * * * * * *
'   * remove record from list box
'  * * * * * * * * * * * * * * * * * * * * * * * * * * * * * *
A% = MAKerMain.List1(ActiveList%).ListIndex
MAKerMain.List1(ActiveList%).RemoveItem A%
'  * * * * * * * * * * * * * * * * * * * * * * * * * * * * * *
'   * clear cFullPath entry for this control
'  * * * * * * * * * * * * * * * * * * * * * * * * * * * * * *
cFullPath(cdel%) = ""
SelectNextVBXInList ActiveList%, A%
End Sub
```

LISTING

MAKER.FRM

```
'  * * * * * * * * * * * * * * * * * * * * * * * * * * * * * *
'   MAKER.FRM
'   Copyright (c) 1993 by Paul Bonner
'   PC Magazine Visual Basic Utilities
'  * * * * * * * * * * * * * * * * * * * * * * * * * * * * * *
VERSION 2.00
Begin Form MAKerMain
    BackColor       =       &H00C0C0C0&
    BorderStyle     =       1  'Fixed Single
    Caption         =       "VB MAKer"
    ClientHeight    =       4485
    ClientLeft      =       1320
    ClientTop       =       2175
    ClientWidth     =       6090
    Height          =       5175
    Icon            =       MAKER.FRX:0000
    Left            =       1260
    LinkTopic       =       "Form2"
    MaxButton       =       0    'False
    ScaleHeight     =       4485
    ScaleWidth      =       6090
    Top             =       1545
    Width           =       6210
    Begin TextBox Text1
        DataSource      =       "Data1"
        Height          =       285
        Left            =       1800
```

```
      MaxLength        =    60
      TabIndex         =    10
      Text             =    "Text1"
      Top              =    3600
      Width            =    3615
   End
   Begin CommonDialog CMDialog1
      Left             =    240
      Top              =    3840
   End
   Begin Data Data1
      Caption          =    "Data1"
      Connect          =    ""
      DatabaseName     =    ""
      Exclusive        =    0     'False
      Height           =    375
      Left             =    1080
      Options          =    0
      ReadOnly         =    0     'False
      RecordSource     =    ""
      Top              =    3960
      Visible          =    0     'False
      Width            =    3135
   End
   Begin CommandButton Command1
      Caption          =    "¬"
      FontBold         =    -1    'True
      FontItalic       =    0     'False
      FontName         =    "Symbol"
      FontSize         =    9.75
      FontStrikethru   =    0     'False
      FontUnderline    =    0     'False
      Height           =    495
      Index            =    1
      Left             =    2640
      TabIndex         =    5
      Top              =    1320
      Width            =    735
   End
   Begin CommandButton Command1
      Caption          =    "®"
      FontBold         =    -1    'True
      FontItalic       =    0     'False
      FontName         =    "Symbol"
      FontSize         =    9.75
      FontStrikethru   =    0     'False
      FontUnderline    =    0     'False
      Height           =    495
      Index            =    0
      Left             =    2640
      TabIndex         =    4
      Top              =    720
      Width            =    735
   End
   Begin ListBox List1
      Height           =    2175
      Index            =    1
      Left             =    3720
      TabIndex         =    3
      Top              =    360
      Width            =    2175
   End
   Begin ListBox List1
      Height           =    2175
```

```
      Index              =    0
      Left               =    240
      Sorted             =    -1   'True
      TabIndex           =    1
      Top                =    360
      Width              =    2175
   End
   Begin Label Label3
      BackColor          =    &H00FFFFFF&
      BackStyle          =    0    'Transparent
      DataSource         =    "Data1"
      Height             =    285
      Left               =    1860
      TabIndex           =    9
      Top                =    3240
      Width              =    3615
   End
   Begin Label Label2
      AutoSize           =    -1   'True
      BackStyle          =    0    'Transparent
      Caption            =    "&Description:"
      Height             =    195
      Index              =    1
      Left               =    600
      TabIndex           =    7
      Top                =    3600
      Width              =    1035
   End
   Begin Label Label2
      AutoSize           =    -1   'True
      BackStyle          =    0    'Transparent
      Caption            =    "Path:"
      Height             =    195
      Index              =    0
      Left               =    600
      TabIndex           =    6
      Top                =    3240
      Width              =    465
   End
   Begin Label SelRecord
      BackColor          =    &H00C0C0C0&
      BackStyle          =    0    'Transparent
      Caption            =    "Selected:"
      Height             =    1215
      Left               =    480
      TabIndex           =    8
      Top                =    2880
      Width              =    5415
   End
   Begin Label Label1
      AutoSize           =    -1   'True
      BackColor          =    &H00C0C0C0&
      Caption            =    "Current &MAK file:"
      Height             =    195
      Index              =    1
      Left               =    3720
      TabIndex           =    2
      Top                =    120
      Width              =    1455
   End
   Begin Label Label1
      AutoSize           =    -1   'True
      BackColor          =    &H00C0C0C0&
      Caption            =    "&Available controls:"
```

```
      Height               =    195
      Index                =    0
      Left                 =    240
      TabIndex             =    0
      Top                  =    120
      Width                =    1590
   End
   Begin Menu fileMenu
      Caption              =    "&File"
      Begin Menu fItem
         Caption           =    "&New"
         Index             =    0
      End
      Begin Menu fItem
         Caption           =    "&Open"
         Index             =    1
      End
      Begin Menu fItem
         Caption           =    "&Save"
         Index             =    2
      End
      Begin Menu fItem
         Caption           =    "Save &As..."
         Index             =    3
      End
      Begin Menu fItem
         Caption           =    "E&xit"
         Index             =    4
      End
      Begin Menu fItem
         Caption           =    "-"
         Index             =    5
      End
      Begin Menu fItem
         Caption           =    "About VB MAKer..."
         Index             =    6
      End
   End
   Begin Menu cMenu
      Caption              =    "&Controls"
      Begin Menu cItem
         Caption           =    "&Add Controls to Database..."
         Index             =    0
         Shortcut          =    ^A
      End
      Begin Menu cItem
         Caption           =    "&Delete Selected Control..."
         Index             =    1
         Shortcut          =    ^D
      End
      Begin Menu cItem
         Caption           =    "-"
         Index             =    2
      End
      Begin Menu cItem
         Caption           =    "&Find by Description..."
         Index             =    3
         Shortcut          =    ^F
      End
      Begin Menu cItem
         Caption           =    "Find &Next"
         Enabled           =    0    'False
         Index             =    4
         Shortcut          =    {F3}
```

```
        End
        Begin Menu cItem
            Caption           =    "-"
            Index             =    5
        End
        Begin Menu cItem
            Caption           =    "C&lear Database"
            Index             =    6
        End
    End
    Begin Menu RunMenu
        Caption           =    "&Run"
        Begin Menu RunItem
            Caption           =    "&Launch Current MAK"
        End
    End
End
Option Explicit
DefInt A-Z

Sub cItem_Click (Index As Integer)
'   * * * * * * * * * * * * * * * * * * * * * * * * *
'   * this routine processes Controls menu selections
'   * * * * * * * * * * * * * * * * * * * * * * * * *

'   * * * * * * * * * * * * * * * * * * * * * * * * * *
'   * post error message if VBX database is empty
'   * * * * * * * * * * * * * * * * * * * * * * * * * *
If List1(0).ListCount + List1(1).ListCount = 0 Then
    If Index <> 0 Then AlertNoDB: Exit Sub
End If
Select Case Index
Case 0    'add controls
    AddControlFrm.Show 1
Case 1    'delete selected control
    If List1(ActiveList%).ListIndex < 0 Then Exit Sub
    DelControl.Show 1
Case 2    'sep
Case 3    'find
'   * * * * * * * * * * * * * * * * * * * * * * * * *
'   * get the text to find
'   * disable FindNext if user cancels input box
'   * otherwise search for text in description field
'   * * * * * * * * * * * * * * * * * * * * * * * * *
    Static FindDes$
  FindDes$ = InputBox("Description text to find:", "VB MAKer", FindDes$)
    If FindDes$ = "" Then
        cItem(4).Enabled = False
    Else
        ItemFinder FindDes$
    End If
Case 4    'find next
    ItemFinder FindDes$
Case 6    'clear database
'   * * * * * * * * * * * * * * * * * * * * * * * * *
'   * confirm action twice just to be sure
'   *
'   * if confirmed both times, clear both list boxes
'   * call the cleardatabase routine
'   * and clear the rsbookmark and rsfullpath arrays
'   * * * * * * * * * * * * * * * * * * * * * * * * *
    Dim X%
    If FileDirty% = True Then
     If Not Confirm%("Abandon changes to current MAK file?") Then Exit Sub
```

```
      End If
   If Not Confirm%("This action will delete all entries in the VBX database!" ⇔
      + CRLF$ + "Are you sure that you wish to do this?") Then Exit Sub
      If Not Confirm%("Clear VBX database now?") Then Exit Sub
      List1(0).Clear
      List1(1).Clear
      ClearDatabase
      ReDim rsBookMark(0)
      ReDim cFullPath(0)
End Select
End Sub

Sub Command1_Click (Index As Integer)
'  * * * * * * * * * * * * * * * * * * * * * * * * * * * *
'  * call button handler
'  * * * * * * * * * * * * * * * * * * * * * * * * * * * *
ArrowButtonHandler Index
End Sub

Sub fItem_Click (Index As Integer)
'  * * * * * * * * * * * * * * * * * * * * * * * * * * * *
'  * process file menu selections
'  * exit if vbx database is empty
'  * * * * * * * * * * * * * * * * * * * * * * * * * * * *
If List1(0).ListCount + List1(1).ListCount = 0 Then
   If Index < 4 Then AlertNoDB: Exit Sub
End If
Dim Ask%
Select Case Index
Case 0   'New
'  * * * * * * * * * * * * * * * * * * * * * * * * * * * *
'  * check file status
'  * if ok, initialize new file
'  * * * * * * * * * * * * * * * * * * * * * * * * * * * *
   If FileDirty% = True Then
      Ask% = Confirm%("Abandon changes to current MAK file?")
      If Ask% = False Then Exit Sub
   End If
   NewFile
Case 1   'Open
'  * * * * * * * * * * * * * * * * * * * * * * * * * * * *
'  * check file status
'  * if ok, disable file menu
'  * * * * * * * * * * * * * * * * * * * * * * * * * * * *
   If FileDirty% = True Then
      Ask% = Confirm%("Abandon changes to current MAK file?")
      If Ask% = False Then Exit Sub
   End If
   fileMenu.Enabled = False
'  * * * * * * * * * * * * * * * * * * * * * * * * * * * *
'  * set up common dialog
'  * * * * * * * * * * * * * * * * * * * * * * * * * * * *
   CMDialog1.Flags = OFN_HIDEREADONLY Or OFN_FILEMUSTEXIST
   CMDialog1.DefaultExt = "MAK"
   CMDialog1.CancelError = True
   On Error Resume Next
ExtenErrorLoop:
   CMDialog1.Filter = "Project files|*.MAK"
'  * * * * * * * * * * * * * * * * * * * * * * * * * * * *
'  * call common dialog box
'  * exit if user cancels
'  * * * * * * * * * * * * * * * * * * * * * * * * * * * *
   CMDialog1.Action = 1
   If Err = CancelButton Then fileMenu.Enabled = True: Exit Sub
```

```
'    * * * * * * * * * * * * * * * * * * * * * * * *
'    * don't accept extension other than MAK
'    * * * * * * * * * * * * * * * * * * * * * * * *
     If CMDialog1.Flags And OFN_EXTENTIONDIFFERENT Then
         Alert "File must have an MAK extension!"
         GoTo ExtenErrorLoop
     End If
     On Error GoTo 0
     MAKfile$ = CMDialog1.Filename
     If MAKfile$ = "" Then Exit Sub
'    * * * * * * * * * * * * * * * * * * * * * * * *
'    * reinit database, then
'    * load file
'    * * * * * * * * * * * * * * * * * * * * * * * *
     NewFile
     GetMAKFile
Case 2    'Save
'    * * * * * * * * * * * * * * * * * * * * * * * *
'    * invoke saveas routine if no current file name
'    * otherwise save to current name
'    * * * * * * * * * * * * * * * * * * * * * * * *
     If MAKfile$ = "" Then
         SaveAs
     Else
         SaveFile
     End If
Case 3    'Save As
     SaveAs
Case 4    'Exit
'    * * * * * * * * * * * * * * * * * * * * * * * *
'    * check file status
'    * unload MAKerMain if ok
'    * * * * * * * * * * * * * * * * * * * * * * * *
     If FileDirty% = True Then
         Ask% = Confirm%("Abandon changes to current MAK file?")
         If Ask% = False Then Exit Sub
     End If
     Unload Me
Case 5    'sep
Case 6    'About
'    * * * * * * * * * * * * * * * * * * * * * * * *
'    * copyright notice
'    * * * * * * * * * * * * * * * * * * * * * * * *
     MsgBox "VB MAKer" + CRLF$ + "Copyright 1993 by Paul Bonner" + CRLF$ + ⇔
     "PC Magazine Visual Basic Utilities" + CRLF$ + "All rights reserved.", ⇔
         64, "VB MAKer"
End Select
fileMenu.Enabled = True
End Sub

Sub Form_Load ()
Dim P$
'    * * * * * * * * * * * * * * * * * * * * * * * *
'    * specify database and table for Data control
'    * * * * * * * * * * * * * * * * * * * * * * * *
P$ = App.Path
P$ = FixPath(P$)
Data1.DatabaseName = P$ + "CONTROLS.MDB"
Data1.RecordSource = "Custom Controls"
Screen.MousePointer = 11
CenterForm Me
CRLF$ = Chr$(13) + Chr$(10)
'    * * * * * * * * * * * * * * * * * * * * * * * *
'    * set up data control and bound controls
```

```
'   *   *   *   *   *   *   *   *   *   *   *   *   *   *   *   *   *   *   *   *
Data1.Connect = ""
Text1.DataField = "Description"
Label3.DataField = "Path"
'   *   *   *   *   *   *   *   *   *   *   *   *   *   *   *   *   *   *   *   *
'   * create an empty record
'   *   *   *   *   *   *   *   *   *   *   *   *   *   *   *   *   *   *   *   *
Data1.Refresh
Data1.UpdateRecord
Data1.Recordset.AddNew
Show
Refresh
ShowFields False
'   *   *   *   *   *   *   *   *   *   *   *   *   *   *   *   *   *   *   *   *
'   * load database records
'   *   *   *   *   *   *   *   *   *   *   *   *   *   *   *   *   *   *   *   *
InitializeDatabase
'   *   *   *   *   *   *   *   *   *   *   *   *   *   *   *   *   *   *   *   *
'   * select first record
'   *   *   *   *   *   *   *   *   *   *   *   *   *   *   *   *   *   *   *   *
If List1(0).ListCount > 0 Then List1(0).ListIndex = 0
ShowFields True
Screen.MousePointer = 0
End Sub

Sub Form_Paint ()
'   *   *   *   *   *   *   *   *   *   *   *   *   *   *   *   *   *   *   *   *
'   * draw 3D panel
'   *   *   *   *   *   *   *   *   *   *   *   *   *   *   *   *   *   *   *   *
Draw3dFrame Me, SelRecord
End Sub

Sub Form_Unload (Cancel As Integer)
End
End Sub

Sub List1_Click (Index As Integer)
'   *   *   *   *   *   *   *   *   *   *   *   *   *   *   *   *   *   *   *   *
'   * call click handler
'   *   *   *   *   *   *   *   *   *   *   *   *   *   *   *   *   *   *   *   *
ControlListClick Index
End Sub

Sub List1_DblClick (Index As Integer)
'   *   *   *   *   *   *   *   *   *   *   *   *   *   *   *   *   *   *   *   *
'   * move selected list item to other list
'   *   *   *   *   *   *   *   *   *   *   *   *   *   *   *   *   *   *   *   *
Command1_Click Index
End Sub

Sub RunItem_Click ()
'   *   *   *   *   *   *   *   *   *   *   *   *   *   *   *   *   *   *   *   *
'   * process Launch MAK command
'   *   *   *   *   *   *   *   *   *   *   *   *   *   *   *   *   *   *   *   *
'
'   *   *   *   *   *   *   *   *   *   *   *   *   *   *   *   *   *   *   *   *
'   * abort if vbx database is empty
'   *   *   *   *   *   *   *   *   *   *   *   *   *   *   *   *   *   *   *   *
If List1(0).ListCount + List1(1).ListCount = 0 Then AlertNoDB: Exit Sub
'   *   *   *   *   *   *   *   *   *   *   *   *   *   *   *   *   *   *   *   *
'   * abort if file needs to be saved
'   *   *   *   *   *   *   *   *   *   *   *   *   *   *   *   *   *   *   *   *
If Not InStr(MAKerMain.Caption, ".MAK") > 0 Then
    Alert "You must save this MAK file before you can launch it."
```

```
        Exit Sub
    End If
    If FileDirty% = True Then
        Alert "Please save changes in this MAK file first."
        Exit Sub
    End If
    ' * * * * * * * * * * * * * * * * * * * * * * * * * *
    ' * look for vb dev environment window
    ' * * * * * * * * * * * * * * * * * * * * * * * * * *
    Dim vbwin%
    vbwin% = SearchWindowList("Microsoft Visual Basic")
    If vbwin% > 0 Then
        Dim winText As String * 255
        Dim y%
        y% = GetWindowText(vbwin%, winText, 255)
    ' * * * * * * * * * * * * * * * * * * * * * * * * * *
    ' * abort if dev environment in run mode
    ' * * * * * * * * * * * * * * * * * * * * * * * * * *
        If InStr(winText, "[run]") Then
            Alert "Can't launch project while VB is in [run] mode."
            Exit Sub
        End If
    ' * * * * * * * * * * * * * * * * * * * * * * * * * *
    ' * instruct dev enviroment to open MAKfile$
    ' * * * * * * * * * * * * * * * * * * * * * * * * * *
        vbwin% = SetFocusAPI(vbwin%)
        SendKeys "%FO" + MAKfile$ + Chr$(13)
        y% = DoEvents()
    ' * * * * * * * * * * * * * * * * * * * * * * * * * *
    ' * create a form if none in project
    ' * * * * * * * * * * * * * * * * * * * * * * * * * *
        If NonVBXData1$ = "" Then SendKeys "%FF"
    Else
    ' * * * * * * * * * * * * * * * * * * * * * * * * * *
    ' * launch vb & MAK if vb not running
    ' * * * * * * * * * * * * * * * * * * * * * * * * * *
     vbwin% = ShellExecute(MAKerMain.hWnd, "Open", MAKfile$, "", "", SW_SHOW)
    ' * * * * * * * * * * * * * * * * * * * * * * * * * *
    ' * abort if can't launch it
    ' * * * * * * * * * * * * * * * * * * * * * * * * * *
        If vbwin% < 32 Then Alert "Can't launch Visual Basic. Please use ⇔
         File Manager to Associate MAK files with VB.EXE": Exit Sub
        y% = DoEvents()
    ' * * * * * * * * * * * * * * * * * * * * * * * * * *
    ' * create a form if none in project
    ' * * * * * * * * * * * * * * * * * * * * * * * * * *
        If NonVBXData1$ = "" Then SendKeys "%FF"
    End If
    ' * * * * * * * * * * * * * * * * * * * * * * * * * *
    ' * minimize VB MAKer
    ' * * * * * * * * * * * * * * * * * * * * * * * * * *
    WindowState = 1
    End Sub
```

LISTING

VBXMIND.FRM

```
'   * * * * * * * * * * * * * * * * * * * * * * * * * * * * *
'   VBXMIND.FRM
'   Copyright (c) 1993 by Paul Bonner
'   PC Magazine Visual Basic Utilities
'   * * * * * * * * * * * * * * * * * * * * * * * * * * * * *
VERSION 2.00
Begin Form NewCFrm
    BackColor       =   &H00C0C0C0&
    BorderStyle     =   3   'Fixed Double
    Caption         =   "Locate Controls"
    ClientHeight    =   2535
    ClientLeft      =   1785
    ClientTop       =   2115
    ClientWidth     =   7635
    Height          =   2940
    Left            =   1725
    LinkTopic       =   "Form1"
    MaxButton       =   0   'False
    MinButton       =   0   'False
    ScaleHeight     =   2535
    ScaleWidth      =   7635
    Top             =   1770
    Width           =   7755
    Begin Timer Timer1
        Interval        =   10
        Left            =   5760
        Top             =   120
    End
    Begin CommandButton bCancel
        Cancel          =   -1  'True
        Caption         =   "Cancel"
        Height          =   280
        Left            =   6000
        TabIndex        =   5
        Top             =   2160
        Width           =   800
    End
    Begin ListBox VBXLister
        Height          =   1395
        Left            =   2880
        MultiSelect     =   2   'Extended
        TabIndex        =   3
        Top             =   720
        Width           =   4575
    End
    Begin CommandButton bAdd
        Caption         =   "&Add to VBX database"
        Height          =   280
        Left            =   3840
        TabIndex        =   4
        Top             =   2160
        Width           =   2055
    End
    Begin DirListBox Dir1
```

```
      Height              =      1605
      Left                =      120
      TabIndex            =      1
      Top                 =      720
      Width               =      2535
   End
   Begin DriveListBox Drive1
      Height              =      315
      Left                =      120
      TabIndex            =      0
      Top                 =      240
      Width               =      2535
   End
   Begin Label Label1
      BackColor           =      &H00C0C0C0&
      BackStyle           =      0    'Transparent
      Caption             =      "Label1"
      Height              =      375
      Left                =      2880
      TabIndex            =      2
      Top                 =      240
      Width               =      3105
      WordWrap            =      -1   'True
   End
End
Option Explicit
DefInt A-Z

Sub bAdd_Click ()
' * * * * * * * * * * * * * * * * * * * * * * * * * * * * *
' * add selected file to database
' * * * * * * * * * * * * * * * * * * * * * * * * * * * * *
Dim cFile$, cPath$, X%, LI%, Y%
' * * * * * * * * * * * * * * * * * * * * * * * * * * * * *
' * abort if no file selected
' * * * * * * * * * * * * * * * * * * * * * * * * * * * * *
If VBXLister.SelCount = 0 Then
   Alert "Please select the controls that you wish to add to the database."
   Exit Sub
End If
Screen.MousePointer = 11
' * * * * * * * * * * * * * * * * * * * * * * * * * * * * *
' * step through selected files
' * do it backwards 'cause you're removing 'em as you go
' * * * * * * * * * * * * * * * * * * * * * * * * * * * * *
For LI% = VBXLister.ListCount - 1 To 0 Step -1
   If VBXLister.Selected(LI%) Then
' * * * * * * * * * * * * * * * * * * * * * * * * * * * * *
' * add new database record
' * * * * * * * * * * * * * * * * * * * * * * * * * * * * *
      MAKerMain.Data1.Recordset.AddNew
' * * * * * * * * * * * * * * * * * * * * * * * * * * * * *
' * break fully qualified file name into path and file
' * * * * * * * * * * * * * * * * * * * * * * * * * * * * *
      cFile$ = VBXLister.List(LI%)
      For X% = Len(cFile$) To 1 Step -1
         If Mid$(cFile$, X%, 1) = "\" Then
            cPath$ = Left$(cFile$, X%)
            cFile$ = Mid$(cFile$, X% + 1)
            Exit For
         End If
      Next
' * * * * * * * * * * * * * * * * * * * * * * * * * * * * *
' * update database record fields
```

```
'  * * * * * * * * * * * * * * * * * * * * * * * * *
       MAKerMain.Data1.Recordset("FileName") = cFile$
       cPath$ = FixPath$(cPath$)
       MAKerMain.Data1.Recordset("Path") = cPath$
       MAKerMain.Data1.Recordset("Description") = ""
       MAKerMain.Data1.UpdateRecord
'  * * * * * * * * * * * * * * * * * * * * * * * *
'  * now remove from list box
'  * * * * * * * * * * * * * * * * * * * * * * * *
     VBXLister.RemoveItem (LI%)
End If
Next LI%
VBXLister.ListIndex = -1
'  * * * * * * * * * * * * * * * * * * * * * * * * *
'  * clear Available Controls list
'  * * * * * * * * * * * * * * * * * * * * * * * * *
MAKerMain.List1(0).Clear
'  * * * * * * * * * * * * * * * * * * * * * * * * *
'  * now reload database to reinitialize arrays
'  * * * * * * * * * * * * * * * * * * * * * * * * *
InitializeDatabase
'  * * * * * * * * * * * * * * * * * * * * * * * * *
'  * remove items from Available Controls that are already in MAK file
'  * * * * * * * * * * * * * * * * * * * * * * * * *
Dim cPat1$
For X% = 0 To MAKerMain.List1(1).ListCount - 1
    cPat1$ = cFullPath(MAKerMain.List1(1).ItemData(X%))
    For Y% = 0 To MAKerMain.List1(0).ListCount - 1
        If cFullPath(MAKerMain.List1(0).ItemData(Y%)) = cPat1$ Then
            MAKerMain.List1(0).RemoveItem Y%
            Exit For
        End If
    Next Y%
Next X%
Screen.MousePointer = 0
'  * * * * * * * * * * * * * * * * * * * * * * * * *
'  * get count of remaining unlisted controls
'  * * * * * * * * * * * * * * * * * * * * * * * * *
X% = VBXLister.ListCount
'  * * * * * * * * * * * * * * * * * * * * * * * * *
'  * move highlight bar
'  * * * * * * * * * * * * * * * * * * * * * * * * *
If LI% < X% Then
    VBXLister.ListIndex = LI%
Else
    VBXLister.ListIndex = LI% - 1
End If
'  * * * * * * * * * * * * * * * * * * * * * * * * *
'  * disable Add Controls button if none remaining
'  * * * * * * * * * * * * * * * * * * * * * * * * *
If X% = 0 Then bAdd.Enabled = False
Screen.MousePointer = 0
End Sub

Sub bCancel_Click ()
Unload Me
End Sub

Sub Dir1_Change ()
'  * * * * * * * * * * * * * * * * * * * * * * * * *
'  * when directory changes, clear Unlisted Controls list
'  * then add unlisted controls in current dir
'  * * * * * * * * * * * * * * * * * * * * * * * * *
VBXLister.Clear
```

```
Dim CurrentDir$
CurrentDir$ = FixPath$(UCase$(Dir1))
FindEm CurrentDir$
End Sub

Sub Drive1_Change ()
'  * * * * * * * * * * * * * * * * * * * * * * * * * *
'  * tell Dir1 that the drive has changed
'  * * * * * * * * * * * * * * * * * * * * * * * * * *
On Error Resume Next
Dir1.Path = Drive1.Drive
Dir1.Refresh
End Sub

Sub Form_Load ()
'  * * * * * * * * * * * * * * * * * * * * * * * * * *
'  * rearrange form if automatic search mode
'  * enable timer to start search
'  * * * * * * * * * * * * * * * * * * * * * * * * * *
If Autosearch% = True Then
    Caption = "Find All VBXs"
    Drive1.Visible = False
    Dir1.Visible = False
    bAdd.Visible = False
    Label1.Left = 300
    VBXLister.Left = 240
    Width = VBXLister.Width + 640
    bAdd.Left = (Width - bAdd.Width) / 2
    bCancel.Left = bAdd.Left + bAdd.Width + 240
    Timer1.Enabled = True
Else
  Label1 = "These VBX files are not currently listed in VB MAKer's database:"
    Timer1.Enabled = False
End If
CenterForm Me
End Sub

Sub Timer1_Timer ()
Dim X%
'  * * * * * * * * * * * * * * * * * * * * * * * * * *
'  * search path for unlisted controls
'  * show Add Controls button if you find any
'  * * * * * * * * * * * * * * * * * * * * * * * * * *
X% = SearchPath%()
Timer1.Enabled = False
Label1 = "These VBX files are not currently listed in VB MAKer's database:"
If VBXLister.ListCount > 0 Then
    bAdd.Visible = True
End If
End Sub

Sub VBXLister_DblClick ()
bAdd_Click
End Sub
```

LISTING

VBXMIND.BAS

```
'  *  *  *  *  *  *  *  *  *  *  *  *  *  *  *  *  *  *  *  *  *  *  *  *
'    VBXMIND.BAS
'    Copyright (c) 1993 by Paul Bonner
'    PC Magazine Visual Basic Utilities
'  *  *  *  *  *  *  *  *  *  *  *  *  *  *  *  *  *  *  *  *  *  *  *  *
Option Explicit
DefInt A-Z
'  *  *  *  *  *  *  *  *  *  *  *  *  *  *  *  *  *  *  *  *  *  *  *  *
'    * API calls to obtain SYSTEM and WINDOWS directories
'  *  *  *  *  *  *  *  *  *  *  *  *  *  *  *  *  *  *  *  *  *  *  *  *
Declare Function GetSystemDirectory Lib "Kernel" (ByVal lpBuffer$, ByVal ⇔
    nSize%) As Integer
Declare Function GetWindowsDirectory Lib "Kernel" (ByVal lpBuffer$, ByVal ⇔
    nSize%) As Integer
'  *  *  *  *  *  *  *  *  *  *  *  *  *  *  *  *  *  *  *  *  *  *  *  *
'    * global variables
'  *  *  *  *  *  *  *  *  *  *  *  *  *  *  *  *  *  *  *  *  *  *  *  *
Global cFullPath() As String
Global rsBookMark() As String
Global CRLF$
Global AutoSearch%
Global ActiveList%
Global Filedirty%
Global NonVBXData1$
Global NonVBXData2$
Global MAKfile$
'  *  *  *  *  *  *  *  *  *  *  *  *  *  *  *  *  *  *  *  *  *  *  *  *
'    * constants used by Common Dialogs VBX
'  *  *  *  *  *  *  *  *  *  *  *  *  *  *  *  *  *  *  *  *  *  *  *  *
Global Const OFN_EXTENTIONDIFFERENT = &H400
Global Const OFN_FILEMUSTEXIST = &H1000
Global Const OFN_HIDEREADONLY = &H4
Global Const CancelButton = 32755
Global Const OFN_OVERWRITEPROMPT = &H2
'  *  *  *  *  *  *  *  *  *  *  *  *  *  *  *  *  *  *  *  *  *  *  *  *
'    * API calls used to launch VB
'  *  *  *  *  *  *  *  *  *  *  *  *  *  *  *  *  *  *  *  *  *  *  *  *
Declare Function ShellExecute Lib "Shell.dll" (ByVal hWnd%, ByVal lpszOp$, ⇔
    ByVal lpszFile$, ByVal lpszParams As Any, ByVal lpszDir$, ByVal ⇔
    fsShowCnd%) As Integer
Declare Function SetFocusAPI Lib "User" Alias "SetFocus" (ByVal hWnd As ⇔
    Integer) As Integer
Declare Function GetWindowText Lib "User" (ByVal hWnd As Integer, ByVal ⇔
    lpString As String, ByVal aint As Integer) As Integer
Global Const SW_SHOW = 5
'  *  *  *  *  *  *  *  *  *  *  *  *  *  *  *  *  *  *  *  *  *  *  *  *
'    * API calls used by SearchWindowList%()
'  *  *  *  *  *  *  *  *  *  *  *  *  *  *  *  *  *  *  *  *  *  *  *  *
Declare Function GetWindow% Lib "USER" (ByVal hWnd%, ByVal wCmd%)
Global Const GW_HWNDFIRST = 0
Global Const GW_HWNDNEXT = 2

Sub Alert (Mess$)
'  *  *  *  *  *  *  *  *  *  *  *  *  *  *  *  *  *  *  *  *  *  *  *  *
```

```
'   * creates an Alert box with an OK button
' * * * * * * * * * * * * * * * * * * * * * * * *
MsgBox Mess$, 48, App.Title
End Sub

Sub AlertNoDB ()
'   * * * * * * * * * * * * * * * * * * * * * * * *
'   * Warning message if VB MAKer's database is empty
'   * * * * * * * * * * * * * * * * * * * * * * * *
Alert "You must add at least one custom control (VBX) to VB MAKer's ⇔
    database before performing this action."
End Sub

Sub ArrowButtonHandler (Index As Integer)
'   * * * * * * * * * * * * * * * * * * * * * * * *
'   * handler for arrow button clicks
'   * * * * * * * * * * * * * * * * * * * * * * * *
Dim Dest%, rSource%
'   * * * * * * * * * * * * * * * * * * * * * * * *
'   * set FileDirty% flag
'   * * * * * * * * * * * * * * * * * * * * * * * *
Filedirty% = True
'   * * * * * * * * * * * * * * * * * * * * * * * *
'   * determine destination list
'   * * * * * * * * * * * * * * * * * * * * * * * *
Dest% = OtherC%(Index)
'   * * * * * * * * * * * * * * * * * * * * * * * *
'   * move item from source control to dest
'   * * * * * * * * * * * * * * * * * * * * * * * *
rSource% = MAKerMain.List1(Index).ListIndex
If rSource% = -1 Then Exit Sub
MAKerMain.List1(Dest%).AddItem MAKerMain.List1(Index)
MAKerMain.List1(Dest%).ItemData(MAKerMain.List1(Dest%).NewIndex) ⇔
    = MAKerMain.List1(Index).ItemData(rSource%)
MAKerMain.List1(Index).RemoveItem rSource%
'   * * * * * * * * * * * * * * * * * * * * * * * *
'   * select next vbx in source list
'   * * * * * * * * * * * * * * * * * * * * * * * *
If MAKerMain.List1(Index).ListCount > 0 Then
    SelectNextVBXInList Index, rSource%
Else
    MAKerMain.List1(Dest%).ListIndex = MAKerMain.List1(Dest%).NewIndex
    ControlListClick Dest%
End If
End Sub

Sub CenterForm (f As Form)
f.Left = (Screen.Width - f.Width) / 2
f.Top = (Screen.Height - f.Height) / 2
End Sub

Sub ClearDatabase ()
'   * * * * * * * * * * * * * * * * * * * * * * * *
'   * routine to delete all records in database
'   * * * * * * * * * * * * * * * * * * * * * * * *
MAKerMain.Data1.Recordset.MoveFirst
BeginTrans
Do While Not MAKerMain.Data1.Recordset.EOF
    MAKerMain.Data1.Recordset.Delete
    MAKerMain.Data1.Recordset.MoveNext
Loop
CommitTrans
MAKerMain.Data1.Recordset.Update
MAKerMain.Data1.Recordset.AddNew
```

```
End Sub

Function CntrlAlreadyListed% (test$)
'    * * * * * * * * * * * * * * * * * * * * * * * * *
'    * searches cFullPath() array
'    * returns True if control already in db
'    * requires fully qualified control name
'    * * * * * * * * * * * * * * * * * * * * * * * * *
CntrlAlreadyListed% = False
Dim X%, ac%
ac% = UBound(cFullPath)
For X% = 0 To ac%
    If cFullPath(X%) = test$ Then
        CntrlAlreadyListed% = True
        Exit For
    End If
Next
End Function

Function Confirm% (Ask$)
'    * * * * * * * * * * * * * * * * * * * * * * * * *
'    * standard yes/no message box
'    * * * * * * * * * * * * * * * * * * * * * * * * *
If MsgBox(Ask$, 52, App.Title) = 6 Then Confirm% = True
End Function

Sub ControlListClick (Index As Integer)
'    * * * * * * * * * * * * * * * * * * * * * * * * *
'    * move current recordset record pointer to point to selected VBX
'    * * * * * * * * * * * * * * * * * * * * * * * * *
If MAKerMain.List1(Index).ListIndex > -1 Then
    ActiveList% = Index
    MAKerMain.Data1.Recordset.Bookmark = rsBookMark⇔
((MAKerMain.List1(Index).ItemData(MAKerMain.List1(Index).ListIndex)))
'    * * * * * * * * * * * * * * * * * * * * * * * * *
'    * remove highlight from other list box
'    * * * * * * * * * * * * * * * * * * * * * * * * *
    MAKerMain.List1(OtherC%(Index)).ListIndex = -1
End If

End Sub

Sub Draw3dFrame (f As Form, C As Label)
'    * * * * * * * * * * * * * * * * * * * * * * * * *
'    * draws a 3D frame around specified label
'    * autosize must be False
'    * label font must be same as form font
'    * * * * * * * * * * * * * * * * * * * * * * * * *
Const White = &HFFFFFF
Const DarkGray = &H808080
Dim X1%, X2%, Y1%, Y2%, FrameHeight%, FrameWidth%, FrameLeft%, FrameTop%
f.DrawWidth = 1
FrameLeft% = C.Left
FrameTop% = C.Top
FrameHeight% = C.Height
FrameWidth% = C.Width
'    * * * * * * * * * * * * * * * * * * * * * * * * *
'    * draw top line to left of label text
'    * * * * * * * * * * * * * * * * * * * * * * * * *
X1% = FrameLeft% - 60
X2% = FrameLeft% - 180
Y1% = FrameTop% + (f.TextHeight(C.Caption) / 2) - 60
f.ForeColor = DarkGray
f.Line (X1%, Y1%)-(X2, Y1%)
```

```
Y1% = Y1% + 20
f.ForeColor = White
f.Line (X1%, Y1%)-(X2, Y1%)
' * * * * * * * * * * * * * * * * * * * * * * * * * *
'  * draw left side
' * * * * * * * * * * * * * * * * * * * * * * * * * *
Y2% = Y1% + FrameHeight%
f.ForeColor = DarkGray
f.Line (X2%, Y1%)-(X2%, Y2%)
X2% = X2% + 20
f.ForeColor = White
f.Line (X2%, Y1%)-(X2%, Y2%)
' * * * * * * * * * * * * * * * * * * * * * * * * * *
'  * draw bottom
' * * * * * * * * * * * * * * * * * * * * * * * * * *
X1% = X2%
X2% = FrameLeft% + FrameWidth%
f.ForeColor = DarkGray
f.Line (X1%, Y2)-(X2%, Y2%)
Y2% = Y2% + 15
f.ForeColor = White
f.Line (X1%, Y2)-(X2%, Y2%)
' * * * * * * * * * * * * * * * * * * * * * * * * * *
'  * draw right
' * * * * * * * * * * * * * * * * * * * * * * * * * *
Y1% = FrameTop% + (f.TextHeight(C.Caption) / 2) - 60
f.Line -(X2%, Y1%)
f.ForeColor = DarkGray
X1% = X2% - 20
f.Line (X1%, Y2% - 20)-(X1%, Y1% + 20)
' * * * * * * * * * * * * * * * * * * * * * * * * * *
'   draw top line to right edge of label text
' * * * * * * * * * * * * * * * * * * * * * * * * * *
X2% = FrameLeft% + f.TextWidth(C.Caption) + 60
f.Line (X1%, Y1% - 15)-(X2%, Y1% - 15)
f.ForeColor = White
f.Line (X1%, Y1%)-(X2%, Y1%)
End Sub

Function FindCntrlIndex% (test$)
' * * * * * * * * * * * * * * * * * * * * * * * * * *
'  * find list box index of specified VBX file
' * * * * * * * * * * * * * * * * * * * * * * * * * *
Dim X%, ac%, fp%, temp$
FindCntrlIndex = -1
ac% = UBound(cFullPath)
If InStr(test$, "\") > 0 Then fp% = True
For X% = 0 To ac%
   If fp% = True Then
      temp$ = cFullPath(X%)
   Else
      temp$ = StripPath$(cFullPath(X%))
   End If
   If temp$ = test$ Then
      FindCntrlIndex% = X%
      Exit For
   End If
Next
End Function

Sub FindEm (CurrentDir As String)
' * * * * * * * * * * * * * * * * * * * * * * * * * *
'  * search specified directory for VBX files
'  * add any not currently in database to VBXLister
```

```
'   *  *  *  *  *  *  *  *  *  *  *  *  *  *  *  *  *  *  *  *  *  *  *  *
Dim X%, Found$
If AutoSearch% Then NewCFrm.Label1 = "Searching " + CurrentDir
CurrentDir$ = FixPath$(CurrentDir$)
Found$ = Dir$(CurrentDir + "*.VBX")
X% = DoEvents()
Do While Len(Found$) <> 0
    If Not CntrlAlreadyListed%(CurrentDir + Found$) Then
        NewCFrm.VBXLister.AddItem CurrentDir + Found$
    End If
    Found$ = Dir$
Loop
End Sub

Function FixAPIString$ (ByVal test$)
'   *  *  *  *  *  *  *  *  *  *  *  *  *  *  *  *  *  *  *  *  *  *  *  *
'   * strips leading and trailing spaces and trailing nulls
'   * from strings returned by API function
'   *  *  *  *  *  *  *  *  *  *  *  *  *  *  *  *  *  *  *  *  *  *  *  *
FixAPIString$ = Trim$(Left$(test$, InStr(test$, Chr$(0)) - 1))
End Function

Function FixPath$ (ByVal test$)
'   *  *  *  *  *  *  *  *  *  *  *  *  *  *  *  *  *  *  *  *  *  *  *  *
'   * sticks a backslash on the end of test$
'   * if there is not one there already
'   *  *  *  *  *  *  *  *  *  *  *  *  *  *  *  *  *  *  *  *  *  *  *  *
If Right$(test$, 1) <> "\" Then test$ = test$ + "\"
FixPath$ = test$
End Function

Sub GetMAKFile ()
'   *  *  *  *  *  *  *  *  *  *  *  *  *  *  *  *  *  *  *  *  *  *  *  *
'   * load MAKfile$
'   *  *  *  *  *  *  *  *  *  *  *  *  *  *  *  *  *  *  *  *  *  *  *  *
Dim ff%, I$, J$, indx%, X%
ff% = FreeFile
Open MAKfile$ For Input As ff%
Do While Not EOF(ff%)
    Line Input #1, I$
'   *  *  *  *  *  *  *  *  *  *  *  *  *  *  *  *  *  *  *  *  *  *  *  *
'   * does input line specify a VBX?
'   *  *  *  *  *  *  *  *  *  *  *  *  *  *  *  *  *  *  *  *  *  *  *  *
    I$ = UCase$(I$)
    If InStr(I$, ".VBX") Then
'   *  *  *  *  *  *  *  *  *  *  *  *  *  *  *  *  *  *  *  *  *  *  *  *
'   * is VBX already listed?
'   *  *  *  *  *  *  *  *  *  *  *  *  *  *  *  *  *  *  *  *  *  *  *  *
    indx% = FindCntrlIndex%(I$)
        If indx% > -1 Then
'   *  *  *  *  *  *  *  *  *  *  *  *  *  *  *  *  *  *  *  *  *  *  *  *
'   * if already listed, find it in Available Controls list
'   *  *  *  *  *  *  *  *  *  *  *  *  *  *  *  *  *  *  *  *  *  *  *  *
            For X% = 0 To MAKerMain.List1(0).ListCount - 1
                If MAKerMain.List1(0).ItemData(X%) = indx% Then
                    MAKerMain.List1(0).ListIndex = X%
                    Exit For
                End If
            Next
'   *  *  *  *  *  *  *  *  *  *  *  *  *  *  *  *  *  *  *  *  *  *  *  *
'   * and copy it to Current MAK File list
'   *  *  *  *  *  *  *  *  *  *  *  *  *  *  *  *  *  *  *  *  *  *  *  *
                ArrowButtonHandler 0
        Else
```

```
'   *  *  *  *  *  *  *  *  *  *  *  *  *  *  *  *  *  *  *  *  *  *
'   *  if not listed, post error message and abort
'   *  *  *  *  *  *  *  *  *  *  *  *  *  *  *  *  *  *  *  *  *  *
            Close #1
            Alert I$ + " is not listed in VB MAKer's database. Please add ⇔
    this control to the database before using VB MAKer to edit this MAK file."
            NewFile
            Exit Sub
         End If
      Else
'   *  *  *  *  *  *  *  *  *  *  *  *  *  *  *  *  *  *  *  *  *  *
'   *  if line doesn't specify a VBX
'   *  *  *  *  *  *  *  *  *  *  *  *  *  *  *  *  *  *  *  *  *  *
         If InStr(I$, ".") And (InStr(I$, Chr$(34)) = 0) Then
'   *  *  *  *  *  *  *  *  *  *  *  *  *  *  *  *  *  *  *  *  *  *
'   *  add it to NonVBXData1$ if it specifies a different file
'   *  *  *  *  *  *  *  *  *  *  *  *  *  *  *  *  *  *  *  *  *  *
            NonVBXData1$ = NonVBXData1$ + I$ + CRLF$
         Else
'   *  *  *  *  *  *  *  *  *  *  *  *  *  *  *  *  *  *  *  *  *  *
'   *  otherwise add it to NonVBXData2$
'   *  *  *  *  *  *  *  *  *  *  *  *  *  *  *  *  *  *  *  *  *  *
            NonVBXData2$ = NonVBXData2$ + I$ + CRLF$
         End If
      End If
      indx% = DoEvents()
Loop
Close #1
Filedirty% = False
'   *  *  *  *  *  *  *  *  *  *  *  *  *  *  *  *  *  *  *  *  *  *
'   *  move highlight bar and update caption
'   *  *  *  *  *  *  *  *  *  *  *  *  *  *  *  *  *  *  *  *  *  *
If MAKerMain.List1(0).ListCount Then MAKerMain.List1(0).ListIndex = 0
MAKerMain.Caption = "VB MAKer -- " + MAKfile$
End Sub


Sub InitializeDatabase ()
'   *  *  *  *  *  *  *  *  *  *  *  *  *  *  *  *  *  *  *  *  *  *
'   *  select first item in db
'   *  *  *  *  *  *  *  *  *  *  *  *  *  *  *  *  *  *  *  *  *  *
On Error Resume Next
MAKerMain.Data1.Recordset.MoveFirst
On Error GoTo 0
'   *  *  *  *  *  *  *  *  *  *  *  *  *  *  *  *  *  *  *  *  *  *
'   *  init arrays
'   *  *  *  *  *  *  *  *  *  *  *  *  *  *  *  *  *  *  *  *  *  *
Dim Arraysize%, Counter%, P$
Arraysize% = 24
ReDim cFullPath(Arraysize%)
ReDim rsBookMark(Arraysize%)
'   *  *  *  *  *  *  *  *  *  *  *  *  *  *  *  *  *  *  *  *  *  *
'   *  read all records
'   *  *  *  *  *  *  *  *  *  *  *  *  *  *  *  *  *  *  *  *  *  *
Do While Not MAKerMain.Data1.Recordset.EOF
      Counter% = Counter% + 1
'   *  *  *  *  *  *  *  *  *  *  *  *  *  *  *  *  *  *  *  *  *  *
'   *  redim preserve arrays if necessary
'   *  *  *  *  *  *  *  *  *  *  *  *  *  *  *  *  *  *  *  *  *  *
      If Counter% = Arraysize% Then
         Arraysize% = Arraysize + 12
         ReDim Preserve cFullPath(Arraysize%)
         ReDim Preserve rsBookMark(Arraysize%)
      End If
'   *  *  *  *  *  *  *  *  *  *  *  *  *  *  *  *  *  *  *  *  *  *
```

```
'    * if you've got a real record, add it to list box
'    * save record's bookmark and path to arrays
'    * * * * * * * * * * * * * * * * * * * * * * * * * * *
    If Not IsNull(MAKerMain.Data1.Recordset("FileName")) Then
      MAKerMain.List1(0).AddItem MAKerMain.Data1.Recordset("FileName")
       rsBookMark(Counter%) = MAKerMain.Data1.Recordset.Bookmark
    MAKerMain.List1(0).ItemData(MAKerMain.List1(0).NewIndex) = Counter%
       P$ = MAKerMain.Data1.Recordset("Path")
       P$ = FixPath$(Trim(P$))
      cFullPath(Counter%) = P$ + MAKerMain.Data1.Recordset("FileName")
    End If
'    * * * * * * * * * * * * * * * * * * * * * * * * * * *
'    * select next record
'    * * * * * * * * * * * * * * * * * * * * * * * * * * *
    MAKerMain.Data1.Recordset.MoveNext
Loop
If MAKerMain.List1(0).ListCount Then MAKerMain.List1(0).ListIndex = 0
End Sub

Sub ItemFinder (ByVal FindMe$)
'    * * * * * * * * * * * * * * * * * * * * * * * * * * *
'    * search for FindMe$ in description field
'    * * * * * * * * * * * * * * * * * * * * * * * * * * *
Dim LI%, iFound%
'    * * * * * * * * * * * * * * * * * * * * * * * * * * *
'    * hide Description and Path fields to speed search
'    * * * * * * * * * * * * * * * * * * * * * * * * * * *
ShowFields False
'    * * * * * * * * * * * * * * * * * * * * * * * * * * *
'    * advance list box index
'    * * * * * * * * * * * * * * * * * * * * * * * * * * *
LI% = MAKerMain.List1(ActiveList%).ListIndex + 1
'    * * * * * * * * * * * * * * * * * * * * * * * * * * *
'    * loop until end of list
'    * * * * * * * * * * * * * * * * * * * * * * * * * * *
Do While LI% < MAKerMain.List1(ActiveList%).ListCount
'    * * * * * * * * * * * * * * * * * * * * * * * * * * *
'    * select list box entry
'    * then compare bound text field to search string
'    * exit search if you find a match
'    * * * * * * * * * * * * * * * * * * * * * * * * * * *
    MAKerMain.List1(ActiveList%).ListIndex = LI%
    If InStr(1,UCase$(MAKerMain.Text1), FindMe$,1) Then
       iFound% = True
       Exit Do
    End If
    LI% = LI% + 1
Loop
'    * * * * * * * * * * * * * * * * * * * * * * * * * * *
'    * enable find next item if you've got a match
'    * otherwise tell the user you failed
'    * * * * * * * * * * * * * * * * * * * * * * * * * * *
If iFound% Then
    MAKerMain.cItem(4).Enabled = True
Else
    MAKerMain.cItem(4).Enabled = False
    Alert "Couldn't find that text."
End If
ShowFields True
End Sub

Sub NewFile ()
'    * * * * * * * * * * * * * * * * * * * * * * * * * * *
'    * save value of fileMenu.Enabled, then disable it
```

```
'   * * * * * * * * * * * * * * * * * * * * * * * * * * *
Dim fe%
fe% = MAKerMain.fileMenu.Enabled
MAKerMain.fileMenu.Enabled = False
'   * * * * * * * * * * * * * * * * * * * * * * * * * * *
'   clean up
'   * * * * * * * * * * * * * * * * * * * * * * * * * * *
NonVBXData1$ = ""
NonVBXData2$ = ""
ShowFields False
Filedirty% = False
MAKerMain.List1(0).Clear
MAKerMain.List1(1).Clear
MAKerMain.Caption = "VB MAKer"
'   * * * * * * * * * * * * * * * * * * * * * * * * * * *
'   * reload database
'   * * * * * * * * * * * * * * * * * * * * * * * * * * *
InitializeDatabase
ShowFields True
'   * * * * * * * * * * * * * * * * * * * * * * * * * * *
'   * restore state of fileMenu.Enabled
'   * * * * * * * * * * * * * * * * * * * * * * * * * * *
MAKerMain.fileMenu.Enabled = fe%
End Sub

Function OtherC% (I%)
'   * * * * * * * * * * * * * * * * * * * * * * * * * * *
'   * given an index number, returns
'   * index of other control in pair
'   * i.e., 0 if passed 1, 1 if passed 0
'   * * * * * * * * * * * * * * * * * * * * * * * * * * *
If I% = 0 Then
    OtherC% = 1
Else
    OtherC% = 0
End If
End Function

Sub SaveAs ()
'   * * * * * * * * * * * * * * * * * * * * * * * * * * *
'   *set Common Dialog flags
'   * * * * * * * * * * * * * * * * * * * * * * * * * * *
    MAKerMain.CMDialog1.Flags = OFN_HIDEREADONLY Or OFN_OVERWRITEPROMPT
    MAKerMain.CMDialog1.DefaultExt = "MAK"
    MAKerMain.CMDialog1.Filter = "Project files|*.MAK"
    On Error Resume Next
'   * * * * * * * * * * * * * * * * * * * * * * * * * * *
'   * call Save dialog
'   * * * * * * * * * * * * * * * * * * * * * * * * * * *
    MAKerMain.CMDialog1.Action = 2
'   * * * * * * * * * * * * * * * * * * * * * * * * * * *
'   * exit if user pressed cancel button
'   * otherwise, force an MAK extension
'   * * * * * * * * * * * * * * * * * * * * * * * * * * *
    If Err = CancelButton Then Exit Sub
    If MAKerMain.CMDialog1.Flags And OFN_EXTENTIONDIFFERENT Then
        Alert "File must have an MAK extension!"
        Exit Sub
    End If
'   * * * * * * * * * * * * * * * * * * * * * * * * * * *
'   * set file name and path variables
'   * call SaveFile routine to save data
'   * * * * * * * * * * * * * * * * * * * * * * * * * * *
    MAKfile$ = MAKerMain.CMDialog1.Filename
```

```
    If MAKfile$ = "" Then Exit Sub
    SaveFile
End Sub

Sub SaveFile ()
MAKerMain.fileMenu.Enabled = False
Dim X, ff%
' * * * * * * * * * * * * * * * * * * * * * * * * * *
' * open file for output
' * * * * * * * * * * * * * * * * * * * * * * * * * *
ff% = FreeFile
Open MAKfile$ For Output As ff%
' * * * * * * * * * * * * * * * * * * * * * * * * * *
' * save nonvbx files
' * * * * * * * * * * * * * * * * * * * * * * * * * *
If NonVBXData1$ <> "" Then Print #ff%, NonVBXData1$;
' * * * * * * * * * * * * * * * * * * * * * * * * * *
' * save all vbxs specified in Current MAK File list
' * * * * * * * * * * * * * * * * * * * * * * * * * *
For X% = 0 To MAKerMain.List1(1).ListCount - 1
    MAKerMain.List1(1).ListIndex = X%
    Print #ff%, cFullPath(MAKerMain.List1(1).ItemData(X%))
Next
' * * * * * * * * * * * * * * * * * * * * * * * * * *
' * save remaining project data
' * * * * * * * * * * * * * * * * * * * * * * * * * *
If NonVBXData2$ <> "" Then Print #ff%, NonVBXData2$
Close #ff%
' * * * * * * * * * * * * * * * * * * * * * * * * * *
' update caption to display file name
' * * * * * * * * * * * * * * * * * * * * * * * * * *
Filedirty% = False
MAKerMain.Caption = "VB MAKer -- " + MAKfile$
End Sub

Function SearchPath% ()
Dim Path As String, CurrentDir As String, Found$
Dim Y%, WinDir$, SystemDir$, SemiColon
Dim sBuffer As String * 254
NewCFrm.bCancel.Enabled = False
' * * * * * * * * * * * * * * * * * * * * * * * * * *
' * search VB MAKer's directory
' * * * * * * * * * * * * * * * * * * * * * * * * * *
CurrentDir = App.Path
FindEm UCase$(CurrentDir)
' * * * * * * * * * * * * * * * * * * * * * * * * * *
' * search SYSTEM and WINDOWS directories
' * * * * * * * * * * * * * * * * * * * * * * * * * *
Y% = GetSystemDirectory(sBuffer, 254)
SystemDir$ = FixAPIString$(sBuffer)
FindEm UCase$(SystemDir$)
Y% = GetWindowsDirectory(sBuffer, 254)
WinDir$ = FixAPIString$(sBuffer)
FindEm UCase$(WinDir$)
' * * * * * * * * * * * * * * * * * * * * * * * * * *
' * search path
' * * * * * * * * * * * * * * * * * * * * * * * * * *
Path = Environ$("PATH")
If Path <> "" Then
    If Right$(Path, 1) <> ";" Then Path = Path + ";"
    SemiColon = InStr(Path, ";")
    Do
        CurrentDir = Left$(Path, SemiColon - 1)
      If CurrentDir <> App.Path And CurrentDir <> SystemDir$ And Current⇔
```

```
      Dir <> WinDir$ Then
            FindEm UCase$(CurrentDir)
        End If
        Path = Right$(Path, Len(Path) - SemiColon)
        SemiColon = InStr(Path, ";")
    Loop While SemiColon <> 0
End If
On Error GoTo 0
'  * * * * * * * * * * * * * * * * * * * * * * * * *
'  * see how many you found
'  * * * * * * * * * * * * * * * * * * * * * * * * *
Y% = NewCFrm.VBXLister.ListCount
Select Case Y%
'  * * * * * * * * * * * * * * * * * * * * * * * * *
'  * tell the user how many you found
'  * * * * * * * * * * * * * * * * * * * * * * * * *
Case 0
    Alert "All VBXs on path are already listed in the database."
    SearchPath% = False
Case Else
 Alert "Found " + Str$(NewCFrm.VBXLister.ListCount) + " unlisted VBX files."
    SearchPath% = True
End Select
NewCFrm.bCancel.Enabled = True
End Function


Function SearchWindowList% (Cap$)
'  * * * * * * * * * * * * * * * * * * * * * * * * *
'  * returns handle of first window that matches partial
'  * caption passed to function
'  * * * * * * * * * * * * * * * * * * * * * * * * *
SearchWindowList% = 0
Dim w%, Y%, winCap As String * 255
'  * * * * * * * * * * * * * * * * * * * * * * * * *
'  * start with first window in window list
'  * * * * * * * * * * * * * * * * * * * * * * * * *
w% = GetWindow%(MAKerMain.hWnd, GW_HWNDFIRST)
'  * * * * * * * * * * * * * * * * * * * * * * * * *
'  * continue until no more top level windows to check
'  * * * * * * * * * * * * * * * * * * * * * * * * *
Do While w% <> 0
'  * * * * * * * * * * * * * * * * * * * * * * * * *
'  * compare window caption to Cap$
'  * * * * * * * * * * * * * * * * * * * * * * * * *
    Y% = GetWindowText(w%, winCap, 254)
'  * * * * * * * * * * * * * * * * * * * * * * * * *
'  * exit if you get a match
'  * * * * * * * * * * * * * * * * * * * * * * * * *
    If Left$(winCap, Len(Cap$)) = Cap$ Then
        SearchWindowList% = w%
        Exit Do
    End If
'  * * * * * * * * * * * * * * * * * * * * * * * * *
'  * try next window
'  * * * * * * * * * * * * * * * * * * * * * * * * *
    w% = GetWindow%(w%, GW_HWNDNEXT)
Loop
End Function


Sub SelectNextVBXInList (ListNum%, rSource%)
Dim Dest%
'  * * * * * * * * * * * * * * * * * * * * * * * * *
'  * select next item in source list if there is one
'  * otherwise select previous item
```

```
'   * * * * * * * * * * * * * * * * * * * * * * * * * * *
If MAKerMain.List1(ListNum).ListCount > 0 Then
    If rSource% < (MAKerMain.List1(ListNum%).ListCount) Then
        MAKerMain.List1(ListNum).ListIndex = rSource%
    Else
        MAKerMain.List1(ListNum).ListIndex = rSource% - 1
    End If
    ControlListClick ListNum
'   * * * * * * * * * * * * * * * * * * * * * * * * * * *
'   * if the source list is empty, select most recently added item in dest
'   * * * * * * * * * * * * * * * * * * * * * * * * * * *
Else
    MAKerMain.List1(Dest%).ListIndex = MAKerMain.List1(Dest%).NewIndex
    ControlListClick Dest%
End If
End Sub

Sub ShowFields (ShowField%)
'   * * * * * * * * * * * * * * * * * * * * * * * * * * *
'   * hide or show the two bound controls
'   * hiding them speeds process of reading entire db
'   * because it eliminates screen updates
'   * * * * * * * * * * * * * * * * * * * * * * * * * * *
MAKerMain.Label3.Visible = ShowField%
MAKerMain.Text1.Visible = ShowField%
End Sub

Function StripPath$ (T$)
'   * * * * * * * * * * * * * * * * * * * * * * * * * * *
'   * strip path from specified file name
'   * * * * * * * * * * * * * * * * * * * * * * * * * * *
Dim X%, ct%
StripPath$ = T$
X% = InStr(T$, "\")
Do While X%
    ct% = X%
    X% = InStr(ct% + 1, T$, "\")
Loop
If ct% > 0 Then StripPath$ = Mid$(T$, ct% + 1)
End Function
```

TOOLS AND RESOURCES

■ CUSTOM CONTROLS AND CODE LIBRARIES

The utilities presented in *PC Magazine Visual Basic Utilities* are designed to stand by themselves. Any Windows 3.*x* user should be able to make use of these utilities, and any Visual Basic 3.0 user should be able to modify or customize them.

In order to meet that goal, I eschewed the use of commercial dynamic link libraries or custom controls in putting together these utilities. This approach had the side benefit of allowing me to demonstrate techniques for achieving many things that one might otherwise turn to a custom control to do. However, this isn't always the most efficient or practical approach to Visual Basic programming. A well-chosen custom control can save you hundreds of hours of coding time and provide access to routines which would be difficult or impossible to implement in Visual Basic code alone. Thus, in working on your own projects you might want to consider making use of some of the custom controls offered by the vendors listed below. I've worked with most of these products, and seen the results obtained with the others, and I can vouch for the fact that each is worth its weight in gold in some situations. Contact the vendors for full product information.

Apex Software   Apex offers Agility/VB, a high-speed database manager custom control for Visual Basic and Visual C++, and TrueGrid, a high-performance data-aware grid control. For more information, contact

Apex Software Corp.
4516 Henry Street
Pittsburgh, PA 15213
412-681-4343

Crescent Software   Crescent supplies several high-quality products for Visual Basic, including QuickPak Professional 3.0, a collection of assembly language subroutines and functions along with two dozen custom controls, many of which are data-aware; and PDQComm for Windows, an enhanced version of Visual Basic's communication control with automatic terminal emulations and support for several binary file transfer protocols. For more information, contact

Crescent Software, Inc.
11 Baily Avenue
Ridgefield, CT 06877
203-438-5300

Desaware   Desaware supplies several packages that extend the capabilities of Visual Basic, including SpyWorks-VB, a collection of custom controls which provide Visual Basic applications with full access to the Windows message stream, support for callback functions, and automatic subclassing capabilities, plus several powerful debugging tools; and CCF-Cursors, a custom control which aids in the creation and display of custom cursors. For more information, contact

Desaware
5 Town & Country Village, #790
San Jose, CA 95128
408-377-4770

FarPoint Technologies   FarPoint offers Spread/VBX, a full-featured data-aware spreadsheet custom control. For more information, contact

FarPoint Technologies, Inc.
585A Southlake Boulevard, Southport Office Park
Richmond, VA 23236
800-645-5913

MicroHelp   MicroHelp offers a broad range of Visual Basic-related products, including VB Tools 3, a collection of more than 40 custom controls, many of which are data aware; 3-D Gizmos 2, a collection of 13 data-aware three-dimensional controls; HighEdit, a word processing control; SpellPro, a spell-checking control; and Network Library, a collection of assembly-language routines for accessing NetBios, Novell and LANtastic network functions from within Visual Basic. For more information, contact

MicroHelp, Inc.
4359 Shallowford Industrial Parkway

Marietta, GA 30066
404-516-0899

Sheridan Software   Sheridan's custom control offerings include Data Widgets, a collection of data-aware controls, and 3D Widgets, a collection of three-dimensional custom controls and custom menus. For more information, contact
Sheridan Software Systems
65 Maxess Road
Melville, NY 11747
516-753-0985

■ OTHER DEVELOPMENT TOOLS

Visual Basic offers a remarkably well-designed integrated development environment, providing simple but efficient tools for achieving the commonly required programming tasks. However, that simplicity has been achieved at the cost of ignoring some areas that are of vital interest to many Visual Basic programmers. Fortunately, many of these gaps in Visual Basic's design environment can be filled with third-party vendor products. The four products that follow, each of which fulfills a unique programming need, are among the best Visual Basic accessories that I've encountered.

RoboHelp 2.0   Blue Sky Software's RoboHelp 2.0 is a powerful and easy-to-use tool for creating Windows Help files. Working in conjunction with Microsoft Word for Windows, it provides access to every capability and function of the Windows Help engine. It also includes a Visual Basic custom control that greatly simplifies the process of linking Help menus and buttons to specific Help file topics. For more information, contact
Blue Sky Software Corp.
7486 La Jolla Blvd, Suite 3
La Jolla, CA 92037
800-677-4WIN

VBAssist 3.0   Sheridan Software's VBAssist 3.0 adds a broad range of new capabilities to the Visual Basic development environment, including toolbar buttons for aligning controls, setting control properties individually or according to stored named styles, and setting control tab orders; plus a code library, quick access to API declarations, a facility for creating scrollable forms and picture boxes, and a facility for creating new databases or data tables and automatically creating forms from tables. For more information, contact

Sheridan Software Systems
65 Maxess Road
Melville, NY 11747
516-753-0985

VB Project Archiver   The Young Software Works's VB Project Archiver is a project management and version control utility for Visual Basic programmers that provides the ability to create archival copies of multiple versions of Visual Basic projects, and to automatically create distribution disks for any archived project with all necessary DLLs and custom controls. For more information, contact

The Young Software Works, Inc.
P.O. Box 185, Cooper Station
New York, NY 10276
212-982-4127

VB XREF   MicroHelp's VB XREF generates a wide variety of printed and on-screen information about the forms and modules in a Visual Basic program, including the current values of any or all control properties, cross-referenced lists of all the variables, procedures, keywords, and external declarations in a project and how each is used, and highly formatted program listings. For more information, contact

MicroHelp, Inc.
4359 Shallowford Industrial Parkway
Marietta, GA 30066
404-516-0899

■ ADDITIONAL RESOURCES

As much as I wish I could say that *PC Magazine Visual Basic Utilities* is the only book you'll ever need to buy for Visual Basic programming, it's just not true. The fact is that Windows programming is just too broad a subject—even when viewed through as relatively sharp a lens as Visual Basic—for any one book to come close to covering all that you need to know. In addition to the standard texts on programming Windows, Visual Basic programmers will find *PC Magazine Visual Basic Programmer's Guide to the Windows API* by Daniel Appleman (Ziff-Davis Press, 1993) particularly valuable. This is an essential reference for anyone who wants to exploit Windows API functions from within Visual Basic. The only API guide written specifically for Visual

Basic programmers, this book provides the declarations for and describes the use of every API function and subroutine, and provides sample applications demonstrating the use of API routines in a wide variety of areas.

COMPANION DISK INSTRUCTIONS

The companion disk in the back of *PC Magazine Visual Basic Utilities* includes the source and compiled code for all eight utilities described in the book, plus additional utilities, code samples and custom controls that will be of interest to readers of this book.

The disk also includes an installation program called Visual Basic Utilities Installer that will install the code from any or all of the projects on the disk. To launch Visual Basic Utilities Installer, place the companion disk in your PC's floppy disk drive and execute the program VBUINST.EXE. One way to do this is by selecting the File Run menu item in Program Manager, and then using the browse button to locate VBUINST.EXE in the root directory of the installation disk.

Visual Basic Utilities Installer offers you the ability to select an individual project to install, or to install the code from all the projects at once. In either case, it will install each project's code in a separate subdirectory under a single parent directory. The program will suggest C:\VBUTILS as the default directory in which to place each of the project subdirectories, but you can change that to any disk or directory you please. If the specified directory does not exist, Visual Basic Utilities Installer will create it.

Once you've specified a directory, you can either select a single project in the list box on the Visual Basic Utilities main screen and click on the Install Selected button, or click on the Install All button to install all the projects from the companion disk. The Install All button will install the source and compiled code from each chapter, plus the bonus code and programs described below.

Once the specified files have been installed, Visual Basic Utilities Installer will offer to create a new Program Manager group called VB Utilities and to install individual items for each .EXE and .MAK file. Click the No button if you don't want it to do so.

Most of the files on the Companion Disk have been compressed and renamed with Microsoft's COMPRESS.EXE utility. Visual Basic Utilities Installer uses VER.DLL and LZEXPAND.DLL to automatically expand and rename these files as it installs them. If you would prefer to manually install some or all of the files from the disk, use the EXPAND.EXE program which you'll find in the SETUPKIT\KITFILES subdirectory of your Visual Basic directory. (Note: This file is included only with the Professional Edition of Visual Basic. Standard Edition users should either use the VB Utilities Installer program or obtain EXPAND.EXE from another source.)

■ COMPANION DISK CONTENTS

This disk contains the source and compiled code for each of the eight projects presented in *PC Magazine Visual Basic Utilities*. In some cases, the code presented on the disk will vary slightly from that described in the text of this book. These variances reflect fixes or improvements made after the text of the chapter was printed, and except as described below, they are relatively minor. Where these variances do exist, you should view the code on the companion disk as the "official" version which will provide the most reliable operation.

■ VB Librarian

Following installation, the files for VB Librarian, the source code library presented in Chapter 1, are located in the VBLIB directory. In addition to the source and compiled code for the project, the VBLIB directory includes a library file containing more than a dozen general purpose routines which may be of value in your programming projects.

■ Title Bar Clock

Following installation, the files for Title Bar Clock, the title bar clock presented in Chapter 2, are located in the VBCLOCK directory.

After the completion of Chapter 2, I made one major change to Title Bar Clock. Further testing revealed that Title Bar Clock could interfere with the operation of a few programs in ways that were hard to predict. Accordingly, I added a routine to Title Bar Clock which reads a private .INI file listing any programs whose windows it should not modify. Title Bar Clock now maintains this list in an array, and consults it before modifying a window's title bar. The READVBC.TXT file that the installation program will copy to the VBCLOCK subdirectory further explains the use of this .INI file.

■ VB Zip Shell

Following installation, the files for VB Zip Shell, the interface to PKZIP and PKUNZIP presented in Chapter 3, are located in the ZIPSHELL directory. In addition, the

ZIPSHELL directory includes a file called PDS_ZIP.BAS containing Neal B. Scott's
PDS 7.1 routines for reading .ZIP files, which I adopted for use in this project.

VB Zip Shell underwent several minor changes following completion of Chapter 3.
Most of these were minor bug fixes to the routines for file handling and for activating
and deactivating command buttons. The most interesting change was the addition of
code to add a horizontal scroll bar to the list box displayed on the UnZipper form.
The code, which is attached to the UnZipper Form_Load procedure, uses the Windows API function SetWindowLong to change the style of the list box so that a horizontal scroll bar appears when the width of any list box item exceeds the width of the
list box. The code which performs this trick follows:

```
Dim wLong&, sWidth%
wLong& = GetWindowLong(List1.hWnd, GWL_STYLE)
wLong& = wLong& Or WS_HSCROLL
wLong& = SetWindowLong(List1.hWnd, GWL_STYLE, wLong&)
sWidth% = (List1.Width * 2) / Screen.TwipsPerPixelX
wLong& = SendMessage(List1.hWnd, LB_SETHORIZONTALEXTENT, sWidth%, 0)
```

One final note about VB Zip Shell. PKZIP.EXE and PKUNZIP.EXE must be on your
DOS path in order for VB Zip Shell to locate them.

■ VB Q

Following installation, the files for VB Q, the print queue facility described in Chapter 4, are located in the VBQ subdirectory, except for DRAGDROP.VBX, which is automatically installed in your WINDOWS\SYSTEM directory.

■ VB Typographer

Following installation, the files for VB Typographer, the font preview utility described
in Chapter 5, are located in the TYPO subdirectory, except for CMDIALOG.VBX,
which is automatically installed in your WINDOWS\SYSTEM directory. (Note: Because VB Utilities Installer makes use of VER.DLL to copy files, it only installs CM-
DIALOG.VBX and other standard Visual Basic controls and libraries if your WINDOWS\
SYSTEM directory does not already contain the file, or if the version of the file found
there is outdated.)

■ Clips

Following installation, the files for Clips, the multidimensional clipboard utility described
in Chapter 6, are located in the CLIPS subdirectory, except for CLPWATCH.DLL and
CMDIALOG.VBX, which are installed in your WINDOWS\SYSTEM directory. In addition to the source and .EXE files for Clips, you'll find a file called CB7.LST, containing
the GFA-BASIC source code listing for CLPWATCH.DLL, in the CLIPS directory.

- **DeskMenu**

  Following installation, the files for DeskMenu, the popup menu utility described in Chapter 7, are located in the DESKMENU directory, except for DMENU.DLL, which is automatically installed in your WINDOWS\SYSTEM directory. You'll find a copy of DESKMENU.LST, the GFA-BASIC source code for DMENU.DLL, in the DESKMENU directory.

- **VB MAKer**

  Following installation, the files for VB MAKer, the .MAK file editor described in Chapter 8, are located in the VBMAKER directory, except for CMDIALOG.VBX and three files required by VB MAKer's data access routines (MSAJT110.DLL, MSAES110.DLL, and VBDB300.DLL), which are installed in your WINDOWS\SYSTEM directory. In addition to VB MAKer's source code and .EXE file, the VBMAKER directory includes CONTROLS.MDB and CONTROLS.LDB, the empty Access tables used by VB MAKer to store its .VBX database.

- **PKZIP**

  Following installation, the files PKZIP.EXE, PKUNZIP.EXE and ORDER.DOC are located in the PKZ110 directory. You'll want to either move these files onto your DOS path or add this directory to your path if you intend to use them with VB Zip Shell. (Note: PKZIP and PKUNZIP are shareware—you are obligated to pay a registration fee to PKWARE, Inc. if you intend to use them. See ORDER.DOC for information on how to do so.)

- **DRAGDROP.VBX**

  Following installation, a sample project file illustrating other uses for the File Manager drag-and-drop client control, DRAGDROP.VBX, is located in the DRAGDROP subdirectory.

- **Window Information Utility**

  Following installation, the source and compiled code for the Window Information Utility described in Chapter 2 is located in the WINFO directory.

- **VB Utilities Installer**

  Following installation, the complete source code for VB Utilities Installer is located in the VBUINST directory.

INDEX

Imagination.
Innovation. Insight.

The How It Works Series from Ziff-Davis Press

". . . a magnificently seamless integration of text and graphics . . ."

Larry Blasko, The Associated Press, reviewing *PC/Computing How Computers Work*

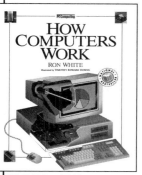

ISBN: 094-7 Price: $22.95

No other books bring computer technology to life like the *How It Works* series from Ziff-Davis Press. Lavish, full-color illustrations and lucid text from some of the world's top computer commentators make *How It Works* books an exciting way to explore the inner workings of PC technology.

PC/Computing How Computers Work

A worldwide blockbuster that hit the general trade bestseller lists! *PC/Computing* magazine executive editor Ron White dismantles the PC and reveals what really makes it tick.

ISBN: 133-1 Price: $24.95
Available: October

ISBN: 129-3 Price: $24.95

How Networks Work

Two of the most respected names in connectivity showcase the PC network, illustrating and explaining how each component does its magic and how they all fit together.

ISBN: 166-8 Price: $15.95 Available: October

How Macs Work

A fun and fascinating voyage to the heart of the Macintosh! Two noted *MacUser* contributors cover the spectrum of Macintosh operations from startup to shutdown.

How Software Works

This dazzlingly illustrated volume from Ron White peeks inside the PC to show in full-color how software breathes life into the PC. Covers Windows™ and all major software categories.

How to Use Your Computer

Conquer computerphobia and see how this intricate machine truly makes life easier. Dozens of full-color graphics showcase the components of the PC and explain how to interact with them.

All About Computers

This one-of-a-kind visual guide for kids features numerous full-color illustrations and photos on every page, combined with dozens of interactive projects that reinforce computer basics, making this an exciting way to learn all about the world of computers.

ISBN: 146-3 Price: $24.95

ISBN: 155-2 Price: $19.95

Available at all fine bookstores or by calling
1-800-688-0448, ext. 100. Call for information
on the Instructor's Supplement, including transparencies,
for each book in the How It Works Series.

ZIFF-DAVIS
ZD
PRESS

© 1993 Ziff-Davis Press

MAXIMIZE YOUR PRODUCTIVITY WITH THE TECHNIQUES & UTILITIES SERIES

Ziff-Davis Press Survey of Readers

Please help us in our effort to produce the best books on personal computing.
For your assistance, we would be pleased to send you a FREE catalog
featuring the complete line of Ziff-Davis Press books.

1. How did you first learn about this book?

Recommended by a friend . . . . ☐ -1 (5)

Recommended by store personnel . . . . ☐ -2

Saw in Ziff-Davis Press catalog . . . . ☐ -3

Received advertisement in the mail . . . . ☐ -4

Saw the book on bookshelf at store . . . . ☐ -5

Read book review in: _____ ☐ -6

Saw an advertisement in: _____ ☐ -7

Other (Please specify): _____ ☐ -8

2. Which THREE of the following factors most influenced your decision to purchase this book? (Please check up to THREE.)

Front or back cover information on book . . . ☐ -1 (6)

Logo of magazine affiliated with book . . . . . . ☐ -2

Special approach to the content . . . . ☐ -3

Completeness of content . . . . ☐ -4

Author's reputation. . . . . ☐ -5

Publisher's reputation . . . . ☐ -6

Book cover design or layout . . . . ☐ -7

Index or table of contents of book . . . . ☐ -8

Price of book . . . . ☐ -9

Special effects, graphics, illustrations . . . . . . ☐ -0

Other (Please specify): _____ ☐ -x

3. How many computer books have you purchased in the last six months? _____ (7-10)

4. On a scale of 1 to 5, where 5 is excellent, 4 is above average, 3 is average, 2 is below average, and 1 is poor, please rate each of the following aspects of this book below. (Please circle your answer.)

Depth/completeness of coverage	5	4	3	2	1 (11)
Organization of material	5	4	3	2	1 (12)
Ease of finding topic	5	4	3	2	1 (13)
Special features/time saving tips	5	4	3	2	1 (14)
Appropriate level of writing	5	4	3	2	1 (15)
Usefulness of table of contents	5	4	3	2	1 (16)
Usefulness of index	5	4	3	2	1 (17)
Usefulness of accompanying disk	5	4	3	2	1 (18)
Usefulness of illustrations/graphics	5	4	3	2	1 (19)
Cover design and attractiveness	5	4	3	2	1 (20)
Overall design and layout of book	5	4	3	2	1 (21)
Overall satisfaction with book	5	4	3	2	1 (22)

5. Which of the following computer publications do you read regularly; that is, 3 out of 4 issues?

Byte . . . . ☐ -1 (23)

Computer Shopper . . . . ☐ -2

Corporate Computing . . . . ☐ -3

Dr. Dobb's Journal . . . . ☐ -4

LAN Magazine . . . . ☐ -5

MacWEEK . . . . ☐ -6

MacUser . . . . ☐ -7

PC Computing . . . . ☐ -8

PC Magazine . . . . ☐ -9

PC WEEK . . . . ☐ -0

Windows Sources . . . . ☐ -x

Other (Please specify): _____ ☐ -y

Please turn page.

6. What is your level of experience with personal computers? With the subject of this book?

	With PCs	With subject of book
Beginner	☐ -1 (24)	☐ -1 (25)
Intermediate	☐ -2	☐ -2
Advanced	☐ -3	☐ -3

7. Which of the following best describes your job title?

Officer (CEO/President/VP/owner)........ ☐ -1 (26)
Director/head............................. ☐ -2
Manager/supervisor....................... ☐ -3
Administration/staff...................... ☐ -4
Teacher/educator/trainer................. ☐ -5
Lawyer/doctor/medical professional....... ☐ -6
Engineer/technician...................... ☐ -7
Consultant............................... ☐ -8
Not employed/student/retired............. ☐ -9
Other (Please specify): _____ ☐ -0

8. What is your age?

Under 20............................. ☐ -1 (27)
21-29................................ ☐ -2
30-39................................ ☐ -3
40-49................................ ☐ -4
50-59................................ ☐ -5
60 or over........................... ☐ -6

9. Are you:

Male................................. ☐ -1 (28)
Female............................... ☐ -2

Thank you for your assistance with this important information! Please write your address below to receive our free catalog.

Name: _____

Address: _____

City/State/Zip: _____

Fold here to mail.

1064-10-13

_____

_____

_____

BUSINESS REPLY MAIL
FIRST CLASS MAIL   PERMIT NO. 1612   OAKLAND, CA

POSTAGE WILL BE PAID BY ADDRESSEE

NO POSTAGE
NECESSARY
IF MAILED IN
THE UNITED
STATES

Ziff-Davis Press
ZD PRESS 5903 Christie Avenue
Emeryville, CA 94608-1925
Attn: Marketing

■ TO RECEIVE 5¼-INCH DISK(S)

The Ziff-Davis Press software contained on the $3^1/_2$-inch disk included with this book is also available in $5^1/_4$-inch format. If you would like to receive the software in the $5^1/_4$-inch format, please return the $3^1/_2$-inch disk with your name and address to:

Disk Exchange
Ziff-Davis Press
5903 Christie Avenue
Emeryville, CA 94608